Microsoft® SQL Server™ 2008

REPORTING SERVICES

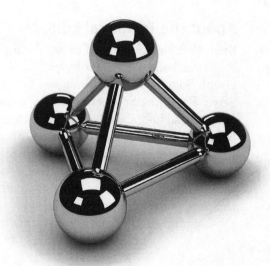

About the Author

Brian Larson is a Phi Beta Kappa graduate of Luther College in Decorah, Iowa, with degrees in physics and computer science. Brian has 23 years of experience in the computer industry and 19 years experience as a consultant creating custom database applications. He is currently the Chief of Technology for Superior Consulting Services in Minneapolis, Minnesota, a Microsoft Consulting Partner for Reporting Services. Brian is a Microsoft Certified Solution Developer (MCSD) and a Microsoft Certified Database Administrator (MCDBA).

Brian served as a member of the original Reporting Services development team as a consultant to Microsoft. In that role, he contributed to the original code base of Reporting Services.

Brian has presented at national conferences and events, including the SQL Server Magazine Connections Conference, the PASS Community Summit, and the Microsoft Business Intelligence Conference, and has provided training and mentoring on Reporting Services across the country. He has been a contributor and columnist for *SQL Server Magazine*. In addition to this book, Brian is the author of *Delivering Business Intelligence with Microsoft SQL Server 2008*, also from McGraw-Hill.

Brian and his wife Pam have been married for 23 years. Pam will tell you that their first date took place at the campus computer center. If that doesn't qualify someone to write a computer book, then I don't know what does. Brian and Pam have two children, Jessica and Corey.

About the Technical Editor

Brian Welcker is a Senior Product Manager in Microsoft's Health Solution Group, helping to build software solutions for hospitals around the world. Before joining the Health Solutions Group, Brian was Group Program Manager for Microsoft SQL Server Reporting Services, where his team was focused on delivering the premier managed, ad hoc, and developer reporting platform as part of SQL Server and Visual Studio. A 12-year Microsoft veteran, Brian was one of the founding members of the Reporting Services team; he has also worked as the lead program manager for SQL Server Meta Data Services, as well as a technical evangelist in Microsoft's Developer Relations Group. He joined Microsoft after working for a healthcare software company in his home town of Raleigh, North Carolina. Brian resides in Seattle, Washington with his wife and two children.

Microsoft® SQL Server™ 2008

REPORTING SERVICES

Brian Larson

New York   Chicago   San Francisco   Lisbon
London   Madrid   Mexico City   Milan
New Delhi   San Juan   Seoul   Singapore
Sydney   Toronto

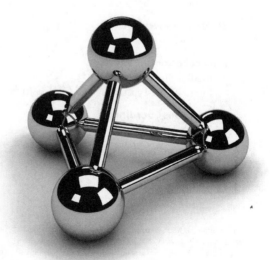

The McGraw·Hill Companies

Library of Congress Cataloging-in-Publication Data

Larson, Brian.
  Microsoft SQL server 2008 : reporting services / Brian Larson.
    p. cm.
  ISBN 978-0-07-154808-3 (alk. paper)
  1. SQL server. 2. Client/server computing. 3. Database management.
I. Title.
  QA76.9.C55L377 2008
  005.75'85—dc22
                              2008034156

McGraw-Hill books are available at special quantity discounts to use as premiums and sales promotions, or for use in corporate training programs. To contact a special sales representative, please visit the Contact Us page at www.mhprofessional.com.

Microsoft® SQL Server™ 2008 Reporting Services

234567890 DOC DOC 1543210

ISBN   978-0-07-154808-3
MHID   0-07-154808-4

Sponsoring Editor
Wendy Rinaldi

Editorial Supervisor
Patty Mon

Project Editor
Madhu Bhardwaj,
International Typesetting and Composition

Acquisitions Coordinator
Mandy Canales

Technical Editor
Brian Welcker

Copy Editor
Lisa McCoy

Proofreader
Bev Weiler

Indexer
Kevin Broccoli

Production Supervisor
Jim Kussow

Composition
International Typesetting and Composition

Illustration
International Typesetting and Composition

Art Director, Cover
Jeff Weeks

This book is dedicated to my family. To my children, Jessica and Corey, who gave up many hours of "dad time" during the writing of this book. And especially to my wife, Pam, who, in addition to allowing me to commit to this project, gave countless hours of her own time to make sure things were done right.

Contents at a Glance

Part I   Getting Started

Chapter 1   Let's Start at the Very Beginning   3

Chapter 2   Putting the Pieces in Place: Installing Reporting Services   23

Part II   Report Authoring

Chapter 3   DB 101: Database Basics   65

Chapter 4   A Visit to Emerald City: The Report Wizard   111

Chapter 5   Removing the Training Wheels: Building Basic Reports   171

Chapter 6   Graphic Expression: Using Charts, Images, and Gauges   219

Chapter 7   Kicking It Up a Notch: Intermediate Reporting   297

Chapter 8   Beyond Wow: Advanced Reporting   365

Chapter 9   A Leading Exporter: Exporting Reports to Other Rendering Formats   441

Part III   Report Serving

Chapter 10   How Did We Ever Manage Without You? The Report Manager   467

Chapter 11   Delivering the Goods: Report Delivery   529

Chapter 12   Extending Outside the Box: Customizing Reporting Services   571

Part IV   Appendixes

Appendix A   Report Item Reference   637

Appendix B   Web Service Interface Reference   709

Appendix C   Ad Hoc Reporting   781

Index   823

Contents

Foreword xvii

Acknowledgments xix

Introduction xxi

The Galactic Database and Other Supporting Materials xxii

Part I   Getting Started

Chapter 1   Let's Start at the Very Beginning   3

Sharing Business Intelligence   5

    The Need to Share   5

    Possible Solutions   6

    Microsoft Reporting Services   8

Report Authoring Architecture   10

    The Business Intelligence Project Type   11

    Report Structure   12

    Report Designer   14

    Standalone Report Builder   16

Report-Serving Architecture   17

    Report Server   18

    Report Delivery   20

Diving In   22

Chapter 2   Putting the Pieces in Place: Installing Reporting Services   23

Preparing for the Installation   24

    The Parts of the Whole   24

    Editions of Reporting Services   27

    Types of Reporting Services Installations   29

    Installation Requirements   34

    Other Installation Considerations   35

The Installation Process   39

    The SQL Server 2008 Installation   39

    The Reporting Services Configuration Manager   49

Common Installation Issues 60

Administrative Rights 60

Server Components Not Shown on the Feature Selection Screen 60

Installation Error 2755 60

Reporting Services and IIS on the Same Server 61

The Repair Utility and Installation Log File 61

Spending Some Time in Basic Training 61

Part II   Report Authoring

Chapter 3   **DB 101: Database Basics** **65**

Database Structure 66

Getting Organized 66

Retrieving Data 76

Galactic Delivery Services 84

Company Background 85

Querying Data 88

The SELECT Query 90

On to the Reports 108

Chapter 4   **A Visit to Emerald City: The Report Wizard** **111**

Obtaining the Galactic Database 112

Your First Report 112

The Customer List Report 113

An Interactive Table Report 137

The Customer-Invoice Report 137

Creating Matrix Reports 153

The Invoice-Batch Number Report 153

Report Parameters 160

The Parameterized Invoice-Batch Number Report 160

Flying Solo 169

Chapter 5   **Removing the Training Wheels: Building Basic Reports** **171**

Riding Down Familiar Roads 172

The Transport List Report 172

The Tablix and Data Regions 195

The Repair Count By Type Report 197

New Territory 205

The Transport Information Sheet 206

Getting Graphical 218

Chapter 6 **Graphic Expression: Using Charts, Images, and Gauges** **219**

Chart Your Course 220
The Deliveries versus Lost Packages Chart 220
The Fuel Price Chart 236
The Fuel Price Chart, Version 2 244
The Business Type Distribution Chart 247
The Days in Maintenance Chart 250
Gauging the Results 257
The Digital Dashboard 257
Image Is Everything 273
Conference Nametags 275
Conference Place Cards 282
The Rate Sheet Report 288
Building Higher 295

Chapter 7 **Kicking It Up a Notch: Intermediate Reporting** **297**

Never Having to Say "I'm Sorry" 298
The Report Template 299
Handling Errors in Reports 306
The Employee Time Report 307
Data Caching During Preview 323
The Employee List Report 324
The Employee Mailing Labels Report 335
The Overtime Report 343
The Revised Employee Time Report 351
Under the Hood 359
Viewing the RDL 359
Practicing Safe Source 361
Using Visual SourceSafe 362
Advance, Never Retreat 364

Chapter 8 **Beyond Wow: Advanced Reporting** **365**

Speaking in Code 366
The Delivery Status Report 367
The Lost Delivery Report 377
The Customer List Report—Revisited 386
Payroll Checks 389

The Weather Report 397

The Delivery Analysis Report 404

Reports Within Reports 411

The Employee Evaluation Report 412

The Invoice Report 424

Interacting with Reports 428

The Invoice Front-End Report 429

The Transport Monitor Report 432

A Conversion Experience 437

The Paid Invoices Report 437

What's Next 440

Chapter 9   **A Leading Exporter: Exporting Reports to Other Rendering Formats** **441**

A Report in Any Other Format Would Look as Good 443

Exporting and Printing a Report 443

Presentation Formats 445

TIFF Image Presentation Format 447

Adobe PDF Presentation Format 450

Web Archive Presentation Format 452

Excel Presentation Format 455

Word Presentation Format 458

Printed Presentation Format 459

Data Exchange Formats 460

Comma-Separated Values (CSV) Data Exchange Format 460

XML Data Exchange Format 461

Call the Manager 464

Part III   Report Serving

Chapter 10   **How Did We Ever Manage Without You? The Report Manager** **467**

Folders 468

The Report Manager 469

Moving Reports and Supporting Files to the Report Server 472

Deploying Reports Using the Report Designer 472

Uploading Reports Using Report Manager 479

Uploading Other Items Using Report Manager 487

Uploading Reports Using .NET Assemblies 491

Modifying Reports from the Report Server 500

Managing Items in Folders 502
 Moving Items Between Folders 502
 Deleting a Folder 503
 Renaming a Folder 504
Seek and Ye Shall Find: Search and Find Functions 504
 Searching for a Report 504
 Finding Text Within a Report 505
Printing from Report Manager 506
 Printing Options 506
Managing Reports on the Report Server 507
 Security 508
Roles 511
Linked Reports 524
 Creating a Linked Report 525
Delivering the Goods 528

Chapter 11 **Delivering the Goods: Report Delivery** **529**
Caching In 530
 Report Caching 531
 Enabling Report Caching 534
Execution Snapshots 539
 Enabling Execution Snapshots 539
Report History 542
 Enabling Report History 542
 Managing Report History Snapshots 546
 Updating Report Definitions and Report History Snapshots 548
Subscriptions 549
 Standard Subscriptions 549
 Managing Your Subscriptions 554
 Data-Driven Subscriptions 555
Site Settings 563
 The General Site Settings Page 563
 Other Pages Accessed from the Site Settings Page 565
 Managing Reporting Services Through the SQL Server Management Studio 566
 Additional Settings 569
A Sense of Style 569
 The ReportingServices Style Sheet 569
Building On 570

Chapter 12 **Extending Outside the Box: Customizing Reporting Services** **571**

Using Reporting Services Without the Report Manager 572
 URL Access 572
 Web Service Access 585
 The Report Viewer Control 589
 SharePoint Web Parts 595
 Reporting Services Utilities 597

Custom Security 608
 Authentication and Authorization 609
 Issues with Custom Security 611
 Creating a Custom Security Extension 613
 Deploying a Custom Security Extension 621
 Using the Custom Security Extension 627
 Other Extensions 629

Best Practices 629
 Report-Authoring Practices 629
 Report Deployment Practices 631

Where Do We Go from Here? 633

Part IV   Appendixes

Appendix A **Report Item Reference** **637**

Report Objects 638
 Layout Areas 638
 Data Regions 639
 Report Items 645

Property Reference 647
 Properties 647

Appendix B **Web Service Interface Reference** **709**

Reporting Services Web Service 710
 Creating a Web Reference 710
 Credentials 711
 Compatibility 712
 ReportExecution2005 Properties 712
 ReportExecution2005 Methods 713
 ReportService2005 Properties 721

ReportService2005 Methods 722

ReportService2006 755

ReportService2005 and ReportExecution2005 Web Service Classes 757

Appendix C   **Ad Hoc Reporting** **781**

The Report Model 782

Creating a Report Model 783

Creating Reports with the Report Builder 800

Report Builder Basics 800

Creating a Table Layout Report 805

Creating a Matrix Layout Report 817

Creating a Chart Layout Report 819

Give It a Try 822

Index **823**

Foreword

At the end of 2005, the Reporting Services development team had some tough decisions to make. Unlike most of the SQL Server development team, who had been working on the 2005 release for close to five years, it had only been a year and a half since we shipped the first version of Reporting Services. In that same timeframe, we shipped two service packs, acquired a new ad hoc reporting tool that we delivered as Report Builder, and built a set of report controls that shipped in Visual Studio 2005. The follow-up release, code-named "Katmai," was scheduled for a relatively quick two- to three-year turnaround.

During this time, we also learned a lot about how people were using Reporting Services. When we started development, our initial assumption was that customers wanted to enable web-based delivery of reports with small to medium-sized data sets. While this was the case for most customers, there was another set of users that wanted to be able to export reports as single documents with up to several thousand pages. As the memory required for generating these reports could be far beyond the actual memory available on the server, supporting this scenario wasn't a trivial task. In fact, it would require a large development effort that would consume most of the schedule allocated for the 2008 release. At the same time, users had also requested a number of smaller features that would make their lives easier and their reports better. We couldn't fit both, so a decision had to be made.

After much debate, we decided to take a long-term approach and build a new engine to support report scalability. New reporting features were put on the back burner until this work was completed. This means that while you won't see as many new "bells and whistles" in the 2008 release, there has been a massive amount of work below the surface to ensure that Reporting Services can handle your biggest reporting workloads. In the end, we did manage to squeeze in quite a few nice features into the release that you will like, even if you aren't pushing the bounds of scalability.

At the end of 2007, it was my turn to make a tough decision. I had been working on the SQL Server team for over ten years, with six of those on Reporting Services. While I was extremely proud of the team that we had assembled and excited by the upcoming release of SQL Server 2008, I felt that it was time to move on to new challenges. This January, I moved to Microsoft's new Health Solutions Group, where I am the product manager for a new line of software applications for hospitals. I still keep in touch with the Reporting Services development team and have been trying out the newest features as the product approaches release.

Brian Larson was one of the early proponents of Reporting Services and completed the first edition of this book just as we wrapped up the work on the first release. While many other Reporting Services books have appeared on the market, I always considered Brian's book to be the best all-around introduction to the product. I enjoyed working with Brian on the first two editions of this book and was excited when he asked me to assist with this update. The new release of Reporting Services is the most powerful and flexible yet. Whether you are a seasoned professional or a first-time user, I hope that you use the information and techniques presented in this book to get the most out of the product.

—Brian Welcker
Senior Product Manager
Microsoft Health Solutions Group

Acknowledgments

A journey of a thousand miles begins with a single step." Perhaps this book project was not a journey of a thousand miles, although it seemed that way in the early hours of the morning with a deadline approaching. Be that as it may, it is possible to identify the first step in this whole process. A coworker of mine at Superior Consulting Services, Marty Voegele, was between assignments, on-the-bench, in consultant-speak. Marty was bored, so he decided to take matters into his own hands. Marty had previously consulted to Microsoft and still had contacts in the SQL Server area. He made a few phone calls and before long, Marty was again consulting to Microsoft, this time creating something called Rosetta.

As additional work was added, I had the opportunity to take on part of this assignment as well. It was both challenging and exciting working on code that you knew would be part of a major product from a major software company. What was perhaps most exciting was that Rosetta seemed to be a tool that would fill several needs we had identified while developing custom applications for our own clients.

As the beta version of what was now called Reporting Services was released, a brief introductory article on Reporting Services appeared in *SQL Server Magazine.* One of the sales representatives here at Superior Consulting Services, Mike Nelson, decided this would be a nice bit of marketing material to have as we trumpeted our involvement with Reporting Services. One thing led to another, and before we knew it, Mike had offered Marty's and my services to write a more in-depth article for *SQL Server Magazine.* This article became the cover article for the December 2003 issue and has become known as the "Delightful" article. (You'll have to read the first paragraph of the article to understand why.) It is now available on MSDN.

This was where I grabbed the map and compass, and decided on the next path. Because the magazine article came out fairly well, I decided to write a book on the topic. Marty informed me that writing a 700-page book would probably make his fingers fall off, so I could take this next step on my own. So, here we are today, one book and two revisions later.

All of this is a rather lengthy way of saying that I owe a big thank you to Marty and Mike. Without a shadow of a doubt, this book would not have happened without them. In addition to the contributions already stated, I want to thank Marty for helping to keep me up-to-speed on Reporting Services information and newsgroup postings. We have learned a great deal preparing presentations on Reporting Services and providing Reporting Services solutions for clients.

I also want to thank John Miller, the owner of Superior Consulting Services. John hired me as his first employee eleven years ago to be Superior's Chief of Technology. He has supported our efforts on Reporting Services and made it a focus area at Superior Consulting. Without John's founding of Superior Consulting Services and his bringing together people such as Marty and Mike, none of this would have come into being.

I need to extend a big thank you to Brian Welcker and the rest of the Reporting Services development team. Their guidance and patience during development is much appreciated. The information they were able to provide during the creation of this book has enhanced the final product you are now holding.

I also want to thank the entire group at McGraw-Hill, especially Wendy Rinaldi, who has worked with me through two books and three revised editions. The assistance, guidance, professionalism, and humor of the editorial staff have made this project much easier. The attention that McGraw-Hill has given this project has been truly overwhelming.

Last, but certainly not least, I want to thank my wife, Pam, for all her efforts and understanding. Not only did she agree to my taking personal time to write and revise this book, but she took it upon herself to proofread every page and work through every sample report. You, as a reader, are greatly benefiting from her efforts.

I also want to thank you, the reader, for purchasing this book. My hope is that it will provide you with an informative overview, steady guide, and quick reference as you use Reporting Services.

Best wishes,
Brian Larson
blarson@teamscs.com

Introduction

Microsoft SQL Server 2000 Reporting Services and Microsoft SQL Server 2005 Reporting Services were exciting products. With the addition of the tablix and gauge data regions, the enhancements to the chart data region, and the complete re-architecting of the rendering engine, Microsoft SQL Server 2008 Reporting Services is even more exciting. Never has there been a product with so much potential for sharing business information with such ease of use and at such a reasonable price. Anyone who has ever struggled to find a way to efficiently share database information across an enterprise will see a reason to be delighted with this product.

Now I will admit that I may not be unbiased when expressing this opinion. I did have the opportunity to create a small piece of what has now become Reporting Services. But my excitement goes beyond that.

The main reason I get excited about Reporting Services is because I have been a database application developer for 19 years. I have fought with various reporting tools. I have struggled to find a way to efficiently share data between far-flung sales offices and the corporate headquarters. I have researched enterprise-wide reporting systems and started salivating when I saw the features they offered, only to have my hopes dashed when I looked at the licensing fees. I have shaken my fist at the computer screen and screamed, "There must be a better way!"

With Reporting Services, there is. During the past five years, my colleagues and I at Superior Consulting Services have had the opportunity to incorporate Reporting Services into custom database solutions. We have worked with a number of organizations, helping them get up-to-speed on the product. We have seen how quickly and easily Reporting Services can improve the data analysis and data distribution capabilities within an enterprise.

At one client, we began implementing Reporting Services on Monday morning. By Wednesday afternoon, reports were being e-mailed around the company. Information was being shared as never before. On Thursday morning, the president of the company emerged from his office to see what all the hoopla was about. As he stared at a newly created Reporting Services report, he began saying things like, "So that's why we're having a problem in this area" and "Now I see why our end-of-month's totals went that direction."

At another client, I was working with a manager to mock up a report in Reporting Services. He seemed to be taking a long time going over the layout, so I assumed we did not have things quite right. When I asked what was wrong with the report, he said, "Nothing's wrong. I'm just seeing information about this year's production that I hadn't seen before." Scenarios like these are enough to make even the most cynical data processing professional sit up and take notice!

This book is designed to help you and your organization achieve those same results. As you work through the examples in this book, I hope you have several of those "ah-ha!" moments—not only moments of discovering new capabilities in Reporting Services, but also moments of discovering how Reporting Services can solve business problems in your organization.

One note about the structure of the book: This book is meant to be a hands-on process. You should never be far from your Reporting Services development installation as you read through these chapters. The book is based on the philosophy that people understand more and remember longer when the learning takes place in an interactive environment. Consequently, the majority of the book is based on business needs and the reports, code, and configurations you will create to fulfill those needs.

The book is dedicated to offering examples demonstrating complete solutions. I have tried to stay away from code snippets as much as possible. Nothing is worse than seeing five lines of code and knowing they are exactly the solution you need, but being unable to implement them because you do not know what code is supposed to come before or after those five lines to make the whole thing work. With the examples in this book, along with the supporting materials available from the book's website, you should always see a solution from beginning to end, and you should be able to turn around and implement that solution to fulfill your organization's business needs.

I have also tried to have a little fun in the book when appropriate. That is why the business scenarios are based on Galactic Delivery Services (GDS), an interplanetary package delivery service. (You might call it the delivery service to the stars.) While GDS is a bit fanciful with its antimatter transports and robotic employees, the business needs discussed will ring true for most organizations.

I hope you find this book a worthwhile tool for getting up-to-speed on Microsoft's exciting new product. I hope you get a chuckle or two from its GDS examples. Most of all, I hope the book enables you to unlock the potential of Reporting Services for your organization.

The Galactic Database and Other Supporting Materials

All of the samples in this book are based on business scenarios for a fictional company called Galactic Delivery Services. The data for these examples comes from the Galactic database. You can download the Galactic database, as well as the image files and other supporting materials, from the book's website on the McGraw-Hill Professional website. This download also includes the complete source code for all of the reports and .NET assemblies used in the book.

The download is found on this book's web page at www.mhprofessional.com. Search for the book's web page using the ISBN, which is 0071548084. Use the "Code" link to download the zip file containing the book's material. Follow the instructions in the zip file to install the Galactic database and the other sample code as needed.

Part I

Getting Started

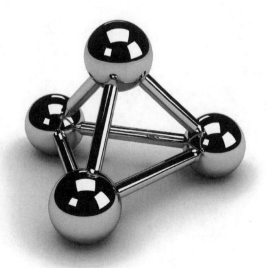

Chapter 1

Let's Start at the Very Beginning

In This Chapter

▶ **Sharing Business Intelligence**

▶ **Report Authoring Architecture**

▶ **Report-Serving Architecture**

▶ **Diving In**

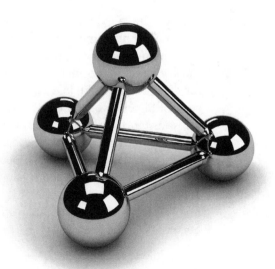

SQL Server 2000 Reporting Services was Microsoft's entry into the web-based reporting arena. This first version of Reporting Services enabled you to easily share business information—what is commonly known as "business intelligence" these days—with management, coworkers, business partners, and customers throughout the world. In an interconnected workplace, it makes sense that your reporting solution should offer company-wide, nationwide, and even worldwide communication.

SQL Server 2005 Reporting Services built on the success of the original. Where almost every other aspect of the SQL Server 2005 release represented a completely new platform, Reporting Services simply added to the solid foundation provided by the earlier version to make a great product even better. The 2005 release provided an additional report-authoring environment, improved report-development features, and enhanced capabilities for distributing reports.

Now, the SQL Server 2008 release brings major changes to Reporting Services. The report processing and rendering engine has been completely rewritten. This allows Reporting Services to be more robust, especially when rendering large reports. This overhaul led to a number of other changes as well.

The report definition structure now includes something called a *tablix*, a report item whose name and functionality represent a combination of the table and matrix report items. The tablix allows for much greater flexibility in report layout while actually simplifying the inner workings of the report-rendering engine. (It has been pointed out that this new object could have just as easily been called a mable. I think the Microsoft team made the right naming decision.)

In previous versions, the Reporting Services report server depended on Internet Information Services (IIS). This dependence is gone in 2008. Instead, the report server now uses the Windows Hypertext Transfer Protocol (HTTP) library for hosting web services.

Reporting Services was code-named Rosetta during its original development at Microsoft. This name comes from the Rosetta Stone, a stone slab found in 1799 that contains an inscription in both Egyptian hieroglyphics and Greek. This stone provided the key piece of information necessary to unlock the mystery of Egyptian hieroglyphics for the modern world. Just as the Rosetta Stone brought key information across 1,400 years of history, Rosetta, or Reporting Services, is designed to bring key information across distances to unlock the mystery of success for your business.

The Rosetta project was originally conceived as a feature of SQL Server 2005. However, as Microsoft told prospective customers about the features in Rosetta and demonstrated the first alpha versions, the reaction was strong: "We need this product and we need it now!" Because of this reaction, Microsoft decided that Rosetta would not wait for 2005, but, instead, would be made its own product to work with SQL Server 2000.

Just what are the features of Reporting Services that got everyone so excited? *Reporting Services* provides an environment for creating a number of different types of reports from a number of different data sources. The reports are previewed and refined using this authoring tool. Once completed, the reports are deployed to a *report server,* which makes the reports available via the Internet in a structured, secure environment. Last, but not least, the report management and distribution portion of Reporting Services is free of charge when installed on a server already running SQL Server.

Why did this set of features generate so much excitement? When you put them all together, the result is a product that facilitates the creation, management, and timely use of business intelligence.

Sharing Business Intelligence

Because you are reading this book, you are probably the keeper of some type of information that is important to your organization. You may have information on sales, finance, production, delivery—or one of a hundred other areas. All this information makes up the business intelligence necessary to keep today's corporate, academic, and governmental entities humming along.

The Need to Share

In addition to maintaining this information, you have a need to share this information with others. This need to share may have come from an important lesson you learned in kindergarten ("The world would be a much happier place if we all learned to share") or, more likely, this need to share your information was probably suggested to you by a manager or executive somewhere higher up the food chain. See if any of these situations sound familiar.

The Production Manager

Your company's order-entry system automatically updates the inventory database every four hours. In your company's line of business, some orders can require a large quantity of a given product. Because of this, it is important that the production manager knows about these changes in the inventory level in a timely manner so he can adjust production accordingly.

The production manager has asked you to provide him with an up-to-date inventory report that is created immediately following each update to the inventory database occurring during business hours. He would like this report to arrive on his PC as quickly as possible, so he can make changes to the production schedule within an hour of the updates. He would also like to be able to print this report so he can add his own notations to the report as he works out his new production schedule.

One more fact to keep in mind: Your company's inventory system is in Cleveland, but the production facility is in Portland!

The Vice President of Sales

You are responsible for maintaining information on the amount of credit your company will extend to each of its clients. This information is updated daily in the company database. A report containing the credit information for all clients is printed weekly at corporate headquarters and mailed to each sales representative.

The vice president of sales has requested that the credit information be made available to the sales staff in a timelier manner. He has asked that this report be accessible over the Internet from anywhere across the country. The sales representatives will print the report when they have access to the Internet, and then carry it with them for those times when they cannot get online. He has also asked that this online version of the report be as up-to-date as possible.

The Chief Executive Officer

The chief executive officer for your company has a hands-on management style. She likes to participate in all facets of the decision-making process and, therefore, needs to stay well informed on all aspects of the company. This includes the corporate balance sheet, inventory and production, and the company's stock price.

The CEO expects all this information to be available on her desktop when she arrives for work each morning at 7:00 A.M. The information must be in a format that's appropriate to print and share with the corporate vice presidents at their meeting each morning at 9:00 A.M. As you search for solutions to this one, remember no budget is allocated for this project—and, of course, your job is on the line.

Possible Solutions

These situations, and a thousand others just like them, confront businesses each day. In our world of massive connectivity, these types of requests are not unreasonable. Even if that is the case, it does not mean these requests are easy to fulfill.

An HTML Solution

The first candidate to explore when you're looking to move information across the Internet is, of course, Hypertext Markup Language (HTML). You could use one of a number of tools for creating data-driven HTML pages. This would include Microsoft's Active Server Pages, Macromedia's ColdFusion, any of a number of Java environments, PHP: Hypertext Preprocessor (PHP)—the list goes on and on.

Each of these environments is good at creating dynamic web content. However, they all take time and a certain level of programming knowledge. With deadlines looming, you may not have the time to create custom web applications to solve each of these problems. If you are used to manipulating data with Crystal Reports or Access reporting, you may not be ready to jump into full-blown application development, and you may not have a desire to do so at any time in the near future.

Even if you did create an application for each of these scenarios, one important requirement in each case is this: The information must be printable. HTML screens can look great in a browser window, but they can cause problems when printed. The content can be too wide to fit on the page, and there is no control of page breaks. In fact, the page can break right in the middle of a line of text, with the top half of the characters on one page and the bottom half of the characters on the next! These types of formatting issues could make the output difficult for the sales representatives and the production manager to read. Asking the CEO to take this type of a report to the executive meeting could get you fired.

Let's look for another option!

A PDF Solution

Because the capability to control the printed output is important, Adobe PDF should be considered. PDF files look good, both on the screen and in print. You can control where the page breaks occur and make sure everything looks great. However, several issues need to be overcome with PDF files.

First of all, you need some type of utility to produce output in a PDF format. This could be Adobe's full version of Acrobat or some other utility. Once this has been obtained, a document must be created that contains the desired database information. This is usually a report created with a reporting tool or development software. After this document is created, it is converted into a PDF document using an export function or a special printer driver.

Once the PDF document has been created, it can be copied to a website for access through the Internet. However, as soon as the PDF document is created, it becomes a static entity. It does not requery the database each time it is requested from the website. To remain up-to-date, the PDF document must be re-created each time the source data is changed. In addition, you may have to return to your programming environment to control access to the PDF documents on the website.

Perhaps there is a better way.

A Third-Party Reporting Environment

Reporting environments from other companies certainly overcome the limitations of our first two options. These third-party products allow reports to be built without requiring large amounts of programming. They can also dynamically generate output in a format such as Adobe PDF that will perform well onscreen and in print.

The problem with third-party reporting environments is the cost. Some products can run into the thousands or tens of thousands of dollars. This can be enough to break the budget—if indeed there is a budget—for reporting projects such as the ones discussed previously.

Microsoft Reporting Services

Now you can begin to see why companies get so excited about Reporting Services. It provides an elegant solution for all three of your demanding users—the production manager, the vice president of sales, and the chief executive officer. Reporting Services does not have the drawbacks inherent in the possible solutions considered previously.

No Programming Required

Reporting Services provides a simple, drag-and-drop approach to creating reports from database information. You can use three different tools to author reports. The Ad Hoc Report Builder enables you to create basic reports, even if you do not know much about databases and query languages. The Standalone Report Builder and the Report Designer let you truly unlock the power of Reporting Services to convey complex information.

You do not need to be a programmer to create Reporting Services reports. However, if you are comfortable with programming constructs, Chapters 7 and 8 include some simple Visual Basic expressions that can be used to spice up your report's presentation. Note, however, these expressions are not necessary to create useful reports. They are also simple enough that even those who are totally new to Visual Basic can master them with ease.

A Server with a View

With Reporting Services, you can view reports in your browser. Reporting Services provides a high-quality presentation of each report using dynamic HTML. Reports are presented in multiple pages with "VCR button" controls for navigating between pages.

Because Reporting Services uses dynamic HTML, it does not require any additional programs to be downloaded on your PC. There is no ActiveX control to install, no Java applet to download. Any browser that supports HTML 4.0 can view reports.

Plays Well with Printers

In addition to presenting reports in your browser using dynamic HTML, Reporting Services can *render* a report in a number of additional formats. These include an Adobe PDF document, a Tagged Image File Format (TIFF) image, an Excel spreadsheet, and even a Word document. All these formats look great onscreen when they are viewed, or on paper when they are printed.

NOTE

When Reporting Services renders a report, it gathers the most recent data from the database, formats the data in the manner the report's author specifies, and outputs the report into the selected format (that is, HTML, PDF, TIFF, and so on).

Even when being output in the PDF or TIFF format for printing, a report can be configured to requery the database every time it is accessed. This ensures the report is always up-to-date.

Special Delivery

Reporting Services provides several different ways to deliver reports to end users. The Report Manager website enables users to access reports via the Internet. It also includes security features, which ensure that users access only the reports they should.

Users can also subscribe to reports they would like to receive on a regular basis. Reporting Services will send out a copy of the report as an e-mail attachment to each subscriber on a regularly scheduled basis. Alternatively, a Reporting Services administrator can send out a copy of the report as an e-mail attachment to a number of recipients on a mailing list. If that isn't enough, reports can be embedded right in .NET applications.

The Price Is Right

For anyone who has a licensed copy of SQL Server 2008, the price of Reporting Services is certainly right. Free! As long as the report server is installed on the same computer as the SQL Server database engine, your SQL Server 2008 license covers everything. With this single server architecture, it will not cost you one additional penny to share your reports with others using Reporting Services.

Reporting Services to the Rescue

Let's take one more look at the three scenarios we considered earlier—the production manager, the vice president of sales, and the chief executive officer. How can you use the features of Reporting Services to fulfill the requests made by each of them?

The production manager wants a report showing the current inventory. It is certainly not a problem to query the inventory data from the database and put it into a report. Next, he wants to get a new copy of the report every time the inventory is updated during business hours. The production manager can subscribe to your inventory report and, as part of the subscription, ask that a new report be delivered at 8:15 A.M., 12:15 P.M., and 4:15 P.M. Finally, the inventory system is in Cleveland, but the production manager is in Portland. Because a subscription to a report can be delivered by e-mail, the Reporting Services server can be set up in Cleveland, produce the report from the local data source, and then e-mail the report to Portland.

The solution for the vice president of sales is even more straightforward. He wants a report with credit information for each client. No problem there. Next, he wants the report available to his sales staff, accessible via the Internet. To achieve this, you can publish the report on the Report Manager website. You can even set up security so only sales representatives with the appropriate user name and password can access the report.

In addition, the vice president of sales wants the report to look good when printed. This is achieved with no additional work on the development side. When the sales representatives retrieve the report from the website, it is displayed as HTML. This looks good in the browser, but it may not look good on paper. To have a report that looks good on paper every time, the sales representatives simply need to export the report to either the PDF or TIFF format and then display and print the exported file. Now they are ready to go knocking on doors!

For the CEO, you can build a report or, perhaps a series of reports, that reflects the state of her company. This will serve to keep her informed on all facets of her business. To have this available on her desktop at 7:00 A.M., you can set up a subscription that will run the reports and e-mail them to her each morning at 6:15 A.M.

Finally, because she wants to print this report and share it with the corporate vice presidents, you can make sure the subscription service delivers the report in either PDF or TIFF format. The best part is that because you already have a SQL Server 2008 license, the Reporting Services solution costs the company nothing. You have earned a number of bonus points with the big boss, and she will make you the chief information officer before the end of the year!

Report Authoring Architecture

As mentioned previously, Reporting Services reports are created using one of three tools: the Ad Hoc Report Builder, the Standalone Report Builder, or the Report Designer. The *Ad Hoc Report Builder* is geared toward those power users and analysts who want to do their own ad hoc reporting without having to learn all the ins and outs of database structure and query creation. The Ad Hoc Report Builder presents report authors with a simplified model of their database, so these authors do not need to know the details of querying databases to create reports. Once the Ad Hoc Report Builder has created a report, that report can be deployed to the report server and will function exactly like a report created with the Standalone Report Builder or the Report Designer.

The Standalone Report Builder is new in SQL Server 2008. This report authoring environment supports the construction of full-featured Reporting Services reports. However, it does not provide all of the program and project organization tools found in the Report Designer.

Because we want to cover the entirety of the rich capabilities found in Reporting Services, this book focuses on report authoring using the Report Designer, rather than the Ad Hoc Report Builder or the Standalone Report Builder. We will look briefly at the Standalone Report Builder when discussing report authoring later in this book. If you are interested in learning more about the Ad Hoc Report Builder, please refer to Appendix C.

The *Report Designer* offers far greater capabilities for creating interesting and highly functional reports used to convey business intelligence to the report users. This book can help you get the most from this incredibly rich report-authoring environment. The Report Designer contains everything necessary to create a wide variety of reports for Reporting Services. Everything you need to select information from data sources, create a report layout, and test your creation is right at your fingertips. Best of all, the Report Builder is found in both the Business Intelligence Development Studio and in Visual Studio.

Both the Business Intelligence Development Studio and Visual Studio are a type of program-authoring software called an integrated development environment (IDE). (In fact, the Business Intelligence Development Studio is a special version of Visual Studio operating under a different name.) *IDEs* came into being when the people who create programming languages thought it would be more convenient if the editor, compiler, and debugger were packaged together. Prior to the advent of integrated development environments, creating and debugging software could be a long and tedious process. With an IDE, however, a programmer can be much more efficient while writing and testing an application.

Even though you will be creating reports rather than writing software, the Report Designer provides you with a friendly working environment. You won't be editing, compiling, and debugging, but you will be selecting data, laying out the report, and previewing the end result. All of this is done quickly and easily within the Report Designer.

The Business Intelligence Project Type

The Business Intelligence Development Studio and Visual Studio can be used for a number of business intelligence and software development tasks. The *Business Intelligence Development Studio* is used to create Integration Services packages for data extract, transform, and load (ETL). It also is used to create Analysis Services, multidimensional data structures. Visual Studio is used to create Windows applications, web applications, and web services.

To facilitate this variety of capabilities, these IDEs support many different types of projects. These project types organize the multitude of solutions that can be created within the IDE into related groups. Reporting Services reports are created using the Business Intelligence project type.

Project Templates

When you choose to create a new project in the IDE, you will see the New Project dialog box shown in Figure 1-1. The Project Types area of the screen shows the one project type you will be concerned with: Business Intelligence Projects. *Business Intelligence Projects* includes templates for a number of different projects.

You will look at three project templates in this book: Report Server Project Wizard, Report Server Project, and Report Model Project. Either of the first two templates will, ultimately, create a report project. The *Report Server Project Wizard* template uses the Report Wizard to guide you through the process of creating the first report in your new report project. The *Report Server Project* template simply creates an empty report project and turns you loose. The *Report Model Project* creates a data model for use with the Ad Hoc Report Builder authoring tool.

Report Structure

A report project can contain a number of reports. Each report contains two distinct sets of instructions that determine what the report will contain. The first is the data definition. The *data definition* controls where the data for the report will come from

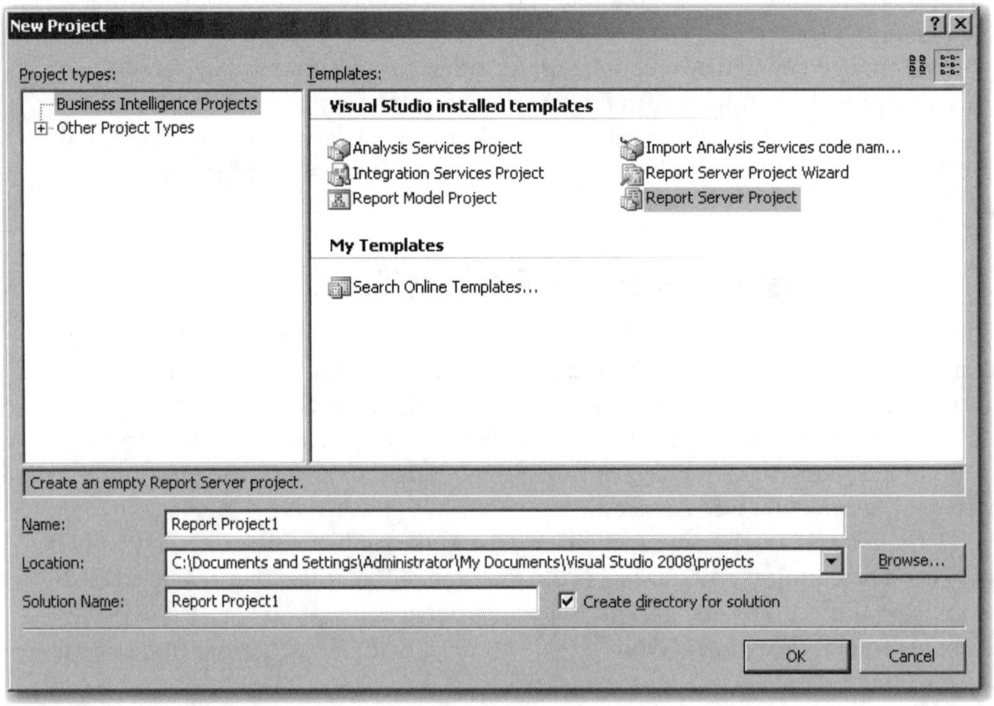

Figure 1-1 *The New Project dialog box*

and what information will be selected from that data. The second set of instructions is the report layout. The *report layout* controls how the information will be presented on the screen or on paper. Both of these sets of instructions are stored using the Report Definition Language.

Figure 1-2 shows this report structure in a little more detail.

Data Definition

The data definition contains two parts: the data source and the dataset. The *data source* is the database server or data file that provides the information for your report. Of course, the data source itself is not included in the report. What is included is the set of instructions the report needs to gain access to that data source. These instructions include the following:

▶ The type of source you will be using for your data (for example, Microsoft SQL Server 2008, Oracle, DB2, Informix, or Microsoft Access). Reporting Services will use this information to determine how to communicate with the data source.

▶ The name of the database server or the path to the data file.

▶ The name of the database.

▶ The login for connecting to this data source, if a login is required.

When the report is executing, it uses the data source instructions contained in the report to gain access to the data source. It then extracts information from the data source into a new format that can be used by the report. This new format is called a *dataset*.

The content of the dataset is defined using a tool called the Query Designer. The *Query Designer* helps you build a database query. The database query may be

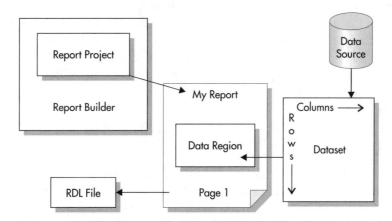

Figure 1-2   *Report structure*

in Transact-Structured Query Language (T-SQL) for querying relational data, Multidimensional Expression language (MDX) for querying multidimensional data, or Data Mining Expression language (DMX) for querying data-mining data. The query provides instructions to the data source, telling it what data you want selected for your report. The query is stored in the report as part of the data definition.

The data selected by the query into the dataset consists of rows and columns. The rows correspond to the records the query selects from the data source. The columns correspond to the fields the query selects from the data source. (MDX queries are flattened into a single table of rows and columns.) Information on the fields to be selected into the dataset is stored in the report as part of the data definition. Only the information on what the fields will be called and the type of data they will hold is stored in the report definition. The actual data is not stored in the report definition, but instead is selected from the data source each time the report is run.

Report Layout

The data that the report has extracted into a dataset is not of much use to you unless you have some way of presenting it to the user. You need to specify which fields go in which locations on the screen or on paper. You also need to add things such as titles, headings, and page numbers. All of this forms the report layout.

In most cases, your report layout will include a special area that interacts with the dataset. This special area is known as a data region. A *data region* displays all the rows in the dataset by repeating a section of the report layout for each row.

Report Definition Language

The information in the data definition and the report layout is stored using the Report Definition Language (RDL). *RDL* is an Extensible Markup Language (XML) standard designed by Microsoft specifically for storing report definitions. This includes the data source instructions, the query information that defines the dataset, and the report layout. When you create a report in the Report Designer, it is saved in a file with an .rdl extension.

If you have not worked with XML, or are not even sure what it is, don't worry. The Report Designer and Reporting Services will take care of all the RDL for you. For those of you who want to learn more about RDL, we'll take a quick peek under the hood in Chapter 7.

Report Designer

Figure 1-3 shows the Report Designer. This is the tool you will use for creating and editing reports throughout this book. We will look at some features of the Report Designer now and discuss them in more detail in Chapter 5 through Chapter 8.

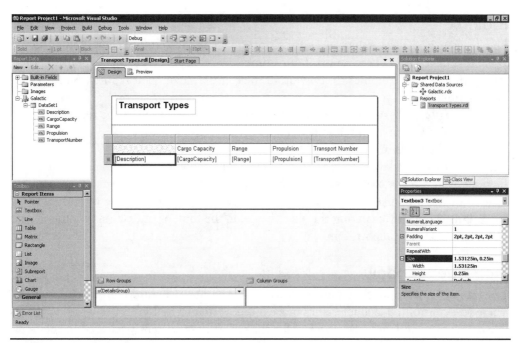

Figure 1-3   *The Report Designer*

Design Surface

The design surface, in the center of Figure 1-3, is where you create your report layout. To do this, you use four of the other areas visible in Figure 1-3: the Report Data window, the Toolbox, the Properties window, and the Grouping pane. You will learn how these work in the following sections. The design surface shares space with the Preview tab. The Preview tab will show you how the report layout and the data combine to create an honest-to-goodness report.

Report Data Window

The Report Data window, in the upper-left corner of Figure 1-3, provides a list of database and other types of fields you can use in your report. The Report Data window makes it easy to add database information to your report layout. Simply drag the desired field from the Report Data window and drop it in the appropriate location on your report layout. The Report Designer takes care of the rest.

Toolbox

The *Toolbox*, in the lower-left corner of Figure 1-3, contains all the report items you use to build your reports. These report items, sometimes called *controls*, are responsible for getting the text and graphics to show up in the right place on your reports. As with any construction project, you can only construct reports properly *after* you learn how to use the tools (report items) in the Toolbox. You learn how to use each of the report items in the Toolbox in Chapters 4, 5, and 6.

As with the fields in the Report Data window, the report items in the Toolbox are placed on the report layout with a simple drag-and-drop. However, whereas fields are pretty much ready to go when they are dropped onto the design surface, report items almost always need some formatting changes to get them just the way you want them. This is done by changing the size, the color, the font, or one of many other characteristics of the report item.

Properties Window

The Properties window, shown in the lower-right corner of Figure 1-3 is the place where you control the characteristics of each report item. The Properties window always shows the characteristics, or *properties*, for the report item currently selected in the design surface. You will see an entry in the Properties window for every aspect of this report item that you can control.

The top of the Properties window shows the name of the selected report item. In Figure 1-3, the text box named "Textbox3" is selected. The left column in the Properties window shows the name of each property that can be changed for that report item. The right column shows the current setting for each of those properties. For example, in Figure 1-3, you can see Textbox3 has a Height of 0.25in.

Grouping Pane

The Grouping pane is at the bottom of the design surface in Figure 1-3. This pane, made up of the row groups area and the column groups area, is where you control how grouping operates within the report. The advanced row grouping and column grouping that are now possible in a report are what make the tablix a powerful tool for creating complex report layouts.

Standalone Report Builder

The Standalone Report Builder is a report authoring environment that exists as its own application, rather than being tucked away inside of the Business Intelligence Development Studio/Visual Studio. The Standalone Report Builder functions

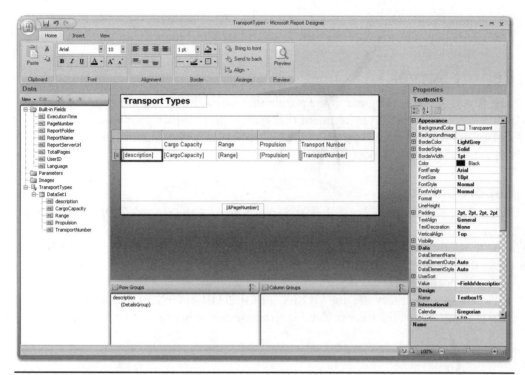

Figure 1-4   *The Standalone Report Builder*

very similar to the Report Designer. Figure 1-4 shows a report being created in the Standalone Report Builder.

The Standalone Report Builder uses the ribbon-style of user interface found in Microsoft Office 2007. This is the main difference between the Report Designer and the Standalone Report Builder. The Standalone Report Builder does not have a Toolbox. Instead, the report items are found on the Insert tab of the ribbon. The other tabs on the ribbon provide additional controls for formatting report items placed on the design surface.

Again, in this book, we will do most of our report authoring using the Report Designer. However, anything you can do in the Report Designer, along the lines of report creation, you can also do in the Standalone Report Builder.

Report-Serving Architecture

Once you finish building your report and have it looking exactly the way you want, it is time to share that report with others. This is the time when your report moves from safe, childhood life inside the Report Designer to its adult life on a Report Server.

This is known as *deploying* or *publishing the report.* Let me assure you, reports pass through deployment much easier than you and I passed through adolescence!

Report Server

The *Report Server* is the piece of the puzzle that makes Reporting Services the product it is. This is the software environment that enables you to share your report with the masses—at least, those masses who have rights to your server. Figure 1-5 shows the basic structure of the Report Server.

Report Catalog

When a report is deployed to a Report Server, a copy of the report's RDL definition is put in that server's Report Catalog. The *Report Catalog* is a set of databases used to store the definitions for all of the reports available on a particular Report Server. It also stores the configuration, security, and caching information necessary for the operation of that Report Server.

Even though you may use any ODBC- or OLE DB-compliant data source to supply data to your reports, the Report Catalog database can only exist in SQL Server 2005

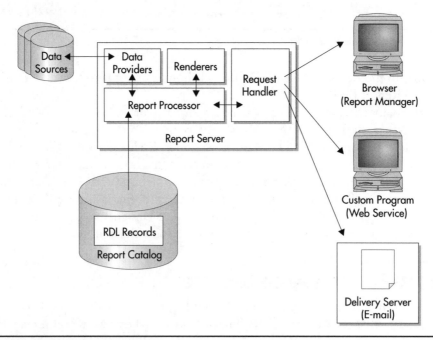

Figure 1-5   *Report Server architecture*

or SQL Server 2008. The Report Catalog database is created as part of the Reporting Services installation process. Except for creating regular backups of any Report Catalog databases, it is probably a good idea to leave the Report Catalog alone.

Report Processor

When a report needs to be executed, the report processor component of the Report Server directs the show. The *report processor* retrieves the report from the Report Catalog and orchestrates the operation of the other components of the Report Server as the report is produced. It takes the output from each of the other components and combines them to create the completed report.

Data Providers

As the report processor encounters dataset definitions in the report RDL, it retrieves the data to populate that dataset. It does this by first following the instructions in the report's data source for connecting to the database server or file that contains the data. The report processor selects a *data provider* that knows how to retrieve information from this type of data source.

The data provider then connects to the source of the data and selects the information required for the report. The data provider returns this information to the report processor, where it is turned into a dataset for use by the report.

Renderers

Once all the data for the report has been collected, the report processor is ready to begin processing the report's layout. To do this, the report processor looks at the format requested. This might be HTML, PDF, TIFF, or one of several other possible formats. The report processor then uses the *renderer* that knows how to produce that format. You will learn more about the capabilities of each of these report formats in Chapter 9.

The renderer works with the report processor to read through the report layout. The report layout is combined with the dataset, and any repeating sections of the report are duplicated for each row in the dataset. This expanded report layout is then translated into the requested output format. The result is a report ready to be sent to the user.

Request Handler

The *request handler* is responsible for receiving requests for reports and passing those requests on to the report processor. Once the report processor has created the requested report, the request handler is also responsible for delivering the completed report. In the next section, you will learn about the various methods the request handler uses for delivering reports.

Report Delivery

We have discussed how a report is created by the Report Server. What we have not discussed is where that report is going after it is created. The report may be sent to a user through the Report Manager website. It may be sent in response to a web service request that came, not from a user, but from another program. It may also be e-mailed to a user who has a subscription to that report.

Report Manager Website

One way for users to request a report from the Report Server is through the *Report Manager* website. This website is created for you when you install Reporting Services. Figure 1-6 shows a screen from the Report Manager website.

The Report Manager website organizes reports into folders. Users can browse through these folders to find the report they need. They can also search the report titles and descriptions to locate a report.

The Report Manager also includes security that can be applied to folders and reports. With this security, the site administrator can create security roles for the users who will be accessing the site. These security roles control which folders and reports a user is allowed to access. You will learn about security when we look at the Report Manager in Chapter 10.

In the Report Manager, reports are always displayed using the HTML format. Once a report has been displayed as an HTML page, the user can then export the report into any of the other available formats.

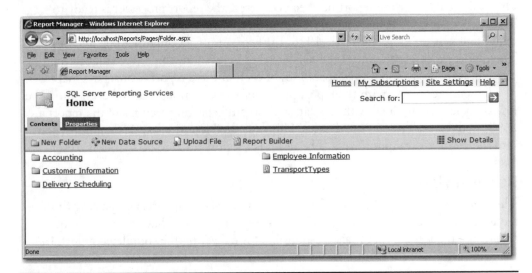

Figure 1-6 *The Report Manager website*

SharePoint/Office Server

SharePoint may also be set up to serve as a means for users to request reports. This can be done in two ways. The first uses the Report Explorer and Report Viewer web parts. These web parts can be used in a SharePoint web application to allow users to navigate report folders and to view reports on a Reporting Services report server.

The Report Explorer and Report Viewer web parts were originally made available as part of SQL Server 2000 Reporting Services Service Pack 2. They were part of SQL Server 2005 Reporting Services as well. The web parts continue to be available in the 2008 release, but their functionality has not been upgraded to take advantage of new features and functionality.

The second means of utilizing Reporting Services through SharePoint involves a tight integration of the two products. In this configuration, a Windows SharePoint Services 3.0 or Office SharePoint Server 2007 installation will actually become the host for the report server's Report Catalog. In addition, the SharePoint user interface replaces the Report Manager website as the user interface for locating and viewing reports, as well as for managing the report server. Accessing reports through SharePoint integration is as easy and intuitive as accessing any other document on the SharePoint site.

Subscription Delivery

If the users do not want to go to the report, the request handler can make the report go to them. In other words, users do not necessarily need to come to the Report Manager website to receive a report. They can have the report delivered to them through a subscription service. The Report Manager enables users to locate a report on the site and then subscribe to it so it will be delivered to them in the future.

When users subscribe to a report, they provide an e-mail address to which the report will be delivered, either as the body of the e-mail or as an e-mail attachment, depending on the requested format. Users can specify the format for the report at the time they create their subscription.

The site administrator can also set up report subscriptions. These function like a mass mailing, using a list of e-mail addresses. Rather than requiring each user to access the Report Manager to create their own subscription, the site administrator can create one subscription that is delivered to every user in the list.

Web Service Interface

In addition to delivering reports to humans, either at their request or on a subscription basis, the request handler can deliver reports to other software applications. This is done through a series of web services. A *web service* is a mechanism that allows programs to communicate with each other over the Internet.

A program calls a web service on the Report Server, requesting a particular report in a particular format. The request handler relays this request to the report processor, just like any other request for a report. The completed report is returned to the program that originated the request as the response to the web service request.

Web services use a standard called Simple Object Access Protocol (SOAP). *SOAP* is supported by both Windows and non-Windows environments, so a program running on a non-Windows computer that supports SOAP can receive a report created by Reporting Services.

Diving In

Now that you have been introduced to all of the capabilities of Reporting Services, I hope you are ready to dive in and make it work for you. In the next chapter, you will learn about the installation and setup of Reporting Services. If Reporting Services has already been installed, you can skip ahead to Chapter 3.

In Chapter 3, we make sure you have a firm understanding of database basics before getting to the actual building of reports in Chapter 4. Chapter 3 also introduces you to Galactic Delivery Services (GDS), the company we use as a case study throughout the remainder of the book. Even if your database skills are tip-top, you should spend a few minutes in Chapter 3 to get to know GDS.

Chapter 2

Putting the Pieces in Place: Installing Reporting Services

In This Chapter

▶ **Preparing for the Installation**

▶ **The Installation Process**

▶ **Common Installation Issues**

▶ **Spending Some Time in Basic Training**

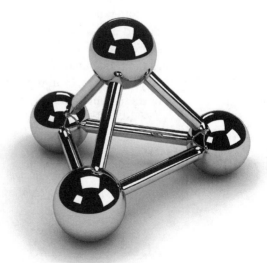

Before you can begin to enjoy all the benefits of Reporting Services discussed in Chapter 1, you of course have to install the Reporting Services software. Reporting Services installs as part of the SQL Server 2008 installation. Before you begin the installation process, however, it is important to understand the structure of Reporting Services.

In this chapter, you will learn about the components that make up Reporting Services and the three licensed editions of Reporting Services offered by Microsoft. Next, you will find out how the components are combined in different types of Reporting Services installations and see how to plan for each installation type. As part of that planning, you will learn about the software that must be in place prior to installing Reporting Services. After considering these preliminaries, we will walk you through the installation process.

Preparing for the Installation

The most important part of the Reporting Services installation is not what you do as you run the setup program, but what you do before you begin. In this section, we discuss the knowledge you need and the steps you should take to prepare for installation. With the proper plan in place, your Reporting Services installation should go smoothly and you can create reports in no time.

The Parts of the Whole

Reporting Services is not a single program that runs on a computer to produce reports. Instead, it is a number of applications, utilities, and databases that work together to create a report management environment. As you plan your Reporting Services installation, it is important that you understand a little bit about each piece of the puzzle and how all these pieces work together to create a complete system.

Figure 2-1 shows all the parts that make up a complete Reporting Services installation. Each part has a specific role to play in the development, management, and delivery of reports, or in the management of the Reporting Services environment itself. All of these items can be installed as part of the SQL Server 2008 installation process.

Let's take a look at each part and see how it fits into the whole.

NOTE

Not all Reporting Services installations include all of the items shown in Figure 2-1. The following sections of this chapter discuss the various types of installations and which components they include.

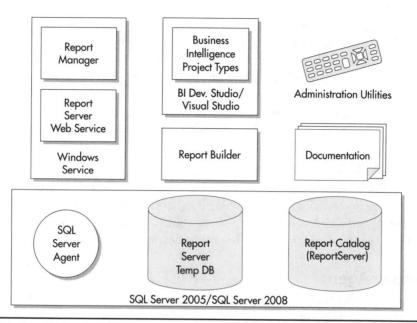

Figure 2-1   *Reporting Services component parts*

The Windows Service

The Reporting Services *Windows service* is the heart of Reporting Services and is, of course, installed as part of the Reporting Services installation. This service is responsible for the two main interfaces with the report server. First, it contains the application that implements the Report Manager website. Second, it provides a web service interface for programmatic interaction with the report server.

As discussed in Chapter 1, the Report Manager website provides a user interface for requesting reports and managing the report server. The Report Server web service provides a programmatic interface for requesting reports. It also provides an interface for report server administration.

In addition to these two interfaces, the Reporting Services Windows service provides the engine responsible for report rendering. This is true whether the report is requested through the Report Manager website, the report server web service, or subscription delivery. As you saw in Figure 1-5 of Chapter 1, this includes fetching the report definition, retrieving the data used in the report, and rendering the report in the desired format.

Administration Utilities

The administration utilities are tools for managing the Reporting Services Windows service and for making changes to its configuration. The main administration utility is the *Reporting Services Configuration Manager*. This tool provides a convenient method for examining and modifying the configuration settings of a Reporting Services installation. You learn about the Reporting Services Configuration Manager in more detail in the section "The Reporting Services Configuration Manager," later in this chapter.

The administration utilities can be run on the computer that is hosting the Reporting Services Windows service to manage the configuration on that computer. Most of the administrative utilities can also be used to manage a Reporting Services Windows service that is running on another computer. This is called *remote administration.*

SQL Server 2005/SQL Server 2008

Either SQL Server 2005 or SQL Server 2008 is required to hold the database where Reporting Services stores its Report Catalog database. Reporting Services also uses the SQL Server Agent, which you will learn about shortly. In addition, databases in SQL Server can be used as data sources for Reporting Services reports.

SQL Server Agent

SQL Server Agent is part of SQL Server and is created as part of the SQL Server installation process. It is used by SQL Server to execute jobs scheduled to run at a certain time. These jobs might back up a database or transfer information from one database to another. Jobs may be scheduled to run once, or they may run on a regular basis, such as once a day or once a week.

Reporting Services also uses the SQL Server Agent to execute scheduled jobs. These jobs are used to run reports and distribute the results. In Chapter 1, you learned about users who subscribe to a report. When users subscribe to a report, they ask for it to be run and delivered to them on a regular basis. When a user creates a subscription, Reporting Services creates a SQL Server Agent job to handle that subscription.

For example, our production manager in Chapter 1 wanted an inventory report to be printed every four hours during the workday. He subscribes to the inventory report and creates a delivery schedule of 8:15 A.M., 12:15 P.M., and 4:15 P.M. When this subscription is created, Reporting Services creates a SQL Server Agent job scheduled to run at 8:15 A.M., 12:15 P.M., and 4:15 P.M. each day. When the job runs, it instructs the Reporting Services Windows service to run the report and e-mail it to the production manager.

The Report Server and Report Server Temp DB Databases

During the Reporting Services installation process, two databases are created within SQL Server: the Report Server and Report Server Temp DB databases. The *Report Server database* is used to store the Report Catalog. (Recall from Chapter 1 that the Report Catalog holds the information about all of the reports deployed to a Report Server.) The Report Server database also holds information about the virtual structure that contains these reports. This includes such things as the folder structure displayed by the Report Manager and the security settings for each folder and report.

As the name implies, the *Report Server Temp DB database* is used as temporary storage for Reporting Services operations. Information can be stored here to track the current users on the Report Manager website. Short-term copies of some of the most recently executed reports are also stored here in what is known as the *execution cache*.

Sample Reports and the AdventureWorks Database

In previous versions of SQL Server, the sample code and sample database could be installed as part of the SQL Server installation process. Beginning with SQL Server 2008, the samples are now downloaded from the Internet. From the Start menu, select All Programs | Microsoft SQL Server 2008 | Documentation and Tutorials | Microsoft SQL Server Sample Overview for instructions on downloading and installation.

Business Intelligence Development Studio/Visual Studio/ Standalone Report Builder

As discussed in Chapter 1, Reporting Services reports are created using the Business Intelligence Development Studio, Visual Studio, or the Standalone Report Builder. All of these report development environments function exactly the same. There is no difference between a report created in the Business Intelligence Development Studio, Visual Studio, or the Standalone Report Builder.

If you are going to use the Business Intelligence Development Studio for creating reports, you need to install it as part of the Reporting Services installation process. The same is true with the Standalone Report Builder. If you plan to create reports using Visual Studio, you need to purchase and install it separately. Visual Studio does not come with Reporting Services.

Documentation

The final piece of Reporting Services is the documentation. The bulk of this documentation is found in the SQL Server Books Online. After Reporting Services is installed, you can view the SQL Server Books Online through your Start menu. You'll find it under All Programs | Microsoft SQL Server 2008 | Documentation and Tutorials | SQL Server Books Online. There is also a set of help screens for the Report Manager interface that can be accessed through the Report Manager website.

Editions of Reporting Services

Reporting Services can be licensed in five different editions: Workgroup Edition, Web Edition, Standard Edition, Enterprise Edition, and Developer Edition. There is also an Evaluation Edition, which does not require a license, but it can only be used for a limited time. We won't be discussing the Evaluation Edition in this book, but you can think of it as essentially being a Developer Edition you get to try out for free.

Reporting Services is licensed as part of your SQL Server 2008 license. Therefore, in a production environment, the Reporting Services edition you are licensed to use is the same as the SQL Server 2008 edition you are licensed to use. For example, if you have a Standard Edition of SQL Server 2008, you are only licensed for the Standard Edition of Reporting Services.

The Workgroup, Web, and Standard Editions

All editions of Reporting Services provide a rich environment for report authoring, report management, and report delivery. The Workgroup Edition of SQL Server is designed for smaller enterprises. It does not include all of the business intelligence and high-availability features you find in the Standard and Enterprise Editions. The Web Edition is to be used in conjunction with web hosting. However, as far as Reporting Services is concerned, the Workgroup, Web, and Standard Editions are almost identical. Just a few of the more advanced features of Reporting Services are not included in the Standard Edition. These advanced features are listed in the following section, "The Enterprise Edition."

The Enterprise Edition

The Enterprise Edition of Reporting Services includes the following advanced features:

▶ **Data-Driven Subscriptions**   Send a report to a number of users from a predefined mailing list. Data-driven subscriptions are discussed in Chapter 11.

▶ **Scale-Out Deployment**   Configure several Reporting Services Windows services running on multiple computers to point to a single SQL Server 2005 or 2008 server hosting the Report Catalog. The scale-out deployment is discussed in the section "Types of Reporting Services Installations."

▶ **Advanced Server Support**   Utilize multiple symmetric multiprocessing to support more than four processors and additional memory support to handle more than 2 gigabytes (GB) of random access memory (RAM).

▶ **Ad Hoc Report Builder Infinite Clickthrough Reports**   Explore data relationships in a model of the underlying database through ad hoc reports. The Ad Hoc Report Builder is discussed in detail in Appendix C.

The Developer Edition

The Developer Edition provides support for all of the features of the Enterprise Edition. The Developer Edition does not, however, require that you have an Enterprise Edition license of SQL Server 2008. Of course, the Developer Edition is only for development and testing. It cannot be used in a production environment.

Types of Reporting Services Installations

Now that you are familiar with the components that make up Reporting Services and the ways that Microsoft licenses it, you can give some thought to just what your Reporting Services installation will look like. The first decision you need to make is which of the components you want to install. Although you can choose to include or exclude items in any combination you like, in the end, only three combinations make sense: the full installation, the server installation, and the report author installation.

In addition to these are a couple of specialized installation types. These are the distributed installation and the scale-out installation. These installations are for high-end, high-volume Reporting Services sites. We will discuss these configurations briefly, so you are familiar with the variety of ways that Reporting Services can be configured.

The Full Installation

The full installation, as the name implies, is the "everything including the kitchen sink" installation. All of the items shown in Figure 2-1 and discussed previously are included in this installation. Nothing is left out.

The full installation is most likely to be used in a development environment. This might be on a server used by a group of developers or on a power workstation used by a single developer. In either case, we want to have all the bells and whistles available to us as we figure out how to best use Reporting Services to suit our business needs.

The Server Installation

The server installation is most likely used when we're setting up Reporting Services on a production server. On a production server, we only want those items that are going to be used to deliver reports or to help us manage Reporting Services. We don't want to include anything that will take up space unnecessarily. Figure 2-2 shows the items included in the server installation.

The server installation includes the Reporting Services Windows service and the administration utilities used to manage it. As we discussed earlier, the Reporting Services Windows service provides the Report Manager website and the Report Server web service for managing and delivering reports. In addition, Reporting Services will need the SQL Server Agent, the Report Server database, and the Report Server Temp DB database for its operations.

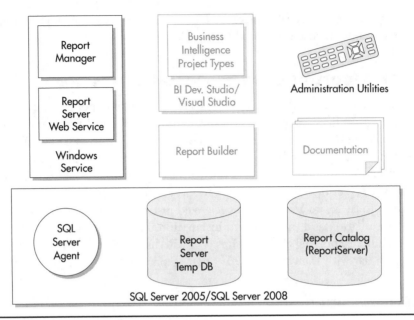

Figure 2-2 *The server installation*

We won't be doing any development work on the production server, so we will not need the Business Intelligence Development Studio, Visual Studio, or the Standalone Report Builder. It is possible that you would want the documentation on the production server for questions on managing Reporting Services. Probably a better idea, though, is to have the documentation handy on a development computer and to keep the production installation as uncluttered as possible. The same can be said for the sample reports and the AdventureWorks database. You may want these on your production server for demonstration purposes, but, again, it is probably better to do this on a different computer and reserve your production server for reports and data required by your users.

The Report Author Installation

The report author installation is for individuals who are creating Reporting Services reports but not doing heavy-duty development. These report authors may even be creating ad hoc reports and require more capabilities than those available in the Ad Hoc Report Builder. Report authors will not be creating full-blown applications that incorporate Reporting Services as part of a larger business system. The items included in the report author installation are shown here.

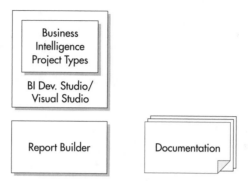

Report authors need the capability to create and preview reports. This capability is found in the Business Intelligence Development Studio, Visual Studio, or the Standalone Report Builder. Report authors may also want access to the Reporting Services Books Online to look up information as they create reports. (Although, in my humble opinion, this book would serve as a better resource.) When report authors have completed their reports and are ready to have others use them, they will deploy the reports to a production Reporting Services server.

The Distributed Installation

In a distributed installation, the Reporting Services items discussed are not installed on a single computer. Instead, they are split between two computers that work together to create a complete Reporting Services system. One computer runs SQL Server 2005 or SQL Server 2008 and hosts the Report Catalog databases. This is the database server. The other computer runs the Reporting Services Windows service. This is the report server.

Figure 2-3 shows a distributed installation. Note that this figure shows the servers and the report designer workstations. It does not show computers used for viewing reports.

The distributed installation has advantages when it comes to scalability. Because the workload of the server applications—SQL Server and the Reporting Services Windows service—is divided between two servers, it can serve reports to a larger number of simultaneous users. The disadvantage of this type of installation is that it is more complex to install and administer. However, if you need a high-volume solution, it is certainly worth the effort to obtain one that will provide satisfactory response times under a heavy workload.

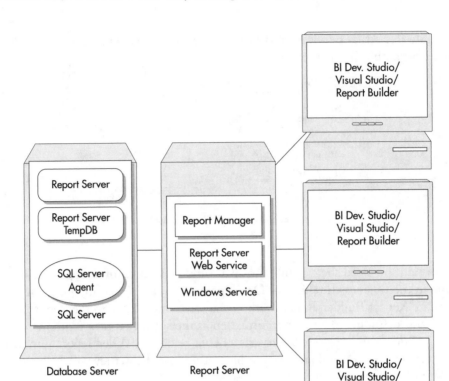

Figure 2-3 *A distributed installation of Reporting Services*

The Scale-Out Installation

The scale-out installation is a specialized form of the distributed installation, as shown in Figure 2-4. In a scale-out installation, a single database server interacts with several report servers. Each of the report servers uses the same Report Catalog databases for its information. By using additional report servers, we can handle even more simultaneous users with the scale-out installation than we could with the distributed installation.

Again, note that Figure 2-4 shows only the servers and the report designer workstations. It does not show computers used for viewing reports.

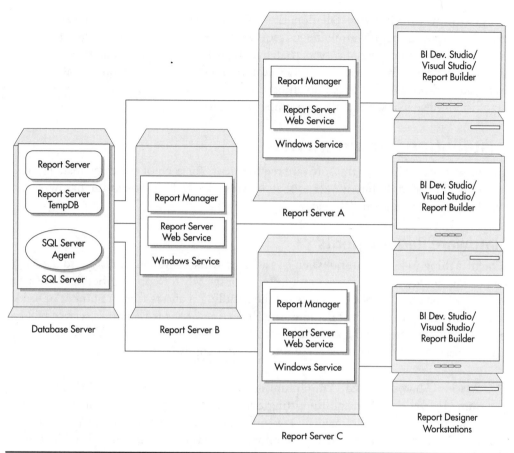

Figure 2-4   *A scale-out installation of Reporting Services*

When report designers create reports, they can deploy them to any of the report servers. No matter which server is used, the reports will end up in the single Report Server database. Once the reports are in the Report Server database, they can be delivered by any of the report servers. In addition, because all of the information about the Report Manager is stored in the Report Server database, any changes to the Report Manager configuration made on one server will take effect on all the servers.

For example, suppose an administrator uses the Report Manager website to access the Report Manager through Report Server A. The administrator creates a new folder in Report Manager called Sales Forecasts 2009, sets the security so the sales staff can access this folder, and places the Sales Forecast report in the folder. Immediately after the administrator is finished, a salesperson brings up Report Manager through Report Server C. The salesperson can browse the contents of the Sales Forecasts 2009 folder and will be able to run the Sales Forecast report.

As with the distributed installation, the scale-out installation provides a way to handle a large number of simultaneous requests for reports. Even though the scale-out installation uses a number of servers to deliver reports, it allows the Report Manager interface to be administered without duplication of effort. The scale-out installation may take additional effort to get up and running, but once it is ready to go, it provides an efficient means of serving a large number of users.

Installation Requirements

In this section, we itemize the software requirements for each of the three installation types just discussed. Before we get to that, however, let's take a look at the hardware requirements for Reporting Services.

Hardware Requirements

The first thing to keep in mind when considering what computer hardware to use for Reporting Services is this: Bigger and faster is better. With Reporting Services, we are dealing with a server application that will be handling requests from a number of users at the same time. In most installations, the Reporting Services Windows service will be sharing processor time and computer memory with SQL Server 2008. We need to have enough server power so both of these systems can happily coexist.

Processor   Microsoft's stated minimum processor is a 600-megahertz (MHz) Pentium III. You should install Reporting Services on this type of computer only if you are a patient person. A more realistic low end is probably a Pentium III at 1 gigahertz (GHz). This is true even for the report author installation. The Business Intelligence Development Studio and Visual Studio demand a fair amount of horsepower to keep them from being sluggish.

Computer Memory   Microsoft's minimum requirement for computer memory is 512 megabytes (MB). This is, indeed, a bare minimum. If you are running the Reporting Services Windows service on the same server with SQL Server, that minimum should probably go up to 2GB.

Disk Space   A server installation of Reporting Services requires a minimum of 120MB of disk space. This does not include the space required for SQL Server 2008. Consult the Microsoft website for information on the disk space requirements for these items.

A report author installation requires a minimum of 1.1GB of disk space. Plan on using an additional 145MB if you are downloading and installing the sample reports. Taken all together, you are going to need a minimum of 1.3GB of disk space for a full installation of Reporting Services.

Remember, these requirements are minimums. Also, keep in mind that they do not include the space required for reports to be deployed to the server or project files created by the Report Designer. A Reporting Services installation is not useful if there is no room for reports.

Software Requirements

SQL Server 2008 Reporting Services will run on the following operating systems:

- ▶ Windows Vista Ultimate Edition (32-bit or 64-bit)
- ▶ Windows Vista Home Premium Edition (32-bit or 64-bit)
- ▶ Windows Vista Home Basic Edition (32-bit or 64-bit)
- ▶ Windows Vista Enterprise Edition (32-bit or 64-bit)
- ▶ Windows Vista Business Edition (32-bit or 64-bit)
- ▶ Windows Server 2008 Standard Edition (32-bit or 64-bit)
- ▶ Windows Server 2008 Data Center Edition (32-bit or 64-bit)
- ▶ Windows Server 2008 Enterprise Edition (32-bit or 64-bit)
- ▶ Windows Server 2003 SP1 (32-bit or 64-bit)
- ▶ Windows Server 2003 Enterprise Edition SP1 (32-bit or 64-bit)
- ▶ Windows XP Professional SP2

The following software must be installed and running properly on your computer before you can complete a server installation:

- ▶ Microsoft Windows Installer 3.1 or later
- ▶ Microsoft Data Access Components (MDAC) 2.8 SP1 or later
- ▶ Microsoft .NET Framework version 3.5

Microsoft .NET Framework 3.5 will be installed as the first step in the SQL Server 2008 installation process if it is not already present on the target computer.

Other Installation Considerations

You need to keep several other tidbits of information in mind as you plan your Reporting Services installation. Many of these items are listed here.

Distributed Installation and Scale-Out Installation Considerations

If you create a distributed installation, the report server and the database server must be in the same domain or in domains that have a trust relationship. If you create a scale-out installation, all the report servers and the database server must be in the same domain or in domains that have a trust relationship.

Database Server Considerations

The following are a couple of things to keep in mind as you are determining which server will host the Reporting Services databases:

▶ The Report Server and Report Server Temp DB databases must be hosted by SQL Server 2005 or SQL Server 2008. They cannot be hosted by an earlier version of SQL Server.

▶ If you do not want to use the default name for the Reporting Services database (ReportServer), you can specify a different name. The database name you specify must be 117 characters or fewer.

E-mail (SMTP) Server

If you are going to allow users to subscribe to reports and have them e-mailed, you need to specify the address of a Simple Mail Transfer Protocol (SMTP) server using the Reporting Services Configuration Manager. *SMTP* is the standard for exchanging e-mail across the Internet. You need to specify the address of an e-mail server that will accept e-mail messages from the report server and send them to the appropriate recipients.

In many cases, the address of your e-mail server is the same as the portion of your e-mail address that comes after the @ sign, prefaced by www. For example, if your e-mail address is MyEmail@Galactic.com, your e-mail server's address is probably either www.Galactic.com or smtp.Galactic.com. Be sure to verify the address of your e-mail server with your e-mail administrator. Also, make sure this e-mail server supports the SMTP protocol and that it will accept and forward mail originating from other servers on your network.

Encrypting Reporting Services Information

One of the options you may specify in the Reporting Services Configuration Manager is a requirement to use a Secure Sockets Layer (SSL) connection when accessing the Report Manager website and the Report Server web service. When an SSL connection is used, all of the data transmitted across the network is encrypted, so it cannot be intercepted and read by anyone else. This is important if your reports contain sensitive personal or financial information.

To use SSL on a server, the server must have a server certificate. Server certificates are purchased from a certificate authority and installed on your server. You can find information on certificate authorities on the Internet.

Each server certificate is associated with a specific Uniform Resource Locator (URL). To use SSL with the Report Manager website and the Report Server web service, your server certificate must be associated with the URL that corresponds to the default website on the server. If www.MyRSServer.com takes you to the default website on your server, then the server certificate must be associated with www.MyRSServer.com. If you plan to require an SSL connection, you should obtain and install the appropriate server certificate prior to installing Reporting Services.

When you require the use of an SSL connection to access the Report Manager website and the Report Server web service, your users must specify a slightly different URL to access these locations. For instance, if the users would normally use http://www.MyRSServer.com/Reports to get to the Report Manager website, they will now have to use https://www.MyRSServer.com/Reports. The https in place of the http creates the SSL connection.

Login Accounts

The login account you are logged in as when you run the setup program must have administrative rights on the computer where the installation is being done. If you are doing a distributed or scale-out installation, the login account must have administrative rights on the computer that will be the report server and have SQL Server administrator rights on the database server.

The login account you are logged in as must also have system administration rights in the SQL Server installation that will contain the Report Catalog. The setup program uses this login to access SQL Server and create the items necessary for the Report Catalog. You may specify a different login, either a SQL login or a Windows login, for the Report Server to use when accessing the Report Catalog after the installation is complete.

You will be asked to specify two other login accounts during the Reporting Services installation and in the Reporting Services Configuration Manager. Make your choices ahead of time and track down any passwords you may need before you begin the installation process.

The Reporting Services Windows Service Account   During the installation process, you will be asked to specify the login account used by the Reporting Services Windows service. If you are installing the SQL Server database engine or other SQL components as part of the same installation, you will be asked for login accounts for each of the necessary Windows services at the same time. You can choose from the following types of accounts:

▶ **The built-in account NT AUTHORITY\SYSTEM (also called the local system account)**   The local system account has access to almost all resources on the local computer and may or may not have access to resources on other computers in the network. You do not need to supply a password if you use this account.

▶ **The built-in account NT AUTHORITY\NETWORK SERVICE (also called the network service account)**   This account exists on Windows server operating systems for running services. The difference between this account and the local service account is that this account has rights on the network and can access other servers on the network. You do not need to supply a password if you use this account.

▶ **A domain user account**   This is a regular user account that exists in the domain in which this server resides. You will need to know both the login name and the password.

Microsoft recommends the network service account be used as the login account for the Report Server service. Using the network service account ensures the Report Server service has all the rights it needs on the local server.

The Report Server Database Credentials   In the Reporting Services Configuration Manager, you can specify the report server database credentials. These credentials are used by the Reporting Services Windows service to log in to SQL Server and to access the Report Server database, the Report Server Temp DB database, and the SQL Server Agent. As noted earlier, this login account is used after the installation is complete. It is not used to access SQL Server during the installation process.

You have two options:

▶ The login account used by the Reporting Services Windows service

▶ A SQL Server login

You need to work with the database administrator of your SQL Server to determine which of these options to use.

NOTE

If a SQL Server login is used, it is recommended that you not use the sa login. The SQL Server login must be added to the RSExecRole role in the ReportServer, ReportServerTempDB, master, and msdb databases. This will be done automatically by the Reporting Services Configuration Manager.

Running the SQL Server Installation Program

When you run the SQL Server installation program, you need to run it under a login that is a member of the local system administrators group. In addition, your login needs to have administrator permissions in SQL Server so you can perform the following tasks:

▶ Create SQL logins

▶ Create SQL roles

▶ Create databases

▶ Assign roles to logins

The Installation Process

Now that you have worked through all of the preparation, it is finally time to install Reporting Services. This is done through the SQL Server 2008 setup program, either at the time SQL Server 2008 is originally installed or later, as an addition to an existing SQL Server installation. In this section, you will see the portions of the SQL Server 2008 installation dealing with Reporting Services and learn about the option selections necessary for the various types of Reporting Services installations discussed earlier in this chapter. You will also look at the Reporting Services configuration, which must be done after the installation is complete. This additional configuration is done using the Reporting Services Configuration Manager.

The SQL Server 2008 Installation

If you are doing a full, server, distributed, or scale-out installation of Reporting Services, the setup program must be run on the computer that will serve as the report server. This is the computer that will be running the Reporting Services Windows service and hosting Report Manager and the Report Server web service. If you are doing a report author installation, the setup program must be run on the computer you will be using for report authoring.

NOTE

If you are creating reports using Visual Studio, you do not need to run the SQL Server 2008 setup on the computer you are using for report authoring. The Business Intelligence project types are installed as part of the Visual Studio setup. You need to run the SQL Server 2008 setup on your report authoring computer only if you are using the Business Intelligence Development Studio or the Standalone Report Builder for report creation.

If you are doing a distributed or scale-out installation, you do not need to run the Reporting Services setup program on the database server. You will, of course, need to install SQL Server 2005 or SQL Server 2008 on the database server prior to doing the Reporting Services installation, but you do not need to run the Reporting Services portion of the setup program on that computer. The Reporting Services setup program on the report server will access the database server and take care of all the necessary installation and setup remotely.

Begin the installation by inserting the SQL Server 2008 installation CD into the CD or DVD drive. In most cases, the autorun process should take you to the Start screen. If this does not happen automatically, double-click the setup.exe file in the Servers folder on the installation CD. Use the Planning page to ensure you have all the necessary hardware and software prerequisites.

When you are ready to begin the actual installation, select New SQL Server stand-alone installation or add features to an existing installation from the Installation page as shown in Figure 2-5.

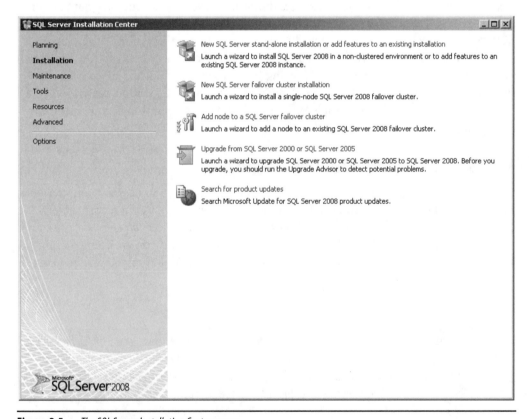

Figure 2-5   *The SQL Server Installation Center screen*

Preliminaries

The setup process begins with the usual preliminaries. You must read and accept the SQL Server licensing agreement. The setup will also double-check to make sure all the prerequisite software is installed and properly configured. Of course, you also need to enter the product key.

The Feature Selection Page

Once all this groundwork is complete, you get to the good stuff. On the Feature Selection page of the Installation Wizard, you can determine which components of SQL Server to install. The following sections show which items to select on the Feature Selection page for each type of installation.

Reporting Services Full Installation   On the Feature Selection page, select the following for a Reporting Services full installation:

- ▶ Database Engine Services, if you do not already have a SQL Server 2005 or a SQL Server 2008 server available to host the Report Catalog

- ▶ Reporting Services

- ▶ Business Intelligence Development Studio

- ▶ Client Tools Connectivity

- ▶ SQL Server Books Online

- ▶ Management Tools - Basic and Management Tools - Complete

The Feature Selection page should appear as shown in Figure 2-6. Click Next to continue with the SQL Server Installation Wizard.

NOTE
You may want to select other items on the Feature Selection page if you are installing other SQL Server components as part of this process. The items documented here represent the minimum for a Reporting Services full installation.

Reporting Services Server Installation   On the Feature Selection page, select the following for a Reporting Services server installation:

- ▶ Database Engine Services, if you do not already have a SQL Server 2005 or a SQL Server 2008 server available to host the Report Catalog

- ▶ Reporting Services

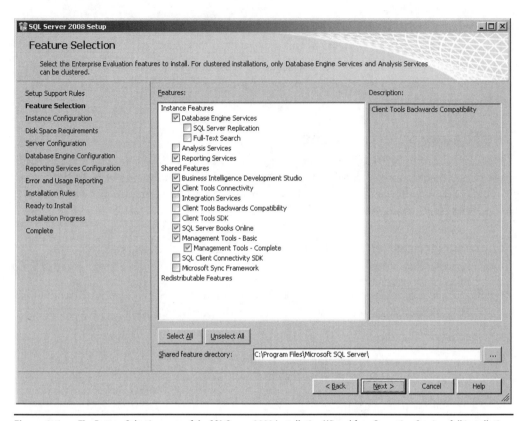

Figure 2-6   *The Feature Selection page of the SQL Server 2008 Installation Wizard for a Reporting Services full installation*

▶   Client Tools Connectivity

▶   Management Tools - Basic and Management Tools - Complete

The Feature Selection page should appear as shown in Figure 2-7. Click Next to continue with the SQL Server Installation Wizard.

NOTE

You may want to select other items on the Feature Selection page if you are installing other SQL Server components as part of this process. The items documented here represent the minimum for a Reporting Services server installation.

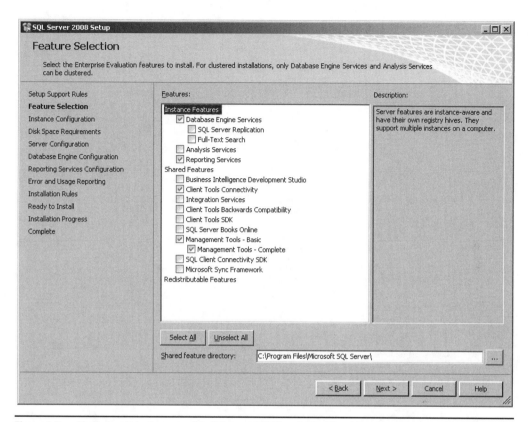

Figure 2-7   *The Feature Selection page of the SQL Server 2008 Installation Wizard for a Reporting Services server installation*

Reporting Services Report Author Installation   On the Feature Selection page, select the following for a Reporting Services report author installation:

▶ Business Intelligence Development Studio

▶ Client Tools Connectivity

▶ SQL Server Books Online

▶ Management Tools - Basic and Management Tools - Complete

The Feature Selection page should appear as shown in Figure 2-8. Click Next to continue with the SQL Server Installation Wizard.

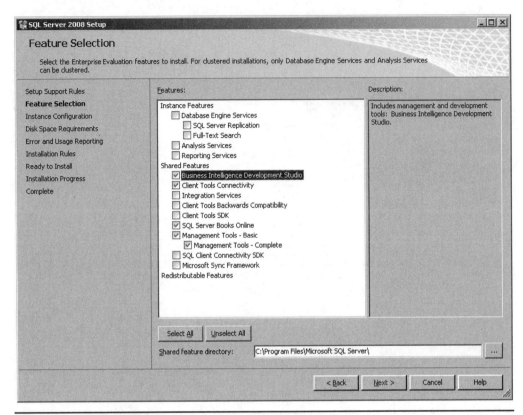

Figure 2-8 *The Feature Selection page of the SQL Server 2008 Installation Wizard for a Reporting Services report author installation*

Reporting Services Distributed Installation and Scale-out Installation Before completing the Reporting Services portion of a distributed or scale-out installation, you must have either SQL Server 2005 or SQL Server 2008 running on the computer that will serve as the database server. Remember, the Enterprise Edition of Reporting Services is required for a scale-out installation. On the Feature Selection page, select the following for a Reporting Services distributed installation or a scale-out installation:

► Reporting Services

► Client Tools Connectivity

► Management Tools - Basic and Management Tools - Complete

The Feature Selection page should appear as shown in Figure 2-9. Click Next to continue with the SQL Server Installation Wizard.

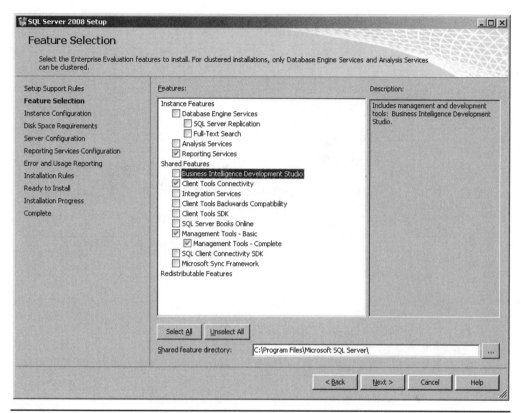

Figure 2-9   *The Feature Selection page of the SQL Server 2008 Installation Wizard for a Reporting Services distributed installation or scale-out installation*

Instance Configuration Page

The Instance Configuration page, shown in Figure 2-10, enables you to choose the name assigned to this instance of the components you are installing, including Reporting Services. The default instance will use Reports as the name of the Report Manager website and ReportServer as the name of the Reporting Services web service. If you specify an instance name, by default an underscore (_) followed by the instance name is appended to the end of the website and web service name. For example, if you specify an instance name of "RS2008," the website will be "Reports_RS2008" and the web service will be "ReportServer_RS2008."

You can see all the instances of SQL Server components currently installed on this computer in the grid at the bottom of the Instance Configuration page. Of course, your new instance name cannot be exactly the same name as any existing instance. Unless you have a reason to change the instance name from the default, such as multiple Reporting Services instances on a single server, it is probably a good idea to stick with the default.

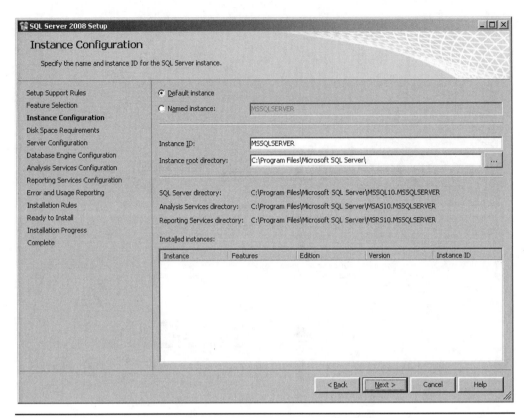

Figure 2-10   *The Instance Configuration page*

After you have entered the instance name, or if you have decided to use the default instance, click Next to continue with the SQL Server Installation Wizard.

Server Configuration Page

The Server Configuration page is shown in Figure 2-11. This page enables you to specify the Windows credentials the Reporting Services Windows service is to run under. The content of this screen will vary, depending on the SQL Server 2008 components you chose to install. The options available here were discussed previously in the "The Reporting Services Windows Service Account" section of this chapter. This page also enables you to select the startup type of each of the services being installed. If SQL Server was included as part of this install, SQL Server Agent should be changed to the Automatic startup type.

After you make your selections on this page, click Next to continue with the SQL Server Installation Wizard.

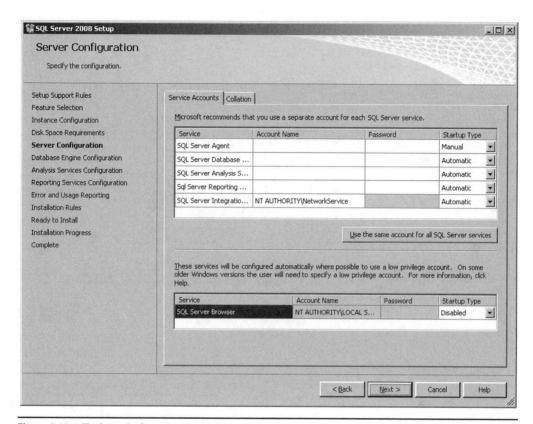

Figure 2-11   *The Server Configuration page*

The Reporting Services Configuration Page

After leaving the Server Configuration page, you may encounter several pages that deal with the setup of the SQL Server database engine and other SQL Server components, depending on the items you selected on the Feature Selection page. Make the appropriate choices for your SQL Server installation. Click Next to move from one page to the next.

Eventually, you will come to the Reporting Services Configuration page, shown in Figure 2-12. If SQL Server was selected on the Feature Selection page and you are installing the default instance, this page provides you with three choices for configuring your Reporting Services installation:

▶   Install the native mode default configuration

▶   Install the SharePoint integrated mode default configuration

▶   Install, but do not configure the report server

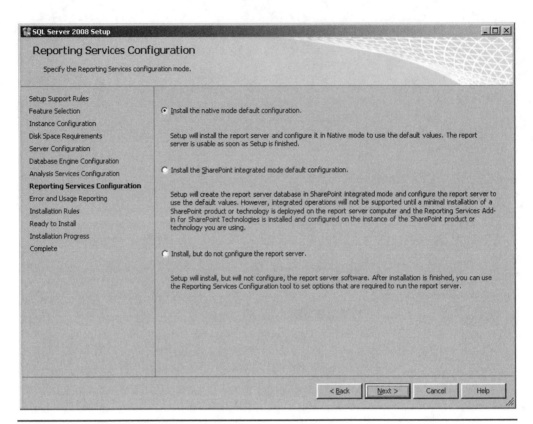

Figure 2-12   *The Reporting Services Configuration page*

If SQL Server was not selected on the Feature Selection page, or if you are not installing the default instance, you will not have a choice; the Install, but do not configure the report server option will be selected for you.

The Install the SharePoint integrated mode default configuration option is used if you intend to use SharePoint integration for hosting Reporting Services. If the Install, but do not configure the report server option is chosen, your new Reporting Services installation will need to be configured using the Reporting Services Configuration Manager utility program. You will learn more about this utility program in the upcoming section, "The Reporting Services Configuration Manager."

This may seem like a rather limiting set of choices, sort of an all-or-nothing proposition, but it is not. For the majority of Reporting Services installations, the native mode default configuration will do just fine. Only rarely, for distributed or scale-out installations, or for non-default instances, do you need to change the default configuration settings.

The default configuration settings are:

▶ Web service name is ReportServer.

▶ Report Manager website is Reports.

▶ The Report Catalog is hosted by the default instance of SQL Server 2008 being created by this installation process. (This is why the choice Install the Native mode default configuration is disabled when you are not installing SQL Server at the same time.)

▶ The login account used by the Reporting Services Windows service is used as the credentials for accessing the report server database (Report Catalog).

After you make your selection on this page, click Next to continue with the SQL Server Installation Wizard.

Completing the SQL Server Installation Wizard

After a couple of summary screens, the SQL Server Installation Wizard has all the information it requires to install the components of SQL Server you requested. Complete the wizard to finish the installation process. Remember, if you chose the Install, but do not configure the report server option, you will need to run the Reporting Services Configuration Manager to complete the final configuration of Reporting Services.

Even if you did use the Reporting Services Native mode default configuration, you should run the Reporting Services Configuration Manager to complete one important task. You should always create a backup of the Reporting Services encryption key as the final step of a Reporting Services installation. See the later section, "Backing Up the Encryption Key," for instructions on completing this task.

The Reporting Services Configuration Manager

As you learned in the previous section of this chapter, the SQL Server Installation Wizard is geared completely toward installing Reporting Services with the Native mode default configuration. If you want to deviate from the Native mode default configuration, you must use another tool to make these nondefault configuration settings. That tool is the Reporting Services Configuration Manager.

The Reporting Services Configuration Manager is found on the Start menu under All Programs | Microsoft SQL Server 2008 | Configuration Tools | Reporting Services Configuration. When this utility starts up, it asks for the name of a server to connect to, as shown in Figure 2-13. Once you enter a server name and click Find, the program

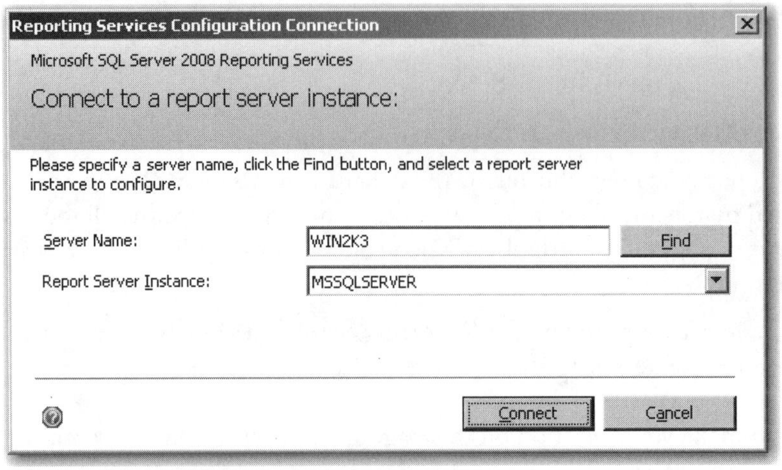

Figure 2-13   *The Reporting Services Configuration Connection dialog box*

finds all instances of Reporting Services 2008 running on that server and displays them in the Report Server Instance drop-down box, as shown in Figure 2-14. You need to select an instance and click Connect to enter the utility program with the configuration information for that Reporting Services instance loaded.

The Reporting Services Configuration Manager contains a number of pages, each geared toward configuring a different aspect of Reporting Services. Let's take a look at each of these pages and learn what they are used for.

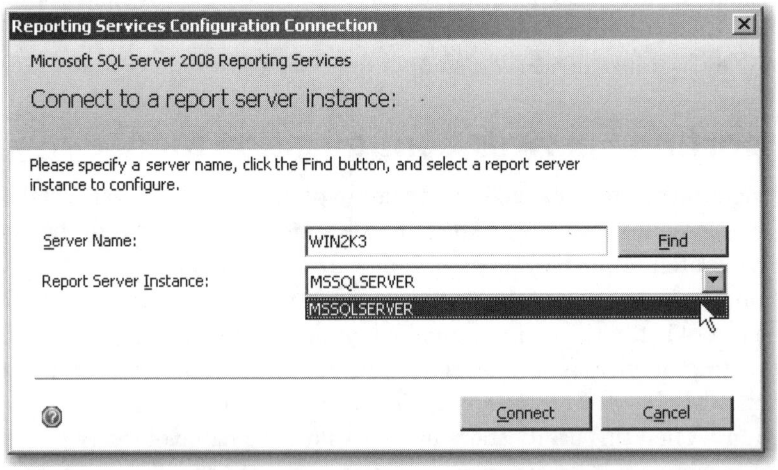

Figure 2-14   *Selecting an instance in the Reporting Services Configuration Connection dialog box*

Server Status Page

The Report Server Status page displays status information about the Report Server instance you selected, as shown in Figure 2-15. There is no configuration information to change on this page. This page does provide buttons to start or stop this instance of Reporting Services.

Service Account Page

The Service Account page enables you to view and change the credentials used to run the Reporting Services Windows service. This is shown in Figure 2-16. These are the same credentials you set on the Server Configuration page of the SQL Server 2008 Installation Wizard. For more information about the possible choices on this page, see the "The Reporting Services Windows Service Account" section of this chapter.

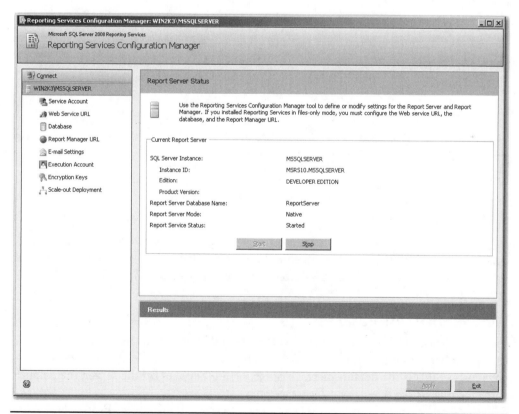

Figure 2-15   *The Report Server Status page of the Reporting Services Configuration Manager*

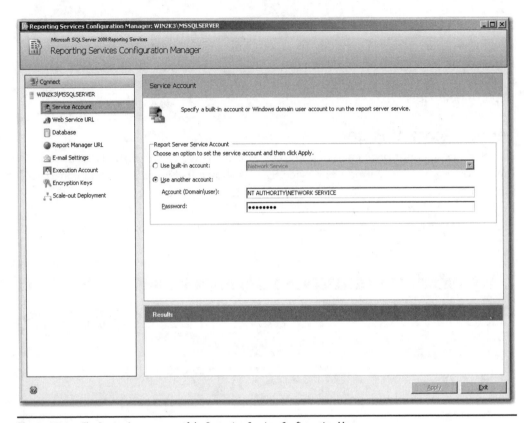

Figure 2-16 *The Service Account page of the Reporting Services Configuration Manager*

NOTE

If you ever need to change the credentials used to run the Reporting Services Windows service, be sure to make that change in the Reporting Services Configuration Manager and not through the Services Management Console snap-in. The Services snap-in will not apply the required database and file permissions to the new credentials.

Web Service URL Page

The Web Service URL page enables you to view and change the URL used by the Reporting Services web service. This page is shown in Figure 2-17. As mentioned previously, if this is the default instance of Reporting Services on the server, the default name for this virtual directory is ReportServer.

The Web Service URL page also enables you to select the Internet Protocol (IP) address and Transmission Control Protocol (TCP) port used by the Report Server web service. You need to make sure the Report Server web service does not conflict with

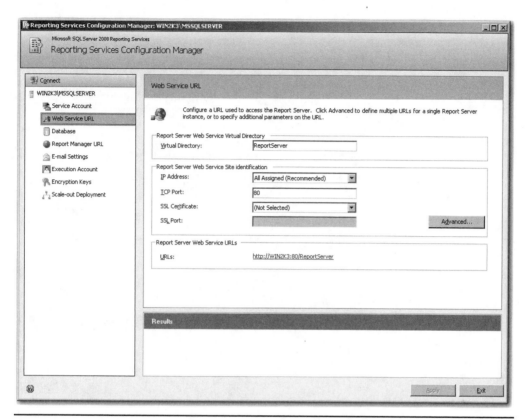

Figure 2-17   *The Web Service URL page of the Reporting Services Configuration Manager*

any other TCP/IP addresses on the network. The IP address setting will default to all IP addresses assigned to the computer, and the TCP port will default to port 80 for Hypertext Transfer Protocol (HTTP) and port 443 for Hypertext Transfer Protocol Secure (HTTPS).

Finally, the Web Service URL page enables you to select whether or not you want to require a Secure Socket Layer (SSL) connection when retrieving data from the Report Server web service. If you have any questions on this option, refer to the section "Encrypting Reporting Services Information." Because a server certificate is required for SSL, this option is disabled if you do not have a server certificate.

Report Server Database Page

The Report Server Database page, shown in Figure 2-18, enables you to select the set of databases that will serve as the Report Catalog. You can select the database server name, the name of the database on that server, and the credentials used to connect to that server. If you are performing a distributed or scale-out installation, this is where you will select

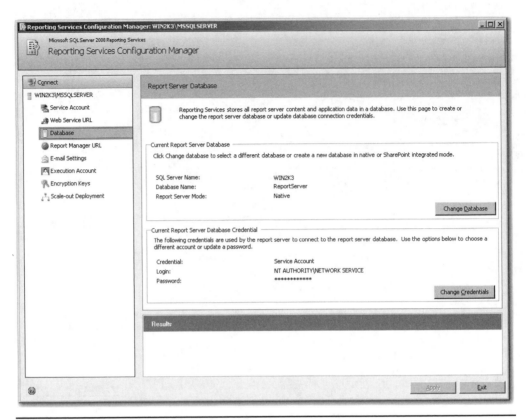

Figure 2-18   *The Report Server Database page of the Reporting Services Configuration Manager*

the remote database server for hosting the Report Catalog. Remember, the database server hosting the Report Catalog must be SQL Server 2005 or SQL Server 2008.

Click the Change Database button to change the database server or database to be used by the report server. You will have the option of creating a new report server database or choosing an existing report server database. In either case, you will need to complete the following steps:

▶   Specify the database server and the credentials to be used to complete the current operation. These credentials are not necessarily the same as those that will be used by the Reporting Services Windows service to connect to the database.

▶   Provide the name of the database and the report server mode: Native or SharePoint.

▶   Specify the credentials used by the Reporting Services Windows service to connect to the database.

Click the Change Credentials button to change only the credentials used by the Reporting Services Windows service to connect to the database.

When you click the Apply button, the following tasks are performed:

▶ **Grant access rights to Report Server accounts**   This task will set the appropriate rights in the databases for the credentials specified to be used by the Reporting Services Windows service.

▶ **Set the connection information**   This task will set this Reporting Services instance to use the specified Report Catalog.

Report Manager URL Page

The Report Manager URL page enables you to view and change the name of the virtual directory used by the Report Manager website. This page is shown in Figure 2-19. As mentioned previously, if this is the default instance of Reporting Services on the server, the default name for this virtual directory is Reports. Clicking the URL shown on this page will open Internet Explorer and take you to the Report Manager website.

E-mail Settings Page

The E-mail Settings page, shown in Figure 2-20, enables you to identify an SMTP server that can be used by Reporting Services. The SMTP server is used for delivering

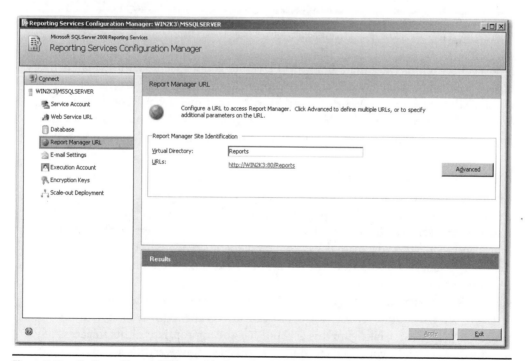

Figure 2-19   *The Report Manager URL page of the Reporting Services Configuration Manager*

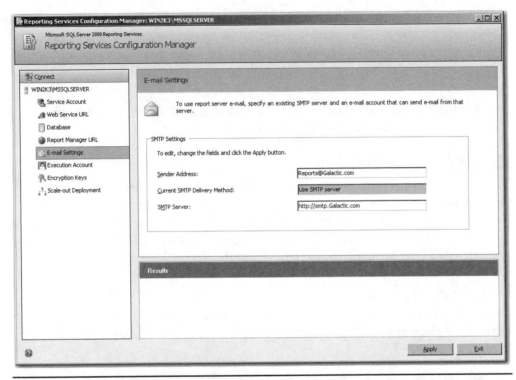

Figure 2-20   *The E-mail Settings page of the Reporting Services Configuration Manager*

report subscriptions via e-mail. If an SMTP server is not specified, the e-mail delivery option will be unavailable when creating report subscriptions.

Enter the name of an SMTP server that will accept mail from Reporting Services. You can also enter an e-mail address for Sender Address. This e-mail address will appear in the From line of any report subscriptions e-mailed from Reporting Services.

Execution Account Page

The Execution Account page, shown in Figure 2-21, enables you to specify a set of login credentials to be used by Reporting Services when it needs to access a file or other resource. For example, suppose you have a report that uses an Access database as its data source and that Access database does not require logon credentials. When it is time for the report to query the data from the Access database, the Execution Account credentials are used to gain rights to the Access MDB file. The Execution Account is also used to gain access to image files, which are pulled from the file system for use in your report.

Using the Execution Account page, you can specify the login account and the password to be used. Make sure this account has the appropriate rights to access any directories that might contain data sources or images. However, this account should

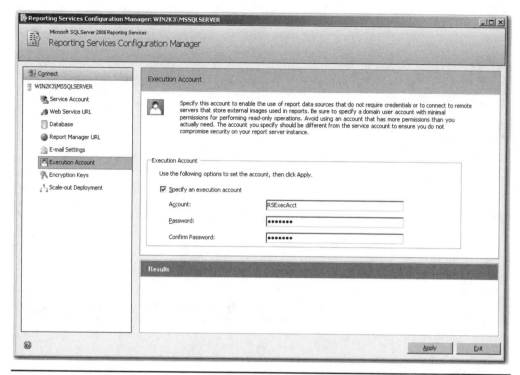

Figure 2-21   *The Execution Account page of the Reporting Services Configuration Manager*

have limited rights throughout the network to prevent it from being used in a malicious manner. If you do not anticipate the need to allow access to data sources or image files in the file system, you do not need to specify an execution account.

Encryption Keys Page

As you have seen, Reporting Services uses various sets of credentials for its operation. Whenever a login account and a password are specified, these credentials are stored as encrypted text. In addition, any credentials you specify in a report or shared data source are also encrypted. To encrypt and, more importantly, to decrypt these credentials, Reporting Services needs to use an encryption key. This encryption key is created as part of the Reporting Services installation.

If this encryption key ever becomes corrupt, none of these encrypted credentials can be decrypted. The credentials become useless, and Reporting Services becomes inoperable. To remedy this situation, you need to have a backup of the encryption key, which can be restored over the top of the corrupt key. This is the purpose of the Encryption Keys page, shown in Figure 2-22.

Use the Backup button to create a backup copy of the encryption key. Use the Restore button to restore a previously created encryption-key backup. Use the Change

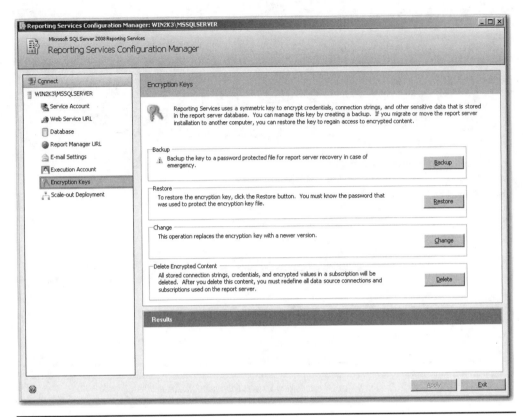

Figure 2-22   *The Encryption Keys page of the Reporting Services Configuration Manager*

button to create a new encryption key for Reporting Services. This should be done if your current encryption key becomes compromised. The current encryption key must be operable (that is, not corrupt) to use the Change function.

If your Reporting Services encryption key does become corrupt and you do not have a current backup, use the Delete button. This will remove all the encrypted credentials and create a new encryption key. After using this option, you will need to use the Report Server Database page of the Reporting Services Configuration Manager to reenter the database credentials. When the Delete button is used, Reporting Services will be inoperable until you enter a new set of database credentials. You will also need to reenter the data source credentials for each report and shared data source deployed on the server.

Backing Up the Encryption Key   To create a backup copy of the encryption key, click the Backup button. Enter a path and a filename for storing the key, and then enter a password to protect the encryption key. You may want to put the key backup on removable media so it can be stored in a safe place. Make sure you keep the password in a safe place as well. The password helps protect your encryption key backup and is required by the restore process.

> **NOTE**
>
> *In previous versions of Reporting Services, the Reporting Services encryption keys had a bad habit of becoming corrupted. If the key does become corrupted, Reporting Services ceases to function and all the encrypted credential information on the server must be reentered. Therefore, it is important to maintain a current backup of your Reporting Services encryption key in a secure location.*

Scale-out Deployment Page

The Scale-out Deployment page, shown in Figure 2-23, is used to add servers to a scale-out installation of Reporting Services. Each server added to the scale-out list uses the same encryption key. In this way, encrypted data stored in the common Report Catalog can be decrypted by any report server in the scale-out installation.

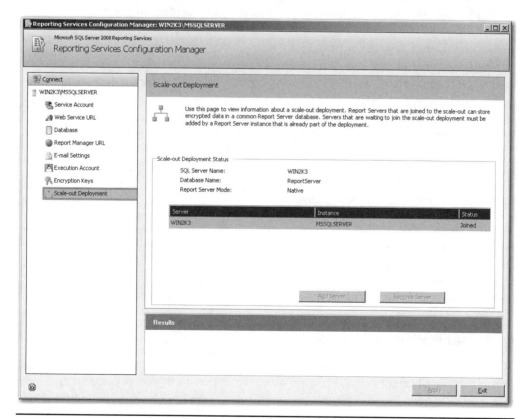

Figure 2-23   *The Scale-out Deployment page of the Reporting Services Configuration Manager*

Menu Bar

The Connect button, at the top of the page's menu area, lets you connect to a different server and then select a Reporting Services instance on that server.

Common Installation Issues

This section lists some of the common problems you may encounter while installing Reporting Services. Suggested solutions are provided to help you resolve these problems.

A new troubleshooting issue with Reporting Services 2008 is the co-existence of Internet Information Services (IIS) and Reporting Services—e.g., if you put Reporting Services on port 80, it will steal requests from IIS, and Reporting Services and IIS can't sit on the same port on Windows XP.

Administrative Rights

One of the most frequent problems with the Reporting Services setup is not using login accounts that have the appropriate rights. If you encounter an error during installation, refer to the earlier section, "Login Accounts," and make sure you are using login accounts that have the appropriate rights.

If you discover you received a setup error because one of the login accounts you used was not adequate to the task, try changing that account using the Reporting Services Configuration Manager. If this does not work, remove the failed installation of Reporting Services and try again. To remove the failed installation, select Add or Remove Programs from the Control Panel and choose to remove Reporting Services.

Server Components Not Shown on the Feature Selection Screen

If you are performing an installation that requires the server components, but they are not present on the Feature Selection screen, this is probably an indication that you are not up-to-date on your Windows service packs. Reporting Services is finicky about this. If you encounter this problem, cancel the installation, install the latest service pack for your version of Windows, and then start the installation process again.

Installation Error 2755

You may receive Error 2755 if you are installing Reporting Services using a Terminal Server session. This will occur if you are using a mapped drive to access the setup files. The Windows Installer service that performs the setup operation is running in a different Windows session, so it may not have the same drive mappings. The error occurs because certain files needed by the installer cannot be found.

To remedy this problem, use a Universal Naming Convention (UNC) path to access the setup files, rather than a mapped drive. Alternatively, you may put the installation CD in a drive that is local to the computer on which you are performing the installation or copy the setup files to a drive that is local to that computer.

Reporting Services and IIS on the Same Server

If you are installing the report server on a computer that is already running IIS, care must be taken to ensure that these two services are not using the same TCP/IP port. Both IIS and the Report Server will default to using port 80 for HTTP requests and port 443 for HTTPS requests. If this occurs, IIS and the Report Server will compete to handle traffic on these ports, resulting in neither service working correctly. If this occurs, simply use the Reporting Services Configuration Manager to direct the Report Server to a different port.

The Repair Utility and Installation Log File

If your installation does not complete successfully, you can try the Repair utility on the Maintenance page of the SQL Server Installation Center. If none of these suggestions solve your installation issues, you may want to consult the installation log files for more information.

The default location for the log files is

```
C:\Program Files\Microsoft SQL Server\100\Setup Bootstrap\Log
```

The log files will be in a folder named for the date and time of the installation.

Spending Some Time in Basic Training

You now have Reporting Services installed and ready to go. As mentioned at the end of Chapter 1, we will take time to ensure that you understand the basics of database architecture and querying before we begin creating reports. Chapter 3 gives you this database basic training. This basic training won't be as tough as Army boot camp, but it will get you ready to attack all those tough data-reporting challenges.

Chapter 3 also introduces you to Galactic Delivery Services (GDS): what it does, how it is structured, and what its data processing systems look like. We use GDS and its business needs for all our sample reports throughout the book.

Part II

Report Authoring

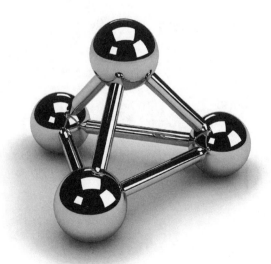

Chapter 3

DB 101: Database Basics

In This Chapter

▶ Database Structure
▶ Galactic Delivery Services
▶ Querying Data
▶ On to the Reports

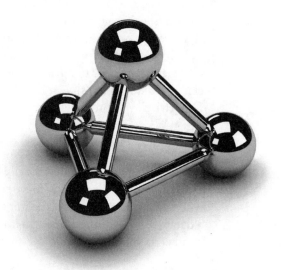

Before you begin creating reports, it is important that you have a good understanding of relational databases. In the first part of this chapter, you will see the tables, rows, and columns that make up relational databases. You will also learn about concepts such as normalization and relationships. These are the characteristics that make a relational database … well, relational.

Once you cover the basics, you are introduced to Galactic Delivery Services (GDS). The business needs of GDS serve as the basis for all the sample reports throughout this book. Even though GDS is a unique company in many respects, you will discover its reporting needs and its uses of Reporting Services are typical of most companies in this galaxy.

For the remainder of the chapter, you will explore the ins and outs of the *SELECT query,* which is what you use to extract data from your data sources for use in your reports. Even though Reporting Services helps you create SELECT queries through a tool called the Query Designer, it is important that you understand how SELECT queries work and how they can be used to obtain the correct data. A report may look absolutely stunning with charts, graphics, special formatting, and snappy colors, but it is completely useless if it contains the wrong data!

Database Structure

Databases are basically giant containers for storing information. They are the electronic crawlspaces and digital attics of the corporate, academic, and governmental worlds. For example, anything that needs to be saved for later use by payroll, inventory management, or the external auditor is placed in a database.

Just like our crawlspaces and attics at home, the information placed in a database needs to be organized and classified. Figure 3-1 shows my attic in its current state. As you can see, it is going to be pretty hard to find those old kids' clothes for the thrift store clothing drive! I know they are up there somewhere.

Without some type of order placed on it, all the stuff in our home storage spaces becomes impossible to retrieve when we need it. The same is true in the world of electronic storage, as shown in Figure 3-2. Databases, like attics, need structure. Otherwise, we won't be able to find anything!

Getting Organized

The first step in getting organized is to have a place for everything and to have everything in its place. To achieve this, you need to add structure to the storage space, whether this is a space for box storage, like my attic, or a space for data storage, like a database. To maintain this structure, you also need to have discipline of one sort or another as you add items to the storage space.

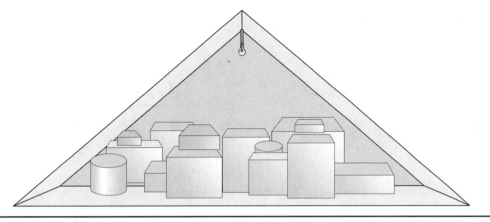

Figure 3-1   *My attic, with no organization*

Tables, Rows, and Columns

To get my attic organized, I need some shelves, a few labels, and some free time, so I can add the much-needed structure to this storage space. To keep my attic organized, I also need the discipline to pay attention to my new signs each time I put another box into storage. Figure 3-3 shows my attic as it exists in my fantasy world, where I have tons of free time and loads of self-discipline.

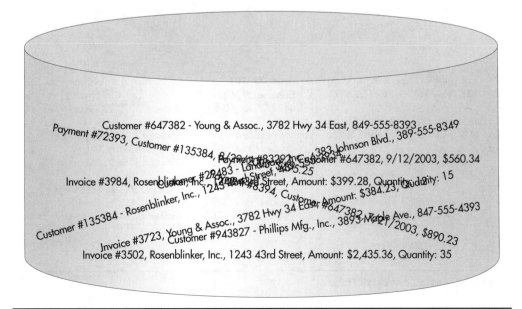

Figure 3-2   *An unorganized database*

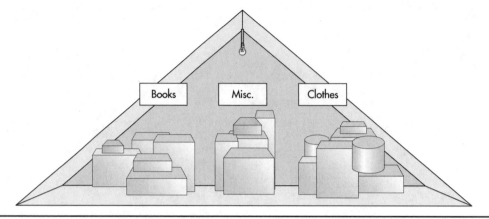

Figure 3-3 *My attic in my fantasy world*

Structure in the database world comes in the form of tables. Each database is divided into a number of tables. These tables store the information. Each table contains only one type of information. Figure 3-4 shows customer information in one table, payment information in another, and invoice header information in a third.

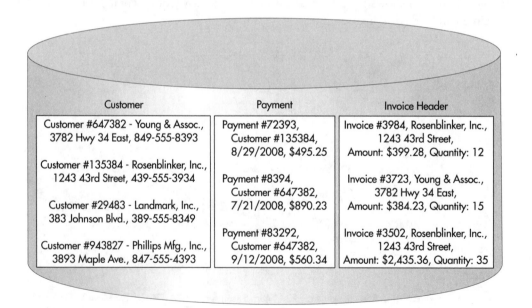

Figure 3-4 *A database organized by tables*

NOTE

Invoice Header is used as the name of the third table for consistency with the sample database that will be introduced in the section "Galactic Delivery Services" and used throughout the remainder of the book. The Invoice Header name helps to differentiate this table from the Invoice Detail table that stores the detail lines of the invoice. The Invoice Detail table is not discussed here, but it will be present in the sample database.

Dividing each table into rows and columns brings additional structure to the database. Figure 3-5 shows the Customer table divided into several rows—one row for each customer whose information is being stored in the table. In addition, the Customer table is divided into a number of columns. Each column is given a name: Customer Number, Customer Name, Address, and Phone. These names tell you what information is being stored in each column.

With a database structured as tables, rows, and columns, you know exactly where to find a certain piece of information. For example, it is pretty obvious that the customer name for customer number 135384 will be found in the Name column of the second row of the Customer table. We are starting to get this data organized, and it was a lot easier than cleaning out the attic!

NOTE

Rows in a database are also called records. Columns in a database are also called fields. Reporting Services uses the terms "rows" and "records" interchangeably. It also uses the terms "columns" and "fields" interchangeably. Don't be confused by this!

Customer

Customer #	Customer Name	Address	Phone
647382	Young & Assoc.	3782 Hwy 34 East	849-555-8393
135384	Rosenblinker, Inc.	1243 43rd Street	439-555-3934
29483	Landmark, Inc.	383 Johnson Blvd.	389-555-8349
943827	Phillips Mfg., Inc.	3893 Maple Ave.	847-555-4393

Figure 3-5   *A database table organized by rows and columns*

Columns also force some discipline on anyone putting data into the table. Each column has certain characteristics assigned to it. For instance, the Customer Number column in Figure 3-5 may only contain strings of digits (0–9); no letters (A–Z) are allowed. It is also limited to a maximum of six characters. In data design lingo, these are known as *constraints*. Given these constraints, it is impossible to store a customer's name in the Customer Number column. The customer's name is likely too long and contains characters that are not legal in the Customer Number column. Constraints provide the discipline to force organization within a database.

Typically, when you design a database, you create tables for each of the things you want to keep track of. In Figure 3-4, the database designer knew that her company needed to track information for customers, payments, and invoices. Database designers call these things *entities*. The database designer created tables for the customer, payment, and invoice header entities. These tables are named Customer, Payment, and Invoice Header.

Once the entities have been identified, the database designer determines what information needs to be known about each entity. In Figure 3-5, the designer identified the customer number, customer name, address, and phone number as the things that need to be known for each customer. These are *attributes* of the customer entity. The database designer creates a column in the Customer table for each of these attributes.

Primary Key

As entities and attributes are being defined, the database designer needs to identify a special attribute for each entity in the database. This special attribute is known as the primary key. The purpose of the *primary key* is to be able to uniquely identify a single entity or, in the case of a database table, a single row in the table.

Two simple rules exist for primary keys. First, every entity must have a primary key value. Second, no two rows in an entity can have the same primary key value. In Figure 3-5, the Customer Number column can serve as the primary key. Every customer is assigned a customer number, and no two customers can be assigned the same customer number.

For most entities, the primary key is a single attribute. However, in some cases, two attributes must be combined to create a unique primary key. This is known as a *composite primary key*. For instance, if you were defining an entity based on presidents of the United States, the first name would not be a valid primary key. John Adams, John Quincy Adams, and John Kennedy all have the same first name. You would need to create a composite key combining first name, middle name, and last name to have a valid primary key.

Normalization

As the database designer continues to work on identifying entities and attributes, she will notice that two different entities have some of the same attributes. For example, in Figure 3-6, both the customer entity and the invoice header entity have attributes of

Customer Name and Address. This duplication of information seems rather wasteful. Not only are the customer's name and address duplicated between the Customer and Invoice Header tables, but they are also duplicated in several rows in the Invoice Header table itself.

The duplicate data also leads to another problem. Suppose that Rosenblinker, Inc. changes its name to RB, Inc. Then, Ann in the data-processing department changes the name in the Customer table because this is where we store information about the customer entity. However, the customer name has not been changed in the Invoice Header table. Because the customer name in the Invoice Header table no longer matches the customer name in the Customer table, it is no longer possible to determine how many invoices are outstanding for RB, Inc. Believe me, the accounting department will think this is a bad situation.

Customer

Customer #	Customer Name	Address	Phone
647382	Young & Assoc.	3782 Hwy 34 East	849-555-8393
135384	Rosenblinker, Inc.	1243 43rd Street	439-555-3934
29483	Landmark, Inc.	383 Johnson Blvd.	389-555-8349
943827	Phillips Mfg., Inc.	3893 Maple Ave.	847-555-4393

Invoice Header

Invoice #	Customer Name	Address	Amount	Quantity
3984	Rosenblinker, Inc.	1243 43rd Street	$399.28	12
3723	Young & Assoc.	3782 Hwy 34 East	$384.23	15
3502	Rosenblinker, Inc.	1243 43rd Street	$2,435.36	35

Figure 3-6   *Database tables with duplicate data*

To avoid these types of problems, database tables are normalized. *Normalization* is a set of rules for defining database tables so each table contains attributes from only one entity. The rules for creating normalized database tables can be quite complex. You can hear database designers endlessly debating whether a proper database should be in 3rd normal form, 4th normal form, or 127th normal form. Let the database designers debate all they want. All you need to remember is this: A normalized database avoids data duplication.

Relations

A *relation* is a tool the database designer uses to avoid data duplication when creating a normalized database. A relation is simply a way to put the duplicated data in one place and then point to it from all the other places in the database where it would otherwise occur. The table that contains the data is called the *parent* table. The table that contains a pointer to the data in the parent table is called the *child* table. Just like parents and children of the human variety, the parent table and the child table are said to be *related*.

In our example, the customer name and address are stored in the Customer table. This is the parent table. A pointer is placed in the Invoice Header table in place of the duplicate customer names and addresses it had contained. The Invoice Header table is the child table.

As mentioned previously, each customer is uniquely identified by their customer number. Therefore, the Customer Number column serves as the primary key for the Customer table. In the Invoice Header table, we need a way to point to a particular customer. It makes sense to use the primary key in the parent table, in this case the Customer Number column, as that pointer. This is illustrated in Figure 3-7.

Each row in the Invoice Header table now contains a copy of the primary key of a row in the Customer table. The Customer Number column in the Invoice Header table is called the foreign key. It is called a *foreign key* because it is not one of the native attributes of the invoice header entity. The customer number is a native attribute of the customer entity. The only reason the Customer Number column exists in the Invoice Header table is to create the relationship.

Let's look back at the name change problem, this time using our new database structure that includes the parent-child relationship. When Rosenblinker, Inc. changes its name to RB, Inc., Ann changes the name in the Customer table as before. In our new structure, however, the customer name is not stored in any other location. Instead, the Invoice Header table rows for RB, Inc. point back to the Customer table row that has the correct name. The accounting department stays happy because it can still figure out how many invoices are outstanding for RB, Inc.

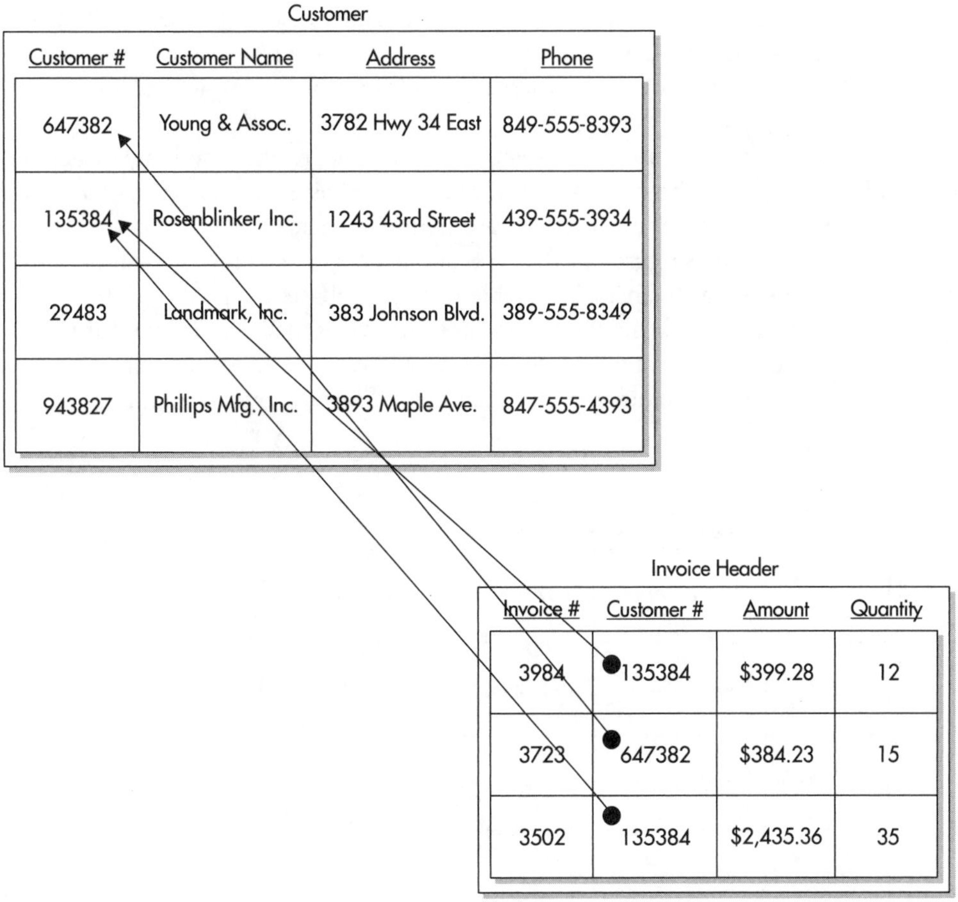

Customer

Customer #	Customer Name	Address	Phone
647382	Young & Assoc.	3782 Hwy 34 East	849-555-8393
135384	Rosenblinker, Inc.	1243 43rd Street	439-555-3934
29483	Landmark, Inc.	383 Johnson Blvd.	389-555-8349
943827	Phillips Mfg., Inc.	3893 Maple Ave.	847-555-4393

Invoice Header

Invoice #	Customer #	Amount	Quantity
3984	135384	$399.28	12
3723	647382	$384.23	15
3502	135384	$2,435.36	35

Figure 3-7 *A database relation*

Cardinality of Relations

Database relations can be classified by the number of records that can exist on each side of the relationship. This is known as the *cardinality* of the relation. For example, the relation in Figure 3-7 is a *one-to-many relation* (in other words, one parent record can have many children). More specifically, one customer can have many invoices.

It is also possible to have a *one-to-one relation*. In this case, one parent record can have only one child. For example, let's say our company rewards customers with a customer loyalty discount. Because only a few customers will receive this loyalty discount, we do not want to set aside space in every row in the Customer table to store the loyalty discount information. Instead, we create a new table to store this information. The new table is related to the Customer table, as shown in Figure 3-8. Our company's business rule says that a given customer can only receive one loyalty discount. Because the Loyalty Discount table has only one Customer Number column, each row can link to just one customer. The combination of the business rule and the table design makes this a one-to-one relation.

It is also possible to have a *many-to-many relation*. This relation no longer fits our parent/child analogy. It is better thought of as a brother/sister relationship. One brother can have many sisters, and one sister can have many brothers.

Suppose we need to keep track of the type of business engaged in by each of our customers. We can add a Business Type table to our database, with columns for the business type code and the business type description. We can add a column for the business type code to the Customer table. We now have a one-to-many relation, where one business type can be related to many customers. This is shown in Figure 3-9.

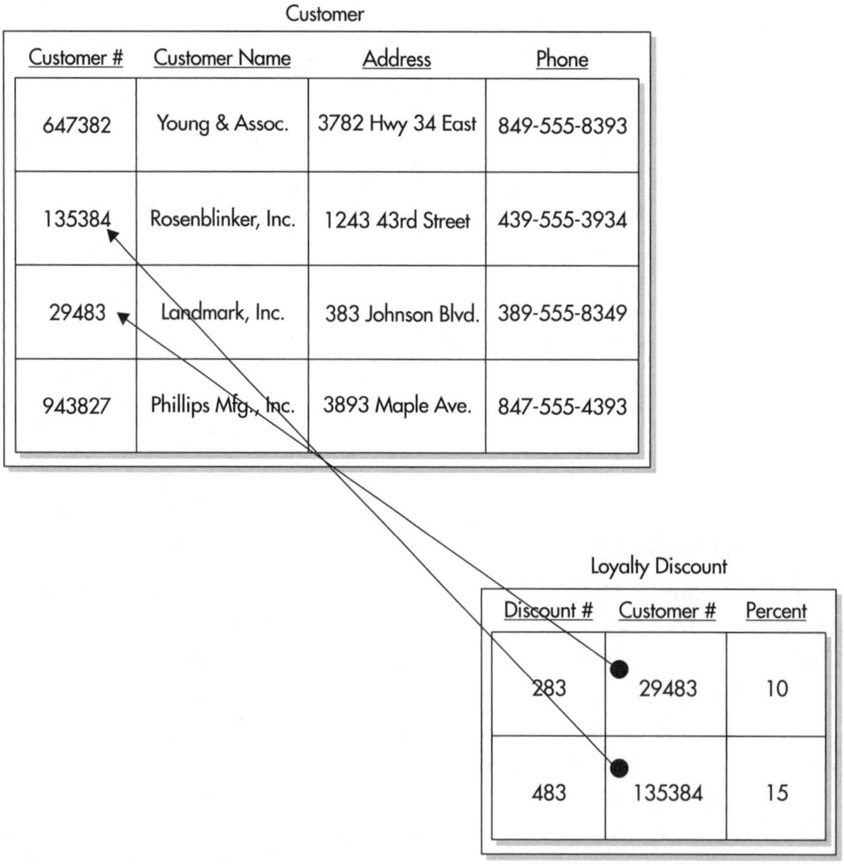

Figure 3-8 *A one-to-one relation*

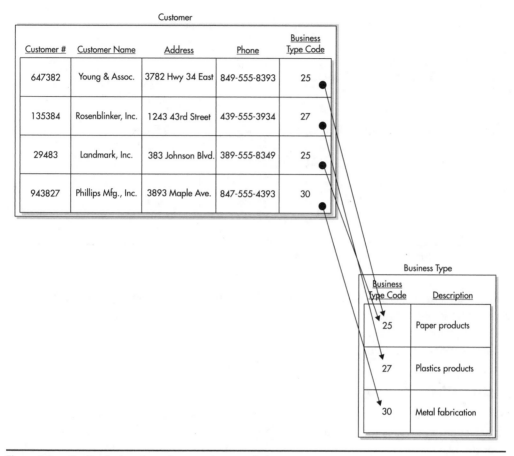

Figure 3-9   *Tracking business type using a one-to-many relation*

The problem with this structure becomes apparent when we have a customer that does multiple things. If Landmark, Inc. only produces paper products, there isn't a problem. We can put the business type code for paper products in the Customer table row for Landmark, Inc. We run into a bit of a snag, however, if Landmark, Inc. also produces plastics. We could add a second business type code column to the Customer table, but this still limits a customer to a maximum of two business types. In today's world of national conglomerates, this is not going to work.

The answer is to add a third table to the mix to create a many-to-many relation. This additional table is known as a *linking table*. Its only purpose is to link two other tables together in a many-to-many relation. To use a linking table, you create the Business Type table just as before. This time, however, instead of creating a new column in the Customer table, we'll create a new table called Customer To Business Type Link. The new table has

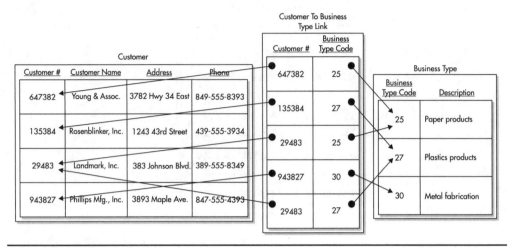

Figure 3-10 *Tracking the business type using a many-to-many relation*

columns for the customer number and the business type code. Figure 3-10 shows how this linking table relates the Customer table to the Business Type table. By using the linking table, we can relate one customer to many business types. In addition, we can relate one business type to many customers.

Retrieving Data

We now have all the tools we need to store our data in an efficient manner. With our data structure set, it is time to determine how we can access that data to use it in our reports. Data that was split into multiple tables must be recombined for reporting. This is done using a database tool called a *join*. In most cases, we will also want the data in the report to appear in a certain order. This is accomplished using a sort.

Inner Joins

Suppose we need to know the name and address of the customer associated with each invoice. This is certainly a reasonable request, especially if we want to send invoices to these clients and have those invoices paid. Checking the Invoice Header table, you can see it contains the customer number, but not the name and address. The name and address is stored in the Customer table.

To print our invoices, we need to join the data in the Customer table with the data in the Invoice Header table. This join is done by matching the customer number in each record of the Invoice Header table with the customer number in the Customer table. In the language of database designers, we are joining the Customer table to the Invoice Header table on the Customer Number column.

The result of the join is a new table that contains information from both the Customer table and the Invoice Header table in each row. This new table is known as a *result set*. The result set from the Customer table-to-Invoice Header table join is shown in Figure 3-11. Note that the result set table contains nearly the same information that was in the Invoice Header table before it was normalized. The result set is a *denormalized* form of the data in the database.

It may seem like we are going in circles, first normalizing the data and then denormalizing it. There is, however, one important difference between the denormalized form of the Invoice Header table that we started with in Figure 3-6 and the result set in Figure 3-11. The denormalized result set is a temporary table: It exists only as long as it is needed; then it is automatically deleted. The result set is re-created each time we execute the join, so the result set is always current.

Let's return once more to Ann, our faithful employee in data processing. We will again consider the situation where Rosenblinker, Inc. changes its name to RB, Inc. Ann makes the change in the Customer table, as in the previous example. The next time we execute the join, this change is reflected in the result set. The result set has the new company name because our join gets a new copy of the customer information from the Customer table each time it is executed. The join finds the information in the Customer table based on the primary key, the customer number, which has not changed. Our invoices are linked to the proper companies, so accounting can determine how many invoices are outstanding for RB, Inc., and everyone is happy!

Outer Joins

In the previous section, we looked at a type of join known as an inner join. When you do an inner join, your result set includes only those records that have a representative

Customer/Invoice Header Join Result Set

Customer #	Customer Name	Address	Phone	Invoice #	Customer #	Amount	Quantity
135384	Rosenblinker, Inc.	1243 43rd Street	439-555-3934	3984	135384	$399.28	12
647382	Young & Assoc.	3782 Hwy 34 East	849-555-8393	3723	647382	$384.23	15
135384	Rosenblinker, Inc.	1243 43rd Street	439-555-3934	3502	135384	$2,435.36	35

Data from the Customer table   Data from the Invoice Header table

Figure 3-11   *The result set from the Customer-table-to-Invoice-Header table join*

on both sides of the join. In Figure 3-11, Landmark, Inc. and Phillips Mfg., Inc. are not represented in the result set because they do not have any Invoice Header table rows linked to them.

Figure 3-12 shows another way to think about joins. Here, the two tables are shown as sets of customer numbers. The left-hand circle represents the set of customer numbers in the Customer table. It contains one occurrence of every customer number present in the Customer table. The right-hand circle represents the set of customer numbers in the Invoice Header table. It contains one occurrence of each customer number present in the Invoice Header table. The center region, where the two sets intersect, contains one occurrence of every customer number present in both the Customer table and the Invoice Header table. Looking at Figure 3-12, you can quickly tell that no customer numbers are present in the Invoice Header table that are not also present in the Customer table. This is as it should be. We should not have any invoice headers assigned to a customer that does not exist in the Customer table.

Figure 3-13 shows a graphical representation of the inner join in Figure 3-11. Only records with customer numbers that appear in the shaded section will be included in the result set. Remember, two rows in the Invoice Header table contain customer number 135384. For this reason, the result set contains three rows—two rows for customer number 135384 and one row for customer number 647382.

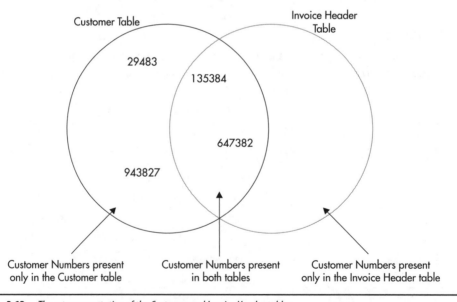

Figure 3-12   *The set representation of the Customer and Invoice Header tables*

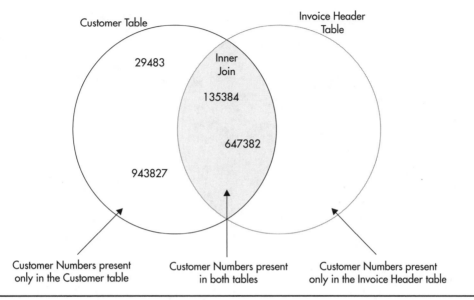

Figure 3-13   *The set representation of the inner join of the Customer table and the Invoice Header table*

The result set in Figure 3-11 enables us to print invoice headers that contain the correct customer name and address. Now let's look at customers and invoice headers from a slightly different angle. Suppose we have been asked for a report showing all customers and the invoice headers that have been sent to them. If we were to print this customers/invoice headers report from the result set in Figure 3-11, it would exclude Landmark, Inc. and Phillips Mfg., Inc. because they do not have any invoices and, therefore, would not fulfill the requirements.

What we need is a result set that includes all the customers in the Customer table. This is illustrated graphically in Figure 3-14. This type of join is known as a *left outer join,* so named because this join is not limited to the values in the intersection of both circles. It also includes the values to the left of the inner, overlapping sections of the circles.

We can also perform a right outer join on two tables. In our example, a *right outer join* would return the same number of rows as the inner join. This is because no customer numbers are to the right of the intersection.

The result set produced by a left outer join of the Customer table and the Invoice Header table is shown in Figure 3-15. Notice the columns populated by data from the Invoice Header table are empty in rows for Landmark, Inc. and Phillips Mfg., Inc. The columns are empty because these two customers do not have any Invoice Header rows to provide data on the right side of the join.

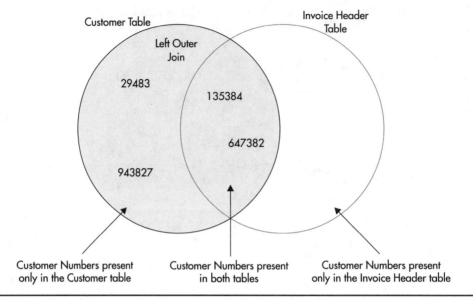

Figure 3-14 *The set representation of the left outer join of the Customer table and the Invoice Header table*

Customer/Invoice Header Left Outer Join Result Set

Customer #	Customer Name	Address	Phone	Invoice #	Customer #	Amount	Quantity
135384	Rosenblinker, Inc.	1243 43rd Street	439-555-3934	3984	135384	$399.28	12
647382	Young & Assoc.	3782 Hwy 34 East	849-555-8393	3723	647382	$384.23	15
135384	Rosenblinker, Inc.	1243 43rd Street	439-555-3934	3502	135384	$2,435.36	35
29483	Landmark, Inc.	383 Johnson Blvd.	389-555-8349				
943827	Phillips Mfg, Inc.	3893 Maple Ave.	847-555-4393				

Data from the Customer table   Data from the Invoice Header table

Figure 3-15 *The result set from the left outer join of the Customer table and the Invoice Header table*

Joining Multiple Tables

Joins, whether inner or outer, always involve two tables. However, in Figure 3-10, you were introduced to a many-to-many relation that involved three tables. How do you retrieve data from this type of relation? The answer is to chain together two different joins, each involving two tables.

Figure 3-16 illustrates the joins required to reassemble the data from Figure 3-10. Here, the Customer table is joined to the Customer To Business Type Link table using the Customer Number column common to both tables. The Customer To Business Type Link table is then joined to the Business Type table using the Business Type Code column present in both tables. The final result set contains the data from all three tables.

Self-Joins

In our previous example, we needed to join three tables to get the required information. Other joins may only require a single table. For instance, we may have a customer that is a subsidiary of another one of our customers. In some cases, we'll want to treat these two separately, so both appear in our result set. This requires us to keep the two customers as separate rows in our Customer table. In other cases, we may want to combine information

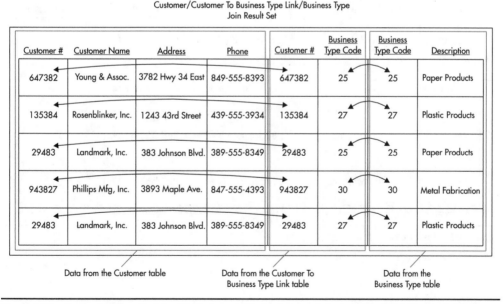

Figure 3-16   *The result set from the join of the Customer table, the Customer To Business Type Link table, and the Business Type table*

from the parent company and the subsidiary into one record. To do this, our database structure must include a mechanism to tie the subsidiary to its parent.

To track a customer's connection to its parent, we need to create a relationship between the customer's row in the Customer table and its parent's row in the Customer table. To do this, we add a Parent Customer Number column to the Customer table, as shown in Figure 3-17. In the customer's row, the Parent Customer Number column will contain the customer number of the row for the parent. In the row for the parent, and in all the rows for customers that do not have a parent, the Parent Customer Number column is empty.

When we want to report from this parent/subsidiary relation, we need to do a join. This may seem like a problem at first because a join requires two tables, and we only have one. The answer is to use the Customer table on one side of the join and a "copy" of the Customer table on the other side of the join. The second occurrence of the Customer table is given a nickname, called an *alias,* so we can tell the two apart. This type of join, which uses the same table on both sides, is known as a *self-join.* Figure 3-18 shows the results of the self-join on the Customer table.

Customer

Customer #	Customer Name	Address	Phone	Parent Customer #
647382	Young & Assoc.	3782 Hwy 34 East	849-555-8393	
135384	Rosenblinker, Inc.	1243 43rd Street	439-555-3934	
29483	Landmark, Inc.	383 Johnson Blvd.	389-555-8349	135384
943827	Phillips Mfg., Inc.	3893 Maple Ave.	847-555-4393	647382

Figure 3-17   *The customer/parent customer relation*

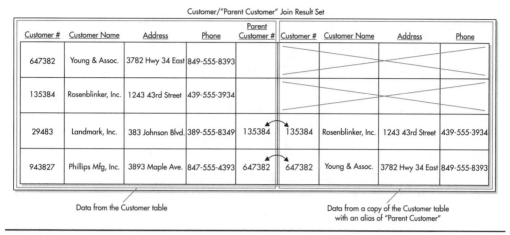

Customer/"Parent Customer" Join Result Set

Customer #	Customer Name	Address	Phone	Parent Customer #	Customer #	Customer Name	Address	Phone
647382	Young & Assoc.	3782 Hwy 34 East	849-555-8393					
135384	Rosenblinker, Inc.	1243 43rd Street	439-555-3934					
29483	Landmark, Inc.	383 Johnson Blvd.	389-555-8349	135384	135384	Rosenblinker, Inc.	1243 43rd Street	439-555-3934
943827	Phillips Mfg, Inc.	3893 Maple Ave.	847-555-4393	647382	647382	Young & Assoc.	3782 Hwy 34 East	849-555-8393

Data from the Customer table   Data from a copy of the Customer table
                                      with an alias of "Parent Customer"

Figure 3-18   *The result set from the Customer table self-join*

Sorting

In most cases, one final step is required before our result sets can be used for reporting. Let's go back to the result set produced in Figure 3-15 for the customer/invoice header report. Looking back at this result set, notice the customers do not appear to be in any particular order. In most cases, users do not appreciate reports with information presented in this unsorted manner. This is especially true when two rows for the same customer do not appear consecutively, as is the case here.

We need to sort the result set as it is being created to avoid this situation. This is done by specifying the columns that should be used for the sort. Sorting by customer name probably makes the most sense for the customer/invoice header report. Columns can be sorted either in ascending order, smallest to largest (A–Z), or descending order, largest to smallest (Z–A). An ascending sort on Customer Name would be most appropriate.

We still have a situation where the order of the rows is left to chance. Because two rows have the same customer name, we do not know which of these two rows will appear first and which will appear second. A second sort field is necessary to break this "tie." All the data copied into the result set from the Customer table will be the same in both of these rows. We need to look at the data copied from the Invoice Header table for a second sort column. In this case, an ascending sort on Invoice Number would be a good choice. Figure 3-19 shows the result set sorted by Customer Name, ascending, and then by Invoice Number, ascending.

Customer/Invoice Header Left Outer Join Result Set

Customer #	Customer Name	Address	Phone	Invoice #	Customer #	Amount	Quantity
29483	Landmark, Inc.	383 Johnson Blvd.	389-555-8349				
943827	Phillips Mfg, Inc.	3893 Maple Ave.	847-555-4393				
135384	Rosenblinker, Inc.	1243 43rd Street	439-555-3934	3502	135384	$2,435.36	35
135384	Rosenblinker, Inc.	1243 43rd Street	439-555-3934	3984	135384	$399.28	12
647382	Young & Assoc.	3782 Hwy 34 East	849-555-8393	3723	647382	$384.23	15

Data from the Customer table   Data from the Invoice Header table

Figure 3-19   *The sorted result set from the left outer join of the Customer table and the Invoice Header table*

Galactic Delivery Services

Throughout the remainder of this book, you will get to know Reporting Services by exploring a number of sample reports. These reports will be based on the business needs of a company called Galactic Delivery Services (GDS). To better understand these sample reports, here is some background on GDS.

Company Background

GDS provides package-delivery service between several planetary systems in the near galactic region. It specializes in rapid delivery featuring same-day, next-day, and previous-day delivery. The latter is made possible by its new Photon III transports, which travel faster than the speed of light. This faster-than-light capability allows GDS to exploit the properties of general relativity and deliver a package on the day before it was sent.

Package Tracking

Despite GDS's unique delivery offerings, it has the same data-processing needs as any more conventional package-delivery service. It tracks packages as they are moved from one interplanetary hub to another. This is important, not only for the smooth operation of the delivery service, but also to allow customers to check on the status of their delivery at any time.

To remain accountable to its clients and to prevent fraud, GDS investigates every package lost en route. These investigations help to find and eliminate problems throughout the entire delivery system. One such investigation discovered that a leaking antimatter valve on one of the Photon III transports was vaporizing two or three packages on each flight.

GDS stores its data in a database called Galactic. Figure 3-20 shows the portion of the Galactic database that stores the information used for package tracking. The tables and their column names are shown. A key symbol in the gray square next to a column name indicates this column is the primary key for that table. The lines connecting the tables show the relations that have been created between these tables in the database. The key symbol at the end of the line points to the primary key column used to create the relation. The infinity sign, at the opposite end of the line to the key symbol, points to the foreign key column used to complete the relation. (The infinity sign looks like two circles or a sideways number 8.)

Each relation shown in Figure 3-20 is a one-to-many relation. The side of the relation indicated by the key is the "one" side of the relation. The side indicated by the infinity sign is the "many" side of the relation. For example, if you look at the line between the Customer table and the Delivery table, you can see that one customer may have many deliveries.

You may want to refer to these diagrams as we create sample reports from the Galactic database. Don't worry if the diagrams seem a bit complicated right now. They will make more sense as we consider the business practices and reporting needs at GDS. Also, our first report examples will contain only a few tables and the corresponding relations, so we will start simple and work our way up.

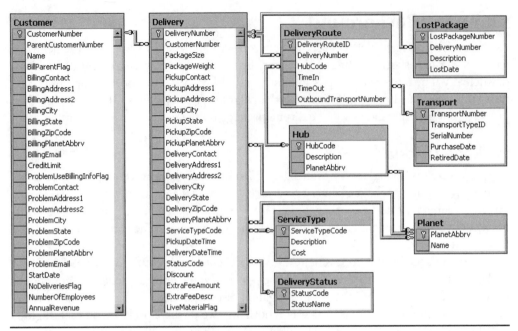

Figure 3-20 *The package tracking tables from the Galactic database*

Personnel

Every business needs a personnel department to look after its employees. GDS is no different. The GDS personnel department is responsible for the hiring and firing of all the robots employed by GDS. This department is also responsible for tracking the hours put in by the robotic laborers and paying them accordingly. (Yes, robots get paid at GDS. After all, GDS is an equal-opportunity employer.)

The personnel department is also responsible for conducting annual reviews of each employee. At the annual review, goals are set for the employee to attain over the coming year. After a year has passed, several of the employee's coworkers are asked to rate the employee on how well it did in reaching those goals. The employee's manager then uses the ratings to write an overall performance evaluation for the employee and establish new goals for the following year.

Figure 3-21 shows the tables in the Galactic database used by the personnel department. Notice that the Rating table has key symbols next to both the EvaluationID column name and the GoalID column name. This means the Rating table uses a composite primary key that combines the EvaluationID column and the GoalID column.

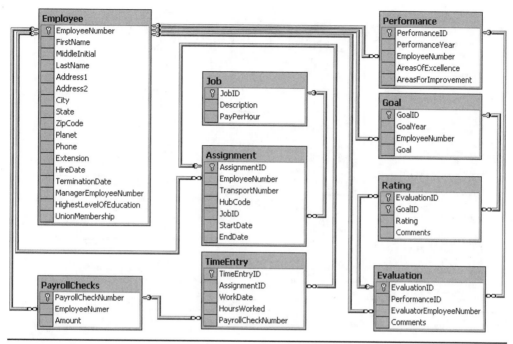

Figure 3-21   *The personnel department tables from the Galactic database*

Accounting

The GDS accounting department is responsible for seeing that the company is paid for each package it delivers. GDS invoices its customers for each delivery completed. The invoices are sent to the customer and payment is requested within 30 days.

Even though GDS delivers its customers' packages at the speed of light, those same customers pay GDS at a much slower speed. "Molasses at the northern pole of Antares Prime" was the analogy used by the current Chief Financial Droid. Therefore, GDS must track when invoices are paid, how much was paid, and how much is still outstanding.

Figure 3-22 shows the tables in the Galactic database used by the accounting department. Notice the Customer table appears in both Figure 3-20 and Figure 3-22. This is the same table in both diagrams. This table is shown in both, because it is a major part of both the package tracking and the accounting business processes.

Transport Maintenance

In addition to all this, GDS must maintain a fleet of transports. Careful records are kept on the repair and preventative maintenance work done on each transport.

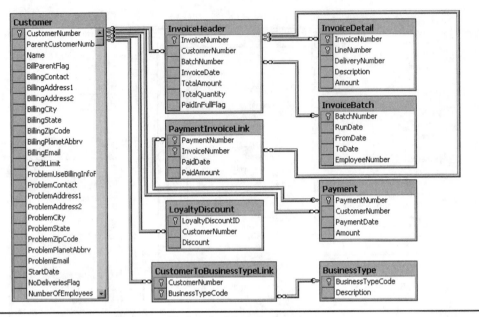

Figure 3-22   *The accounting department tables from the Galactic database*

GDS also has a record of each flight a transport makes, as well as any accidents and mishaps involved.

Maintenance records are extremely important, not only to GDS itself, but also to the Federation Space Flight Administration (FSFA). Without proper maintenance records on all its transports, GDS would be shut down by the FSFA in a nanosecond. You may think this is an exaggeration, but the bureaucratic androids at the FSFA have extremely high clock rates.

Figure 3-23 shows the transport maintenance tables in the Galactic database.

Querying Data

You have now looked at the database concepts of normalization, relations, and joins. You have also been introduced to the Galactic database. We use this relational database throughout the remainder of this book for our examples. Now, it is time to look more specifically at how you retrieve the data from the database into a format you can use for reporting. This is done through the database query.

A *query* is a request for some action on the data in one or more tables. An *INSERT query* adds one or more rows to a database table. An *UPDATE query* modifies the data in one or more existing rows of a table. A *DELETE query* removes one or more rows

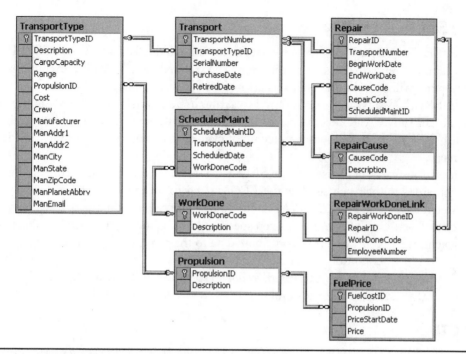

Figure 3-23   *The transport maintenance tables from the Galactic database*

from a table. Because we are primarily interested in retrieving data for reporting, the query we are going to concern ourselves with is the *SELECT query,* which reads data from one or more tables (it does not add, update, or delete data).

We will look at the various parts of the SELECT query. This is to help you become familiar with this important aspect of reporting. The good news is Reporting Services provides a tool to guide you through the creation of queries, including the SELECT query. That tool is the Query Designer.

If you are familiar with SELECT queries and are more comfortable typing your queries from scratch, you can bypass the Query Designer and type in your queries directly. If SELECT queries are new to you, the following section can help you become familiar with the SELECT query and what it can do for you. Rest assured: The Query Designer enables you to take advantage of all the features of the SELECT query without having to memorize syntax or type a lot of code.

NOTE

If you have another query-creation tool you like to use instead of the Query Designer, you can create your queries with that tool and then copy them into the appropriate locations in the report definition.

The SELECT Query

The SELECT query is used to retrieve data from tables in the database. When a SELECT query is run, it returns a result set containing the selected data. With few exceptions, your reports will be built on result sets created by SELECT queries.

The SELECT query is often referred to as a *SELECT statement*. One reason for this is because it can be read like an English sentence or statement. As with a sentence in English, a SELECT statement is made up of clauses that modify the meaning of the statement.

The various parts, or clauses, of the SELECT statement enable you to control the data contained in the result set. Use the *FROM clause* to specify which table the data will be selected from. The *FIELD LIST* permits you to choose the columns that will appear in the result set. The *JOIN clause* lets you specify additional tables that will be joined with the table in the FROM clause to contribute data to the result set. The *WHERE clause* enables you to set conditions that determine which rows will be included in the result set. Finally, you can use the *ORDER BY clause* to sort the result set, and the *GROUP BY clause* and the *HAVING clause* to combine detail rows into summary rows.

NOTE

The query statements shown in the remainder of this chapter all use the Galactic database. If you want to try out the various query statements as they are being discussed, open a query window for the Galactic database in the SQL Server Management Studio. If you are not familiar with SQL Server Management Studio, you can try out the queries in the Reporting Services Generic Query Designer. To do this, turn to Chapter 5 and follow the steps for Task 1 of the Transport List Report, but stop after Step 29. You will be in the Generic Query Designer. You can enter the query statements in the upper portion of the Generic Query Designer and execute them by clicking the toolbar button with the exclamation point (!). When you are finished, close the application without saving your changes.

The FROM Clause

The SELECT statement in its simplest form includes only a FROM clause. Here is a SELECT statement that retrieves all rows and all columns from the Customer table:

```
SELECT *
FROM dbo.Customer
```

The word "SELECT" is required to let the database know this is going to be a SELECT query, as opposed to an INSERT, UPDATE, or DELETE query. The asterisk (*) means all columns will be included in the result set. The remainder of the statement is the

FROM clause. It says the data is to be selected from the Customer table. We will discuss the meaning of "dbo." in a moment.

As stated earlier, the SELECT statement can be read as if it were a sentence. This SELECT statement is read, "Select all columns from the Customer table." If we run this SELECT statement in the Galactic database, the results would appear similar to Figure 3-24. The SELECT query is being run in the Query Designer window of Visual Studio. Note the scroll bars on the right and on the bottom of the result set area indicate that not all of the rows and columns returned can fit on the screen.

Note the table name, Customer, has "dbo." in front of it. The dbo is the name of the owner of the table. Usually, this is the user who created the table. Here, dbo stands for database owner, meaning the user who owns the database is also the user who owns the table. The dbo abbreviation is also another name for the system administrator login. In many cases, an administrative user, logged into the database, will create the database tables. Because of this, the table owner will more than likely be dbo.

In the Galactic database, the dbo.Customer table was created by the system administrator. If another user with a database login of User2 also has rights to create tables in the Galactic database, they could also create a Customer table. This second table would be known as User2.Customer.

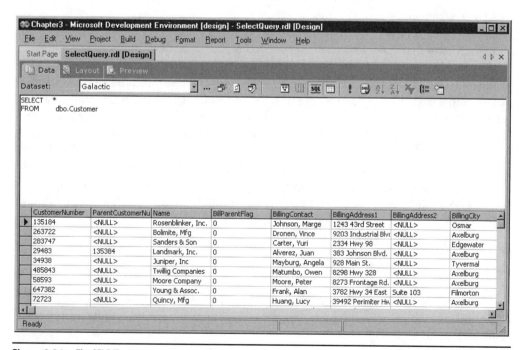

Figure 3-24   *The SELECT statement in its simplest form*

This situation, with two tables of the same name in the same database, does not happen often and is probably not a great idea. It can quickly lead to confusion and errors. Even though this is a rare occurrence, the Query Designer needs to account for this situation. The Query Designer uses both the name of the table owner and the name of the table itself in the queries it builds and executes for you.

The FIELD LIST

In the previous example, the result set created by the SELECT statement contained all of the columns in the table. In most cases, especially when creating reports, you only need to work with some of the columns of a table in any given result set. Including all of the columns in a result set when only a few columns are required wastes computing power and network bandwidth.

A FIELD LIST provides the capability you need to specify which columns to include in the result set. When a FIELD LIST is added to the SELECT statement, it appears similar to the following:

```
SELECT CustomerNumber, Name, BillingCity
FROM dbo.Customer
```

The bold portion of the SELECT statement indicates changes from the previous SELECT statement.

This statement returns only the CustomerNumber, Name, and BillingCity columns from the Customer table. The result set created by this SELECT statement is shown in Figure 3-25.

In addition to the names of the fields to include in the result set, the FIELD LIST can contain a word that influences the number of rows in the result set. Usually, there is one row in the result set for each row in the table from which you are selecting data. However, this can be changed by adding the word "DISTINCT" at the beginning of the FIELD LIST.

When you use DISTINCT in the FIELD LIST, you are saying that you only want one row in the result set for each distinct set of values. In other words, the result set from a DISTINCT query will not have any two rows that have exactly the same values in every column. Here is an example of a DISTINCT query:

```
SELECT DISTINCT BillingCity
FROM dbo.Customer
```

This query returns a list of all the billing cities in the Customer table. A number of customers have the same billing city, but these duplicates have been removed from the result set, as shown in Figure 3-26.

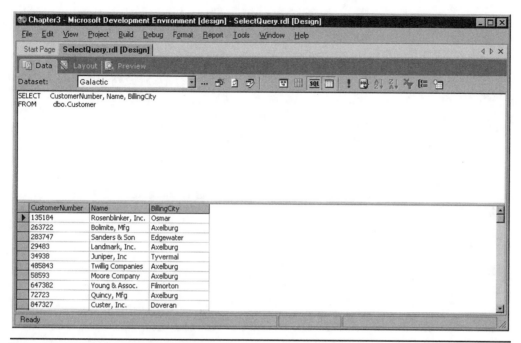

Figure 3-25   *A SELECT statement with a FIELD LIST*

The JOIN Clause

When your database is properly normalized, you are likely to need data from more than one table to fulfill your reporting requirements. As discussed earlier in this chapter, the way to get information from more than one table is to use a join. The JOIN clause in the SELECT statement enables you to include a join of two or more tables in your result set.

The first part of the JOIN clause specifies which table is being joined. The second part determines the two columns that are linked to create the join. Joining the Invoice Header table to the Customer table looks like this:

```
SELECT dbo.Customer.CustomerNumber,
    dbo.Customer.Name,
    dbo.Customer.BillingCity,
    dbo.InvoiceHeader.InvoiceNumber,
    dbo.InvoiceHeader.TotalAmount
FROM dbo.Customer
INNER JOIN dbo.InvoiceHeader
 ON dbo.Customer.CustomerNumber = dbo.InvoiceHeader.CustomerNumber
```

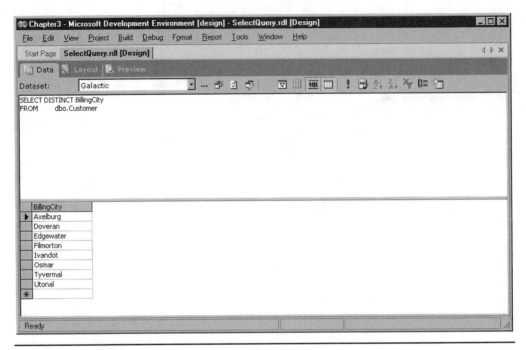

Figure 3-26 *A DISTINCT query*

With the Customer table and the Invoice Header table joined, you have a situation where some columns in the result set have the same name. For example, a CustomerNumber column is in the Customer table, and a CustomerNumber column is in the Invoice Header table. When you use the FIELD LIST to tell the database which fields to include in the result set, you need to uniquely identify these fields using both the table name and the column name.

If you do not do this, the query will not run and you will receive an error. Nothing prevents you from using the table name in front of each column name, whether it is a duplicate or not, as in this example. Using the table name in front of each column name makes it immediately obvious where every column in the result set is selected from. The result set created by this SELECT statement is shown in Figure 3-27.

You can add a third table to the query by adding another JOIN clause to the SELECT statement. This additional table can be joined to the table in the FROM clause or to the table in the first JOIN clause. In this statement, we add the Loyalty Discount table and join it to the Customer table:

```
SELECT dbo.Customer.CustomerNumber,
    dbo.Customer.Name,
    dbo.Customer.BillingCity,
```

```
    dbo.InvoiceHeader.InvoiceNumber,
    dbo.InvoiceHeader.TotalAmount,
    dbo.LoyaltyDiscount.Discount
FROM dbo.Customer
INNER JOIN dbo.InvoiceHeader
 ON dbo.Customer.CustomerNumber = dbo.InvoiceHeader.CustomerNumber
INNER JOIN dbo.LoyaltyDiscount
 ON dbo.Customer.CustomerNumber = dbo.LoyaltyDiscount.CustomerNumber
```

The result set from this SELECT statement is shown in Figure 3-28. Notice that the result set is rather small. This is because Landmark, Inc. is the only customer currently receiving a loyalty discount. Because an INNER JOIN was used to add the Loyalty Discount table, only customers that have a loyalty discount are included in the result set.

To make our result set a little more interesting, let's try joining the Loyalty Discount table with an OUTER JOIN rather than an INNER JOIN. Here is the same statement,

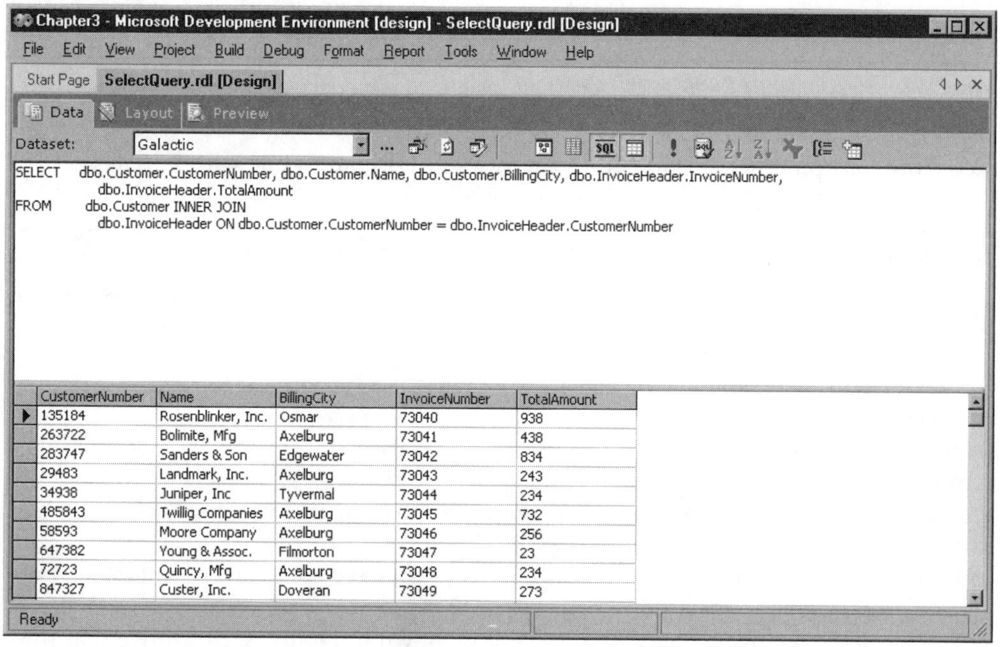

Figure 3-27 *A SELECT statement with a JOIN clause*

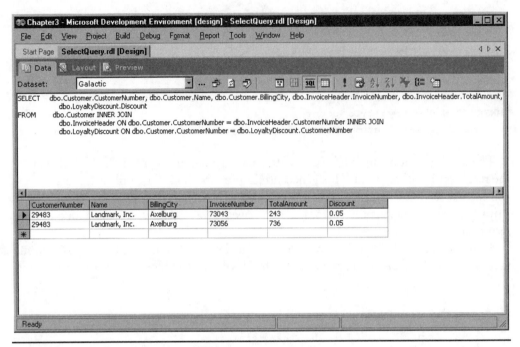

Figure 3-28 *A SELECT statement with two JOIN clauses*

except the Customer table is joined to the Loyalty Discount table with a LEFT OUTER JOIN:

```
SELECT dbo.Customer.CustomerNumber,
    dbo.Customer.Name,
    dbo.Customer.BillingCity,
    dbo.InvoiceHeader.InvoiceNumber,
    dbo.InvoiceHeader.TotalAmount,
    dbo.LoyaltyDiscount.Discount
FROM dbo.Customer
INNER JOIN dbo.InvoiceHeader
 ON dbo.Customer.CustomerNumber = dbo.InvoiceHeader.CustomerNumber
LEFT OUTER JOIN dbo.LoyaltyDiscount
 ON dbo.Customer.CustomerNumber = dbo.LoyaltyDiscount.CustomerNumber
```

The result set for this SELECT statement is shown in Figure 3-29. Notice that the value for the Discount column is NULL in the rows for all of the customers except for Landmark, Inc. This is to be expected, because there is no record in the Loyalty Discount table to join with these customers. When no value is in a column, the result set will contain a NULL value.

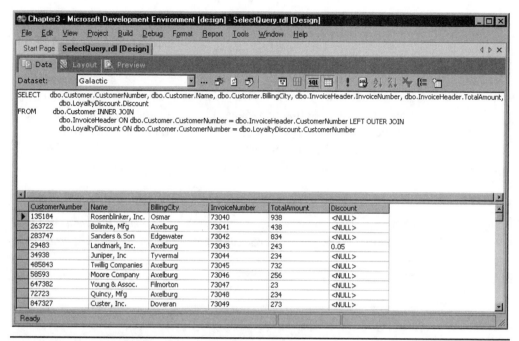

Figure 3-29   *A SELECT statement with an INNER JOIN and an OUTER JOIN*

The WHERE Clause

Up to this point, the result sets have included all of the rows in the table or all of the rows that result from the joins. The FIELD LIST limits which columns are being returned in the result set. Nothing, however, placed a limit on the rows.

To limit the number of rows in the result set, you need to add a WHERE clause to your SELECT statement. The WHERE clause includes one or more logical expressions that must be true for a row before it can be included in the result set. Here is an example of a SELECT statement with a WHERE clause:

```
SELECT dbo.Customer.CustomerNumber,
    dbo.Customer.Name,
    dbo.Customer.BillingCity,
    dbo.InvoiceHeader.InvoiceNumber,
    dbo.InvoiceHeader.TotalAmount,
    dbo.LoyaltyDiscount.Discount
FROM dbo.Customer
INNER JOIN dbo.InvoiceHeader
```

```
ON dbo.Customer.CustomerNumber = dbo.InvoiceHeader.CustomerNumber
LEFT OUTER JOIN dbo.LoyaltyDiscount
ON dbo.Customer.CustomerNumber = dbo.LoyaltyDiscount.CustomerNumber
WHERE (dbo.Customer.BillingCity = 'Axelburg')
```

The word 'Axelburg' (enclosed in single quotes) is a string constant. A *string constant*, also known as a *string literal*, is an actual text value. The string constant instructs SQL Server to use the text between the single quotes as a value rather than the name of a column or a table. In this example, only customers with a value of Axelburg in their BillingCity column will be included in the result set, as shown in Figure 3-30.

NOTE

Microsoft SQL Server 2008, in its standard configuration, insists on single quotes around string constants, such as 'Axelburg' in the previous SELECT statement. SQL Server 2008 assumes that anything enclosed in double quotes is a field name.

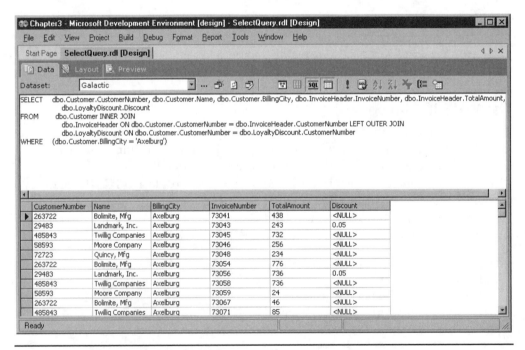

Figure 3-30   *A SELECT statement with a WHERE clause*

To create more complex criteria for your result set, you can have multiple logical expressions in the WHERE clause. The logical expressions are linked together with an AND or an OR. When an AND is used to link logical expressions, the logical expressions on both sides of the AND must be true for a row in order for that row to be included in the result set. When an OR is used to link two logical expressions, either one or both of the logical expressions must be true for a row in order for that row to be included in the result set.

This SELECT statement has two logical expressions in the WHERE clause:

```
SELECT dbo.Customer.CustomerNumber,
    dbo.Customer.Name,
    dbo.Customer.BillingCity,
    dbo.InvoiceHeader.InvoiceNumber,
    dbo.InvoiceHeader.TotalAmount,
    dbo.LoyaltyDiscount.Discount
FROM dbo.Customer
INNER JOIN dbo.InvoiceHeader
 ON dbo.Customer.CustomerNumber = dbo.InvoiceHeader.CustomerNumber
LEFT OUTER JOIN dbo.LoyaltyDiscount
 ON dbo.Customer.CustomerNumber = dbo.LoyaltyDiscount.CustomerNumber
WHERE (dbo.Customer.BillingCity = 'Axelburg')
AND (dbo.Customer.Name > 'C')
```

Only customers with a value of Axelburg in their BillingCity column *and* with a name that comes after C will be included in the result set. This result set is shown in Figure 3-31.

The ORDER BY Clause

Up to this point, the data in the result sets has shown up in any order it pleases. As discussed previously, this will probably not be acceptable for most reports. You can add an ORDER BY clause to your SELECT statement to obtain a sorted result set. This statement includes an ORDER BY clause with multiple columns:

```
SELECT dbo.Customer.CustomerNumber,
    dbo.Customer.Name,
    dbo.Customer.BillingCity,
    dbo.InvoiceHeader.InvoiceNumber,
    dbo.InvoiceHeader.TotalAmount,
    dbo.LoyaltyDiscount.Discount
FROM dbo.Customer
INNER JOIN dbo.InvoiceHeader
```

```
 ON dbo.Customer.CustomerNumber = dbo.InvoiceHeader.CustomerNumber
LEFT OUTER JOIN dbo.LoyaltyDiscount
 ON dbo.Customer.CustomerNumber = dbo.LoyaltyDiscount.CustomerNumber
WHERE (dbo.Customer.BillingCity = 'Axelburg')
AND (dbo.Customer.Name > 'C')
ORDER BY dbo.Customer.Name DESC, dbo.InvoiceHeader.InvoiceNumber
```

The result set created by this SELECT statement, shown in Figure 3-32, is first sorted by the contents of the Name column in the Customer table. The DESC that follows dbo.Customer.Name in the ORDER BY clause specifies the sort order for the customer name sort. DESC means this sort is done in descending order. In other words, the customer names will be sorted from the end of the alphabet to the beginning.

Several rows have the same customer name. For this reason, a second sort column is specified. This second sort is only applied within each group of identical customer names. For example, Twillig Companies has three rows in the result set. These three rows are sorted by the second sort, which is invoice number. No sort order is specified for the invoice number sort, so this defaults to an ascending sort. In other words, the invoice numbers are sorted from lowest to highest.

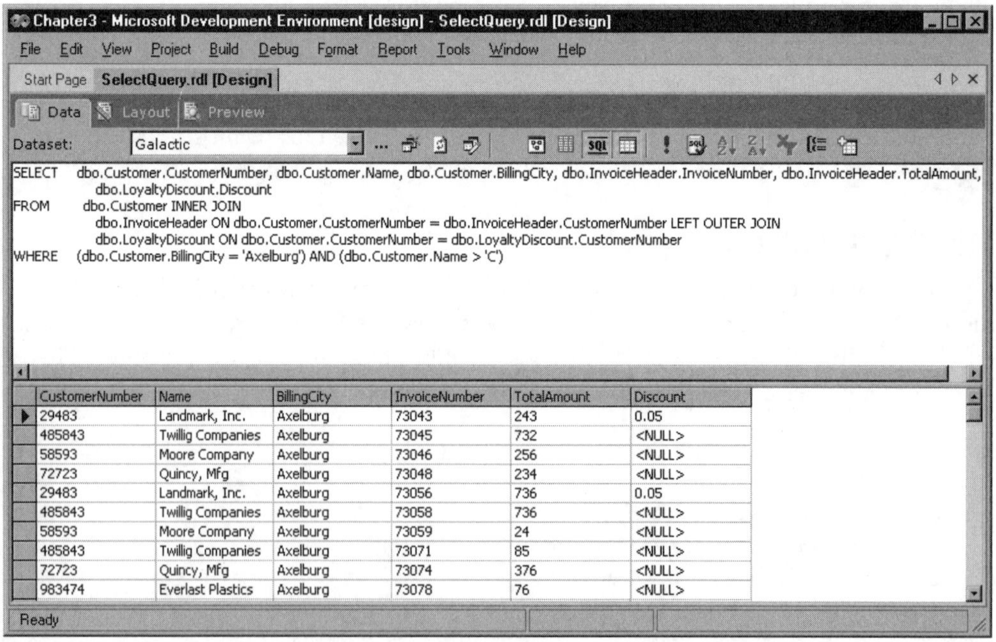

Figure 3-31   *A SELECT statement with two logical expressions in the WHERE clause*

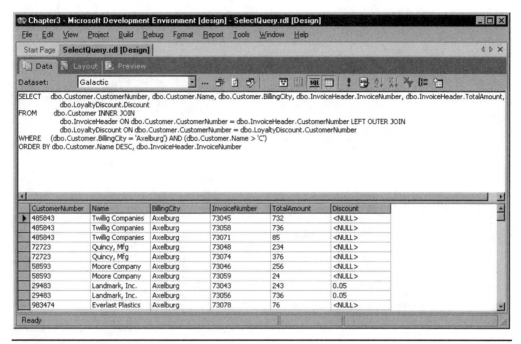

Figure 3-32   *A SELECT statement with an ORDER BY clause*

Constant and Calculated Fields

Our SELECT statement examples thus far have used an asterisk symbol or a FIELD LIST that includes only columns. A FIELD LIST can, in fact, include other things as well. For example, a FIELD LIST can include a constant value, as is shown here:

```
SELECT dbo.Customer.CustomerNumber,
    dbo.Customer.Name,
    dbo.Customer.BillingCity,
    dbo.InvoiceHeader.InvoiceNumber,
    dbo.InvoiceHeader.TotalAmount,
    dbo.LoyaltyDiscount.Discount,
    'AXEL' AS ProcessingCode
FROM dbo.Customer
INNER JOIN dbo.InvoiceHeader
 ON dbo.Customer.CustomerNumber = dbo.InvoiceHeader.CustomerNumber
LEFT OUTER JOIN dbo.LoyaltyDiscount
 ON dbo.Customer.CustomerNumber = dbo.LoyaltyDiscount.CustomerNumber
WHERE (dbo.Customer.BillingCity = 'Axelburg')
AND (dbo.Customer.Name > 'C')
ORDER BY dbo.Customer.Name DESC, dbo.InvoiceHeader.InvoiceNumber
```

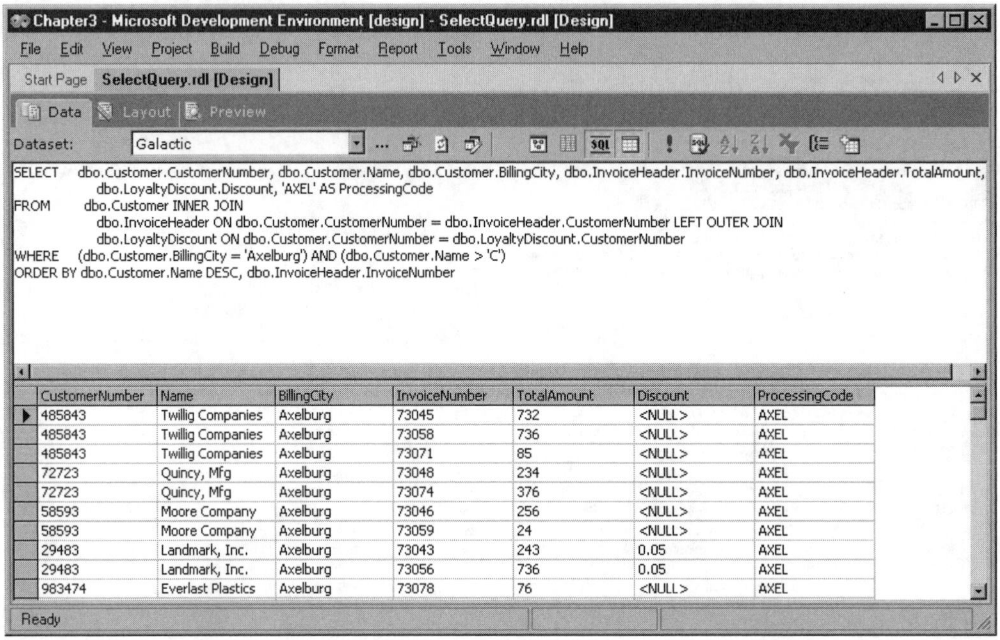

Figure 3-33   *A SELECT statement with a constant in the FIELD LIST*

The string constant 'AXEL' has been added to the FIELD LIST. This creates a new column in the result set with the value AXEL in each row. By including AS ProcessingCode on this line, we give this result set column a column name of ProcessingCode. Constant values of other data types, such as dates or numbers, can also be added to the FIELD LIST. The result set for this SELECT statement is shown in Figure 3-33.

In addition to adding constant values, you can include calculations in the FIELD LIST. This SELECT statement calculates the discounted invoice amount based on the total amount of the invoice and the loyalty discount:

```
SELECT dbo.Customer.CustomerNumber,
    dbo.Customer.Name,
    dbo.Customer.BillingCity,
    dbo.InvoiceHeader.InvoiceNumber,
    dbo.InvoiceHeader.TotalAmount,
    dbo.LoyaltyDiscount.Discount,
    dbo.InvoiceHeader.TotalAmount -
      (dbo.InvoiceHeader.TotalAmount *
           dbo.LoyaltyDiscount.Discount)
             AS DiscountedTotalAmount
```

```
FROM dbo.Customer
INNER JOIN dbo.InvoiceHeader
 ON dbo.Customer.CustomerNumber = dbo.InvoiceHeader.CustomerNumber
LEFT OUTER JOIN dbo.LoyaltyDiscount
 ON dbo.Customer.CustomerNumber = dbo.LoyaltyDiscount.CustomerNumber
WHERE (dbo.Customer.BillingCity = 'Axelburg')
AND (dbo.Customer.Name > 'C')
ORDER BY dbo.Customer.Name DESC, dbo.InvoiceHeader.InvoiceNumber
```

The result set for this SELECT statement is shown in Figure 3-34. Notice the value for the calculated column, DiscountedTotalAmount, is NULL for all the rows that are not for Landmark, Inc. This is because we are using the value of the Discount column in our calculation. The Discount column has a value of NULL for every row except for the Landmark, Inc. rows.

A NULL value cannot be used successfully in any calculation. Any time you try to add, subtract, multiply, or divide a number by NULL, the result is NULL. The only way to receive a value in these situations is to give the database a valid value to use in

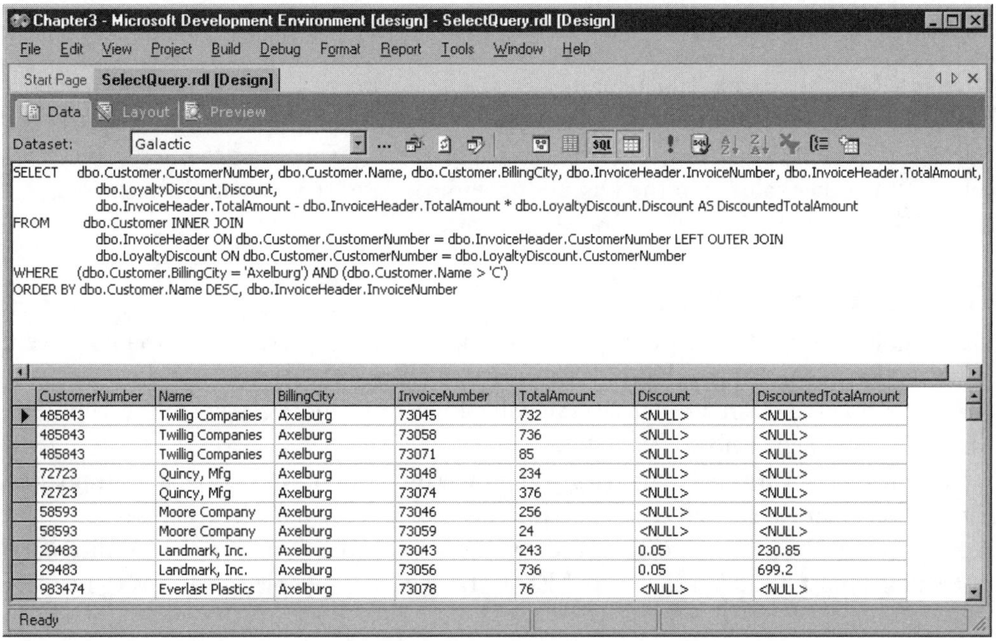

Figure 3-34   *A SELECT statement with a calculated column in the FIELD LIST*

place of any NULLs it might encounter. This is done using the ISNULL( ) function, as shown in the following statement:

```
SELECT dbo.Customer.CustomerNumber,
    dbo.Customer.Name,
    dbo.Customer.BillingCity,
    dbo.InvoiceHeader.InvoiceNumber,
    dbo.InvoiceHeader.TotalAmount,
    dbo.LoyaltyDiscount.Discount,
    dbo.InvoiceHeader.TotalAmount -
       (dbo.InvoiceHeader.TotalAmount *
          ISNULL(dbo.LoyaltyDiscount.Discount, 0.00))
                    AS DiscountedTotalAmount
FROM dbo.Customer
INNER JOIN dbo.InvoiceHeader
 ON dbo.Customer.CustomerNumber = dbo.InvoiceHeader.CustomerNumber
LEFT OUTER JOIN dbo.LoyaltyDiscount
 ON dbo.Customer.CustomerNumber = dbo.LoyaltyDiscount.CustomerNumber
WHERE (dbo.Customer.BillingCity = 'Axelburg')
AND (dbo.Customer.Name > 'C')
ORDER BY dbo.Customer.Name DESC, dbo.InvoiceHeader.InvoiceNumber
```

Now, when the database encounters a NULL value in the Discount column while it is performing the calculation, it substitutes a value of 0.00 and continues with the calculation. The database only performs this substitution when it encounters a NULL value. If any other value is in the Discount column, it uses that value. The result set from this SELECT statement is shown in Figure 3-35.

The GROUP BY Clause

Our sample SELECT statement appears to resemble a run-on sentence. You have seen, however, that each of these clauses is necessary to change the meaning of the statement and to provide the desired result set. We will add just two more clauses to the sample SELECT statement before we are done.

At times, as you are analyzing data, you only want to see information at a summary level, rather than viewing all the detail. In other words, you want the result set to group together the information from several rows to form a summary row. Additional instructions must be added to our SELECT statement in two places for this to happen.

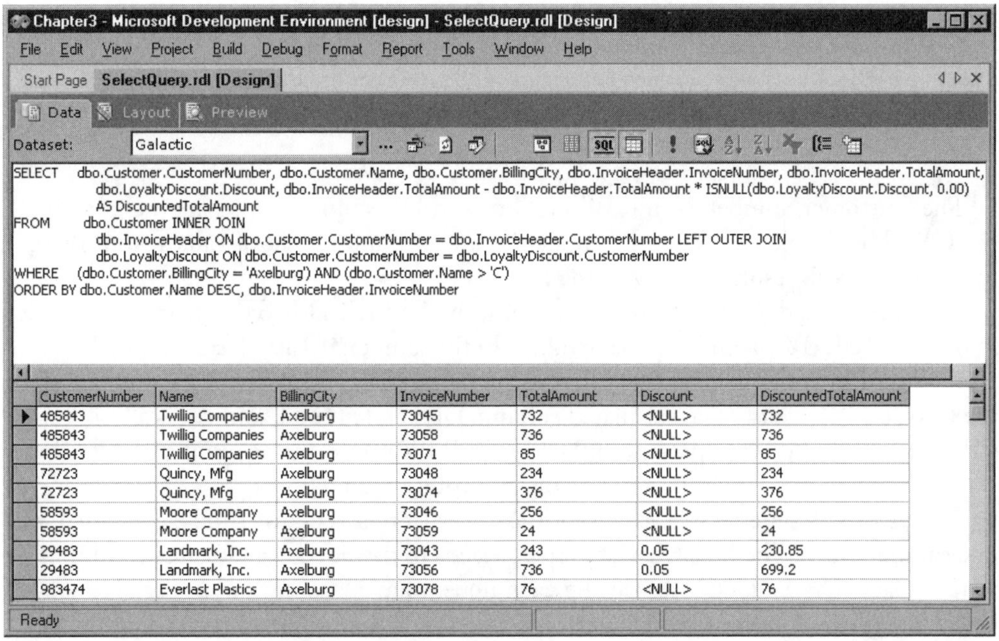

Figure 3-35   *A SELECT statement using the ISNULL() function*

First, you need to specify which columns are going to be used to determine when a summary row will be created. These columns are placed in the GROUP BY clause. Consider the following SELECT statement:

```
SELECT dbo.Customer.CustomerNumber,
    dbo.Customer.Name,
    dbo.Customer.BillingCity,
    COUNT(dbo.InvoiceHeader.InvoiceNumber) AS NumberOfInvoices,
    SUM(dbo.InvoiceHeader.TotalAmount) AS TotalAmount,
    dbo.LoyaltyDiscount.Discount,
    SUM(dbo.InvoiceHeader.TotalAmount -
      (dbo.InvoiceHeader.TotalAmount *
        ISNULL (dbo.LoyaltyDiscount.Discount, 0.00)) )
                AS DiscountedTotalAmount
FROM dbo.Customer
INNER JOIN dbo.InvoiceHeader
 ON dbo.Customer.CustomerNumber = dbo.InvoiceHeader.CustomerNumber
LEFT OUTER JOIN dbo.LoyaltyDiscount
 ON dbo.Customer.CustomerNumber = dbo.LoyaltyDiscount.CustomerNumber
```

```
WHERE (dbo.Customer.BillingCity = 'Axelburg')
AND (dbo.Customer.Name > 'C')
GROUP BY dbo.Customer.CustomerNumber, dbo.Customer.Name,
    dbo.Customer.BillingCity, dbo.LoyaltyDiscount.Discount
ORDER BY dbo.Customer.Name DESC
```

The CustomerNumber, Name, BillingCity, and Discount columns are included in the GROUP BY clause. When this query is run, each unique set of values from these four columns will result in a row in the result set.

Second, you need to specify how the columns in the FIELD LIST that are not included in the GROUP BY clause are to be handled. In the sample SELECT statement, the InvoiceNumber and TotalAmount columns are in the FIELD LIST, but are not part of the GROUP BY clause. The calculated column, DiscountedTotalAmount, is also in the FIELD LIST, but it is not present in the GROUP BY clause. In the sample SELECT statement, these three columns are the non-group-by columns.

The SELECT statement is asking for the values from several rows to be combined into one summary row. The SELECT statement needs to provide a way for this combining to take place. This is done by enclosing each non-group-by column in a special function called an *aggregate function,* which performs a mathematical operation on values from a number of rows and returns a single result. Aggregate functions include:

▶ **SUM( )**   Returns the sum of the values

▶ **AVG( )**   Returns the average of the values

▶ **COUNT( )**   Returns a count of the values

▶ **MAX( )**   Returns the largest value

▶ **MIN( )**   Returns the smallest value

The SELECT statement in our GROUP BY example uses the SUM( ) aggregate function to return the sum of the invoice amount and the sum of the discounted amount for each customer. It also uses the COUNT( ) aggregate function to return the number of invoices for each customer. The result set from this SELECT statement is shown in Figure 3-36. Note when an aggregate function is placed around a column name in the FIELD LIST, the SELECT statement can no longer determine what name to use for that column in the result set. You need to supply a column name to use in the result set, as shown in this SELECT statement.

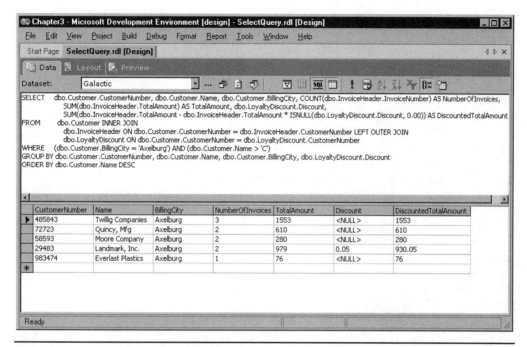

Figure 3-36   *A SELECT statement with a GROUP BY clause*

NOTE

When you're using a GROUP BY clause, all columns in the FIELD LIST must either be included in the GROUP BY clause or be enclosed in an aggregate function. In the sample SELECT statement, the CustomerNumber column is all that is necessary in the GROUP BY clause to provide the desired grouping. However, because the Name, BillingCity, and Discount columns do not lend themselves to being aggregated, they are included in the GROUP BY clause along with the CustomerNumber column.

The HAVING Clause

The GROUP BY clause has a special clause that can be used with it to determine which grouped rows will be included in the result set. This is the HAVING clause. The HAVING clause functions similarly to the WHERE clause. The WHERE clause limits the rows in the result set by checking conditions at the row level. The *HAVING* clause limits the rows in the result set by checking conditions at the group level.

Consider the following SELECT statement:

```
SELECT dbo.Customer.CustomerNumber,
    dbo.Customer.Name,
    dbo.Customer.BillingCity,
    COUNT(dbo.InvoiceHeader.InvoiceNumber) AS NumberOfInvoices,
    SUM(dbo.InvoiceHeader.TotalAmount) AS TotalAmount,
    dbo.LoyaltyDiscount.Discount,
    SUM(dbo.InvoiceHeader.TotalAmount -
      (dbo.InvoiceHeader.TotalAmount *
        ISNULL(dbo.LoyaltyDiscount.Discount,0.00)))
                   AS DiscountedTotalAmount
FROM dbo.Customer
INNER JOIN dbo.InvoiceHeader
 ON dbo.Customer.CustomerNumber = dbo.InvoiceHeader.CustomerNumber
LEFT OUTER JOIN dbo.LoyaltyDiscount
 ON dbo.Customer.CustomerNumber = dbo.LoyaltyDiscount.CustomerNumber
WHERE (dbo.Customer.BillingCity = 'Axelburg')
AND (dbo.Customer.Name > 'C')
GROUP BY dbo.Customer.CustomerNumber, dbo.Customer.Name,
    dbo.Customer.BillingCity, dbo.LoyaltyDiscount.Discount
HAVING COUNT(dbo.InvoiceHeader.InvoiceNumber) >= 2
ORDER BY dbo.Customer.Name DESC
```

The WHERE clause says that a row must have a BillingCity column with a value of Axelburg and a Name column with a value greater than C before it can be included in the group. The HAVING clause says a group must contain at least two invoices before it can be included in the result set. The result set for this SELECT statement is shown in Figure 3-37.

On to the Reports

Good reporting depends more on getting the right data out of the database than it does on creating a clean report design and delivering the report in a timely manner. If you are feeling a little overwhelmed by the workings of relational databases and SELECT queries, don't worry. Refer to this chapter from time to time if you need to.

Also, remember Reporting Services provides you with the Query Designer tool to assist with the query-creation process. You needn't remember the exact syntax for the LEFT OUTER JOIN or a GROUP BY clause. What you do need to know are the capabilities of the SELECT statement so you know what to instruct the Query Designer to create.

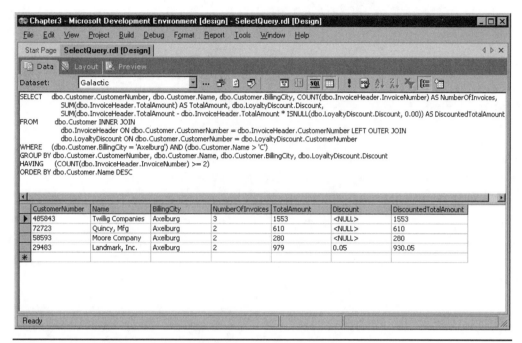

Figure 3-37   *A SELECT statement with a HAVING clause*

Finally, when you are creating your queries, use the same method that was used here: In other words, build them one step at a time. Join together the tables you will need for your report, determine what columns are required, and then come up with a WHERE clause that gets you only the rows you are looking for. After that, you can add in the sorting and grouping. Assemble one clause, and then another and another, and pretty soon, you will have a slam-bang query that will give you exactly the data you need!

Now, on to the reports....

Chapter 4

A Visit to Emerald City: The Report Wizard

In This Chapter

- ▶ **Obtaining the Galactic Database**
- ▶ **Your First Report**
- ▶ **An Interactive Table Report**
- ▶ **Creating Matrix Reports**
- ▶ **Report Parameters**
- ▶ **Flying Solo**

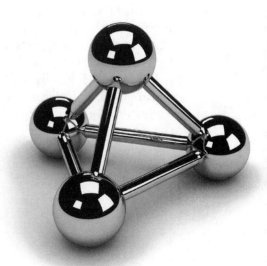

I f the relational database concepts of Chapter 3 were new to you, you may feel like you have been through a twister and are not in Kansas anymore. You can take heart, knowing you have completed the preliminaries and are now ready to start building reports. So, without further ado, strap on your ruby slippers and follow the yellow-brick road, because you are off to see the wizard!

That wizard is, of course, the Report Wizard found in Visual Studio and the Business Intelligence Development Studio. Like the ruler of the Emerald City, the Report Wizard is not all-powerful. For example, the Report Wizard will not let you make use of all the features available in Reporting Services. The wizard is, however, a great place to get a feel for the way reports are constructed.

Obtaining the Galactic Database

Beginning with this chapter, we will create sample reports using the Galactic database. If you have not done so already, download the sample code from this book's web page at www.mhprofessional.com. Search for the book's web page using the ISBN, which is 0071548084, and then use the "Code" link to download the zip file containing the book's material. Follow the instructions in the zip file to install the Galactic database and the other sample code as needed.

Your First Report

Once you have installed the Galactic database, you are ready to build your first Reporting Services report. Of course, few people build reports just for the fun of it. Usually, there is some business reason for this endeavor. In this book, as stated in the previous chapter, we use the business needs of Galactic Delivery Services (GDS) as the basis for our sample reports.

Each of the sample reports used in this book is presented in a manner similar to what you see in this section. The report is introduced with a list of the Reporting Services features it highlights. This is followed by the business need of our sample company, Galactic Delivery Services, which this report is meant to fill. Next is an overview of the tasks that must be accomplished to create the report.

Finally, there are the steps to walk through for each task, step by step. In addition to the step-by-step description, each task includes a few notes to provide additional information on the steps you just completed. Follow the step-by-step instructions to complete the task, and then read through the task notes to gain additional understanding of the process you have just completed. You can complete the step-by-step instructions using either the Business Intelligence Development Studio or Visual Studio.

The Customer List Report

Here is our first attempt at creating a report: the Customer List Report.

Features Highlighted

▶ Creating a data source

▶ Using the Query Designer to create a dataset

▶ Using the Report Wizard to create a table report

Business Need   The accounting department at Galactic Delivery Services would like an e-mail directory containing all the billing contacts for its customers. The directory should be an alphabetical list of all GDS customers. It must include the customer name, along with a billing contact and a billing e-mail address for each customer.

Task Overview

1. Begin a New Project in the Business Intelligence Development Studio or Visual Studio
2. Create a Data Source
3. Create a Dataset
4. Choose the Report Layout

Customer List Report, Task 1: Begin a New Project in the Business Intelligence Development Studio or Visual Studio

1. Run the Business Intelligence Development Studio or Visual Studio. The Start page appears, as shown here.

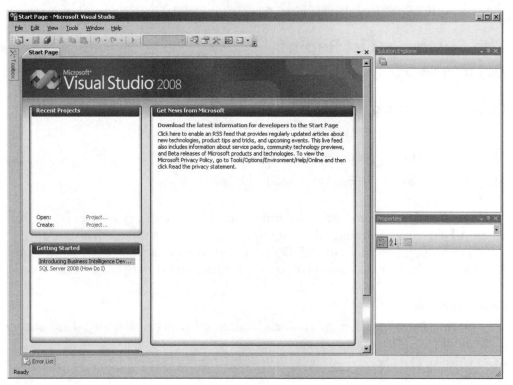

NOTE

The first illustration shows the default configuration of The Business Intelligence Development Studio. Your screen may vary if this configuration has been changed.

2. Click the New Project toolbar button to create a new project. This displays the New Project dialog box, as shown in the following illustration. (You can create a new project in three different ways: Select File | New | Project from the Main menu, click the New Project toolbar button, or click the Create: Project link on the Start page.)

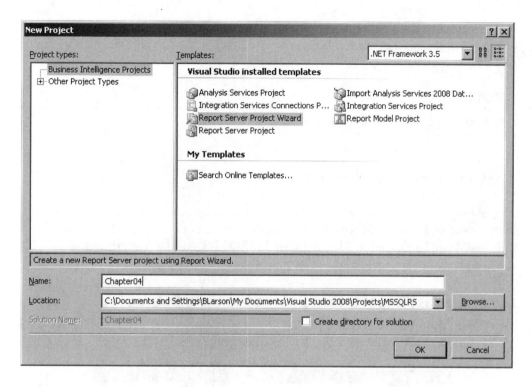

3. Select Business Intelligence Projects in the Project Types area of the dialog box.

4. Select Report Server Project Wizard in the Templates area of the dialog box.

5. Type **Chapter04** for the project name. This project will contain all the reports you create in this chapter.

6. Click Browse to open the Project Location dialog box.

7. The dialog box should default to the My Documents/Visual Studio 2008/Projects folder. If it does not, navigate to this folder.

8. Click the Make New Folder button.

9. Enter **MSSQLRS** for the name of the new folder. This folder will contain all the projects you create for this book. Press ENTER.

10. Click OK in the Project Location dialog box.

11. Make sure the Create directory for solution check box is unchecked. The New Project dialog box should now look like the second illustration.

Task Notes   We have now established a name and location for this project. This must be done for every project you create. Because the Business Intelligence Development Studio and Visual Studio use the project name to create a folder for all the project files, the project name must be a valid Windows folder name. You can use the Browse button to browse to the appropriate location, as we did here, or you can type the path in the Location text box.

> **NOTE**
>
> *Valid folder names can contain any character, except the following:*
>
> */ ? : & \ * " < > | # %*
>
> *In addition, a folder cannot be named "." or ".."*

The project name is appended to the end of the location path to create the full path for the folder that will contain the new project. In our example, a folder called Chapter04 will be created inside the folder MSSQLRS. All the files created as part of the Chapter04 project will be placed in this folder.

Customer List Report, Task 2: Create a Data Source

1. Click OK in the New Project dialog box to start the Report Wizard. The Welcome to the Report Wizard page appears, as shown here.

2. Click Next. The Select the Data Source page appears.
3. Type **Galactic** for the data source name.
4. Select Microsoft SQL Server from the Type drop-down list, if it is not already selected.
5. Click Edit. The Connection Properties dialog box appears.
6. Type the name of the Microsoft SQL Server database server that is hosting the Galactic database. If the Galactic database is hosted by the computer you are currently working on, you may type **(local)** for the server name.
7. Click the Use SQL Server Authentication radio button.
8. Type **GalacticReporting** for the user name.
9. Type **gds** for the Password.
10. Check the Save my password check box.
11. Select Galactic from the Select or Enter a Database Name drop-down list. The Connection Properties dialog box should now look like this:

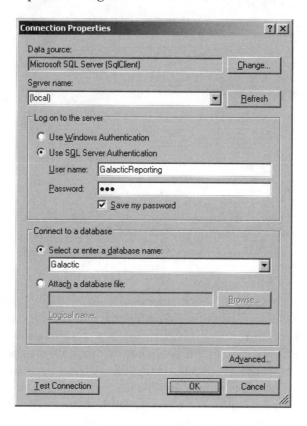

12. Click the Test Connection button. If the message "Test connection succeeded" appears, click OK. If an error message appears, make sure the name of your database server, the user name, the password, and the name of your database were entered properly. If your test connection still does not succeed, make sure you have correctly installed the Galactic database.

13. Click OK to return to the Select the Data Source page of the Report Wizard.

14. Check the Make this a shared data source check box. This page should now look like this:

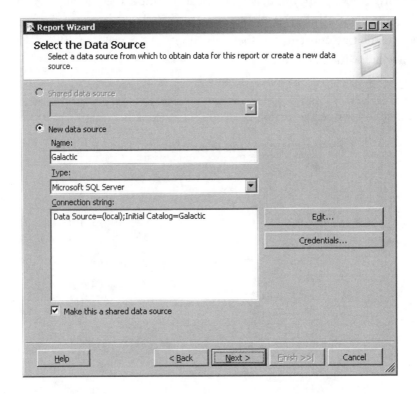

Task Notes   As discussed in Chapter 1, the data source is a set of instructions for connecting to the database server or the data file that will provide the information for your report. This set of instructions is also known as a *connection string*. In this sample report, we used the Connection Properties dialog box to build the connection string. Those of you who memorize connection strings can type the appropriate string on the Select the Data Source page without using the Connection Properties dialog box at all. The rest of us will continue to use the Connection Properties dialog box when building future reports to have the connection string created for us.

CAUTION

If you do type your own connection string, do not include the login and password information. The connection string is stored as plain text in the report definition file, so a password stored as part of the connection string is easy to discover. Instead, use the Credentials button on the Select the Data Source page to enter the login and password so they are stored in a more secure fashion.

Reporting Services can utilize data from a number of different databases and data files, but you need to tell the wizard what type of database or data file the report will be using. You did this using the Type drop-down list in Step 4 of the previous task. This selection tells Reporting Services which data provider to use when accessing the database or data file. When you select Microsoft SQL Server, Reporting Services uses the .NET Framework Data Provider for SQL Server. This data provider knows how to retrieve information from a SQL Server database.

The Type drop-down list on the Select the Data Source page includes only a few of the possible types of data sources. If you are using data from a data source other than a Microsoft SQL Server database, you need to click the Change button on the Connection Properties dialog box. This displays the Change Data Source dialog box shown in the following illustration.

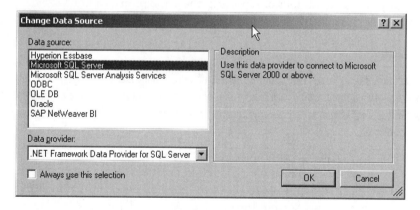

Use this dialog box to select the appropriate data source type.

Each data provider requires slightly different bits of information to create the connection string. The Connection Properties dialog box changes to suit the selected data provider. This means Steps 6 through 11 will vary when you use a data source type other than Microsoft SQL Server. Simply provide the information requested on the Connection Properties dialog box. Be sure to use the Test Connection button to make sure everything is entered properly before leaving the Connection Properties dialog box.

Checking the Save My Password check box on the Connection Properties page allows the data source credentials to be saved with the data source definition. The *data source credentials* are the user name and password information required to access that data source. The credentials are encrypted before they are saved to help protect them. If you are not comfortable having the credentials stored in this manner, leave both the user name and password fields blank. You will be prompted for the credentials every time you execute the report or modify the dataset.

NOTE

If you leave the data source credentials blank and your selected data source requires a login, you will be prompted for database credentials when you click Next on the Select the Data Source page. The credentials you enter here are used to create a connection to the data source for the Design the Query page and for the Query Designer. These credentials are not stored with the data source.

A data source can be used by a single report, or it can be shared by several reports in the same project. Checking the Make This a Shared Data Source check box allows this data source to be used by many reports. Shared data sources are stored separately from the reports that use them. Nonshared data sources are stored right in the report definition. If you have a number of reports in the same project that utilize data from the same database or the same data files, you will save time by using a shared data source.

CAUTION

Even though the data source credentials are encrypted, it is never a good idea to use the system administrator account or any other database login with system administrator privileges to access data for reporting. Always create a database login that has only the privileges required for reporting operations and use this login as the reporting credentials.

Some companies require that reports use data from a development database server while they are being developed and a production database server when the reports are completed. Using a shared data source in this type of an environment makes it easier to switch a number of reports from the development database server to the production database server. The change is made once to the shared data source, and all the reports are ready to go.

Customer List Report, Task 3: Create a Dataset

1. Click Next. The Design the Query page of the Report Wizard appears.
2. Click Query Builder. The Query Designer window opens with the Graphical Query Designer active as shown in this illustration.

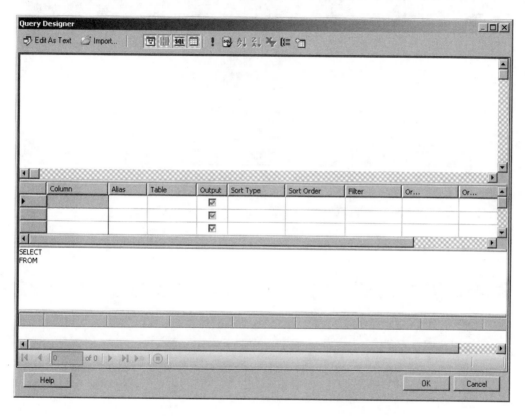

3. The Graphical Query Designer is divided into four horizontal sections. The top section is called the *diagram pane*. Right-click in the diagram pane. You see the Context menu, as shown here.

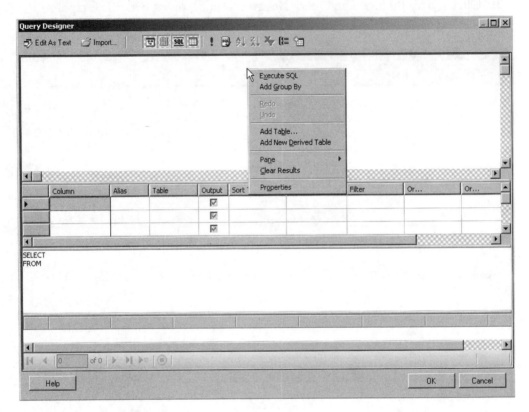

4. Select Add Table from the Context menu. This displays the Add Table dialog box shown here. This dialog box contains a list of all the tables, views, and functions that return datasets, which are found in the data source.

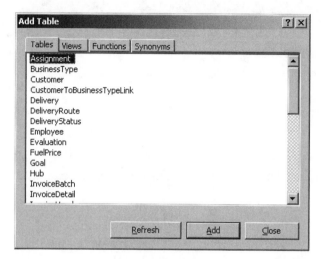

5. Double-click Customer in the list of tables. The Customer table is added to the query.

6. Click Close to exit the Add Table dialog box.

7. A list of the fields in the Customer table is displayed. Check the check box next to the Name field.

8. Scroll down the list of fields, and check the BillingContact and BillingEmail fields as well.

9. The section of the Query Designer directly below the diagram pane is called the *criteria pane.* In the criteria pane, type **1** in the Sort Order column across from the Name field. Or, you can click in the Sort Order column across from the Name field and select 1 from the drop-down list.

10. The section of the Query Designer directly below the criteria pane is the *SQL pane*. Right-click in the SQL pane. You see the Context menu shown here.

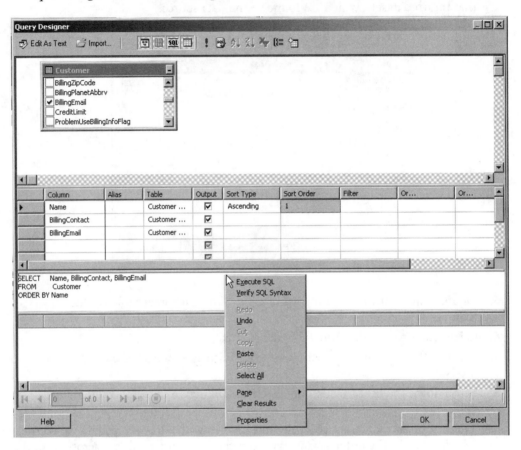

11. Select Execute SQL from the context menu. This runs the query and displays the results in the bottom section of the Query Designer. This bottom section is called the *results pane*. The Query Designer should now look like this:

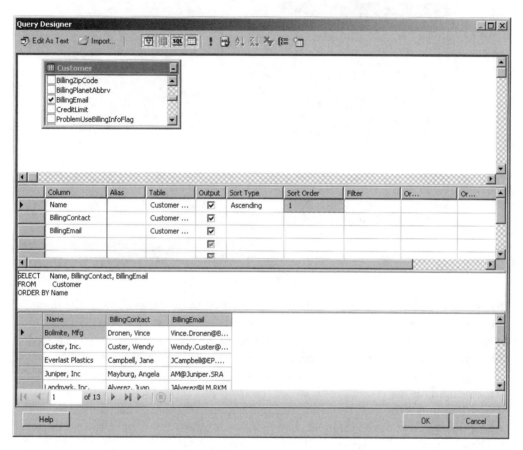

12. Click OK to return to the Design the Query page of the Report Wizard. This page should now look like the following illustration.

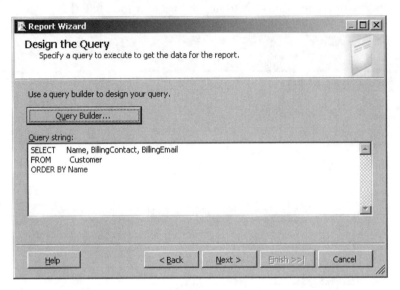

Task Notes The dataset represents the information to be retrieved from the data source and used in your report. The dataset consists of two parts. The first part is the database command used to retrieve data. This is the SELECT statement you created using the Query Designer. This database command is called the *query string*.

The second part is the list of the columns in the result set created by executing the query string. This list of columns is called the *structure* or *schema* of the result set. Visual Studio determines the field list by executing the query string in a special manner so it returns the structure of the result set, but it does not return any rows in the result set.

Those of you familiar with your data source and also familiar with the SELECT statement can type your SELECT statement in the Query String text box on the Design the Query page. This is especially appropriate when you are executing a stored procedure to retrieve data rather than using a SELECT statement. A *stored procedure* is a program saved inside the database itself that can be used to modify or retrieve data. Using stored procedures in a query string is discussed more in Chapter 7.

It is a good idea to run the query yourself before exiting the Query Designer. We did this in Steps 10 and 11 of this task. This ensures no errors exist in the SQL statement the Query Designer created for you. It also lets you look at the result set in the results pane so you can make sure you are getting the information you expected.

Customer List Report, Task 4: Choose the Report Layout

1. Click Next. The Select the Report Type page of the Report Wizard appears.

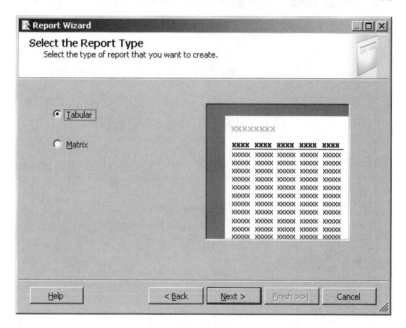

2. Make sure the Tabular radio button is selected, and click Next. The Design the Table page of the Report Wizard appears.

3. With the Name field highlighted in the Available fields list, click Details. The Name field moves to the Displayed fields list.

4. Do the same thing with the BillingContact and BillingEmail fields. The Design the Table page should now look like the following illustration.

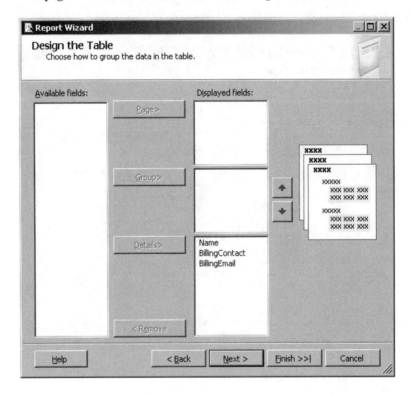

5. Click Next. Select the Generic style in the style list. The Choose the Table Style page of the Report Wizard appears as shown here.

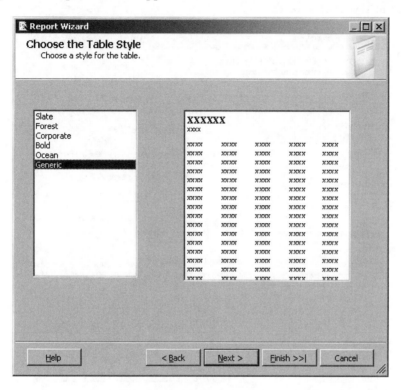

6. Click Next. The Choose the Deployment Location page of the Report Wizard appears. (This page of the wizard will be skipped under certain circumstances. See the Task Notes for this task.)

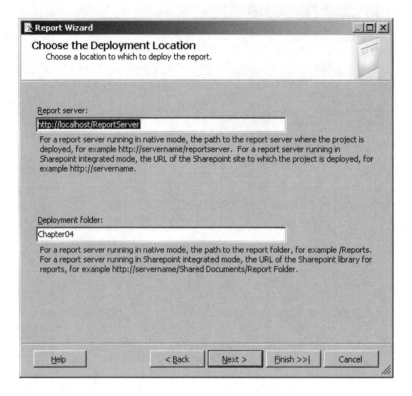

7. Click Next. The Completing the Wizard page appears.

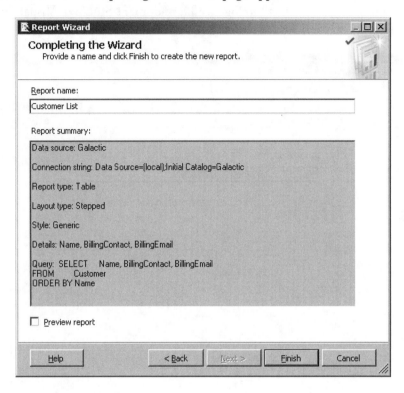

8. Type **Customer List** for the report name.
9. Click Finish. The Business Intelligence Development Studio or Visual Studio window appears with the Report Designer active.

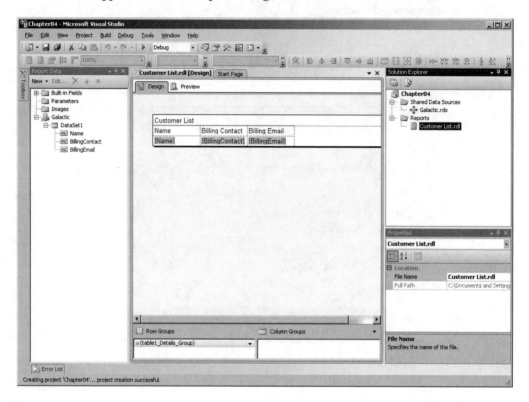

10. Click the Preview tab located near the middle of the screen just above the report layout. A preview of your report appears.

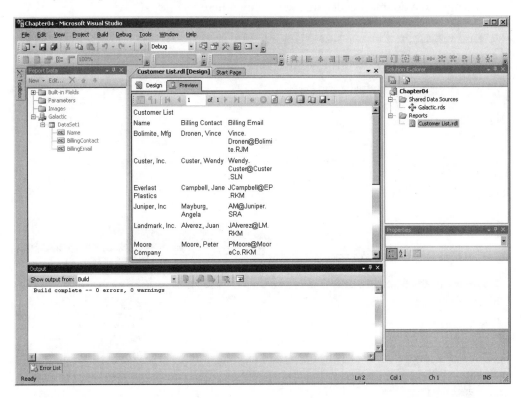

11. Click the Design tab.
12. The Report Wizard created columns in our report that seem a bit too narrow. We can improve the report by widening the columns. Click the Name heading ("Name" in a cell without square brackets around it).

13. Place your mouse pointer on the line separating the gray box above the Name heading and the gray box above the Billing Contact heading. Your mouse pointer changes to a double-headed arrow, as shown here.

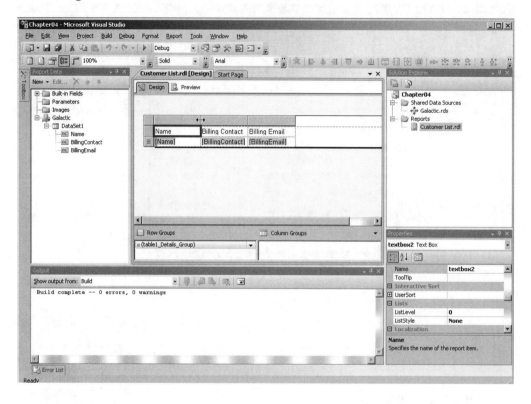

14. Hold down the left mouse button, and move the mouse pointer to the right. This makes the Name column wider.

15. Follow the technique described in Step 14 of this task to widen the Billing Contact and Billing Email columns as well.

16. Click the Preview tab. Your report should appear as shown here.

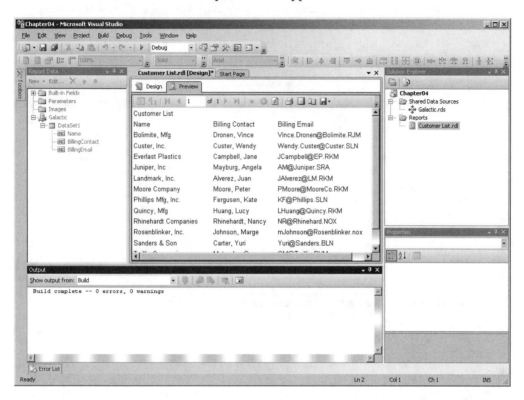

17. Repeat Steps 11 through 16 until you are satisfied with the appearance of the report.

18. When you are satisfied with the report, click the Save All button on the toolbar. This saves the project, the shared data source, and the report files. The Save All button is highlighted in the following illustration.

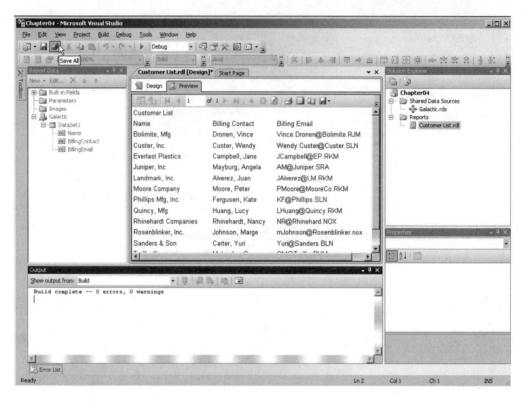

Task Notes   As you may have noticed, the Choose the Table Style page offers several table style choices (refer to the illustration in Step 5). You can try these different table styles as you complete the other sample reports in this chapter and as you create your own reports using the Report Wizard. For ease of comparison between sample reports, the figures in this book will continue to use the Generic style.

The report server and deployment folder items on the Choose the Deployment Location page (refer to the illustration in Step 6) are used when the report is moved from the development environment to a report server. These items are saved with the project, not with an individual report. For this reason, the Deployment Location page is only displayed by the Report Wizard for the first report created in a project. We discuss report deployment in Chapter 10.

You probably had to repeat Steps 11 through 16 of this task several times to get the report just the way you wanted it to look. This is not a problem. Most reports you create require multiple trips between the Layout and Preview tabs before everything is laid out as it should be. Knowing you can move between layout and preview with such ease is a real plus of the Report Designer.

Congratulations! You have now completed your first report.

An Interactive Table Report

Now that you have a taste of how the Report Wizard works and what it can do, let's try something a bit more complex. Let's create a table report that implements an interactive feature called *drilldown*. With the drilldown type of report, only the high-level, summary information is initially presented to the viewers. They can then click a special area of the report (in our case, that area is designated by a plus (+) sign) to reveal part of the lower-level, detail information. The viewers drill down through the summary to get to the detail.

The Customer-Invoice Report

Features Highlighted

- ▶ Using a shared data source
- ▶ Linking tables in the Graphical Query Designer
- ▶ Assigning columns for page breaks and grouping
- ▶ Enabling subtotals and drilldown

Business Need   The accounting department would like a report listing all GDS customers. The customers need to be grouped by billing city, with each city beginning on a new page. The report allows a viewer to drill down from the customer level to see the invoices for that customer.

Task Overview

1. Reopen the Chapter04 Project.
2. Create a New Report in the Chapter04 Project, Select the Shared Data Source, and Create a Dataset.
3. Choose the Report Layout.

Customer-Invoice Report, Task 1: Reopen the Chapter04 Project

If you have not closed the Chapter04 project since working on the previous section of this chapter, skip to Step 8. Otherwise, follow these steps, starting with Step 1:

1. Run the Business Intelligence Development Studio or Visual Studio.
2. If a link to the Chapter04 project is visible on the Start page, click this link, and the Chapter04 project opens. Proceed to Step 8. If a link to the Chapter04 project is not visible on the Start page, continue with Step 3.
3. Select File | Open | Project/Solution.
4. Click Projects.
5. Double-click MSSQLRS.
6. Double-click Chapter04.
7. Double-click Chapter04.sln. (This is the file that contains the solution for Chapter04.)
8. If the CustomerList report is displayed in the center of the screen, click the X button in the upper-right corner of the center section of the screen to close this report.

Task Notes   Opening the Chapter04 solution (Chapter04.sln) and opening the Chapter04 project (Chapter04.rptproj) produce the same end result, so you can do either. Only one project is in the Chapter04 solution, so that project is automatically opened when the solution is opened. When the Chapter04 project is opened, the last report you worked on is displayed in the center of the screen. In this case, it is probably the Customer List report.

You do not need to close one report before working on another. In fact, you can have multiple reports open at one time and use the tabs containing the report names to move among them. In most cases, however, I find that a philosophy of "the less clutter, the better" works well when creating reports. For this reason, I recommend you close all unneeded reports as you move from one report to the next.

Customer-Invoice Report, Task 2: Create a New Report in the Chapter04 Project, Select the Shared Data Source, and Create a Dataset

1. In the Solution Explorer on the right side of the screen, right-click the Reports folder. You see the context menu shown here.

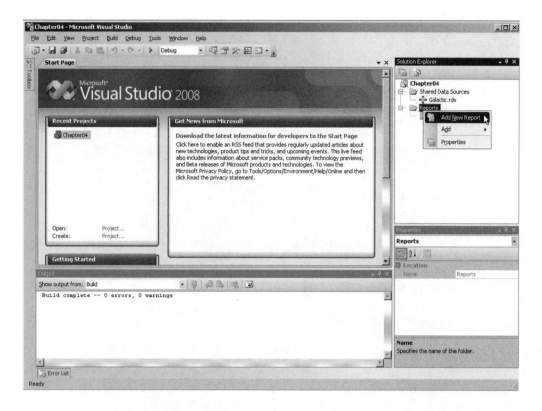

2. Select the Add New Report command from the context menu. This starts the Report Wizard, enabling you to create another report in the current project.
3. Click Next. The Select the Data Source page appears.

4. Make sure the Shared data source radio button is selected and the Galactic data source is selected in the drop-down list, as shown here. Click Next. The Design the Query page appears.

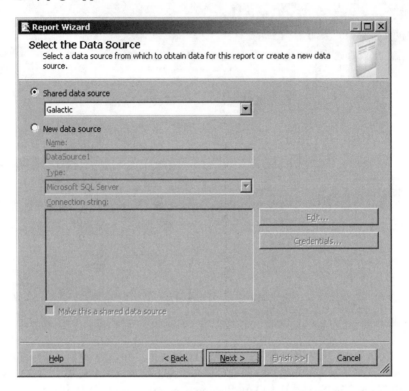

5. Click Query Builder. The Graphical Query Designer appears.
6. Right-click in the diagram pane (the upper area) of the Query Designer screen. You see the Diagram Pane context menu.
7. Select Add Table from the context menu.
8. Double-click Customer in the list of tables. The Customer table is added to the query.

9. Double-click InvoiceHeader in the list of tables. Make sure you select InvoiceHeader and *not* InvoiceDetail. The InvoiceHeader table is added to the query.

10. Click Close to exit the Add Table dialog box. Notice the Query Designer automatically creates the INNER JOIN between the Customer and the InvoiceHeader tables, as shown in the following illustration.

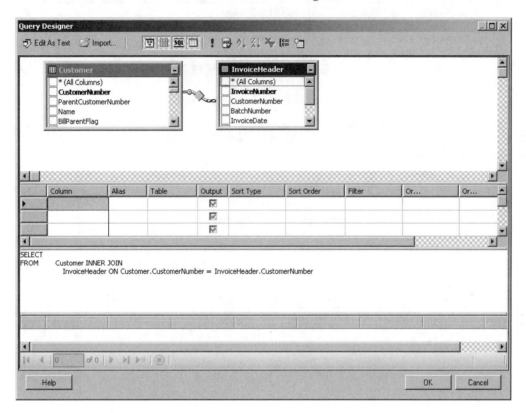

11. Right-click the gray diamond in the middle of the link joining the Customer and the InvoiceHeader tables. The Join Context menu is displayed, as shown in the following illustration.

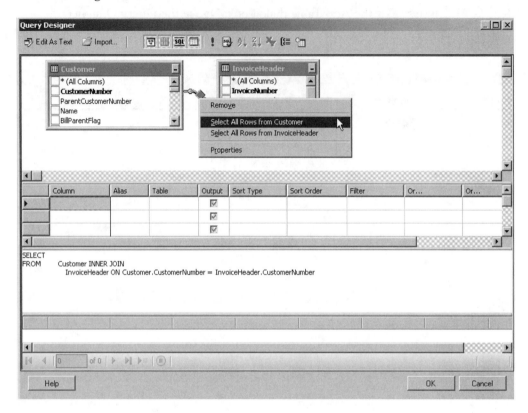

12. Choose the Select All Rows from Customer option from the context menu. The diamond symbol changes, as shown in the next illustration.

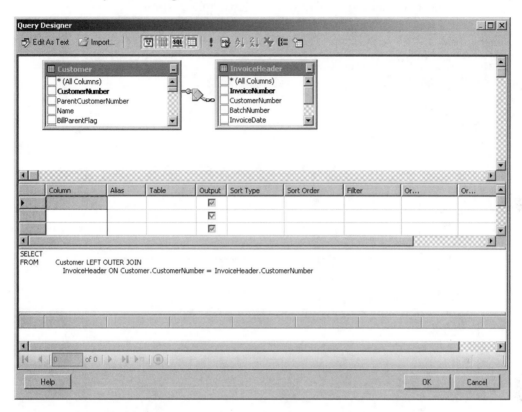

13. Scroll down in the list of columns for the Customer table until the BillingCity column name is visible.

14. Check the box next to the BillingCity column in the Customer table.

15. Scroll up in the list of columns for the Customer table, and check the box next to the Name column. This places the Name field after the BillingCity field in the resulting SQL query.

16. In the list of columns for the InvoiceHeader table, check the boxes next to the InvoiceNumber, InvoiceDate, and TotalAmount columns.

17. Place a 1 in the Sort Order column for the BillingCity field either by typing in the cell or using the drop-down list.

18. Place a 2 in the Sort Order column for the Name field.

19. Place a 3 in the Sort Order column for the InvoiceNumber field.

20. Right-click in the SQL pane, and select Execute SQL from the context menu. The query executes, and the result set is displayed in the results pane. The Query Designer should appear similar to the following illustration.

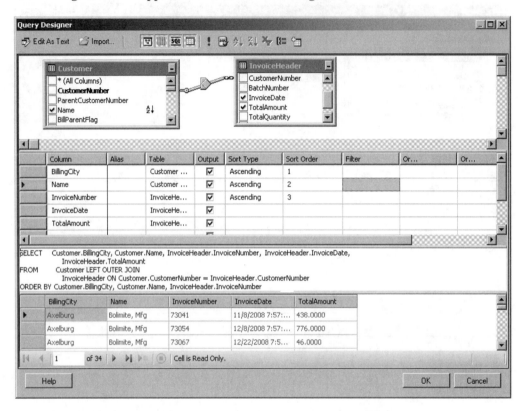

21. Click OK. This returns you to the Design the Query page.

Task Notes   The Galactic data source you created in the first report is a shared data source. As such, the wizard defaults to using this shared data source on the Select the Data Source page any time a new report is created.

In the Query Designer, when a second table is added to the query, the column names from each table are compared. If the Query Designer finds two columns with the same name and data type, it will create a JOIN based on those columns. You saw this in Steps 8 through 10 in this task.

The business need for this report states that the report should include all GDS customers. As you saw in Chapter 3, some customers may not have invoices, so to include all the customers in the report, you need to use a LEFT OUTER JOIN between the Customer table and the InvoiceHeader table. You can accomplish this by choosing Select All Rows from Customer, as you did in Step 12 of this task.

Customer-Invoice Report, Task 3: Choose the Report Layout

1. Click Next. The Select the Report Type page of the Report Wizard appears.
2. Make sure the Tabular radio button is selected, and click Next. The Design the Table page of the Report Wizard appears.
3. With the BillingCity field highlighted in the Available Fields list, click Page. The BillingCity field is moved to the Displayed Fields list.
4. With the Name field highlighted in the Available Fields list, click Group. The Name field is moved to the Displayed Fields list.
5. With the InvoiceNumber field highlighted in the Available Fields list, click Details. The InvoiceNumber field is moved to the Displayed Fields list.
6. With the InvoiceDate field highlighted in the Available Fields list, click Details. The InvoiceDate field is moved to the Displayed Fields list.
7. With the TotalAmount field highlighted in the Available Fields list, click Details. The TotalAmount field is moved to the Displayed Fields list. The Design the Table page appears as shown here.

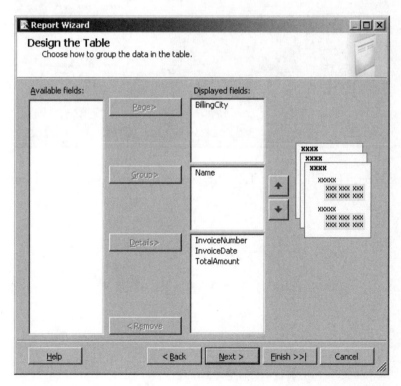

8. Click Next. The Choose the Table Layout page of the Report Wizard appears. This page appears in the Report Wizard because we put fields in the Group area on the Design the Table page.

9. Check the Include subtotals check box.

10. Check the Enable drilldown check box. The Choose the Table Layout page appears as shown.

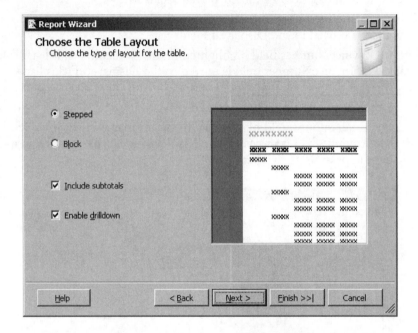

11. Click Next. The Choose the Table Style page of the Report Wizard appears.

12. Select Generic in the style list, and then click Next. The Completing the Wizard page appears.

13. Type **Customer-Invoice Report** for the report name.

14. Click Finish. The Report Designer window opens as shown here.

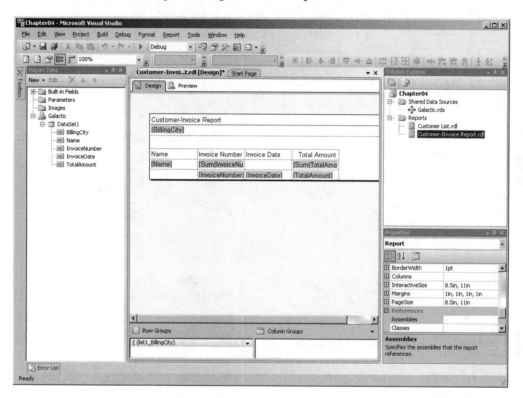

15. Widen the Name column, as you did with the previous report.

16. Click the table cell directly under the Invoice Number heading. This cell is highlighted, as shown in the illustration.

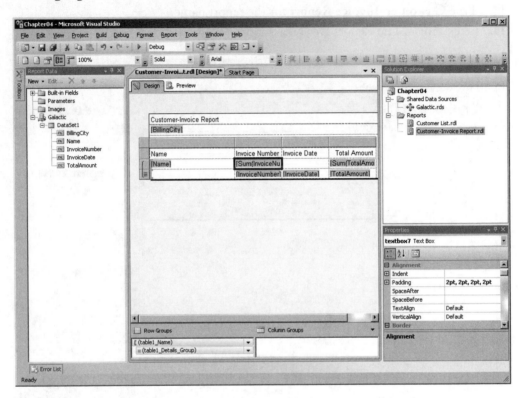

17. Press DELETE on your keyboard to remove the nonsensical totaling of the invoice numbers.

18. Click the Preview tab. A preview of your report appears.

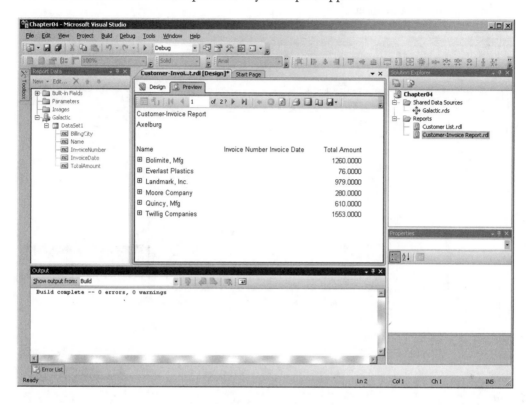

19. Click the plus sign in front of Bolimite, Mfg to view the invoices for this company, as shown here.

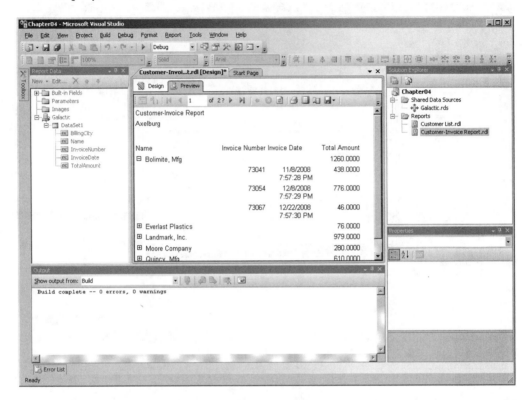

20. Click the Next Page button (the blue triangle just below the Preview tab) to advance to the next page of the report. The Next Page button is highlighted in the following illustration.

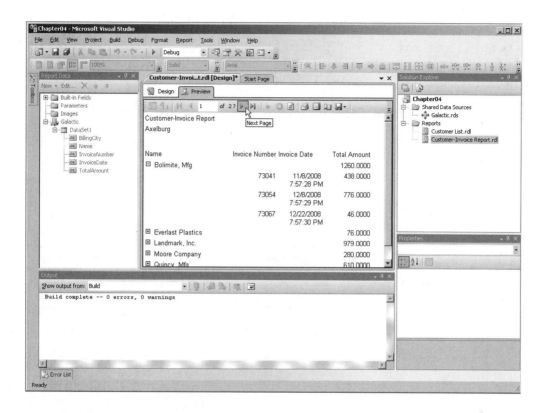

21. You can continue to work with the report preview to get a feel for the way report navigation and drilldown works. (For instance, you may want to try clicking the minus (–) sign.)

22. Click the Save All button on the toolbar.

Task Notes   When we created the Customer List report, we put all the columns from the dataset into the detail line of the report. This time, we put the BillingCity column in the Page area of the table layout. Because of this, the Report Wizard created a report that begins a new page every time there is a new value in the BillingCity column. In addition, the value of the BillingCity column appears at the top of each report page.

The following illustration shows the dataset used in the Customer-Invoice report. The first 13 rows have a value of Axelburg for the BillingCity column. Therefore, Axelburg appears at the top of Page 1 of the report. All the rows with Axelburg in the BillingCity column will be on Page 1 of the report.

Groupings on the Customer-Invoice Report

Page Grouping On BillingCity	Table Grouping on Name	Dataset				
		BillingCity	Name	InvoiceNumber	InvoiceDate	TotalAmount
Page 1: Axelburg	Bolimite, Mfg	Axelburg	Bolimite, Mfg	73041	11-08-2008	438.00
		Axelburg	Bolimite, Mfg	73054	12-08-2008	776.00
		Axelburg	Bolimite, Mfg	73067	12-22-2008	46.00
	Everlast Plastics	Axelburg	Everlast Plastics	73078	12-22-2008	76.00
	Landmark, Inc.	Axelburg	Landmark, Inc.	73043	11-08-2008	243.00
		Axelburg	Landmark, Inc.	73056	12-08-2008	736.00
	Moore Company	Axelburg	Moore Company	73046	11-08-2008	256.00
		Axelburg	Moore Company	73059	12-08-2008	24.00
	Quincy, Mfg	Axelburg	Quincy, Mfg	73048	11-08-2008	234.00
		Axelburg	Quincy, Mfg	73074	12-22-2008	376.00
	Twillig Companies	Axelburg	Twillig Companies	73045	11-08-2008	732.00
		Axelburg	Twillig Companies	73058	12-08-2008	736.00
		Axelburg	Twillig Companies	73071	12-22-2008	85.00
Page 2: Doveran	Custer, Inc.	Doveran	Custer, Inc.	73049	11-08-2008	273.00
		Doveran	Custer, Inc.	73062	12-08-2008	243.00
		Doveran	Custer, Inc.	73075	12-22-2008	368.00
		Edgewater	Sanders & Son	73042	11-08-2008	834.00

Using the Report Wizard, we put the Name column in the Group area of the table layout. This means the report will create a new group each time the value of the Name column changes. Again, looking at the preceding illustration, you can see the first three rows have a value of Bolimite, Mfg in the Name column. Therefore, these three rows will be combined in the first group on Page 1 of the report.

By checking the Enable Drilldown check box, you told the Report Wizard to create a report in which the detail lines for each grouping are initially hidden. The detail lines for a group become visible when the plus sign for that group is clicked. By checking the Include Subtotals check box, you told the Report Wizard to total any numeric columns in the detail and to show those totals in the group header for each group.

Let's look again at the first few rows of the dataset shown in the preceding illustration. The first three rows have a value of Bolimite, Mfg in the Name column. Because of this, these three rows are grouped together for the report shown after Step 18 in Task 3. In this report, the number 1260.0000 appears across from Bolimite, Mfg. This is the total of all the invoices in the detail rows for Bolimite, Mfg.

Because the Report Wizard tried to add up any and all numeric columns, it also created an entry in the grouping for a total of the invoice numbers. Adding up the invoice numbers does not result in a meaningful value, so we deleted this grouping entry in Steps 16 and 17 of this task.

Creating Matrix Reports

You have now seen much of what the Report Wizard can do for you when it comes to tabular reports. Now, let's look at the other report type the Report Wizard can produce for you. Prepare yourself. You are going to enter the matrix.

What Reporting Services calls a matrix report is referred to as a *crosstab* or a *pivot table report* elsewhere. In a tabular report, you have columns from a result set across the top and rows from a result set going down the page. In a matrix report, you have row values going across the top and down the page. Matrix reports are much easier to grasp once you have seen one in action, so let's give it a try.

The Invoice-Batch Number Report

Feature Highlighted

▶   Using the matrix report type

Business Need   The accounting department processes invoices in batches. Once a week, the accounting department creates invoices to send to their customers for the deliveries made over the previous week. A batch number is assigned to each invoice as it is created. All the invoices created on the same day are given the same batch number.

The new report requested by the accounting department shows the total amount of the invoices created in each batch. The report also allows batches to be broken down by billing city and by customer. To allow this type of analysis, you need to use a matrix report.

Task Overview

1.   Reopen the Chapter04 Project, Create a New Report in the Chapter04 Project, Select the Shared Data Source, and Create a Dataset.

2.   Choose the Report Layout.

Invoice-Batch Number Report, Task 1: Reopen the Chapter04 Project, Create a New Report in the Chapter04 Project, Select the Shared Data Source, and Create a Dataset

1.   If you closed the Chapter04 project, reopen it. (If you need assistance with this, see Task 1 of the previous report.) If you have not yet done so, close the Customer-Invoice Report.

2.   In the Solution Explorer on the right side of the screen, right-click the Reports folder.

3. Select the Add New Report command from the context menu. This starts the Report Wizard, enabling you to create an additional report in the current project.

4. Click Next. The Select the Data Source page appears.

5. Make sure the Shared Data Source radio button is selected and the Galactic data source is selected in the drop-down list. Click Next.

6. Click Query Builder. The Graphical Query Designer appears.

7. Right-click in the diagram pane (the upper area) of the Query Designer screen. You see the Diagram pane context menu.

8. Select Add Table from the context menu.

9. Add the following tables to the query:

   Customer
   InvoiceHeader

10. Click Close to exit the Add Table dialog box.

11. Check the following columns in the Customer table in the order shown here:

    BillingCity
    Name

12. Check the following columns in the InvoiceHeader table in the order shown here:

    BatchNumber
    InvoiceNumber
    TotalAmount

13. Right-click in the SQL pane, and select Execute SQL from the context menu. The query executes, and the result set is displayed in the results pane. The Query Designer should appear similar to the illustration.

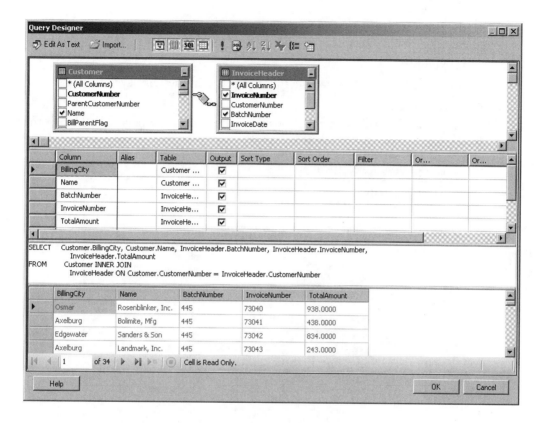

14. Click OK. You return to the Design the Query page.

Task Notes Your dataset contains the columns we need to create the matrix report. Note, we did not specify any sort order for the dataset. The matrix itself takes care of sorting the dataset and displaying things in the correct order. It presents the data in the rows and in the columns in ascending order.

Invoice-Batch Number Report, Task 2: Choose the Report Layout

1. Click Next. The Select the Report Type page of the Report Wizard appears.
2. Select the Matrix radio button.
3. Click Next. The Design the Matrix page of the Report Wizard appears.
4. Use the Columns button to place the following fields in the Displayed fields list:
   BillingCity
   Name

5. Use the Rows button to place the following fields in the Displayed fields list:
   BatchNumber
   InvoiceNumber

6. Use the Details button to place the following field in the Displayed fields list:
   Total Amount

7. Check the Enable drilldown check box at the bottom of the page. The Design the Matrix page should appear as shown.

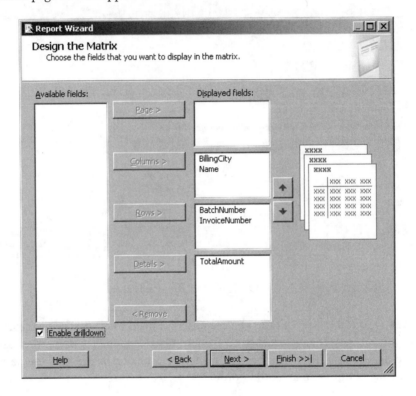

8. Click Next. The Choose the Matrix Style page of the Report Wizard appears.
9. Select Generic in the style list, and click Next. The Completing the Wizard page appears.
10. Type **Invoice-Batch Number Report** for the report name.
11. Click Finish. The Report Designer window opens.

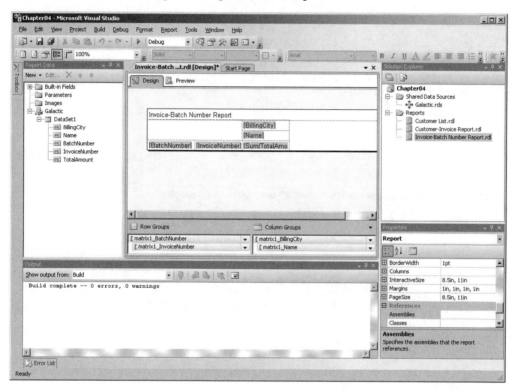

12. Widen the column on the far right of the matrix, as shown in the illustration.

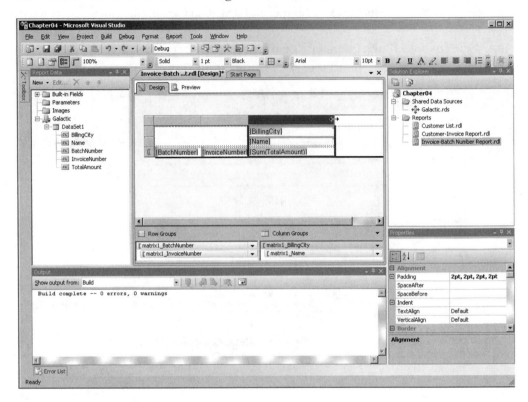

13. Click the Preview tab. A preview of your report appears.

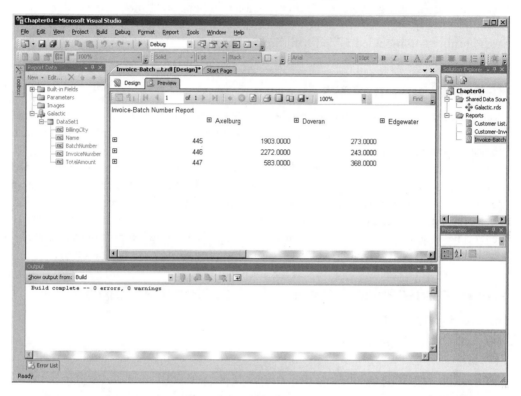

14. Click the Save All button in the toolbar.

Task Notes   The Invoice-Batch Number Report contains a column for each billing city and a row for each batch number. You need to scroll to the right to see all the columns in the report. The numbers in the matrix are the totals for each batch number in each billing city. For example, $1,903 was invoiced to companies in Axelburg in batch number 445.

The column headings are left-justified, whereas the numeric values are right-justified. This makes the report a bit hard to read. We discuss how to correct these types of formatting issues in Chapter 5.

Clicking the plus sign next to a batch number shows you all the invoices in that batch. If you expand batch number 445, you can see that invoice number 73040 included $938 for companies in Osmar, and invoice number 73041 included $438 for companies in Axelburg.

Clicking the plus sign next to a billing city shows you all the customers in that city. If you expand Axelburg, you can see that invoice number 73041 included $438 for Bolimite, Mfg. If you click the minus sign next to batch number 445, you can see that batch number 446 included $776 for Bolimite, Mfg.

Report Parameters

From the users' standpoint, all our sample reports up to this point have been "what you see is what you get." These reports each ran a predetermined query to create the dataset. No user input was requested.

In the real world, this is not the way things work. Most reports require the user to specify some criteria that can help determine what information is ultimately in the report. The user may need to enter a start and an end date, or they may need to select the department or sales region to be included in the report. Users like to have control over their reports so they receive exactly the information they are looking for. Our next report demonstrates how Reporting Services enables you to get user input by using report parameters.

The Parameterized Invoice-Batch Number Report

Feature Highlighted

▶ Using report parameters

Business Need The accounting department is pleased with the Invoice-Batch Number Report. Like most users, when they are happy with something, they want to change it. No software or report is ever really completed. It only reaches a resting point until users think of another enhancement.

The accounting department would like to be able to view the Invoice-Batch Number Report for one city at a time. And, they would like to pick the city from a list of all the cities where they have customers. They would also like to specify a start date and an end date, and only view batches that were run between those dates.

We can modify the Invoice-Batch Number Report to include these features. We can add a WHERE clause to the SELECT statement that creates the dataset. Then we can send the user's selections for city, start date, and end date to the WHERE clause using report parameters.

Task Overview

1. Reopen the Chapter04 Project, Open the Invoice-Batch Number Report, and Add Parameters to the Query in the Original Dataset.
2. Create a Second Dataset Containing a List of Cities.
3. Customize the Report Parameters.

Parameterized Invoice-Batch Number Report, Task 1: Reopen the Chapter04 Project, Open the Invoice-Batch Number Report, and Add Parameters to the Query in the Original Dataset

1. If you closed the Chapter04 project, reopen it. (If you need assistance with this, see Task 1 of the Customer-Invoice Report.)

2. If the Invoice-Batch Number Report is open, make sure the Design tab, not the Preview tab, is selected. If the Invoice-Batch Number Report is not open, double-click the entry for the Invoice-Batch Number Report in the Solution Explorer on the right side of the screen.

3. Right-click the DataSet1 entry in the Report Data window. You will see the context menu, as shown here.

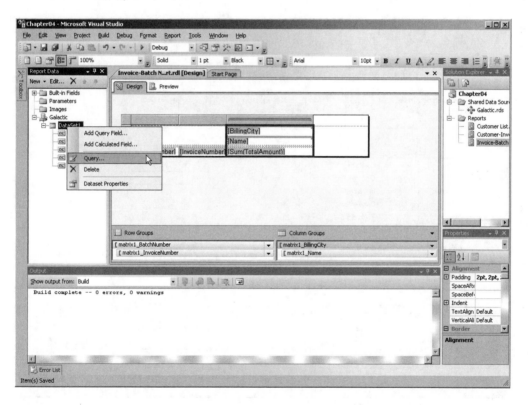

4. Select Query from the context menu. You see the Query Designer screen with the query built for this report while running the Report Wizard.

5. Right-click in the diagram pane, and select Add Table from the context menu.

6. The accounting department wants to specify a date range based on the date each batch was run. This date is stored in the InvoiceBatch table. We need to join this table with the InvoiceHeader table. Double-click InvoiceBatch in the list of tables. The Graphical Query Designer automatically creates the JOIN for us.

7. Click Close to exit the Add Table dialog box.

8. In the InvoiceBatch table, check the check box next to the RunDate field. This adds RunDate to the criteria pane.

9. Now we can create the portion of the WHERE clause involving the billing city. In the criteria pane, click the cell across from BillingCity and under Filter. The cursor moves to that cell. Type **=@City** and press ENTER. The Graphical Query Designer appears as shown in the following illustration. Notice the SQL statement in the SQL pane now includes a WHERE clause.

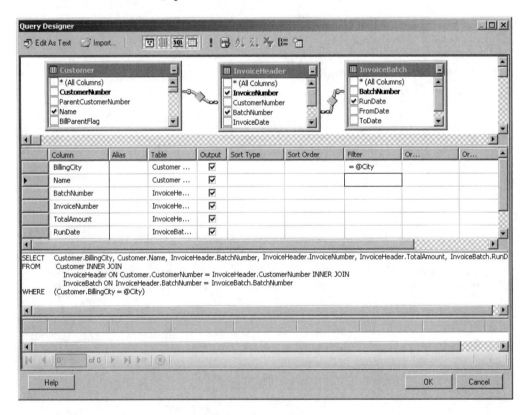

10. Next, we create the portion of the WHERE clause involving the RunDate. Scroll down in the criteria pane until RunDate is visible, if necessary. Click the cell across from RunDate and under Filter. Type **>= @StartDate AND < DATEADD(dd, 1, @EndDate)** and press ENTER. The Query Designer portion

of the screen appears as shown in the following illustration. Notice the addition to the WHERE clause in the SQL pane. We discuss why we are using the DATEADD() function in the task notes.

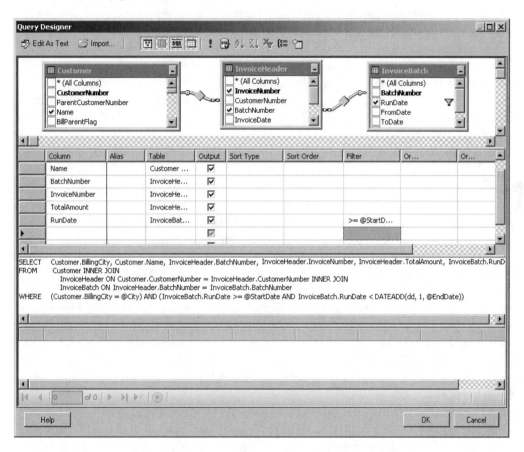

11. We needed to include RunDate in the WHERE clause, but we do not need to include it in the FIELD LIST of the SELECT statement. Click in the cell across from RunDate and under Output to remove the check mark. The RunDate field is no longer in the FIELD LIST for the SELECT statement in the SQL pane.

12. Right-click in the SQL pane, and select Execute SQL from the context menu.

13. The Query Designer requires values for the three parameters you just created to run the query. You see the Query Parameters dialog box. Enter **Axelburg** for @City, **12/01/2008** for @StartDate, and **12/31/2008** for @EndDate. Click OK.

14. After viewing the result set, click OK to exit the Query Designer window. The Define Query Parameters dialog box appears. Click OK to exit the Define Query Parameters dialog box.

Task Notes   You have now added three parameters to the WHERE clause of the SELECT statement. Only rows where the City column has a value equal to the value of @City will be displayed in the result set. When you ran the query in the Query Designer just now, you gave the @City parameter a value of Axelburg. Therefore, only rows with Axelburg in the City column were included in the result set.

One of the trickiest things about working with datetime data types in SQL Server is remembering that they consist of both a date and a time. The RunDate field we are working with here is a datetime. When the invoice batches are run at GDS, the invoicing program assigns both the date and the time the batch was run. For instance, batch 447 was run on 12/31/2008 at 7:54:49 P.M. It has a value of 12/31/2008 7:54:49 P.M. stored in its RunDate column by the invoicing program.

When a user is asked to enter a date, most of the time, they enter the date without a time. When you were asked for a value for @EndDate, you entered 12/31/2008, without any time specified. Because SQL Server is dealing with a date and a time together, it adds on a time value for you. The default value it uses is 00:00:00 A.M., or midnight. Remember, midnight is the start of the new day. This means when you're comparing datetime values, midnight is less than any other time occurring on the same day.

Let's think about the comparison created in the WHERE clause involving @EndDate. Assume, for a moment, that instead of using RunDate < DATEADD(dd, 1, @EndDate), we used the more obvious RunDate <= @EndDate. When the user enters 12/31/2008 for the end date, they expect the result set to include batches run on 12/31/2008. However, when SQL Server compares the value of RunDate (12/31/2008 7:54:49 P.M.) with the value of @EndDate (12/31/2008 00:00:00 A.M.), it finds that RunDate is not less than or equal to @EndDate. This is because 7:54:49 P.M., the time portion of RunDate, is greater than 00:00:00 A.M., the time portion of @EndDate. Batch 447 would not be included in this result set.

To include batches that occur on the day specified by @EndDate, you need to use RunDate < DATEADD(dd, 1, @EndDate). What this expression does is add one day to the value of @EndDate and check to see if RunDate is less than this calculated value. Let's look at our example with Batch 447. This time, SQL Server compares the value of RunDate (12/31/2008 7:54:49 P.M.) with the calculated value (12/31/2008 00:00:00 A.M. + 1 day = 1/1/2009 00:00:00 A.M.). Now it is true that RunDate is less than our calculated value, so Batch 447 is included in the result set.

Parameterized Invoice-Batch Number Report, Task 2: Create a Second Dataset Containing a List of Cities

1. The accounting department wants to be able to select a value for the @City parameter from a list of billing cities. You need to create a second dataset in the report that provides that list for the users. Right-click the Galactic entry in the Report Data window, and select Add Dataset from the context menu. The Dataset Properties dialog box appears.

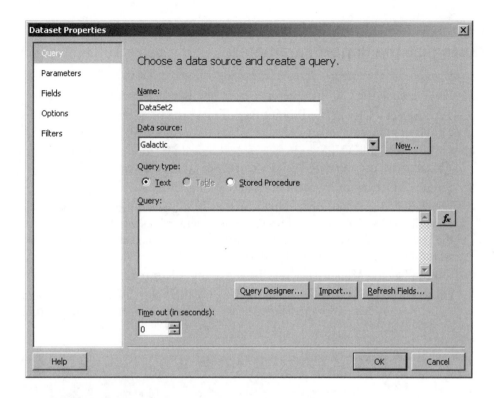

2. Type **BillingCities** for the name. The Galactic data source is already selected for you in the Data source drop-down list, so this does not need to be changed.

NOTE

Make sure you type BillingCities without a space between the two words. Spaces are not allowed in dataset names.

3. Based on what you learned in Chapter 3, we'll compose the query for this dataset without the Query Designer. We want a list of all the billing cities for GDS customers. It also makes sense that each city name should only show up once in the list. Click in the Query text box, and enter the following SQL statement:

```
SELECT DISTINCT BillingCity FROM Customer
```

4. Click OK to exit the Dataset Properties dialog box.

Task Notes   Remember, the word DISTINCT means we want SQL Server to remove duplicates for us. To do this, SQL Server automatically sorts the result set. For this reason, you don't need to specify an ORDER BY clause for the SELECT statement.

Parameterized Invoice-Batch Number Report, Task 3: Customize the Report Parameters

1. Expand the Parameters entry in the Report Data window.
2. Double-click the City parameter entry in the Report Data window.
3. Type **Select a City** in the Prompt field. This is the prompt the user sees when running the report.
4. On the Available Values page, select the Get values from a query radio button. This lets you use the BillingCities dataset to create a drop-down list.
5. From the Dataset drop-down list, select BillingCities.
6. From the Value field drop-down list, select BillingCity. From the Label field drop-down list, select BillingCity. The Value field determines what value is assigned to the parameter. The Label field determines what the user sees in the drop-down list when selecting a value. In this case, they are one and the same thing.
7. On the Default Values page, select the Specify values radio button.
8. Click Add. Type **Axelburg** in the text box for the Value. This serves as the default value for the City parameter. The Report Parameter Properties dialog box should now look like this:

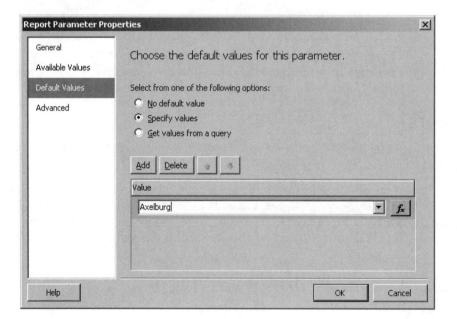

9. Click OK to exit the Report Parameter Properties dialog box.

10. Double-click the StartDate entry in the Report Data window. The Report Parameter Properties dialog box appears.

11. Type **Enter a Start Date** in the Prompt field.

12. Select Date/Time from the Data type drop-down list.

13. Click OK to exit the Report Parameter Properties dialog box.

14. Double-click the EndDate entry in the Report Data window. The Report Parameter Properties dialog box appears.

15. Type **Enter an End Date** in the Prompt field.

16. Select Date/Time from the Data type drop-down list.

17. Click OK to exit the Report Parameter Properties dialog box.

18. Click the Preview tab.

19. The prompts for the three report parameters appear at the top of the preview area. No report is displayed until a value is entered for each parameter. Axelburg is selected from the Select a City drop-down list because you made this the default. Type or use the date picker to select **12/01/2008** for Enter a Start Date. Type or use the date picker to select **12/31/2008** for Enter an End Date.

20. Click View Report. The report, based on the parameter values you entered, now appears. The report, with all the rows and columns expanded, is shown here.

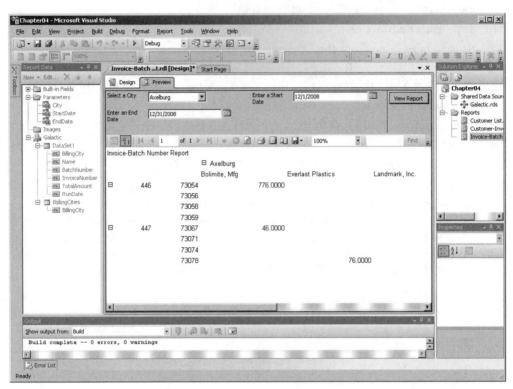

NOTE

You can change the size of the Solution Explorer window, the Report Data window, and the other windows around the outside of the Report Designer to make more room in the center for your report. Just click the separator between the window and drag in the desired direction.

21. Click the Save All button in the toolbar.

Task Notes Each time you added a parameter to the query in the dataset, the Report Designer created a corresponding report parameter for you. When the report is viewed, the values entered for the report parameters are automatically passed on to the query parameters before the query is executed. In this way, the user can enter information and have it used in the WHERE clause of the SELECT statement to affect the contents of the report.

The Report Parameters dialog box enables you to control the user's interaction with the report parameters. You can change the prompts the user sees. You can specify the data type of a parameter. You can even determine the default value for a parameter.

One of the most powerful features of the Report Parameters dialog box is the capability to create a drop-down list from which the user can select a value for a parameter. In many cases, the user will not know values, such as department codes, part numbers, and so forth without looking them up. This capability to enable the user to select valid values from a list makes the reports much more user-friendly.

Flying Solo

You have now seen what the Report Wizard can do for you. It can provide you with a great starting place for a number of reports. However, the Report Wizard does have its limitations and, in most cases, you need to make additions to the reports it generates before they are ready for the end user. In the next chapter, you begin learning how to make those enhancements. In addition, you learn how to create reports without the aid of the Report Wizard.

Chapter 5

Removing the Training Wheels: Building Basic Reports

In This Chapter

- ▶ **Riding Down Familiar Roads**
- ▶ **The Tablix and Data Regions**
- ▶ **New Territory**
- ▶ **Getting Graphical**

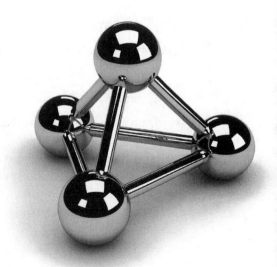

I n Chapter 4, you built your first reports using the Report Wizard. This is like learning to ride your first two-wheeler with the training wheels on. Now it is time for the training wheels to come off so you can see what this baby can really do! We are going to begin building reports from scratch. We hope these next few chapters provide the handholding you need, and then you can learn to ride sans training wheels without getting skinned knees.

First, we work with the two types of reports you were introduced to in Chapter 4. We begin by building a table report without the use of the Report Wizard. From there, we do the same with a matrix report. After that, we look at a new report type—the list report. We end the chapter by working with some of the basic report items that make up each report—namely, the line control, the text box control, and the rectangle control. Along the way, you learn more about the Report Builder that serves as our development platform.

So, the training wheels are off and the wrenches have been put away. Don your helmets; it's time to ride!

Riding Down Familiar Roads

We cover some familiar territory as we begin building reports without the Report Wizard. In Chapter 4, you used the Report Wizard to create table reports (the Customer List Report and the Customer-Invoice Report) and matrix reports (the Invoice-Batch Number Report). We create these types of reports once more, but, this time, without the aid of the wizard.

Again, we look at the business needs of Galactic Delivery Services (GDS) and create reports to satisfy those business needs.

The Transport List Report

Features Highlighted

▶ Building a GROUP BY clause using the Graphical Query Designer

▶ Creating a table report from scratch

▶ Using the Expression dialog box

Business Need The transport maintenance department at Galactic Delivery Services needs a list of all the transports currently in service. They want this list to be grouped by transport type. The list includes the serial number, the purchase date, and the date the transport was last in for repairs. The list also includes the cargo capacity and range of each transport type.

Task Overview

1. Create the Chapter05 Project, Create a Shared Data Source, and Create a New Report in the Chapter05 Project.
2. Create a Dataset.
3. Place a Table Item on the Report and Populate It.
4. Add Table Grouping and Other Report Formatting.

Transport List Report, Task 1: Create the Chapter05 Project, Create a Shared Data Source, and Create a New Report in the Chapter05 Project

1. Run the Business Intelligence Development Studio or Visual Studio 2008. The Start page is displayed (or select File | Close Project from the menu if a solution is already open).
2. Click New Project to create a new project. This displays the New Project dialog box. (Remember, you can create a new project in three different ways: Select File | New | Project from the main menu, click the New Project toolbar button, or click the Create Project link on the Start page. All these actions achieve the same result.)
3. Click the Report Server Project icon in the Templates area of the New Project dialog box. (Be sure to click the Report Server Project icon and *not* the Report Server Project Wizard icon.)
4. Type **Chapter05** for the project name. This project will contain all the reports you create in this chapter.
5. Click Browse to open the Project Location dialog box.
6. Under My Documents, navigate to the Visual Studio 2008\Projects\MSSQLRS folder.
7. Select the MSSQLRS folder and click OK.

8. Make sure the Create directory for solution check box is unchecked. The New Project dialog box should now look like this:

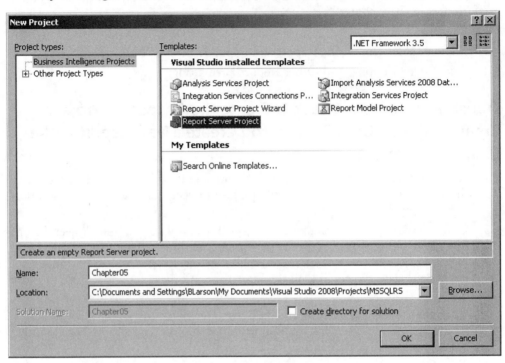

9. Click OK in the New Project dialog box. A new project is created.
10. In the Solution Explorer on the right side of the screen, right-click the Shared Data Sources folder. Select Add New Data Source from the context menu, as shown here.

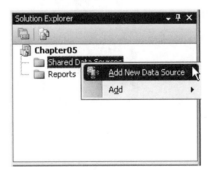

11. Type **Galactic** for Name. Click Edit. The Connection Properties dialog box appears.

12. Type the name of the Microsoft SQL Server database server hosting the Galactic database in the Server or file name text box. If the Galactic database is hosted by the computer you are currently working on, you may type **(local)** for the server name.

13. Select the Use SQL Server Authentication radio button.

14. Type **GalacticReporting** for the user name.

15. Type **gds** for the password.

16. Check the Save my password check box.

17. Select Galactic from the Select or enter a database name drop-down list.

18. Click Test Connection. If the message, "Test connection succeeded" appears, click OK. If an error message appears, make sure the name of your database server, the user name, the password, and the database are entered properly. If your test connection still does not succeed, make sure you have correctly installed the Galactic database.

19. Click OK to exit the Connection Properties dialog box. Click OK again to exit the Shared Data Source Properties dialog box. A new shared data source called Galactic.rds is created in the Chapter05 project.

20. In the Solution Explorer, right-click the Reports folder.

21. Put your mouse pointer over Add in the context menu, and wait for the submenu to appear. Select the New Item command from the context menu, as shown here.

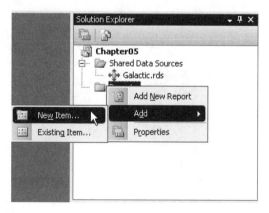

22. The Add New Item - Chapter05 dialog box appears. Make sure the Report icon is selected in the Templates area. Enter **Transport List** for the name. The dialog box appears as follows:

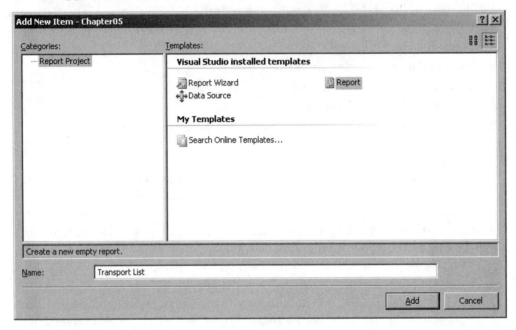

23. Click Add. A new report called TransportList.rdl is created in the Chapter05 project.

24. In the Report Data window, click the New drop-down menu. Select Data Source from the menu that appears. The Data Source Properties dialog box appears.

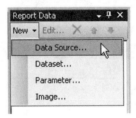

25. Enter **Galactic** for the name.

26. Select the Use shared data source reference radio button, and select Galactic from the drop-down list below it. Click OK. An entry for the Galactic data source appears in the Report Data window.

27. In the Report Data window, right-click the entry for the Galactic data source, and select Add Dataset from the context menu. The Dataset Properties dialog box appears.

28. Enter **TransportList** for the name.

NOTE

The dataset name must not contain any spaces.

29. Click the Query Designer button. The Query Designer window opens, displaying the Generic Query Designer. We use the Generic Query Designer in Chapter 6. For now, we switch to the Graphical Query Designer and all the helpful tools it provides.

30. Click the Edit As Text button in the toolbar, as shown in the following illustration. This unselects the Generic Query Designer and switches to the Graphical Query Designer.

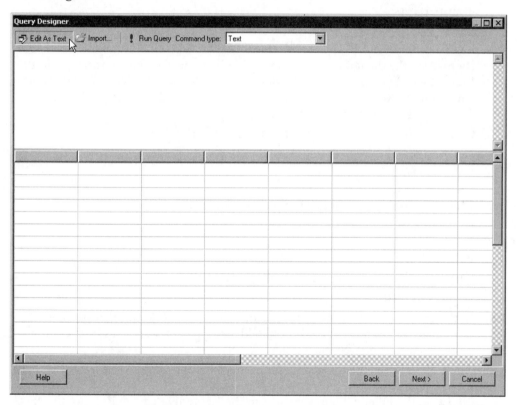

Task Notes   Because we are creating several reports in the Chapter05 project, all of which select data from the Galactic database, we began by creating a shared data source. This saves us time as we create each of the reports. We continue this practice throughout the remaining chapters.

In Step 20 through Step 23, we are adding a report to the project. In Chapter 4, you saw that selecting Add New Report from the context menu causes the new report to be created with the Report Wizard. In this chapter, we are looking to build our reports from scratch, which is why we used Add | New Item in Step 21.

Transport List Report, Task 2: Create a Dataset

1. Right-click in the diagram pane (the upper area) of the Graphical Query Designer screen. Select Add Table from the context menu.

2. Add the following tables to the query:

   Transport
   TransportType
   Repair

3. Click Close to exit the Add Table dialog box.

4. Right-click the diamond on the connection between the Transport table and the Repair table. You may need to rearrange the TransportType table, the Transport table, and the Repair table to see this diamond. Select the Select All Rows from Transport item from the context menu.

5. Check the following columns in the TransportType table:

   Description
   CargoCapacity
   Range

6. Check the following columns in the Transport table:

   SerialNumber
   PurchaseDate
   RetiredDate

7. Check the following column in the Repair table:

   BeginWorkDate

8. In the criteria pane (the second area from the top), type **1** in the Sort Order column across from the Description field and type **2** in the Sort Order column across from the SerialNumber field.

9. The business need for this report states it is to include only active transports. That means we only want to include transports that do not have a retired date. Type **IS NULL** in the Filter column across from the RetiredDate field. Remove the check mark under the Output column across from the RetiredDate field.

10. Right-click in the SQL pane (the third area from the top), and select Execute SQL from the context menu. In the results pane (the bottom area), notice that several records appear for serial number P-348-23-4532-22A. Your screen should look like the following illustration.

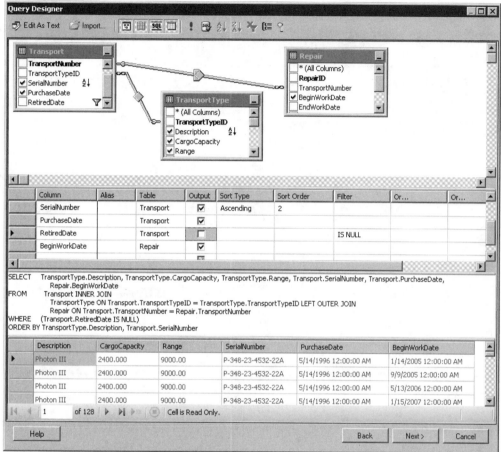

NOTE

You can also run the query by clicking the Run button (the one with a red exclamation point) in the Query Designer window toolbar.

11. Right-click in the diagram pane of the Graphical Query Designer screen. Select Add Group By from the context menu. A new column called Group By is added to the criteria pane.

12. In the criteria pane, click in the Group By column across from BeginWorkDate.

13. Use the drop-down list in this cell to select Max, as shown here.

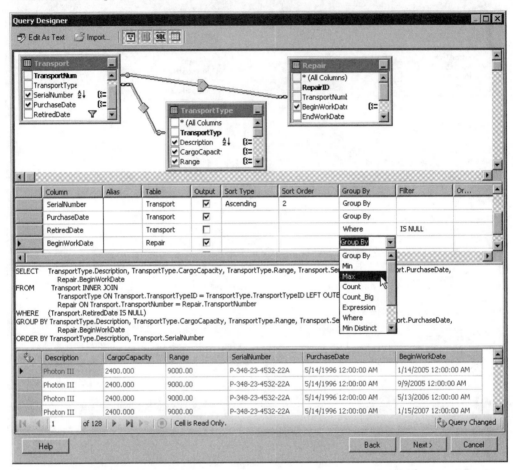

14. When you move your cursor out of the Group By column, Expr 1 will be assigned as the alias for BeginWorkDate. Replace Expr1 with **LatestRepairDate** in the Alias column across from BeginWorkDate.

15. Right-click in the SQL pane, and select Execute SQL from the context menu. Notice that now only one record appears for serial number P-348-23-4532-22A.

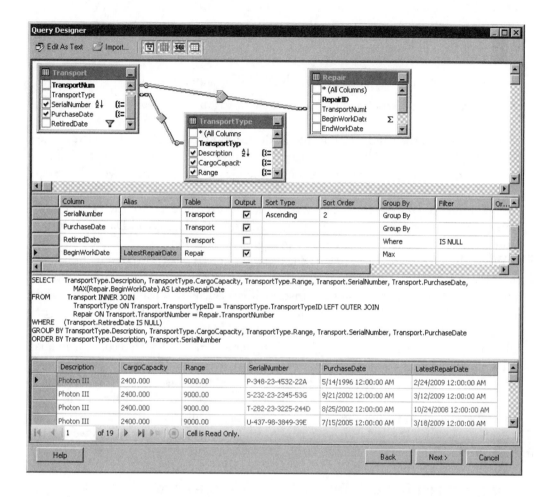

Task Notes The relationship between the Transport table and the Repair table is a one-to-many relationship. One transport may have many repairs. When you join these two tables, you get one record in the result set for each match between records in the Transport table and the Repair table. Because transport P-348-23-4532-22A has been in for repairs ten times, it generates ten records in the result set.

This is not exactly what the business requirements call for. Instead, we want to have one record for transport P-348-23-4532-22A with the latest repair date. To accomplish this, we use the GROUP BY clause. In Step 11, we instruct the Graphical Query Designer to group together records in the result set that have the same value.

When you use the GROUP BY clause, all the fields in the FIELD LIST must fit into one of the following two categories:

▶ The field must be included in the GROUP BY clause.

▶ The field must be enclosed in an aggregate function.

Any fields with the words "Group By" in the Group By column are included in the GROUP BY clause. These fields also have a special Group By symbol next to them in the diagram pane. By selecting Max under the Group By column, as we did in Step 13, we enclose BeginWorkDate in the MAX() aggregate function. This returns the maximum BeginWorkDate (in other words, the latest repair date) for each transport. Note a special symbol, the Greek letter sigma, next to the BeginWorkDate field in the diagram pane to signify it is enclosed in an aggregate function.

When the BeginWorkDate field is enclosed in the MAX() aggregate function, it becomes a calculated field. It is not simply the value of the BeginWorkDate field that is returned as a column in the result set. Instead, it is a calculation using the value of the BeginWorkDate field that makes up this column of the result set. The Graphical Query Designer needs a name for this calculated column. This is known as the *alias* for the column. By default, the Graphical Query Designer assigns a calculated column an alias of Expr1 or something similar. To better remember what is in this result set column when the time comes to use it in a report, we changed the alias to LatestRepairDate.

As soon as we click OK in the following task, the Report Builder will save the dataset we created as part of the report. It will automatically name this dataset "DataSet1" when it is saved. We learn how to explicitly name datasets when we create the Transport Information Sheet report later in this chapter.

Transport List Report, Task 3: Place a Table Item on the Report and Populate It

1. Click OK to exit the Query Designer window. Click OK to exit the Dataset Properties dialog box and begin working on the report layout.

NOTE

Your installation of the Report Designer may be using a feature called Auto-Hide with the Toolbox. Auto-Hide is used to provide more screen space for your report layout. When Auto-Hide is active for the Toolbox, the Toolbox is only represented on the screen by a tab containing a tool icon and the word "Toolbox" at the extreme left side of the window. To view the actual Toolbox, place your mouse pointer on top of this tab. After a second or two, the Toolbox appears. Once your mouse pointer moves off the Toolbox, it is automatically hidden again.

2. Click the Table report item in the Toolbox. The mouse pointer changes to a table icon and crosshairs when you move your mouse pointer over the report layout area, as shown in the next illustration.

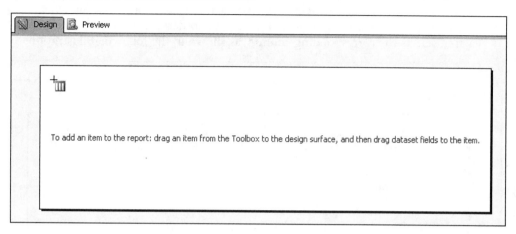

3. Drag the mouse over the lower three-quarters of the design surface, as shown in the following illustration.

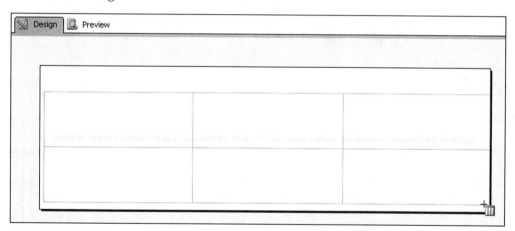

4. When you release the mouse button after dragging, a table is created to occupy the area you just defined. By default, every cell in the table is occupied by an empty text box. Click in each cell of the table, and note the name and type of report item shown at the top of the Properties window.

5. Let's take a few moments to go over the methods for selecting various parts of the table. You have already seen how to select individual cells. When you click the table, gray borders appear on top of and to the left of the table item. These borders provide handles for selecting other parts of the table. Click the table, and then click any of the gray rectangles in the border above the table item. This action selects the corresponding column, as shown in the following illustration.

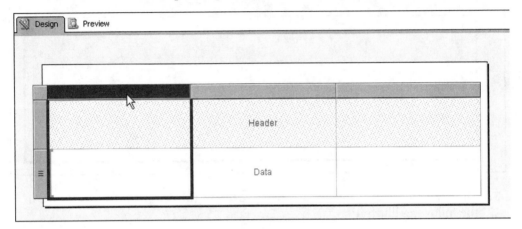

6. Click any of the gray rectangles in the border to the left of the table item. This action selects a row, as shown here.

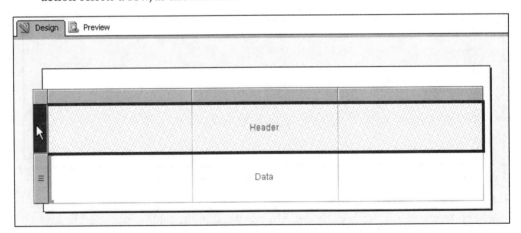

7. Click the gray square in the upper-left corner of the border. This action selects the entire table. When the entire table is selected, the gray border is replaced by the sizing handles (the small white squares) for the table. You must select the entire table before you can move and size the table item. Note in the Properties window the item is called a tablix rather than a table. We will discuss this in the section called "The Tablix and Data Regions" later in this chapter.

8. Hover your cursor over the lower-left table cell. A small icon representing the Field Selector will appear, as shown here.

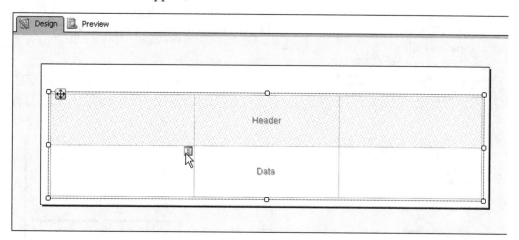

9. Click the icon. The Field Selector, a list of the fields defined in your dataset, is displayed, as shown here.

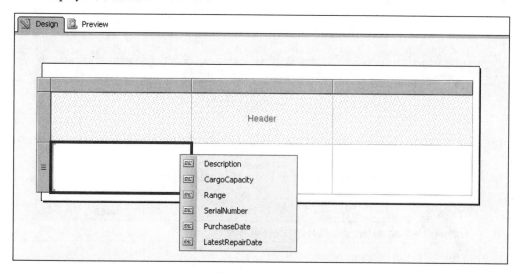

10. Select the SerialNumber field from the Field Selector. An expression that returns the value of the SerialNumber field is placed in the text box that occupies the lower-left table cell. This is represented by the name of the field enclosed in square brackets. The name of the field is also used to create a column heading in the upper-left table cell.

11. Repeat this process in the lower cell in the center column of the table to select the PurchaseDate field from the Field Selector.

12. Repeat the process once more in the lower-right table cell to select the LatestRepairDate field from the Field Selector. The report layout should now appear as shown.

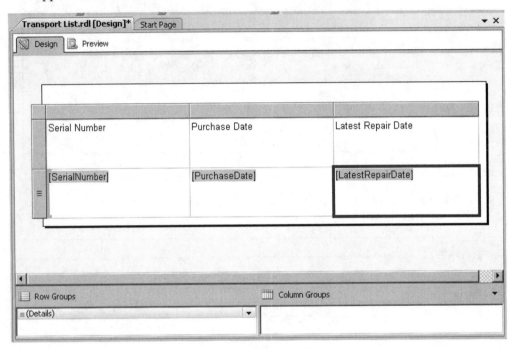

13. Select the header row (the top row) by clicking the gray rectangle in the border to the left of the row.

14. Make the following changes in the Properties window:

Property	New Value
FontWeight (expand the Font property to find the FontWeight property)	Bold
TextDecoration	Underline

15. In the gray border to the left of the table, click the line between the header row and the data row. Drag it to reduce the height of the header row.

16. In the gray border to the left of the table, click the bottom of the data row rectangle. Drag it to reduce the height of the data row.

17. Click the center cell in the data row. Hold down SHIFT and click the right cell in the data row. Both of these cells are now selected. Make the following changes in the Properties window:

Property	New Value
Format	MM/dd/yyyy
TextAlign	Left

NOTE

Make sure you use uppercase letter M's in the Format property. MM is the placeholder for month in a format string, whereas mm is the placeholder for milliseconds.

18. Click the Preview tab to preview the report. The report should appear as shown here.

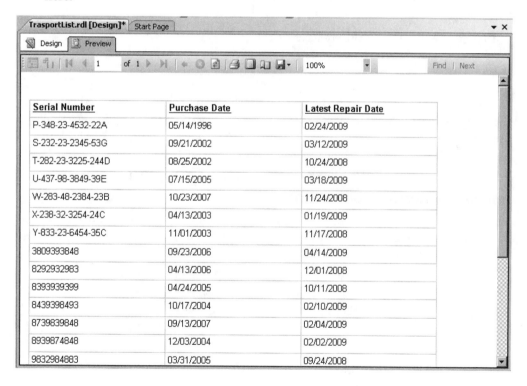

Task Notes   In the Properties window are several instances where a group of related properties are combined under a summary property. For instance, the FontStyle, FontFamily, FontSize, and FontWeight properties are combined under the Font property. The Font property serves as a summary of the other four.

Initially, only the summary property is visible in the Properties window. A plus (+) sign to the left of a property tells you it is a summary property and has several detail properties beneath it. The summary property has a value that concatenates the values of all the detail properties underneath it.

For example, suppose the FontFamily, FontSize, FontStyle, and FontWeight properties have the following values:

FontFamily:	Arial
FontSize:	10pt
FontStyle:	Normal
FontWeight:	Bold

In that case, the Font property has this value:

Font:	Arial, 10pt, Normal, Bold

You can change the value of a detail property by editing the concatenated values in the summary property, or you can expand the summary property and edit the detail properties directly.

Transport List Report, Task 4: Add Table Grouping and Other Report Formatting

1. Click the Design tab. Notice there is one entry in the Row Groups section of the Grouping pane at the bottom of the Design tab. We will add a second row group to display the transport type.

2. Click the drop-down arrow in the Row Groups pane, as shown here.

3. From the menu that appears, select Add Group | Parent Group. The Tablix Group dialog box appears.

4. Select [Description] from the Group by drop-down list.

5. Check the Add group header check box.

6. Click OK. A new column and a new row are added to the table. Note that a default group name, Group1, is used to create a header for this new column. The

field we selected as the group expression provides the value in this new column. In addition, there is now a Group1 entry in the Row Groups pane.

7. Select the cell containing the Group1 header. Click the cell a second time so the blinking text-edit cursor appears in that cell.

8. Delete Group1 and type the following:

   `Transport Type`

   (Don't worry about the fact that it wraps to a second line.)

9. Select the table cell containing the Description field.

10. Make the following changes in the Properties window:

Property	New Value
FontWeight	Bold

11. Click the empty table cell immediately below the Serial Number heading. Hold down SHIFT, and then click the center and the rightmost cells in the same row. Right-click in any of the selected cells, and select Merge Cells from the Tablix section of the context menu, as shown here.

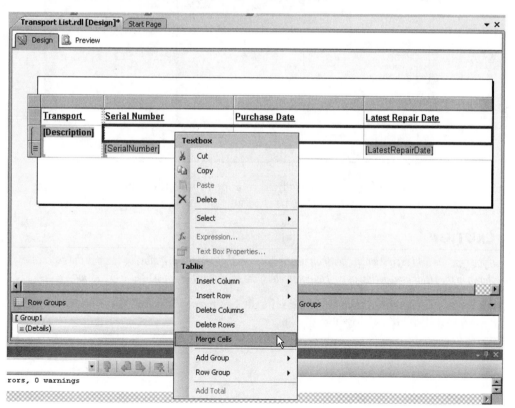

12. Right-click in the newly merged cells, and select Expression from the Textbox section of the context menu. The Expression dialog box appears.

13. Type the following after the equal sign (=), including the quotation marks, in the Set expression for: Value area:

```
"Cargo Capacity: " & CStr(
```

14. Select the Fields (TransportList) entry in the tree view, as shown here. Note the fields in the selected dataset appear in the lower-right list box.

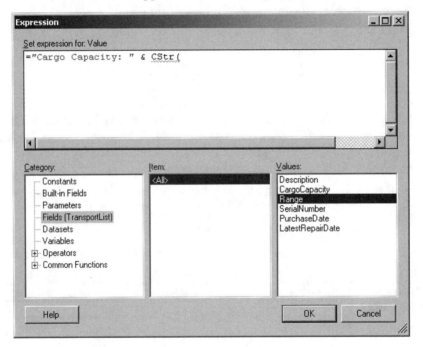

15. Double-click the CargoCapacity field to append it to the expression. Note an expression is created, which returns the value of the CargoCapacity field.

CAUTION

If you type the field expression, rather than selecting it from the Fields area, it must be typed in the exact case shown in the Fields area. Fields, as well as parameters, are case-sensitive when used in expressions.

16. Type) at the end of the expression in the Set expression for: Value area and press ENTER. Type the following:

```
& vbCrLf & "Range: " & CStr(
```

17. Double-click the Range field to append it to the expression in the Set expression for: Value area. Type a) at the end of the expression. The Expression dialog box should appear as shown.

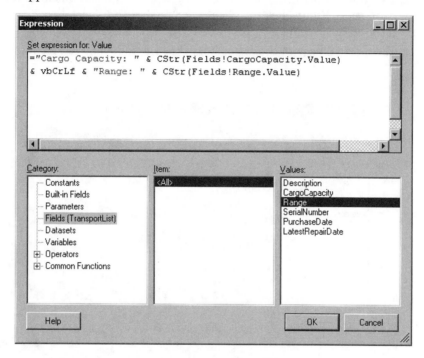

18. Click OK. Note the "<<Expr>>" in the merged cells indicates the value being displayed in this area of the report does not come from a single field, but from an expression.

19. With the merged cells still selected, make the following changes in the Properties window:

Property	New Value
BorderColor/Default (expand the BorderColor property to find the Default property)	Black
BorderWidth/Default	2pt
FontWeight	Bold

20. Click the Textbox report item in the Toolbox. The mouse pointer changes to a text box icon and crosshairs when you move your mouse pointer over the design surface.

21. Drag the mouse cursor over the entire area above the table on the design surface.

22. When you release the mouse button after dragging, a text box is created to occupy the area you just defined. Click on the "<<Expr>>" entry in this text box to select the expression. Right-click the selected expression and select Text Box Properties from the context menu. The Text Box Properties dialog box appears.

23. On the General page of the dialog box, Type the following for Value:

    ```
    Transport List
    ```

24. On the Alignment page of the dialog box, select Center from the Horizontal drop-down list.

25. On the Font page of the dialog box, make the following changes:

Property	New Value
Size	16pt
Style	Bold

26. Click OK to exit the Text Box Properties dialog box.

27. Click the Preview tab. The report should appear as shown here.

| Transport List.rdl [Design]* | Start Page | ▾ ✕ |

Design | Preview

◀ 1 of 1 ▶ ▶│ ◀ ⊘ 💾 🖨 ▣ 📖 🖫 ▾ 100% ▾   Find | Next

Transport List

Transport Type	Serial Number	Purchase Date	Latest Repair Date
Photon III	**Cargo Capacity: 2400.000** **Range: 9000.00**		
	P-348-23-4532-22A	05/14/1996	02/24/2009
	S-232-23-2345-53G	09/21/2002	03/12/2009
	T-282-23-3225-244D	08/25/2002	10/24/2008
	U-437-98-3849-39E	07/15/2005	03/18/2009
	W-283-48-2384-23B	10/23/2007	11/24/2008
	X-238-32-3254-24C	04/13/2003	01/19/2009
	Y-833-23-6454-35C	11/01/2003	11/17/2008
Star Lifter	**Cargo Capacity: 5000.000** **Range: 18000.00**		
	3809393848	09/23/2006	04/14/2009
	8292932983	04/13/2006	12/01/2008
	8393939399	04/24/2005	10/11/2008

28. Click Save All in the toolbar.

Task Notes When we added the grouping, we selected a field for the group expression in Step 4. The selected field determines when a new group begins in the report. In the Transport List report, we used the Description field from the TransportType table as the group expression. Because our first sort in the dataset was on the Description column in the TransportType table, all the Photon III transports came first in the dataset, followed by the StarLifter transports, and finally, the Warp Hauler transports. Each time the value of the group expression changes, a new value appears in the group column and a new group header is added to the report.

Be sure you do not confuse the grouping in the report with the GROUP BY clause we used in SQL SELECT statements. The SQL GROUP BY clause takes a number of records and combines them into a single record in the result set. The grouping in the report takes a number of records in the dataset and surrounds them with a group column, along with a possible group header and/or group footer when they are output in the report.

In Steps 12–18, we combined the fields that need to be in the group header into one expression. This was done so we could create a multiline group header, and also to concatenate or combine the labels (Cargo Capacity: and Range:) and the contents of the two fields (CargoCapacity and Range) into one string. The three columns of the group header were merged together to create room for the resulting expression. The Visual Basic concatenation operator (&) is used to combine the values into one long string. The Visual Basic constant vbCrLf is used to put a carriage return and linefeed in the middle of the string. This causes everything following the carriage return and linefeed to be placed on the next line down, giving us a two-line group header. The CStr() function is used to convert the CargoCapacity and Range numeric values to strings so they can be concatenated with the string constants.

Remember, table cells are always occupied by a report item. If no other report item has been placed in a cell, the cell is occupied by a text box. When multiple cells are merged, the report item in the leftmost cell expands to fill the merged table cell. The report items in the other cells involved in the merge are automatically deleted.

We created a border around the text box in the merged cells to set off our group heading. This is easier and more efficient than adding a line or a rectangle report item to the report to get the same result. This is especially true when you are trying to set off something in the middle of a table, such as our group header.

When you typed the text in Step 8, it looked like you were entering the text directly into the text box. What you *were* doing is changing the Value property of the text box. You can change the Value property of a text box by typing directly into the text box in the design surface or by typing in the Value field on the General page of the Text Box Properties dialog box.

In addition, the Expression dialog box can be used to change the Value property of a text box, as well as many other report item properties. In Step 12, we used the context menu to bring up the Expression dialog box. The Expression dialog box can also be accessed by clicking the *fx* button, as the following illustration shows. In addition to the Value property of the text box, the Expression dialog box can be used to change a number of properties of various report items. We discuss this in more detail in Chapter 7.

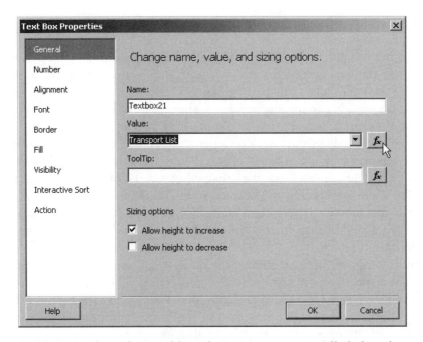

You probably noticed a red, jagged line that appears occasionally below the expression as you typed it in the Expression dialog box. If you have ever used Microsoft Word, then you know this means something is wrong with the text you have typed. In Word, this red line indicates a spelling error. In the Expression dialog box, this means a problem exists with the syntax of your expression. Hovering over the red line provides you with a brief description of the problem.

The Tablix and Data Regions

In the report you just completed, you saw when we dragged a table from the Toolbox onto the design surface, we actually ended up with a report item called a tablix. As mentioned in Chapter 1, a tablix provides the capabilities of a table and a matrix combined into one. When we selected a table from the toolbox, what we really did was select a template that creates a tablix that functions like a table. When we select a matrix from the toolbox, as we will do in our next report, we really select a template that creates a tablix that functions like a matrix. In the same manner, the list is a template that creates a tablix that functions like a freeform list.

In the previous report, you saw how the tablix, when functioning like a table, starts with a predefined number of columns. It then adds a data row to the resulting report for each record in the dataset. The tablix, when functioning like a matrix, creates both rows and columns based on the contents of the dataset. You see this demonstrated in our next report. The tablix, when functioning like a freeform list, is not limited to rows and columns. It creates a whole section, perhaps a whole page, of layout for each record in the dataset. We create a report using the list template later in this chapter.

These templates help us start work on a particular type of report layout, table, matrix, or list. The templates do not, however, change the functionality of the tablix that appears as part of our report. They just help configure some of the initial settings for the tablix so it looks a certain way. We could start with the table template and end up with a tablix that functions more like a matrix. Or we could start with a matrix template and end up with a tablix that functions more like a table. Underneath it all, a tablix is a tablix is a tablix.

The tablix is one of three special report items designed specifically for working with datasets. These special report items are called *data regions*. The other data regions are the chart and the gauge. (It could also be considered correct to refer to the table, the matrix, and the list as data region items in the Toolbox, even though we now know these are simply templates for creating the tablix data region.)

Data regions are able to work with multiple records from a dataset. The data region reads a record from the dataset, creates a portion of the report using the data found in that record, and then moves on to the next record. It does this until all the records from the dataset have been processed. The tablix creates mainly textual layout for each record in the dataset. The chart and gauge data regions create mainly graphical layout for the records in the dataset.

Each data region item has a property called DataSetName. This property contains the name of the dataset used by the data region. In the Transport List report you just created, the DataSetName property of the tablix has the value TransportList (see the following illustration). Each data region always works with one and only one dataset. However, a given dataset can be used by multiple data regions within the same report. For example, you could create a report containing both a tablix data region and a chart data region to present the data from a single dataset in both a textual and a graphical layout.

Now let's move down the road a little further and create a matrix report without the wizard.

The Repair Count By Type Report

Features Highlighted

▶ Creating a matrix report from scratch

▶ Using the Property Pages button

Business Need   GDS needs to purchase several new transports to update their delivery fleet. The company must decide which type of transport to purchase. One factor in the decision is the amount of time the new transports will spend in the maintenance hangar for repairs and preventative maintenance.

Upper management has asked the GDS maintenance department to provide a report showing the number of each type of repair required by each type of transport. The report should include statistics from all transports, both active and retired. Also, the report should group the repairs by their cause.

Task Overview

1. Reopen the Chapter05 Project, Create a New Report in the Chapter05 Project, Select the Shared Data Source, and Create a Dataset.
2. Place a Matrix Item on the Report and Populate It.
3. Add Column Grouping and Other Report Formatting.

Repair Count By Type Report, Task 1: Reopen the Chapter05 Project, Create a New Report in the Chapter05 Project, Select the Shared Data Source, and Create a Dataset

1. If you closed the Chapter05 project, reopen it.
2. In the Solution Explorer on the right side of the screen, right-click the Reports folder.
3. Put your mouse pointer over Add in the context menu, and wait for the submenu to appear. Select New Item from the context menu. This displays the Add New Item - Chapter05 dialog box.
4. Make sure the Report icon is selected in the Templates area. Enter RepairCountByType for the name.
5. Click Add. A new report called RepairCountByType.rdl is created in the Chapter05 project.

6. In the Report Data window, click the New drop-down menu. Select Data Source from the menu that appears. The Data Source Properties dialog box appears.

7. Enter **Galactic** for the name.

8. Select the Use shared data source reference radio button. and select Galactic from the drop-down list below it. Click OK. An entry for the Galactic data source appears in the Report Data window.

9. In the Report Data window, right-click the entry for the Galactic data source, and select Add Dataset from the context menu. The Dataset Properties dialog box appears.

10. Enter **RepairsByType** for the name.

11. Click the Query Designer button. The Query Designer window opens, displaying the Generic Query Designer.

12. Click the Edit As Text button in the toolbar to unselect the Generic Query Designer and switch to the Graphical Query Designer.

13. Right-click in the diagram pane of the Graphical Query Designer screen. Select Add Table from the context menu.

14. Add the following tables to the query:

    Repair
    Transport
    TransportType
    RepairWorkDoneLink
    WorkDone
    RepairCause

15. Click Close to exit the Add Table dialog box.

16. Check the following column in the Repair table:

    RepairID

17. Check the following column in the TransportType table:

    Description

18. In the criteria pane, type **TypeOfTransport** in the Alias column in the Description row.

19. Check the following column in the WorkDone table:

    Description

20. In the criteria pane, type **TypeOfWork** in the Alias column in the Description row for the WorkDone table.

21. Check the following column in the RepairCause table:

    Description

22. In the criteria pane, type **RepairCause** in the Alias column in the Description row for the RepairCause table.

23. Type **1** in the Sort Order column for RepairCause. Type **2** in the Sort Order column for TypeOfWork.

24. Right-click in the SQL pane, and select Execute SQL from the context menu. The Graphical Query Designer should appear similar to this:

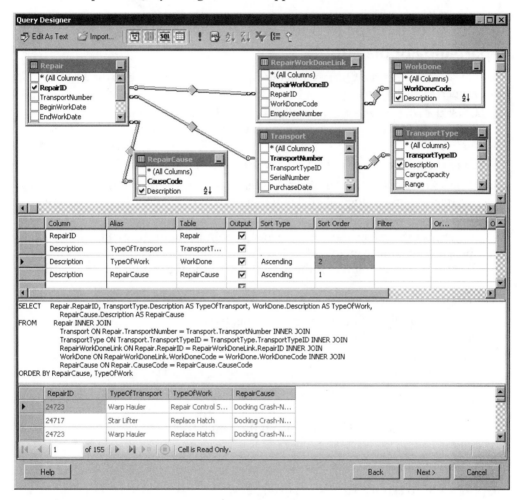

Task Notes   Although this report is a pretty straightforward request, we need to link together a number of tables to collect the necessary data. What we are interested in is repairs, so we start with the Repair table. However, none of the fields we need in the result set are in the Repair table. To find the type of transport being repaired, we need to join the Transport table with the Repair table and then join the TransportType table to the

Transport table. To find the type of work done, we need to join the RepairWorkDoneLink table to the Repair table and then join the WorkDone table to the RepairWorkDoneLink table. Finally, to group by the cause of the repair, we need to join the RepairCause table to the Repair table. If you get confused by all of this, refer to Figure 3-23 in Chapter 3.

Repair Count By Type Report, Task 2: Place a Matrix Item on the Report and Populate It

1. Click OK to exit the Query Designer window. Click OK to exit the Dataset Properties dialog box.
2. Click the Matrix report item in the Toolbox. The mouse pointer changes to a matrix icon and crosshairs when you move the mouse pointer over the design surface.
3. Drag the mouse cursor over the lower three-quarters of the design surface.
4. When you release the mouse button after dragging, a matrix is created to occupy the area you just defined. By default, every cell in the matrix is occupied by an empty text box.
5. Hover over the cell containing the word "Columns" until the Field Selector icon appears. Click the icon and select the TypeOfTransport field. The values in the TypeOfTransport column of the dataset determine the columns in the matrix report.
6. Use the same process in the cell containing the word "Rows" to select the TypeOfWork field. The values in the TypeOfWork column of the dataset determine the rows in the matrix report.
7. Use the same process once more in the cell containing the word "Data" to select the RepairID field.
8. Right-click the cell you worked on in Step 7, and select Expression from the Textbox section of the context menu. The Expression dialog box appears.
9. Change the word "Sum" to "Count" so the contents of the expression appear as follows:

   ```
   =Count(Fields!RepairID.Value)
   ```

10. Click OK to exit the Expression dialog box.
11. With this cell still selected, change the following property in the Properties window:

Property	New Value
TextAlign	Center

12. Reduce the width and height of the columns in the matrix. When you finish, your report design should look similar to this:

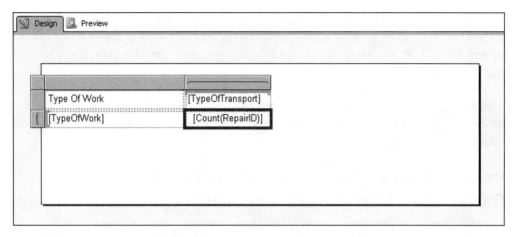

13. Click the Preview tab. Your report should look similar to the following illustration. The rows and columns in your report may appear in a different order from those shown here.

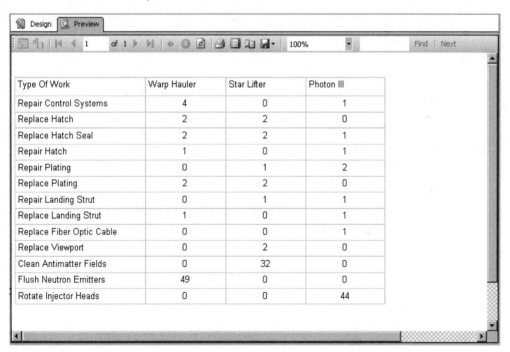

Task Notes Because the matrix report always groups a number of records from the dataset to create the entries in the matrix, the field that supplies the data for the matrix must be enclosed in some type of aggregate function. If the field placed in the data cell is a number, Report Designer encloses the field in the Sum() aggregate function.

The RepairID field, which we placed in the data cell in Step 7, is a number. However, it does not make sense to add up the RepairIDs. Instead, we want to count the number of RepairIDs. For this reason, we changed the Sum() aggregate function to the Count() aggregate function.

We have been referring to this as a matrix report because it was created from the matrix template in the Toolbox. We also refer to this as a matrix report because it will function like a matrix when it is completed. However, we know that the data region being used is actually a tablix.

Repair Count By Type Report, Task 3: Add Column Grouping and Other Report Formatting

1. Click the Design tab to return to the report layout.
2. In the Rows Groups area of the Grouping pane, click the drop-down arrow and select Add Group | Parent Group from the menu. The Tablix group dialog box appears.
3. Select [RepairCause] from the Group by drop-down list. Click OK.
4. Select the cell containing the Group1 header. Click the cell a second time so the blinking text-edit cursor appears in that cell.
5. Delete Group1 and type the following:

   Repair Cause

6. The report layout should appear as follows.

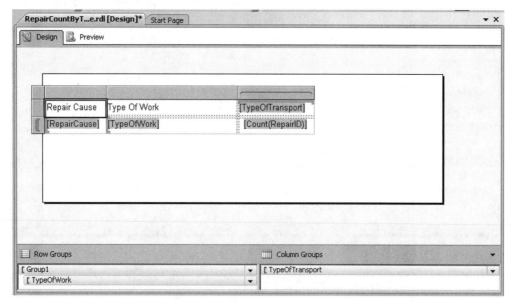

7. Make the Repair Cause group column approximately twice as wide as its default width.

8. Select the text box containing the RepairCause field (*not* the text box where you just typed "Repair Cause" as a heading).

9. In the Properties window, click the Property Pages button shown in the following illustration. The Text Box Properties dialog box appears.

10. Replace the current content of Name with **txtRepairCause**. Click OK. We give this text box an explicit name because we reference it in just a moment.

11. In the Row Groups area, right-click the TypeOfWork entry and select Group Properties from the context menu. The Group Properties dialog box appears.

12. Select the Visibility page. Set the When the report is initially run radio buttons group to Hide. Check the Display can be toggled by this report item check box, and select txtRepairCause from the associated drop-down list. The Group Properties dialog box should appear as shown.

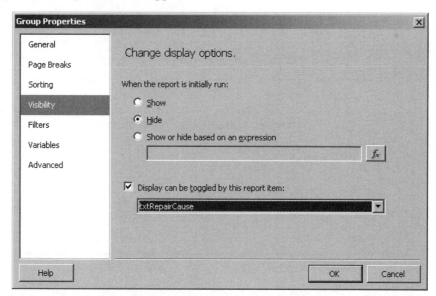

13. Click OK in the Group Properties dialog box.

14. Click the gray rectangle to the left of the upper row in the tablix to select this entire row. Change the following properties in the Properties window:

Property	New Value
FontWeight	Bold
TextDecoration	Underline

15. Click the Textbox report item in the Toolbox. Drag the mouse cursor over the area above the matrix on the design surface. When you release the mouse button after dragging, a text box is created to occupy the area you just defined. Double-click the text box and type the following:

```
Repair Count By Type Report
```

16. Press ESC to leave text-edit mode and select the text box. Make the following changes in the Properties window:

Property	New Value
FontSize	16pt
FontWeight	Bold
TextAlign	Center

17. Your report layout should appear similar to the illustration.

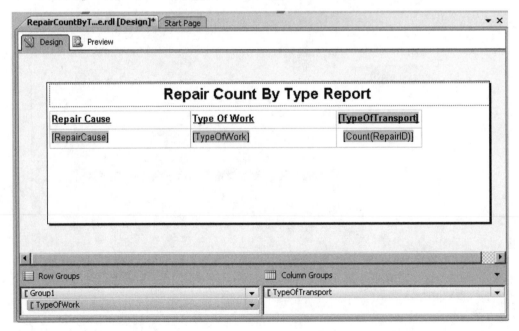

18. Click the Preview tab. Try expanding some of the drilldown sections. The report should appear as follows.

RepairCountByT...e.rdl [Design]*	Start Page				▼ ✕
🖻 Design	🔍 Preview				

		of 1		100%	Find | Next

Repair Count By Type Report

Repair Cause	Type Of Work	Warp Hauler	Star Lifter	Photon III
⊟ Docking Crash-No Fault	Repair Control Systems	1	0	0
	Replace Hatch	1	1	0
	Replace Hatch Seal	1	1	0
⊞ Docking Crash-Pilot Fault		4	0	3
⊟ Landing Crash-No Fault	Repair Control Systems	1	0	0
	Repair Landing Strut	0	1	0
	Replace Landing Strut	1	0	0
	Replace Plating	0	1	0
⊞ Landing Crash-Pilot Fault		0	0	4
⊞ Midair Collision-No Fault		3	0	1
⊞ Midair Collision-Pilot Fault		0	6	0
⊞ Scheduled Maintenance		49	32	44

19. Click Save All in the toolbar.

Task Notes   The Property Pages button in the Properties window provides an alternative way to access the properties dialog box for a report item. The properties dialog box can make it much easier to modify the properties of a report item. As we saw in the previous report, you can also access the properties dialog box by right-clicking a report item and selecting Properties from the context menu.

New Territory

Now that you have created the table and matrix reports without the aid of the Report Wizard, it is time to venture into new territory. We will move on to create a *list report*. List reports are used when you need to repeat a large area of content—perhaps even an entire page—for each record in the dataset. They are often used to create forms. List reports function similarly to a mail merge in a word-processing program, such as Microsoft Word.

The Transport Information Sheet

Feature Highlighted

▶   Creating a list report

Business Need   The GDS maintenance department needs an efficient way to look up general information about a particular transport that comes in for repair. The user should be able to select the serial number from a drop-down list and see all the basic information about the transport. This transport information sheet should also include the date of the next scheduled maintenance appointment for this transport.

Task Overview

1.   Reopen the Chapter05 Project, Create a New Report in the Chapter05 Project, Select the Shared Data Source, and Create the TransportSNs Dataset.
2.   Create the TransportInfo Dataset.
3.   Place a List Item on the Report and Populate It.

Transport Information Sheet, Task 1: Reopen the Chapter05 Project, Create a New Report in the Chapter05 Project, Select the Shared Data Source, and Create the TransportSNs Dataset

1.   If you closed the Chapter05 project, reopen it.
2.   In the Solution Explorer on the right side of the screen, right-click the Reports folder. Select Add | New Item. This displays the Add New Item-Chapter05 dialog box.
3.   Make sure the Report icon is selected in the Templates area. Enter **TransportInfoSheet** for the name. Click Add.
4.   In the Report Data window, click the New drop-down menu. Select Data Source from the menu that appears. The Data Source Properties dialog box appears.
5.   Enter **Galactic** for the name.
6.   Select the Use shared data source reference radio button, and select Galactic from the drop-down list below it. Click OK. An entry for the Galactic data source appears in the Report Data window.
7.   In the Report Data window, right-click the entry for the Galactic data source, and select Add Dataset from the context menu. The Dataset Properties dialog box appears.
8.   Enter **TransportSNs** for the name.

9. Click the Query Designer button. The Query Designer window opens, displaying the Generic Query Designer.

10. Enter the following in the upper portion of the Generic Query Designer window:

```
SELECT SerialNumber FROM Transport WHERE RetiredDate IS NULL ORDER BY
SerialNumber
```

11. Click the Run toolbar button (the red exclamation mark). The Generic Query Designer window should appear similar to the following.

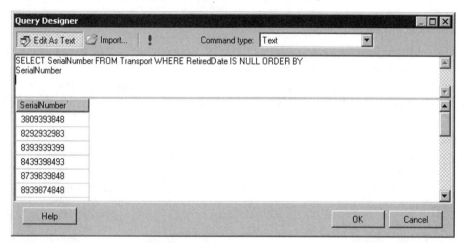

12. Click OK to exit the Query Designer window. Click OK to exit the Dataset Properties dialog box.

Task Notes The TransportSNs dataset provides a list of the serial numbers for all the active transports at GDS. This dataset is used to populate the drop-down list from which the user selects the transport for which the Transport Information Sheet will be printed. Because the query for this dataset is relatively straightforward, it is faster to type the query string by hand rather than build it using the Graphical Query Designer.

This is not the case with the query string for the second dataset required by this report, as you shall see in the next task.

Transport Information Sheet, Task 2:
Create the TransportInfo Dataset

1. Right-click the Galactic data source entry in the Report Data window, and select Add Dataset from the context menu The Dataset Properties dialog box appears.

2. Enter **TransportDetail** for the name.

3. Click the Query Designer button to display the Query Designer window.

4. Click the Edit As Text toolbar button to switch from the Generic Query Designer to the Graphical Query Designer.

5. Right-click in the diagram pane of the Graphical Query Designer screen. Select Add Table from the context menu. Add the following tables to the query:

   Transport
   TransportType
   ScheduledMaint
   Repair

6. Click Close to exit the Add Table dialog box.

7. Right-click the link between the Transport and the Repair tables, and then select Remove from the context menu. (You may have to rearrange the tables in the diagram pane to make this visible.)

8. Right-click the diamond in the middle of the link between the Repair table and the ScheduledMaint table. Choose Select All Rows from ScheduledMaint in the context menu.

9. Find the diamond in the middle of the link between the Transport and ScheduledMaint tables. (You may have to rearrange the tables in the diagram pane to make this visible.) Right-click this diamond and choose Select All Rows from Transport from the context menu. With a bit of rearranging, your diagram pane should look similar to the illustration.

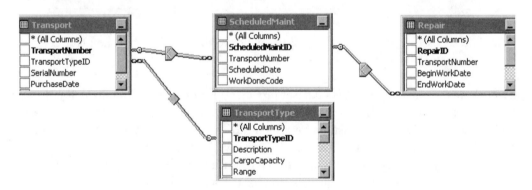

10. Check the following columns in the Transport table:
    SerialNumber
    PurchaseDate

11. Check the following columns in the TransportType table:
    Description
    CargoCapacity
    Range
    Cost
    Crew
    Manufacturer
    ManAddr1
    ManAddr2
    ManCity
    ManState
    ManZipCode
    ManPlanetAbbrv
    ManEmail

12. Check the following column in the ScheduledMaint table:
    ScheduledDate

13. Check the following column in the Repair table:
    RepairID

14. In the criteria pane, type the following in the Filter column for SerialNumber:

    `= @SerialNumber`

15. In the Filter column for RepairID, type this:

    `IS NULL`

16. Right-click in the diagram pane, and select Add Group By from the context menu.

17. In the criteria pane, in the Group By column for ScheduledDate, select Min from the drop-down list.

18. In the Alias column for ScheduledDate, change Expr1 to NextMaintDate.

19. Right-click in the SQL pane, and select Execute SQL from the context menu. Enter **3809393848** for the @SerialNumber parameter, and click OK. The Graphical Query Designer should appear similar to the next illustration.

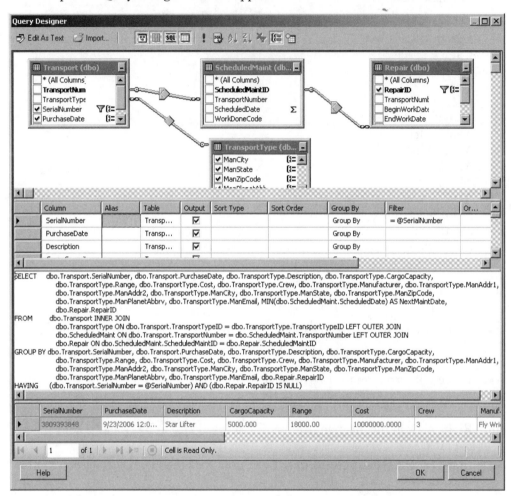

Task Notes The TransportDetail dataset must include all the information about a selected transport. This is not complicated, except for the last item noted in the business need for this report: the date of the next scheduled maintenance for this transport. You need a little background on the way the Galactic database functions regarding scheduled maintenance to understand this query.

Records are added to the ScheduledMaint table for each time a transport needs to come into a maintenance facility for preventative maintenance. These are considered appointments for preventative maintenance. They are scheduled for dates in the future. Transports may have more than one pending preventative maintenance appointment. The ScheduledMaint table records are linked to a transport by the TransportNumber field.

When a transport comes in for preventative maintenance, a record is added to the Repair table. This indicates an appointment for preventative maintenance has been fulfilled. The record in the Repair table is linked to the record in the ScheduledMaint table by the ScheduledMaintID field. If a scheduled appointment is missed, the appointment is rescheduled by changing the value in the ScheduledMaint.ScheduleDate field to a value in the future.

Given these business rules, records in the ScheduledMaint table for a given transport that do not have corresponding records in the Repair table represent pending preventative maintenance appointments. The record that has the minimum value in the ScheduledDate field represents the next appointment. To find this record, we are joining the ScheduledMaint table to the Repair table using a left outer join. Because we require the RepairID to be NULL, our result set only includes the pending appointments (that is, the records in the ScheduledMaint table that do not have a matching record in the Repair table).

Because a transport may have more than one pending appointment, we could end up with more than one record for a given transport. We need to use GROUP BY to consolidate these into one record. The MIN() aggregate function is used to find the ScheduledDate field with the lowest value (that is, the next scheduled appointment).

The "= @SerialNumber" we put in the Filter column for SerialNumber allows the user to specify a serial number at the time the report is run. The user will select a transport serial number from a drop-down list, and that serial number will be fed into the query in place of the @SerialNumber. This is called parameterizing the query. We next do a bit of work to make sure the parameter functions the way we intend it to.

Transport Information Sheet, Task 3: Place a List Item on the Report and Populate It

1. Click OK to exit the Query Designer window. Click OK to exit the Dataset Properties dialog box.
2. In the Report Data window, expand the Parameters folder.
3. Right-click the entry for SerialNumber, and select Parameter Properties from the context menu. The Report Parameter Properties dialog box appears.
4. Select the Available Values page.
5. Select the Get values from a query radio button.
6. Select TransportSNs from the Dataset drop-down list.
7. Select SerialNumber from the Value field drop-down list. Select SerialNumber from the Label field drop-down list as well. The Report Parameter Properties dialog box should appear as shown.

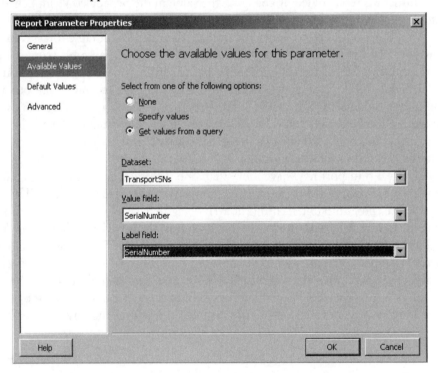

8. Click OK to exit the Report Parameter Properties dialog box.
9. Move your mouse pointer to the bottom of the white design surface so it changes from the regular mouse pointer to the double-headed arrow, as shown in the following illustration. The white design surface is the body of the report.

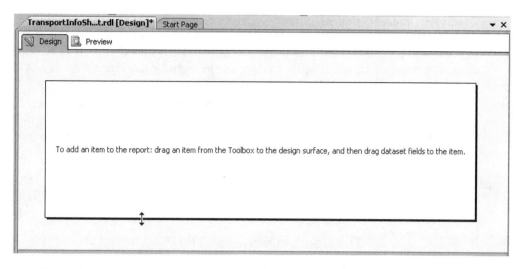

10. Drag the bottom of the report body down to create more room to lay out the list report.

11. Select the Toolbox window, and click the List report item. The mouse pointer changes to a list icon and crosshairs when you move your mouse pointer over the design surface.

12. Drag the mouse cursor over the entire report body.

13. When you release the mouse button after dragging, a list is created to occupy the area you just defined.

14. Drag a text box from the Toolbox, and drop it inside the list at the top. The list will become selected as you drag the text box on to it. This text box will be the title.

15. Double-click this new text box so the blinking text-edit cursor appears. Type **Transport Information Sheet** in the textbox. Press ESC to leave text-edit mode and select the text box.

16. As an alternative to the Properties window, font and text alignment properties can be set using the toolbar buttons similar to working in Microsoft Word or Microsoft Excel. Use the toolbar to set the properties of the text box as follows:

Property	Value
FontSize	16pt
FontWeight	Bold
TextAlign	Center

17. Drag a second text box from the Toolbox and place it under the existing title. Type **Serial Number:** in this text box. Size the text box so it just fits this text. This serves as the label for the Serial Number field.

18. In the Report Data window, expand the Galactic data source and the TransportDetail dataset. Drag the SerialNumber field from the Report Data window and place it to the right of the text box that was added in Step 17. Click the sizing handle (the small white square) on the right side of this new text box to make it approximately twice its original size.

19. Now use the positioning handle (the square with the four arrow heads) to position the text box relative to the text box containing the "Serial Number:" label. When the two text boxes are aligned, you will see alignment lines appear between the two text boxes, as shown here.

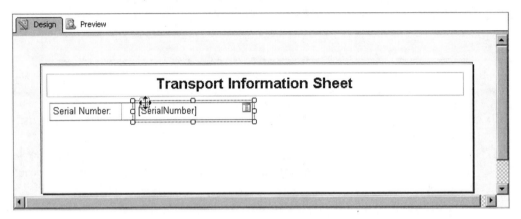

20. Drag a line from the Toolbox, and drop it inside the list below the text box containing the "Serial Number:" label.

21. Drag the end points of the line so it goes across the entire list below the Serial Number: text boxes.

22. Repeat Step 17 through Step 19 for each of the following fields, creating a label for the field and then placing the field to the right of the label. (Hint: You may want to create all the labels first and then add all the fields so you are not switching back and forth between the Toolbox window and the Report Data window.)

Label	Field
Purchase Date:	PurchaseDate
Transport Type:	Description
Cargo Capacity:	CargoCapacity
Range:	Range
Cost:	Cost
Crew:	Crew
Next Maint:	NextMaintDate

23. Use either the Report Formatting toolbar or the Properties window to set the properties for these fields as follows (these properties are for the fields themselves, not the labels):

Field	Property	Value
PurchaseDate	Format	MM/dd/yyyy
PurchaseDate	TextAlign	Left
CargoCapacity	TextAlign	Left
Range	TextAlign	Left
Cost	Format	###,###,##0.00
Cost	TextAlign	Left
Crew	TextAlign	Left
NextMaintDate	Format	MM/dd/yyyy
NextMaintDate	TextAlign	Left

24. Drag a rectangle from the Toolbox, and drop it inside the list below the bottom-most text box. Size the rectangle so it covers the remaining area of the list.

25. Use the Report Borders toolbar, shown here, to set the properties for the border of the rectangle. Make sure the toolbar items are set to Solid, 1pt, and Black.

26. Click the Outside Border toolbar button, indicated here by the mouse pointer, to create a solid, 1-point-wide, black border on all sides of the rectangle.

27. Drag a text box from the Toolbox, and place a text box in the upper-left corner of the rectangle. Type **Manufacturer:** in this text box. This is the manufacturer label.

28. Drag the Manufacturer field from the Report Data window, and place it inside the rectangle to the right of the manufacturer label. Align the Manufacturer field text box with the manufacturer label text box, and size the field text box so it goes almost all the way to the right side of the rectangle. If you drag too far to the right, the Report Designer automatically increases the size of the body of the report. If this happens, simply reduce the width of the body of the report.

29. Place the ManAddr1 and ManAddr2 fields below the Manufacturer field. Make these new fields the same size as the Manufacturer field.

30. Place the ManCity field inside the rectangle, below the ManAddr2 field. Make this new field the same size as the ManAddr2 field.

31. Click on "[ManCity]" in the text box added in step 30 to select that text, and then right-click on this selected text. Select Expression from the context menu. The Expression dialog box appears.

    Type the following expression in the Set expression for: Value area:

    ```
    =Fields!ManCity.Value & ", " & Fields!ManState.Value & " " &
    Fields!ManZipCode.Value & " " &Fields!ManPlanetAbbrv.Value
    ```

32. Click OK to exit the Expression dialog box.

33. Drag the ManEmail field from the Report Data window, and place it inside the rectangle under the text box added in Step 26. Make this text box as wide as the text boxes above it.

34. Your report layout should appear similar to the following illustration:

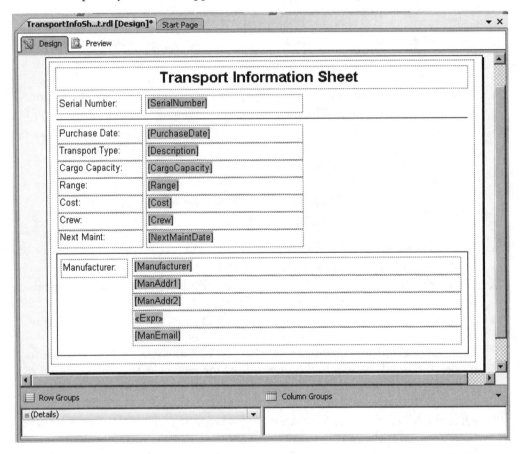

35. Click the Preview tab.

36. Select the first serial number from the Serial Number drop-down list, and click View Report. Your report should appear similar to the illustration.

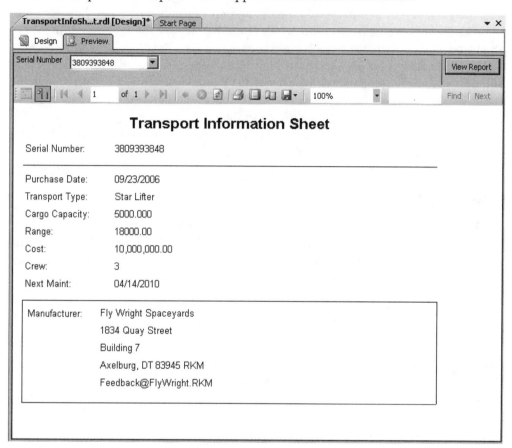

37. Click the Save All button on the toolbar.

Task Notes   As you saw in the Transport Information Sheet report, the List item enables you to place information anywhere. Text boxes, lines, and rectangles can be placed anywhere within the List item to create complex forms. This type of report is good for presenting a large amount of information about a single entity, as we did in this report.

As stated earlier, the contents of the List item are repeated for each record in the dataset. The TransportInfo dataset selects only a single record based on the user's selection of a serial number. Therefore, our report only has one page.

The Line report item is used simply to help format the report. It helps separate information on the report to make it easier for the user to understand. When working with the Table report item, we could use the borders of the text boxes in the table cells to create lines. In the more freeform layout of the List report, the Line report item often works better than using cell borders.

The Rectangle report item serves two purposes. When its border is set to something other than None, it becomes a visible part of the report. Therefore, it can serve to help visibly separate information on the report in the same manner as the Line report item. This is how we are using the Rectangle report item in this report.

The Rectangle report item can also be used to keep together other items in the report. We examine this use of rectangles in Chapter 7.

Getting Graphical

You have now seen the tablix data region, along with its table, matrix, and list templates in action. In the next chapter, you learn about the final two data regions—the chart and the gauge. We also look at the Image report item and its uses for adding graphics to a report. Finally, in Chapter 6, you learn about ways to control the properties of a report item using Visual Basic expressions.

Chapter 6

Graphic Expression: Using Charts, Images, and Gauges

In This Chapter

▶ **Chart Your Course**
▶ **Gauging the Results**
▶ **Image Is Everything**
▶ **Building Higher**

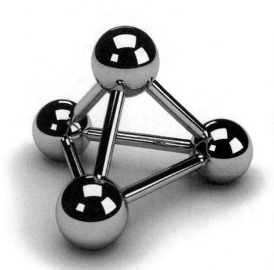

We live in a world today where image is everything. Color and graphics are used to add interest and convey meaning. This is true not only for TV, newspapers, and magazines, but also for some of the reports you create. Reports going to managers or executives need to provide the quick, concise communication of charts and graphs. Reports shared with customers need the polish provided by a well-placed image or two. Reporting Services has the tools you need to effectively communicate and impress in each of these situations.

In this chapter, we explore the final data regions, the chart and the gauge, and how they can be used to summarize and express data. We also use the image report item to add graphics to our reports. Finally, we end this chapter by looking at properties that can be used to format the report output and creative ways to control those properties.

Chart Your Course

In many cases, the best way to convey business intelligence is through business graphics. Bar charts, pie charts, and line graphs are useful tools for giving meaning to endless volumes of data. They can quickly reveal trends and patterns to aid in data analysis. They compress lines upon lines of numbers into a format that can be understood in a moment.

In addition, charts can increase the reader's interest in your information. A splash of color excites the reader. Where endless lines of black on white lull people to sleep, bars of red and blue, and pie wedges of purple and green wake people up.

You create charts in Reporting Services using the chart report item. The chart report item is a data region like the tablix. This means the chart can process multiple records from a dataset. The tablix enables you to place other report items in a row, a column, or a list area, which is repeated for every record in the dataset. The chart, on the other hand, uses the records in a dataset to create bars, lines, or pie wedges. You cannot place other report items inside a chart item.

In the next sections of this chapter, we explore the many charting possibilities provided by the chart report item.

The Deliveries versus Lost Packages Chart

Features Highlighted

- ▶ Creating a report using the chart report item
- ▶ Using multiple series
- ▶ Copying an existing report into the same project

▶ Using scale breaks

▶ Using multiple chart areas

▶ Using a secondary value axis

Business Need   Galactic Delivery Services (GDS) needs to determine if there is a correlation between the number of deliveries in a month and the number of lost packages in that same month. The best way to perform this analysis is by creating a chart of the number of deliveries and the number of lost packages over time.

Task Overview

1. Create the Chapter06 Project, a Shared Data Source, a New Report, and Two Datasets.
2. Place a Chart Item on the Report and Populate It.
3. Explore Alternate Ways to Present the Deliveries and Lost Packages Together.

Deliveries versus Lost Packages Chart, Task 1: Create the Chapter06 Project, a Shared Data Source, a New Report, and Two Datasets

1. Create a new Reporting Services project called Chapter06 in the MSSQLRS folder. (If you need help with this task, see Chapter 5.)
2. Create a shared data source called Galactic for the Galactic database. (Again, if you need help with this task, see Chapter 5.)
3. Add a blank report called DelvLostPkgChart to the Chapter06 project. (Do not use the Report Wizard.)
4. In the Report Data window, click the New drop-down menu. Select Data Source from the menu that appears. The Data Source Properties dialog box appears.
5. Enter **Galactic** for the name.
6. Select the Use shared data source reference radio button and select Galactic from the drop-down list. Click OK.
7. In the Report Data window, right-click the entry for the Galactic data source and select Add Dataset from the context menu. The Dataset Properties dialog box appears.
8. Enter **TransportList** for the name.
9. Click the Query Designer button. The Query Designer window opens displaying the Generic Query Designer.

10. Enter the following in the SQL pane (upper portion) of the Generic Query Designer window:

```
SELECT Delivery.DeliveryNumber,
    LostPackage.LostPackageNumber,
    MONTH(PickupDateTime) AS Month
FROM Delivery
LEFT OUTER JOIN LostPackage
    ON Delivery.DeliveryNumber = LostPackage.DeliveryNumber
WHERE YEAR(PickupDateTime) = 2008
ORDER BY MONTH(PickupDateTime)
```

11. Click the Run Query button on the Generic Query Designer toolbar to run the query and make sure no errors exist. Correct any typos that may be detected. Click OK to exit the Query Designer window. Click OK to exit the Dataset Properties dialog box.

Task Notes   We created the dataset for this report by typing a query in the SQL pane of the Generic Query Designer. The graphical tools of the Graphical Query Designer are helpful if you are still learning the syntax of SELECT queries, or if you are unfamiliar with the database you are querying. However, it is more efficient to simply type the query into the SQL pane or the Dataset Properties dialog box. In addition, some complex queries must be typed in because they cannot be created through the Graphical Query Designer.

Throughout the remainder of this book, we type our SELECT statements rather than create them using the Graphical Query Designer. This enables us to quickly create the necessary datasets and then concentrate on the aspects of report creation that are new and different in each report. As you create your own reports, use the interface—Graphical Query Designer or Generic Query Designer—with which you are most comfortable.

In the query for this report, we join the Delivery table, which holds one record for each delivery, with the LostPackage table, which holds one record for each package lost during delivery. Because only some Delivery table records have associated LostPackage table records (at least we hope so), we need to use the LEFT OUTER JOIN to get all of the Delivery records joined with their matching LostPackage records. In our chart, we can count the number of DeliveryNumbers and the number of LostPackageNumbers to determine the number of deliveries and the number of lost packages.

Deliveries versus Lost Packages Chart, Task 2: Place a Chart Item on the Report and Populate It

1. Drag the edges of the design surface to make it larger so the design surface fills the available space on the screen.
2. Select the chart report item in the Toolbox window. Click and drag to place the chart on the design surface. The chart should cover almost the entire design surface because it will be the only item on the report.

3. After you place the chart on the report, the Select Chart Type dialog box appears. As you can see, the chart report item is extremely flexible. Click the first item in the Line row as shown here. This creates a simple line graph.

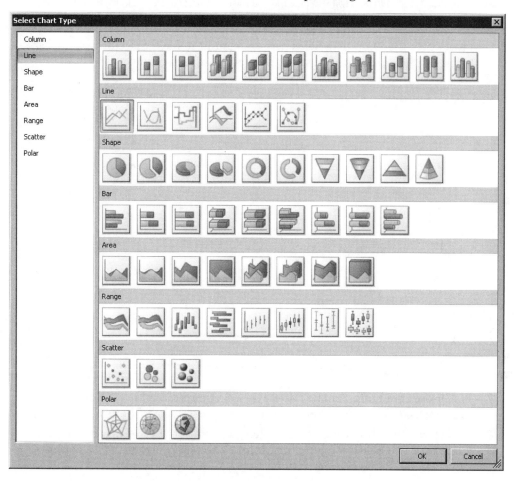

4. Click OK to exit the Select Chart Type dialog box. You will see a representation of the chart on the design surface.

5. Click anywhere on the chart. Three drop areas appear. They are: Drop data fields here, Drop series fields here, and Drop category fields here. You may need to scroll the layout window to see each of the drop areas.

NOTE

You make the drop areas disappear by clicking somewhere on the Design tab that is not covered by the graph. After that, clicking the chart once will select the chart so you can move and size it. Clicking the chart a second time will cause the drop areas to reappear.

6. Hover over the Drop data fields here area until the Field Selector icon appears. Click the Field Selector and select DeliveryNumber as shown.

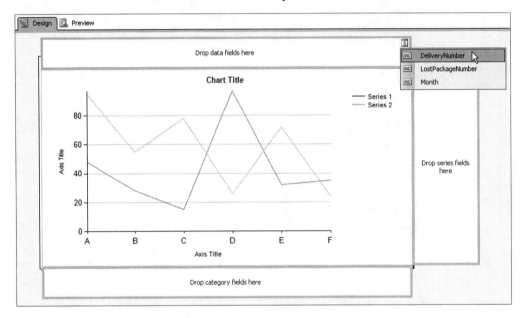

7. Hover over the Drop data fields here area again until the Field Selector icon reappears. Click the Field Selector and select LostPackageNumber.

8. Hover over the Drop category fields here area until the Field Selector appears. Click the Field Selector and select Month. The report layout should appear similar to the following illustration.

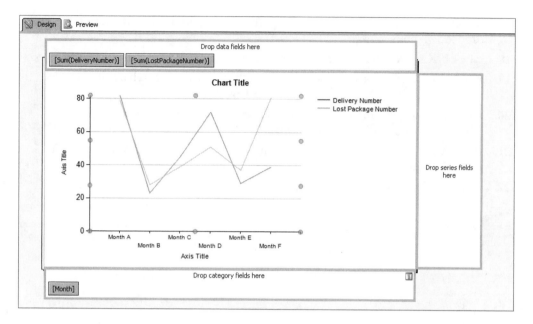

9. Right-click the [Sum(DeliveryNumber)] item in the Drop data fields here area and select Series Properties from the context menu. The Series Properties dialog box appears.

10. Change the Value field to **[Count(DeliveryNumber)]**.

11. Select the Legend page of the Series Properties dialog box. Type **Deliveries** in the Custom legend text box.

12. Select the Fill page of the Series Properties dialog box. Select Green from the Color drop-down color picker.

13. Click OK to exit the Select Properties dialog box.

14. Right-click the [Sum(LostPackageNumber)] item in the Drop data fields here area and select Series Properties from the context menu. The Series Properties dialog box appears.

15. Change the Value field to **[Count(LostPackageNumber)]**.

16. Select the Legend page of the Series Properties dialog box. Type **Lost Packages** in the Custom legend text text box.

17. Select the Fill page of the Series Properties dialog box. Select Red from the Color drop-down color picker.

18. Click OK to exit the Select Properties dialog box.

19. Double-click the words "Chart Title" to edit the text of the chart title. Replace the words "Chart Title" with **Deliveries and Lost Packages**.

20. Double-click the words "Axis Title" below the horizontal axis (the axis with Month A, Month B, etc.). Replace the words "Axis Title" with **Month**.

21. Right-click the words "Axis Title" to the left of the vertical axis (the axis with numeric values). Select Show Axis Title from the context menu to uncheck this item.

22. Click the Preview tab. Your report appears similar to this:

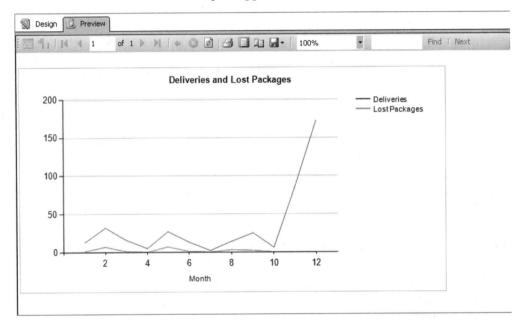

Task Notes You have now seen how easy it is to create a chart using the chart report item. Simply select the type of chart you want, select the fields from your dataset into the appropriate drop areas, and you have a functioning chart. In the next sections, we explore ways to manipulate the properties of the chart to create more complex results.

The fields you select in the data fields area, DeliveryNumber and LostPackageNumber in this report, provide the values for the data points on the chart. Each field creates a series of data points—in this case, a single line—on the graph. The scale for these values is along the vertical axis in this line chart. Therefore, the vertical axis is known as the *value axis*.

The fields you select in the category fields area, Month in this report, provide the labels for the horizontal axis of the chart. This axis is called the *category axis*. These category fields also group the rows from the dataset into multiple categories. One data point is created on the category axis for each category in each series.

Because the category fields create groups, we need to use aggregate functions with the values we are charting. Because the DeliveryNumber and LostPackageNumber fields are numeric data types, Visual Studio uses the Sum() aggregate function by default. Of course, the sum of the Delivery Numbers or the Lost Package Numbers makes no sense. Instead, we want to count the number of deliveries and the number of lost packages. For this reason, we changed both to the Count() aggregate function.

Notice in our graph the number of deliveries jumps up to over 150 in month 12. This makes it difficult to see the line for the lost packages. In Task 3, we explore three alternatives for dealing with this issue. We will make three copies of the DelvLostPkgChart report to try out these three alternatives.

Deliveries versus Lost Packages Chart, Task 3: Explore Alternate Ways to Present the Deliveries and Lost Packages Together

1. Close the DelvLostPkgChart report.
2. Click Save All on the toolbar.
3. Right-click the DelvLostPkgChart.rdl entry in the Solution Explorer window and select Copy from the context menu.
4. Right-click the Chapter06 entry in the Solution Explorer window and select Paste from the context menu. A copy of the DelvLostPkgChart report is added to the project.
5. Repeat Step 4 twice more so the project contains the original report plus three more.
6. Double-click the Copy of DelvLostPkgChart.rdl entry in the Solution Explorer window. The Design tab for this report is displayed.

7. Right-click the value axis on this chart and select Axis properties from the context menu. The Value Axis Properties dialog box appears, as shown here.

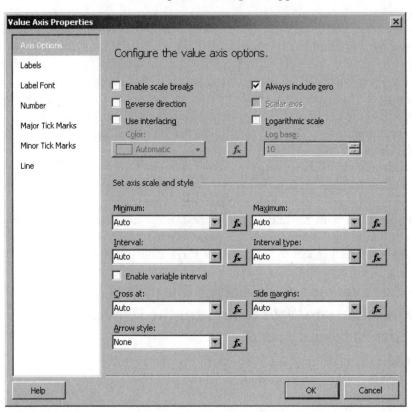

8. Check the Enable scale breaks check box.
9. Click OK to exit the Value Axis Properties dialog box.
10. Click the Preview tab. The value axis now contains two scale breaks.

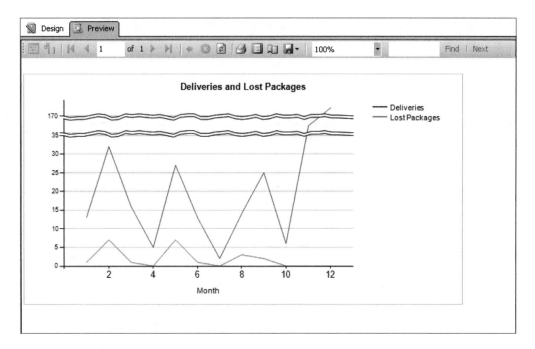

11. Click Save All on the toolbar.
12. Close the Copy of DelvLostPkgChart report.
13. Double-click the Copy (2) of DelvLostPkgChart.rdl entry in the Solution Explorer window. The Design tab for this report is displayed.

14. Right-click the center of the chart and select Chart | Add New Chart Area from the context menu. The chart splits into two regions: one above and one below. The lower portion appears as an empty rectangle, as shown. The upper chart area is known as the Default area and the lower chart area is given the name ChartArea1.

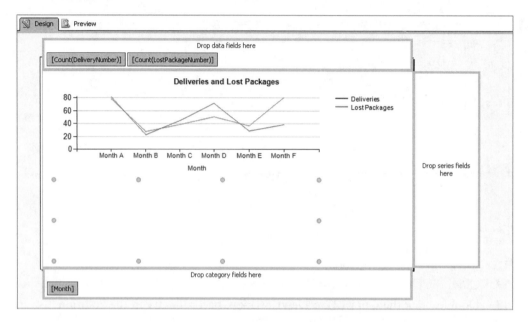

15. Right-click the Count(LostPackageNumber) entry in the Drop data fields here area. Select Series Properties from the context menu. The Series Properties dialog box appears.

16. Select the Axes and Chart Area page of the dialog box.

17. The Chart area drop-down list determines which chart area this series will appear in. Select ChartArea1 from the Chart area drop-down list. This is shown in the following illustration.

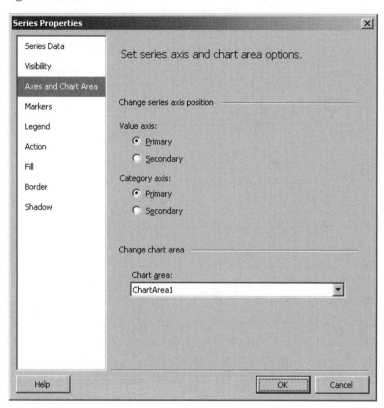

18. Click OK to exit the Series Properties dialog box.

19. Click the Preview tab. The report appears as shown.

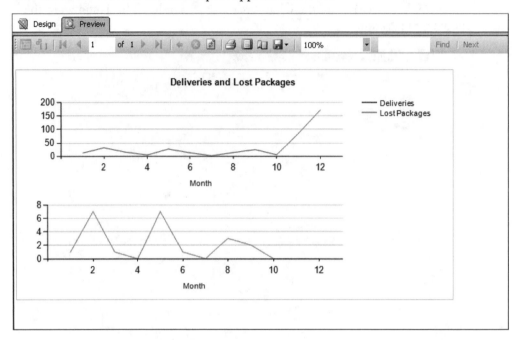

20. Click Save All on the toolbar.

21. Close the Copy (2) of DelvLostPkgChart report.

22. Double-click the Copy (3) of DelvLostPkgChart.rdl entry in the Solution Explorer window. The Design tab for this report is displayed.

23. Click twice on the chart so the drop area tabs are displayed.

24. Right-click the Count(LostPackageNumber) entry in the Drop data fields here area. Select Series Properties from the context menu. The Series Properties dialog box appears.

25. Select the Axes and Chart Area page of the dialog box.

26. Select Secondary from the Value axis radio buttons.

27. Click OK to exit the Series Properties dialog box. A secondary value axis appears on the right side of the chart, as shown here.

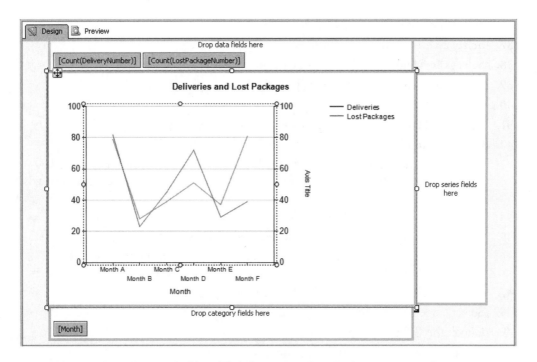

28. Double-click the words "Axis Title" associated with the new, secondary axis.
29. Replace the words "Axis Title" with **Lost Packages**. Press ENTER.
30. Right-click the words "Lost Packages" and select Axis Title Properties from the context menu. The Axis Title Properties dialog box appears.
31. Select the Font page of the Axis Title Properties dialog box.

NOTE

If you ended up with a different default color scheme for your chart and the deliveries line is a color other than green or the lost packages line is a color other than red, simply adapt the following steps to pick the appropriate colors for the two axes.

32. Select Red from the Color drop-down color picker.
33. Check the Bold check box.
34. Click OK to exit the Axis Title Properties dialog box.
35. Right-click the secondary value axis itself (the axis on the right side). Select Axis Properties from the context menu. The Secondary Value Axis Properties dialog box appears.

36. Select the Label Font page of the dialog box.

37. Select Red from the Color drop-down color picker.

38. Select the Major Tick Marks page of the dialog box.

39. Select Red from the Line color drop-down color picker.

40. Select the Line page of the dialog box.

41. Select Red from the Line color drop-down color picker.

42. Click OK to exit the Secondary Value Axis Properties dialog box.

43. Right-click the value axis on the left side of the chart. Select Show Axis Title from the context menu to check this item. The title for the left-side, primary axis appears.

44. Double-click the words "Axis Title" associated with the primary axis.

45. Replace the words "Axis Title" with **Deliveries**. Press ENTER.

46. Right-click the word "Deliveries" that you just added and select Axis Title Properties from the context menu. The Axis Title Properties dialog box appears.

47. Select the Font page of the Axis Title Properties dialog box.

48. Select Green from the Color drop-down color picker.

49. Check the Bold check box.

50. Click OK to exit the Axis Title Properties dialog box.

51. Right-click the value axis next to the Deliveries label (the axis on the left side). Select Axis Properties from the context menu. The Value Axis Properties dialog box appears.

52. Select the Label Font page of the dialog box.

53. Select Green from the Color drop-down color picker.

54. Select the Major Tick Marks page of the dialog box.

55. Select Green from the Line color drop-down color picker.

56. Select the Line page of the dialog box.

57. Select Green from the Line color drop-down color picker.

58. Click OK to exit the Value Axis Properties dialog box.

59. Right-click the legend area where "Deliveries" appears next to a green line and "Lost Packages" appears next to a red line. Select Delete Legend from the context menu. The legend disappears.

60. Click the Preview tab. The report appears as shown.

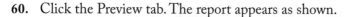

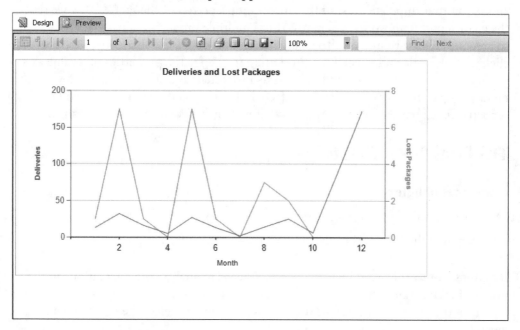

61. Click Save All on the toolbar.

Task Notes   In this task, we see three methods for analyzing two series with different value ranges on the same chart. In the first copy of the DelvLostPkgChart, we enabled scale breaks. Scale breaks allow portions of the scale that do not contain any values to be skipped over in the chart. On our chart, there are no values between 32 and 86 nor between 86 and 172, so these portions of the scale are eliminated from the chart.

In the second copy of the DelvLostPkgChart, we use a second chart area to display one of the two series. Each chart area has its own value axis, so each axis can size itself appropriately. Of course, a similar effect could be achieved by placing two chart items on a single report, one below the other. Using a single chart report item with two chart areas enables us to label both series in a single legend and ensures the category axes of both chart areas will stay aligned.

For the third copy of the DelvLostPkgChart, we use a secondary value axis to display the scale for one of the two series. As with the second chart area, this approach allows each series to have its own scale that will adapt to its own range of values. Using a secondary axis can make the chart confusing unless we provide enough visual cues to tell the user which series goes with which axis. This is why we took the time to color-code all of the various parts of the two value axes.

In the previous chapter, you saw the tablix has a single property dialog box that allows you to manipulate most of the important properties of the tablix. Now we see the chart report item works differently. It has multiple property dialog boxes that correspond to its various parts. To change the properties of the chart title, we right-click the chart title and select Title Properties; to change the properties of a value axis, we right-click that value axis and select Axis Properties; and so on. When you want to modify a particular item in a chart, right-click that item and odds are there will be a property dialog box available right there that will enable you to make the change.

The Fuel Price Chart

Features Highlighted

▶ Using a series group

▶ Refining the look of the chart to best present the information

Business Need Galactic Delivery Services needs to analyze the fluctuations in the price of fuel from month to month. The best way to perform this analysis is by creating a chart of the price over time. The user needs to be able to select the year from a drop-down list.

Task Overview

1. Create a New Report and Two Datasets.
2. Place a Chart Item on the Report and Populate It.
3. Refine the Chart.

Fuel Price Chart, Task 1: Create a New Report and Two Datasets

1. Add a blank report called FuelPriceChart to the Chapter06 project. (Do not use the Report Wizard.)
2. In the Report Data window, click the New drop-down menu. Select Data Source from the menu that appears. The Data Source Properties dialog box appears.
3. Enter **Galactic** for the name.
4. Select the Use shared data source reference radio button and select Galactic from the drop-down list. Click OK.
5. In the Report Data window, right-click the entry for the Galactic data source and select Add Dataset from the context menu. The Dataset Properties dialog box appears.
6. Enter **FuelPrices** for the name.

7. Click the Query Designer button. The Query Designer window opens displaying the Generic Query Designer.

8. Enter the following in the SQL pane (upper portion) of the Generic Query Designer window:

```
SELECT Description AS FuelType,
       PriceStartDate,
       Price
FROM FuelPrice
INNER JOIN Propulsion
       ON FuelPrice.PropulsionID = Propulsion.PropulsionID
WHERE (YEAR(PriceStartDate) = @Year)
ORDER BY FuelType, PriceStartDate
```

9. Click the Run Query button in the Generic Query Designer toolbar to run the query and make sure no errors exist. Correct any typos that may be detected. When the query is correct, the Define Query Parameters dialog box appears. Enter **2007** for the @Year parameter and click OK.

10. Click OK to exit the Query Designer window. Click OK to exit the Dataset Properties dialog box.

11. The business needs for the report specified the user should select the year from a drop-down list. We need to define a second dataset to populate this drop-down list. In the Report Data window, right-click the Galactic entry and select Add Dataset from the context menu. The Dataset Properties dialog box appears.

12. Enter **Years** for the name of the dataset.

13. Galactic is selected for the data source by default. Enter the following in the Query entry area of the Dataset Properties dialog box:

```
SELECT DISTINCT YEAR(PriceStartDate) AS Year FROM FuelPrice
```

14. Click OK to exit the Dataset Properties dialog box. The Years dataset will appear in the Report Data window along with the FuelPrices dataset.

15. We did not have a chance to test the query, so let's see how to go back and do that. In the Report Data window, right-click the Years dataset and select Query from the context menu. The Query Designer window opens with the Generic Query Designer containing the dataset query.

16. Run the query to make sure it is correct. You see a list of the distinct years from the FuelPrice table.

17. When the query is working properly, click OK to exit the Query Designer window.

Task Notes We created two datasets in the FuelPriceChart report—one to populate the Year drop-down list and the other to provide data for the chart. For the previous report, we created our query without the aid of the Graphical Query Designer. Here we are even more daring. We create our second query right in the Query entry area of the Dataset Properties dialog box. This is the fastest way to create a straightforward query.

Fuel Price Chart, Task 2: Place a Chart Item on the Report and Populate It

1. Expand the Parameters item in the Report Data window. You see an entry for the Year parameter. This report parameter was created to correspond to the @Year parameter in the FuelPrices dataset.

2. Double-click the Year parameter entry. The Report Parameter Properties dialog box appears.

3. Go to the Available Values page of the dialog box.

4. Select the Get values from a query radio button.

5. In the Dataset drop-down list, select Years. Select Year from both the Value field drop-down list and the Label field drop-down list. Your screen should appear similar to the illustration shown here.

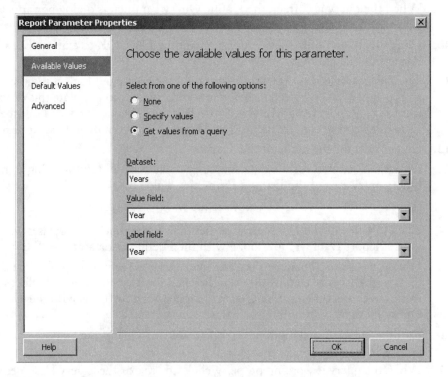

6. Click OK to exit the Report Parameter Properties dialog box.

7. Drag the edges of the design surface so it fills the available space on the screen.

8. Select the chart report item in the Toolbox window and place it on the design surface. The chart should cover almost the entire design surface because it will be the only item on the report. The Select Chart Type dialog box appears.

9. Select the Line with Markers graph, as shown here.

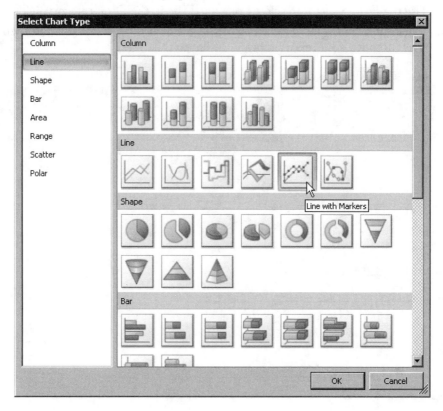

10. Click OK to exit the Select Chart Type dialog box. You will see a representation of the chart on the design surface.

11. Click anywhere on the chart to activate the three drop areas for the chart.

12. Hover over the Drop data fields here area until the Field Selector icon appears. Click the Field Selector and select Galactic | FuelPrices | Price as shown.

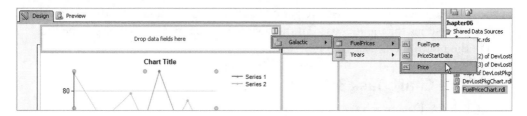

13. Use the Field Selector to select FuelType in the Drop series fields here area.

14. Use the Field Selector to select PriceStartDate in the Drop category fields here area.

15. Click the Preview tab. Select 2007 from the Year drop-down list, and then click View Report. Your report appears similar to this:

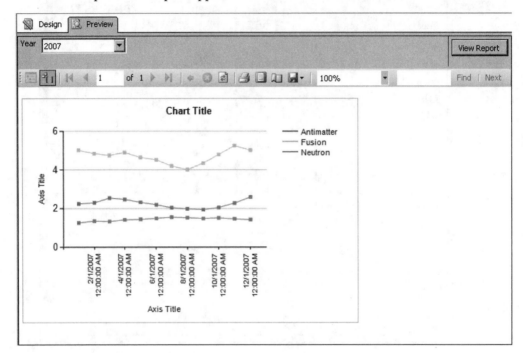

Task Notes   For the previous report, we used multiple series values to create multiple lines on our graph. For this report, we use a different approach. The FuelType field in the Drop series fields here area serves as the grouping value to create a series group. In the tablix report item, we get one group for each distinct value in the grouping field. Similarly, in the chart we get one series, one line on the graph, for each distinct value in the grouping field. In this case, we get one series for the fuel used in the antimatter engines, one series for the fuel used in the fusion engines, and one series for the fuel used in the neutron engines.

Fuel Price Chart, Task 3: Refine the Chart

1. Click the Design tab.

2. Double-click the words "Chart Title" to edit the text of the chart title. Replace the words "Chart Title" with **Fuel Prices**. Press ENTER to leave the text edit mode. The blinking text cursor will disappear and the chart itself will be selected.

3. Right-click the Fuel Prices title and select Chart | Add New Title from the context menu. A second title line is added to the chart.

4. Click on this new title so the edit cursor appears. Replace "New Title" with **Monthly Fuel Survey.**

5. Right-click the Fuel Prices title and select Title Properties from the context menu. The Chart Title Properties dialog box appears.

6. Select the Font page of the Chart Title Properties dialog box.

7. Set the following properties:

Property	Value
Size	12pt
Effects	Underline

8. Click OK to exit the Chart Title Properties dialog box.

9. Right-click the title for the category axis and select Axis Title Properties from the context menu. The Axis Title Properties dialog box appears.

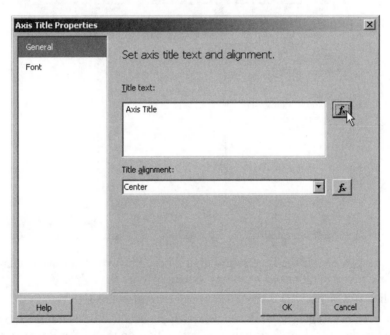

10. Click the *fx* button next to the Title text entry area as shown here. The Expression dialog box appears.

11. Replace the words "Axis Title" in the Set expression for: Title entry area with the following:

    =

12. Select Parameters in the Category tree view. The report parameters appear in the Values pane of the dialog box. (Year is the only report parameter defined for this report.)

13. Double-click the Year parameter entry in the lower-right pane of the dialog box. The dialog box should appear as shown.

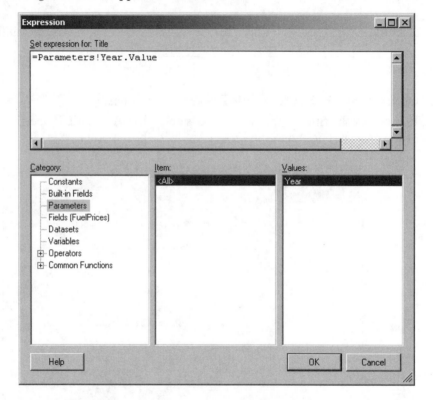

14. Click OK to exit the Expression dialog box. The expression we just created for the Title text is symbolized by the shorthand: [@Year].

15. Click OK to exit the Axis Title Properties dialog box.

16. Select the category axis. When selected, the axis will be surrounded by a dashed rectangle and Chart Axis will be displayed at the top of the Properties window as shown.

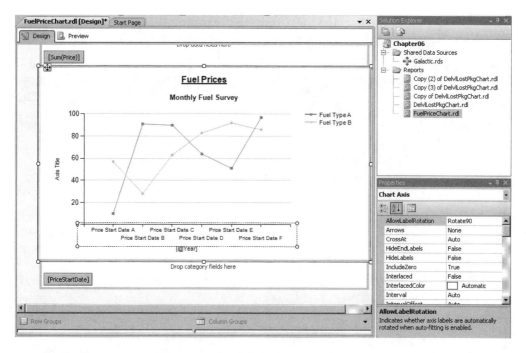

17. In the Properties window, set the following property:

Property	Value
LabelsFormat	MMM

18. Double-click the value axis title. Replace the words "Axis Title" with **Price in Dollars** and press ENTER to leave the text edit mode.
19. Right-click the value axis and select Axis Properties from the context menu. The Value Axis Properties dialog box appears.
20. Set the following properties in the Set axis scale and style area on the Axis Options page:

Property	Value
Minimum	0
Maximum	6
Interval	1

21. Click OK to exit the Value Axis Properties dialog box.

22. Click the Preview tab. Select 2007 from the Year drop-down list, and then click View Report. Your report appears similar to the illustration.

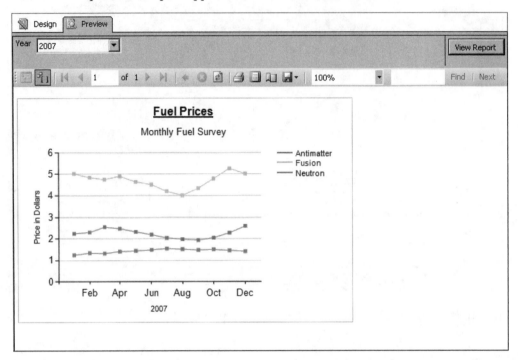

23. Click Save All on the toolbar.

Task Notes   The format code MMM is a date-formatting code. It causes the chart to use only the first three characters of the month name for the category axis labels.

The Fuel Price Chart, Version 2

Features Highlighted

▶ Using the union operator in a SELECT statement

▶ Using a WHERE clause to return records of one type or of all types

Business Need   GDS would now like to be able to select a single fuel type or all fuel types from a drop-down list to view in the report.

Task Overview

1. Create a New Dataset for the Second Drop-down List and Revise the FuelPrices Dataset to Allow for Fuel Type Selection.

Fuel Price Chart, Version 2, Task 1: Create a New Dataset for the Second Drop-down List and Revise the FuelPrices Dataset to Allow for Fuel Type Selection

1. Reopen the Chapter06 project, if it was closed. Double-click the FuelPriceChart report in the Solution Explorer, if it does not open automatically. If the FuelPriceChart report is open and being previewed, click the Design tab to return to the report layout.

2. Right-click the entry for the Galactic data source in the Report Data window. Select Add Dataset from the context menu. The Dataset Properties dialog box appears.

3. Enter **FuelTypes** for Name.

4. Galactic is selected for the Data source by default. Click the Query Designer button. The Generic Query Designer appears in the Query Designer window.

5. Type the following in the SQL pane:

```
SELECT 'All' AS FuelType, '_All' AS SortField
UNION
SELECT Description, Description FROM Propulsion ORDER BY SortField
```

6. Run the query to make sure it is correct. You see a list of the distinct fuel types from the FuelPrice table. There is also a record for "All".

7. Click OK to exit the Query Designer window. Click OK to exit the Dataset Properties dialog box.

8. Right-click the entry for the FuelPrices dataset in the Report Data window. Select Query from the context menu.

9. Change the SELECT statement to the following (the only change is in the second half of the WHERE clause, shown in bold):

```
SELECT Description AS FuelType,
     PriceStartDate,
     Price
FROM FuelPrice
INNER JOIN Propulsion
     ON FuelPrice.PropulsionID = Propulsion.PropulsionID
WHERE (YEAR(PriceStartDate) = @Year)
     AND ((Description = @PropulsionType)
     OR (@PropulsionType = 'All'))
ORDER BY FuelType, PriceStartDate
```

10. Run the query to make sure it is correct. The Define Query Parameters dialog box appears. Enter **2007** for the @Year parameter, **All** for the @PropulsionType parameter, and click OK.

11. Click OK to exit the Query Designer window.

12. Expand the Parameters item in the Report Data window. A report parameter called PropulsionType is created to correspond to the @PropulsionType parameter from the FuelPrices dataset. Double-click the PropulsionType entry in the Report Data window. The Report Parameter Properties dialog box appears.

13. Select the Available Values page.

14. Select the Get values from a query radio button.

15. In the Dataset drop-down list, select FuelTypes. In the Value field drop-down list, select FuelType. In the Label field drop-down list, select FuelType. Click OK to exit the Report Parameter Properties dialog box.

16. Click the Preview tab. Select 2007 from the Year drop-down list, select Antimatter from the Propulsion Type drop-down list, and then click View Report. Your report appears similar to the illustration.

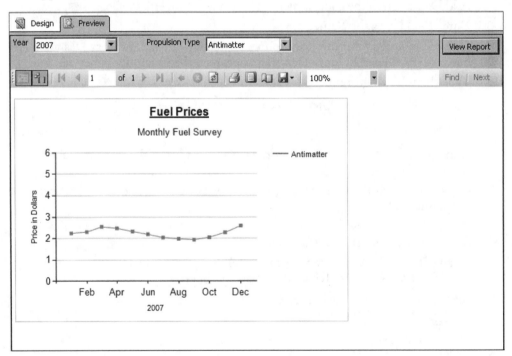

17. Click Save All on the toolbar.

Task Notes   The query that creates the FuelTypes dataset is two SELECT statements combined to produce one result set. The first SELECT statement returns a single row with the constant value "All" in the FuelType column and a constant value of "_All" in the SortField. The underscore is placed in front of the word "All" in SortField to make sure it sorts to the top of the list. The second SELECT statement returns a row for each record in the Propulsion table. The two result sets are unified into a single result set by the UNION operator in between the two SELECT statements.

When result sets are *unioned,* the names of the columns in the result set are taken from the first SELECT statement in the union. That is why the FuelTypes dataset has two columns named FuelType and SortField rather than Description. When SELECT statements are unioned, only the last SELECT statement can have an ORDER BY clause. This ORDER BY clause is used to sort the entire result set after it has been unified into a single result set.

The UNION operator can be used with any two SELECT statements as long as the following is true:

▶ The result set from each SELECT statement has the same number of columns.

▶ The corresponding columns in each result set have the same data type.

In fact, the UNION can be used to combine any number of SELECT statements into a unified result set as long as these two conditions hold true for all the SELECT statements in the UNION.

The Business Type Distribution Chart

Features Highlighted

▶ Creating a report using a pie chart

▶ Using the Data Label property

▶ Changing the chart palette

▶ Using the 3-D effect

Business Need The Galactic Delivery Services marketing department needs to analyze what types of businesses are using GDS for their delivery services. This information should be presented as a pie chart.

Task Overview

1. Create a New Report and a Dataset.
2. Place a Chart Item on the Report and Populate It.

Business Type Distribution Chart, Task I:
Create a New Report and a Dataset

1. Reopen the Chapter06 project, if it was closed. Close the FuelPriceChart report.
2. Add a blank report called BusinessTypeDistribution to the Chapter06 project. (Do not use the Report Wizard.)
3. In the Report Data window, click the New drop-down menu. Select Data Source from the menu that appears. The Data Source Properties dialog box appears.
4. Enter **Galactic** for the name.
5. Select the Use shared data source reference radio button and select Galactic from the drop-down list. Click OK.
6. In the Report Data window, right-click the entry for the Galactic data source and select Add Dataset from the context menu. The Dataset Properties dialog box appears.
7. Enter **CustomerBusinessTypes** for the name.
8. Click the Query Designer button. The Query Designer window opens displaying the Generic Query Designer.
9. Enter the following in the SQL pane (upper portion) of the Generic Query Designer window:

```
SELECT Name AS CustomerName,
     Description AS BusinessType
FROM Customer
INNER JOIN CustomerToBusinessTypeLink
     ON Customer.CustomerNumber
          = CustomerToBusinessTypeLink.CustomerNumber
INNER JOIN BusinessType
     ON CustomerToBusinessTypeLink.BusinessTypeCode
          = BusinessType.BusinessTypeCode
```

10. Run the query to make sure no errors exist. Correct any typos that may be detected.
11. Click OK to exit the Query Designer window. Click OK to exit the Dataset Properties dialog box.

Task Notes   The CustomerBusinessTypes dataset simply contains a list of customer names and their corresponding business type. Remember, some customers are linked to more than one business type. That means some of the customers appear in the list more than once.

This dataset is used to populate a pie chart in the next task. The BusinessType field is used to create the categories for the pie chart. The items in the CustomerName field are counted to determine how many customers are in each category.

Business Type Distribution Chart, Task 2: Place a Chart Item on the Report and Populate It

1. Drag the edges of the design surface larger so it fills the available space on the screen.

2. Select the chart report item in the Toolbox window and place it on the design surface. The chart should cover almost the entire design surface because it will be the only item on the report. The Select Chart Type dialog box appears.

3. Select the pie chart from the Shape area.

4. Click OK to exit the Select Chart Type dialog box. You will see a representation of the pie chart on the design surface.

5. Click anywhere on the chart to activate its three drop areas.

6. In the Drop data fields here area, use the Field Selector to select CustomerName.

7. In the Drop category fields here area, use the Field Selector to select BusinessType.

8. Right-click BusinessType in the Drop category fields here area and select Category Group Properties from the context menu. The Category Group Properties dialog box appears.

9. Click the *fx* button next to the Label drop-down list. The Expression dialog box appears.

10. Enter the following in the Set expression for: Label entry area:

```
=Fields!BusinessType.Value & vbcrlf &
"(" & CStr(Count(Fields!CustomerName.Value)) & ")"
```

Remember you can select the fields using the Fields(CustomerBusinessType) entry in the Category pane along with the Field list in the lower-right pane of the dialog box.

11. Click OK to exit the Expression dialog box.

12. Click OK to exit the Category Group Properties dialog box.

13. Change the Chart Title to **Customer Business Types**.

14. Right-click the pie chart and select 3 D Effects from the context menu. The Chart Area Properties dialog box appears.

15. Check the Enable 3 D check box.

16. Set Rotation to **50**.

17. Set Inclination to **50**.

18. Click OK to exit the Chart Area Properties dialog box.

19. Click the Preview tab. Your report appears similar to the illustration.

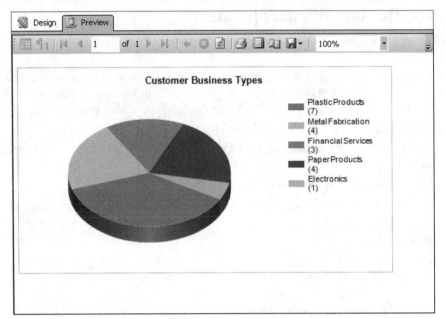

20. Click Save All on the toolbar.

Task Notes By default, the pie chart uses a legend, located to the side of the chart, to provide labels for each wedge in the pie. The Label item in the Category Group Properties dialog box determines what is displayed as the legend for each category group (pie wedge). In the Business Type Distribution chart, we added to the label expression so it not only showed the name of the category, the business type, but also the number of customers in that category. The expression concatenates the business type and the count of the number of customers with a carriage return/linefeed (vbcrlf) in between. The carriage return/linefeed causes the business type and the count to each appear on its own line.

In this chart, we are also using the 3 D effect. The 3 D effect can help to add interest to a chart by taking a flat graphic and lifting it off the page.

Now let's try one more chart before looking at incorporating images in reports.

The Days in Maintenance Chart

Feature Highlighted

▶ Creating a report using a 3-D, stacked column chart

Business Need   The Galactic Delivery Services transport maintenance department is looking to compare the total maintenance downtime for each year. They would also like to know how that maintenance time is distributed among the different transport types. They would like a graph showing the number of days that each type of transport spent "in for repairs." This information should be presented as a 3-D, stacked column chart. The underlying data should be displayed as a label on each column in the chart.

Task Overview

1.   Create a New Report, Create a Dataset, Place a Chart Item on the Report, and Populate It.

Days in Maintenance Chart, Task 1: Create a New Report, Create a Dataset, Place a Chart Item on the Report, and Populate It

1.   Reopen the Chapter06 project, if it was closed. Close the BusinessTypeDistribution report.
2.   Add a blank report called DaysInMaint to the Chapter06 project. (Do not use the Report Wizard.)
3.   In the Report Data window, click the New drop-down menu. Select Data Source from the menu that appears. The Data Source Properties dialog box appears.
4.   Enter **Galactic** for the name.
5.   Select the Use shared data source reference radio button and select Galactic from the drop-down list. Click OK.
6.   In the Report Data window, right-click the entry for the Galactic data source and select Add Dataset from the context menu. The Dataset Properties dialog box appears.
7.   Enter **DaysInMaint** for the name.
8.   Click the Query Designer button. The Query Designer window opens displaying the Generic Query Designer.
9.   Enter the following in the SQL pane (upper portion) of the Generic Query Designer window:

```
SELECT Description AS PropulsionType,
     YEAR(BeginWorkDate) AS Year,
     DATEDIFF(dd, BeginWorkDate, EndWorkDate) AS DaysInMaint
FROM Repair
INNER JOIN Transport
     ON Repair.TransportNumber = Transport.TransportNumber
INNER JOIN TransportType
     ON Transport.TransportTypeID = TransportType.TransportTypeID
ORDER BY PropulsionType, Year
```

10. Run the query to make sure there are no errors. Correct any typos that may be detected.

11. Click OK to exit the Query Designer window. Click OK to exit the Dataset Properties dialog box.

12. Click the design surface. The body of the report will be selected in the Properties window. Set the following properties of the body in the Properties window:

Property	Value
Size: Width	7.5in
Size: Height	4.375in

13. Select the chart report item in the Toolbox window and place it on the report layout. The chart should cover almost the entire report layout because it is the only item on the report. The Select Chart Type dialog box appears.

14. Select the 3-D Stacked Column chart from the Column area.

15. Click OK to exit the Select Chart Type dialog box. You will see a representation of the 3-D stacked column chart on the design surface.

16. Click anywhere on the chart to activate its three drop areas. You may need to scroll the window to work with each of the drop areas.

17. In the Drop data fields here area, use the Field Selector to select DaysInMaint.

18. In the Drop series fields here area, use the Field Selector to select PropulsionType.

19. In the Drop category fields here area, use the Field Selector to select Year.

20. Change the chart title to Days In Maintenance.

21. Right-click the PropulsionType entry in the series area. Select Series Group Properties from the context menu. The Series Group Properties dialog box appears.

22. Click the *fx* button next to the Label drop-down list. The Expression dialog box appears.

23. Enter the following in the Set expression for: Label entry area:

```
=Fields!PropulsionType.Value & " (All Yrs) - "
   & CStr(Sum(Fields!DaysInMaint.Value))
```

24. Click OK to exit the Expression dialog box. Click OK to exit the Series Group Properties dialog box.

25. Right-click the Year entry in the category area. Select Category Group Properties from the context menu. The Category Group Properties dialog box appears.

26. Click the *fx* button next to the Label drop-down list. The Expression dialog box appears.

27. Enter the following in the Set expression for: Label entry area:

```
="Total Maint. Days - " & CStr(Sum(Fields!DaysInMaint.Value))
  & vbcrlf & Fields!Year.Value
```

28. Click OK to exit the Expression dialog box. Click OK to exit the Category Group Properties dialog box.

29. Right-click the chart area. Select Show Data Labels from the context menu. Numbers will appear on the columns.

30. Right-click the chart legend. Select Legend Properties as shown here.

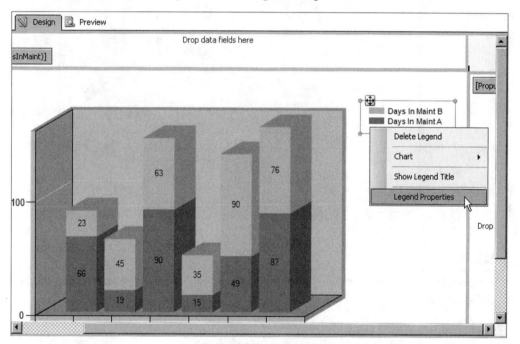

31. In the Legend Properties dialog box, select Tall table from the Layout drop-down box.

32. Select the legend position in the center bottom of the Legend position circle as shown.

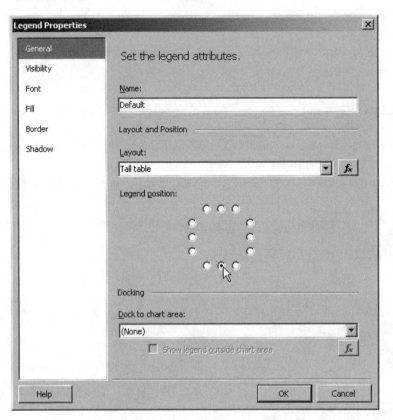

NOTE

You can also change the position of the legend by selecting it and using the positioning handle to drag it to the desired location.

33. Select the Border page of the dialog box.
34. Select Solid from the Line style drop-down box.
35. Select the Shadow page of the dialog box.
36. Click the up arrow of the Shadow offset entry area until the shadow offset is set to 1 pt.
37. Select Silver from the Shadow color drop-down color picker.
38. Click OK to exit the Legend Properties dialog box.
39. Change the category axis title to **Year**.

40. Right-click the value axis title and select Axis Title Properties from the context menu. The Axis Title Properties dialog box appears.

41. Click the *fx* button next to the Title text entry area. The Expression dialog box appears.

42. Enter the following in the Set expression for: Title area:

    ```
    ="Days in" & vbcrlf & "Maintenance Hanger"
    ```

43. Click OK to exit the Expression dialog box. Click OK to exit the Axis Title Properties dialog box.

44. Click the Preview tab. Your report appears similar to this:

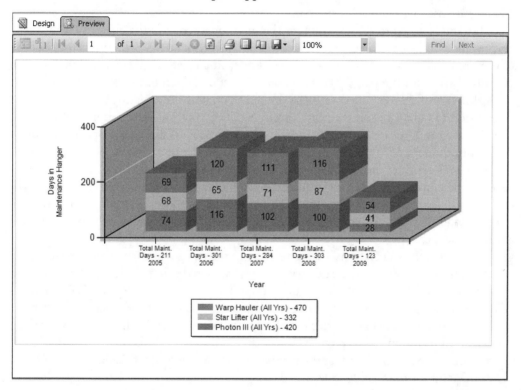

45. Click Save All on the toolbar.

Task Notes   The stacked column chart is a good choice to fulfill the business needs for this report, because it can graphically illustrate two different pieces of information at the same time. Each colored section of the graph shows the number of maintenance days for a given propulsion type. In addition, the combined height of the three sections of the column shows the fluctuations in the total maintenance days from year to year.

Above and beyond the graphical information provided in the chart, several additional pieces of information are provided numerically. This includes the category labels along the X axis, the legend at the bottom of the graph, and the detail data displayed right on the column sections themselves. The values on the columns are the result of the expression being charted, which is SUM(DaysInMaint).

This expression uses the SUM() aggregate function to add up the values from the DaysInMaint field. It may seem this sum should give us the total for the DaysInMaint field for the entire dataset. After all, there is nothing in this expression that references the category or series groups. The reason this does not occur is because of the scope in which this expression is evaluated. The *scope* sets boundaries on which rows from the dataset are used with a given expression.

The data label expression operates at the innermost scope in the chart. This means expressions in the data label are evaluated using only those rows that come from both the current category and the current series. For example, let's look at the column section for Star Lifters for the year 2005. This column section is part of the Star Lifter series. It is also part of the year 2005 category. When the report is evaluating the data label expression to put a label on the Star Lifter/year 2005 column section, it uses only those rows in the result set for the Star Lifters in the year 2005. Using this scope, the report calculates the sum of DaysInMaint for Star Lifters in the year 2005 as 68 days.

Next, let's consider the summary data that appears in the labels along the category axis. These entries are the result of the expression entered for the label in the category groups. This expression also uses the SUM() function to add up the values from the DaysInMaint column. However, it calculates different totals because it is operating in a different scope.

In this case, the calculations are being done in the category scope, which means the expression for the label in the category group is evaluated using all the records from the current category. For example, let's look at the category label for the year 2005 column. This column is part of the year 2005 category. When the report is evaluating the label expression to put a label below this column, it uses all the rows in the result set for the year 2005. The propulsion type of each row does not make a difference, because it is not part of this scope. Using the year 2005 category scope, the report calculates the sum of DaysInMaint for the year 2005 as 211 days.

Finally, we come to the summary data that appears in the legend below the chart. These entries are the result of the expression entered for the label in the series groups. Yet again, this expression uses the SUM() function to add up the values from the DaysInMaint column. And yet again, we get different numbers because it is working in a different scope. Here, the calculations are being done in the series scope. That means the expressions are evaluated using all the records from the current series. For example, let's look at the entry in the legend for the Star Lifter series. When the report is evaluating the series group label expression, it uses all the rows in the result set for Star Lifters.

The year of each row does not make a difference, because it is not part of this scope. Using the Star Lifter series scope, the report calculates the sum of DaysInMaint for the Star Lifters as 332 days.

In several expressions used in this chart, we are concatenating several strings to create the labels we need. This is being done using the Visual Basic string concatenation operator (&). You may notice several of the fields being concatenated are numeric rather than string fields. The reason these concatenations work is the & operator automatically converts numeric values to strings. In this way, we can take "Total Maint. Days -" and concatenate it with 211 to get the first lines of the year 2005 column label. The 211 is converted to "211" and then concatenated with the rest of the string.

The final noteworthy item on this report is the expression used to create the label on the Y axis. To have this label fit nicely along the Y axis, we used our old friend the carriage return/linefeed to split the label onto two lines. Because the text is rotated 90 degrees, the first line of the label is farthest from the value axis and the second line is to the right of the first line.

Gauging the Results

One of the current trends in business intelligence is the digital dashboard. The dashboard on a car tells the driver the current state of the car's operations: current speed, current amount of gas in the tank, etc. The gauges and displays on the dashboard allow the driver to take in this current information at a glance.

In the same manner, the digital dashboard tells a decision maker the current state of the organization's operations. This digital dashboard also uses gauges and other easy-to-understand displays. The digital dashboard makes it easy for the decision maker to get current information at a glance.

Reporting Services provides the gauge data region for building reports that serve as digital dashboards.

The Digital Dashboard

Features Highlighted

► Using the gauge data region

Business Need   Three key indicators of the health of Galactic Delivery Services are the number of deliveries in the past four weeks, the number of lost packages in the past four weeks, and the number of transport repairs in the past four weeks. The GDS executives would like a digital dashboard showing these three key performance indicators using easy-to-read gauges.

Task Overview

1. Create a New Report along with a Dataset and Present the Data on a Gauge.
2. Refine the Appearance of the Gauge.
3. Modify the Dataset and Add a Second Gauge.

Digital Dashboard, Task 1: Create a New Report along with a Dataset and Present the Data on a Gauge

1. Reopen the Chapter06 project, if it was closed. Close the DaysInMaint report.
2. Add a blank report called DigitalDashboard to the Chapter06 project.
3. In the Report Data window, click the New drop-down menu. Select Data Source from the menu that appears. The Data Source Properties dialog box appears.
4. Enter **Galactic** for the name.
5. Select the Use shared data source reference radio button and select Galactic from the drop-down list. Click OK.
6. In the Report Data window, right-click the entry for the Galactic data source and select Add Dataset from the context menu. The Dataset Properties dialog box appears.
7. Enter **PickupsAndLost** for the name.
8. Click the Query Designer button. The Query Designer window opens displaying the Generic Query Designer.
9. Enter the following in the SQL pane (upper portion) of the Generic Query Designer window:

```
SELECT COUNT(Delivery.DeliveryNumber) AS NumOfPickups,
    COUNT(LostPackage.LostPackageNumber) AS NumLost
FROM Delivery
LEFT OUTER JOIN LostPackage
    ON Delivery.DeliveryNumber = LostPackage.DeliveryNumber
WHERE PickupDateTime BETWEEN DATEADD(d, -28, @GaugeDate) AND @GaugeDate
```

10. Click the Run Query button on the Generic Query Designer toolbar to run the query and make sure no errors exist. Correct any typos that may be detected. When the query is correct, the Define Query Parameters dialog box appears. Enter **3/1/2008** for the @GaugeDate parameter and click OK.
11. Click OK to exit the Query Designer window.
12. The Define Query Parameters dialog box appears again. The Report Designer uses the value entered here to determine the fields in this dataset. Again, enter **3/1/2008** for the @GaugeDate parameter and click OK.
13. Click OK to exit the Dataset Properties dialog box.

NOTE

The following uses a more abbreviated format for specifying which properties need to be changed in a given dialog box. A table is provided for each dialog box with the page names and properties along with the desired property values. Simply select the appropriate page of the dialog box and change the items specified.

14. Click the design surface. The body of the report will be selected in the Properties window. Set the following properties of the body in the Properties window:

Property	Value
Size: Width	8.5in
Size: Height	5in

15. Select the gauge report item in the Toolbox window and place it on the report layout. The gauge should cover almost the entire report layout because it is the only item on the report. The Select Gauge Type dialog box appears.

16. Select the Radial-Two Scales gauge as shown here.

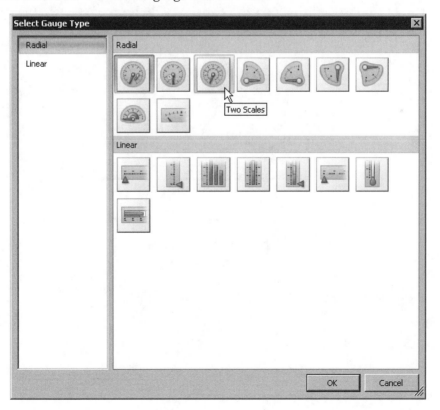

17. Click OK to exit the Select Gauge Type dialog box. You will see a representation of the gauge on the design surface.

18. Click anywhere on the gauge to activate its data fields area. This appears above the gauge and works the same as the data drop areas of the chart.

19. There is an item in the data fields area labeled RadialPointer1. This item allows you to associate a dataset field with the large pointer on the gauge. Hover over the RadialPointer1 item and a Field Selector will appear. Use the Field Selector to select NumOfPickups as shown.

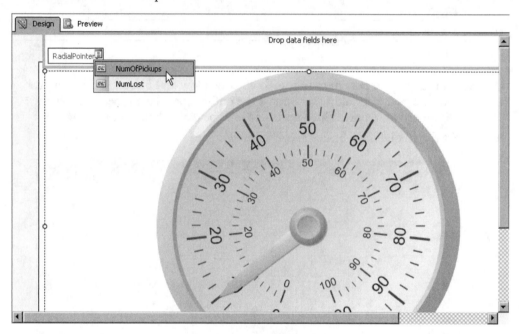

20. Right-click anywhere on the chart and select Add Pointer For | RadialScale2, as shown.

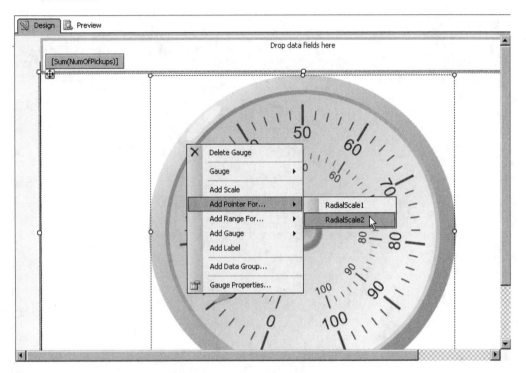

21. A second item, labeled RadialPointer2, appears in the data fields area. Hover over this new item and a Field Selector will appear. Use the Field Selector to select NumLost. This field will be associated with the small pointer on the gauge.

22. Click the Preview tab. Type **3/1/2008** for Gauge Date and click View Report. Your report should appear as shown here.

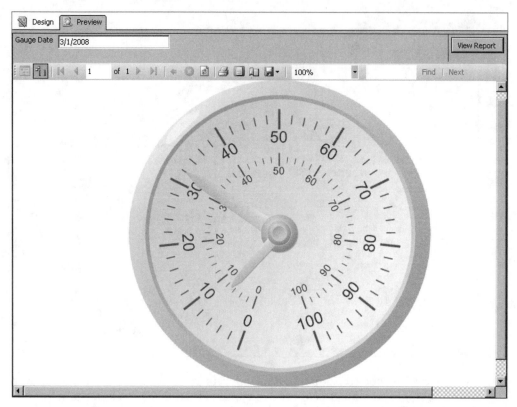

Task Notes Unlike the chart, which presents values grouped into categories, often days, months, or years, the gauge presents a single value. Well, in this task, it actually presents two values, because our gauge has two needles. So, more precisely, the gauge presents one value per needle or other indicator.

Most often, a gauge is going to present the current value of some field. Therefore, the query that creates the dataset for the gauge will use the GETDATE() function to calculate the time period to report on. However, to make this report more interesting with our static database, it has a parameter so you can enter a date and view the gauge as it changes from month to month.

Digital Dashboard, Task 2: Refine the Appearance of the Gauge

1. Click the Design tab.

2. Right-click the large outer scale and select Scale Properties from the context menu. The Radial Scale Properties dialog box appears.

3. Set the following properties of the dialog box:

Property	Value
General page:	
Maximum value	200
Interval	20
Layout page:	
Scale radius	31
Labels page:	
Rotate labels with scale	Unchecked
Placement	Outside
Minor Tick Marks page:	
Interval	5

4. Click OK to exit the Radial Scale Properties dialog box.
5. Right-click the small inner scale and select Scale Properties from the context menu. The Radial Scale Properties dialog box appears.
6. Set the following properties of the dialog box:

Property	Value
General page:	
Maximum value	30
Interval	2
Layout page:	
Scale Bar width	6
Labels page:	
Rotate labels with scale	Unchecked
Label Font page:	
Color	Red
Minor Tick Marks page:	
Interval	1
Fill page:	
Fill style	Gradient
Color	Yellow
Secondary color	Red
Gradient style	Left right

7. Click OK to exit the Radial Scale Properties dialog box.
8. Click the large pointer to select it.
9. Right-click the large pointer and select Pointer Properties from the context menu. The Radial Pointer Properties dialog box appears.
10. Set the following properties of the dialog box:

Property	Value
Pointer Options page:	
Needle style	Tapered with tail
Shadow page:	
Shadow offset	3pt

11. Click OK to exit the Radial Pointer Properties dialog box.
12. Right-click the small pointer and select Pointer Properties from the context menu. The Radial Pointer Properties dialog box appears.
13. Set the following properties of the dialog box:

Property	Value
Pointer Fill page:	
Secondary color	Red
Shadow page:	
Shadow offset	6pt

14. Click OK to exit the Radial Pointer Properties dialog box.
15. Right-click the outer edge of the gauge and select Add Range For | RadialScale1 from the context menu. A range appears on the gauge as shown.

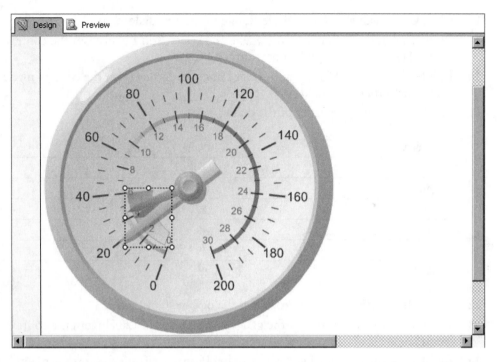

16. Right-click the range and select Range Properties from the context menu. The Radial Scale Range Properties dialog box appears.

17. Set the following properties in the dialog box:

Property	Value
General page:	
Start range at scale value	0
End range at scale value	20
Placement relative to scale	Outside
Fill page:	
Color	Red
Secondary color	White
Border page:	
Line style	None

18. Click OK to exit the Radial Scale Range Properties dialog box.
19. Right-click the outer edge of the gauge and select Add Label from the context menu. The word "Text" will appear on the gauge.
20. Right-click the word "Text" and select Label Properties from the context menu. The Label Properties dialog box appears.
21. Set the following properties of the dialog box:

Property	Value
General page:	
Text	Deliveries
Top	80
Left	40
Width	19
Height	9

22. Click OK to exit the Label Properties dialog box.
23. Right-click the outer edge of the gauge and select Add Label from the context menu.
24. Right-click the new label and select Label Properties from the context menu. The Label Properties dialog box appears.
25. Set the following properties of the dialog box:

Property	Value
General page:	
Text	Lost
Top	71
Left	45
Width	21
Height	6
Font page:	
Color	Red

26. Click OK to exit the Label Properties dialog box.
27. Click the Preview tab.

28. Enter **3/1/2008** for Gauge Date and click View Report. Your report should appear as shown.

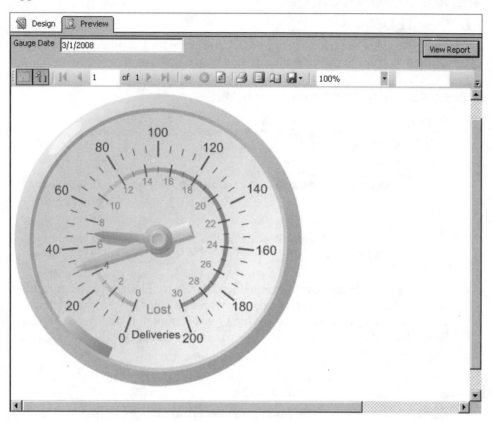

Task Notes   As with the chart report item, the gauge uses several properties dialog boxes, which enable you to change its configuration. There are properties dialog boxes to configure each pointer, each scale, each range, and one for the gauge itself. The chart and the gauge are also similar in that we can add new items to build a rich data presentation for the user. On the chart, we can add titles and legends, and even new chart areas. On the gauge, we can add scales, pointers, ranges, labels, and, as we will see in the next task, even new gauges.

On a gauge, it is often helpful to provide the user with visual clues for interpreting the data. We do this in two ways on our gauge. First, we use the range with the outer scale to indicate when deliveries are getting to be too few and far between. Second, we use the bar with the inner scale. The gradient shading from yellow to red aids the user in determining when the number of lost packages approaches an unacceptable level.

Digital Dashboard, Task 3: Modify the Dataset and Add a Second Gauge

1. Click the Design tab.

2. In the Report Data window, right-click the entry for PickupAndLost and select Query from the context menu. The Query Designer window opens.

3. Change the SELECT statement to the following (the only change is the subquery in the field list, shown in bold):

```
SELECT COUNT(Delivery.DeliveryNumber) AS NumOfPickups,
    COUNT(LostPackage.LostPackageNumber) AS NumLost,
    (SELECT COUNT(*)
     FROM Repair
     WHERE BeginWorkDate
         BETWEEN DATEADD(d, -28, @GaugeDate) AND @GaugeDate) AS
NumRepairs
FROM Delivery
LEFT OUTER JOIN LostPackage
    ON Delivery.DeliveryNumber = LostPackage.DeliveryNumber
WHERE PickupDateTime BETWEEN DATEADD(d, -28, @GaugeDate) AND @
GaugeDate
```

4. Click the Run Query button on the Generic Query Designer toolbar to run the query and make sure no errors exist. Correct any typos that may be detected. When the query is correct, the Define Query Parameters dialog box appears. Enter **3/1/2008** for the @GaugeDate parameter and click OK.

5. Click OK to exit the Query Designer window.

6. The Define Query Parameters dialog box appears again. Enter **3/1/2008** for the @GaugeDate parameter and click OK.

7. Right-click the edge of the gauge and select Add Gauge | Adjacent from the context menu. The Select Gauge Type dialog box appears.

8. Select the Three Color Range gauge from the Linear list as shown here.

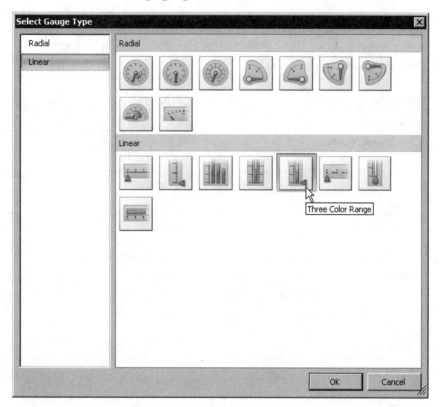

9. Click OK to exit the Select Gauge Type dialog box.
10. Right-click the new gauge and select Gauge Properties from the context menu. The Linear Gauge Properties dialog box appears.
11. Set the following properties of the dialog box:

Property	Value
General page:	
Auto-fit all gauges in panel	unchecked
X position	71
Y position	0
Width	20
Height	100
Aspect ratio	0.3

12. Click OK to exit the Linear Gauge Properties dialog box.

13. Click the red portion of the scale range on the new linear gauge to select it. Now right-click the red portion of the scale range and select Range Properties from the context menu. The Linear Scale Range Properties dialog box appears.

14. Set the following properties in the dialog box:

Property	Value
General page:	
End range at scale value	6
Fill page:	
Fill style	Gradient
Color	Green
Secondary color	Yellow

15. Click OK to exit the Linear Scale Range Properties dialog box.

16. Right-click the yellow portion of the scale range and select Range Properties from the context menu. The Linear Scale Range Properties dialog box appears.

17. Set the following properties in the dialog box:

Property	Value
General page:	
Start range at scale value	6
End range at scale value	14
Fill page:	
Fill style	Gradient
Color	Yellow
Secondary color	Orange

18. Click OK to exit the Linear Scale Range Properties dialog box.

19. Right-click the green portion of the scale range and select Range Properties from the context menu. The Linear Scale Range Properties dialog box appears.

20. Set the following properties in the dialog box:

Property	Value
General page:	
Start range at scale value	14
End range at scale value	20
Fill page:	
Fill style	Gradient
Color	Orange
Secondary color	Red

21. Click OK to exit the Linear Scale Range Properties dialog box.
22. Right-click the scale and select Scale Properties from the context menu. The Linear Scale Properties dialog box appears.
23. Set the following property in the dialog box:

Property	Value
General page:	
Maximum value	20

24. Click OK to exit the Linear Scale Properties dialog box.
25. Right-click the gauge and select Add Label from the context menu. The word "Text" is added to the gauge.
26. Right-click the word "Text" and select Label Properties from the context menu. The Label Properties dialog box appears.
27. Set the following properties in the dialog box:

Property	Value
General page:	
Text	Repairs
Text alignment	Center
Vertical alignment	Middle
Top	27
Left	47
Width	63
Height	45
Angle	270

28. Click OK to exit the Label Properties dialog box.
29. In the Drop data fields here area there is a new entry for LinearPointer1. Use the Field Selector to select the NumRepairs field for the linear gauge as shown.

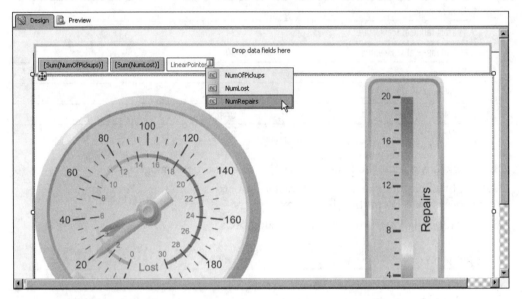

30. Click the Preview tab.
31. Enter **3/1/2008** for Gauge Date and click View Report. Your report should appear as shown.

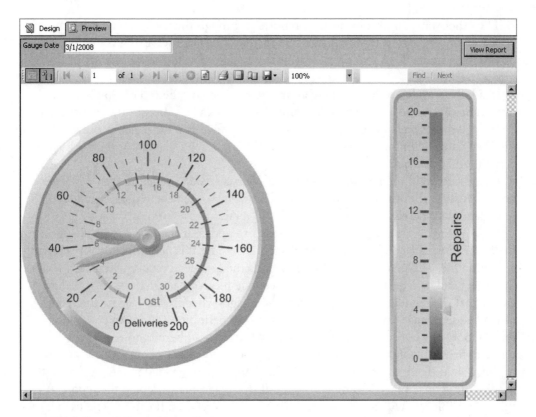

32. Click Save All on the toolbar.

Task Notes   The modification we made to the SELECT statement may look a bit strange. We are adding the count of repairs to the result set. However, repairs are not related to deliveries. The only thing they have in common is the fact that we are using the same date range. Therefore, we add the count of repairs by simply adding a subquery in the field list. This works, in this case, because we are only expecting a single row in the result set.

Image Is Everything

You have seen in the previous sections that charts and gauges allow us to create some pretty flashy output in a short time. Now it is time to turn our attention to two other methods for adding color to a report. One way is through the use of borders and background colors. Almost all report items have properties you can use to specify borders and background colors.

The other way to add color to your reports is through the use of images. Images can be placed on a report using the image report item. They can serve as a background for other report items. They can even serve as the background to the main body of the report itself.

In addition to determining where an image is placed on the report, you have to determine where the image will come from. Images can be stored in the report project, embedded in the report itself, pulled from a binary field in a database, or obtained from the Web using a Uniform Resource Locator (URL). Each image location has its own benefits and drawbacks.

Images stored in the report project are, of course, saved as separate files. They are not stored as part of the report definition. This means when the report is rendered, the renderer must find each of these image files to render the report correctly.

Images stored in the report project are easier to update if they have to be changed in the future. You can simply modify the image file because it is not embedded in a report definition file. These images can also be shared among several reports. However, because the report and its required images exist as separate files, some care has to be taken to ensure that the renderer can always locate the images when it is rendering the report.

Embedded images are stored right in the report definition file. With embedded images, only one file is required for rendering the report. There is no risk of the renderer being unable to find a required image. The downside of embedded images is it is more difficult to update an image. To change an embedded image, you need to modify the source image, re-embed the modified image, and redeploy the report. Also, it is impossible to share an embedded image between reports. It can only be used by the report in which it is embedded.

Images stored in a database file can be shared among reports and are easy to track down when a report is rendered. In addition, when images are stored with the data in the database, it is possible to use a different image in your report for each row in the dataset. This is more difficult to do with project or embedded images.

Images in the database do pose two concerns. First, retrieving images from the database puts an additional load on your database server. Care must be taken to make sure your server can handle this additional load without degradation in response time. Second, managing large binary objects, such as images, in database records is not always a trivial task.

Images obtained through the Internet have a number of advantages. They can be easily shared among tens or even hundreds of reports; all the reports simply reference the same URL. They can be easily updated; just post a new image to the web server and all the reports are referencing this new version. In addition, web servers are designed for serving images, so there should not be an issue with additional load on the web server, unless it is extremely busy already.

The downside to obtaining images from a web server is this: The renderer must take the time to make a Hypertext Transfer Protocol (HTTP) request for each image it needs to put in the report. If the image's URL points to the report server itself or if it points to another server on the same internal network, this may not be a big deal. If, on the other hand, the URL points to a server across the Internet from the report server, the time required for rendering will increase. You also need to ensure that the report server can always connect to the web server hosting the image.

As a rule of thumb, images to be shared among many reports, such as company logos, should be kept either in the report project or accessed through a URL. These shared images should be put in one central location so they can be accessed by the reports when they are needed. Images that have a strong association with data in a particular record in a database table should be stored in the database itself. For example, a picture of a particular employee has a strong association with that employee's record in the Employee table. We are only interested in displaying the picture of a particular employee when the row in the dataset for that employee is being processed. Any images that do not fall into these two categories should be embedded in the report to ease deployment issues.

Conference Nametags

Features Highlighted

▶   Using background colors on report items

▶   Using borders on report items

▶   Placing an image on a report

Business Need   Galactic Delivery Services is preparing for its annual customer conference. The billing contact for each customer has been invited to the conference. As part of the preparations, the GDS art department must create nametags for the conference attendees. Because the names of all the billing contacts are available in the Galactic database, and this database can easily be accessed from Reporting Services, the art department has decided to use Reporting Services to create the nametags.

The conference nametags should include the name of the attendee and also the name of the company they work for. The art department would like the nametags to be bright and colorful. They should include the GDS logo.

NOTE

The image files used in the reports in this chapter are available on the website for this book. If you have not done so already, go to www.mhprofessional.com. Search for the book's web page using the ISBN, which is 0071548084, and then use the "Code" link to download the zip file containing the book's material. Follow the instructions to unzip the image files.

Task Overview

1. Create a New Report, Create a Dataset, and Place the Report Items on the Report.

Conference Nametags, Task 1: Create a New Report, Create a Dataset, and Place the Report Items on the Report

1. Find the GDS.gif file in the materials downloaded for this book. (It is in ImagesFiles.Zip inside of the main zip file.) Copy this to a location on your computer.

2. Reopen the Chapter06 project, if it was closed. Close the DigitalDashboard report.

3. Right-click the Reports entry in the Solution Explorer window and select Add | Existing Item from the context menu. The Add Existing Item - Chapter06 dialog box appears.

4. Select All Files (*.*) from the Objects of type drop-down list.

5. Browse to the copy of the GDS.gif file you just saved. Select the GDS.gif file and click Add. The GDS.gif file is added to the Chapter06 project.

6. Add a blank report called Nametags to the Chapter06 project.

7. In the Report Data window, click the New drop-down menu. Select Data Source from the menu that appears. The Data Source Properties dialog box appears.

8. Enter **Galactic** for the name.

9. Select the Use shared data source reference radio button and select Galactic from the drop-down list. Click OK.

10. In the Report Data window, right-click the entry for the Galactic data source and select Add Dataset from the context menu. The Dataset Properties dialog box appears.

11. Enter **BillingContacts** for the name.

12. Click the Query Designer button. The Query Designer window opens displaying the Generic Query Designer.

13. Enter the following in the SQL pane (upper portion) of the Generic Query Designer window:

```
SELECT BillingContact, Name
FROM Customer
ORDER BY BillingContact
```

14. Run the query to make sure no errors exist. Correct any typos that may be detected.

15. Click OK to exit the Query Designer window. Click OK to exit the Dataset Properties dialog box.

16. Select the list report item in the Toolbox window and drop it onto the design surface. This will create a tablix report item using the list template. Modify the following properties of the tablix in the Properties window:

Property	Value
BackgroundColor	DarkOrange (Either type DarkOrange in place of "No Color" in the Properties window or use the color picker drop-down list in the Properties window and select the More colors link.)
Location: Left	0.125in
Location: Top	0.125in
Size: Width	4.75in
Size: Height	2.125in

We are using the list template to create the tablix for this report because it is going to have a freeform layout, rather than the rows and columns of a table or matrix.

17. In the Report Data window, drag the BillingContact field onto the tablix. Click the BillingContact text box to select it and use the Properties window to modify the following properties:

Property	Value
BackgroundColor	Gold
BorderColor: Default	DarkBlue
BorderStyle: Default	Solid
BorderWidth	4pt
Color	DarkBlue
Font: FontSize	20pt
Font: FontWeight	Bold
Location: Left	0.125in
Location: Top	0.125in
Size: Width	4.5in
Size: Height	0.5in
TextAlign	Center
VerticalAlign	Middle

18. Drag the Name field from the Report Data window onto the tablix. Click the Name text box to select it and using the Properties window, modify the following properties:

Property	Value
BackgroundColor	Gold
BorderColor: Default	DarkBlue
BorderStyle: Default	Solid
BorderWidth	4pt
Color	DarkBlue
Font: FontSize	16pt
Font: FontWeight	Bold
Location: Left	0.125in
Location: Top	0.875in
Size: Width	4.5in
Size: Height	0.375in
TextAlign	Center
VerticalAlign	Middle

19. Drag a text box from the Toolbox onto the tablix. Click the resulting text box to select it and modify the following properties:

Property	Value
Font: FontSize	23pt
Location: Left	1in
Location: Top	1.375in
Size: Width	3.625in
Size: Height	0.625in
TextAlign	Center
VerticalAlign	Middle

20. Click this text box again so the blinking edit cursor appears. Type **GDS Conference 2009**.

21. Drag a line from the Toolbox onto the tablix. Click the resulting line to select it and modify the following properties of the line *in this order*:

Property	Value
Location: Left	0in
Location: Top	2.125in
EndPoint: Horizontal	4.75in
EndPoint: Vertical	2.125in
LineColor	DarkBlue
LineWidth	10pt

22. Drag an image report item from the Toolbox onto the list. The Image Properties dialog box appears.
23. In the Select the image source drop-down list, select External.
24. In the Use this image drop-down list, select GDS.gif. This is the image file you added to the project in Step 3 through Step 5.
25. Click OK to exit the Image Properties dialog box.
26. Click the image to select it and modify the following properties using the Properties window:

Property	Value
Location: Left	0.125in
Location: Top	1.375in
Sizing	AutoSize

27. Check to make sure the tablix is still the correct size. Select the tablix, and then use the Properties window to change the dimensions to match the following, if necessary:

Property	Value
Size: Width	4.75in
Size: Height	2.125in

NOTE

Clicking the orange background will select the rectangle in the tablix cell, not the tablix itself. To select the tablix, click the gray square in the upper-left corner of the tablix.

28. Click in the design surface outside of the tablix. This causes the report body to be selected in the Properties window. Modify the following properties of the report body:

Property	Value
BackgroundColor	DarkBlue
Size: Width	5in
Size: Height	2.25in

29. Click the Preview tab. The nametags are ready to be printed, cut apart, and placed in nametag holders, as shown here.

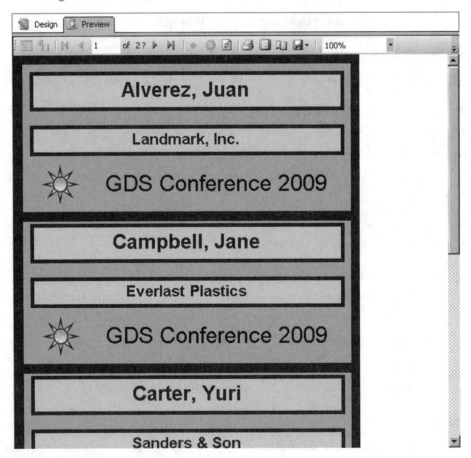

30. Click Save All on the toolbar.

Task Notes   We used several properties of the report items in our Conference Nametags report to add color. The BackgroundColor property controls the color in the background of the report item. This defaults to Transparent, meaning that whatever is behind the item shows through. When the BackgroundColor property is set to a color rather than Transparent, that color fills in and covers up everything behind the item.

The BorderColor property controls the color of the border around the outside of the report item. BorderColor works in cooperation with two other properties: BorderStyle and BorderWidth. The BorderStyle property defaults to None. When BorderStyle is None, the border is invisible. No matter what color you set for BorderColor, it does not show up when the BorderStyle is set to None.

To have a visible border around an item, you must change the BorderSyle property to a solid line (Solid), a dotted line (Dotted), a dashed line (Dashed), a double line (Double), or one of the other settings in the BorderStyle drop-down list. Once you select one of these visible settings for the BorderStyle property, you can set the color of the border using the BorderColor property and the thickness of the border using the BorderWidth property.

The border settings for each side of a report item can be controlled separately or altogether. If you expand any of the three border properties, you can see they have separate entries for Default, Left, Right, Top, and Bottom. The Default property is, as it says, the default value for all four sides of the report item. When the Left, Right, Top, or Bottom property is blank, the setting for that particular side is taken from the Default property. For example, if the BorderStyle: Default property is set to None and BorderStyle: Left, BorderStyle: Right, BorderStyle: Top, and BorderStyle: Bottom are all blank, then there is no border around the report item. If the BorderStyle: Bottom property is set to Double, this overrides the default setting and a double line appears across the bottom of the item. The border on the other three sides of the item (left, right, and top) continues to use the default setting.

The Color property controls the color of the text created by a report item. You find the Color property on a text box, which is expected, because the main purpose of a text box is to create text. You also find the Color property on the tablix data region. The tablix can create a text message when no rows are in the dataset attached to it. The Color property specifies the color of the text in this special "no rows" message when it is displayed. (We discuss the "no rows" message more in Chapter 7.)

The final color property we used in the Conference Nametags report is the LineColor property. This property exists only for line report items. It should come as no surprise that this property controls the color of the line.

We used the TextAlign property to adjust the way text is placed horizontally inside a text box (left, center, or right). In this report, we also used the VerticalAlign property to adjust the way text is placed vertically inside a text box (top, middle, or bottom).

The vertical alignment of text in a text box is not usually an issue unless the border of the text box is visible and you can see where the text is being placed relative to the top and bottom of the text box.

Conference Place Cards

Features Highlighted

- ► Using background images on report items
- ► Using an embedded image
- ► Using the WritingMode property of a text box

Business Need   Galactic Delivery Services is continuing its preparations for the annual customer conference. In addition to the nametags, the GDS art department must create place cards for the conference attendees. The place cards are going to be put on the table in front of each attendee during roundtable discussions. As with the nametags, place cards should be created for all the billing contacts.

The conference place cards should include the name of the attendee and the name of the company they work for. The art department would like the place cards to continue the color scheme set by the nametags, but with a more intricate pattern. They should include the GDS logo.

Task Overview

1. Create a New Report, Create a Dataset, and Place the Report Items on the Report.

Conference Place Cards, Task 1: Create a New Report, Create a Dataset, and Place the Report Items on the Report

1. Find the GDSBackOval.gif, GDSBackRect.gif, and GDSBig.gif files in the materials downloaded for this book. (They are in ImagesFiles.Zip inside of the main zip file.) Copy these files to a location on your computer.
2. Reopen the Chapter06 project, if it was closed. Close the Nametags report.
3. Add a blank report called PlaceCards to the Chapter06 project.
4. In the Report Data window, click the New drop-down menu. Select Data Source from the menu that appears. The Data Source Properties dialog box appears.

5. Enter **Galactic** for the name.

6. Select the Use shared data source reference radio button and select Galactic from the drop-down list. Click OK.

7. In the Report Data window, right-click the entry for the Galactic data source and select Add Dataset from the context menu. The Dataset Properties dialog box appears.

8. Enter **BillingContacts** for the name.

9. Click the Query Designer button. The Query Designer window opens displaying the Generic Query Designer.

10. Enter the following in the SQL pane (upper portion) of the Generic Query Designer window:

```
SELECT BillingContact, Name
FROM Customer
ORDER BY BillingContact
```

11. Run the query to make sure no errors exist. Correct any typos that may be detected.

12. Click OK to exit the Query Designer window. Click OK to exit the Dataset Properties dialog box.

13. In the Report Data window, right-click the Images entry and select Add Image from the context menu. The Open dialog box appears.

14. Select GIF files from the Files of type drop-down list. Navigate to the location where you stored the images in Step 1. Select the GDSBackOval.gif file and click Open. This image is now embedded in the report. It will be encoded as part of the Report Definition Language (RDL) file.

15. In the Report Data window, right-click the Images entry again and select Add Image from the context menu. The Open dialog box appears.

16. Select GIF files from the Files of type drop-down list. Navigate to the location where you stored the images in Step 1. Select the GDSBackRect.gif image file and click Open. This image is also embedded in the report.

17. In the Report Data window, right-click the Images entry again and select Add Image from the context menu. The Open dialog box appears.

18. Select GIF files from the Files of type drop-down list. Navigate to the location where you stored the images in Step 1. Select the GDSBig.gif image file and click Open. This image is also embedded in the report.

19. Click the design surface. This causes the report body to be selected in the Properties window. Modify the following properties of the report body:

Property	Value
BackgroundColor	DarkOrange
BackgroundImage: Source	Embedded
BackgroundImage: Value	GDSBackRect (The drop-down list shows all the images embedded in the report.)
Size: Width	8.875in
Size: Height	3.2in

20. Drag a list from the Toolbox onto the report layout. Modify the following properties of the resulting tablix:

Property	Value
Location: Left	0in
Location: Top	0in
Size: Width	8.75in
Size: Height	3.2in

21. In the Report Data window, drag the BillingContact field onto the tablix. Click the BillingContact text box to select it and use the Properties window to modify the following properties:

Property	Value
BackgroundImage: Source	Embedded
BackgroundImage: Value	GDSBackOval
Font: FontSize	30pt
Font: FontWeight	Bold
Location: Left	2.5in
Location: Top	1.75in
Size: Width	6.125in
Size: Height	0.625in
TextAlign	Center
VerticalAlign	Middle

22. Drag the Name field from the Report Data window onto the tablix. Click the Name text box to select it and, using the Properties window, modify the following properties:

Property	Value
BackgroundImage: Source	Embedded
BackgroundImage: Value	GDSBackOval
Color	DarkBlue
Font: FontSize	30pt
Font: FontWeight	Bold
Location: Left	2.5in
Location: Top	2.5in
Size: Width	6.125in
Size: Height	0.625in
TextAlign	Center
VerticalAlign	Middle

23. In the Report Data window, select the entry for the GDSBig image. Drag this item onto the tablix near the top. The Image Properties dialog box appears.
24. Click OK to exit the Image Properties dialog box.
25. Click the image to select it and modify the following properties of the image in the Properties window:

Property	Value
BorderStyle: Default	Double
BorderWidth	3pt
Location: Left	0.3in
Location: Top	1.715in
Size: Width	1.625in
Size: Height	1.375in
Sizing	Fit

26. Make sure the tablix is selected, and then drag a text box from the Toolbox onto the tablix.
27. Double-click the text box so the blinking edit cursor appears. Type **GDS Conference 2009** and then press ESC.

28. The text box should be selected. Modify the following properties of this text box:

Property	Value
Font: FontSize	9pt
Font: FontWeight	Bold
Location: Left	0.05in
Location: Top	1.715in
Size: Width	0.25in
Size: Height	1.375in
TextAlign	Center
WritingMode	Vertical

29. Make sure the tablix is selected, and then drag a second text box from the Toolbox onto the tablix.

30. Double-click this text box so the blinking edit cursor appears. Type **GDS Conference 2009** and then press ESC.

31. The text box should be selected. Modify the following properties of this text box:

Property	Value
Font: FontSize	9pt
Font: FontWeight	Bold
Location: Left	1.925in
Location: Top	1.715in
Size: Width	0.25in
Size: Height	1.375in
TextAlign	Center
VerticalAlign	Bottom
WritingMode	Vertical

32. Click the Preview tab. The place cards are ready to be printed, cut apart, folded, and placed on the tables, as shown here.

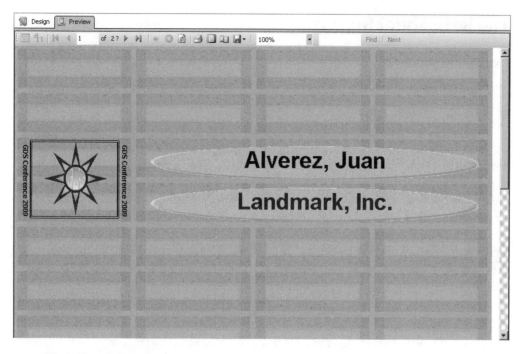

33. Click Save All on the toolbar.

Task Notes   In this report, we used embedded images instead of external images, as we did in the previous report. Remember, the method of storing the image has nothing to do with the way the image is used in the report. External images can be used as background images. Embedded images can be used in image report items.

The Images entry in the Report Data window enables you to manage the images embedded in the report. Remember, an embedded image remains in the report even if no report item is referencing it. The only way to remove an embedded image from a report is to delete it from the Report Data window. Always remove embedded images from the report if they are not being used. This way, the report definition does not become any larger than it needs to be.

In this report, we also used the WritingMode property to rotate the contents of two text boxes by 90 degrees. The normal writing mode for English text in a text box is horizontal. We changed this default writing mode and told these two text boxes to output our text vertically. The WritingMode property was implemented to allow Reporting Services to work with languages written from top to bottom and right to left, a vertical writing format rather than the horizontal format we are used to with English. However, that does not prevent us from using the WritingMode property to produce a fancy effect with our English text.

The Rate Sheet Report

Features Highlighted

▶ Using database images

▶ Using rectangle report items within table cells

Business Need The Galactic Delivery Services marketing department needs to produce a new rate sheet. The rate sheet needs to include a description of each type of delivery service provided by GDS. Each type has its own image to help customers remember the three types of service. The rate sheet also includes the name of each service type with a longer description below it and the cost of each service type off to the right side of the page.

Because all the information on the three types of service is available in the database, the marketing department wants to produce the rate sheet from a report, rather than creating or updating a document each time the rates change.

Task Overview

1. Create a New Report, Create a Dataset, and Place the Report Items on the Report.
2. Refine the Report Layout.

Rate Sheet Report, Task 1: Create a New Report, Create a Dataset, and Place the Report Items on the Report

1. Reopen the Chapter06 project, if it was closed. Close the PlaceCards report.
2. Add a blank report called RateSheet to the Chapter06 project.
3. In the Report Data window, click the New drop-down menu. Select Data Source from the menu that appears. The Data Source Properties dialog box appears.
4. Enter **Galactic** for the name.
5. Select the Use shared data source reference radio button and select Galactic from the drop-down list. Click OK.
6. In the Report Data window, right-click the entry for the Galactic data source and select Add Dataset from the context menu. The Dataset Properties dialog box appears.
7. Enter **ServiceTypes** for the name.
8. Click the Query Designer button. The Query Designer window opens displaying the Generic Query Designer.

9. Enter the following in the SQL pane (upper portion) of the Generic Query Designer window:

```
SELECT Description, LongDescription, Cost, PriceSheetImage
FROM ServiceType
ORDER BY Cost
```

10. Run the query to make sure no errors exist. Correct any typos that may be detected.

11. Click OK to exit the Query Designer window. Click OK to exit the Dataset Properties dialog box.

12. Make the design surface larger, and then drag an image report item from the Toolbox onto the report layout. The Image Properties dialog box appears.

13. In the Select the image source drop-down list, select External.

14. In the Use this image drop-down list, select GDS.gif.

15. Click OK to exit the Image Properties dialog box.

16. Modify the following properties of the image:

Property	Value
Location: Left	0in
Location: Top	0in
Sizing	AutoSize

17. Drag a text box from the Toolbox onto the report layout. Modify the following properties of this text box:

Property	Value
Color	DarkBlue
Font: FontSize	30pt
Font: FontWeight	Bold
Location: Left	0.875in
Location: Top	0in
Size: Width	6in
Size: Height	0.625in
VerticalAlign	Middle

18. Click this text box again so the blinking edit cursor appears. Type **Galactic Delivery Services**.

19. Drag a text box from the Toolbox onto the report layout. Modify the following properties of this text box:

Property	Value
Color	DarkOrange
Font: FontSize	25pt
Font: FontWeight	Bold
Location: Left	0.875in
Location: Top	0.625in
Size: Width	6in
Size: Height	0.5in
VerticalAlign	Middle

20. Click this text box again so the blinking edit cursor appears. Type **Type of Service**.

21. Drag a text box from the Toolbox onto the report layout. Modify the following properties of this text box:

Property	Value
Color	Gold
Font: FontSize	20pt
Font: FontWeight	Bold
Format	MMMM d, yyyy
Location: Left	0.875in
Location: Top	1.125in
Size: Width	6in
Size: Height	0.5in
TextAlign	Left
VerticalAlign	Middle

22. Right-click the last text box added to the report and select Expression from the context menu. The Expression dialog box appears.
23. Click Built-in Fields in the Category pane.
24. Double-click ExecutionTime in the Item pane.
25. Click OK to exit the Expression dialog box.
26. Drag a table from the Toolbox onto the report layout to create a tablix.

27. Click the tablix to activate the gray sizing rectangles.
28. Right-click in the gray rectangle to the left of the header row. Select Delete Rows from the context menu. This removes the header row.
29. Click the gray square in the upper-left corner of the tablix. This selects the tablix. Modify the following properties of the tablix:

Property	Value
DataSetName	ServiceTypes
Location: Left	0.875in
Location: Top	1.75in
Size: Width	6.25in
Size: Height	2.125in

30. Drag an image report item from the Toolbox onto the leftmost table cell. The Image Properties dialog box appears.
31. In the Select the image source drop-down list, select Database.
32. In the Use this field drop-down list, select [PriceSheetImage].
33. In the Use this MIME type drop-down list, select image/gif.
34. Click OK to exit the Image Properties dialog box.
35. Click the center table cell, and then select the Description field from the Field Selector. Modify the following properties of the text box in this cell:

Property	Values
BorderStyle: Default	None
Color	DarkBlue
Font: FontSize	14pt
Font: FontWeight	Bold
Size: Width	2.45in

36. Click the rightmost table cell, and then select the Cost field from the Field Selector. Modify the following properties of the text box in this cell:

Property	Values
BorderStyle	None
Font: FontSize	14pt
Format	$###,##0.00
VerticalAlign	Middle

37. Click the Preview tab. Your report appears similar to the illustration.

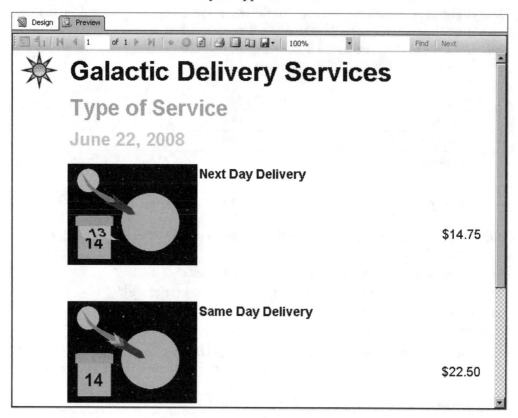

Task Notes   In the Rate Sheet Report, we used image data stored in a database table. As we discussed earlier in the chapter, this allows the report to have a different image for each row in the table report object. The Next Day Delivery row, the Same Day Delivery row, and the Previous Day Delivery row each have their own unique image on the report.

We have one requirement left to fulfill. The business needs specified that the long description of the service type should come below the name of that service type. Let's reformat our report to include the long description in the report.

Rate Sheet Report, Task 2: Refine the Report Layout

1. Click the Design tab.
2. Click the center table cell. This selects the text box in the cell.
3. Press DELETE to remove the text box.
4. Drag a rectangle from the Toolbox onto the center table cell. A rectangle report item is now in the center table cell.
5. Drag the Description field from the Report Data window onto the rectangle you just created.
6. Click the resulting text box to select it and modify the following properties:

Property	Value
Color	DarkBlue
Font: FontSize	14pt
Font: FontWeight	Bold
Location: Left	0.125in
Location: Top	0.125in
Size: Width	2.3in
Size: Height	0.375in

7. Drag the LongDescription field from the Report Data window onto the same rectangle that contains the text box for the Description field. Click the resulting text box to select it and modify the following properties:

Property	Value
Location: Left	0.125in
Location: Top	0.625in
Size: Width	2.3in
Size: Height	0.875in

8. Click the Preview tab. Your report appears similar to the illustration.

9. Click Save All on the toolbar.

Task Notes   In reviewing this task, you can see the rectangle allowed us to do some creative formatting within a table cell. The business needs specified the long description of the service type should appear below the name of the service type. We could accomplish this by putting a rectangle in the center table cell, and then putting two text boxes inside the rectangle.

This is similar to what happens when we use the list template to create a tablix. The tablix has a single cell, which is filled with a rectangle. This rectangle then enables the freeform layout we expect from a list.

The Rate Sheet report is ready to go.

Building Higher

We have now covered all the basic aspects of creating reports in Reporting Services. In the next two chapters, we continue to look at report creation, but we move to the intermediate and advanced levels. Building on what you have learned so far, we create more complex reports with more interactivity.

With each new feature you encounter, you gain new tools for turning data into business intelligence.

Chapter 7

Kicking It Up a Notch: Intermediate Reporting

In This Chapter

▶ **Never Having to Say "I'm Sorry"**

▶ **Handling Errors in Reports**

▶ **Data Caching During Preview**

▶ **Under the Hood**

▶ **Practicing Safe Source**

▶ **Advance, Never Retreat**

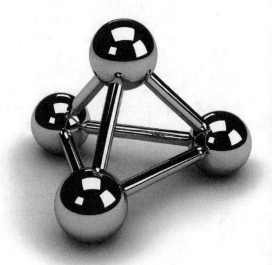

Basic training is at an end. Boot camp is over. You now know the basics of building reports in Reporting Services. You should be able to create reports, both with the Report Wizard and from scratch. When needed, you can spice up your reports with color, images, charts, and gauges.

In the last chapter, you learned how to add punch to your reports with color and graphics. In this chapter, you learn how to add value to your reports through summarizing and totaling, and added interactivity. All this enhances the users' experience and allows them to more readily turn information into business intelligence.

We begin the chapter, however, by looking for a way to enhance your experience as a report developer. In the first section, we create a report template that can be used to standardize the look of your reports. The report template can also take care of some of the basic formatting tasks so they do not need to be repeated for each report.

Never Having to Say "I'm Sorry"

Users can be particular about the way their reports are laid out. In many cases, you will be creating new reports to replace existing ones. It may be that the user was getting a report from a legacy system, from an Access report or a spreadsheet, or from a ledger book. Whatever the case, the user is used to seeing the data presented in a certain way, with everything arranged just so.

Now you come along with Microsoft SQL Server 2008 Reporting Services, telling the user that the new reporting system is infinitely better than the old way—more efficient, more timely, and with more delivery options. That is all well and good with the user, but, invariably, the question will arise, "Can you make the report look the same as what I have now?" No matter how antiquated or inefficient the current reporting system might be, it is familiar, perhaps even comforting, to your users. Change is difficult. The irony of the human race is this: On a large scale, we like change, but on an individual level, we mainly want things to stay the same.

Even if Reporting Services is well established and you are not converting reports from an existing system, users still have preconceived notions. They have a vision for the way a new report should be laid out. These visions need to be respected. After all, the report developer is not the one who has to look at the report every day, week, or month—the user is! The user is the one who probably knows how to best turn the data into something useful.

What the users don't want to hear is, "I'm sorry, but we can't do it that way in Reporting Services." You will be miles ahead if you spend your time fulfilling your users' vision, rather than trying to convince them that Reporting Services is a great tool, despite the fact that it cannot do what they want it to. The techniques in this section, and also in parts of Chapter 8, can help you to make Reporting Services reports do exactly what your users want them to. After all, if your users ain't happy, ain't nobody happy!

Successful report development means never having to say, "I'm sorry."

The Report Template

Features Highlighted

▶ Creating a reusable template for reports

▶ Using values from the Built-in Fields collection

Business Need   Galactic Delivery Services (GDS) is looking to increase the efficiency of its report developers. GDS would like a template that can be used for each new report created. The report template is to include the GDS logo and the company name in a header across the top of each page. The template is also to include a footer across the bottom of each page showing the date and time the report was printed, who printed the report, the current page number, and the total number of pages in the report.

Task Overview

1. Create the Template Project and the Template Report with a Page Header.
2. Create the Page Footer on the Template Report.
3. Copy the Template to the Report Project Directory.

Report Template, Task 1: Create the Template Project and the Template Report with a Page Header

1. Create a new Reporting Services project called Template in the MSSQLRS folder. (If you need help with this task, see Chapter 5.)
2. Add a blank report called GDSReport to the Template project.
3. From the main menu, select Report | Add Page Header. A space for the page header layout appears at the top part of the design surface.
4. From the Toolbox, place an image item in the layout area for the page header. The Image Properties dialog box appears.
5. Click the Import button. The Open dialog box appears.
6. Select GIF files from the Files of type drop-down list.
7. Navigate to the GDS.gif image file and select it. (This is the same image file you used in Chapter 6.) Click Open.
8. Click OK to exit the Image Properties dialog box. The image is embedded in the report and used by the image report item you placed in the page header.

NOTE

From this point on, the book will not give specific instructions for setting the values of object properties. You can set the properties in the Properties window or in the properties dialog box specific to that object, whatever you are most comfortable with.

9. Modify the following properties of the image:

Property	Value
Location: Left	0in
Location: Top	0in
Size: Width	0.75in
Size: Height	0.625in
Sizing	Fit

10. Place a text box in the layout area for the page header. Modify the following properties of the text box:

Property	Value
Color	DarkBlue
Font: FontSize	30pt
Font: FontWeight	Bold
Location: Left	0.75in
Location: Top	0in
Size: Width	5.75in
Size: Height	0.625in
Value (See the following note.)	Galactic Delivery Services
VerticalAlign	Middle

NOTE

The Value property is not found in the Properties window. It can be set by entering the text directly into the text box, using the Text Box Properties dialog box, or using the Expression dialog box.

11. Click in the page header layout area outside the text box and image. Page Header is selected in the drop-down list at the top of the Properties window.

12. Modify the following property for the page header:

Property	Value
Height	0.75in

Task Notes   Reporting Services reports have a page header layout area that can be used to create a page heading for the report. The page header has properties, so it can be turned off on the first page or the last page of the report. Aside from these options, if the page header is turned on in the Report menu, it appears on each report page.

The page header can be populated with images, text boxes, lines, and rectangles. You cannot, however, place any data regions, tables, matrixes, lists, or charts in a page header. You can place a text box that references a field from a dataset in the page header. As with any other field expression placed outside of a data region, the value will not change from page to page.

In the previous task, you made the logo image in the report header an embedded image. This was done for reasons of convenience for these exercises. In an actual template created for your company, retrieving images from an Internet or intranet site is probably a good idea. As discussed previously, this allows for the image to be used in a multitude of reports while being stored in a single location. This also makes it easy to update the image the next time the marketing department gives it a makeover.

Report Template, Task 2: Create the Page Footer on the Template Report

1. Click anywhere on the design surface.
2. From the main menu, select Report | Add Page Footer. A space for the page footer layout appears below the layout area for the body of the report.
3. In the Report Data window, expand the Built-in Fields entry. Select ReportName and drag it onto the page footer layout area.
4. Modify the following properties of the text box that results:

Property	Value
Font: FontSize	8pt
Location: Left	0in
Location: Top	0.125in
Size: Width	2.25in
Size: Height	0.25in

5. Place a text box in the layout area for the page footer. Modify the following properties of the text box:

Property	Value
Font: FontSize	8pt
Location: Left	2.75in
Location: Top	0.125in
Size: Width	1in
Size: Height	0.25in

6. Right-click this text box and select Expression from the context menu. The Expression dialog box appears.

7. Type the following in the Set expression for: Value area after the equals (=) sign:

`"Page " &`

A space should be typed both before and after the ampersand character (&).

8. Select Built-in Fields in the Category pane.

9. Double-click PageNumber in the Item pane to append it to the expression. The expression to return PageNumber from the Globals collection is added to the Expression area. (Globals and Built-in Fields are two different names for the same group of items.)

10. After the PageNumber expression, type the following:

`& " of " &`

A space should be typed both before and after each ampersand.

11. Double-click TotalPages in the Item pane. The expression to return TotalPages from the Globals collection is added to the Expression area.

12. Click OK to exit the Expression dialog box.

13. In the Report Data window, select ExecutionTime and drag it onto the page footer layout area.

14. Modify the following properties of the text box that results:

Property	Value
Font: FontSize	8pt
Location: Left	4.25in
Location: Top	0.125in
Size: Width	2.25in
Size: Height	0.25in
TextAlign	Right

15. Click in the page footer layout area outside of the three text boxes so Page Footer is selected in the Properties window. Modify the following property of the page footer:

Property	Value
Height	0.375in

Your report layout should appear similar to Figure 7-1.

16. Click the Preview tab. Your report should appear similar to Figure 7-2.

17. For a better look at what the header and footer will look like on a printed report, click the Print Layout button, as shown in Figure 7-3.

18. Finally, let's set the margins for the report. Click the Design tab.

19. In the main menu, select Report | Report Properties. The Report Properties dialog box appears.

20. Modify the following values:

Property	Value
Margins: Left	1in
Margins: Right	1in
Margins: Top	0.5in
Margins: Bottom	0.5in

Figure 7-1   *The report template layout*

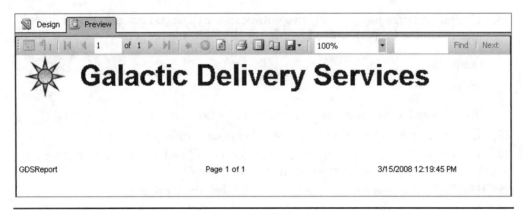

Figure 7-2 *The report template on the Preview tab*

21. Click OK to exit the Report Properties dialog box.
22. Click the Preview tab. The header and footer should appear to be positioned better on the page.
23. Click the Print Layout button to exit the print layout mode.
24. Click Save All on the toolbar.

Task Notes Reporting Services provides a number of global or built-in fields you can use in your reports, including the following:

ExecutionTime	The date and time the report was executed. (This is not the time it takes for the report to run, but rather, the time at which the report was run.)
Language	The language the report is output in.
PageNumber	The current page number within the report.
ReportFolder	The report server folder the report resides in. Report Folder is blank in the development environment.
ReportName	The name of the report.
ReportServerUrl	The Uniform Resource Locator (URL) of the Internet server hosting the report.
TotalPages	The total number of pages in the report.
UserID	The network user name of the person executing the report.

These global fields are commonly used in the page header and page footer areas of the report. It is possible, however, to use them anywhere in the report.

The report has its own properties that can be modified. You are most likely to use the Report Properties dialog box to modify the orientation, page size, and the margins. In Chapter 8, however, we explore some of the other properties available in this dialog box.

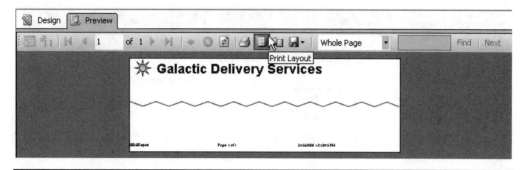

Figure 7-3   *The report template in Print Layout Mode*

Report Template, Task 3: Copy the Template to the Report Project Directory

1. From the main menu, select File | Close Project to close the project and its associated solution.
2. Open Windows Explorer and navigate to the folder you created for the Template project. From the My Documents folder, the path should be the following:

    ```
    Visual Studio 2008\Projects\MSSQLRS\Template
    ```

3. In the Template folder, highlight the file GDSReport.rdl. This is the template report we just created. Make sure you highlight GDSReport.rdl and *not* GDSReport.rdl.data.
4. Press CTRL-C to copy this file.
5. Navigate to the directory where the Report Designer stores its templates. In a default installation, this is

    ```
    C:\Program Files\Microsoft Visual Studio 9.0\Common7\IDE\
                          PrivateAssemblies\ProjectItems\
                          ReportProject
    ```

6. Select the ReportProject folder.
7. Press CTRL-V to paste the copied file in this directory.
8. Close Windows Explorer.

Task Notes   When we add a new item to a report project, the Report Designer looks in the ProjectItems\ReportProjects folder. Any report files (.rdl) it finds in this folder are included in the Templates area of the Add New Item dialog box. This is shown in Figure 7-4.

In the remainder of this chapter, we use our new template to create reports.

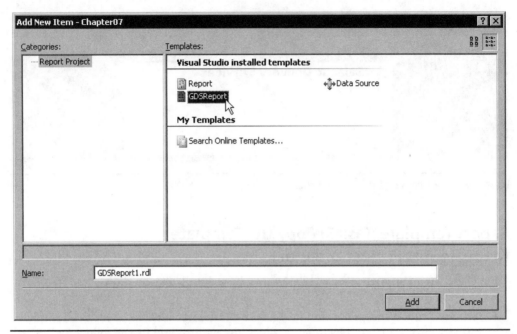

Figure 7-4   *The Add New Item dialog box with a custom template*

Handling Errors in Reports

As you create more complex reports and use more intricate expressions in those reports, you increase the chance of introducing errors. The Report Designer lets you know you have an error when you try to preview a report. You receive a message in the Preview tab saying, "An error occurred during local report processing."

Fortunately, the Report Designer also provides tools for dealing with errors. A list of detailed error messages is displayed in both the Build section of the Output window and in the Error List window. (You may need to select Error List from the View menu to see the Error List Window.) In most cases, these error messages provide a pretty good description of the problem. In many cases, the problem is a syntax error in an expression you constructed in a property of a report item.

If you double-click an error entry in the Error List window, you return to the Design tab (if you are not already there) and the report item that contains the offending expression is selected. You can then use the error message to determine which property contains the error and you can fix the problem. In some cases, if you open the Properties dialog box for the report item, the property containing the error has an exclamation mark surrounded by a red circle placed next to it.

Once you make changes to remedy each error listed in the Error List window, you can click the Preview tab to run the report. If all the errors have been corrected, the Build section of the Output window shows 0 errors and all the entries are cleared out of the Error List window. If you still have errors, continue the debugging process by double-clicking an Error List window entry and try again to correct the error.

The Employee Time Report

Features Highlighted

- ▶ Using a report template
- ▶ Putting totals in headers and footers
- ▶ Using scope to affect aggregate function results
- ▶ Toggling visibility

Business Need   The Galactic Delivery Services personnel department needs a report showing the amount of time entered by its employees on their weekly timesheets. The report should group the time by job, employee, and week, with totals presented for each grouping. The groups should be collapsed initially, and the user should be able to drill down into the desired group. Group totals should be visible even when the group is collapsed.

Task Overview
1. Create the Chapter07 Project, a Shared Data Source, a New Report, and a Dataset.
2. Populate the Report Layout.
3. Add Drilldown Capability.
4. Add Totaling.

Employee Time Report, Task 1: Create the Chapter07 Project, a Shared Data Source, a New Report, and a Dataset
1. Create a new Reporting Services project called Chapter07 in the MSSQLRS folder. (If you need help with this task, see Chapter 5.)
2. Create a shared data source called Galactic for the Galactic database. (Again, if you need help with this task, see Chapter 5.)
3. Right-click Reports in the Solution Explorer. Select Add | New Item from the context menu. The Add New Item dialog box appears.

4. Single-click GDSReport in the Templates area to select it. Change the Name to EmployeeTime and click Add.

5. Create a data source called "Galactic" in this new report. This new data source should reference the Galactic shared data source. (If you need help with this task, see Chapter 5.)

6. Create a dataset called "EmployeeTime" with the following query:

```
SELECT Description AS Job,
    Employee.EmployeeNumber,
    FirstName,
    LastName,
    CONVERT(char(4),DATEPART(yy, WorkDate))+'-'+
        CONVERT(char(2),DATEPART(wk, WorkDate)) AS Week,
    WorkDate,
    HoursWorked
FROM TimeEntry
INNER JOIN Assignment
    ON TimeEntry.AssignmentID = Assignment.AssignmentID
INNER JOIN Employee
    ON Assignment.EmployeeNumber = Employee.EmployeeNumber
INNER JOIN Job
    ON Assignment.JobID = Job.JobID
ORDER BY Job, Employee.EmployeeNumber, Week, WorkDate
```

Task Notes If you need to, refer to the database diagram for the personnel department in Chapter 3 to see how the TimeEntry, Assignment, Employee, and Job tables are related. Our query joins these four tables to determine what work hours were entered for each employee and what job they held.

We are using a combination of the CONVERT() and DATEPART() functions to create a string containing the year and the week number for each time entry. This enables us to group the time into workweeks. Note, the year comes first in this string, so it sorts correctly across years.

When you created the new report, content was already in the page header and page footer. This, of course, is because we used our new GDSReport template to create the report. By using our report template, we have a consistent header and footer on our reports without having to work at it.

Employee Time Report, Task 2: Populate the Report Layout

1. Place a text box onto the body of the report. Modify the following properties of this text box:

Property	Value
Font: FontSize	25pt
Font: FontWeight	Bold

Property	Value
Location: Left	0in
Location: Top	0in
Size: Width	2.875in
Size: Height	0.5in
Value	Employee Time

2. Use the table template from the Toolbox to place a tablix onto the body of the report immediately below the text box you just added.

3. In the Report Data window, drag the WorkDate field into the data row in the center column of the tablix.

4. Drag the HoursWorked field into the data row in the right-hand column of the table.

5. Select the entire header row in the tablix. Modify the following property:

Property	Value
Font: TextDecoration	Underline

6. Right-click anywhere in the lower row of the tablix and hover over the Add Group item in the Tablix area of the context menu. Select the Parent Group item from the Row Group area of the submenu. The Tablix group dialog box appears.

7. Select [Week] from the Group by drop-down list.

8. Check the Add group header check box and the Add group footer check box.

9. Click OK to exit the Tablix group dialog box.

10. Right-click the cell containing the [Week] field and select Tablix: Add Group | Row Group: Parent Group from the context menu. The Tablix group dialog box appears.

11. Select [EmployeeNumber] from the Group by drop-down list.

12. Check the Add group header check box and the Add group footer check box.

13. Click OK to exit the Tablix group dialog box.

14. Right-click the cell containing the [EmployeeNumber] field and select Tablix: Add Group | Row Group: Parent Group from the context menu. The Tablix group dialog box appears.

15. Select [Job] from the Group by drop-down list.

16. Check the Add group header check box and the Add group footer check box.

17. Click OK to exit the Tablix group dialog box. The report layout should appear as shown in Figure 7-5.

Figure 7-5 *Three groups added to the Employee Time report layout*

18. In addition to the header and footer rows for each group, we have a header column for each group. These are the columns to the left of the double dashed line. We show this form of group headings in the TransportList report in Chapter 5. For this report, we are going to try a different format. Click the gray rectangle above the Group3 column and hold down the mouse button. Drag the mouse pointer to the gray rectangle above the Group1 column and release the mouse button. All three group columns to the left of the double dashed lines should be selected.

19. Right-click in the gray rectangle above the Group1 column and select Delete Columns from the context menu. This deletes the grouping columns, but it does not delete the groups or the group header and footer rows.

20. The symbols in the gray boxes to the left of the tablix identify the three groupings and the detail row. The detail row has the gray box with the three horizontal lines. Immediately above the detail row is the header for the innermost group. Immediately below the detail row is the footer for the innermost group. The innermost group is Group1. The innermost group is surrounded by the header and footer for the middle group, which is Group2. The middle group is surrounded by

the header and footer for the outermost group, which is Group3. At the very top of the tablix is a tablix header row for column headings (see Figure 7-6). Hover over the leftmost cell in the top group header row. (This is the second row from the top.) Select the Job field from the Field Selector.

21. Modify the following property of this cell:

Property	Value
Font: FontWeight	Bold

22. Right-click anywhere in the leftmost column in the table. Select Tablix: Insert Column | Right from the context menu.

23. Hover over the cell in the middle group header row in the column you just created. Select the EmployeeNumber field from the Field Selector.

24. Modify the following property of this cell:

Property	Value
Font: FontWeight	Bold

25. Drag the width of the leftmost column in the table until the column is just wide enough for the word "Job" in the table header cell.

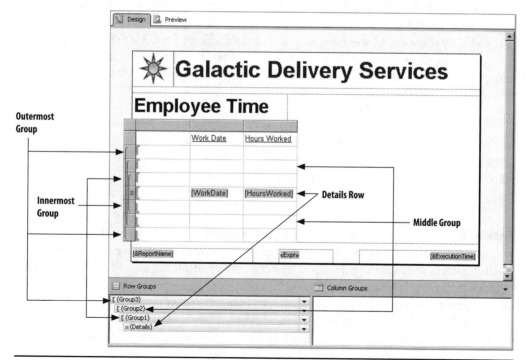

Figure 7-6   *The group header and footer rows in the EmployeeTime report*

26. Select the two leftmost cells in the row for the outermost group header, right-click and select Tablix: Merge Cells from the context menu. (Click and drag or hold down SHIFT while clicking to select multiple cells at the same time.)

27. Right-click anywhere in the second-from-the-left column in the table. Select Tablix: Insert Column | Right from the context menu.

28. Hover over the cell in the column you just created in the innermost group header row. Select the Week field from the Field Selector.

29. Modify the following property of this cell:

Property	Value
Font: FontWeight	Bold

30. Drag the width of the second column from the left until it is just wide enough for the words "Employee Number" in the tablix header cell.

31. Drag the width of the third column from the left until it is about twice as wide as the word "Week" in the tablix header cell.

32. Drag the width of the fourth column from the left until it is about twice as wide as the words "Work Date" in the tablix header cell.

33. Select the cell containing "[Sum(EmployeeNumber)]" (you may not be able to see all of this expression on the screen). In addition, select the two cells to the right of this cell. Right-click this group of cells and select Tablix: Merge Cells from the context menu.

34. Modify the value of the merged cell that results from Step 33. Select Expression from the drop-down list to make editing easier. (You can select the field expressions from the Fields area and use Append to add them to the Expression area. Remember, the Globals, Parameters, and Fields expressions are case-sensitive!) Set the value to the following:

```
=Fields!EmployeeNumber.Value & "-" &
Fields!FirstName.Value & " " & Fields!LastName.
Value
```

35. Your report layout should appear similar to Figure 7-7.

36. Click the Preview tab. Your report should appear similar to Figure 7-8.

Task Notes   We placed a table on our report to contain the employee time information. We created three groups within the table to contain the groups required by the business needs for this report. The detail information is grouped into weeks. The week groups are grouped into employees. The employee groups are grouped into jobs. By merging cells in the grouping rows, we can give the report a stepped look, the same as we had in the TransportList report in Chapter 5. However, this approach, along with the merged cells, allows each group heading to flow across the top of the information below it. This provides more room for the detail information.

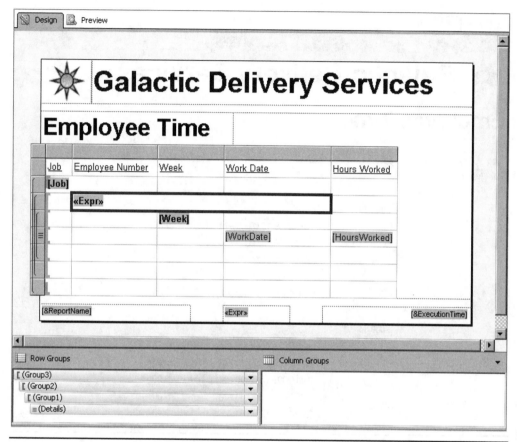

Figure 7-7 *Employee Time Report layout after Task 2*

Employee Time Report, Task 3: Add Drilldown Capability

1. Click the Design tab.
2. Using the drop-down menu for Group2 in the Row Groups pane, select Group Properties, as shown in Figure 7-9. The Group Properties dialog box appears.
3. Select the Visibility page.
4. Select the Hide radio button under the When the report is initially run: prompt.
5. Check the Display can be toggled by this report item check box.
6. Select Job from the drop-down list immediately below this check box.
7. Click OK to exit the Group Properties dialog box.
8. Using the drop-down menu for Group1 in the Row Groups pane, select Group Properties. The Group Properties dialog box appears.

Figure 7-8 *Employee Time Report preview after Task 2*

9. Select the Visibility page.
10. Select the Hide radio button under the When the report is initially run: prompt.
11. Check the Display can be toggled by this report item check box.
12. Select EmployeeNumber from the drop-down list immediately below this check box.
13. Click OK to exit the Group Properties dialog box.
14. Using the drop-down menu for the Details group in the Row Groups pane, select Group Properties. The Group Properties dialog box appears.
15. Select the Visibility page.
16. Select the Hide radio button under the When the report is initially run: prompt.
17. Check the Display can be toggled by this report item check box.
18. Select Week from the drop-down list immediately below this check box.

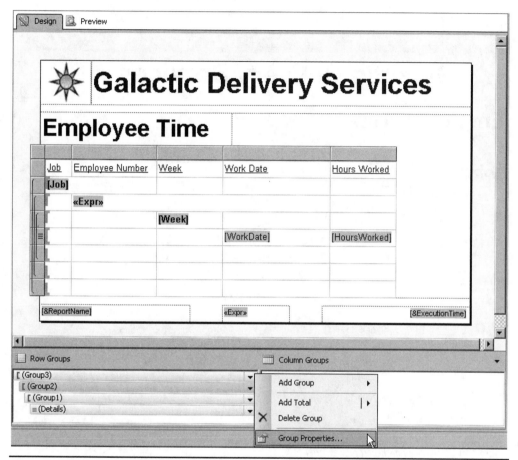

Figure 7-9   *Selecting Group Properties from the drop-down menu in the Row Groups pane*

19. Click OK to exit the Group Properties dialog box.
20. Click the Preview tab. Your report should appear similar to Figure 7-10 after expanding the top few groups.

Task Notes   We now have the drilldown capability working as required for this report. This was done using the visibility and toggling properties of the groupings in the tablix. The visibility of each group is set to be toggled by a report item in the group above it. Therefore, the Employee group, Group2, is set to be toggled by the Job report item and the Week group, Group1, is set to be toggled by the EmployeeNumber report item. The detail row of the table is treated as a group and is called the *details group*. The details group is set to be toggled by the Week report item.

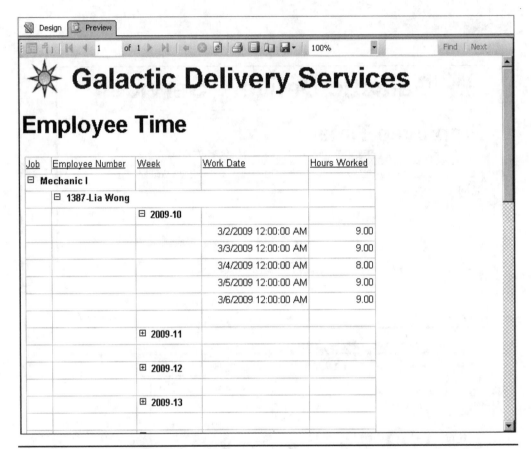

Figure 7-10   *Employee Time Report preview after Task 3*

The Employee group, the Week group, and the details group all have their initial visibility set to Hide. This means when you run the report in the Preview tab, you do not see any of these groups. Only the top group, the Job group (Group3), is visible.

Remember, in data regions, the items are repeated according to the rows in the dataset. Therefore, the report contains a number of Job group rows, one for each distinct job contained in the dataset. Each Job group contains sets of Employee group rows, Week group rows, and the details group rows.

The first Job group contains a Job report item (text box) with a value of Mechanic I. There is a small plus (+) sign in front of Mechanic I because it controls the visibility of the Employee group rows in the Mechanic I Job group. Clicking the plus sign changes the visibility of all the Employee group rows in the Mechanic I Job group from Hide to Show. The Employee group rows in the Mechanic I Job group now show up on the report.

When the Employee group rows are visible in the Mechanic I Job group, the plus sign next to Mechanic I changes to a minus sign. Clicking the minus (−) sign will again change the visibility of all the Employee group rows in the Mechanic I Job group, this time from Show to Hide. The Employee group rows in the Mechanic I Job group now disappear from the report.

Click the plus and minus signs to change the visibility of various groups and detail rows in the report. Make sure you have a good understanding of how visibility and toggling are working in the report. We make it a bit more complicated in Task 4.

Employee Time Report, Task 4: Add Totaling

1. Click the Design tab.
2. Right-click the rightmost cell in the header row for the outermost group (the Job group) and select Textbox: Text Box Properties from the context menu. The Text Box Properties dialog box appears.
3. Type the following for Value:

   `=Sum(Fields!HoursWorked.Value)`

4. Select the Visibility page of the dialog box.
5. Check the Display can be toggled by this report item check box.
6. Select Job from the drop-down list immediately below this check box. (We are leaving the Show radio button selected.)
7. Click OK to exit the Text Box Properties dialog box.
8. Right-click the rightmost cell in the header row for the middle group (the Employee group) and select Textbox: Text Box Properties from the context menu. The Text Box Properties dialog box appears.
9. Type the following for Value:

   `=Sum(Fields!HoursWorked.Value)`

10. Select the Visibility page of the dialog box.
11. Check the Display can be toggled by this report item check box.
12. Select EmployeeNumber from the drop-down list immediately below this check box. (We are leaving the Show radio button selected.)
13. Click OK to exit the Text Box Properties dialog box.
14. Right-click the rightmost cell in the header row for the innermost group (the Week group) and select Textbox: Text Box Properties from the context menu. The Text Box Properties dialog box appears.
15. Type the following for Value:

    `=Sum(Fields!HoursWorked.Value)`

16. Select the Visibility page of the dialog box.

17. Check the Display can be toggled by this report item check box.

18. Select Week from the drop-down list immediately below this check box. (We are leaving the Show radio button selected.)

19. Click OK to exit the Text Box Properties dialog box.

20. Click the gray square for the footer row of the outermost group. Modify the following properties for this footer row using the Properties window:

Property	Value
Hidden	True
ToggleItem	Job

21. Click the gray square for the footer row of the middle group. Modify the following properties for this footer row using the Properties window:

Property	Value
Hidden	True
ToggleItem	EmployeeNumber

22. Click the gray square for the footer row of the innermost group. Modify the following properties for this footer row using the Properties window:

Property	Value
Hidden	True
ToggleItem	Week

23. Select the rightmost cell in the footer row of the innermost group. Modify the following properties for this text box using the Properties window:

Property	Value
BorderColor: Top	Black
BorderStyle: Top	Solid
Font: FontWeight	Bold
Value (Right-click the text box and select Expression from the drop-down list to make it easier to enter this value.)	=Sum(Fields!HoursWorked.Value)

24. Repeat Step 23 for the rightmost cell in the footer row of the middle group.

25. Repeat Step 23 for the rightmost cell in the footer row of the outermost group.

26. Right-click anywhere in the last row of the tablix and select Tablix: Insert Row | Outside Group - Below from the context menu. A row that will serve as a tablix footer row is added.

27. Select the rightmost cell in this new tablix footer row. Modify the following properties for this text box using the Properties window:

Property	Value
BorderColor: Top	Black
BorderStyle: Top	Double
BorderWidth: Top	3pt
Font: FontWeight	Bold
Value (Right-click the text box and select Expression from the drop-down list to make it easier to enter this value.)	=Sum(Fields!HoursWorked.Value)

28. Your report layout should appear similar to Figure 7-11.

29. Click the Preview tab. Your report should appear similar to Figure 7-12 when the top few groups are expanded.

30. Click Save All on the toolbar.

Task Notes   Now we not only have a report with group totals, we have a report that keeps its group totals where they ought to be. When the group is collapsed, the group total is on the same line with the group header. When the group is expanded, the group total moves from the group header to the group footer.

When you think about it, this is how you would expect things to work. When the group is collapsed, we expect it to collapse down to one line. Therefore, the group total should be on the line with the group header. When the group is expanded, we see a column of numbers in the group. We would naturally expect the total for that column of numbers to be below it. Therefore, the group total should move to the group footer.

We achieved this functionality by using our toggle items to control the visibility of three other items at the same time. In the previous section, we discussed the fact that Mechanic I controls the visibility of the Employee Group rows in the Mechanic I Job Group. Now, Mechanic I also controls the visibility of the Hours Worked total in the group header and the Hours Worked total in the group footer. The Hours Worked total in the group header is initially set to Visible. The Hours Worked total in the group footer is initially set to Hidden.

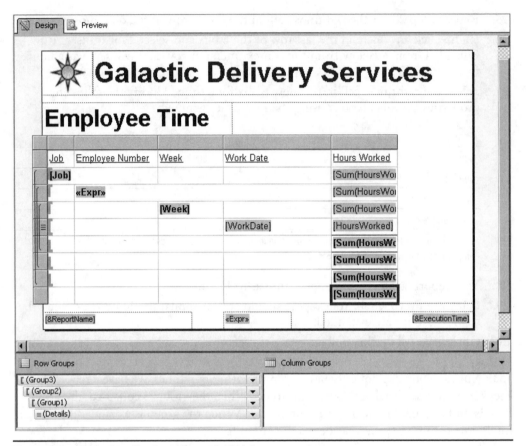

Figure 7-11   *The Employee Time Report layout after Task 4*

When the plus sign next to Mechanic I is clicked, three things occur:

► The Employee Group rows are set to Visible.

► The Hours Worked total in the group header is set to Hidden.

► The Hours Worked total in the group footer is set to Visible.

When the minus sign next to Mechanic I is clicked, the reverse takes place. This same behavior occurs at each level. Again, you can click the plus and minus signs to change the visibility of various groups and detail rows in the report. Make sure you understand how the visibility and toggle items interrelate.

Figure 7-12 *The Employee Time Report preview after Task 4*

The other feature of note used in this task is the Sum( ) aggregate function. If you were paying attention, you noticed we used the following expression in a number of different locations:

```
= Sum(Fields!HoursWorked.Value)
```

If you were paying close attention, you also noticed this expression yields a number of different results. How does this happen? It happens through the magic of scope.

Scope is the data grouping in which the aggregate function is placed. For example, the Sum() function placed in the Job Group header row (the outermost header row) uses the current Job Group as its scope. It sums hours worked only for those records in the current Job Group data grouping. The Sum() function placed in the Employee Group header row (the middle header row) uses the current Employee Group as its scope. It sums the hours worked only for those records in the current Employee Group data grouping. The Sum() function placed in the footer row at the bottom of the tablix is not within any data grouping, so it sums the hours worked in the entire dataset.

As you have seen in this report, it does not make a difference whether the aggregate function is placed in the group header or the group footer—either way, the aggregate function acts on all the values in the current data grouping. At first, this may seem a bit counterintuitive. It is easy to think of the report being processed sequentially, from the top of the page to the bottom. In this scenario, the total for a group would only be available in the group footer after the contents of that group are processed. Fortunately, this is not the way Reporting Services works. The calculation of aggregates is separate from the rendering of the report. Therefore, aggregates can be placed anywhere in the report.

Finally, it is important not to confuse the aggregate functions within Reporting Services with the aggregate functions that exist within the environs of SQL Server. Many of the Reporting Services aggregate functions have the same names as SQL Server aggregate functions. Despite this, Reporting Services aggregate functions and SQL Server aggregate functions work in different locations.

SQL Server aggregate functions work within a SQL Server query. They are executed by SQL Server as the dataset is being created by the database server. SQL Server aggregate functions do not have a concept of scope. They simply act on all the data that satisfies the WHERE clause of the query. As just discussed, Reporting Services aggregate functions are executed after the dataset is created, as the report is executing and are dependent on scope.

Here is a list of the Reporting Services aggregate functions:

Avg()	Calculates the average of the values in a scope.
Count()	Counts the number of values in a scope.
CountDistinct()	Counts the number of unique values in a scope.
CountRows()	Counts the number of rows in a scope.
First()	Returns the first value in the scope.
Last()	Returns the last value in the scope.
Max()	Returns the maximum value in the scope.
Min()	Returns the minimum value in the scope.
StDev()	Calculates the standard deviation of the values in the scope.
StDevP()	Calculates the population standard deviation of the values in the scope.
Sum()	Calculates the sum of the values in the scope.
Var()	Calculates the variance of the values in the scope.
VarP()	Calculates the population variance of the values in the scope.

Each of the aggregate functions in the previous table returns a single result for the entire scope. The following two functions are known as running aggregates. The *running aggregates* return a result for each record in the scope. That result is based on a value in the current row and all of the previous rows in the scope.

The running aggregate functions are:

RowNumber()	Returns the number of the current row, starting at 1 and counting upward.
RunningValue()	Returns the running sum of the values.

Data Caching During Preview

You switched between layout and preview a number of times during the development of the Employee Time report. If you were to look on your SQL Server, however, you would find the rather complex query that provides the data for this report was only executed once. This is because the data returned for the dataset the first time the report was run is stored in a cache file. Any time after that, when the same report is run in the Report Designer with the same query, same parameters, and same data access credentials, the cached data is used.

This data caching helps to make your report development sessions more efficient. Even if you have a report based on a query that takes a fair amount of time to run, you only have to wait for it once. Any time you preview the report after that, the data is pulled from the cache file with no delay. This caching process also substantially decreases the load on your SQL server. This can be important if you are following the frowned-upon practice of developing reports against a production database server.

The drawback to the data-caching process comes when you are making changes to the data at the same time you are developing a report. If you insert new records or update existing records after the first time you preview the report, and then expect to see those changes in your report the next time you preview it, you are going to be confused, disappointed, or perhaps both. The report is rendered from the cached data that does not include the changes.

To remedy this situation, click the Refresh toolbar button, shown in Figure 7-13. This will cause the Report Builder to re-run the queries in the report and create a new cache file. The cache file is in the same folder as the report definition file and has the same name, with a .data on the end. For example, MyReport.rdl has a cache file located in the same folder called MyReport.rdl.data.

Remember, this data-caching process is only used by the Report Builder during report development. A different data-caching scheme operates on the report server after the report has been put into production. We discuss that caching scheme in Chapter 11.

Figure 7-13 *The Refresh toolbar button*

The Employee List Report

Features Highlighted

▶ Implementing user-selectable grouping

▶ Implementing interactive sorting

▶ Using explicit page breaks

▶ Using a floating header

Business Need   The Galactic Delivery Services personnel department wants a flexible report for listing employee information. Rather than having a number of reports for each of their separate grouping and sorting needs, they want a single report where they can choose the grouping and sort order each time the report is run. The report should be able to group on job, hub, or city of residence. The report should be able to sort by employee number, last name, or hire date. Also, each new group should start on a new page. The header information should remain visible even when the user scrolls down the report page.

Task Overview

1. Create a New Report and a Dataset.
2. Create the Report Layout.
3. Add Interactive Sorting and a Floating Header.

Employee List Report, Task 1: Create a New Report and a Dataset

1. Reopen the Chapter07 project, if it was closed. Close the EmployeeTime report, if it is still open.
2. Right-click Reports in the Solution Explorer and select Add | New Item from the context menu. The Add New Item - Chapter07 dialog box appears.

3. Single-click GDSReport in the Templates area to select it. Change the name to EmployeeList and click Add.

4. Create a data source called "Galactic" in this new report. This new data source should reference the Galactic shared data source.

5. Create a dataset called "Employees" with the following query:

```
SELECT Job.Description AS Job,
       Hub.Description AS Hub,
       Employee.EmployeeNumber,
       FirstName,
       LastName,
       Address1,
       City,
       State,
       ZipCode,
       HireDate,
       HighestLevelOfEducation,
       UnionMembership
FROM Employee
INNER JOIN Assignment
       ON Employee.EmployeeNumber = Assignment.EmployeeNumber
INNER JOIN Job
       ON Assignment.JobID = Job.JobID
INNER JOIN Hub
       ON Assignment.HubCode = Hub.HubCode
```

Task Notes Notice no ORDER BY clause is in our SELECT statement. In most cases, this would cause a problem. Users like to have their information show up in something other than a random sort order. In this case it is fine, because we are sorting the data within the report itself according to what the user selects as report parameters.

Employee List Report, Task 2: Create the Report Layout

1. Place a text box onto the body of the report. Modify the following properties of this text box:

Property	Value
Font: FontSize	25pt
Font: FontWeight	Bold
Location: Left	0in
Location: Top	0in
Size: Width	2.875in
Size: Height	0.5in
Value	Employee List

2. Use the table template to place a tablix onto the body of the report immediately below the text box you just added.

3. Hover over the leftmost field in the data row of the tablix and select the EmployeeNumber field from the Field Selector.

NOTE

From this point on, the steps will simply instruct you to select a given field in a given cell. You should use the Field Selector to make these selections.

4. Select the FirstName field in the middle cell in the data row of the tablix.

5. Select the LastName field in the rightmost cell in the data row of the tablix.

6. Drag the Address1 field from the Report Data window onto the right edge of the tablix, as shown in Figure 7-14. This will create a new column in the tablix.

7. Repeat Step 6 for the City, State, ZipCode, HireDate, HighestLevelOfEducation, and UnionMembership fields. As the tablix grows wider, the report body will also grow wider to accommodate it.

Figure 7-14   *Dragging a field to add a new column to a tablix*

8. Right-click the cell in the detail row containing the HireDate and select Textbox: Text Box Properties from the context menu. The Text Box Properties dialog box appears.

9. Modify the following properties:

Property	Value
Number page:	
Category	Date
Type	January 31, 2000
Alignment page:	
Horizontal	Left

10. Click OK to exit the Text Box Properties dialog box.

11. Size each column appropriately. Use the Preview tab to check your work. Continue switching between the Design tab and the Preview tab until you have the table columns sized correctly.

12. Drag the right edge of the report body layout area until it is just touching the right side of the tablix.

13. Click the gray square for the table header row to select the entire row. Modify the following property:

Property	Value
Font: TextDecoration	Underline

14. In the Report Data window, right-click the Parameters entry and select Add Parameter from the context menu. The Report Parameter Properties dialog box appears.

15. Type **GroupOrder** for Name and **Group By** for Prompt.

16. Select the Available Values page.

17. Select the Specify values radio button.

18. Add the following items to the list. (Click Add to create each new entry.)

Label	Value
Job	Job
Hub	Hub
City	City

19. Select the Default Values page.

20. Select the Specify values radio button.
21. Add the following item to the list. (Click Add to create a new entry.)

Value
Job

22. Click OK to exit the Report Parameter Properties dialog box.
23. Right-click in the gray square in the upper-right corner of the tablix and select Tablix Properties from the context menu. The Tablix Properties dialog box appears.
24. In the Column Headers section of the General page, check the Repeat header rows on each page check box. (Make sure you are in the Column Headers section and not the Row Headers section of the General page.)
25. Click OK to exit the Tablix Properties dialog box.
26. Right-click anywhere in the detail row of the tablix and select Tablix: Add Group | Row Group: Parent Group. The Tablix group dialog box appears.
27. Click the *fx* button. The Expression dialog box appears.
28. Type the following in the Set expression for: GroupExpression area:

```
= IIF(Parameters!GroupOrder.Value = "Job", Fields!Job.Value,
      IIF(Parameters!GroupOrder.Value = "Hub", Fields!Hub.Value,
          Fields!City.Value))
```

NOTE

Use the Parameters and Fields entries in the Expression dialog box to help build expressions, such as the previous one. Double-click the desired parameter or field to add it to the expression you are building.

29. Highlight the entire expression you just entered and press CTRL-C to copy this text.
30. Click OK to exit the Expression dialog box.
31. Check the Add group header check box.
32. Click OK to exit the Tablix group dialog box.
33. In the Row Groups pane, use the drop-down menu for Group1 to select Group Properties. The Group Properties dialog box appears.
34. Select the Page Breaks page.
35. Check the Between each instance of a group check box.
36. Select the Sorting page.
37. Click the *fx* button. The Expression dialog box appears. Note the tablix is automatically set to sort by our grouping expression.

38. Click OK to exit the Expression dialog box.

39. Leave the Order set to "A to Z." Click OK to exit the Group Properties dialog box.

40. In the Row Groups pane, use the drop-down menu for Details to select Group Properties. The Group Properties dialog box appears.

41. Select the Sorting page.

42. Click Add to create a new sorting entry.

43. Select [EmployeeNumber] from the Sort by drop-down list.

44. Leave the Order set to "A to Z." Click OK to exit the Group Properties dialog box.

45. Click the cell containing the "<<Expr>>" expression placeholder. Press DELETE to remove the text box in this cell. Repeat this with the cell containing the "Group1" heading. Size the leftmost column so it is as narrow as possible.

46. Right-click the cell containing the [EmployeeNum] placeholder and select Tablix: Insert Column | Left.

47. Right-click the detail row of this new column and select Tablix: Add Group | Column Group: Parent Group. The Tablix group dialog box appears.

48. Enter =**1** for Group by and check the Add group header check box. Click OK to exit the Tablix group dialog box.

49. Click the cell containing the "<<Expr>>" expression placeholder. Press DELETE to remove the text box in this cell. Size the two leftmost columns so they are as narrow as possible.

50. Select the three leftmost cells in the group header row. (This is the third row from the top in the tablix.) Right-click these cells and select Tablix: Merge Cells from the context menu.

51. Right-click these cells again and select Textbox: Expression from the context menu. The Expression dialog box appears.

52. Delete the equals sign from the Set expression for: Value area and press CTRL-V to paste the expression into the Expression area. This should be the same expression you entered in Step 28.

53. Click OK to exit the Expression dialog box.

54. Modify the following property of the merged cells:

Property	Value
Font: Weight	Bold

55. Click the text box containing the Employee Number header (only the "Employee" portion may be visible) and hold down the mouse button. Drag the mouse pointer over to the text box containing the Union Membership header (again, only the "Union" portion may be visible). This will select all of the header text boxes.

56. Press CTRL-X to cut these text boxes.

57. Press UP ARROW to select a text box in the top row of the tablix.

58. Press CTRL-V to paste the header text boxes in the top row of the tablix.

59. Right-click the gray box to the right of the empty row (the row from which we just removed the header text boxes) and select Delete Rows from the context menu. Your report layout should appear similar to Figure 7-15.

60. Click the Preview tab. Your report should appear similar to Figure 7-16. Experiment with changing the grouping. Remember to click View Report each time to refresh the report.

61. Click Save All on the toolbar.

Task Notes   In this report, the report parameter is used to control properties within the report rather than as a parameter to a SQL query. Because of this, we needed to create this report parameter manually, rather than having it created automatically from the dataset query. We also manually constructed a list of valid values and provided a default value. We were then able to use the values selected for this parameter to change the grouping and the group sorting of the tablix in the report.

We are able to change the grouping and group sorting of the tablix because of the IIF() function. This function has three parameters. The first parameter is a Boolean expression (in other words, an expression that results in either a true or false value).

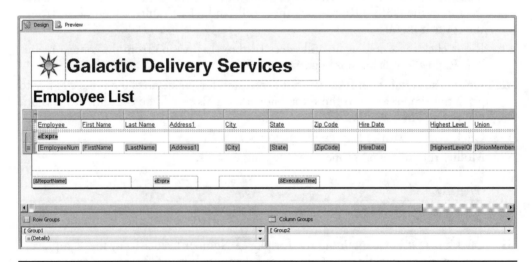

Figure 7-15   *The Employee List report layout after Task 2*

Figure 7-16 *The Employee List report preview after Task 2*

The second parameter is the value returned if the Boolean expression is true. The third parameter is the value returned if the Boolean expression is false.

Let's take a look at our expressions using the IIF() function:

```
= IIF( Parameters!GroupOrder.Value = "Job", Fields!Job.Value,
       IIF(Parameters!GroupOrder.Value = "Hub", Fields!Hub.Value,
            Fields!City.Value))
```

This expression uses two IIF() functions, one nested inside the other. The first parameter of the outer IIF() function is

```
Parameters!GroupOrder.Value = "Job"
```

If Job is selected for the grouping, the value of the second parameter is returned by the function. In this case, the second parameter is

```
Fields!Job.Value
```

Therefore, if Job is selected for the grouping, the value of the Job field is used.

If Job is not selected for the grouping, the value of the third parameter is returned. The value of this third parameter is another complete IIF() function:

```
IIF(Parameters!GroupOrder.Value = "Hub", Fields!Hub.Value,
            Fields!City.Value)
```

In this second IIF() function, if Hub is selected for the grouping, the second parameter of this IIF() function is returned. Here, the second parameter is

```
Fields!Hub.Value
```

Therefore, if Hub is selected for the grouping, the value of the Hub field is used.

Finally, if Hub is not selected for the grouping, the value of the third parameter of this IIF() function is returned. Here, the third parameter is

```
Fields!City.Value
```

Therefore, if Hub is not selected for the grouping, the value of the City field is used.

We used the same expression for both the grouping and the group sorting. The group sorting property sorts the groups themselves so they come out in the proper order. We also set the sorting for the DetailsGroup. This provided a default sort order for the rows within each group. In other words, it provided a sorting at the detail level.

In many cases, a report needs to start each new group on a new page. We used the Between each instance of a group page break option in the Tablix Group Properties dialog box to force the report to start a new page between each grouping. Additional page break options can be set to force a page break before the first grouping or after the last grouping. Page breaks can also be set for other report items. For instance, you can force a page break before the beginning of a tablix or after the end of a tablix. We created what amounts to a dummy column group in the tablix. This dummy group uses a grouping expression of "=1" that will have a value of 1 for every record in the data set. Therefore, all of the records will be in the same group. This dummy group allows us to create a set of column headers that will be repeated on each page and will also remain visible while scrolling down a page (see Step 3 in the next section). In Figure 7-15, notice the double-dashed line separating the top row from the rest of the tablix. The rows above the double-dashed line are recognized as column header rows. The repeat header rows and headers remain visible properties only apply to these special column header rows. The same is true with the equivalent settings for row header columns.

Employee List Report, Task 3: Add Interactive Sorting and a Floating Header

1. Click the Design tab.
2. Bring up the Tablix Properties dialog box.
3. In the Column Headers section of the General page, check the Header should remain visible while scrolling check box. (Make sure you are in the Column Headers section and not the Row Headers section of the General page.)
4. Click OK to exit the Tablix Properties dialog box.

5. Click anywhere on the tablix. Click the gray square for the header row. Modify the following property:

Property	Value
BackgroundColor	White

6. Right-click the Employee Number text box in the tablix header row and select Text Box Properties from the context menu. The Text Box Properties dialog box appears.

7. Select the Interactive Sort page.

8. Check the Enable interactive sort on this text box check box.

9. Make sure the Detail rows radio button is selected.

10. Select [EmployeeNumber] from the Sort by drop-down list.

11. Click OK to exit the Text Box Properties dialog box.

12. Right-click the Last Name text box in the tablix header row and select Text Box Properties from the context menu. The Text Box Properties dialog box appears.

13. Select the Interactive Sort page.

14. Check the Enable interactive sort on this text box check box.

15. Make sure the Detail rows radio button is selected.

16. Click the Expression button (the button with *fx* on it) next to the Sort by drop-down list. The Expression dialog box appears.

17. Type the following in the Set expression for: SortExpression area:

```
=Fields!LastName.Value & " " & Fields!FirstName.Value
```

18. Click OK to exit the Expression dialog box.

19. Click OK to exit the Text Box Properties dialog box.

20. Right-click the Hire Date text box in the tablix header row and select Text Box Properties from the context menu. The Text Box Properties dialog box appears.

21. Select the Interactive Sort page.

22. Check the Enable interactive sort on this text box check box.

23. Make sure the Detail rows radio button is selected.

24. Select [HireDate] from the Sort by drop-down list.

25. Click OK to exit the Text Box Properties dialog box.

26. Click the Preview tab.

27. Click the Interactive Sort button next to the Last Name column, as shown in Figure 7-17.

28. Page through the report and note that, within each group, the rows are now sorted by last name in ascending order.

Figure 7-17 *The Employee List Report with interactive sorting*

29. Click the Interactive Sort button next to the Last Name column again. You return to the first page of the report. Again, page through the report and note that the rows are now sorted by last name in descending order.

30. Click the Interactive Sort button next to the Hire Date column heading. You return to the first page of the report.

31. Page through the report once more. The rows are now sorted by hire date in ascending order.

32. Go to Page 5 of the report.

33. Scroll the page up and down, and notice the table headers always remain visible at the top of the page.

34. Click Save All on the toolbar.

Task Notes The interactive sort feature enables the user viewing the report to choose the sort order they would like to see. This could also be done using a report parameter passed as part of the query that creates the dataset. This scheme requires the query to be re-run every time the sort order is changed. Interactive sorting, on the other hand, redisplays the report in the newly selected sort order without re-running the dataset query. The sorting is all done within the report renderer, using the data already collected from the data source.

The Interactive Sort page of the Text Box Properties dialog box, shown in Figure 7-18, gives us a number of options for the interactive sort. In our report, we chose to have the interactive sort work on the detail rows of the tablix. This option changes the order of

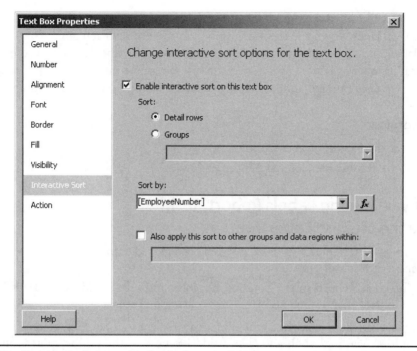

Figure 7-18 *The Interactive Sort page of the Text Box Properties dialog box*

the detail records within each of the groups in the tablix. There is also a radio button that enables the sorting of groups themselves within the tablix. In addition, there is an option to enable the sorting of other groups and data regions based on this interactive sort selection.

The floating header does, indeed, seem to float over the columns of the report as you scroll down the page. For this reason, the background of a floating header row should be set to something other than transparent. If this is not done, the column data shows right through the header, making it rather difficult to read.

The Employee Mailing Labels Report

Features Highlighted

▶ Enable multiple columns

▶ Put information from the database into the report header

Business Need The Galactic Delivery Services personnel department has a new version of the employee manual. The personnel department needs mailing labels to send the new manual out to each employee. The mailing labels are to be printed on a 2½-inches wide and 1-inch high label. The label sheet has three labels across the sheet and ten labels down the sheet, with no margin between each label.

The labels should be sorted by ZIP code and then last name. It would also be helpful if the total number of labels is printed in the top margin of the first page printed. Finally, a sequence number should be printed in the lower-right corner of each label.

Task Overview

1. Create the Mailing Label Content.
2. Add the Report Header and Multiple Columns.

Employee Mailing Labels Report, Task 1: Create the Mailing Label Content

1. Reopen the Chapter07 project, if it has been closed. Close the Employee List Report, if it is still open.
2. Right-click Reports in the Solution Explorer and select Add | New Item from the Context menu. The Add New Item dialog box appears.
3. Single-click Report in the Templates area to select it. Change the name to EmployeeMailingLabels and click Add. (Do not use the GDSReport template.)
4. Create a data source called "Galactic" in this new report. This new data source should reference the Galactic shared data source.
5. Create a dataset called "Employees" with the following query:

```
SELECT FirstName + ' ' + LastName AS Name,
    Address1,
    City + ', ' + State + ' ' + ZipCode AS CSZ
FROM Employee
WHERE TerminationDate IS NULL
ORDER BY ZipCode, LastName, FirstName
```

6. Use the List template to place a tablix onto the body of the report. Modify the following properties of the tablix:

Property	Value
Location: Left	0in
Location: Top	0in
Size: Width	2.5in
Size: Height	1in

7. In the Report Data window, select the Name field and drag it onto the tablix. Select the resulting text box and set the following properties:

Property	Value
Location: Left	0in
Location: Top	0in
Size:Width	2.25in
Size:Height	0.25in

8. Drag the Address1 field onto the tablix and set the following properties of the resulting text box:

Property	Value
Location: Left	0in
Location: Top	0.25in
Size:Width	2.25in
Size:Height	0.25in

9. Drag the CSZ field onto the tablix and set the following properties of the resulting text box:

Property	Value
Location: Left	0in
Location: Top	0.5in
Size:Width	2.25in
Size:Height	0.25in

10. Drag a text box onto the list and set the following properties of the text box:

Property	Value
Font: FontSize	8 pt
Location: Left	1.125in
Location: Top	0.75in
Size:Width	1.375in
Size:Height	0.25in
TextAlign	Right
VerticalAlign	Bottom

11. Right-click the text box you just added and select Expression from the context menu. The Expression dialog box appears.

12. Expand the Common Functions item in the Category pane and select Miscellaneous. The Item list in the center contains the miscellaneous functions available in Reporting Services.

13. Double-click RowNumber in the Item list to add the RowNumber aggregate to the expression.

14. The parameter information for the RowNumber aggregate function appears, as shown in Figure 7-19.

15. To complete the expression, type **"Tablix1")** after the (.

16. Click OK to exit the Expression dialog box.

17. Adjust the size of the tablix, if it grew during the creation of the layout.

Property	Value
Size:Width	2.5in
Size:Height	1in

18. Adjust the report body so it is exactly the same size as the tablix report item.

19. Click the Preview tab. Your report should appear similar to Figure 7-20.

20. Click Save All on the toolbar.

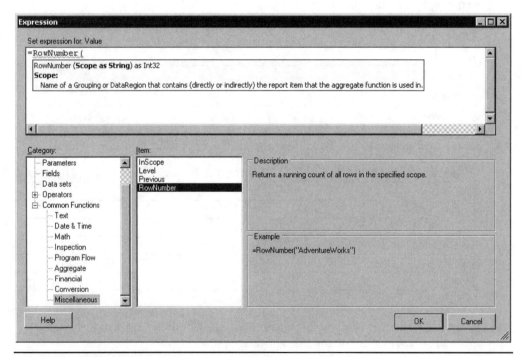

Figure 7-19   *The Expression dialog box with parameter information*

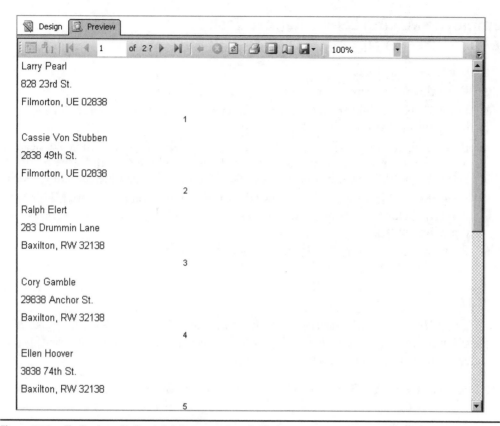

Figure 7-20   *The Employee Mailing Labels Report preview after Task 1*

Task Notes   The Expression dialog box provides assistance in building expressions. Earlier, we talked about the syntax checking done as you type an expression and the jagged red line that indicates an error. The Expression dialog box enables you to add global variables, parameters, fields, and even common functions to an expression with a double-click. Finally, we saw in Step 14 how the Expression dialog box provides information on the parameters expected by a function.

The business requirements call for a sequence number on each label. To do this, we look to the functions available in Reporting Services. The RowNumber function provides just what is needed.

In the next section, you finalize the formatting of the mailing labels. One of the business requirements was for the count of the number of employees at the top of the first page of labels. The Employees dataset returns the employee count, so we have the information we need. The only place we can put this employee count without messing up the label layout is in the page header.

Employee Mailing Labels Report, Task 2: Add the Report Header and Multiple Columns

1. Click the Design tab.
2. From the main menu, select Report | Add Page Header.
3. Drag the Name field from the Report Data window and drop it in the page header layout area.
4. Position the text box created in Step 3 in the upper-left corner of the page header. Make the text box as wide as the Name, Address1, and CSZ fields in the report body. A blue alignment line will appear when these text boxes are the same width.
5. Drag the page header so it is only as tall as the text box you just created. This is done by clicking the dotted line between the page header and the report body and dragging upward.
6. Right-click the text box in the page header and select Expression from the context menu. The Expression dialog box appears.

NOTE

The Name field was placed on the report layout outside of a data region. Therefore, the Report Builder must place the field inside an aggregate function to get a single value. By default, a numeric field is placed inside a Sum() aggregate and a non-numeric field is placed inside a First() aggregate.

7. Replace the word "First" with **Count** to get a count of the number of records in the dataset.
8. Modify the expression so it appears as follows:

```
="Total Employees: " & CStr(Count(Fields!Name.Value, "Employees"))
```

9. Click OK to exit the Expression dialog box.
10. Right-click the text box in the page header and select Text Box Properties from the context menu. The Text Box Properties dialog box appears.
11. Select the Visibility page.
12. Select the Show or hide based on an expression radio button under the When the report is initially run prompt.
13. Click the Expression button below and to the right of the radio button you just selected. The Expression dialog box appears.
14. Expand Common Functions in the Category pane and select Program Flow in the list on the left.
15. Double-click IIf in the Item pane.
16. Select Built-in Fields in the Category pane.
17. Double-click PageNumber in the Item pane.
18. Type **> 1, true, false)** at the end of the expression.

19. Click OK to exit the Expression dialog box.
20. Click OK to exit the Text Box Properties dialog box.
21. In the Properties window, select Report from the drop-down list at the top of the window.
22. Modify the following properties of the report:

Property	Value
Columns: Columns	3
Columns: ColumnSpacing	0in

23. Click anywhere in the tablix. From the main menu, select Report | Report Properties. The Report Properties dialog box appears.
24. Modify the following properties:

Property	Value
Margins: Left	0.5in
Margins: Right	0.5in
Margins: Top	0.25in
Margins: Bottom	0.5in

25. Click OK to exit the Report Properties dialog box. Your report layout should appear similar to Figure 7-21.
26. Click the Preview tab, and then click the Print Layout toolbar button. The report appears similar to Figure 7-22 when viewed at 100%.
27. Click Save All on the toolbar.

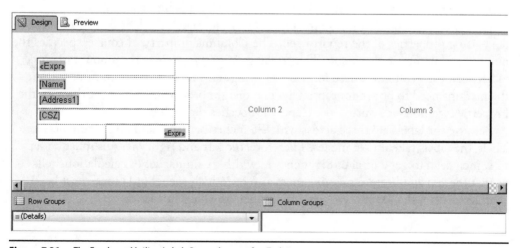

Figure 7-21   *The Employee Mailing Labels Report layout after Task 2*

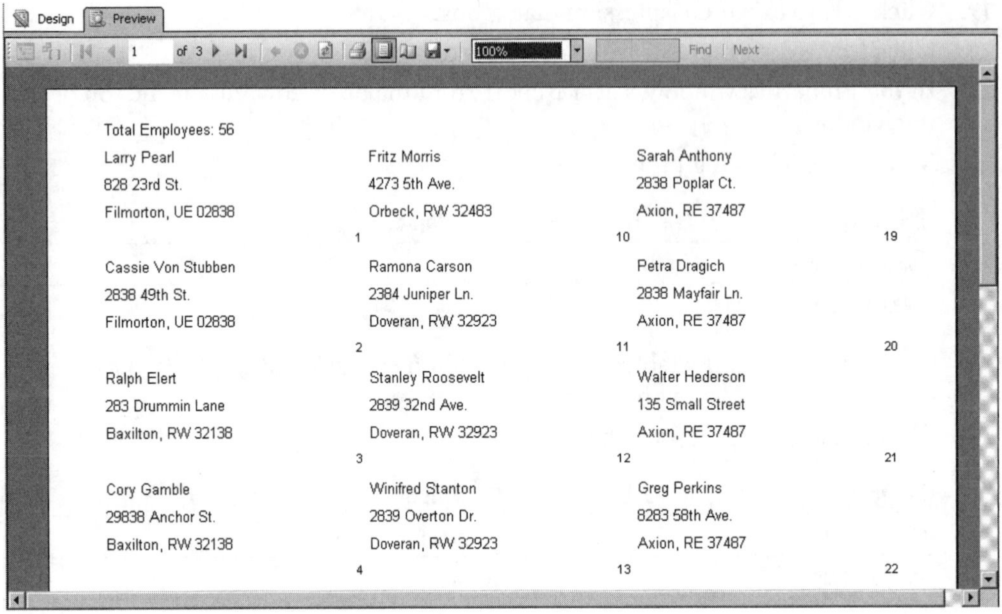

Figure 7-22 *The Employee Mailing Labels Report print layout preview after Task 2*

Task Notes The business requirements specify that the employee count should only be displayed on the first page. The page header has properties that hide it on the first page or the last page. There is no option to have it display only on the first page. To accomplish this, you created an expression to control the visibility of the text box in the page header. If the page number is less than or equal to 1, the employee count is visible. If the page number is greater than 1, the employee count is hidden.

In addition, you need to set up the report layout to match the label sheet. This is done using properties of the report itself. The Columns property, of course, specifies the number of columns in the report. The Spacing property specifies the amount of space in between each column. These must be set using the Properties window. In addition, the margins need to be set appropriately. The margin properties can be set through the Properties window or by using the Report Properties dialog box.

Because the labels are three across with 2½ inches per label and no spacing between labels, the labels take up 7½ inches. Therefore, the left and right margins must be set to ½ inch each to get a total of 8½ inches in width. A similar set of calculations tells us that the top and bottom margins must also be ½ inch each, but ¼ inch must be subtracted from the top margin to accommodate the page header.

The Overtime Report

Features Highlighted

► Implementing cascading parameters

► Using SQL stored procedures

► Using table filters

► Using the NoRows property

Business Need   The Galactic Delivery Services personnel department needs to monitor the amount of overtime put in at each of its repair and distribution hubs to determine when additional personnel must be hired. The personnel department needs a report that lists the employees with over 45 hours worked in a given week at a given hub. The report should have two sections. The first section should list employees with more than 45 hours and less than 55 hours worked for the selected week. The second section should list employees with more than 55 hours worked for the selected week.

The user should be able to select a work week from a drop-down list, and then see a second drop-down list, showing the hubs that have one or more employees with more than 45 hours for the selected week. The user selects a hub from this second list, and then sees the report for that hub.

Two stored procedures in the Galactic database should be used for retrieving data. The stp_HubsOver45 stored procedure returns a list of hubs with one or more employees who have over 45 hours worked for the selected week. The stp_EmployeesOver45 stored procedure returns a list of employees who have over 45 hours worked for the selected week at the selected hub. We discuss stored procedures in the Task Notes.

Task Overview

1.   Create a New Report and Three Datasets.
2.   Create the Report Layout.

Overtime Report, Task 1:
Create a New Report and Three Datasets

1.   Reopen the Chapter07 project, if it was closed. Close the Employee Mailing Labels Report, if it is open.
2.   Right-click Reports in the Solution Explorer and select Add | New Item from the context menu. The Add New Item dialog box appears.
3.   Single-click GDSReport in the Templates area to select it. Change the name to **Overtime** and click Add.

4. Create a data source called "Galactic" in this new report. This new data source should reference the Galactic shared data source.

5. Create a dataset called "Weeks" with the following query:

```
SELECT DISTINCT CONVERT(char(4), DATEPART(yy,WorkDate))+'-'+
    RIGHT('0'+CONVERT(varchar(2), DATEPART(wk,WorkDate)),2) as Week
FROM TimeEntry
ORDER BY Week
```

6. Right-click the Galactic entry in the Report Data window. Select Add Dataset from the context menu. The Dataset Properties dialog box appears.

7. Enter **HubsOver45** for the name in the Dataset dialog box.

8. Select the Stored Procedure radio button under the Query type prompt.

9. Select stp_HubsOver45 from the Select or enter stored procedure name drop-down list.

10. Click OK to exit the Dataset Properties dialog box. An entry for the HubsOver45 dataset appears in the Report Data window.

11. Right-click the Galactic entry in the Report Data window. Select Add Dataset from the context menu. The Dataset Properties dialog box appears.

12. Enter **EmployeesOver45** for the name in the Dataset dialog box.

13. Select the Stored Procedure radio button under the Query type prompt.

14. Select stp_EmployeesOver45 from the Select or enter stored procedure name drop-down list.

15. Click OK to exit the Dataset Properties dialog box. An entry for the EmployeesOver45 dataset appears in the Report Data window.

Task Notes   For two of our three datasets, we used stored procedures rather than queries. A *stored procedure* is a query or a set of queries given a name and stored in the database itself. You can think of a stored procedure as a data-manipulation program created and kept right inside the database.

Stored procedures have several advantages over queries:

▶ **Speed**   A certain amount of preprocessing must be done on any query before it can be run in the database. This preprocessing creates an execution plan. Essentially, SQL Server selects the approach it will use to actually execute the query. Stored procedures are preprocessed when they are created, and the resulting query plan is saved with the stored procedure. This means when you execute a stored procedure, you do not need to wait for the preprocessing. The result is faster execution time.

▶ **Simplicity**   A developer or database administrator can create a stored procedure that uses a number of intricate queries. When you execute the stored procedure, you do not need to understand, or even see, this complexity. All you need to do is execute the stored procedure to get the result set you need.

▶ **Security**   When you query a set of tables, you must be given rights to see any and all data in each of the tables. However, when a stored procedure is used, you only need rights to execute the stored procedure. You do not need rights to any of the tables being queried by the stored procedure. The stored procedure can then control which rows and columns can be seen by each user.

▶ **Reusability**   A single stored procedure can be used by a number of reports. Therefore, complex queries do not have to be created over and over again when a number of reports need to use the same data.

▶ **Maintainability**   When changes are made to the database structure, the developer or database administrator can make the corresponding changes in the stored procedure, so the stored procedure continues to return the same result set. Without stored procedures, a change in the database structure could result in a number of reports needing to be edited.

For these reasons, it is often advantageous to use stored procedures rather than queries for your datasets.

NOTE

Querying against database views has a number of the same benefits as stored procedures and is also a good choice as the source for your datasets. Because querying views is much the same as querying tables (they present fields to the Query Builder just as tables do), we will not spend time discussing views.

When you are using a stored procedure for your dataset, all you need to do is set Query Type to Stored Procedure and select the name of the stored procedure. The Report Designer can figure out the parameters required by the stored procedure and add them to the report. Can't get much simpler than that!

Overtime Report, Task 2: Create the Report Layout

1. Expand the Parameters entry in the Report Data window. Notice two parameters, Week and HubCode, were created automatically for us based on the parameters required by the stored procedures we selected.

2. Right-click the entry for the Week parameter in the Report Data window and select Parameter Properties from the context menu. The Report Parameter Properties dialog box appears.

3. Select the Available Values page.

4. Select the Get values from a query radio button.

5. Select Weeks from the Dataset drop-down list. Select Week from the Value field drop-down list. Select Week from the Label field drop-down list.

6. Click OK to exit the Report Parameter Properties dialog box.

7. Right-click the entry for the HubCode parameter in the Report Data window and select Parameter Properties from the context menu. The Report Parameter Properties dialog box appears.

8. Change Prompt to **Hub**.

9. Select the Available Values page.

10. Select the Get values from a query radio button.

11. Select HubsOver45 from the Dataset drop-down list. Select HubCode from the Value field drop-down list. Select Hub from the Label field drop-down list.

12. Click OK to exit the Report Parameter Properties dialog box.

13. Place a text box onto the body of the report. Modify the following properties of this text box:

Property	Value
Font: FontSize	25pt
Font: FontWeight	Bold
Location: Left	0in
Location: Top	0in
Size: Width	2in
Size: Height	0.5in
Value	Overtime

14. Place a second text box onto the body of the report. Modify the following properties of this text box:

Property	Value
Font: FontSize	16pt
Location: Left	0in
Location: Top	0.5in
Size: Width	5.25in
Size: Height	0.375in

15. Right-click this text box and select Expression from the context menu.

16. Type the following in the Set expression for: Value area:

```
= "Week: " &  Parameters!Week.Value &
"      Hub: " &  Parameters!HubCode.Value
```

17. Click OK to exit the Expression dialog box.

18. Place a third text box onto the body of the report. Modify the following properties of this text box:

Property	Value
Font: FontSize	16pt
Font: FontWeight	Bold
Location: Left	0in
Location: Top	1.125in
Size: Width	5.25in
Size: Height	0.375in
Value	Employees with 45 to 55 hours for this week

19. Use the table template to place a tablix onto the body of the report immediately below the third text box.

20. Place the EmployeeNumber field from the EmployeesOver45 dataset in the leftmost cell in the detail row of the tablix.

21. Place the FirstName field from the EmployeesOver45 dataset in the center cell in the detail row of the tablix.

22. Place the LastName field from the EmployeesOver45 dataset in the rightmost cell in the detail row of the tablix.

23. Drag the HoursWorked field from the EmployeesOver45 dataset in the Report Data window and use it to add a new column on the right side of the tablix.

24. Select the tablix header row. Modify the following property:

Property	Value
TextDecoration	Underline

25. Select the leftmost table column. Modify the following property:

Property	Value
TextAlign	Left

NOTE

Remember, you can use the items in the Report Formatting toolbar to do things such as turning on underlining and changing the text alignment.

26. Right-click the gray box in the upper-left corner of the tablix and select Tablix Properties from the context menu. The Tablix Properties dialog box appears.

27. Select the Filters page.

28. Click Add to create a new filter entry.

29. Select [HoursWorked] from the Expression drop-down list.

30. Select <= from the Operator drop-down list.

31. Type =**55** for Value.

32. Click OK to exit the Tablix Properties dialog box.

33. Modify the following property of the tablix using the Properties window:

Property	Value
NoRowsMessage	No Employees

34. Select both the tablix and the text box with the string "Employees with 45 to 55 hours for this week." Press CTRL-C to copy these two report items. We are going to paste a copy of these two items and use them to create the layout for the Employees over 55 Hours.

35. Drag the report body larger. Do this by dragging the dashed line between the report body and the page footer.

36. Press CTRL-V to paste a copy of the two report items. Drag the two new items so they are below the originals.

37. Select the new text box by itself. Change the value of the text box to **Employees with over 55 hours for this week**.

38. Click anywhere in the new tablix, right-click any of the gray boxes above or to the left of the tablix and select Tablix Properties from the context menu. The Tablix Properties dialog box appears.

39. Select the Filters page.

40. Select > from the Operator drop-down list.

41. Click OK to exit the Tablix Properties dialog box. Your report layout should appear similar to Figure 7-23.

42. Click the Preview tab.

43. Notice the Week drop-down list is enabled, but the Hub drop-down list is disabled. Select 2009–15 from the Week drop-down list.

44. Once a week is selected, the Hub drop-down list is enabled. Select Borlaron Repair Base from the Hub drop-down list. Click the View Report button. Your report should appear similar to Figure 7-24.

45. Select 2009–10 from the Week drop-down list. Borlaron Repair Base is still selected in the Hub drop-down list. Click the View Report button. Note the text under the Employees with Over 55 Hours for This Week heading.

46. Click Save All on the toolbar.

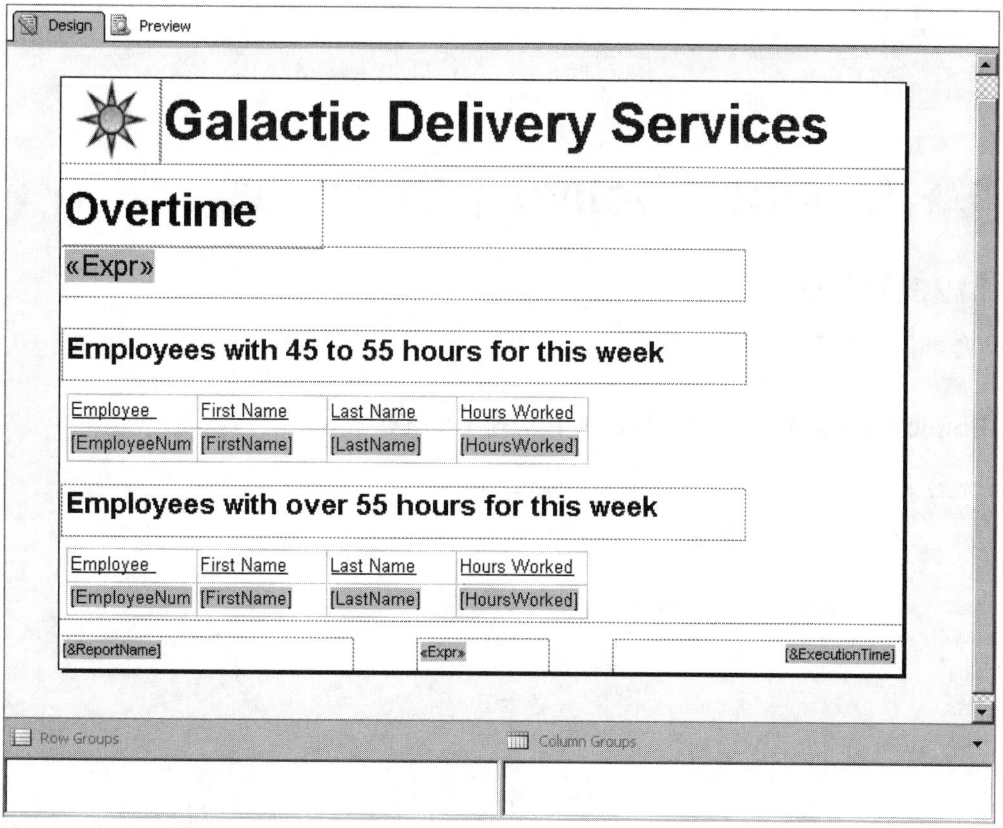

Figure 7-23   *The Overtime Report layout*

Task Notes   In this report, we used the same dataset to populate two tablixes. We got different information in the two tablixes by applying different filters on each. The filter for the upper table on the report says we only want records in this tablix where the number of hours worked is less than or equal to 55. The filter for the lower tablix on the report says we only want records in this tablix where the number of hours worked is greater than 55. In this way, we can divide the data in the dataset to fulfill the business requirements of the report.

You may have noted that we used an equals sign in front of the number 55 in the Value field for our filter expressions. This is due to the fact that the Value, without an equals sign in front of it, is interpreted as a string constant. In other words, without the equals sign, the report would have been trying to compare an integer database field with the string "55" which results in an error. When we place the equals sign in front of the value, Reporting Services interprets this as an expression. The expression "=55" results in an integer value of 55 which is just what we want for our comparison.

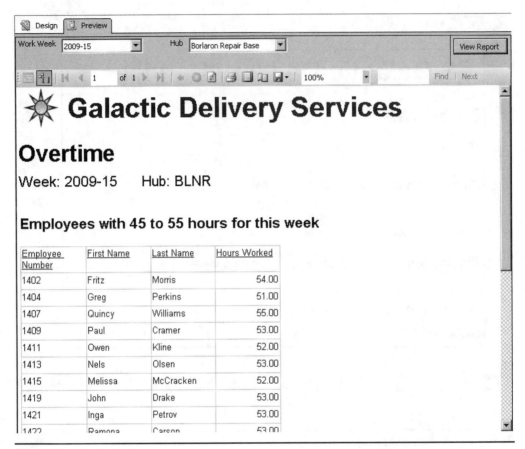

Figure 7-24   *The Overtime Report preview*

In addition to what you saw here, filters can be applied to data in other locations. A dataset can have a filter applied to it after it has been selected from the database. Individual groups within a table, matrix, or chart can also utilize filters.

Filters work well in situations like the one in this report where we want to use one dataset to provide a slightly different set of records to multiple data regions. They can also be useful for taking data from a stored procedure that provides almost, but not quite, the result set you need. It is usually best, however, to have your filtering done by your select query or stored procedure, rather than by the report. The reason is, in most cases, it is considerably faster and more efficient if the database does the filtering as it executes the query or stored procedure. It does not make sense to have your query select 1,000 records from the database if your report is going to filter out all but ten of these records. Filters are a good tool to have; just remember to use them wisely.

In the Overtime Report, we used two drop-down lists to let the user select the parameters for our report. The Week drop-down list enables the user to select the week of the year for which the report should be run. This drop-down list is populated by the Week dataset. The Hub drop-down list lets the user select the hub for which the report should be run. This drop-down list is populated by the HubsOver45 dataset. The HubsOver45 dataset requires a value from the Week drop-down list before it can return a list of the hubs with employees working over 45 hours for that week. In this way, the data that populates the Hub drop-down list is dependent on the value selected in the Week drop-down list.

Reporting Services is smart enough to recognize this dependency and act accordingly. If no value is selected in the Week drop-down list, the Hub drop-down list cannot be populated, so it is disabled. Every time the selected value in the Week drop-down list changes, the Hub drop-down list is repopulated.

Finally, in this report we used the NoRows property of each of the tablixes. This property enables you to define a string that is output when there are no rows to populate the tablix. When the filter on either tablix in the report filters out all the rows in the dataset, the content of the NoRows property is displayed. This is more helpful to the user than simply having a blank space where a tablix should be. The NoRows property is available on any of the data region report items.

The Revised Employee Time Report

Features Highlighted

▶ Implementing fixed and dynamic columns and rows in the same tablix

▶ Using the Switch() function

Business Need The Galactic Delivery Services personnel department is finding the Employee Time Report to be useful. To make the report even more useful, they would like to add summary information to the report. To the right of the current report, they would like to summarize the hours worked by the day of the week—in other words, how many hours were put in on Mondays, Tuesdays, Wednesdays, etc. They would like a summary of the hours worked at each delivery hub specified by hub code.

Finally, at the bottom of the report, they would like a summary of the hours worked by job type. Our database does not contain a definition of job type. Job type is an ad hoc classification that the personnel department uses for some analysis. All levels of mechanics, both I and II, form one job type. All levels of sorters, both I and II, form a second job type, while transport pilots and transport copilots make up the third job type.

Task Overview

1. Copy and Rename the Existing Report, Modify the Dataset, Modify Layout.

Revised Employee Time Report, Task 1: Copy and Rename the Existing Report, Modify the Dataset, Modify Layout

1. Reopen the Chapter07 project, if it was closed. Close the Overtime Report, if it is open.

2. Right-click the EmployeeTime Report in the Solution Explorer and select Copy from the context menu.

3. Right-click the Chapter07 project in the Solution Explorer and select Paste from the context menu. A copy of the report appears in the Solution Explorer.

4. Right-click this new copy and select Rename from the context menu. Rename the report **RevisedEmployeeTime.rdl**.

5. Double-click the entry for the RevisedEmployeeTime report to open this report for editing.

6. In the Report Data window, right-click EmployeeTime and select Query from the context menu. The Query Designer window opens.

7. Add the HubCode field to the end of the field list, as shown here in bold:

```
SELECT Description AS Job,
     Employee.EmployeeNumber,
     FirstName,
     LastName,
     CONVERT(char(4),DATEPART(yy, WorkDate))+'-'+
         CONVERT(char(2),DATEPART(wk, WorkDate)) AS Week,
     WorkDate,
     HoursWorked,
     HubCode
FROM TimeEntry
INNER JOIN Assignment
     ON TimeEntry.AssignmentID = Assignment.AssignmentID
INNER JOIN Employee
     ON Assignment.EmployeeNumber = Employee.EmployeeNumber
INNER JOIN Job
     ON Assignment.JobID = Job.JobID
ORDER BY Job, Employee.EmployeeNumber, Week, WorkDate
```

8. Run the query to make sure no errors exist. Correct any typos that may be detected.

9. Click OK to exit the Query Designer window.

10. Right-click in the bottom row of the tablix. Select Tablix: Insert Row | Below from the context menu. A new static row is added at the bottom of the tablix.

11. Right-click in the row you just added and select Tablix: Add Group | Adjacent Below from the context menu. The Tablix group dialog box appears.

12. Select [HubCode] from the Group by drop-down list.

13. Click OK to exit the Tablix group dialog box. A new row group is added at the bottom of the tablix.

14. Merge the leftmost three cells in the bottom row of the tablix.
15. Select the HubCode field in the newly merged cells.
16. Merge all of the cells in the second-from-the-bottom row in the tablix.
17. Set the following properties of this newly merged cell:

Property	Value
BorderColor: Top	Black
BorderWidth: Top	4pt
Font: TextDecoration	Underline

18. In the cell in the lower-right corner of the tablix, select the HoursWorked field. This field will automatically be enclosed in a Sum() aggregate function.
19. Set the following property of this cell:

Property	Value
BorderStyle: Top	None

20. Click the Preview tab. The bottom of your report should appear as shown in Figure 7-25.
21. Click the Design tab.
22. Right-click in the bottom row of the tablix. Select Tablix: Insert Row | Outside Group - Below from the context menu. A new static row is added at the bottom of the tablix.
23. Right-click in the row you just added and select Tablix: Add Group | Row Group: Adjacent Below from the context menu. The Tablix group dialog box appears.
24. Click the Expression button next to the Group by drop-down list. The Expression dialog box appears.
25. Enter the following in the Set expression for: GroupExpression area:

```
=Switch(LEFT(Fields!Job.Value, 8) = "Mechanic", "Mechanics",
    LEFT(Fields!Job.Value, 6) = "Sorter", "Sorters",
    LEFT(Fields!Job.Value, 9) = "Transport", "Pilots")
```

26. Highlight the entire expression you just entered and press CTRL-C to copy this text.
27. Click OK to exit the Expression dialog box.
28. Click OK to exit the Tablix group dialog box. A new row group is added at the bottom of the tablix.
29. Merge the leftmost three cells in the bottom row of the tablix.
30. Right-click in the newly merged cells and select Textbox: Expression from the context menu. The Expression dialog box appears.

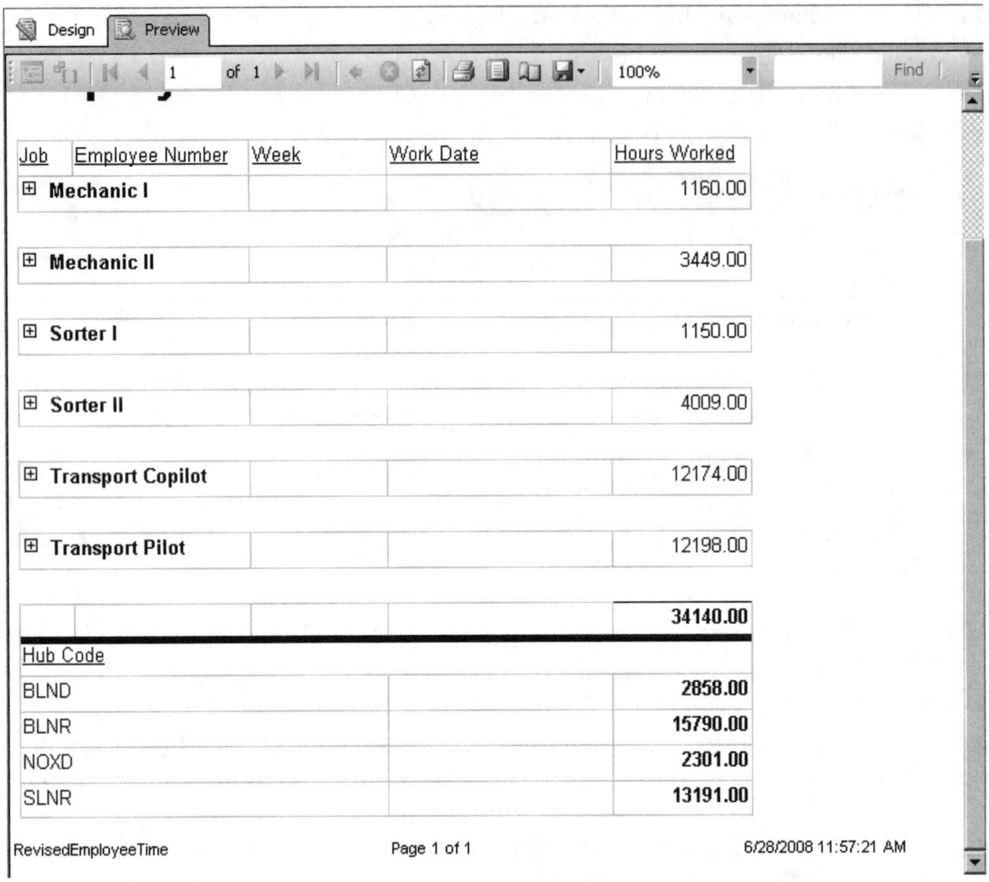

Job	Employee Number	Week	Work Date	Hours Worked
⊞ **Mechanic I**				1160.00
⊞ **Mechanic II**				3449.00
⊞ **Sorter I**				1150.00
⊞ **Sorter II**				4009.00
⊞ **Transport Copilot**				12174.00
⊞ **Transport Pilot**				12198.00
				34140.00

Hub Code			
BLND			**2858.00**
BLNR			**15790.00**
NOXD			**2301.00**
SLNR			**13191.00**

RevisedEmployeeTime   Page 1 of 1   6/28/2008 11:57:21 AM

Figure 7-25   *The Revised Employee Time Report with hub code summary*

31. Delete the equals sign from the Set expression for: Value area and press CTRL-V to paste the expression you entered in Step 25.
32. Click OK to exit the Expression dialog box.
33. Merge all of the cells in the second-from-the-bottom row in the tablix.
34. Set the following properties of this newly merged cell:

Property	Value
BorderColor: Top	Black
BorderWidth: Top	4pt
Font: TextDecoration	Underline
Value	Job Type

35. In the cell in the lower-right corner of the tablix, select the HoursWorked field. This field will automatically be enclosed in a Sum() aggregate function.

36. Click the Preview tab. The bottom of your report should appear as shown in Figure 7-26.

37. Click the Design tab.

38. Right-click in the rightmost column in the tablix and select Tablix: Insert Column | Right from the context menu. A new column is added to the right of the tablix.

39. Size the new column so it is approximately one-fourth its original width.

40. Right-click in the new column and select Tablix: Add Group | Column Group: Adjacent Right from the context menu. The Tablix group dialog box appears.

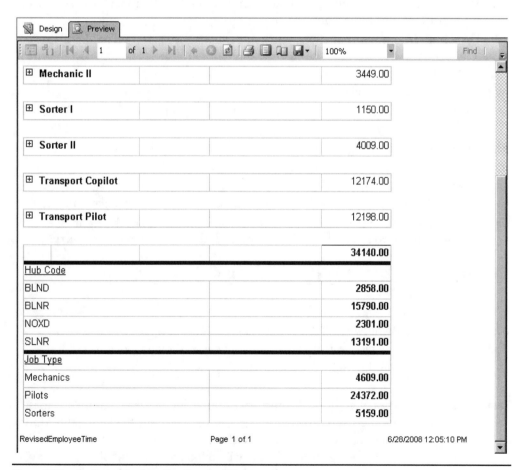

Figure 7-26   *The Revised Employee Time Report with job type summary*

41. Click the Expression button next to the Group by drop-down list. The Expression dialog box appears.
42. Expand the Common Functions entry in the Category pane. Select the Date & Time entry in the Category pane. Double-click the Weekday entry in the Item pane.
43. Select Fields (EmployeeTime) in the Category pane. Double-click the WorkDate field in the Field pane.
44. Type) at the end of the expression.
45. Click OK to exit the Expression dialog box.
46. Click OK to exit the Tablix group dialog box. A new column group is added at the right of the tablix.
47. Right-click the upper cell in the new column and select Textbox: Expression from the context menu. The Expression dialog box appears.
48. Expand the Common Functions entry in the Category pane. Select the Date & Time entry in the Category pane. Double-click the WeekdayName entry in the Item pane.
49. Double-click the Weekday entry in the Item pane.
50. Select Fields (EmployeeTime) in the Category pane. Double-click the WorkDate field in the Field pane.
51. Type)) at the end of the expression.
52. Click OK to exit the Expression dialog box.
53. Select the HoursWorked field in each of the three cells below the cell you just modified. In each case, the field will be enclosed in a Sum() aggregate function.
54. Click the gray rectangle at the top of the second column from the right (the narrow column) to select the entire column. Modify the following property:

Property	Value
BackgroundColor	Silver

55. The tablix layout should appear as shown in Figure 7-27.
56. Click the Preview tab. Your report should appear as shown in Figure 7-28.
57. Click Save All on the toolbar.

Task Notes   The types of additional summary information requested in the business need for this report are the reason the tablix came along. Without the tablix, this kind of formatting was difficult, if not impossible. With the tablix, it is straightforward to create, if perhaps a bit confusing at first. The key is to look at the symbols in the gray boxes across the top and down the left side of the tablix, along with the entries in the Row Groups and Column Groups areas. As was discussed previously, these symbols in

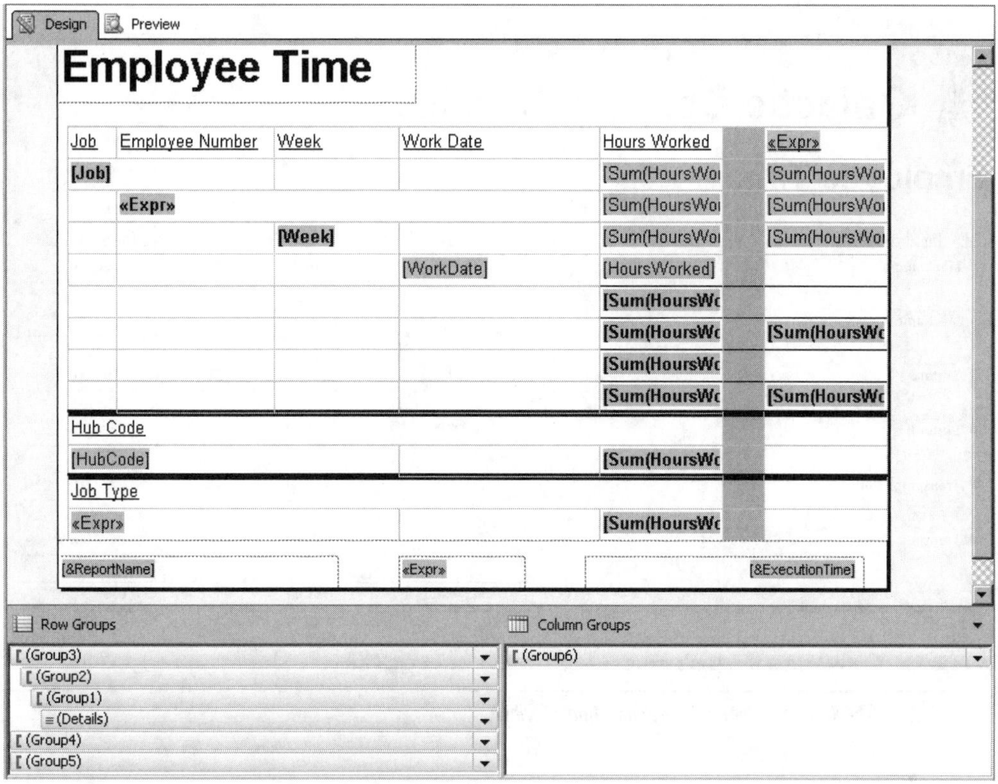

Figure 7-27   *The Revised Employee Time Report final layout*

the gray boxes tell you which columns and rows are static and which are dynamic. The entries in the Row Groups and Column Groups areas allow you to edit the properties of each dynamic grouping.

Static rows and static columns appear once in the tablix. The first row in the tablix containing the column headings is an example of a static row. The narrow column containing the gray background is an example of a static column. Each appears only once in the rendered report.

Dynamic rows and columns repeat, depending on the data in the dataset used to populate the tablix. The group header rows are examples of dynamic rows. The rightmost day of the week group column is an example of a dynamic column. We don't know how many of these rows or columns will appear in the report until it is actually rendered.

Dynamic groups can be nested one inside the other. This is the case with the original version of the Employee Time Report, where we had Job, Employee, Week, and Detail groupings nested one inside the other. Dynamic groups can also be adjacent to one another, as our hub code and job type groups were in the revised version of the report.

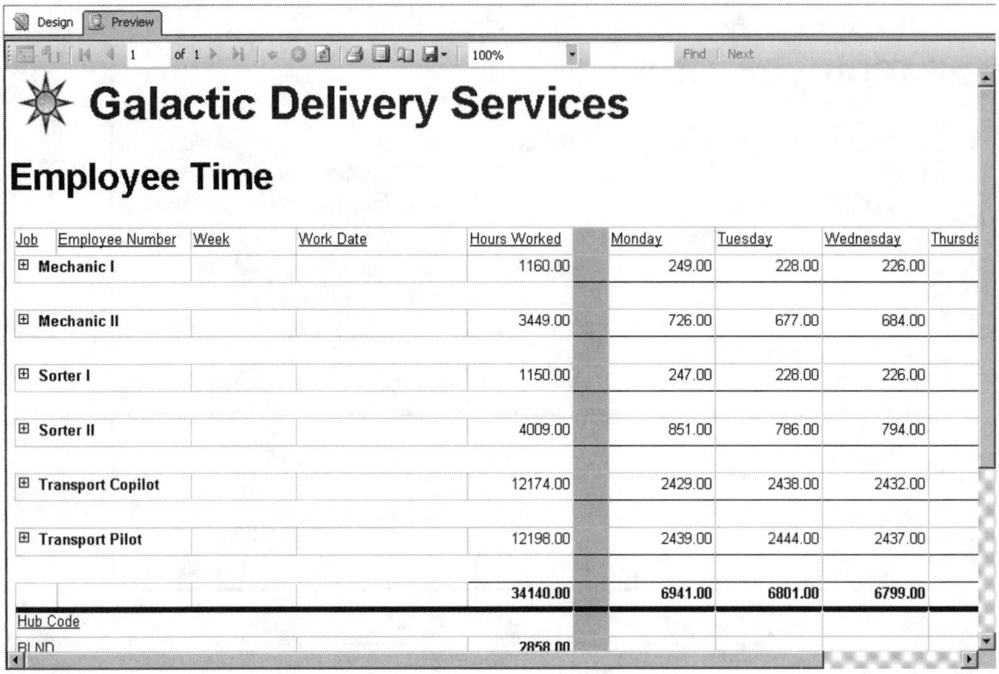

Figure 7-28 *The Revised Employee Time Report final preview*

To create the job type group, we used the Switch() function. The Switch() function is similar to the IIF() function. The IIF() function enables us to test a single Boolean (true/false) statement and return one value if it is true and another if it is false. The Switch() function allows us to test multiple Boolean statements in a specific order. The function will return the value associated with the first Boolean statement that turns out to be true.

Here is the expression we used in the report:

```
=Switch(LEFT(Fields!Job.Value, 8) = "Mechanic", "Mechanics",
    LEFT(Fields!Job.Value, 6) = "Sorter", "Sorters",
    LEFT(Fields!Job.Value, 9) = "Transport", "Pilots")
```

The Switch() function first tests to see if the left eight characters of the Job field are equal to the word Mechanic. If so, the string "Mechanics" is returned by the function. If it is not, the function tests to see if the left six characters of the Job field are equal to the word Sorter. If so, the string "Sorters" is returned by the function. Finally, the function tests to see if the left nine characters of the Job field are equal to the word Transport. If so, the string "Pilots" is returned by the function.

Under the Hood

In Chapter 1, we talked about the fact that the report definitions are stored using the Report Definition Language (RDL). RDL was created by Microsoft specifically for Reporting Services. It was one of the first published Extensible Markup Language (XML) document standards created by Microsoft.

Microsoft has gone public with the specifications for RDL. Third parties can create their own authoring environments for creating report definitions. If the RDL from these third-party tools conforms to the RDL standard, the reports created by these tools can be managed and distributed by Reporting Services.

Because RDL is an XML document, you can look at a report definition in its raw form. If you were so inclined, you could use Notepad to open an RDL file and look at its contents. In fact, you don't even need Notepad. You can look at the contents of an RDL file right in the Report Builder.

Viewing the RDL

Right-click the entry for Overtime.rdl in the Solution Explorer, and then select View Code from the context menu. You see a new tab in the layout area called Overtime.rdl. This tab contains the actual RDL of the report, as shown in Figure 7-29.

XML Structure

Because the RDL is an XML document, it is made up of pairs of tags. A begin tag is at the beginning of an item and an end tag is at the end of the item. A *begin tag* is simply a string of text, the tag name, with < at the front and > at the back. An *end tag* is the same string of text with </at the front and > at the back. This pair of tags creates an XML element. The information in between the two tags is the value for that element. In the following example, the Height element has a value of 0.625in:

```
<Height>0.625in</Height>
```

There can never be a begin tag without an end tag, and vice versa. In fact, it can be said that XML is the Noah's Ark of data structures, because everything must go two by two.

In addition to simple strings of text, XML elements can contain other elements. In fact, a number of elements can nest one inside the other to form complex structures. Here's an example:

```
<Textbox>
  <Style>
    <Color>DarkBlue</Color>
  </Style>
</Textbox>
```

Figure 7-29 *The RDL for the Overtime Report*

In some cases, begin tags contain additional information as attributes. An *attribute* comes in the form of an attribute name, immediately following the tag name, followed by an equals sign (=) and the value of the attribute. In this example, the Textbox element has an attribute called Name with a value of "Textbox1":

```
<Textbox Name="Textbox1">...</Textbox>
```

The RDL contains several sections: the page header, the body, the data sources, the datasets, the embedded images, the page footer, and the report parameters. Each section starts with a begin tag and is terminated by an end tag. For example, the page header section of the RDL starts with <PageHeader> and is terminated by </PageHeader>.

In Figure 7-29, you can see the entire XML structure for the Galactic data source. The begin tag of the data source includes a Name attribute. This corresponds to the Name property of the data source. In between the begin and end tags of the data source element are additional elements, such as the DataSourceReference. These elements correspond to the other properties of this data source. Only those properties that have been changed from their default values are stored in the RDL.

Editing the RDL

One other interesting thing about viewing the RDL in the Report Builder is you can make changes to the RDL and have them affect the report design. Use the text find capabilities of this RDL editor to find the "ReportParameters" section of the RDL. Find the Prompt element within the Week report parameter element, as shown in Figure 7-30. Replace "Week" with "Work Week" and click Save All on the toolbar. Right-click the entry for Overtime.rdl in the Solution Explorer, and then select View Designer from the context menu. Click the Preview tab. You notice the prompt has been changed to Work Week.

If you do find a reason to make modifications directly to the RDL, do so with care. If you break up a begin/end pair or enter an invalid value for a property element (such as puce for a color), you can end up with a report that will not load in the Report Designer. Save your work immediately before making changes directly to the RDL. In just about every case, however, the designer works better for making changes to a report layout, so do your editing there.

Practicing Safe Source

The Report Builder works with source control tools, such as Visual SourceSafe (VSS) or Team Services source control. These tools control access to source code, such as report definitions. This can prevent two report designers from trying to modify the same report at the same time. Even if you do not have multiple report designers, source control can provide a consistent location where all your reporting projects can be found. Each of these source control tools stores all the source code entrusted to its safekeeping in its own library database. If this library database is located on a network, you have a central location where all the source code can be backed up regularly.

Source control has one more valuable feature. It keeps multiple versions of your source code. When you check in your source code, the source control tool does not write over the previous version. Instead, it keeps both the older version and the new version. You continue to work with the newest version of the source code, unless there is a problem and you ask to go back to an earlier version. This can be a lifesaver when you make those massive formatting changes to a report, and then you or your users decide it was better the way it was.

```
                    <Width>5.25in</Width>
                    <ZIndex>5</ZIndex>
                    <Style>
                      <Border>
                        <Style>None</Style>
                      </Border>
                      <PaddingLeft>2pt</PaddingLeft>
                      <PaddingRight>2pt</PaddingRight>
                      <PaddingTop>2pt</PaddingTop>
                      <PaddingBottom>2pt</PaddingBottom>
                    </Style>
                  </Textbox>
                </ReportItems>
                <Height>3.29875in</Height>
                <Style />
              </Body>
              <ReportParameters>
                <ReportParameter Name="Week">
                  <DataType>String</DataType>
                  <Prompt>Week</Prompt>
                  <ValidValues>
                    <DataSetReference>
                      <DataSetName>Weeks</DataSetName>
                      <ValueField>Week</ValueField>
                      <LabelField>Week</LabelField>
                    </DataSetReference>
                  </ValidValues>
                </ReportParameter>
                <ReportParameter Name="HubCode">
                  <DataType>String</DataType>
                  <Prompt>Hub</Prompt>
                  <ValidValues>
                    <DataSetReference>
                      <DataSetName>HubsOver45</DataSetName>
                      <ValueField>HubCode</ValueField>
```

Figure 7-30   *The Prompt element of the Week report parameter*

Using Visual SourceSafe

VSS is tightly integrated with the Report Designer. Once VSS is installed and configured on your PC, you can probably do almost all your interaction with VSS through the Report Designer menus. In this section, we look at adding a reporting project to VSS control, checking reports into and out of VSS, and reverting to an older version of a report.

Adding a Reporting Project to Source Control

Once source control is set up on your PC, adding a reporting project to source control is simple. Right-click the solution or the project in the Solution Explorer and select Add Solution to Source Control. You are prompted to log in to your source control system and to specify the source control database you want to use. Provide this login information and click OK.

You see a dialog box displaying the project folder hierarchy in your source control database. Modify the project name, if desired, and then browse to the appropriate location in the project folder hierarchy and click OK.

Check In, Check Out, and Get Latest Version

Once the solution has been added to source control, a small lock icon appears next to each entry in the Solution Explorer. This indicates each file is checked into source control. The local copy of each of these files is marked as read-only. The file cannot be modified until it has been checked out.

To check out a report definition file, right-click the entry for that report in the Solution Explorer and select Check Out from the context menu. If you choose, you can enter a comment stating why the report is being checked out. The most recent version of the report is then copied from the source control database to your PC. It is no longer read-only but, instead, is ready to accept changes. The lock icon is replaced by a small check mark in the Solution Explorer to indicate the report is checked out. Only one person may have a report checked out at any given time.

Once you complete your changes to the report definition, you need to check the report back into the source control database. Right-click the entry for the report in the Solution Explorer and select Check In from the context menu. Again, you can enter a comment summarizing the changes you made. This is helpful if you ever have to revert to an older version of a report.

If you want to get the latest version of a report someone else is working on, without checking out the report, you can use the Get Latest Version feature. Right-click the entry for the report in the Solution Explorer, and then select Get Latest Version from the context menu. A read-only copy of the latest version of the report is then copied to your PC.

Getting a Previous Version

Retrieving an earlier version of a report from source control is straightforward. Select the report in the Solution Explorer, and then select File | Source Control | History. The History Options dialog box appears. You can enter a range of dates to see the history of the report within that date range. You can also enter a user to see the versions checked in by that user. To see the entire history of the report, leave everything blank and click OK.

The History Of dialog box appears. Here, you can scroll through the previous versions of the report. Click Get to retrieve a copy of a previous version. This previous version then becomes your current copy of the report. Any previous versions of the report checked in after the version you just retrieved continue to reside in the source control database. Click Rollback to retrieve a copy of a previous version and to delete any versions of the report that were checked in after the version you just retrieved.

Advance, Never Retreat

In this chapter, we continued to unlock additional features of Reporting Services. We're always working toward the goal of giving you the tools you need to meet your reporting needs. You should now be well on your way to being able to say, "Yes, I can do that!"

In the next chapter, we look at some of the advanced features of Reporting Services. After that, we take a brief look at the different formats for rendering reports, and then we move on to report serving.

Chapter 8

Beyond Wow: Advanced Reporting

In This Chapter

► **Speaking in Code**
► **Reports Within Reports**
► **Interacting with Reports**
► **A Conversion Experience**
► **What's Next**

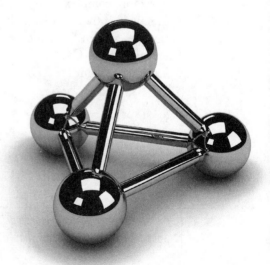

I n this chapter, we explore some of the flashy features of Reporting Services. These are the features that get us techies excited. If you do not say "Wow!" after seeing at least one of these features in the reports created in this chapter, then we (the developers at Microsoft and I) are not doing our jobs. Just to clarify, the "Wow!" does not need to be said out loud. Simply thinking "Wow!" in your head counts just as much.

Getting you to say, or think, "Wow!" is not ultimately the goal of the Microsoft developers who created Reporting Services or the goal of this author as he writes this chapter. The developers who create games for Microsoft can be satisfied with eliciting a "Wow!" from their clientele and consider it a job well done. The developers who create business intelligence tools for Microsoft have to aim a bit higher.

If you develop business intelligence tools, you need to go beyond the "Wow!" to the "Ah-ha!" The "Wow!" comes when you see a feature of a software product and think, "Wow! That is really cool!" The "Ah-ha!" comes when you see a feature of a software product and say, "Ah-ha! That is how we can make that report work just the way we need it to," or "Ah-ha! That is how we can turn that bit of data into meaningful business intelligence." Only when we hear the "Ah-ha!" can we be satisfied.

So, don't be shy when that moment comes along. When you get to that "Ah-ha!" feature you have been searching for, say it nice and loud. I want to hear it so I can go home happy.

Speaking in Code

One of the features of Reporting Services that gives it a tremendous amount of power and flexibility is its capability to speak in code—Visual Basic .NET code, that is. Valid Visual Basic .NET expressions can be used to control many of the properties of report items. They can even be used to control the query you are using to create your dataset.

For more complex tasks, you can embed whole Visual Basic .NET functions in your report. If that isn't enough, you can access methods from .NET assemblies. These assemblies are not limited to Visual Basic .NET. They can be written in any .NET language, such as C#.

Let's write some

```
-.-. --- -.. .
```

and have some

```
..-. ..- -.
```

NOTE

For those of you who may not be familiar with it, the previous sentence contains two words in Morse code. If you want to know what it says, do what I did: Look it up on the Internet.

The Delivery Status Report

Features Highlighted

▶ Using the label property of a parameter

▶ Using multiline headers and footers

▶ Using Visual Basic .NET expressions to control properties

▶ Specifying scope in aggregate functions

Business Need   The customer service department at Galactic Delivery Services (GDS) would like a report to check on the status of deliveries for a customer. The customer service representative should be able to select a customer and a year, and then see all the deliveries for that customer in that year. The hubs each package went through as it was in transit should be listed.

The status for packages that have been delivered should show up in green. The status for packages still en route should be blue. The status for packages that have been lost should be red. In case of a problem, the name and email address of the person to be contacted at that customer site should appear below the entry for each lost package.

Task Overview

1. Create the Chapter08 Project, a Shared Data Source, a New Report, and Two Datasets.
2. Set Up the Report Parameters and Place the Titles on the Report Layout.
3. Add a Tablix to the Report.
4. Add the Expressions.

Delivery Status Report, Task 1: Create the Chapter08 Project, a Shared Data Source, a New Report, and Two Datasets

1. Create a new Reporting Services project called Chapter08 in the MSSQLRS folder.
2. Create a shared data source called Galactic for the Galactic database.
3. Create a new report called DeliveryStatus using the GDSReport template.
4. Create a new data source called Galactic that references the Galactic shared data source.
5. Create a new dataset called DeliveryStatus that calls the stp_DeliveryStatus stored procedure.
6. Create a second dataset called Customers that uses the following query:

```
SELECT CustomerNumber, Name FROM Customer ORDER BY Name
```

Task Notes You probably noticed the instructions are a bit sketchy here. Now that you have reached the level of advanced report authoring, you can handle these basic tasks on your own. If you have any trouble with these steps, refer to the previous chapters for a refresher.

Delivery Status Report, Task 2: Set Up the Report Parameters and Place the Titles on the Report Layout

1. The stored procedure triggered the creation of two report parameters. Use the Report Data window to configure the properties of the CustomerNumber parameter as follows:

Property	Value
General page:	
Prompt	Customer
Available Values page:	
Select from one of the following options	Get values from a query
Dataset	Customers
Value field	CustomerNumber
Label field	Name

2. Click OK to exit the Report Parameters dialog box.

3. Use the Report Data window to configure the properties of the Year parameter as follows:

Property	Value
Available Values page:	
Select from one of the following options	Specify values
(Enter the values from the Available Values table that follows)	
Default Values page:	
Select from one of the following options	Specify values
(Enter the value from the Default Values table that follows)	

On the Available Values page, add the following rows to the grid at the bottom of the dialog box:

Label	Value
2007	2007
2008	2008
2009	2009

On the Default Values page, add the following row to the grid at the bottom of the dialog box:

Value
2008

4. Click OK to exit the Report Parameters dialog box.

5. Place a text box onto the body of the report. Modify the following properties of this text box:

Property	Value
Font: FontSize	16pt
Font: FontWeight	Bold
Location: Left	0in
Location: Top	0in
Size: Width	3.5in
Size: Height	0.375in
Value	="Delivery Status for " & Parameters!Year.Value

6. Place a second text box onto the body of the report. Modify the following properties of this text box:

Property	Value
Font: FontSize	16pt
Font: FontWeight	Bold
Location: Left	0in
Location: Top	0.375in
Size: Width	4.75in
Size: Height	0.375in

7. Right-click this text box and select Expression from the context menu. The Expression dialog box appears.

8. Select Parameters in the Category pane and double-click CustomerNumber in the Parameter pane.

9. Use the BACKSPACE key to remove the word "Value" at the end of the expression. (Do not delete the period.) You see a context menu showing you the available properties of the CustomerNumber parameter.

10. Double-click Label in the context menu.

11. Click OK to exit the Expression dialog box.

Task Notes We have two parameters for this report. The CustomerNumber parameter is selected from a drop-down list created by a dataset. The customer names are displayed in the drop-down list because Name was chosen as the Label field. However, the customer number is the value assigned to this parameter because CustomerNumber is chosen as the Value field. The Year parameter is selected from a drop-down list created by a static list of values we entered. The Label and Value are the same for each entry in this list.

The items placed on the report thus far were put there to provide a heading for the report and to indicate which parameters were selected to create the report. This is pretty straightforward for the Year parameter. All we need is a text box that displays the value of this parameter, with a little explanatory text thrown in for good measure.

The CustomerNumber parameter presents a bit of a problem, though. When we select a parameter in an expression, the value property of the parameter is selected by default. The value property of the CustomerNumber parameter contains the customer number of the selected customer. However, it makes more sense to the user if the customer's name is displayed at the top of the report. To accomplish this, we use the label property rather than the value property. The label property contains the text that appears in the parameter drop-down list for the selected item. In this case, the label property contains the customer's name.

Delivery Status Report, Task 3: Add a Tablix to the Report

1. Use the table template to add a tablix to the body of the report immediately below the text boxes.

2. In the leftmost cell in the data row of the tablix, select the Hub field from the DeliveryStatus dataset.

3. In each of the two remaining cells in the data row of the tablix, select the TimeIn and TimeOut fields.

4. Right-click anywhere in the data row and select Tablix: Add Group | Row Group: Parent Group from the context menu. The Tablix group dialog box appears.

5. Select [DeliveryNumber] from the Group by drop-down list. We are now grouping the information in the table by the values in the DeliveryNumber field.

6. Check the Add group header and Add group footer check boxes.

7. Click OK to exit the Tablix group dialog box.

8. A group header cell is added along the left side of the tablix. This cell contains a text box, which, in turn, contains the DeliveryNumber field. (Don't confuse this with the group header row across the top of the tablix.) Modify the following properties of the text box containing the DeliveryNumber field:

Property	Value
Font: FontWeight	Bold
TextAlign	Left

   Remember, you can set these text box properties using the Properties window or the toolbar buttons.

9. We need to move some of the labels in the table header row to the group header row. Select the text box that contains the word "Hub" (not the text box containing the field reference "[Hub]"). Do this by clicking once in this text box. If you can see a text-editing cursor blinking in this cell, you clicked too many times. If you see the blinking cursor, click elsewhere, and then try again.

10. Press CTRL-X to cut the text box from this table header cell. Click in the group header cell immediately below it and press CTRL-V to paste the text box there.

11. Repeat this for the text boxes containing Time In and Time Out.

12. Right-click the gray square to the left of the table header row. (This row now only contains the text "Group1.") Select Delete Rows from the context menu. This removes the table header row from this table.

13. Right-click anywhere in the group header row and select Tablix: Insert Row | Inside Group - Above from the context menu. An additional group header row appears. This is not a new grouping, but rather, an additional row for the current grouping.

14. Select the ServiceType field in the leftmost cell in the new group header row.

15. Select the StatusName field in the next cell in the new group header row.

16. Right-click anywhere in the new group header row and select Tablix: Insert Row | Inside Group - Above from the context menu. Another new group header row appears.

17. Double-click the leftmost cell in the new group header row and type **Pickup:**.

18. Select the PickupPlanet field in the next cell to the right in the new group header row.

19. Select the PickupDateTime field in the rightmost cell in the new group header row.

20. Double-click in the group footer cell below the [Hub] field and type **Delivery:**.

21. Select the DeliveryPlanet field in the next cell to the right in the group footer row.

22. Select the DeliveryDateTime field in the rightmost cell in the group footer row.

23. Right-click anywhere in the group footer row and select Tablix: Insert Row | Inside Group - Below from the context menu. A new group footer row appears.

24. Double-click in the group footer cell below Delivery and type **Problem Contact:**.

25. Select the ProblemContact field in the next cell to the right in the new group footer row.

26. Select the ProblemEMail field in the rightmost cell in the new group footer row.

27. Right-click anywhere in the new group footer row and select Tablix: Insert Row | Inside Group - Below from the context menu. A new group footer row appears. This row is left blank.

28. Click in the leftmost cell of the top group header row and hold down the mouse button. Drag the mouse to the rightmost cell of the bottom group header row and release the mouse button. You have selected the nine cells in the three group header rows.

29. Modify the following property for these cells:

Property	Value
Font: FontWeight	Bold

30. Repeat Steps 28 and 29 for the six cells in the two group footer rows.

31. Click in the rightmost cell of the top group header row and hold down the mouse button. Drag the mouse to the lower-left corner of the tablix and release the mouse button. You have selected all of the cells in the tablix.

32. Modify the following properties for these cells:

Property	Value
BorderColor	Black
BorderStyle	None

33. Click the gray box in the upper-left corner of the tablix to select the entire tablix. Use the sizing handle on the right side of the tablix to make it as wide as the design surface. Your report layout should appear similar to Figure 8-1.

34. Click the Preview tab. Select Bolimite, Mfg from the Customer drop-down list. Select 2008 from the Year drop-down list. (The year 2008 is already selected for you because you set it up as the default value for the Year parameter.) Click View Report.

35. You may want to return to the Design tab and adjust the size of some of the columns so the data does not wrap within text boxes. Hint: The DeliveryNumber column can be made narrow in order to gain space for some of the other columns. After making size adjustments, your report should appear similar to Figure 8-2.

Figure 8-1 *The Delivery Status Report layout after Task 3*

Task Notes The default behavior for the tablix is to create a light gray border around all of the cells. In our previous reports, we have stuck with that behavior. For this report, we are going to deviate from that approach and not have any border around most cells. The approach you use for your report authoring depends on the preference of you and your report users. What is appropriate and looks the best will probably vary from report to report.

We were able to add rows to both the group header and footer. This let us create more complex group header and footer layouts. In the same fashion, you can add rows to the table header, table footer, or data lines, as needed.

We now have the proper layout for our report, but we do not have the proper behavior of some of the report items. The delivery status is supposed to appear in color. The problem contact information is only supposed to be displayed with lost deliveries. Some additional formatting lines would also make the report more readable. All of this is accomplished in the next task with the aid of expressions.

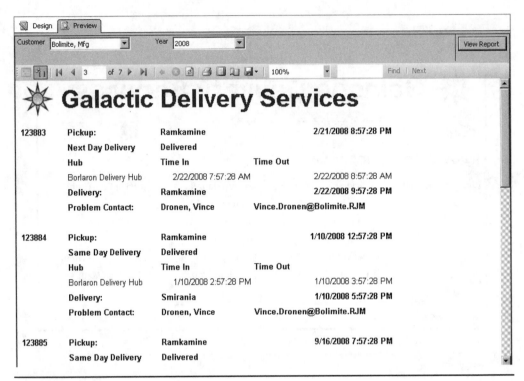

Figure 8-2   *The Delivery Status Report preview after Task 3*

Delivery Status Report, Task 4: Add the Expressions

1. Click the Design tab.
2. Select the entire tablix, if it is not selected already. Modify the following properties of the tablix:

Property	Value
BorderStyle: Top	Double
BorderStyle: Bottom	Double
BorderWidth	6pt

3. Enter the following expression for the Color property of the cell containing the StatusName field:

```
= IIF(Fields!StatusName.Value = "Delivered", "Green",
      IIF(Fields!StatusName.Value = "In Route", "Blue", "Red"))
```

NOTE

When entering each of the expressions, you probably want to select <Expression…> from the drop-down list for the property and enter this expression in the Expression dialog box. Also, remember the Expression dialog box offers help for finding the correct function and for inserting fields and parameters. Expressions involving the Globals, Parameters, and Fields collections are case-sensitive.

4. Click the gray square to the left of the top group header row so the entire row is selected. Modify the following properties for these cells:

Property	Value
BorderStyle: Top	=IIF(Fields!DeliveryNumber.Value = First(Fields!DeliveryNumber.Value, "DeliveryStatus"), "None", "Solid")
BorderWidth: Top	4pt

5. Click and hold down the left mouse button in the cell containing the word "Hub." Continue to hold down the left mouse button and drag the cursor through the Time In cell to the Time Out cell. All three cells should now be selected. Modify the following property for these cells:

Property	Value
BorderStyle: Bottom	Solid

6. Select the following three cells using the same method as in Step 5: "Delivery:", "[DeliveryPlanet]", "[DeliveryDateTime]". Modify the following properties for these cells:

Property	Value
BorderStyle: Top	Solid
BorderStyle: Bottom	= IIF(Fields!StatusName.Value = "Lost", "None", "Solid")
BorderWidth: Bottom	2pt

NOTE

"StatusName" is case-sensitive in this expression.

7. Select the following three cells: "Problem Contact:", "[ProblemContact]",
   "[ProblemEmail]". Modify the following properties for these cells:

Property	Value
BorderStyle: Bottom	= IIF(Fields!StatusName.Value <> "Lost", "None", "Solid")
BorderWidth: Bottom	2pt
Hidden	= IIF(Fields!StatusName.Value = "Lost", false, true)

8. Click the Preview tab. Select Bolimite, Mfg from the Customer drop-down list
   and 2008 from the Year drop-down list, if they are not already selected. Click
   View Report. Your report should appear similar to Figure 8-3.

9. Select Save All on the toolbar.

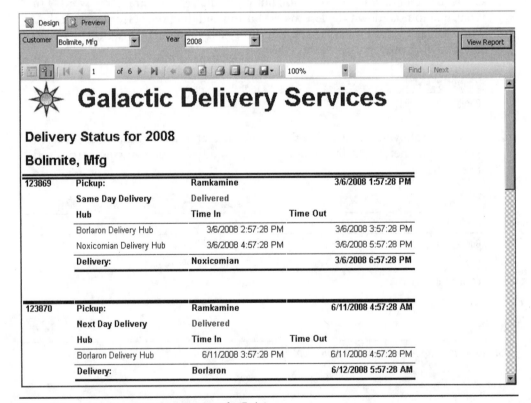

Figure 8-3 *The Delivery Status Report preview after Task 4*

Task Notes   If you scroll through the pages of the report, you see the report now meets the business needs specified. Let's look at what each expression is doing. The expression entered in Step 3 returns green when the status is Delivered, and blue when the status is In Route. Otherwise, it returns red.

The expression in Step 4 is a bit more complex. It checks whether the current value of the DeliveryNumber field is equal to the first value of the DeliveryNumber field in the DeliveryStatus dataset. As you saw in Chapter 7, aggregate functions act within a scope. By default, the First() aggregate function would return the value for the first record in the current scope. Because this expression is in the group header, by default, it would return the value for the first record in each group.

However, in this expression, the First() aggregate function includes a second parameter that specifies the scope it should use. This parameter specifies that the First() aggregate function should use the scope of the entire DeliveryStatus dataset rather than just the current group. Therefore, it returns the first record in the dataset. When the current delivery number is equal to the first delivery number in the dataset, no border is created across the top of these text boxes. This prevents the border across the top of the text boxes from interfering with the border across the top of the tablix. When the current delivery number is not equal to the first delivery number in the dataset, a border is created across the top of the text boxes.

The expression in Step 6 and the first expression in Step 7 use the value of the StatusName field to control the border across the bottom of each grouping. If the problem contact text boxes are displayed, the border should appear across the bottom of these text boxes. However, if the problem contact text boxes are not displayed, the border should appear across the bottom of the text boxes in the row above. The second expression in Step 7 controls whether the text boxes containing the problem contact are displayed. This is also based on the value of the StatusName field.

As you can see, expressions can be useful when the formatting, or even the visibility, of a report item needs to change depending on some condition in the report. Expressions can also be used to calculate the values to appear in a text box, as you see in the next report.

The Lost Delivery Report

Features Highlighted

▶   Using Visual Basic .NET expressions to calculate values in a text box

▶   Adding static columns to a tablix functioning as a matrix

▶   Adding totals to a tablix functioning as a matrix

Business Need The quality assurance department at Galactic Delivery Services would like a report to help them analyze the packages lost during delivery. The report should show the number of packages lost each year at each processing hub. It should break down these numbers by the cause for each loss. It should also show the number of losses by cause as a percentage of the total number of packages lost for each hub.

Task Overview
1. Create a New Report, Create a Dataset, and Add a Tablix to the Report.
2. Add a Calculated Column to the Tablix.
3. Add Totals to the Tablix.

Lost Delivery Report, Task 1: Create a New Report, Create a Dataset, and Add a Tablix to the Report
1. Reopen the Chapter08 project, if it was closed.
2. Create a new report called LostDelivery using the GDSReport template.
3. Create a new data source called Galactic that references the Galactic shared data source.
4. Create a new dataset called LostDelivery that calls the stp_LostDeliveries stored procedure.
5. Use the matrix template to place a tablix onto the body of the report. Select the DeliveryNumber field in the Data cell. Use the Expression dialog box to edit the aggregate function in the resulting expression by changing it from Sum to Count.
6. Select the Cause field in the Rows cell. Select the Hub field in the Columns cell.
7. Click in the upper-left cell of the tablix. Hold down the mouse button and drag the mouse pointer to the lower-right cell. All four cells in the tablix should be selected.
8. Modify the following properties of the selected cells:

Property	Value
BorderColor	Black
BorderStyle	None

9. Click outside of the tablix to unselect the cells.
10. Right-click the Hub cell and select Tablix: Add Group | Column Group | Parent Group. The Tablix group dialog box appears.

11. Click the Expression (*fx*) button. The Expression dialog box appears.

12. Type the following in the Set expression for: GroupExpression area to group the values by year:

```
=Year(Fields!PickupDateTime.Value)
```

13. Click OK to exit the Expression dialog box.

14. Click OK to exit the Tablix group dialog box.

15. Select the empty cell in the upper-left corner of the tablix. Hold down the SHIFT key and click the cell immediately below it. Right-click in this same cell and select Tablix: Merge Cells from the context menu.

16. Modify the following properties of the text box in the merged cell you just created:

Property	Value
BackgroundColor	LightGray
Font: FontSize	18pt
Font: FontWeight	Bold
Size: Width	2in
Size: Height	0.75in
Value	Lost Deliveries by Cause

17. Modify the following property of the text box in the lower-left corner of the tablix:

Property	Value
BackgroundColor	LightGray

18. Modify the following properties of the text box in the upper-right corner of the tablix:

Property	Value
BackgroundColor	LightGray
BorderStyle: Left	Solid
Font: FontSize	14pt
Font: FontWeight	Bold
TextAlign	Center

19. Modify the following properties of the text box in the center of the right-hand column of the tablix:

Property	Value
BackgroundColor	Light Gray
BorderStyle: Left	Solid
BorderStyle: Bottom	Solid
Font: FontWeight	Bold
TextAlign	Center

20. Modify the following property of the text box in the lower-right corner of the matrix:

Property	Value
BorderStyle: Left	Solid

Task Notes   So far, we have a fairly straightforward matrix report. Let's see what happens when we add another column and totals to the matrix.

Lost Delivery Report, Task 2: Add a Calculated Column to the Tablix

1. Right-click the text box in the lower-right corner of the matrix and select Tablix: Insert Column | Inside Group - Right from the context menu. A new column is created inside of the Hub group.

2. Right-click the same text box and select Tablix: Insert Row | Outside Group - Above from the context menu. A new row appears above the Cause group.

3. Modify the following properties of the new text box in the lower-right corner of the tablix:

Property	Value
BorderStyle: Left	Solid
Format	##0.00%
TextAlign	Right
Value	=Count(Fields!DeliveryNumber.Value)/ Count(Fields!DeliveryNumber.Value, "Hub")

4. Modify the following properties of the text box immediately above the text box modified in Step 3:

Property	Value
BorderStyle: Left	Solid
Font: FontWeight	Normal
Font: TextDecoration	Underline
TextAlign	Right
Value	% of Column

5. Modify the following properties of the text box immediately to the left of the text box modified in Step 4:

Property	Value
BorderStyle: Left	Solid
Font: TextDecoration	Underline
TextAlign	Right
Value	# Lost

6. Your report layout should appear similar to Figure 8-4.
7. Click the Preview tab. Your report should appear similar to Figure 8-5.

Task Notes   In the previous report, we created a multirow group header and a multirow group footer. In this report, we created a multicolumn detail section. We did this by adding a second column inside of the column groupings. We also created headings for our columns by adding a new row outside of the row grouping. We want one set of columns for each column grouping. However, we only want one set of headings at the top of each row group.

The row containing the column headings is a static row in the tablix. We took our first look at static rows and columns in Chapter 7. Here they are, back again, to help us do more creative formatting within our tablix. In Task 3 of this report, we will use an additional static row and a static column to provide totals in our tablix.

Our new column takes the count from the current row and calculates it as a percentage of the total for the column. This is done, once again, through the magic of scope. The first Count() aggregate function does not have a scope parameter, so it defaults to the scope of the current cell. In other words, it counts the number of lost deliveries in the current cell.

The second Count() aggregate function has a scope parameter of Hub. This is the name of the column group that creates the column for each hub. Therefore, this aggregate function counts the number of lost deliveries in the entire column. We then divide and use the ###.00% format string to create a percentage.

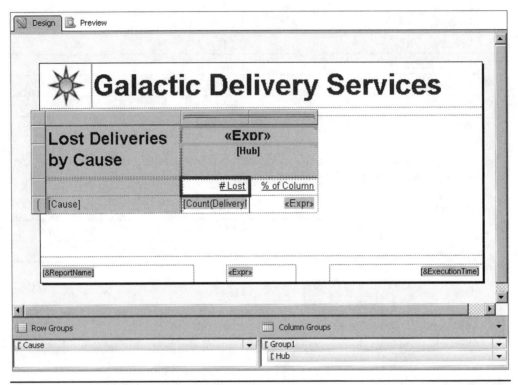

Figure 8-4 *The Lost Delivery Report layout after Task 2*

Lost Delivery Report, Task 3: Add Totals to the Tablix

1. Click the Design tab.
2. Right-click the text box in the lower-left corner of the matrix and select Tablix: Add Total | After from the context menu. A total row is added at the bottom of the tablix.

NOTE

The Report Designer was nice enough to put the word "Total" in this column row for us, but it did not create the total expression for each of the data columns. We will have to do that ourselves.

3. Modify the following properties of the text box containing the word "Total":

Property	Value
BorderStyle: Top	Solid
BorderWidth	2pt

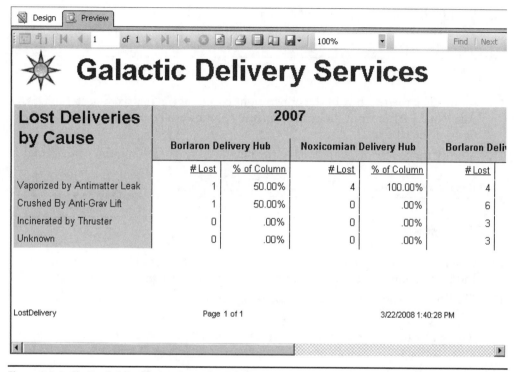

Figure 8-5   *The Lost Delivery Report preview after Task 2*

4. Select the text box immediately below the cell containing "# Lost." Press CTRL-C to copy this text box.

5. Click in the cell immediately below the text box you just copied. Press CTRL-V to paste a copy of the text box into this cell.

6. Modify the following property of the text box you just pasted into the cell:

Property	Value
BorderStyle: Top	Solid

7. Select the text box immediately below the cell containing "% of Column." Press CTRL-C to copy this text box.

8. Click in the cell immediately below the text box you just copied. Press CTRL-V to paste a copy of the text box into this cell.

9. Modify the following property of the text box you just pasted into the cell:

Property	Value
BorderStyle: Top	Solid

10. Right-click the text box in the upper-right corner of the matrix. Select Tablix: Add Total | After from the context menu. A set of total columns is added at the right of the tablix.

11. Modify the following properties of the new text box containing the word "Total":

Property	Value
BorderStyle: Left	Solid
BorderStyle: Bottom	Solid

12. One by one, copy each of the six cells with a white background that contain text and paste them into their corresponding positions in the new total area.

13. Modify the expression in each of the two % of Column cells in the total area to the following:

```
=Count(Fields!DeliveryNumber.Value)/ Count(Fields!DeliveryNumber.Value,
                              "LostDelivery")
```

The change is the scope parameter in the second Count() aggregate function.

14. When completed, your report layout should appear similar to Figure 8-6.
15. Click the Preview tab. Your report should appear similar to Figure 8-7.
16. Select Save All on the toolbar.

Task Notes   Adding totals to our report involves creating additional static rows and columns in our tablix. We first added a total row at the bottom of the tablix. The cells in this total row are inside of the column groupings on year and hub, but outside of the row grouping on repair cause. Therefore, these cells give us the totals for all hub across all of the repair causes as we expect. The second set of totals we added are inside of the row grouping on repair cause, but outside of the column groupings on hub and year. These cells give us the totals for a repair cause across all hubs and years. The two cells in the lower-right corner of the tablix are outside of all column and row groupings, so they provide totals for the entire tablix.

We had to use a different scope for the totals in the rightmost columns because, as we just said, these columns are outside of the hub grouping. An aggregate function must be inside of a scope in order for it to be used as the scope parameter. Instead of using the hub grouping, we use the scope of the entire LostDelivery dataset to create these totals.

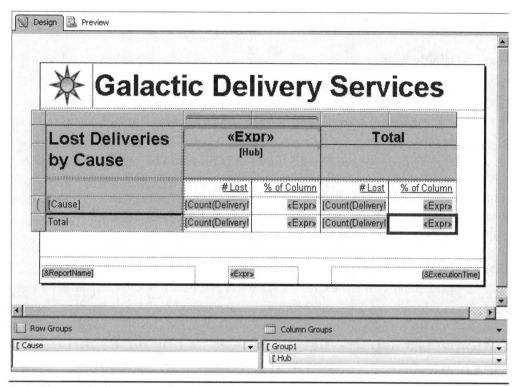

Figure 8-6   *The Lost Delivery Report layout after Task 3*

Lost Deliveries by Cause	2007				2008				Total	
	Borlaron Delivery Hub		Noxicomian Delivery Hub		Borlaron Delivery Hub		Noxicomian Delivery Hub			
	# Lost	% of Column	# Lost	% of Column	# Lost	% of Column	# Lost	% of Column	# Lost	% of Column
Vaporized by Antimatter Leak	1	50.00%	4	100.00%	4	25.00%	5	83.33%	14	50.00%
Crushed By Anti-Grav Lift	1	50.00%	0	.00%	6	37.50%	1	16.67%	8	28.57%
Incinerated by Thruster	0	.00%	0	.00%	3	18.75%	0	.00%	3	10.71%
Unknown	0	.00%	0	.00%	3	18.75%	0	.00%	3	10.71%
Total	2	100.00%	4	100.00%	16	100.00%	6	100.00%	28	100.00%

LostDelivery   Page 1 of 1   3/22/2008 2:51:15 PM

Figure 8-7   *The Lost Delivery Report preview after Task 3*

The Customer List Report—Revisited

Features Highlighted

▶   Copying a report between projects

▶   Using Visual Basic .NET expressions to specify a dataset query

Business Need   The Customer List Report you developed for the Galactic Delivery Services accounting department (in Chapter 4) has proved to be popular. Several other departments would like similar reports to help them track their own lists of email contacts. Rather than create separate reports for each department, which would be hard to maintain, the IT manager has asked for one report that enables the user to select which type of contact they want to view.

Task Overview

1.   Copy the Report from the Chapter04 Project and Add It to the Chapter08 Project.
2.   Add a Report Parameter and Modify the Dataset to Use the Report Parameter.

Customer List Report—Revisited, Task 1: Copy the Report from the Chapter04 Project and Add It to the Chapter08 Project

1.   Use Windows Explorer to copy the report definition file for the Customer List Report (Customer List.rdl) from the Chapter04 project folder and paste it in the Chapter08 project folder. Both of these folders should be found under My Documents in the Visual Studio 2008\Projects\MSSQLRS folder.
2.   In Report Designer, reopen the Chapter08 project, if it was closed.
3.   Right-click the Reports folder in the Solution Explorer and select Add | Existing Item from the context menu. The Add Existing Item–Chapter08 dialog box appears.
4.   Make sure you are looking at the Chapter08 folder in the dialog box and select the Customer List.rdl file. Click Add to exit the Add Existing Item–Chapter08 dialog box.
5.   Double-click the Customer List.rdl entry in the Solution Explorer to open the report definition.
6.   Click the Preview tab to show this report is functioning properly in the Chapter08 project.

Task Notes   Because the entire definition of a report is contained within a single Report Definition Language (RDL) file, it is easy to copy reports to different locations. As you saw here, we can even add them to a project other than the project within which they were originally created. The Customer List Report uses a shared data source called Galactic. We did not need to copy the shared data source, because we already have a shared data source with the same name and the same properties in the Chapter08 project. If this was not the case, we could have copied the shared data source file (Galactic.rds), along with the report file and added that to our new project as well.

Customer List Report—Revisited, Task 2: Add a Report Parameter and Modify the Dataset to Use the Report Parameter

1. Click the Design tab.
2. Right-click the Parameters item in the Report Data window. Select Add Parameter from the context menu. The Report Parameter Properties dialog box appears.
3. Modify the properties for this new report parameter as follows:

Property	Value
General page:	
Name	ListType
Prompt	Select a List
Available Values page:	
Select from one of the following options:	Specify values
(Enter the values from the Available Values table that follows)	

On the Available Values page, add the following rows to the grid at the bottom of the dialog box:

Label	Value
Billing Contacts	B
Manufacturer Contacts	M
Problem Contacts	P

4. Click OK to exit the Report Parameter Properties dialog box.
5. In the Report Data window, right-click the entry for the DataSet1 and select Query from the context menu. The Query Designer window opens, with the Graphical Query Designer displayed.
6. Click Edit As Text in the toolbar to switch to the Generic Query Designer.

7. Replace the entire select statement with the following expression:

```
=IIF(Parameters!ListType.Value="B", "EXEC stp_BillingContacts",
    IIF(Parameters!ListType.Value="M",
        "EXEC stp_ManufacturerContacts",
        "EXEC stp_ProblemContacts"))
```

CAUTION

If you use this method to build a SQL statement by concatenating parameter values into the query text, you must take care to guard against query injection attacks on your SQL server.

8. Click OK to exit the Query Designer window. You may receive an error message indicating the query cannot be parsed. Ignore this error message and click OK to continue.

9. In the Report Data window, right-click the entry for the DataSet1 and select Dataset Properties from the context menu. The Dataset Properties dialog box appears. Note, the only way to edit our query expression now is to click the expression (*fx*) button next to the Query area on this dialog box.

10. Select the Fields page.

11. Change the table on the Fields page to match the following:

Field Name	Field Source
Name	Name
Contact	Contact
Email	Email

12. Click OK to exit the Dataset Properties dialog box.

13. In the text box that currently says "[BillingContact]," select the Contact field using the Field Selector.

14. Double-click the table header cell directly above the text box from Step 13 and change the text to **Contact**.

15. In the text box that currently says "[BillingEmail]," select the Email field using the Field Selector.

16. Double-click the table header cell directly above the text box from Step 15 and change the text to **Email**.

17. Select Save All on the toolbar.

18. Click the Preview tab. Try selecting each of the list types. Remember to click View Report each time after changing your parameter selection.

NOTE

The database does not contain a contact name for each manufacturer, so no contact names are in the manufacturer list.

Task Notes   Rather than specifying the query in the Generic Query Designer, we used an expression to choose among three possible queries (in this case, three stored procedure calls). This is known as a *dynamic query*. The name comes from the fact that the query that is run depends on input from the user at the time the report is run.

Because the content of the query is not known until run time, the Report Designer cannot "pre-run" the query to determine the fields that will result. Instead, we need to manually specify the fields that will result from our dynamic query. All the possible queries that could be run must return result sets with the same field names for your report to work properly.

At this point, you may be ready to suggest two or three alternative approaches to creating this report. It is certainly not unusual to come up with a number of possible ways to meet the business needs of a report. When this happens, use the following criteria to evaluate the possible solutions:

▶   Efficiency of operation

▶   Your comfort with implementing and debugging a given solution in a reasonable amount of time

▶   Maintainability

▶   Your need to illustrate a certain point in a book chapter

Well, maybe that last point won't apply to you, but it was, in fact, the overriding reason for choosing this approach for this particular report.

Payroll Checks

Features Highlighted

▶   Using Visual Basic .NET functions embedded in the report to create reusable code

▶   Using a stored procedure that updates data

▶   Grouping in the details row of a data region

▶   Using nested data regions

Business Need   The Galactic Delivery Services accounting department needs a report to print payroll checks for its hourly employees. The checks should have the check portion in the top one-third of the page and the check register in the bottom two-thirds of the page. The check register should list the work hours included in this check. The user should be able to select a week for which unpaid time is entered and receive the payroll checks for that week. The planetary system tax amount (25 percent) and state tax amount (5 percent) must be deducted from the amount being paid.

Task Overview

1. Create a New Report, Create Two Datasets, Add a Tablix to the Report Layout, and Populate It.
2. Add a Second Tablix to the Report Layout and Populate It.
3. Configure the Report Parameter and Add Embedded Code to the Report.

Payroll Checks, Task 1: Create a New Report, Create Two Datasets, Add a Tablix to the Report Layout, and Populate It

1. Reopen the Chapter08 project, if it was closed.
2. Create a new report called PayrollChecks. Do *not* use the GDSReport template.
3. Create a new data source called Galactic that references the Galactic shared data source.
4. Create a new dataset called PayrollChecks that calls the stp_PayrollChecks stored procedure.
5. Create a new dataset called WeekNumbers that calls the stp_WeekNumbers stored procedure.
6. Use the list template to place a tablix onto the body of the report. Modify the following properties of this tablix in the Properties window:

Property	Value
BackgroundColor	LightGreen
BorderStyle	Solid
DataSetName	PayrollChecks
PageBreak	Start

7. In the Row Group pane, select Group Properties from the (Details) drop-down menu. The Group Properties dialog box appears.
8. On the General page, click Add to add an item to the group expression.
9. Select [PayrollCheckNumber] from the Group on drop-down list.

10. Click OK to exit the Group Properties dialog box.

11. Add text boxes to the list to get the layout shown in Figure 8-8. Make sure the list is selected each time before you drag a field or text box onto it. Remember, the square brackets around an item indicate that a field is being displayed in that text box. You can create text boxes containing fields by dragging the fields from the Report Data window. You can create a text box containing a constant string by dragging a text box from the Toolbox and typing the constant string in the new text box. Enlarge the report body and the tablix, if necessary.

12. Click the text box containing the PayrollCheckNumber field to select it. Right-click the text box and select Expression from the context menu. The Expression dialog box appears.

13. Remove the Sum() aggregate function so the expression is as follows:

    ```
    =Fields!PayrollCheckNumber.Value
    ```

14. Click OK to exit the Expression dialog box.

15. Right-click the text box containing the LineAmount field and select Textbox Properties from the context menu. The Text Box Properties dialog box appears.

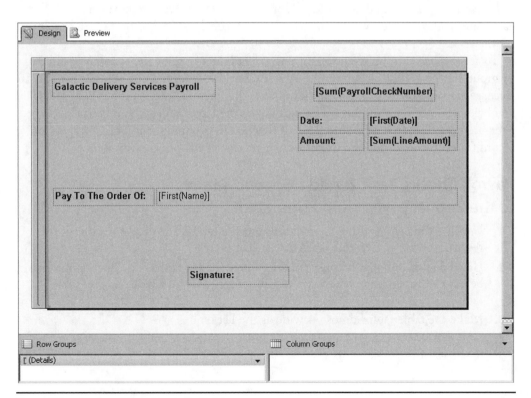

Figure 8-8   *The Payroll Check layout after Task 1*

16.   Modify the following properties of this text box:

Property	Value
Number page:	
Category	Currency
Use 1000 separator check box	checked

17.   Click OK to exit the Text Box Properties dialog box.

Task Notes   Our payroll check has two separate parts: the check itself and the check register. The check register contains a line showing the amount paid for each day worked during the selected workweek. The *check* is essentially a summary of the information in the check register. The *check amount* is the sum of the amount to be paid for all the days worked.

We could use two different datasets to provide data to these two areas. To be a little more efficient with our database resources, however, we are going to use a single dataset. The dataset includes all the detail information required by the check register. It is going to have one row for each date worked. However, we do not want to create a check for each date worked. We only want one check for all the days worked by a given employee in the week.

To accomplish this, we need to group the detail data to print the check. We did this by grouping the DetailsGroup on the PayrollCheckNumber field in Steps 7 through 10. Because we want one check per check number, the PayrollCheckNumber field seems an obvious choice for grouping. (The number in the PayrollCheckNumber field is generated by the stored procedure.) With this details grouping, our tablix receives one record for each check number; therefore, we get one check per check number.

Payroll Checks, Task 2: Add a Second Tablix to the Report Layout and Populate It

1.   Increase the height of the report body and the tablix. For the remainder of the report, we will refer to this tablix as the "list tablix."

2.   Use the table template to place a tablix *inside* the list tablix. The new tablix should be below the signature text box. We will refer to this new tablix as the "table tablix."

3.   Make the table tablix almost as wide as the list tablix.

4.   Select the WorkDate, HoursWorked, and LineAmount fields in the cells in the data row of the table tablix.

5. Right-click anywhere in the lower row of the table tablix and select Tablix: Insert Row | Outside Group - Below from the context menu. This new row will serve as a total row.

6. Select the LineAmount field in the rightmost cell of the row we just added to the table tablix. Set the following properties for the text box in this cell:

Property	Value
BorderColor: Top	Black
Format	C

7. Set the following property for the text box in the cell immediately above the cell modified in Step 6:

Property	Value
Format	C

NOTE

Entering C for the Format property is the same as selecting Currency in the Text Box Properties dialog box.

8. Set the following properties for the table tablix:

Property	Value
BackgroundColor	White
PageBreak	End

9. Drag the bottom of the list tablix and the bottom of the report body up so they are the same as the bottom of the table tablix. Your report layout appears similar to Figure 8-9.

Task Notes   In Task 1, we created a tablix from a list template with a detail grouping to create the check portion of our payroll checks. In Task 2, we created a tablix from a table template to provide the detail information for the check register. The table tablix data region must be nested inside of the list tablix data region so that we get one set of detail information for each check. If the table was placed below the list, we would get all the checks first and then all the check register information at the end.

The PageBreak property was set to End on the table tablix, so there is a page break immediately after the table. This keeps our output to one check per page.

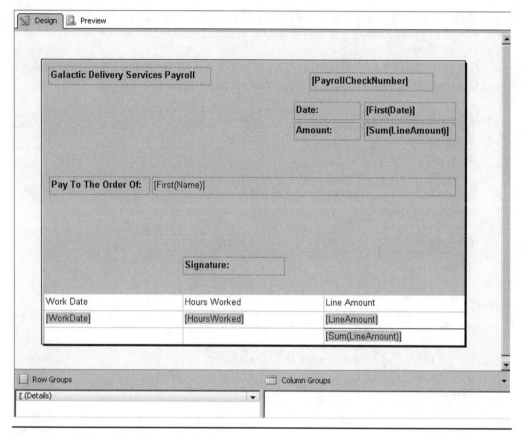

Figure 8-9 *The Payroll Check layout after Task 2*

Payroll Checks, Task 3: Configure the Report Parameter and Add Embedded Code to the Report

1. Expand the Parameters entry in the Report Data window.
2. Right-click the WeekNumber entry and select Parameter Properties from the context menu. The Report Parameter Properties dialog box appears.
3. Modify the following properties for the WeekNumber parameter:

Property	Value
Available Values page:	
Select from one of the following options:	Get values from a query
Dataset	WeekNumbers
Value field	WeekNumber
Label field	WeekNumber

4. Click OK to exit the Report Parameter Properties dialog box.

5. Click anywhere on the report layout to activate the Report menu.

6. Select Report | Report Properties to open the Report Properties dialog box.

7. Select the Code page.

8. Enter the following in the Custom code area:

```
' State and Planetary System Tax Deductions
Public Function TaxDeductions(ByVal Amount As Double) As Double
        ' Planetary System Tax = 25%
        ' State Tax = 5%
        TaxDeductions = Amount * .25 + Amount * .05
End Function
```

9. Click OK to exit the Report Properties dialog box.

10. Right-click the text box in the list tablix (but not in the table tablix) containing the [Sum(LineAmount)] value and select Expression from the context menu. The Expression dialog box appears.

11. Replace the contents of the Set expression for: Value area with the following:

```
=Sum(Fields!LineAmount.Value) -
      Code.TaxDeductions(Sum(Fields!LineAmount.Value))
```

Ignore the red line under "TaxDeductions" indicating a syntax error.

12. Click OK to exit the Expression dialog box.

13. Repeat Steps 10 through 12, with the text box in the table tablix containing the sum of the LineAmount values.

14. Right-click the text box in the details row of the table tablix containing the LineAmount field and select Expression from the context menu. The Expression dialog box appears.

15. Replace the contents of the Set expression for: Value area with the following:

```
=Fields!LineAmount.Value - Code.TaxDeductions(Fields!LineAmount.Value)
```

16. Click OK to exit the Expression dialog box.

17. Click the Preview tab.

18. Select 10-2009 from the Week Number drop-down list and click View Report. Your report should appear similar to Figure 8-10. Remember, once checks have been run for a given week, you cannot produce checks for that week again. Each time you enter the report, the Week Number drop-down list only contains entries for weeks that have not been run. (The check number you see on the first page in your preview may be different from the check number shown in the figure. This is normal.)

19. Select Save All on the toolbar.

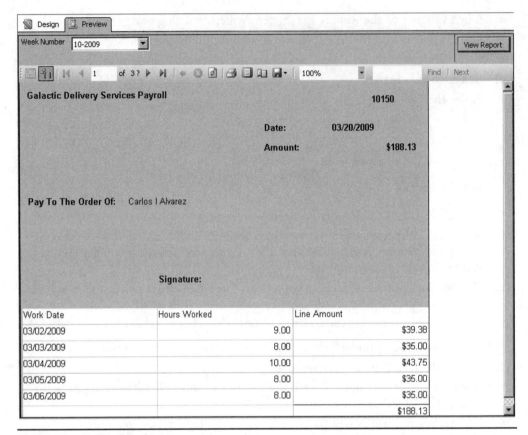

Figure 8-10   *The Payroll Check preview*

Task Notes   Payroll tax calculations are straightforward on the planets where Galactic Delivery Services operates. Everyone pays 25 percent of their pay to the planetary system government and 5 percent of their pay to the state government. Even though this is a simple formula, we need to use it in three different places. Using the embedded code feature of Reporting Services, we are able to put this formula in one location and use it in several locations. This also makes things easier to change when one or the other of these tax rates is increased.

We created a function called TaxDeductions on the Code page in the Report Properties dialog box. This is simply a valid Visual Basic .NET function definition. We access this function by using the key word "Code" followed by a period and the name of the function. You can see this in the expression we entered in Step 11.

The Weather Report

Features Highlighted

▶ Referencing .NET assemblies in the report

▶ Using a multivalued parameter

Business Need The Galactic Delivery Services flight control department needs a way to quickly list the current weather conditions at selected planets served by GDS. (After all, space transports have to go through the atmosphere to take off and land.) One of the GDS programmers has created a .NET assembly that uses a web service to get the weather from various locations. The user should be able to select one or more planets from a list and see the weather for all selected planets. A call must be made to a method of the .NET assembly for each of the selected planets and the results must be incorporated into the report.

Task Overview

1. Copy the .NET Assembly into the Appropriate Location, Create a New Report, and Create a Reference to the Assembly.
2. Create a Dataset, Add a Tablix to the Report Layout, and Populate It.

Weather Report, Task 1: Copy the .NET Assembly into the Appropriate Location, Create a New Report, and Create a Reference to the Assembly

1. If you have not already done so, download the WeatherInfo.dll assembly from the website for this book.
2. Copy this file to the Report Designer folder. The default path for the Report Designer folder is

   ```
   C:\Program Files\Microsoft Visual Studio 9.0\Common7\IDE\PublicAssemblies
   ```

3. We need to make some additions to the Report Builder's security configuration to provide our custom assembly with the rights it needs to execute. The security configuration for the Report Builder is in the RSPreviewPolicy.configfile. The default path for this file is

   ```
   C:\Program Files\Microsoft Visual Studio 9.0\Common7\IDE\
   PrivateAssemblies
   ```

   This file contains the code-access security information in an Extensible Markup Language (XML) structure. We will talk more about code-access security in Chapter 10.

CAUTION

Make a backup copy of the RSPreviewPolicy.config file before making any modifications to it. If you accidentally create an invalid XML structure or otherwise cause a problem with the security configuration, the report server cannot execute any reports.

4. Open the RSPreviewPolicy.config file in Notepad or another text editor.

5. The XML structure in the RSPreviewPolicy.config file can be divided into three sections: Security Classes, Named Permission Sets, and Code Groups. We only need to make changes to the Code Groups section of the document. Scroll down until you locate the Code Group portion of the document. The Code Group portion of the document starts on the line after the closing XML tag for the named permission sets:

```
</NamedPermissionSets>
```

6. The first code group is the parent code group, which makes use of the AllMembershipCondition to assign the Nothing permission to all .NET assemblies and web services. We add a new child code group right beneath this. Insert this new code group as shown. (Add the lines shown in bold.) Alternatively, you can copy the text to be inserted from the "First Code-Access Security Insert.txt" file in the Code Access Modifications folder included with the download materials for this book.

```
   .
   .
   .
<CodeGroup
        class="FirstMatchCodeGroup"
        version="1"
        PermissionSetName="Nothing">
    <IMembershipCondition
            class="AllMembershipCondition"
            version="1"
    />
    <CodeGroup
            class="UnionCodeGroup"
            version="1"
            PermissionSetName="Execution"
            Name="WeatherWebServiceCodeGroup"
            Description="Code group for the Weather Web Service">
        <IMembershipCondition class="UrlMembershipCondition"
                version="1"
                Url="http://live.capescience.com/*"
        />
    </CodeGroup>
    <CodeGroup
        class="UnionCodeGroup"
        version="1"
        PermissionSetName="Execution"
        Name="Report_Expressions_Default_Permissions"
```

```
Description="This code group grants default permissions for
            code in report expressions and Code element. ">
```

.
.
.

7. Another parent code group uses ZoneMembershipCondition to assign Execution permissions to all .NET assemblies and web services in the MyComputer zone. We add a new child code group right beneath this. Insert this new code group as shown. (Add the lines shown in bold.) Note, the Description and PublicKeyBlob should each be entered on one line. Alternatively, you can copy the text to be inserted from the "Second Code-Access Security Insert.txt" file included with the download materials for this book.

.
.
.

```
<CodeGroup
      class="FirstMatchCodeGroup"
      version="1"
      PermissionSetName="Execution"
      Description="This code group grants MyComputer code
      Execution permission. ">
  <IMembershipCondition
        class="ZoneMembershipCondition"
        version="1"
        Zone="MyComputer"/>
<CodeGroup
      class="UnionCodeGroup"
      version="1"
      PermissionSetName="FullTrust"
      Name="MSSQLRSCodeGroup"
      Description="Code group for the MS SQL RS Book Custom
                                          Assemblies">
    <IMembershipCondition
          class="StrongNameMembershipCondition"
          version="1"
          PublicKeyBlob="00240000048000009400000006020000
                  0024000052534131300040000010001000B9F7
                  4F2D5B0AAD33AA619B00D7BB8B0F767839
                  3A0F4CD586C9036D72455F8D1E85BF635C
                  9FB1DA9817DD0F751DCEE77D9A47959E87
                  28028B9B6CC7C25EB1E59CB3DE01BB516D
                  46FC6AC6AF27AA6E71B65F6AB91B957688
                  6F2EF39417F17B567AD200E151FC744C6D
                  A72FF5882461E6CA786EB2997FA968302B
                  7B2F24BDBFF7A5"
                  />
</CodeGroup>
<CodeGroup
      class="UnionCodeGroup"
      version="1"
```

```
PermissionSetName="FullTrust"
Name="Microsoft_Strong_Name"
Description="This code group grants code signed with the
                            Microsoft strong name full trust. ">
<IMembershipCondition
        class="StrongNameMembershipCondition"
        version="1"
        PublicKeyBlob="00240000048000009400000006020000000
                        240000525341310004000001000100070D1
                        FA57C4AED9F0A32E84AA0FAEFD0DE9E8FD
                        6AEC8F87FB03766C834C99921EB23BE79A
                        D9D5DCC1DD9AD236132102900B723CF980
                        957FC4E177108FC607774F29E8320E92EA
                        05ECE4E821C0A5EFE8F1645C4C0C93C1AB
                        99285D622CAA652C1DFAD63D745D6F2DE5
                        F17E5EAF0FC4963D261C8A12436518206D
                        C093344D5AD293"
        />
    </CodeGroup>
```

.
.
.

8. Save the modified file and exit your text editor.
9. Reopen the Chapter08 project in the Report Designer, if it was closed.
10. Create a new report called WeatherReport using the GDSReport template.
11. Open the Report Properties dialog box and select the References page.
12. Click Add under the Add or remove assemblies heading. Click the … button that appears. The Add Reference dialog box appears.
13. Scroll down to the entry for the WeatherInfo assembly and select it. Click OK to exit the Add Reference dialog box. Click OK to exit the Report Properties dialog box.

Task Notes   For a custom assembly to be used in our reports, it must be in a location where it can be found by the Report Designer. When you are designing reports, the assembly must be either in the Public Assemblies folder or in the Global Assembly Cache. We placed the WeatherInfo.dll assembly in the Public Assemblies folder in Step 2. Consult your .NET documentation for information on placing an assembly in the Global Assembly Cache.

We are using a class from the WeatherInfo assembly called PlanetaryWeather and a method from that class called GetWeather. The GetWeather method is a shared method. This means you do not need to create an instance of the PlanetaryWeather class to use the GetWeather method.

To use a method that is not a shared method, you need to use the Classes area of the References page of the Report Properties dialog box. First, create a reference in the References area, as we did in Steps 12 and 13. Then, under Class name, specify the name of the class within that assembly you want to instantiate. Finally, provide a name for the instance of that class. Reporting Services creates an instance of the class with the name you provide when the report is run.

Once the assembly is in the correct location and you have created a reference to that assembly, you can use the methods of this assembly in your reports. When referencing a shared method in an assembly, use the following syntax:

```
Namespace.ClassName.MethodName(Parameters…)
```

For the WeatherInfo assembly, the syntax is

```
WeatherInfo.PlanetaryWeather.GetWeather(PlanetAbbrv)
```

To use a nonshared method from a class you instantiated, use the syntax

```
Code.InstanceName.MethodName(Parameters…)
```

Weather Report, Task 2: Create a Dataset, Add a Tablix to the Report Layout, and Populate It

1. Create a new data source called Galactic that references the Galactic shared data source.

2. Create a new dataset called Planets. Use the following for the query string:

   ```
   SELECT Name, PlanetAbbrv FROM Planet ORDER BY Name
   ```

3. In the Report Data window, right-click the Parameters entry and select Add Parameter from the context menu. The Report Parameter Properties dialog box appears.

4. Set the properties of this new parameter as follows:

Property	Value
General page:	
Name	Planets
Prompt	Select Planets
Allow multiple values	checked
Available Values page:	
Select from one of the following options:	Get values from query
Dataset	Planets
Value field	PlanetAbbrv
Label field	Name

Click OK to exit the Report Parameter Properties dialog box.

5. Place two text boxes onto the body of the report. Then use the table template to place a tablix onto the body of the report. The expression in the second text box should be:

```
="Here is the current weather for the " & Parameters!Planets.Count &
                                        " planet(s) you selected"
```

6. Complete your report layout so it is similar to Figure 8-11. The expression in the right-hand detail cell should be:

```
=WeatherInfo.PlanetaryWeather.GetWeather(Fields!PlanetAbbrv.Value)
```

7. Open the Tablix Properties dialog box. Select the Filters page.
8. Click Add.
9. Enter the following for Expression:

```
=Array.IndexOf(Parameters!Planets.Value, Fields!PlanetAbbrv.Value)
```

10. Select >= from the Operator drop-down list.
11. Enter the following expression for Value:

```
=0
```

12. Click OK to exit the Tablix Properties dialog box.
13. Click the Preview tab.
14. Use the Select Planets drop-down list to check Borlaron and Stilation. Click View Report. Your report should appear similar to Figure 8-12.

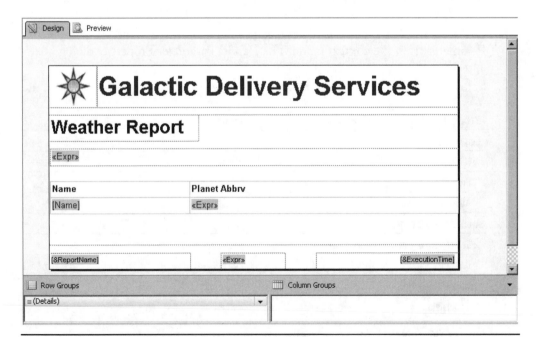

Figure 8-11 *Weather Report layout*

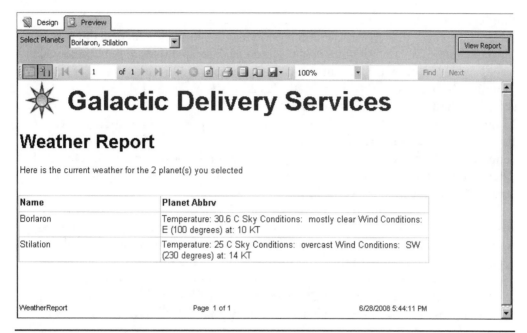

Figure 8-12   *Weather Report preview*

NOTE

Remember, the GetWeather method is going out to the Internet and retrieving weather conditions when you run the report. Because of this, you must be connected to the Internet when you run this report. This process may take some time if you are using a slow Internet connection and have selected a number of planets to report on. Also, the weather conditions you see in your report vary from those shown in Figure 8-12. Finally, some locations may show "null" for a certain condition if that condition has not been reported in the past hour.

15.   Select Save All on the toolbar.

Task Notes   The Weather Report makes use of a special type of parameter that allows for more than one value to be selected. Rather than requiring the user to select a single value from the Available Values drop-down list, a multivalued parameter enables the user to check off a number of values to be used when creating the report. Then, it is up to the Report Designer to figure out how to use those multiple values to return a report with the desired information.

The properties of the report parameter change when that parameter becomes multivalued. Instead of containing single values, the Value and Label properties become arrays. The arrays have one element for each of the items selected by the user. If the user checks three items in the drop-down list, the Value and Label arrays each have three elements. (These are zero-based arrays, so they are elements 0, 1, and 2 in this case.) The Length property of each array contains the number of elements in that array.

In this report, we used the multivalue parameter in a table filter to determine which records would be output. (Later in this chapter, we use a multivalue parameter in the Transport Monitor report to create a WHERE clause in a query.) We are using a shared method of the Array class called IndexOf, which searches an array for a value. In this case, the IndexOf method is searching for each planet abbreviation in the Parameters!Planets.Value array. If the abbreviation is found, the index of the element that contains the abbreviation is returned by the IndexOf method; otherwise, it returns −1. Therefore, we want only those records where the IndexOf method returns a value greater than or equal to 0 to be included in the table.

When you first encountered filters in Chapter 7, you were cautioned to use them wisely. The filter makes sense here for three reasons. First, the dataset we are filtering is small. Selecting just two or three records versus selecting all six is not a significant time savings. Second, as with the example in Chapter 7, the filter enables us to use the same dataset to populate the drop-down list and the table in the report body. It would be inefficient to run two database queries, one without a WHERE clause to get the list of planets for the drop-down list and one with a WHERE clause to get the planets selected for the table in the report. Finally, the most time-consuming part of the report is not the database interaction, but the calls to the web service over the Internet. Because our filter is applied before we step through the table and make the web service call, we are in good shape.

The Delivery Analysis Report

Features Highlighted

▶ Using an Analysis Services cube as a data source via a Multidimensional Expression (MDX) query

▶ Parameterizing an MDX query

▶ Localizing the label strings in a report

Business Need The Galactic Delivery Services long-range planning committee is working on forecasting the equipment and work force needs necessary for future growth. They need a report showing the number of deliveries and the average weight of those deliveries grouped by customer by quarter. They would also like to select whether the data includes next day deliveries, same day deliveries, previous day deliveries, or some combination of the three. The data for this report should come from the GalacticDeliveriesDataMart cube hosted by Microsoft SQL Server Analysis Services.

There are committee members from a number of planets. Most speak English, but the committee does include several Spanish-speaking members. (I know it is rather strange that people in a galaxy far, far away should speak English and Spanish, but work with me here!)

Task Overview

1. Copy the .NET Assembly into the Appropriate Location, Create a New Report, Create a Reference to the Assembly, and Create a Dataset Using the MDX Query Designer.

2. Add a Tablix to the Report Layout, Populate It, and Localize the Report Strings.

Delivery Analysis Report, Task 1: Copy the .NET Assembly into the Appropriate Location, Create a New Report, Create a Reference to the Assembly, and Create a Dataset Using the MDX Query Designer

> **NOTE**
>
> You need to download the GalacticOLAP project from the website for this book and deploy it to a SQL Server Analysis Services server before you can complete this report. If you do not have access to Analysis Services, skip this report and continue with the "Reports Within Reports" section of this chapter.

1. If you have not already done so, download the ReportUtil.dll assembly and the accompanying ES folder from the website for this book.

2. Copy the file and the folder to the Report Designer folder. The default path for the Report Designer folder is

   ```
   C:\Program Files\Microsoft Visual Studio 9\Common7\IDE\PublicAssemblies
   ```

3. Reopen the Chapter08 project in the Report Designer, if it was closed.

4. Create a new report called DeliveryAnalysis using the GDSReport template.

5. Open the Report Properties dialog box and select the References page.

6. Click Add under the Add or remove assemblies heading. Click the ... button that appears. The Add Reference dialog box appears.

7. Scroll down to the entry for ReportUtil Assembly and select it. Click OK to exit the Add Reference dialog box. Click OK to exit the Report Properties dialog box.

8. In the Report Data window, select New | Data Source from the menu. The Data Source Properties dialog box appears.

9. Enter **GalacticDM** for the Name. Select Microsoft SQL Server Analysis Services from the Type drop-down list.

10. Click Edit next to the Connection String text box. The Connection Properties dialog box appears.

11. Enter the name of the SQL Server Analysis Services server for Server name.

12. Select GalacticOLAP from the Select or enter a database name drop-down list. You can test the connection if you like, but if GalacticOLAP shows up in the drop-down list, the connection has already been tested.

13. Click OK to exit the Connection Properties dialog box. Click OK to exit the Data Source Properties dialog box.

14. Right-click the GalacticDM entry in the Report Data window and select Add Dataset from the context menu. The Dataset Properties dialog box appears.

15. Enter **DeliveryInfo** for the Name.

16. Click the Query Designer button. The MDX Query Designer appears as shown in Figure 8-13.

17. Expand the Measures entry in the Metadata pane. Expand the Delivery measure group and then expand the Delivery entry within it.

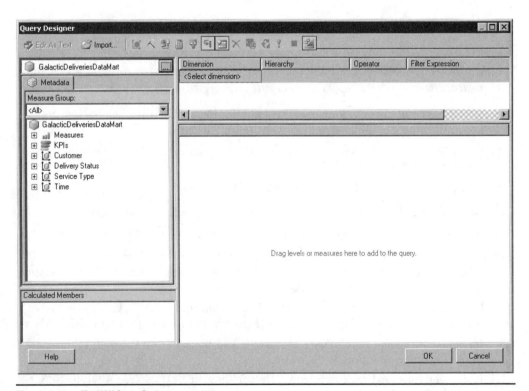

Figure 8-13 *The MDX Query Designer*

18. Drag the Delivery Count measure onto the Results pane (the pane with the words "Drag levels or measures here to add to the query" in the center). The total count of all deliveries currently in the GalacticDeliveriesDataMart cube is shown in the Results pane.

19. Expand the Customer dimension in the Metadata pane. Drag the CustomerName attribute onto the Results pane to the left of the Delivery Count. The Results pane now shows the total count of all deliveries for each customer.

20. Expand the Time dimension in the Metadata pane. Drag the DeliveryQuarter attribute onto the Results pane to the left of the CustomerName column. The Results pane now shows the total count of all deliveries for each customer for each quarter.

21. Right-click in the Calculated Members pane and select New Calculated Member from the context menu. The Calculated Member Builder dialog box appears.

22. Enter **AvgWeight** for the Name.

23. In the Expression area, enter **ROUND(**. Expand the Measures in the Metadata area, expand the Delivery measure group, and then expand the Delivery entry within it. Double-click Package Weight to add it to the expression.

24. Enter **/** at the end of the expression. Double-click Delivery Count to add it to the expression.

25. Enter **,2)** at the end of the expression and click Check to check the syntax of the expression. Click OK to close the Check Syntax dialog box. Make any corrections to the expression, if a syntax error is encountered.

26. Click OK to exit the Calculated Member Builder dialog box.

27. Drag the AvgWeight calculated member onto the Results pane to the right of the Delivery Count.

28. In the Filter pane (the pane in the upper-right corner of the MDX Query Designer), select Service Type from the drop-down list in the Dimension column.

29. Select Description from the drop-down list in the Hierarchy column.

30. Equal should be selected from the drop-down list in the Operator column.

31. Examine the values in the drop-down window in the Filter Expression column, but do not make a selection. The Filter Expression column enables us to select one or more values for the right side of our filter expression. Instead of doing this at design time, we let our users make the selection at run time. Click Cancel to exit the drop-down window.

32. Check the box in the Parameters column. This selection enables the user to select the values of the filter expression at run time. The MDX Query Designer should appear as shown in Figure 8-14.

33. Click OK to exit the Query Designer window. Click OK to exit the Dataset Properties dialog box.

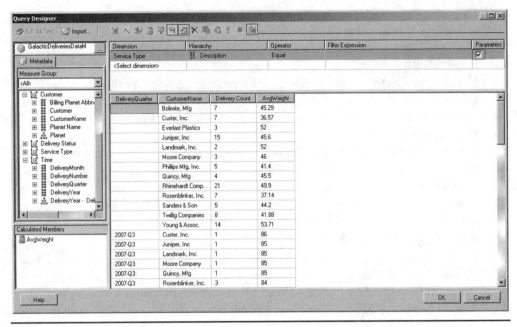

Figure 8-14 *The MDX Query Designer containing the query for the Delivery Analysis Report*

Task Notes   The assembly we are using for this report does not try to venture outside of its sandbox. Therefore, we do not need to make any code-access security changes in order for it to function. We will talk more about what this assembly actually does in the next set of Task Notes.

The MDX Query Designer works almost entirely through drag-and-drop. We drag measures, dimensions, and hierarchies from the Metadata Browser pane and drop them in the Results pane to create our query. We can define calculated members and add them to the Results pane as well.

At the top of the Metadata pane is the name of the cube being queried. To select a different cube, click the … button and make a selection from the Cube Selection dialog box that appears.

The toolbar button with the pickaxe icon switches from the MDX Query Designer to the Data Mining Expression (DMX) Query Designer. The toolbar button with the *X* axis and *Y* axis switches back to the MDX Query Designer. Where the MDX Query Designer is used to query cubes in an Analysis Services database, the DMX Query Designer is used to query data mining models in an Analysis Services database. Because the same Analysis Services database may contain both cubes and data mining models, the Report Designer may not be able to tell which query designer you need simply by examining the database. Therefore, it is necessary to have a way to switch between the two.

The Show Empty Cells toolbar button toggles between showing and hiding empty cells in the Results pane. An empty cell is a combination of dimension and hierarchy members that have a null value for every measure, calculated or otherwise, in the Results pane. If empty cells are hidden in the Results pane, they are also hidden in the final report query. The Design Mode toolbar button enables you to toggle between the design view and the query view of the MDX query. If you are comfortable with MDX query syntax, you may want to type your queries into the query view rather than creating them through the drag-and-drop programming method of the design view. The Auto Execute toolbar button toggles autoexecute mode in the Query Designer. When autoexecute mode is on, the cube is requeried and the Results pane is updated every time an item is added to or removed from the Results pane.

The Filter pane enables us either to hardcode filter expressions at design time or use report parameters for the user to make selections at run time. When the Parameters check box is checked, a parameterized filter is created. Several things happen when we exit the MDX Query Designer dialog box for the first time after a parameterized filter has been added to the query. When this occurs, the Report Designer creates a new dataset for each item being used in a parameterized filter. This dataset includes all the valid members of that item.

In addition to the datasets, new report parameters are created for each parameterized filter. The datasets are used to populate the available values for these report parameters. The report parameters are multivalued. Using this mechanism, the user is allowed to select one or more valid members to be used in the parameterized filters at the time the report is executed.

Delivery Analysis Report, Task 2: Add a Tablix to the Report Layout, Populate It, and Localize the Report Strings

1. Place a text box onto the body of the report and set its properties as follows:

Property	Value
Font:FontSize	20pt
Font: FontWeight	Bold
Location: Left	0in
Location: Top	0in
Size: Width	5.875in
Size: Height	0.375in

2. Set the content of the text box to the following expression:

```
=ReportUtil.Localization.LocalizedString("DeliveryReportTitle",
User!Language)
```

3. Use the matrix template to place a tablix onto the report body.

4. Select the DeliveryQuarter field from the DeliveryInfo dataset in the Columns cell. Click the Bold button and the Center button on the toolbar.

5. Select the CustomerName field in the Rows cell. Click the Bold button on the toolbar.

6. Select the Delivery_Count field in the Data cell.

7. In the Report Data window, drag the AvgWeight field into the same cell where Delivery_Count was placed. Drag to the right side of the cell. This creates a second data column to the right of the first.

8. Right-click the cell that was just created and select Tablix: Insert Row | Outside Group - Above from the context menu.

9. Enter the following expression in the text box above the cell containing the DeliveryCount field:

```
=ReportUtil.Localization.LocalizedString("DeliveryCountColHead",
User!Language)
```

10. Enter the following expression in the text box above the cell containing the AvgWeight field:

```
=ReportUtil.Localization.LocalizedString("AvgWeightColHead",
User!Language)
```

11. Select the cell in the upper-left corner of the tablix and press DELETE to remove the heading created here.

12. Expand the Parameters entry in the Report Data window.

13. Right-click the ServiceTypeDescription entry in the Report Data window and select Parameter Properties from the context menu.

14. Enter **Select Service Types** for the Prompt.

15. Click OK to exit the Report Parameter Properties dialog box.

16. Click the Preview tab. Check All in the Select Service Types drop-down list and click View Report.

17. Select Save All on the toolbar.

Task Notes   You may have noticed we did not type text strings for the report title and the two column headings on the report. Instead, we used expressions that call the LocalizedString method of the Localization class in the ReportUtil assembly. (*Localization* refers to the process of making a report or computer program appear in the language of a certain location.) This method requires two parameters: the name of the string to localize and the language it should be localized into. The string name is hardcoded in each expression. The language comes from the User!Language global variable. This global variable is populated with the language of the client application requesting the report.

The ReportUtil assembly uses multiple resource files to manage the localization. There is one resource file for each language it must support. In the demonstration code supplied for this example, the ReportUtil assembly only has two resource files: one for English and one for Spanish. To support another language, you simply need to add another resource file and rebuild the project.

We used the LocalizedString method to get localized versions of the report title and the two column headers. The remainder of the report content is either proper names or numeric. Neither of these needs to be translated. If you are sharp, you will notice the report parameter prompt and the items in the report parameter drop-down list have not been localized. We cannot use expressions for either of these items, so we cannot use our nifty LocalizedString method.

The drop-down list content is selected from the Analysis Services cube, so some localization of the data could be done on the data in the cube itself. That, unfortunately, is beyond the scope of this book. The report parameter is a bigger problem. In fact, the current version of Reporting Services does not have a nice way to deal with this.

Reports Within Reports

Thus far, we have placed report items within report items and data regions within data regions. In this section, we look at putting whole reports inside one another. This is done using the subreport report item; the only item in the Toolbox that we have not yet used.

The *subreport item* is simply a placeholder in a report. It sits in the parent report and shows the space to be occupied by another report when the parent report is run. Nothing is special about a report placed in a subreport item. Any report can be used as a subreport.

The report placed in the subreport can even contain parameters. These parameter values can be passed from the parent report to the subreport. Any field value, parameter value, or expression in the parent report can be used as a parameter in the subreport.

Subreports are used for many reasons. They can provide an easy way to reuse a complex report layout within a parent report. They can also be used to implement a more complex form of drilldown.

The following subreports are anything but subpar!

The Employee Evaluation Report

Features Highlighted

- ▶ Using a subreport as reusable code
- ▶ Using the page width and page height properties for a landscape report
- ▶ Using a rectangle for grouping
- ▶ Using rich formatting

Business Need   The Galactic Delivery Services personnel department has created an application for employees to conduct peer reviews as part of each employee's annual review process. They are also collecting a review and comments from each employee's manager. They need a report that can be used to present the results of the peer review at the employee's meeting with their supervisor.

The manager's review and comments should be noted as coming from the manager. The peer reviews, however, should be presented anonymously.

Task Overview

1. Create a New Report, Create a Dataset, Add a Tablix to the Report Layout, and Populate It.
2. Create a New Report, Create a Dataset, and Populate the Report Layout.
3. Add a Rectangle.
4. Add Rich Formatting.

Employee Evaluation Report, Task 1: Create a New Report, Create a Dataset, Add a Tablix to the Report Layout, and Populate It

1. Reopen the Chapter08 project, if it was closed.
2. Create a new report called EvalDetail. Do *not* use the GDSReport template.
3. Create a new data source called Galactic that references the Galactic shared data source.
4. Create a new dataset called EvalRatings that calls the stp_EvalRatings stored procedure.
5. Use the table template to place a tablix onto the body of the report.
6. Select the Goal, Rating, and GoalComment fields in the data row of the table.
7. Add a parent row group to the table using grouping by EvaluatorEmployeeNumber. The group should have a group header and a group footer.

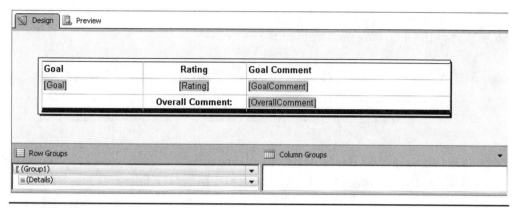

Figure 8-15   *The Employee Evaluation Detail Report layout*

8. Complete your report layout so it is similar to Figure 8-15. The top row has the BorderColor: Top property set to Black. The bottom row has the BorderColor: Bottom property set to Black and the BorderWidth: Bottom property set to 5pt. Also note that the table header row was deleted.

9. Select Save All on the toolbar.

Task Notes   The EvalDetail report is going to be used in two subreports in our parent report. It is going to be used in one location to display the peer reviews and in another location to display the manager review. We can create this layout for displaying review information and then use it in multiple places.

Subreports have several uses. One use is to serve as reusable layout, as we are doing here. Second, subreports can create nested reports from multiple data sources. Finally, subreports can be used to display multiple one-to-many relationships.

Subreports, however, can be inefficient if overused. Every time a subreport executes, its dataset queries must be run. When a subreport is embedded in a data region, it can be executed many times, perhaps once for each record in the parent report. This can result in a long-running report that puts a good deal of stress on your database server. So use those subreports, but use them wisely.

Employee Evaluation Report, Task 2: Create a New Report, Create a Dataset, and Populate the Report Layout

1. Create a new report called EmployeeEval using the GDSReport template.

2. Create a new data source called Galactic that references the Galactic shared data source.

3. Create a new dataset called EvalPerformance that calls the stp_EvalPerformance stored procedure.

4. Open the Report Properties dialog box.

5. Modify the following properties of the report:

Property	Value
Orientation	Landscape
Margins: Left	0.5in
Margins: Right	0.5in

6. Click OK to exit the Report Properties dialog box.

7. Click the design surface to select the report body. Set the following property of the report body:

Property	Value
Size: Width	10in

8. Drag the EmployeeName field onto the report body. Modify the following properties of the text box that results:

Property	Value
Font: FontSize	20pt
Font: FontWeight	Bold
Location: Left	0in
Location: Top	0in
Size: Width	6.875in
Size: Height	0.5in

9. Place a text box onto the report body. Modify the following properties of this text box:

Property	Value
Font: FontSize	20pt
Font: FontWeight	Bold
Location: Left	8.25in
Location: Top	0in
Size: Width	1.625in
Size: Height	0.5in
Value	=Parameters!Year.Value

10. Place a text box onto the report body. Modify the following properties of this text box:

Property	Value
Font: FontSize	16pt
Font: FontWeight	Bold
Location: Left	0in
Location: Top	0.625in
Size: Width	2.75in
Size: Height	0.375in
Value	Peer Evaluations

11. Place a subreport onto the report body immediately below the text box. Modify the following properties of this subreport:

Property	Value
Location: Left	0in
Location: Top	1in
Size: Width	6.875in
Size: Height	1.125in

12. Right-click the subreport and select Subreport Properties from the context menu. The Subreport Properties dialog box appears.
13. Select EvalDetail from the Use this report as a subreport drop-down list.
14. Select the Parameters page.
15. Click Add to add parameters to the grid. Configure the parameters as shown here:

Name	Value
EmpNum	=Parameters!EmpNum.Value
Year	=Parameters!Year.Value
MgrFlag	=0

You can use the drop-down list to select the parameter names. You can use the Expression dialog box to select the parameter values.

16. Click OK to exit the Subreport Properties dialog box.
17. Select the Peer Evaluations text box and the subreport. Press CTRL-C to copy these two items. Press CTRL-V to paste a copy of these items on the report body. Drag the two copied items so they are immediately below the original subreport.

18. Modify the new text box to read "Manager Evaluation." Adjust the width of the text box as needed.

19. Open the Subreport Properties dialog box for the new subreport and select the Parameters page.

20. Change the parameter value for MgrFlag from = 0 to = 1. This causes the second subreport to contain the manager's evaluation rather than the peer evaluations.

21. Click OK to exit the Subreport Properties dialog box.

22. Place a text box onto the report body. Modify the following properties of this text box:

Property	Value
Font: FontWeight	Bold
Location: Left	7.125in
Location: Top	1in
Size: Width	2in
Size: Height	0.25in
Value	Areas of Excellence

23. Drag the AreasOfExcellence field onto the report body. Modify the following properties of the text box that results:

Property	Value
Location: Left	7.125in
Location: Top	1.375in
Size: Width	2.75in
Size: Height	0.25in

24. Place a text box onto the report body. Modify the following properties of this text box:

Property	Value
Font: FontWeight	Bold
Location: Left	7.125in
Location: Top	1.875in
Size: Width	2in
Size: Height	0.25in
Value	Areas for Improvement

25. Drag the AreasForImprovement field onto the report body. Modify the following properties of the text box that results:

Property	Value
Location: Left	7.125in
Location: Top	2.25in
Size: Width	2.75in
Size: Height	0.25in

26. Click the Preview tab. Enter **1394** for EmpNum and **2008** for Year, and then click View Report. Your report should appear similar to Figure 8-16.

Task Notes   We used the Report Properties dialog box to change this report's orientation from portrait to landscape. When you are creating your report templates, you may want to create one template for portrait reports and another template for landscape reports.

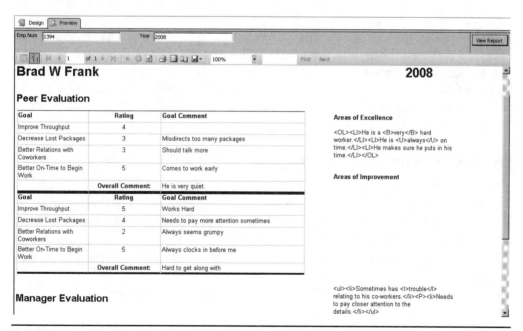

Figure 8-16   *The Employee Evaluations Report preview after Task 2*

Two steps are required to get each subreport item ready to use. First, you have to specify which report is going to be used within the subreport item. Once this is done, you need to specify a value for each of the parameters in the selected report. With these two tasks completed, your subreports are ready to go.

In this report, we are using several fields outside of a data region: the EmployeeName field, the AreasOfExcellence field, and the AreasForImprovement field. Remember, data regions are set up to repeat a portion of their content for each record in the result set. When a field value occurs outside of a data region, it is not repeated; it occurs only once. Therefore, one record must be selected by the Report Designer for display in these fields. It happens that the first record in the dataset is selected in these situations.

In this particular report, the EvalPerformance dataset has only one record. Of course, the Report Designer does not know at design time how many records the dataset will have at run time. (Even if the dataset has only one record at design time, it could have 100 records at run time.) Therefore, the Report Builder always uses the first record for references outside of a data region.

Finally, you may have noticed a little problem with the text box that contains the contents of the AreasForImprovement field. (Not the HTML formatting tags, we will deal with those in Task 4.) It seems to be sliding down the page. In actuality, it was pushed down the page when the subreport grew.

The text boxes that contain the Areas of Excellence title, the AreasOfExcellence field value, and the Areas for Improvement title are all even with the first subreport. However, the text box containing the value of the AreasForImprovement field starts below the bottom of the first subreport. When the subreport grows because of its content, the text box is pushed further down the report, so it remains below the bottom of the subreport.

In Task 3, you see a way to prevent this problem.

Employee Evaluation Report, Task 3: Add a Rectangle

1. Click the Design tab.
2. Select the Areas of Excellence text box, the AreasOfExcellence field value text box, the Areas for Improvement text box, and the AreasForImprovement field value text box. Press CTRL-X to cut these four text boxes.
3. Select a rectangle from the Toolbox and place it in the area just vacated by these four text boxes.
4. With the rectangle still selected, press CTRL-V to paste the four text boxes into the rectangle.
5. Arrange the rectangle and the four text boxes as needed. Your layout should appear similar to Figure 8-17.
6. Click the Preview tab. Enter **1394** for EmpNum and **2008** for Year, and then click View Report. Your report should appear similar to Figure 8-18.
7. Select Save All on the toolbar.

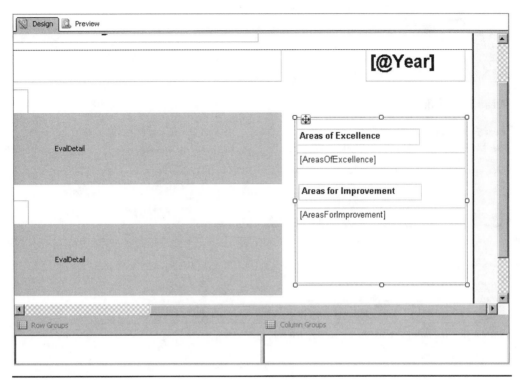

Figure 8-17   *The Employee Evaluation Report layout with a rectangle*

Task Notes   The rectangle report item comes to your rescue here. Once the four text boxes are inside the rectangle, they remain together no matter how much the subreport grows. As your report designs become more complex, rectangles are often necessary to keep things right where you want them.

Employee Evaluation Report, Task 4: Add Rich Formatting

1. Click the Design tab.
2. Double-click the text box containing the expression for the employee name (the large text box right below the Galactic Delivery Services logo and heading). The text edit cursor will be to the left of the "<<Expr>>" placeholder in the text box.
3. Type **Employee:** as shown in Figure 8-19.
4. Highlight the text just entered in Step 3.
5. Click the bold button on the toolbar to unbold the selected text.

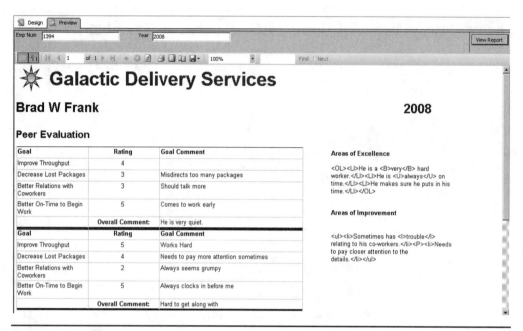

Figure 8-18 *The Employee Evaluation Report preview with a rectangle*

6. Select "12pt" from the font size drop-down list in the toolbar. See Figure 8-20.

7. Double-click the text box containing the Year parameter. The text edit cursor will be to the left of the "[@Year]" placeholder.

8. Type **Year:** and press ENTER.

9. Highlight the text entered in Step 8.

10. Click the bold button on the toolbar to unbold the selected text.

11. Select "12pt" from the font size drop-down list in the toolbar.

12. Click outside of the Year parameter text box to unselect it. Single-click the Year parameter text box to select the text box.

13. Modify the following property of this text box:

Property	Value
TextAlign	Center

14. Double-click the text box for the AreasOfExcellence field.

15. Click "<<Expr>>" to highlight it.

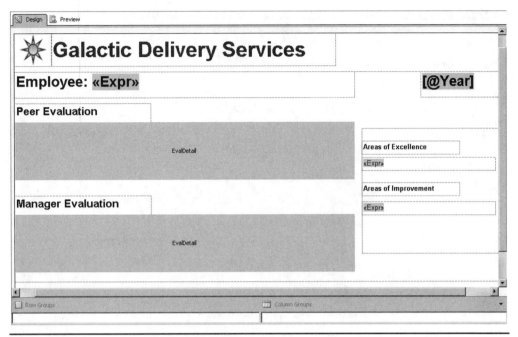

Figure 8-19   *Adding text to the Employee field text box*

16. Right-click the highlighted text and select Placeholder Properties from the context menu as shown in Figure 8-21. The Placeholder Properties dialog box appears.

17. On the General page, select the HTML - Interpret HTML tags as styles radio button.

18. Click OK to exit the Placeholder Properties dialog box.

19. Repeat Step 14 through Step 18 for the AreasForImprovement field text box.

20. Click the Preview tab. Enter **1394** for EmpNum and **2008** for Year, and then click View Report. Your report should appear similar to Figure 8-22.

21. Select Save All on the toolbar.

Task Notes   In previous reports, we have used Visual Basic expressions to combine static text, such as labels, with dynamic text from fields and parameters. As an alternative, we can type text into the text box before or after the field, parameter, or expression *placeholder*. In fact, we can combine several placeholders in a single text box, just as we have sometimes combined several fields in a Visual Basic Expression. To manually add a placeholder to a text box, right-click while editing text in the text box and select Create Placeholder from the context menu.

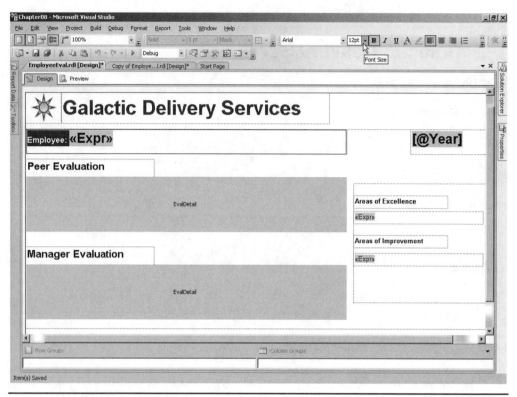

Figure 8-20   *Adding rich formatting to text*

Use either the Visual Basic expressions or the combination of static text and placeholders. Either method works just fine. Note, however, once you use a placeholder/static text combination in a text box, you can no longer view the Expression dialog box for that text box.

In addition to combining static text and placeholders in a single text box, we combined different formatting within a single text box. This is called *rich formatting*. Rich formatting enables us to treat different parts of the contents of a text box as distinct items and allows us to apply different formatting to each of these items.

One of the bits of formatting we can apply to a placeholder in a text box is the ability to interpret HTML tags embedded in the content of the field or parameter represented by that placeholder. In our report, the content of the AreasOfExcellence field is:

```
<OL><LI>He is a <B>very</B> hard worker.</LI><LI>He is <U>always</U> on
time.</LI><LI>He makes sure he puts in his time.</LI></OL>
```

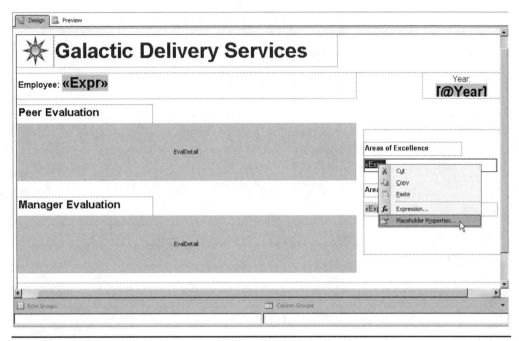

Figure 8-21   *Setting placeholder properties*

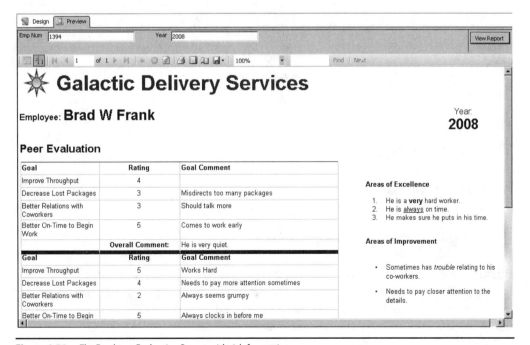

Figure 8-22   *The Employee Evaluation Report with rich formatting*

Note the embedded HTML formatting tags. By selecting the HTML - Interpret HTML tags as styles radio button in the Properties dialog for this placeholder, we can have the HTML tags embedded in this text used as formatting characters. The result is a numbered list containing bold and underlined text. The content of the AreasForImprovement field is:

```
<ul><li>Sometimes has <I>trouble</I> relating to his co-workers.</li>
<P><li>Needs to pay closer attention to the details.</li></ul>
```

These HTML tags produce a bulleted list with italicized text and a paragraph break. The following HTML tags are handled by Reporting Services rich formatting:

<A href></A>	Hyperlink
<FONT></FONT>	Font
<H*n*></H*n*>	Header
<DIV></DIV>	Division
<SPAN></SPAN>	Inline Element Grouping
<P></P>	Paragraph
<B></B>	Bold
<I></I>	Italics
<U></U>	Underline
<S></S>	Strikethrough
<OL></OL>	Numbered List
<UL></UL>	Bulleted List
<LI></LI>	List Item

The Invoice Report

Features Highlighted

▶ Using a subreport in a table

▶ Using a subreport to facilitate drilldown

Business Need   The Galactic Delivery Services accounting department wants an interactive Invoice Report. The Invoice Report needs to show the invoice header and invoice detail information. The user can then expand an invoice detail entry to view information on the delivery that created that invoice detail.

Task Overview

1. Create a New Report, Create a Dataset, and Copy the Layout from the DeliveryStatus Report.
2. Create a New Report, Create a Dataset, and Populate the Report Layout.

Invoice Report, Task 1: Create a New Report, Create a Dataset, and Copy the Layout from the DeliveryStatus Report

1. Reopen the Chapter08 project, if it was closed.
2. Create a new report called DeliveryDetail. Do *not* use the GDSReport template.
3. Create a new data source called Galactic that references the Galactic shared data source.
4. Create a new dataset called DeliveryStatus that calls the stp_DeliveryDetail stored procedure.
5. Double-click the entry for the DeliveryStatus report in the Solution Explorer to open this report.
6. Select the tablix in the DeliveryStatus report and press CTRL-C to copy it. (Make sure you have the entire tablix selected and not just a single cell in the tablix.)
7. Close the DeliveryStatus report and return to the DeliveryDetail report.
8. Press CTRL-V to paste the tablix into the report body.
9. Move the tablix to the upper-left corner of the report body. Size the report body so it exactly contains the table.

Task Notes   Instead of re-creating a layout for the delivery detail, we borrowed a layout created previously in another report. This works because the stp_DeliveryDetail stored procedure returns the same columns as the stp_DeliveryStatus stored procedure used for the previous report. The other requirement needed to make this cut-and-paste operation successful was to use the same name for the dataset in both reports.

When you have a layout that is nice and clean, reusing it whenever possible is always a good idea. Even better would be to modify the DeliveryStatus report to use our new DeliveryDetail report in a subreport. That way, we would only need to maintain this layout in one location.

Consider that an extra credit project.

Invoice Report, Task 2: Create a New Report, Create a Dataset, and Populate the Report Layout

1. Create a new report called Invoice using the GDSReport template.
2. Create a new data source called Galactic that references the Galactic shared data source.

3. Create a new dataset called InvoiceHeader that calls the stp_InvoiceHeader stored procedure.

4. Create a second dataset called InvoiceDetail that calls the stp_InvoiceDetail stored procedure.

5. Use the list template to place a tablix onto the report body.

6. Size the tablix and add fields to create the layout shown in Figure 8-23. The fields come from the InvoiceHeader dataset. The black line across the bottom is a solid bottom border on the tablix with a border width of 10 points.

7. Drag the report body to make it larger.

8. Use the table template to place a tablix onto the report body immediately below the existing tablix.

9. Select the LineNumber, Description, and Amount fields from the InvoiceDetail dataset in the data row of the tablix.

10. Size the table columns appropriately. Type the letter **C** for the Format property of the text box containing the Amount field value.

Figure 8-23　*The Invoice Report layout with an invoice header*

11. Delete the table header row.
12. Select all three of the remaining cells in the tablix and set the following property:

Name	Value
BorderStyle	None

13. Add a second details row below the existing data row. (In other words, insert a second row inside the details group.)
14. Merge the three cells in this new details row.
15. Place a subreport in the merged cell.
16. Open the Subreport Properties dialog box. Set the subreport to use the DeliveryDetail report.
17. Select the Parameters page and configure it as follows:

Name	Value
DeliveryNumber	[DeliveryNumber]

18. Click OK to exit the Subreport Parameters dialog box.
19. Click the gray box to the left of the row containing the subreport. Modify the following properties for this table row using the Properties window:

Property	Value
Hidden	True
ToggleItem	LineNumber

20. Click the Preview tab. Type **73054** for InvoiceNumber and click View Report.
21. Expand one of the invoice detail entries and observe how the subreport appears. Your report should appear as shown in Figure 8-24.
22. Select Save All on the toolbar.

Task Notes In the Invoice Report, we placed our subreport right in a table cell. A field from the table's dataset is used as the parameter for the subreport. Because of this, the subreport is different for each detail row in the table.

We chose to have the subreport initially hidden in our report. The reason for this is the subreport contains a large amount of detail information. This detail would overwhelm the users if it were displayed all at once. Instead, the users can selectively drill down to the detail they need.

In our next report, you look at another way to manage large amounts of detail by using the drillthrough feature of Reporting Services.

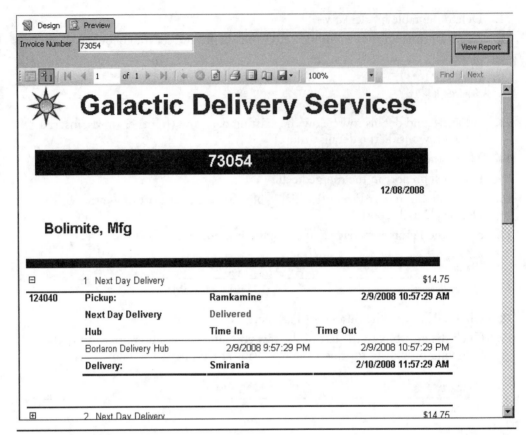

Figure 8-24   *The Invoice Report preview*

Interacting with Reports

In many cases, your reports can be much more effective when users can view them electronically. Reporting Services offers a number of options for enabling the user to interact with the reports when viewed in this way. You have already seen several examples of drilldown interactivity. This type of interactivity hides detail information until it is needed by the user.

In this section, you learn additional methods for navigating within reports and even moving between reports. You also see how to link a report to Internet content. Finally, you look at a way for your report to interact with you by always keeping its data current.

So don't be shy: interact!

The Invoice Front-End Report

Features Highlighted

▶ Using drill-through navigation to move between reports

▶ Using the document map to navigate within a report

▶ Using bookmarks to navigate within a report

▶ Using links to navigate to Internet content

Business Need   The Galactic Delivery Services accounting department is pleased with the Invoice Report. They would now like a front end to make the Invoice Report easier to use. The front-end report should list all invoices by customer and let the user click an invoice to see the complete Invoice Report. The front end should have each customer start on a new page. In addition, the front end should provide a quick way to navigate to the page for a particular customer, and a way to move from a customer to the page for its parent company. Finally, the front end should include a link to the customer's website for further information on the customer.

Task Overview

1. Create a New Report, Create a Dataset, and Populate the Report Layout.
2. Add the Navigation.

Invoice Front-End Report, Task 1: Create a New Report, Create a Dataset, and Populate the Report Layout

1. Reopen the Chapter08 project, if it was closed.
2. Create a new report called FrontEnd using the GDSReport template.
3. Create a new data source called Galactic that references the Galactic shared data source.
4. Create a new dataset called CustomerInvoices that calls the stp_CustomerInvoices stored procedure.
5. Use the table template to place a tablix onto the report body.
6. Select the InvoiceNumber, InvoiceDate, and TotalAmount fields in the Data row of the table.
7. Type the letter **C** for the Format property for the text box containing the TotalAmount field value.
8. Delete the table header row.

9. Add a parent group to the table using the CustomerName as the group expression. The group should have a group header, but not a group footer. Use the Page Breaks page of the Group Properties dialog box to set a page break between each instance of a group.

10. Drag the cell containing the CustomerName field wide enough to contain the customer name without wrapping. Set the FontWeight property of this cell to Bold.

11. Merge the left and center cells in the group header row. Select the ParentName field in the newly merged cells.

Task Notes We have the layout for the Invoice Front-End Report. However, it is not really a front end because it does not lead anywhere yet. Let's continue to the good stuff.

Invoice Front-End Report, Task 2: Add the Navigation

1. Right-click the cell containing the Invoice Number field and select Textbox: Text Box Properties from the context menu. The Text Box Properties dialog box appears.

2. Select the Action page.

3. Select the Go to report option under the Enable as a hyperlink prompt.

4. Select Invoice from the Select a report from the list drop-down list.

5. Click Add in the parameters area and configure the parameter as follows:

Name	Value
InvoiceNumber	[InvoiceNumber]

6. Click OK to exit the Text Box Properties dialog box.

7. In the Row Groups pane, use the Group1 drop-down menu to select Group Properties. The Group Properties dialog box appears.

8. Select the Advanced page.

9. Select [CustomerName] from the Document map drop-down list.

10. Click OK to exit the Group Properties dialog box.

11. Select the cell containing the CustomerName field. Set the following property in the Properties window:

Name	Value
Bookmark	=Fields!CustomerName.Value

12. Right-click the cell containing the ParentName field and select Textbox: Text Box Properties from the context menu. The Text Box Properties dialog box appears.

13. Select the Action page.
14. Select the Go to bookmark option under the Enable as a hyperlink prompt.
15. Select [ParentName] from the Select bookmark drop-down list.
16. Click OK to exit the Text Box Properties dialog box.
17. Right-click the rightmost cell in the group header row and select Textbox: Text box Properties from the context menu. The Text Box Properties dialog box appears.
18. Type **Website Link** for Value.
19. Select the Action page.
20. Select the Go to URL option under the Enable as a hyperlink prompt.
21. Select [CustomerWebsite] from the Select URL drop-down list.
22. Click OK to exit the Text Box Properties dialog box.
23. Click the Preview tab. Your report should appear similar to Figure 8-25.
24. Select Save All on the toolbar.

Task Notes   When you look at the report preview, you notice a new feature to the left of the report. This is the *document map,* which functions like a table of contents for your report. We created entries in the document map when we selected a field from the Document map drop-down list in Step 9.

Because you used CustomerName as the document map field, you see a list of all the customer names in the document map. When you click a customer name in the document map, you are taken directly to the page for that customer.

If you are not using the document map, you can hide it by clicking the Document Map button in the Report Viewer toolbar. The Document Map button is the leftmost button in the toolbar. Clicking this button a second time causes the document map to return.

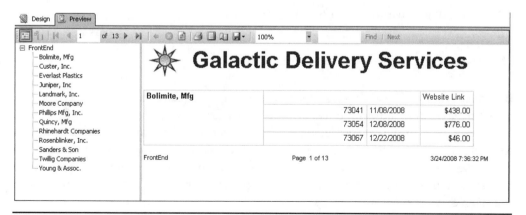

Figure 8-25   *The Front-End Report*

In addition to creating document map entries for each customer name, we created bookmarks for each customer name. This was done in Step 11. We are using these bookmarks to link child companies to their parent company. We are creating a Go to bookmark link using the value of the ParentName field. This was done in Steps 14 and 15.

When a customer has a value in the ParentName field, a Go to bookmark link is created on that parent name. The bookmark link jumps to the page for the customer with the matching name. To try this out, use the document map to jump to the page for Everlast Plastics. Everlast's parent company is Young & Assoc. Click the link for Young & Assoc., and you will jump to the page for Young & Assoc.

We also created a Go to URL link for each customer. This link was placed in the cell that reads Website Link and was created in Steps 20 and 21. Clicking this cell is supposed to take you to the website for each customer. However, we are unable to connect to the Inter-galactic-net used by GDS and its customers. Instead, clicking this link opens a browser and takes you to the McGraw-Hill website.

Earlier in the process, we created a Go to report link. This was done in Steps 2 through 6. Clicking an invoice number jumps you to the Invoice Report and passes the invoice number as a parameter. This enables you to see the detail information for the invoice. When you finish looking at the invoice, you can return to the Invoice Front-End Report by clicking the Back to Parent Report button in the Report Viewer toolbar.

The Transport Monitor Report

Features Highlighted

▶ Using a chart as the data section of a tablix

▶ Indicating values over a set maximum on a chart

▶ Using the autorefresh report property

▶ Using a multivalued parameter with a WHERE clause

Business Need   The Galactic Delivery Services maintenance department needs a report to assist in monitoring transport operations. Each transport feeds real-time sensor data back to the central database. The maintenance department needs a report to display this information for a selected set of transports. Because the sensor data is updated every minute, the report should refresh every minute. The sensor data should be displayed in a graphical form, with a highlight of any values that are above the normal maximums.

Task Overview

1. Create a New Report, Create a Dataset, Populate the Report Layout, and Set Report Properties.

Transport Monitor Report, Task 1: Create a New Report, Create a Dataset, Populate the Report Layout, and Set Report Properties

1. Reopen the Chapter08 project, if it was closed.
2. Create a new report called TransportMonitor. Do *not* use the GDSReport template.
3. Create a new data source called Galactic that references the Galactic shared data source.
4. Create a new dataset called TransportMonitor that calls the stp_TransportMonitor stored procedure.
5. Create a second dataset called TransportList that calls the stp_TransportList stored procedure.
6. Configure the TransportNumber Report Parameter as follows:

Property	Value
General page:	
Prompt	Transports
Allow multiple values	Checked
Available Values page:	
Select from one of the following options	Get values from a query
Dataset	TransportList
Value field	TransportNumber
Label field	TransportNumber

7. Click OK to exit the Report Parameter Properties dialog box.
8. Place a text box on the report body and set its properties as follows:

Property	Value
Font: FontSize	20pt
Font: FontWeight	Bold
Location: Left	0in
Location: Top	0in
Size: Width	3in
Size: Height	0.375in
Value	Transport Monitor

9. Use the matrix template to place a tablix onto the report body. Set the properties of the tablix as follows:

Property	Value
Location: Left	0in
Location: Top	0.5in

10. Select the TransportNumber field from the TransportMonitor dataset in the Rows cell. Set the following properties of the text box created in that cell:

Property	Value
BackgroundColor	White
Font: FontWeight	Bold
VerticalAlign	Middle

11. Select the Item field in the Columns cell. Set the following properties of the text box created in that cell:

Property	Value
BackgroundColor	White
Font: FontWeight	Bold
TextAlign	Center

12. Open the Tablix Properties dialog box. Set the following properties:

Property	Value
Row Headers: Header should remain visible while scrolling	checked
Column Headers: Header should remain visible while scrolling	checked

13. Click OK to exit the Tablix Properties dialog box.

14. Select the Data cell of the tablix and set the following property:

Property	Value
Size: Width	2.25in
Size: Height	1.625in

15. Place a chart in the Data cell. The Select Chart Type dialog box appears.

16. Select the stacked column chart and click OK.

17. Click the chart to activate the drop areas. Select the Value field in the Drop data fields here area.

18. Select the Reading field in the Drop category fields here area. Select the ReadingPortion field in the Drop series fields here area.

19. In the Chart Properties dialog box, set the following property:

Property	Value
Color palette	Excel

20. In the Value Axis Properties dialog box, set the following property:

Property	Value
Maximum	100

21. Right-click the chart title and select Delete Title from the context menu.

22. Right-click the legend area of the chart and select Delete Legend from the context menu.

23. Right-click the category axis title and select Show Axis Title from the context menu. This will uncheck this option and hide the axis title.

24. Right-click the value axis title and select Show Axis Title from the context menu. This will uncheck this option and hide the axis title.

25. Select Report in the drop-down list at the top of the Properties window and set the following property:

Property	Value
Autorefresh	60

26. Click the Preview tab.

27. Select several transport numbers from the drop-down list and click View Report. Your report appears similar to Figure 8-26.

28. Select Save All on the toolbar.

Task Notes A number of interesting things are going on in this report. First, a multivalued parameter is being sent to SQL Server for use in a stored procedure. The stored procedure uses the contents of this multivalued parameter to build a query string on the fly. The SELECT statement in the stored procedure is a bit complicated because

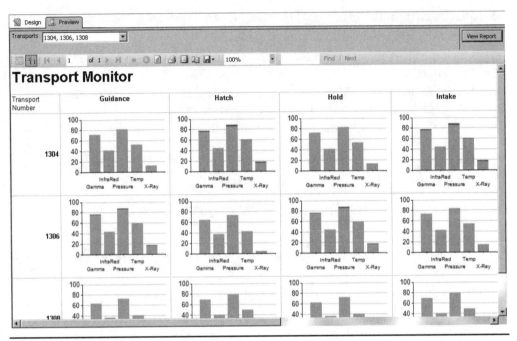

Figure 8-26 *The Transport Monitor Report preview*

it is using some random number generation to simulate the Transport telemetry. Here is a more straightforward version of the content of the stored procedure:

```
DECLARE @DynamicQuery varchar(8000)
SET @DynamicQuery = 'SELECT TransportNumber, Item, Reading, Value '
SET @DynamicQuery = @DynamicQuery + 'FROM transMonitor '
SET @DynamicQuery = @DynamicQuery + 'WHERE TransportNumber IN
                                    ('+@TransportNumber+') '

EXEC (@DynamicQuery)
```

This stored procedure code builds the SELECT statement in the @DynamicQuery variable. It uses the IN operator to look for the content of the TransportNumber field in a list of values. The values must be comma-separated and enclosed in parentheses to be used with the IN operator. The values in the multivalued parameter are being passed to the @TransportNumber stored procedure parameter. Because these values are already comma-separated, all we have to do is place them inside the parentheses to use them with the IN operator.

We placed a chart in the data portion of the matrix data region. Because the data portion of a matrix is an aggregate, the chart has a set of values to use for charting.

When the report is rendered, the chart is repeated in each data cell in the matrix. Each chart then acts within the scope of its data cell and charts the data in that scope.

The chart contains two series. The first series is a value up to the maximum normal value for that reading. The second series is the amount of the reading above the maximum normal value. The second series value is 0 if the reading is below or at its maximum normal value. The stacked column chart puts these two series one on top of the other. The result is any readings that are above their maximum normal value have a maroon section at the top of the column. This should be enough to get the attention of any technician monitoring the readings.

Finally, we used autorefresh to meet the business requirements of the report. When the AutoRefresh property is set, the report is automatically re-run on the schedule you specify.

A Conversion Experience

Reporting Services is not the first report-authoring environment to come along. Hundreds of thousands of reports have been created using other tools. If you have legacy reports and are looking to switch to Reporting Services, these legacy reports need to be re-created—that is, unless your legacy reports were written in Microsoft Access. If that is the case, you are in luck.

The Report Designer includes an import tool for taking Access reports and making them into Reporting Services reports. Not everything in your Access reports imports directly into Reporting Services. Even so, this import tool gives you a leg up on having to rebuild each entire report from scratch.

We now go through a sample report import to give you an introduction to the import tool. You can consult the Reporting Services Books Online for more information on exactly which features the Access report import tool will and won't import.

The Paid Invoices Report

Feature Highlighted

▶ Importing an Access report

Business Need   The Galactic Delivery Services accounting department has an Access report that lists paid invoices. The accounting department would like to convert this report to Reporting Services and eliminate the InvoiceInfo.mdb file. The MDB file uses linked tables to pull data from the SQL Server database.

NOTE

The Access import can only be done if you have Microsoft Access installed on the PC where you are running Reporting Services.

Task Overview

1. Import the Access Report and Change the Data Source.

Paid Invoices Report, Task 1: Import the Access Report and Change the Data Source

1. If you have not already done so, download the InvoiceInfo.mdb file from the website for this book.

2. Create a System ODBC data source called Galactic that points to the Galactic database. Use GalacticReporting for the SQL login and gds for the password. This ODBC data source is used by the linked tables in InvoiceInfo.mdb to access the Galactic database in SQL Server. This Open Database Connectivity (ODBC) data source must be in place for the conversion to function properly.

CAUTION

This is a Windows ODBC data source, not a Reporting Services data source. Use the ODBC Data Source Administrator under Administrative Tools in the Control Panel to create this data source.

3. Reopen the Chapter08 project, if it was closed.

4. Right-click the Reports folder in the Solution Explorer and select Import Reports | Microsoft Access from the context menu. The Open dialog box appears.

5. Browse to the InvoiceInfo.mdb file, select it, and click Open. The Report Designer imports any reports it finds in the selected MDB file.

6. When the import is complete, you have a new report called PaidInvoices.rdl in your Solution Explorer. Double-click this report to open it. The import brought in the layout from the Access report. All you need to do now is add the SQL query.

7. Create a new data source in the PaidInvoices report called Galactic that references the Galactic shared data source.

8. Create a new dataset called PaidInvoices with the following query:

```
SELECT InvoiceHeader.CustomerNumber, InvoiceHeader.InvoiceNumber,
       InvoiceHeader.TotalAmount, PaymentInvoiceLink.PaidDate,
       PaymentInvoiceLink.PaidAmount
FROM InvoiceHeader
```

```
INNER JOIN PaymentInvoiceLink
        ON InvoiceHeader.InvoiceNumber = PaymentInvoiceLink.InvoiceNumber
INNER JOIN Payment
        ON PaymentInvoiceLink.PaymentNumber = Payment.PaymentNumber
WHERE (InvoiceHeader.PaidInFullFlag = 1)
ORDER BY InvoiceHeader.CustomerNumber, InvoiceHeader.InvoiceNumber,
        PaymentInvoiceLink.PaidDate
```

9. Select the tablix called GroupLevel0. Set the following property of the tablix:

Property	Value
DataSetName	PaidInvoices

10. The import initially creates the imported report without a dataset. Therefore, the import creates parameters to replace every field. We need to replace these parameters with the fields from our new result set. Right-click PaidInvoices in the Solution Explorer window and select View Code from the context menu.

11. From the main menu, select Edit | Find and Replace | Quick Replace. The Find and Replace dialog box appears.

12. Enter **Parameters!** for Find what. Enter **Fields!** for Replace with.

13. Click Replace All.

14. Click OK when the find-and-replace operation is complete. Close the Find and Replace dialog box.

15. Select Save All on the toolbar.

16. Close the PaidInvoices.rdl code tab.

17. Expand the Parameters entry in the Report Data window.

18. Delete each of the parameters.

19. Click the Preview tab.

20. Make any additional formatting changes necessary to get the report looking as it should. (You might want to start by moving the column headers into a more appropriate location.)

21. Select Save All on the toolbar when the report is completed.

Task Notes   You can see the column headings from the Access report were placed in the page header in the Reporting Services report. This looks rather strange, but it is nothing a minute or two of additional formatting can't fix. The import does not create a perfect replica of your Access report in Reporting Services. It does, however, save you a lot of time over rebuilding each report from scratch.

What's Next

We have now touched on almost all the report-authoring features for Reporting Services. It is time to move on from report development to report deployment and delivery. We take a quick look at the various formats available for Reporting Services reports and then move on into the world of the Report Manager.

Chapter 9

A Leading Exporter: Exporting Reports to Other Rendering Formats

In This Chapter

▶ **A Report in Any Other Format Would Look as Good**

▶ **Presentation Formats**

▶ **Data Exchange Formats**

▶ **Call the Manager**

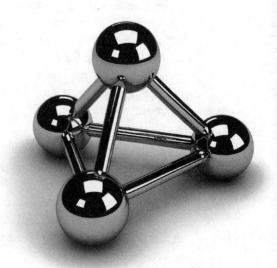

Up to this point, we have been viewing reports in the preview format. The preview format works great during report development for checking out your report layout and interactivity. However, when you want to present your report to users who do not have the Report Designer, you need something other than the preview format to do the job.

In place of the preview format, Reporting Services lets you export your report to other rendering formats so it can be presented to a user. These *presentation rendering formats* retain the layout, fonts, colors, and graphics of the report. The presentation rendering formats are as follows:

▶ TIFF Image

▶ Adobe PDF

▶ MHTML (web archive)

▶ Excel

▶ Word

▶ Print

▶ HTML

The presentation rendering formats can be further divided into three groups. The *interactive presentation rendering formats,* preview and Hypertext Markup Language (HTML), support all of the interactive features of Reporting Services. The *physical page presentation formats,* TIFF Image, Adobe PDF, and print, are primarily concerned with fitting content on a specific page size that can become a printout on a physical piece of paper. The *logical page presentation formats,* MHTML (web archive), Excel, and Word, are primarily concerned with formatting the content for viewing on a screen.

Reporting Services also lets you export your report to two additional formats, which are used primarily for rendering report data into a form that can be used by other computer programs. These *data exchange rendering formats* contain the data portion of the report, along with a minimal amount of formatting. Here are the data exchange rendering formats:

▶ Comma-Separated Values (CSV)

▶ Extensible Markup Language (XML)

During development, most of these rendering formats can be generated from the Preview tab in the Report Builder using the Export toolbar button. This enables you to render a report to a file or to a printer and manually distribute it to your users. It also lets you verify what the report will look like when your users choose to receive your report rendered in one of these formats. We discuss how report users utilize these rendering formats in Chapters 10 through Chapter 12.

In this chapter, we look at each of these rendering formats, which report features they support, and how they can best be used. To demonstrate each rendering format, we use a report project that contains a set of reports with many of the layout and interactivity characteristics discussed in the previous chapters. If you want to "play along at home," you can download the Chapter09 report project from the website for this book and try exporting the report to each rendering format yourself.

A Report in Any Other Format Would Look as Good

If Reporting Services only enabled you to view reports in the preview format when using the Report Designer and in a browser when using the Report Manager, it would be an interesting tool. The fact that reports can be delivered in a number of other presentation formats while maintaining their basic look and feel makes Reporting Services a powerful tool. Adding the capability to transfer information using a pair of data exchange formats further enhances the flexibility of Reporting Services.

Exporting and Printing a Report

We look at each of the export formats in detail in the "Presentation Formats" and "Data Exchange Formats" sections. First, let's look at how the export process works in the Report Designer. We try exporting a report, and then displaying it with the appropriate viewer. Then, we print the report from the Report Designer.

Exporting a Report

Follow these steps to export a report.

1. If you have downloaded the Chapter09 project, open this project, double-click the RenderingTest report, and click the Preview tab. (You may need to re-enter the password in the shared data source in this project before you can preview the report.) If you have not downloaded the Chapter09 project, open your favorite report project from one of the previous chapters, double-click a report, and click the Preview tab. The report is displayed in the preview format.

2. Expand the Bolimite row and the 2007 column in the tablix on the first page.

3. Click the Export button in the Report Designer toolbar. You see a drop-down list showing all the available export formats, as shown in Figure 9-1.

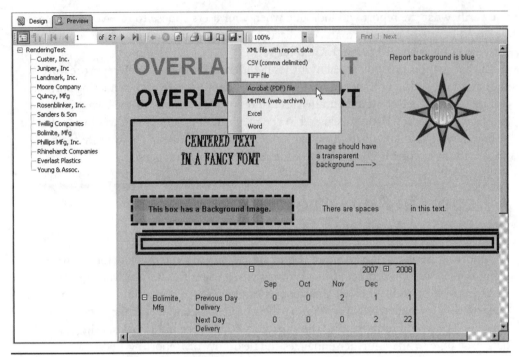

Figure 9-1   *The Export menu on the Preview tab*

4. Select any of the available formats. (Choose one of the presentation formats to make this a more interesting example.) The Exporting dialog box appears.

5. After a few moments, the Save As dialog box appears over the top of the Exporting dialog box. Select the folder where you want the export file to be created. Modify the filename if you would like. Click Save.

6. The Export dialog box disappears after the export file is created. The report has now been exported or rendered in the selected format.

Viewing the Exported Report

Follow these steps to view the report.

1. To view the export file, open Windows Explorer.

2. Navigate to the folder where the export file was created.

3. Double-click the export file. Windows opens the export file using the appropriate application for viewing this type of file. (We cover viewer requirements as we discuss each export format in the "Presentation Formats" and "Data Exchange Formats" sections.)

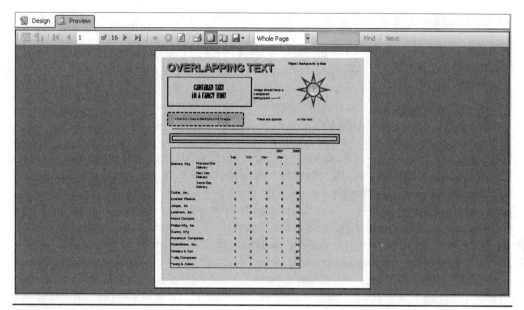

Figure 9-2   *The print layout*

Printing a Report

Follow these steps to print the report.

1. Return to the Preview tab in the Report Designer.
2. Click the Print Layout button on the Report Designer toolbar. The contents of the Preview tab are replaced by the print layout, as shown in Figure 9-2.
3. Use the drop-down list in the Report Designer toolbar to zoom in or zoom out, as needed.
4. Click the Print button just to the left of the Print Layout button. The Print dialog box appears.
5. Select the appropriate printer, set the necessary printer properties, and then click OK. Your report is printed.
6. Click the Print Layout button again to exit the print layout mode.

Presentation Formats

Most of the export or rendering formats provided by Reporting Services are presentation formats. They are intended to reproduce, as faithfully as possible, the format and the interactivity of your report as it appears in the preview format. The degree to which each presentation format can duplicate these things depends, in large part, on the features available in and the limitations of the viewer used by each format. For instance, a TIFF image viewer does not provide any hyperlinks, so the TIFF export does not support the navigation features.

In this section, we look at the viewer required to display each format. Also, the features supported and the features not supported by each presentation format are listed. We also discuss how each presentation format can best be utilized.

We use the RenderingTest report from the Chapter09 report project to examine some of the features supported by each presentation format. As mentioned earlier, you may download this report project from the website for this book if you want to perform the exports and make the comparisons yourself. Our standard is the appearance and behavior of this report in the Preview tab in the Report Designer. The top of the first page of the RenderingTest report in the Preview tab is shown in Figure 9-3. As we look at each presentation format, we can compare it to the way the report looks in this figure.

Note, I used a font called Juice ITC for the text box containing the words "Centered Text in a Fancy Font." This was done to demonstrate the behavior of a font that may not be available on other computers. However, because of this, you may not actually see a fancy font in this text box. Instead, you see the font the Report Designer chooses to substitute for the requested font, which is unavailable. If this is the case, you have to trust the text and the figures to show you the behavior of this text box.

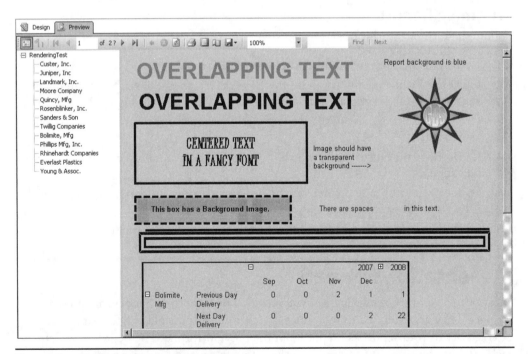

Figure 9-3   *The RenderingTest report in the Preview tab*

Note, too, the preview format does not pay strict attention to the physical page size specified for the report. The preview format allows a page to grow wider than a report page. The preview format does create page breaks based on the length of the page, but it does this only as an approximation. It does not strictly adhere to the page size specified for the report. Therefore, the page breaks found in the preview format differ from the page breaks found in formats that exactly follow the size properties of the report.

TIFF Image Presentation Format

TIFF is an acronym for Tagged Image File Format. *TIFF* is a file standard for storing images on personal computers, similar to the BMP and PCX formats. Unlike these formats, a TIFF file can store a number of images as multiple pages of a single document. This feature makes TIFF a popular format for storing fax documents.

When a report is rendered to a TIFF file, each page of the report is converted to a bitmap image. When we view the image, we see letters and numbers. However, the TIFF file itself contains only a series of dots. Because the entire report is stored as a bitmap image, TIFF files tend to be rather large.

Viewing TIFF Documents

On most Windows systems, TIFF files can be viewed using the Windows Picture and Fax Viewer. The Windows Picture and Fax Viewer has features for moving between pages, printing, and zooming in and out. This viewer also enables you to add annotations, including highlighting, drawing, text, and "sticky notes," as shown in Figure 9-4. These annotations can be helpful if reports are distributed electronically while they are being analyzed.

If you do not have the Windows Picture and Fax Viewer available, TIFF viewers are available for nearly any personal computer platform. In many cases, a TIFF viewer can be obtained for a minimal charge as shareware or freeware. Note, not all TIFF viewers include the annotation features found in the Windows Picture and Fax Viewer.

Features Supported by the TIFF Format

The top of the first page of the RenderingTest report exported to a TIFF file is shown in Figure 9-5. As you can see, the TIFF image provides a faithful representation of the report as it is seen in the preview layout. It includes colors, images (including background images), and charts. It preserves strings of text, including embedded new lines and multiple spaces in a row. (You soon see this causes a problem in another file format.)

The TIFF format preserves the font for all text rendered in the report. This is true even if a font used in the report is not present on the computer being used to view the report.

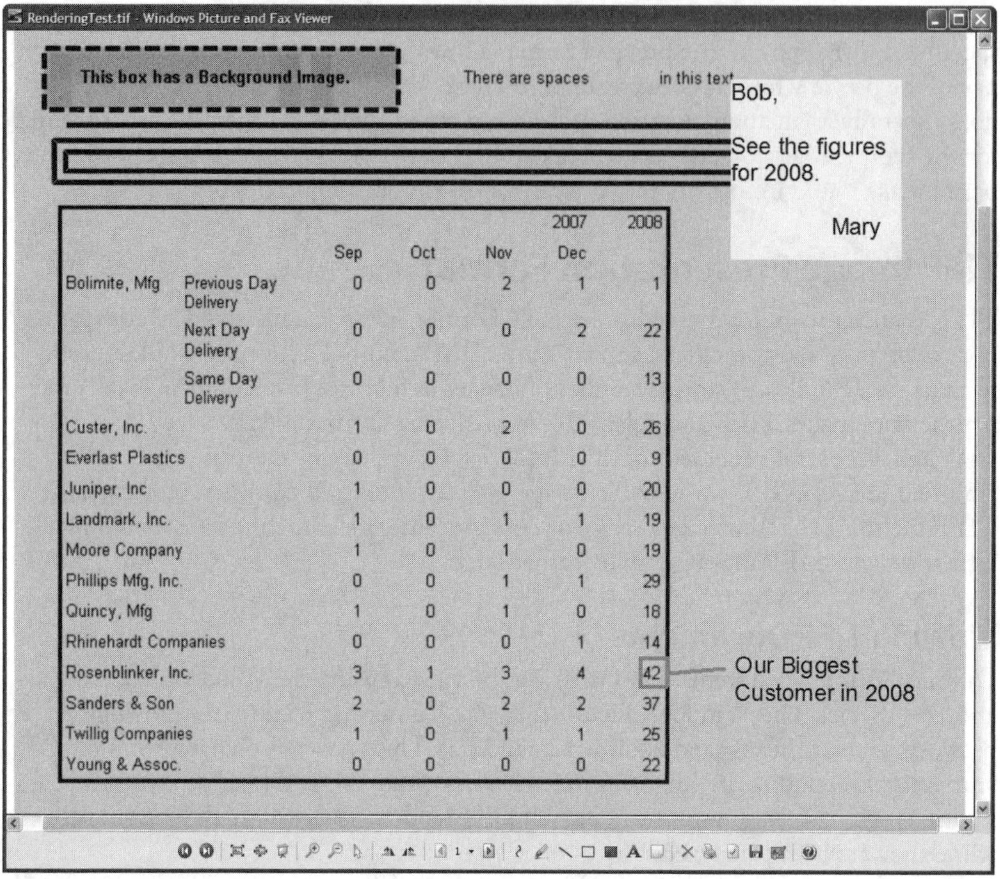

					2007	2008
		Sep	Oct	Nov	Dec	
Bolimite, Mfg	Previous Day Delivery	0	0	2	1	1
	Next Day Delivery	0	0	0	2	22
	Same Day Delivery	0	0	0	0	13
Custer, Inc.		1	0	2	0	26
Everlast Plastics		0	0	0	0	9
Juniper, Inc		1	0	0	0	20
Landmark, Inc.		1	0	1	1	19
Moore Company		1	0	1	0	19
Phillips Mfg, Inc.		0	0	1	1	29
Quincy, Mfg		1	0	1	0	18
Rhinehardt Companies		0	0	0	1	14
Rosenblinker, Inc.		3	1	3	4	42
Sanders & Son		2	0	2	2	37
Twillig Companies		1	0	1	1	25
Young & Assoc.		0	0	0	0	22

Figure 9-4 *The Windows Picture and Fax Viewer with an annotated report*

This is the only presentation format that possesses this characteristic. Also, the TIFF format preserves the exact location of each report item relative to other report items. This is true even if report items overlap one another—something not even the preview layout does properly.

Physical pages are supported by the TIFF format. This means when a report is exported to a TIFF file, the renderer pays attention to the physical page size specified for the report and does not let a page grow beyond that size. When a report page is taller or wider than the physical page size, the TIFF renderer splits it into multiple pages.

Because physical pages are supported, the TIFF format can be printed with the assurance that the printed report is going to match the report on the screen in both layout and pagination.

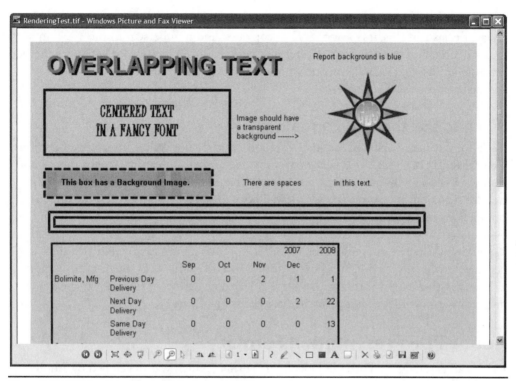

Figure 9-5   *The RenderingTest report exported to a TIFF file*

NOTE

When you're exporting a report to TIFF or any of the other formats that support physical pages, it is important that your report is not wider than the report page. Be sure to include the page margins when you are calculating how wide the body of your report can be.

Features Not Supported by the TIFF Format

The TIFF format does not support any of the interactive features of a report. You cannot use drilldown functionality to expand rows and columns in a tablix. The rows and columns that were expanded when the report was exported are also expanded in the resulting TIFF file. The rows and columns that were hidden when the report was exported are not included in the resulting TIFF file.

In addition, the TIFF format does not support navigation within a report, between reports, or to a web page. Bookmarks, drillthrough functionality, and links to a Uniform Resource Locator (URL) do not work in a TIFF file. The document map does not show up in the TIFF file, even if it is part of the report in the preview format.

Finally, as stated earlier, the TIFF file is simply a series of dots that make up an image. Because of this, it is impossible to copy text and numbers from the TIFF image to paste into another document. Therefore, the TIFF format does not work as a method for passing information to someone who wants to cut and paste it into a spreadsheet and do their own ad hoc analysis.

When to Use the TIFF Format

TIFF format files work well for smaller reports that do not utilize interactive functions. The capability of some TIFF viewers to provide annotation features makes this a good choice for sharing analysis among a number of people. The TIFF format also works well for situations where reports are viewed both onscreen and in print. However, users cannot copy numbers from the report to paste into another application to perform their own analysis.

Because the entire content of the report is stored as a bitmap image, TIFF files become very large very fast. A report exported to a TIFF file is as much as ten times as large as other export formats. Use the TIFF export with care so as not to create monstrous export files that are unwieldy to deliver and use.

Adobe PDF Presentation Format

PDF is an acronym for Portable Document Format, which was developed by Adobe Systems, Inc. *PDF* was designed so a document could be moved from one computer to another—even between computers with different operating systems—and appear exactly the same on both computers.

When a report is rendered to a PDF file, its formatting is stored using a language similar to the PostScript description language. Images that appear in the report are stored right within the PDF file. Text entries in the report remain text; they are not converted to images, as they are with the TIFF format.

Viewing PDF Documents

PDF files are viewed using the Adobe Acrobat Reader. The Acrobat Reader is available as a free download from the Adobe website at www.adobe.com. Versions of the Acrobat Reader are available for Windows, Mac, Solaris Sun, Linux, several flavors of UNIX, and even for handheld devices. The Acrobat Reader has features for moving between pages, printing, and zooming in and out.

Features Supported by the PDF Format

The top of the first page of the RenderingTest report exported to a PDF file is shown in Figure 9-6. (Other versions of Adobe Acrobat Reader may appear slightly different.)

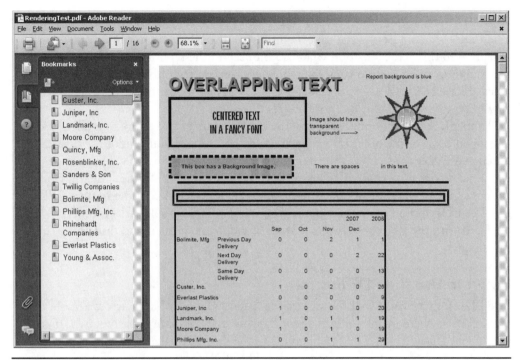

Figure 9-6   *The RenderingTest report exported to a PDF file*

As with the TIFF format, the PDF format provides a faithful representation of the report as it is seen in the preview layout. It includes colors, images (including background images), and charts. It also preserves strings of text, including embedded new lines and multiple spaces in a row. PDF also enables report items to overlap.

Just as in the TIFF format, physical pages are supported by the PDF format. When a report page is taller or wider than the physical page size, the PDF renderer splits it into multiple pages. Because physical pages are supported, the PDF format can be printed with the assurance that the printed report will match the report on the screen in both layout and pagination.

The PDF format supports some of the navigation features available in Reporting Services reports. The report's document map entries become PDF bookmarks. In addition, links to URLs are supported. Also, because the PDF format does retain text and numbers as such, you can copy these items. Therefore, users can copy and paste information from the PDF format into a spreadsheet and do their own ad hoc analysis.

Features Not Supported by the PDF Format

The PDF format preserves the font for almost all text rendered in the report. The exception to this is the situation where a font used in the report is not present on the computer being used to view the report. As you can see in Figure 9-6, the text "CENTERED TEXT IN A FANCY FONT" did not appear in a fancy font when viewed on a computer that did not have that font loaded.

Although the PDF format supports the document map and a link to a URL, it does not support any of the other interactive features of a report. You cannot use drill-down functionality to expand rows and columns in a tablix. The rows and columns expanded when the report was exported are expanded in the resulting PDF file. The rows and columns hidden when the report was exported are not included in the resulting PDF file. The PDF format does not support Reporting Services bookmarks (not to be confused with the PDF bookmarks that act as a document map) and drill-through functionality.

When to Use the PDF Format

The PDF format works well for reports that need to be distributed across a variety of platforms, where maintaining the report layout and pagination are required. If an investment is made in Adobe Standard or Adobe Professional, the PDF format can be used when annotation features are required. The PDF format works well for both large and small reports, and in situations where reports are viewed both on the screen and in print. The PDF format does enable users to copy numbers from a report and paste them into another application to do ad hoc analysis.

The PDF format does not work for reports where drilldown or drill-through functionality is required. It is also not appropriate for situations where one or more fonts that may not be available on the end user's computer are used in the report and these fonts must be preserved in the report output.

Web Archive Presentation Format

The web archive is a special form of web page. In addition to the HTML formatting code, the web archive file contains all the supporting files required by the page. The supporting files are the images referenced by the HTML. As the name implies, the *web archive* can be used to gather all the necessary parts of a web page in one place, so it can be easily moved to a different location and archived. This also makes it an excellent candidate for distributing reports in an HTML format.

The extension on web archive files is .mhtml.

Viewing Web Archive Documents

Because web archive documents are self-contained web pages, they are viewed using a web browser. Having a web browser available on a computer is usually not an issue these days, so web archive documents can be distributed across multiple computer platforms. Web archive documents can also be displayed in many e-mail programs that support HTML e-mail messages.

Features Supported by the Web Archive Format

The top of the first page of the RenderingTest report exported to a web archive file is shown in Figure 9-7. The web archive format provides a somewhat faithful

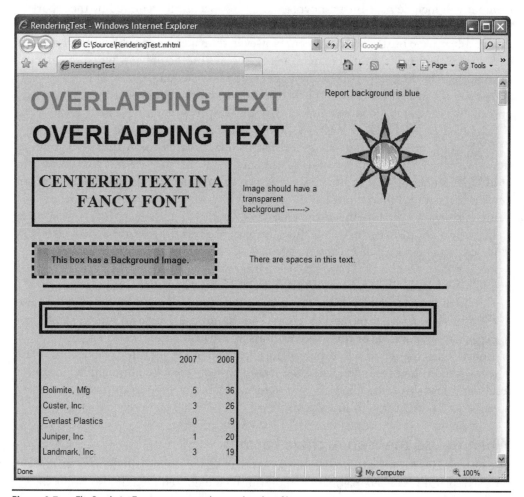

Figure 9-7   *The RenderingTest report exported to a web archive file*

representation of the report as it is seen in the preview layout. It includes colors, images (including background images), and charts.

The web archive format retains only one of the navigation features in Reporting Services reports. It allows for links to URLs to be embedded in the report. Also, because the web archive format retains text and numbers as such, you can copy these items. Therefore, users can copy and paste information from the web format into a spreadsheet and do their own ad hoc analysis.

Features Not Supported by the Web Archive Format

In the web archive format, physical pages are not supported. Instead, the report is presented as one continuous web page. When you print from Internet Explorer, the printout will include page breaks anyplace they are specifically required by the report format (i.e., before the "Page Break Before This Item" rectangle). Horizontal lines mark these explicit page breaks on the screen. However, to make the page breaks that actually occur when the page is printed match the page breaks on the preview tab, some manual manipulation of the Internet Explorer page setup must be done.

You can see in Figure 9-7 that the web archive format does not preserve strings of text, including embedded new lines and multiple spaces in a row. (The text "CENTERED TEXT IN A FANCY FONT" should have a new line after the word "TEXT." The sentence "There are spaces in this text," located below the GDS graphic, should have a gap between the word "spaces" and the word "in.") This is a characteristic of HTML rendering that compresses white space (such as multiple spaces) and ignores new lines. Another HTML limitation is the inability to support overlapping report items, as shown by the top line of the report.

Like the PDF format, the web archive format preserves the font for almost all text rendered in the report. The exception, again, is the situation where a font used in the report is not present on the computer being used to view the report. In Figure 9-7, the text "CENTERED TEXT IN A FANCY FONT" is no longer in a fancy font.

Although the web archive format supports a link to a URL, it does not support any of the other interactive features of a report. You cannot use drilldown functionality to expand rows in a table or rows and columns in a matrix. The rows and columns expanded when the report was exported are expanded in the resulting web archive file. The rows and columns hidden when the report was exported are not included in the resulting web archive file. The web archive format does not support document maps, bookmarks, or drill-through functionality.

When to Use the Web Archive Format

The web archive format works well for reports that need to be distributed across a variety of platforms, where pagination and printing are not required. It also works well for situations where the content of the report is to be embedded in an e-mail message.

The web archive format works well for both large and small reports. The web archive format does let users copy numbers from a report and paste them into another application for ad hoc analysis.

The web archive format does not work well in situations where the report's exact formatting must be preserved. Its limitations also make it a bad choice in situations where pagination and printing capabilities are needed. Finally, it does not work when drilldown, drill-through, or other navigation features are required.

Excel Presentation Format

Excel, of course, is Microsoft's spreadsheet application. The Excel presentation format is simply an Excel workbook file. The workbooks created from Reporting Services reports have multiple tabs or spreadsheets to represent the document map and the logical pages in the report.

Viewing Excel Documents

Naturally, Excel documents are viewed using Microsoft Excel. The initial version of SQL Server 2000 Reporting Services required Excel 2002 (version 10) or Excel 2003 (version 11) to display reports exported in the Excel format. SQL Server 2000 Reporting Services SP2, as well as SQL Server 2005 Reporting Services and SQL Server 2008 Reporting Services, however, work with earlier versions of Excel.

Features Supported by the Excel Format

The document map portion of the RenderingTest report as it appears in the Excel file is shown in Figure 9-8. The top of the first page of the RenderingTest report as it appears in the Excel file is shown in Figure 9-9. The Excel format provides as faithful a representation of the report as it can within the confines of spreadsheet rows and columns. It includes colors, foreground images, and charts. Note, if your report contains any charts, they are exported as images by the Excel export. They are not exported as chart objects, so they cannot be modified in Excel.

The Excel format does not create page breaks based on the page size of the report. It does split the report up into separate tabs at locations where your report logic says there should be page breaks. For example, if a grouping on your report has the PageBreak property set, each new instance of this grouping would begin on a new tab in Excel.

The Excel format does include several of the navigation features in Reporting Services reports. It supports the document map, as well as bookmarks. It also allows for links to URLs to be embedded in the report. The Excel format does preserve strings of text, including embedded new lines and multiple spaces in a row.

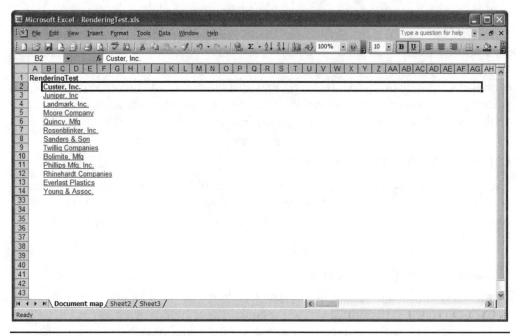

Figure 9-8   *The document map from the RenderingTest report exported to an Excel file*

The Excel format is a series of spreadsheets, so naturally, it allows for ad hoc analysis to be done on its contents. The contents of most cells are represented as text or numeric constants. However, in some cases, the cell may contain a formula. This results if the value of one report item is a calculation utilizing the value of another report item.

Features Not Supported by the Excel Format

In the Excel format, physical pages are not supported. Only logical page breaks are supported, as mentioned previously. Because of this, the Excel format does not work well when printing a report. As with several of the previous formats, the Excel format preserves the font, except when a font used in the report is not present on the computer being used to view it. Even though the Excel format supports foreground images, it does not support background images.

Although the Excel format supports several navigation features, it does not support the drilldown columns in our example. The columns in a tablix appear exactly as they did in the Preview tab, either expanded or contracted, when the export was created. Excel does support the drilldown rows in our example. The Excel format does not support drill-through functionality.

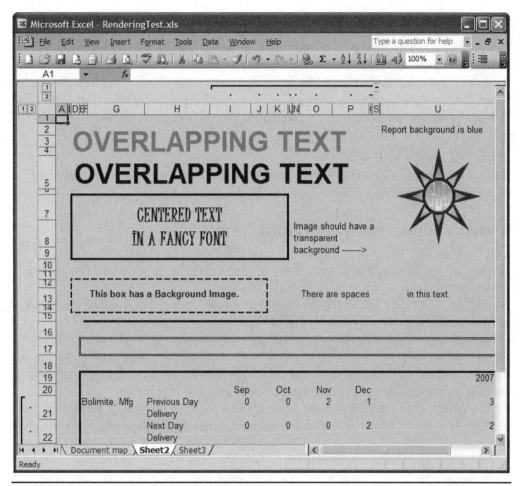

Figure 9-9   *The RenderingTest report exported to an Excel file*

When to Use the Excel Format

The Excel format works well for situations when the end user wants to perform some ad hoc analysis after they receive the report. The Excel format generates much smaller file sizes in the SQL Server 2008 version than in past versions. Therefore, it can now be used for large reports as well as small and medium-size reports. The Excel format does not work well in situations where the report's exact formatting must be preserved. Also, the Excel format is inappropriate in situations where pagination and printing are required. Finally, it does not work when drilldown or drill-through functionality is needed.

Word Presentation Format

The new addition to the export formats in SQL Server 2008 Reporting Services is the Microsoft Word format. This export format, as one might expect, creates a Word document. The document that results depends heavily on tables to reproduce the report layout. As with the Excel export, the goal of the Word export format is to reproduce the look of the report when printed or when viewing in print preview mode.

Viewing Word Documents

Word documents are viewed using Microsoft Word. The documents created by the Reporting Services export can be viewed by Word 2000 and later.

Features Supported by the Word Format

The Word export format provides a good reproduction of the report seen on the Preview tab in the Report Designer. There are just a few things missing. Most obvious, the background of the report is white, not blue. Also, the background image is missing from the text box. As with Excel, the chart is an image, rather than an object that can be modified. The Word export is shown in Figure 9-10.

Because a Word document, by its very nature, is page-based, the Word export is paginated. Not only does it insert page breaks where you define them, but it also forces all of the content to fit on the page size defined for the report. The Word export uses the page size, page orientation, and margins configured for the report.

The Word export does implement some of the navigation features of Reporting Services. It supports bookmarks to move within a report. It also supports hyperlinks to navigate to a URL.

Aside from the charts, the content of the Word export is text. Users can cut and paste items from the reports. Users can also do some elementary analysis, summing or averaging, right in the tables created in Word.

Features Not Supported by the Word Format

Like the Excel format, the Word format also falls short in the area of interactivity. The Word format does not support drilldown functionality. The rows and columns expanded at the time of export are displayed in the report; hidden rows are not present. The Word format does not support drill-through functionality or the document map.

When to Use the Word Format

Microsoft Word is widely available, so most users will be able to display this format. It provides a faithful representation of the report in a format that prints out nicely and supports cut and paste, as well as editing. Having a format that enables editing can be

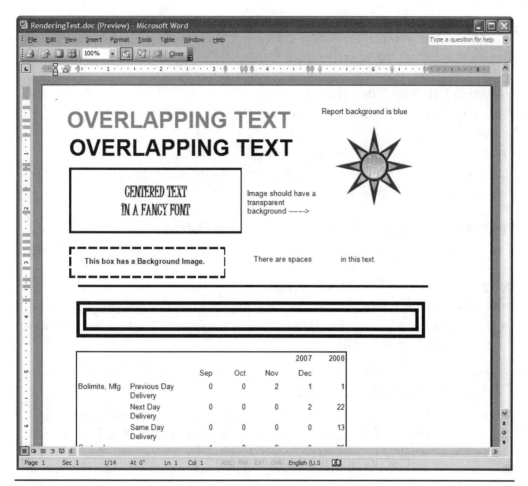

Figure 9-10   *The RenderingTest report exported to a Word document*

a good thing. It allows the user to tweak the formatting, add their own content, and perhaps copy and paste whole sections of the report into other documents. However, having an editable report can be a drawback as well. The user can actually change the data! Something to keep in mind with both the Excel and Word formats.

Printed Presentation Format

At first, it may not seem like printing the report on paper belongs in the same category as the other presentation formats. But, if you think about it, rendering the report to hard copy and delivering that printed paper to your users is a valid way to deliver a report.

In fact, it was the first way and, for many years, the only way to deliver a report. It seems only fitting, if for no other reason than to give a nod to history, that we include this format along with all the others.

Viewing Printed Documents

Printed documents are viewed on paper. Enough said.

Features Supported by the Printed Format

The printed format faithfully captures all the report formatting, along with both physical and logical page breaks.

Features Not Supported by the Printed Format

The only navigation supported by the printed format requires a thumb and forefinger.

When to Use the Printed Format

The printed format should only be used when your end user requires information to be on paper and is not interested in any of the navigation features or ad hoc analysis made available by the other formats.

Data Exchange Formats

The two remaining export or rendering formats provided by Reporting Services are data exchange formats. They are intended to take the data in a report and put it into a format that can be used by another computer program. In this section, we look at the basic structure of each of these formats. We also discuss the customization that can be done with each.

We continue to use the RenderingTest report from the Chapter09 report project to examine the data output by each format.

Comma-Separated Values (CSV) Data Exchange Format

The Comma-Separated Values (CSV) format has been around for a number of years. The CSV format is used to represent tabular data. Each line in the file represents one row in the tablix. Each value between two commas represents a column in the tablix. If a column value contains a comma (for example, "Bolimite, Mfg"), the value is enclosed in quotation marks.

CSV exports include the data contained within every tablix in your report. All the data from the table, matrix, or list is included in the CSV export, even if a column or a row is hidden. The first row of data from a given tablix contains column names based on the names of the text boxes in the tablix that generate the data in those columns. CSV exports do not contain values from charts or text boxes that are not within a table, matrix, or list.

Reports to be exported using the CSV format should be kept simple. Only one tablix should be placed on the report. When reports with more than one tablix are exported using the CSV format, the resulting file can be complex and confusing.

If you open the CSV file that results from the RenderingTest report in Notepad, it appears as follows. (A CSV file opens in Excel by default.) This represents the values from the tablix near the top of the report. If we were going to be importing this data into another computer system, it would probably be a good idea to give meaningful names to all of the text boxes in the tablix. You can also use the DataElementName property to provide column names. You will see an example of this as we look at the XML format in the next section.

```
CustomerName,textbox6,Year,textbox5,DeliveryNumber
"Bolimite, Mfg",Previous Day Delivery,2007,Sep,0
"Bolimite, Mfg",Previous Day Delivery,2007,Oct,0
"Bolimite, Mfg",Previous Day Delivery,2007,Nov,2
"Bolimite, Mfg",Previous Day Delivery,2007,Dec,1
"Bolimite, Mfg",Previous Day Delivery,2008,Jan,0
```

XML Data Exchange Format

In Chapter 7, we discussed XML and the fact that reports are stored in an XML format called Report Definition Language (RDL). Here, we are looking at XML as a means of exchanging data between programs. In both cases, the XML files are simply text files with information organized between XML tags.

By default, XML exports include the data contained within tablixes and charts in your report. All the data from the tablix or chart is included in the XML export, even if a column or a row is hidden. XML exports do not contain values from text boxes that are not within a tablix.

Because each item in the XML export is labeled with an XML tag, reports to be exported using the XML format can be more complex than those exported using the CSV format. Because of this, reports to be exported using the XML format may have more than one tablix or chart.

The following is a section of the XML file that results from the RenderingTest report:

```
<Report xsi:schemaLocation=... >
 <matrix1>
  <matrix1_CustomerName_Collection>
   <matrix1_CustomerName CustomerName="Bolimite, Mfg">
```

```
<matrix1_RowGroup2_Collection>
 <matrix1_RowGroup2 textbox6="Previous Day Delivery">
  <matrix1_Year_Collection>
   <matrix1_Year Year="2007">
    <matrix1_ColumnGroup2_Collection>
     <matrix1_ColumnGroup2 textbox5="Sep" DeliveryNumber="0" />
     <matrix1_ColumnGroup2 textbox5="Oct" DeliveryNumber="0" />
     <matrix1_ColumnGroup2 textbox5="Nov" DeliveryNumber="2" />
     <matrix1_ColumnGroup2 textbox5="Dec" DeliveryNumber="1" />
    </matrix1_ColumnGroup2_Collection>
   </matrix1_Year>
```

You can quickly see how the XML structure follows the report layout. The Report tag provides information about the report as a whole. After that tag is a series of tags containing the data in the tablix near the top of the report. Again, note that by default, the text boxes at the top of the report are not included in the XML export.

Customizing the XML Data Exchange Format

You can customize the XML export to fit your needs. Let's change the XML export to include the contents of the text box that reads "CENTERED TEXT IN A FANCY FONT." We can also change the matrix1_RowGroup2_Collection tag to DeliveryTypes and the matrix1_RowGroup2 tag to DeliveryType. Finally, we remove the DeliveryNumber altogether.

If you have downloaded the Chapter09 project, open the project and try this procedure:

1. Open the RenderingTest report.
2. Select the text box containing "CENTERED TEXT IN A FANCY FONT."
3. In the Properties window, look at the Font: FontFamily property. If the Juice ITC font is not in the drop-down list, select a font present in the list. (You are unable to save the changes made in this dialog box unless a valid font is selected.)
4. Set the following properties for this text box:

Property	Value
DataElementName	FancyFont
DataElementOutput	Output
DataElementStyle	Element

5. Click anywhere in the tablix near the top of the report.

6. Click the entry for RowGroup2 in the Row Groups pane. (Click the item to select it. Do not click the down arrow to activate the drop-down menu. It will say Tablix Member in the drop-down list at the top of the Properties window when this is selected.)

7. Set the following properties for the row group in the Properties window:

Property	Value
DataElementName	DeliveryType
DataElementOutput	Output

8. Select the text box in the lower-right corner of the tablix.

9. Set the following properties for this text box:

Property	Value
DataElementOutput	NoOutput

This causes this item not to be output in the XML.

10. Click the Preview tab.

11. Select XML file with report data from the Export drop-down list.

12. Select a location to store this export, enter a filename, and then click Save.

13. Use the Windows Explorer to find the file you just created, and then double-click the file to open it.

14. The first few lines of the XML file appear similar to the following:

```
<Report xsi:schemaLocation=... >
 <FancyFont>CENTERED TEXT IN A FANCY FONT</FancyFont>
 <matrix1>
  <matrix1_CustomerName_Collection>
   <matrix1_CustomerName CustomerName="Bolimite, Mfg">
    <DeliveryTypes>
     <matrix1_RowGroup2 textbox6="Previous Day Delivery">
      <matrix1_Year_Collection>
       <matrix1_Year Year="2007">
        <matrix1_ColumnGroup2_Collection>
         <matrix1_ColumnGroup2 textbox5="Sep" />
         <matrix1_ColumnGroup2 textbox5="Oct" />
         <matrix1_ColumnGroup2 textbox5="Nov" />
         <matrix1_ColumnGroup2 textbox5="Dec" />
        </matrix1_ColumnGroup2_Collection>
       </matrix1_Year>
```

The values on the DataElementName, DataElementOutput, and DataElementStyle properties of each item in your report can be used in this way to completely customize the XML output generated by the report.

Call the Manager

Now, it is time to move on to the Report Manager. In the next chapters in this book, we look at ways to put your reports into the Report Manager and ways to administer those reports once they are there.

Part III

Report Serving

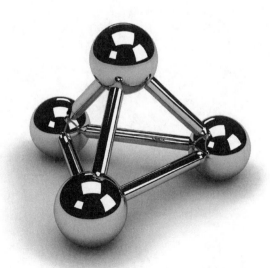

Chapter 10

How Did We Ever Manage Without You? The Report Manager

In This Chapter

- ▶ Folders
- ▶ Moving Reports and Supporting Files to the Report Server
- ▶ Managing Items in Folders
- ▶ Seek and Ye Shall Find: Search and Find Functions
- ▶ Printing from Report Manager
- ▶ Managing Reports on the Report Server
- ▶ Roles
- ▶ Linked Reports
- ▶ Delivering the Goods

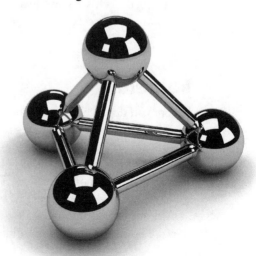

I n Part II of this book, we focused on report authoring. You learned fancy techniques for creating whiz-bang reports. However, the fact is, even the whiz-bangiest of reports are not much good if you cannot easily share them with end users.

In this chapter, you learn how to do just that. We move from authoring to managing reports and delivering them to the end users. This is done through the report server and its Report Manager web interface.

> **NOTE**
>
> *If you are using the SharePoint integration for hosting Reporting Services, these management tasks can be performed through the SharePoint user interface.*

We took a brief look at the report server and the Report Manager in Chapter 1. Now, we take a more detailed look. Much of our examination focuses on the Report Manager and how it is used to access and control the report server.

The first step is moving your report definitions and supporting files from the development environment to the Report Catalog. Recall that the Report Catalog is the SQL Server database where the report server keeps all its information. This information includes the definitions of the reports it is managing. We look at several ways to accomplish this report deployment.

Once your reports are available through the report server, you need to control how they are executed. We use the report server's security features to control who can access each report, and we use the caching and report history to control how a report is executed each time it is requested by a user. Finally, we control all these report server features using the Report Manager.

In short, in this chapter, we take your reports from a single-user development environment to a secure, managed environment where they can be executed by a number of users.

Folders

Before you deploy reports to the report server, you need to have an understanding of the way the report server organizes reports in the Report Catalog. In the Report Catalog, reports are arranged into a system of folders similar to the Windows or Mac file system. Folders can contain reports, supporting files (such as external images and shared data sources), and even other folders. The easiest way to create, view, and maintain these folders is through the Report Manager.

Although the Report Catalog folders look and act like Windows file system folders, they are not actual file system folders. You cannot find them anywhere in the file system on the computer running the report server. *Report Catalog folders* are screen representations of records in the Report Catalog database.

Each folder is assigned a name. Folder names can include just about any character, including spaces. However, folder names cannot include any of the following characters:

```
; ? : @ & = + $ , \ * < > | " /
```

Also, a folder name cannot consist exclusively of dots or spaces.

In addition to a name, folders can be assigned a description. The description can contain a long explanation of the contents of the folder. The description can help users determine what types of reports are in a folder without having to open that folder and look at the contents. Both the folder name and the description can be searched by a user to help them find a report.

The Report Manager

The Report Manager web application provides a straightforward method for creating and navigating folders in the Report Catalog. When you initially install Reporting Services, the Home folder is created by default. This is the only folder that exists at first.

The default Uniform Resource Locator (URL) for accessing the Report Manager site on the computer running Reporting Services is:

```
http://ComputerName/reports
```

In this case, ComputerName is the name of the computer where Reporting Services was installed. If you are using a secure connection to access the Report Manager site, replace http: with https:. If you are on the same computer where Reporting Services is running, you can use the following URL:

```
http://localhost/reports
```

No matter how you get there, when you initially access the Report Manager, it appears similar to Figure 10-1.

Notice the URL shown in Figure 10-1 is a bit different from the URLs given previously. This is because the Report Manager web application redirects you to the Pages/Folder.aspx web page. The Folder.aspx page is used to display folder contents.

NOTE

Figure 10-1 shows the Report Manager as it appears for a user with content manager privileges. If you do not see the New Folder, New Data Source, Upload File, and Report Builder buttons in the toolbar on the Contents tab, you do not have content manager privileges and will be unable to complete the exercises in this section of the chapter. If possible, log out and log in with a Windows login that has local administration privileges on the computer running the report server.

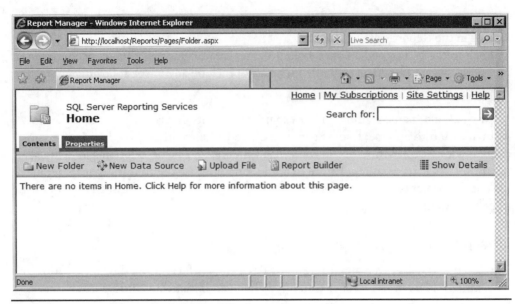

Figure 10-1   *The Report Manager with no folders defined*

To use the Report Manager, you must be using Microsoft Internet Explorer 7.0, Internet Explorer 6.0 with Service Pack 1 (SP1), or Internet Explorer 5.5 with Service Pack 2 (SP2). For all of these, you must have scripting enabled.

Adding a New Folder Using the Report Manager

Let's create a new folder into which we will deploy some of the Galactic Delivery Services reports from the previous chapters. Here are the steps to follow:

NOTE

Examples showing report deployment throughout this chapter assume the Galactic Delivery Services folder is created in the Home folder. If you already have other folders created in your Report Catalog, be sure you are in the Home folder when you complete the following steps.

1. Click the New Folder button in the toolbar on the Contents tab. The New Folder page appears, as shown in Figure 10-2.
2. Type **Galactic Delivery Services** for Name and **Reports created while learning to use Reporting Services** for Description.
3. Click OK to create the new folder and return to the Home folder.

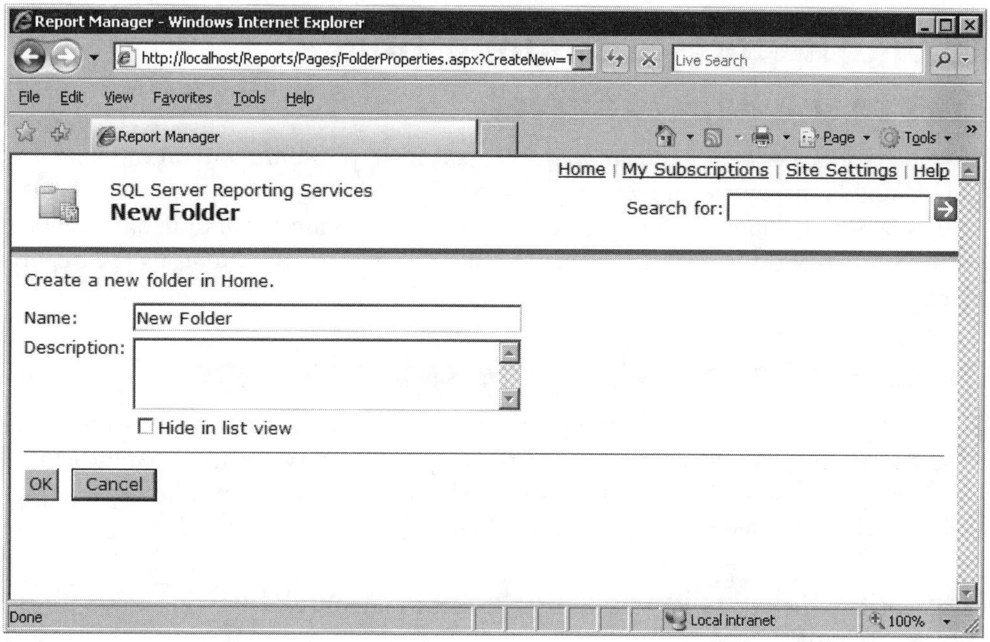

Figure 10-2 *The New Folder page*

You see an entry for your new folder with its name and description on the Contents tab of the Home folder. The text !NEW next to the folder name remains there for 48 hours. This helps to notify users of new content added to your report server.

If you were observant, you noticed one item on the New Folder page we did not use. (If you missed it, look at Figure 10-2.) This is the Hide in List View check box. When the Hide in List View check box is checked, the new folder does not appear on the Contents tab. This is useful when you want to make the reports in a folder available through a custom interface, but unavailable through the Report Manager. We discuss this in detail in Chapter 12.

To view the contents of the new folder, click the folder name. The name of the current folder appears in bold text near the top of the page. Immediately above the name of the current folder is the path from the Home folder to the current folder. Because the Galactic Delivery Services folder is in the Home folder, the path only contains Home >. You can return to any folder in the current path by clicking that folder name in the path shown near the top of the page. You can return to the Home folder by clicking Home at the beginning of the current path or by clicking Home in the upper-right corner of the page.

Moving Reports and Supporting Files to the Report Server

Now that you know how to create folders, it is time to put some content in those folders. You do this by moving reports and their supporting files from the development environment to the report server. This can be done using a number of different methods. We look at two of those methods now: using the Report Designer and using the Report Manager.

Deploying Reports Using the Report Designer

The most common method of moving reports to the report server is by using the Report Designer. Once you are satisfied with a report you developed, you can make it available to your users without leaving the development environment. This capability to create, preview, and deploy a report from a single authoring tool is a real plus.

Deploying Reports in the Chapter09 Project Using the Report Designer

Let's try deploying the report project from Chapter 9. To do so, follow these steps:

1. Start Visual Studio or the Business Intelligence Development Studio, and open the Chapter09 project.

2. Select Project | Chapter09 Properties from the main menu. The Chapter09 Property Pages dialog box appears.

3. Type **Galactic Delivery Services/Chapter 09** for TargetDataSourceFolder and TargetReportFolder. This is the folder into which the report is going to be deployed.

4. Type **http://ComputerName/ReportServer** for TargetServerURL, where ComputerName is the name of the computer where the report server is installed. You should replace http: with https: if you are using a secure connection. You can use localhost in place of the computer name if the report server is installed on the same computer you are using to run Visual Studio (see Figure 10-3).

NOTE

If your report server does not have the Reporting Services web service configured in its default location, you will need to modify the URL in Step 4 appropriately.

5. Click OK to exit the Chapter09 Property Pages dialog box.

6. Right-click the Chapter09 project entry in the Solution Explorer, and select Deploy from the context menu.

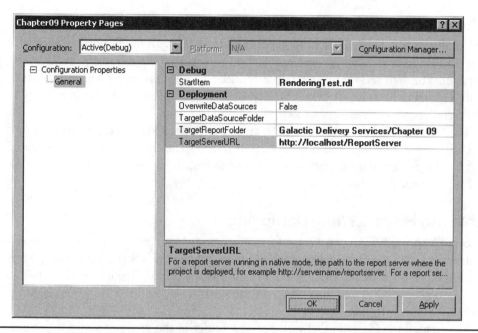

Figure 10-3 *The Chapter09 Property Pages dialog box*

7. The Report Designer builds all the reports in the project and then deploys all the reports, along with their supporting files, to the report server. (During the build process, the Report Designer checks each report for any errors that would prevent it from executing properly on the report server.) The results of the build and deploy are shown in the Output window.

8. Open the Report Manager in your browser. Click the Galactic Delivery Services folder to view its contents. You see that Visual Studio created a new folder in the Galactic Delivery Services folder called Chapter 09.

9. Click the Chapter 09 folder to view its content. All the items in the Chapter09 project—three reports and a shared data source—were deployed.

10. Click the RenderingTest report. You see the Hypertext Markup Language (HTML) version of the RenderingTest report.

NOTE

You can also deploy the contents of a project by selecting Build | Deploy {Project Name} from the main menu.

Working Through the Web Service

When the Report Designer deploys reports, it works through the Reporting Services web service. The Report Manager web application provides a human interface to Reporting Services. The web service provides an interface for other programs to communicate with Reporting Services. Because the Report Designer falls into the latter of these two categories, it uses the web service to deploy reports.

The web service has a different URL from the Report Manager. You must enter the URL for the web service and not the Report Manager in the Properties Pages dialog box for the deployment to work properly. The default URL for the web service is shown in Step 4 in the previous section.

Creating Folders While Deploying

In Steps 2 through 5, you entered information into properties of the Chapter09 project. These values tell the Report Designer where to put the reports and supporting items when the project is deployed. In this case, you instructed the Report Designer to put our reports and shared data source in the Chapter 09 folder within the Galactic Delivery Services folder.

You created the Galactic Delivery Services folder in the previous section. You did not create the Chapter 09 folder. Instead, the Report Designer created that folder for us as it deployed the items in the project. In fact, the Report Designer creates folders for any path you specify.

Deploying a Single Report

In Step 6, you used the project's context menu to deploy all the items in the project. Alternatively, you could have right-clicked a report and selected Deploy from the report's context menu. However, this would have deployed only this report, not the entire project.

On some occasions, you might want to deploy a single report rather than the entire project. At times, one report is going to be completed and ready for deployment, while the other reports in the project are still under construction. At other times, one report will be revised after the entire project has already been deployed. In these situations, it is only necessary to redeploy the single revised report.

Deploying Shared Data Sources

Even when a single report is deployed, any shared data sources used by that report are automatically deployed along with it. This only makes sense. A report that requires shared data sources does not do much if those shared data sources are not present.

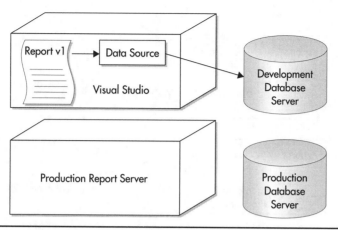

Figure 10-4   *A report and a shared data source ready to deploy*

If you look back at Figure 10-3, you notice an OverwriteDataSources item in the dialog box. This controls whether a shared data source that has been deployed to the report server is overwritten by subsequent deployments. In most cases, shared data sources do not change, so they do not need to be overwritten. For this reason, OverwriteDataSources is set to False, meaning do not overwrite existing data sources.

Aside from saving unnecessary effort, not overwriting data sources also helps out in another way. Consider the environment shown in Figure 10-4. In this environment, reports are developed in Visual Studio using a shared data source that points to a development database server. Once the first version of the report is completed, it is deployed to a production report server, as shown in Figure 10-5. As soon as the deployment is complete,

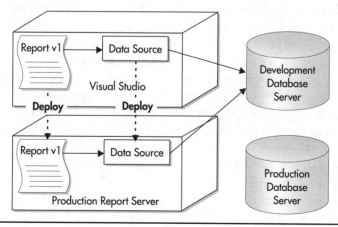

Figure 10-5   *Deploying the report and the shared data source*

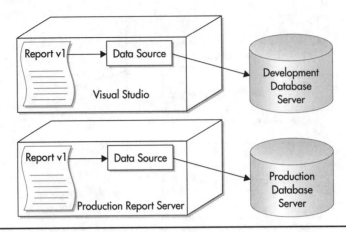

Figure 10-6 *Modifying the shared data source to point to the production database server*

the shared data source on the production report server needs to be changed to point to the production database server. This is shown in Figure 10-6.

Now, as time has passed, a new version of the report (version 2) is created in the development environment. This time, when version 2 of the report is deployed to the production report server, the shared data source already exists there.

If OverwriteDataSources is set to True, the data source from the development environment would overwrite the data source in the production environment, and we would be back to the situation in Figure 10-5. With this setting, we would have to redirect the shared data source each time a report is deployed.

To avoid this, OverwriteDataSources is set to False. Now, when version 2 of the report (and subsequent versions) is deployed to the production report server, the shared data source is not overwritten. It remains pointing to the production database server. This is shown in Figure 10-7. We have saved a bit of extra effort with each deployment.

As you will see throughout this chapter, folders are used to organize reports on the report server and help manage security for those reports. You can, if you are managing your report server properly, have reports deployed in a number of different folders. A number of these reports use the same database as the source for their data. Rather than having a number of shared data sources scattered throughout the folders on your report server, it makes more sense to have the reports all reference a single data source or a set of data sources stored in one central folder. This is accomplished through the use of the TargetDataSourceFolder.

Just as the TargetReportFolder property enables you to specify a path to a report server folder where a report is to be deployed, the TargetDataSourceFolder property, on the Property Pages dialog box, lets you specify a path to a report server folder where the

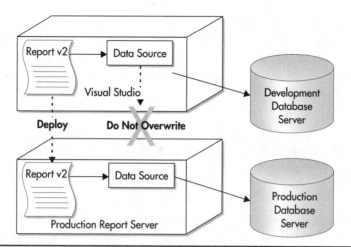

Figure 10-7 *A subsequent deployment with OverwriteDataSources set to False*

shared data source should be deployed or found, if it already exists there. If no folder path is specified, the TargetDataSourceFolder defaults to the TargetReportFolder. The OverwriteDataSources flag applies, whether the shared data source is being deployed to the TargetReportFolder or the TargetDataSourceFolder.

Additional Properties in the Property Pages Dialog Box

If you look back at Figure 10-3, you can see a couple additional items in the Property Pages dialog box that we have not discussed. We look at those two items now.

Maintaining Multiple Configurations At the top of the dialog box is the Configuration drop-down list. This drop-down list enables you to maintain several different deployment configurations for the same project. Each configuration has its own values for TargetDataSourceFolder, TargetReportFolder, TargetServerURL, and the other settings in the dialog box.

This is useful if you need to deploy the reports in a project to more than one report server. Perhaps you have the report server loaded on your PC for your own testing, a development report server where the report undergoes quality assurance testing, and a production report server where the report is to be made available to the end users. You can enter the properties for deploying to the report server on your PC in the DebugLocal configuration, the properties for deploying to the development report server in the Debug configuration, and the properties for deploying to the production report server in the Production configuration.

You can then easily switch between deploying to each of these report servers as new versions of your reports go from your own testing to quality assurance testing and are then made available to the users. You can change the configuration you are using for deployment through the Solution Configuration drop-down list in the Report Designer toolbar, as shown in Figure 10-8.

NOTE

Active(Debug) in the Configuration drop-down list simply refers to the Debug configuration that is currently the selected or active configuration.

Running a Report Project The final item we want to look at in the Project Property Pages dialog box is StartItem, which is used when running your report project. Use the StartItem drop-down list to select which report from your project should be executed

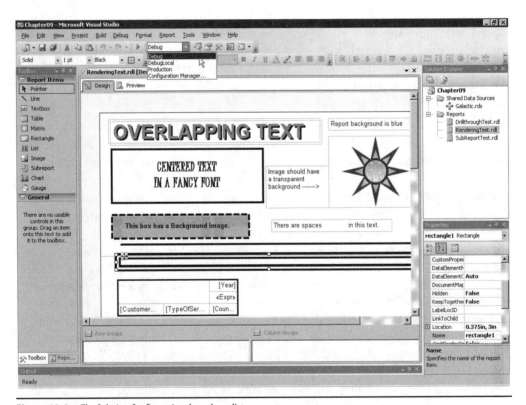

Figure 10-8 *The Solution Configuration drop-down list*

when you run the project. The report selected as the start item is displayed in a browser window in HTML format.

When you run a report project, you deploy all the reports, shared data sources, and other supporting information in the project to the target server and target folders in your active configuration. Once the deployment is complete, the report specified as the start item is executed in a browser window. You can then debug this report, making sure it looks correct and functions properly in HTML format. You can run the project by clicking the Start Debugging button on the toolbar (to the left of the Solution Configuration drop-down list) or by selecting any of the following items from the Debug menu (or by pressing any of the shortcut keys that correspond to these menu items):

▶ Start Debugging

▶ Start Without Debugging

▶ Step Over

There is no such thing as stepping over a report. These menu items simply run the project. The report selected as the start item is executed in a browser window from start to finish.

Uploading Reports Using Report Manager

Another common method of moving a report to the report server is by using the Report Manager. This is known as *uploading* the report. Deploying reports from the Report Designer can be thought of as pushing the reports from the development environment to the report server, whereas uploading reports from the Report Manager can be thought of as pulling the reports from the development environment to the report server.

You may need to use the Report Manager upload feature in situations where your report authors do not have rights to deploy reports on the report server. The report authors create their reports and test them within the Report Designer. When a report is completed, the report author can place the Report Definition Language (RDL) file for the report in a shared directory or send it as an e-mail attachment to the report server administrator. The report server administrator can upload the RDL file to a quality assurance report server and test the report for clarity, accuracy, and proper use of database resources. Once the report has passed this review, the report server administrator can upload the report to the production report server.

Uploading Reports in the Chapter06 Project Using the Report Manager

Let's try uploading some of the reports from the Chapter06 report project.

1. Open the Report Manager in your browser. Click the Galactic Delivery Services folder to view its contents.

2. Create a new folder called **Chapter 06**.

3. Select the new folder to view its contents.

4. Click the Upload File button in the toolbar on the Contents tab. The Upload File page appears, as shown in Figure 10-9.

5. Click Browse. The Choose file dialog box appears.

6. Navigate to the folder where you created your solution for Chapter 6. If this folder is in the default location, you can find it under the following path:

   ```
   My Documents\Visual Studio 2008\Projects\MSSQLRS\Chapter06
   ```

7. Select the Nametags report (Nametags.rdl), and click Open to exit the Choose file dialog box.

8. Click OK to upload the file. The Nametags report has been uploaded to the Chapter 06 folder.

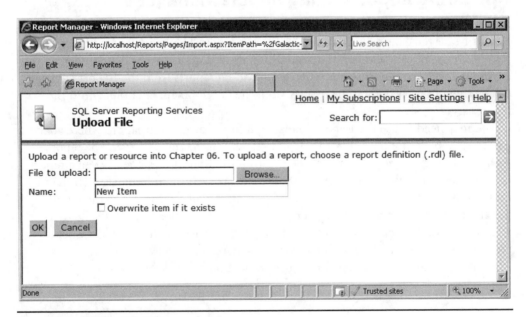

Figure 10-9   *The Upload File page*

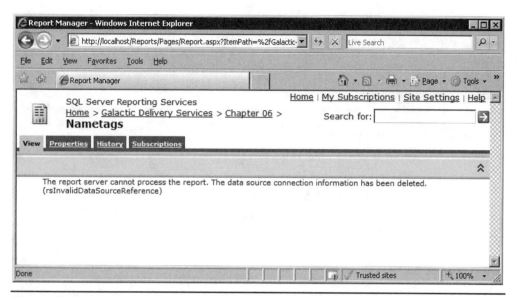

Figure 10-10 *The Reporting Services error page*

9. Click the Nametags report to execute it. You see an error similar to the one in Figure 10-10. You received this because, unlike the deployment from the Report Designer, the upload in Report Manager did not bring the shared data source along with the report.

10. Click the link to the Chapter 06 folder at the top of the page.

Creating a Shared Data Source in the Report Manager

To get the Nametags report functioning, you need to provide it with a shared data source. One way to do this is to create a new shared data source using the Report Manager. Follow these steps:

1. Click the New Data Source button in the toolbar on the Contents tab. The New Data Source page for a shared data source appears, as shown in Figure 10-11.

2. Type **Galactic** for Name.

3. Type **Connection to the Galactic Database** for Description.

4. Make sure Microsoft SQL Server is selected in Data Source Type. Other options here include OLE DB, Microsoft SQL Server Analysis Services, Oracle, ODBC, and XML.

5. Type **data source=(local);initial catalog=Galactic** for Connection String. If the Galactic database is not on the report server, but is on a different computer, put the name of that computer in place of (local) in the connection string.

Report Manager - Windows Internet Explorer

http://localhost/Reports/Pages/DataSource.aspx?CreateNew=True&ItemsParentPa | Live Search

Report Manager | Page ▾ Tools ▾

Home | My Subscriptions | Site Settings | Help

SQL Server Reporting Services
New Data Source

Search for:

Name:

Description:

☐ Hide in list view

☑ Enable this data source

Data Source Type: Microsoft SQL Server

Connection string:

Connect using:

⦿ Credentials supplied by the user running the report

Display the following text to prompt user for a user name and password:

Type or enter a user name and password to access the data sou

☐ Use as Windows credentials when connecting to the data source

◯ Credentials stored securely in the report server

User name:

Password:

☑ Use as Windows credentials when connecting to the data source

☑ Impersonate the authenticated user after a connection has been made to the data source

◯ Windows integrated security

◯ Credentials are not required

OK | Cancel

Figure 10-11 *The New Data Source page*

NOTE

Do not include the parentheses if you use a computer name in place of (local).

6. Select the Credentials stored securely in the report server option.
7. Type **GalacticReporting** for User Name.
8. Type **gds** for Password.
9. Click OK to save the data source and return to the Chapter 06 folder.

10. Click the Nametags report to execute it. You receive the same error message page because we have not yet told the report to use our new data source.

11. Click the Properties tab. The properties page for the Nametags report appears.

12. Click the Data Sources link on the left side of the screen. The Data Sources page for an individual report appears.

13. A shared data source should be selected. Click Browse. The Select a Shared Data Source page appears.

14. Expand each folder in the tree view under Location until you can see the Galactic shared data source in the Chapter 06 folder. Click the Galactic shared data source. The path to the Galactic shared data source is filled in Location. (You can also type this path into Location if you do not want to use the tree view.)

15. Click OK to exit the Select a Shared Data Source page.

16. Click Apply at the bottom of the page.

NOTE

It is easy to forget to click Apply when making changes to a report's data sources. If you do not click Apply, none of your changes are saved. This can lead to confusion, frustration, and wasted troubleshooting time. At least, that is what I have been told.

17. Click the View tab to view the report. The report now generates using the new shared data source. (A red X is where the GDS logo should be. We deal with this in the section "Uploading External Report Images.")

18. Once the report has completed generating, click the Chapter 06 link at the top of the page.

Hiding an Item

Figure 10-12 shows the list view of the Chapter 06 folder. The Galactic shared data source appears in the left column. Shared data sources have an icon consisting of a cylinder and four arrows. The Nametags report appears in the right column. Reports have an icon showing a piece of paper with columns of data and a bar chart.

When users are browsing through folders to find a report, you may not want other items, such as shared data sources, cluttering things up. It makes more sense to have the shared data sources where the reports can use them, but out of sight of the users. Fortunately, Report Manager provides a way to do just that.

1. Click the Galactic data source. The Data Source Properties page appears.

2. Check the Hide in list view check box.

3. Click Apply to save this change.

4. Click the Chapter 06 link at the top of the page.

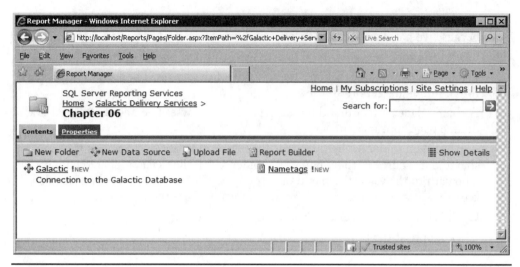

Figure 10-12   *The Chapter 06 folder list view*

The Galactic data source is no longer visible in the list view. You can use this same technique to hide reports you do not want to have generally available to users browsing through the folders.

If you do need to edit the Galactic data source, you can view it by using the detail view of the folder. Follow these steps:

1. Click the Show Details button in the toolbar on the Contents tab. The Galactic data source is now visible in this detail view, as shown in Figure 10-13. By default, the detail view is in alphabetical order by name.
2. Click the Type column heading. The detail view is now sorted by type in ascending order. (In an ascending sort by type, the reports are at the top of the list, with supporting items, such as shared data sources, at the bottom.) Note the downward, black arrow is now next to the Type column heading on your screen.
3. Click the Type column heading again. The detail view is now sorted by type in descending order. Now the black arrow is pointing upward next to the column heading.

NOTE

The name of the sort order (ascending or descending) and the direction of the black arrow may seem opposite to one another. Remember this: In an ascending sort, you move from smaller values (A, B, C . . .) to larger values (. . . X, Y, Z). When you move through the list in the direction of the arrow, you also move from smaller values to larger values.

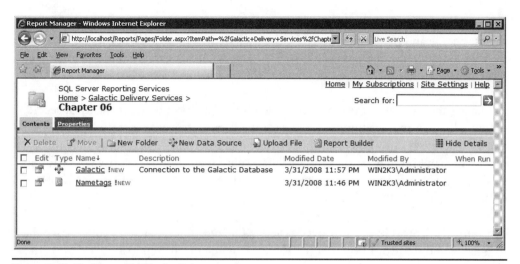

Figure 10-13 *The Chapter 06 folder detail view*

4. Click the Modified Date column heading. The detail view is sorted by modified date in ascending order. You can sort the detail view by Type, Name, Description, Modified Date, Modified By, or When Run, in either ascending or descending order.

5. Click the Hide Details button in the toolbar on the Contents tab. You are back to the list view.

Connect Using Options

When you are accessing data from a server-based database, such as SQL Server or Oracle, you need to provide some type of credentials, usually a user name and password, to show you have rights to access the data. Keeping these credentials secure is an important concern. The shared data sources created on the report server provide several methods for specifying these credentials.

When entering the connection string into a shared data source, it is best not to include the credentials in the connection string itself. The connection string is displayed as plain text to anyone who views the Data Source Properties page. To better protect password information, always enter the credential information under one of the Connect Using options described here.

Credentials Supplied by the User   The first Connect Using option is to have the user enter the credentials required by the data source each time the report is run. This is the "Credentials supplied by the user running the report" option. You can specify the prompt to be presented each time the user must enter these credentials. If the Use as

Windows Credentials When Connecting to the Data Source check box is checked, the user name and password entered by the user are treated as a Windows login. This means the user name and password provide database access using Windows integrated security. If this check box is not checked, the user name and password are treated as a database login.

Having the user enter the credentials each time the report is run is the most secure option. No login information is stored with the data source, but most users are not pleased with a system where they must enter login information each time they run a report. This option may be appropriate when your organization's security policy forbids storing login information in any way. In most other cases, the other Connect Using options provide a better solution.

Credentials Stored in the Report Server The next option enables you to have the user name and password stored in the Report Catalog on the report server. This is the "Credentials stored securely in the report server" option. The user name and password entered with this option are encrypted when they are stored in the Report Catalog. Also, the password is not displayed to the user in the Data Source Properties page.

This Connect Using option is convenient for the user because they do not need to remember and enter credentials to run reports using this data source. It also provides the required security for most situations through the measures noted in the previous paragraph.

As with the first Connect Using option, there is a Use as Windows Credentials When Connecting to the Data Source check box here as well. If this check box is checked, the user name and password stored in the Report Catalog are treated as a Windows login. If this check box is not checked, the user name and password are treated as a database login.

The second check box under this Connect Using option is Impersonate the Authenticated User After a Connection Has Been Made to the Data Source. If this check box is checked, the data source can use these credentials to impersonate this user. This feature is supported by the SQL Server relational database engine and SQL Server Analysis Services.

Integrated Security If you are not comfortable storing credentials in the Report Catalog, but you do not want your users entering credentials every time a report is run, integrated security may be the solution for you. The "Windows integrated security" option does not require the user to enter credentials. Instead, it takes the Windows login credentials that let the user access the Report Manager and passes them along to the database server. Your database server, of course, needs to be set up to accept these credentials.

Integrated security always works when the data source exists on the same server as the report server. It may run into problems, however, if the data source is on another server. The problems are caused by the way integrated security works between servers.

For a better understanding of the problems with integrated security, let's look at an example of the way integrated security works. The user logs in to their computer. This computer knows everything about this user because the original authentication occurred here.

When the user accesses the Report Manager application, the user's credentials are passed from the original computer to the computer hosting the report server. However, using standard Windows security, not everything about this login is passed to the report server computer—only enough information to authenticate the user. Some sensitive information does not make this hop across the network.

When the user runs a report with a data source using integrated security, the report server must pass on the credentials to the database server. However, the report server does not have the complete credentials to pass along. In fact, it does not know enough about the user to successfully authenticate them on the database server. The authentication on the database server fails. Using standard Windows security, integrated security only works across one hop, from the original authenticating computer to a second computer. In the case of the Report Manager, this is the hop from the user's computer to the report server.

To get integrated security to work across more than one hop, your Windows domain must use a special kind of security known as Kerberos, which allows authentication across multiple hops. Using Kerberos security, integrated security works across any number of servers in the network.

Credentials Not Required   The final Connect Using option is for data sources that do not require any authentication. This option would be used for connection to some Access databases, FoxPro databases, and others that do not require any login or password. This option could also be used if you insist, despite prior warnings here, on putting your credentials right in the connection string.

Uploading Other Items Using Report Manager

In addition to reports and shared data sources, other items can be uploaded to report server folders. External images needed as part of the reports can be uploaded, for example, as well as documentation and other supporting materials.

Uploading External Report Images

If you look closely at the Nametags report when it comes up in Report Manager, you notice this report has a problem. The GDS logo that should appear in the lower-left corner of each nametag is missing. You see the broken-link *X* symbol instead of the GDS logo.

This image was stored as an external image in the Chapter06 project. We need to upload this image to the report server. Once the image is uploaded into the same folder as the report, the report can find it. Here are the steps to follow to do this:

1. Return to the Chapter 06 folder in the Report Manager.
2. Click Upload File in the Contents tab toolbar. The Upload File page appears.
3. Click Browse. The Choose File dialog box appears.
4. Navigate to the folder containing the Chapter06 project. Select the GDS.gif file, and click Open to exit the Choose File dialog box.
5. Leave the name as gds.gif. The image needs to keep this name so it can be found by the report. Click OK to upload this file.
6. Click the Nametags report to execute it. If the broken-link *X* is still visible, click the Refresh Report button in the Report Viewer toolbar, as shown in Figure 10-14.

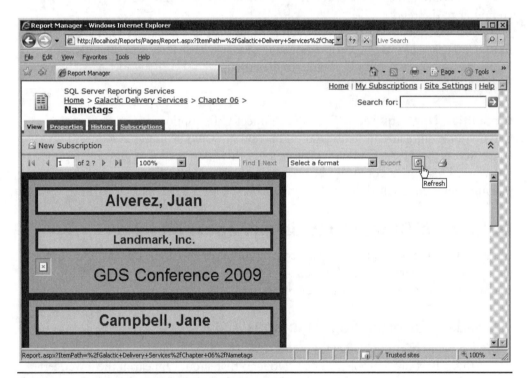

Figure 10-14 *The Refresh Report button in the Report Viewer toolbar*

NOTE

When you need to have Report Manager refresh a report, always use the Refresh Report button in the Report Viewer toolbar. Do not use the browser's Refresh button. The browser's Refresh button causes the page to be refreshed, but it does not cause the report to be reexecuted.

7. Click the link for the Chapter 06 folder.
8. The entry for the GDS.gif image shows in the list view of the Chapter 06 folder. As with the Galactic shared data source, you probably don't want entries for supporting resources cluttering up your list view. Click the entry for GDS.gif. The GDS.gif image is displayed.
9. Click the Properties tab.
10. Check the Hide in List View check box.
11. Click Apply.
12. Click the link for the Chapter 06 folder.

Uploading Supporting Materials

In some cases, you need to provide your users with documentation on one or more reports in the form of either a text file, or a Word or HTML document. Supporting materials may also be created in other applications. For example, you may have a PowerPoint presentation or a Visio diagram that aids in the interpretation and understanding of a set of reports. These materials can be uploaded as a folder item just like report files.

A text file or an HTML document can be displayed right in the browser without any additional software. For other types of documents, if the appropriate application is installed on the user's computer, the documents can be viewed right in the browser as well. These documents can also be downloaded and saved to the user's computer, if desired.

Now, we'll create a simple text document and then upload it to the Chapter 06 folder.

1. Open Notepad or another text editor.
2. Type the following in the text editor:

   ```
   The items in this folder are for the GDS Conference.
   ```

3. Save this as ReportReadMe.txt in a temporary location on your computer.
4. Return to your browser with the Report Manager viewing the Chapter 06 folder. Click Upload File in the Contents tab toolbar. The Upload File page appears.
5. Click Browse. The Choose File dialog box appears.
6. Navigate to the ReportReadMe.txt file, and click Open to exit the Choose File dialog box.
7. Click OK to upload this file.

8. Select the ReportReadMe.txt entry in the Chapter 06 folder. You see the contents of the text file displayed within the Report Manager.

9. Click the link for the Chapter 06 folder.

10. Let's add a second line to our text file. Open the ReportReadMe.txt file in your text editor, and add the following as a second line:

```
These items were created for the GDS Art Department.
```

11. Save the changes and close your text editor.

12. Return to your browser with the Report Manager viewing the Chapter 06 folder. Click Upload File in the Contents tab toolbar. The Upload File page appears.

13. Click Browse. The Choose File dialog box appears.

14. Navigate to the ReportReadMe.txt file, and click Open to exit the Choose File dialog box.

15. Check the Overwrite Item If It Exists check box. If you fail to check this check box, the new version of the text file does not overwrite the older version on the report server.

16. Click OK to upload this file.

17. Select the ReportReadMe.txt entry in the Chapter 06 folder. You see the new version of the text file.

18. Click the Properties tab.

19. Type **The purpose of these reports** ... for the description.

20. Click Apply to save your changes.

21. Click the link for the Chapter 06 folder. The description shows up under the entry for ReportReadMe.txt.

22. Let's make another change to our text file and look at another way to overwrite an entry on the report server. Open the ReportReadMe.txt file in your text editor, and add the following as a third line:

```
These items were created for all billing contacts.
```

23. Save the changes and close your text editor.

24. Return to your browser with the Report Manager viewing the Chapter 06 folder. Select the ReportReadMe.txt entry.

25. Click the Properties tab.

26. Click Replace.

27. Click Browse. The Choose File dialog box appears.

28. Navigate to the ReportReadMe.txt file, and click Open to exit the Choose File dialog box.

29. Click OK to upload this file.

30. Click the View tab. You see the latest version of the text file.
31. Click the link for the Chapter 06 folder.
32. Delete the ReportReadMe.txt file on your computer.

Uploading Reports Using .NET Assemblies

In addition to external images, reports can reference .NET assemblies. You saw this in the Weather Report and the Delivery Analysis Report created in Chapter 8. Let's look at the steps necessary to move these reports to the report server.

Copying the .NET Assembly to the Report Server

For a report to access a .NET assembly, it must be in the application folder of the report server. No fancy deployment, upload, or installation routine is required here. Simply copy the assembly's DLL file to the appropriate directory. We can give this a try using the Weather Report and its .NET assembly, WeatherInfo.dll, as well as the Delivery Analysis Report and its .NET assembly, ReportUtil.dll. Here are the steps to follow:

1. Locate the WeatherInfo.dll and ReportUtil.dll files. You also need the ES folder that contains the Spanish version of the ReportUtil.dll. This Spanish version is called ReportUtil.resources.dll. (The folder name, ES, is the two-letter code for Español.) If you do not have them anywhere else, they should be in the Public Assemblies folder on your development computer. The default path for the Public Assemblies folder is

   ```
   C:\Program Files\Microsoft Visual Studio 9.0\Common7\IDE\PublicAssemblies
   ```

2. Copy these files and the ES folder.
3. Paste the files and the ES folder into the report server application folder on the computer acting as your report server computer. You may receive a warning because a folder called ES already exists. Click Yes to continue. The default path for the report server application folder is

   ```
   C:\Program Files\Microsoft SQL Server\MSRS10.MSSQLSERVER\Reporting Services
                                                         \ReportServer\bin
   ```

Code Access Security

Because Reporting Services is a .NET application, it uses *code access security* to determine what execution permissions are possessed by each assembly. A *code access* group associates assemblies with specific permissions. The criteria for membership in a code access group are determined by a *security class,* and the permissions are determined by *named permission sets.*

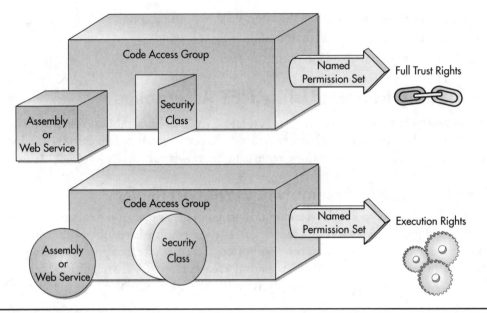

Figure 10-15 *Code access security*

Figure 10-15 provides an illustration of code access security. A .NET assembly or web service can gain entry into a code access group only if it matches the criteria specified by the security class. Once the .NET assembly or web service is allowed into a code access group, it can use the named permission set associated with that code access group to gain rights. These rights allow the .NET assembly or web service to perform tasks on a computer. Full trust rights and execution rights are the two types of rights we use with the Weather report. A number of different types of rights, however, can be included in a named permission set.

Code access groups can be nested inside one another. A .NET assembly or web service can be allowed into a parent group and gain its permissions; then it can try to gain membership in child code access groups to accumulate additional rights. A code access group can be a *first match code group,* where a .NET assembly or web service can only gain membership in one code access group—the first one it matches. Or, a code access group can be a *union code group,* where a .NET assembly or web service is allowed to gain membership in a number of code access groups, joining together the permissions from each group.

For our Weather report to execute properly, we will have to create a code access group that provides permissions to the WeatherInfo.dll assembly. Also, we will have to create a second code access group to provide permissions to the web service that we are using to get our weather information. Even though this web service is not executing on our server, our WeatherInfo.dll assembly is executing some of its methods, so it needs to have permission to execute.

Security Classes   A security class describes the conditions a .NET assembly or web service needs to meet to get into a code access group. We use two different types of security classes with the Weather report. The UrlMembershipCondition security class is used with the web service, and the StrongNameMembershipCondition security class is used with the WeatherInfo.dll and ReportUtil.dll assemblies.

The UrlMembershipCondition security class says that any assembly or web service being executed from a specified URL is to be included in a particular code access group. The URL that must be matched is listed in each code access group using the UrlMembershipCondition security class. For example, the GDSServer code access group may use UrlMembershipCondition and give http://GDSServer/* as the URL that must be matched. Any web service running on the GDSServer would be included in this code access group.

The StrongNameMembershipCondition security class uses the strong name associated with an assembly to identify it. The *strong name*, which is a long string of hexadecimal digits that uniquely identifies an assembly, is assigned to the assembly when it is created. The StrongNameMembershipCondition security class is a good way to ensure that only the intended assembly is allowed into your code access group.

You see a couple of other security classes in the report server security configuration. The AllMembershipCondition security class allows in all .NET assemblies and web services. The ZoneMembershipCondition security class allows in .NET assemblies and web services that originate in a particular zone. Some sample zones are MyComputer, intranet, and Internet.

Named Permission Sets   Named permission sets group together the permissions to be assigned by code access groups. The security configuration used by the report server contains three named permission sets. The *Nothing permission*, which grants no rights, is used to initially take away all rights from a .NET assembly or web service before specific rights are added back by subsequent code access groups. This ensures each .NET assembly or web service has only the rights it should have.

The *Execution permission* grants execution rights to a .NET assembly or web service. This means the .NET assembly or web service can be run. The .NET assembly or web service does not, however, have rights to access any protected resources, such as the file system, the registry, or the Internet.

The *FullTrust permission* grants the .NET assembly or web service access to everything. This includes access to all the protected resources. FullTrust permission should only be granted to .NET assemblies and web services that you trust not to mess up your computer!

Modifying the Report Server's Security Configuration

Now that you have a basic understanding of code access security, we can modify the report server's security configuration to allow the WeatherInfo.dll and the ReportUtil. dll to run.

CAUTION

Consult with your Reporting Services or network administrator before making any changes to server security.

We need to make some additions to the report server's security configuration to provide our custom assemblies with the rights they need to execute. The security configuration for the report server is in the rssrvpolicy.config file. The default path for this file is

```
C:\Program Files\Microsoft SQL Server\MSRS10.MSSQLSERVER\Reporting Services
                                                              \ReportServer
```

This file contains the code access security information in an Extensible Markup Language (XML) structure.

CAUTION

Make a backup copy of the rssrvpolicy.config file before making any modifications to it. If you accidentally create an invalid XML structure or otherwise cause a problem with the security configuration, the report server cannot execute any reports.

The XML structure in the rssrvpolicy.config file can be divided into three sections: Security Classes, Named Permission Sets, and Code Groups. We only need to make changes to the Code Groups section of the document. Here are the steps to follow:

1. Open the rssrvpolicy.config file in Notepad or another text editor.
2. Scroll down until you locate the Code Group portion of the document. The Code Group portion starts on the line after the closing XML tag for the named permission sets:

```
</NamedPermissionSets>
```

3. The first code group is the parent code group, which makes use of the AllMembershipCondition to assign the Nothing permission to all .NET assemblies and web services. We add a new child code group right beneath this. Insert this new code group as shown. (Add the lines shown in bold.) Alternatively, you can copy the text to be inserted from the "First Code-Access Security Insert.txt" file included with the download materials for this book.

```
    .
    .
    .
<CodeGroup
        class="FirstMatchCodeGroup"
        version="1"
        PermissionSetName="Nothing">
    <IMembershipCondition
            class="AllMembershipCondition"
            version="1"
    />
    <CodeGroup
            class="UnionCodeGroup"
            version="1"
            PermissionSetName="Execution"
            Name="WeatherWebServiceCodeGroup"
            Description="Code group for the Weather Web Service">
        <IMembershipCondition class="UrlMembershipCondition"
                version="1"
                Url="http://www.webserviceX.NET/*"
        />
    </CodeGroup>
    <CodeGroup
        class="UnionCodeGroup"
        version="1"
        PermissionSetName="Execution"
        Name="Report_Expressions_Default_Permissions"
        Description="This code group grants default permissions for
                    code in report expressions and Code element. ">
    .
    .
    .
```

4. Another parent code group uses ZoneMembershipCondition to assign Execution permissions to all .NET assemblies and web services in the MyComputer zone. We add a new child code group right beneath this. Insert this new code group as shown here (add the lines shown in bold). Note the Description and PublicKeyBlob should each be entered on one line. Alternatively, you can copy the text to be inserted from the "Second Code-Access Security Insert.txt" file included with the download materials for this book.

```
    .
    .
    .
```

```
<CodeGroup
     class="FirstMatchCodeGroup"
     version="1"
     PermissionSetName="Execution"
     Description="This code group grants MyComputer code
     Execution permission. ">
  <IMembershipCondition
          class="ZoneMembershipCondition"
          version="1"
          Zone="MyComputer"/>
  <CodeGroup
          class="UnionCodeGroup"
          version="1"
          PermissionSetName="FullTrust"
          Name="MSSQLRSCodeGroup"
          Description="Code group for the MS SQL RS Book Custom
                                              Assemblies">
     <IMembershipCondition
             class="StrongNameMembershipCondition"
             version="1"
             PublicKeyBlob="00240000048000009400000006020000000
                      2400005253413100040000010001000B9F7
                      4F2D5B0AAD33AA619B00D7BB8B0F767839
                      3A0F4CD586C9036D72455F8D1E85BF635C
                      9FB1DA9817DD0F751DCEE77D9A47959E87
                      28028B9B6CC7C25EB1E59CB3DE01BB516D
                      46FC6AC6AF27AA6E71B65F6AB91B957688
                      6F2EF39417F17B567AD200E151FC744C6D
                      A72FF5882461E6CA786EB2997FA968302B
                      7B2F24BDBFF7A5"
                     />
  </CodeGroup>
  <CodeGroup
          class="UnionCodeGroup"
          version="1"
          PermissionSetName="FullTrust"
          Name="Microsoft_Strong_Name"
          Description="This code group grants code signed with the
                          Microsoft strong name full trust. ">
          <IMembershipCondition
                  class="StrongNameMembershipCondition"
                  version="1"
                  PublicKeyBlob="00240000048000009400000006020000000
                            2400005253413100040000010001007D1
                            FA57C4AED9F0A32E84AA0FAEFD0DE9E8FD
                            6AEC8F87FB03766C834C99921EB23BE79A
                            D9D5DCC1DD9AD236132102900B723CF980
                            957FC4E177108FC607774F29E8320E92EA
                            05ECE4E821C0A5EFE8F1645C4C0C93C1AB
                            99285D622CAA652C1DFAD63D745D6F2DE5
```

F17E5EAF0FC4963D261C8A12436518206D
C093344D5AD293"

```
                    />
        </CodeGroup>
```

5. Save the modified file, and exit your text editor.

> **NOTE**
>
> *Looking at the rssrvpolicy.config file, you can see that expressions written within a report are granted Execute permissions. Because the WeatherInfo.GetWeather method is called from a report expression, by default, it should only be able to get Execute permissions. .NET Security says a process cannot get rights that exceed the rights granted to processes further up the stack. The GetWeather method needs FullTrust rights to make the web service call. The GetWeather method uses a special process to assert that it needs to exceed the rights of the calling process and gain FullTrust rights. If you downloaded the source code for the WeatherInfo.dll, you can look to see how the assert is accomplished.*

Uploading the Report

You are now ready to upload the Weather report. Complete the following steps using the Report Manager:

1. Create a folder called **Chapter 08** in the Galactic Delivery Services folder.
2. Open the Chapter 08 folder and upload the WeatherReport.rdl file from the Chapter08 project folder.
3. Click the report WeatherReport to execute it. The report produces an error because the shared data source does not exist.
4. Click the Properties tab. The properties page for WeatherReport appears.
5. Click the Data Sources link on the left side of the screen. The Data Sources page for an individual report appears.
6. A shared data source should be selected. Click Browse. The Select a Shared Data Source page appears.
7. Rather than create another shared data source, we are going to use the existing shared data source in the Chapter 06 folder. Expand each folder in the tree view under Location until you can see the Galactic shared data source in the Chapter 06 folder. Click the Galactic shared data source.
8. Click OK to exit the Select a Shared Data Source page.
9. Click Apply at the bottom of the page.

10. Click the View tab to view the report. Select one or more planets, and click View Report. The report now generates. (Remember, the .NET assembly calls a web service, so it requires an Internet connection.)

Try the Deploy One More Time

This last report upload required us to manually point the report to a shared data source in a different folder. This is because we do not want to have a shared data source in every report folder. If we had numerous shared data sources spread across a number of report folders, this would defeat much of the purpose of having shared data sources. When the database server name changes or the login credentials need to be updated, we would still have a major headache.

Instead, we want to have just one shared data source for each unique connection needed by our reports. This small group of shared data sources should be placed in one central location. That still leaves us with the task of manually pointing each report at the central group of shared data sources after each report upload.

You may recall there was a property on the report project's Property Pages dialog box specifying the folder path where the shared data source is to be deployed. Let's try deploying the Delivery Analysis Report from the Report Designer and see if this property can help us avoid all of the manual updating. Try the following:

1. Open the Chapter08 project in Visual Studio or the Business Intelligence Development Studio.
2. From the main menu, select Project | Properties. The Chapter08 Property Pages dialog box appears.
3. Enter **/Galactic Delivery Services/Chapter 06/** for TargetDataSourceFolder.
4. Enter **/Galactic Delivery Services/Chapter 08/** for TargetReportFolder.
5. Enter **http://ComputerName/ReportServer** for TargetServerURL. Substitute the appropriate value for ComputerName as you did earlier in this chapter.
6. Click OK to close the Chapter08 Property Pages dialog box.
7. Select Save All from the toolbar.
8. Right-click the entry for the DeliveryAnalysis report in the Solution Explorer window, and select Deploy from the context menu.
9. Notice in the Output window that the Report Designer attempted to deploy the shared data source from this project along with the report. This did not work because there is already a shared data source with the same name in the Chapter 06 folder and the OverwriteDataSources property is set to False. What, you may ask, did we accomplish by putting a path in TargetDataSourceFolder? In addition to trying to deploy the shared data source to a specific folder, this process instructs the deployed report to look in that same folder for the data sources it needs.

10. Switch to the browser, and navigate to the Chapter 08 folder.

11. Execute the DeliveryAnalysis report.

12. Select a number of service types from the drop-down list, and click View Report. The report displays using the shared data source found in the Chapter 06 folder.

A Look at Localization

You may recall we used the ReportUtil.dll assembly to present the report labels in both English and Spanish. (If you do not recall this, look at the instructions for this report in Chapter 8.) We passed the User!Language parameter to the LocalizedString method to retrieve a report label in the appropriate language. The User!Language parameter contains the language setting for the application requesting the report. When we are using the Report Manager, the browser is that application.

Let's try changing the language setting of the browser and see if our localization works the way it should. (The following directions apply to Internet Explorer.)

1. Select Tools | Internet Options from Internet Explorer's main menu. The Internet Options dialog box appears.

2. Click Languages. The Language Preference dialog box appears.

3. If an entry for Spanish (Mexico) [es-MX] is not in the Language list, click Add. The Add Language dialog box appears.

4. Highlight Spanish (Mexico) [es-MX] in the Language list, and click OK to exit the Add Language dialog box.

5. Highlight Spanish (Mexico) [es-MX] in the Language list, and click Move Up as many times as necessary to move the Spanish entry to the top of the list.

6. Click OK to exit the Language Preference dialog box. Click OK to exit the Internet Options dialog box.

7. Click the link for the Chapter 08 folder, and then reexecute the Delivery Analysis report. The User!Language parameter now has a value of es-MX because you set the primary language of your browser to Spanish (Mexico). Because of this, the title of the report and the column headings are now Spanish.

8. Use the Language Preference dialog box to remove the Spanish entry, if you created it in Steps 3 and 4. Make sure you return the correct language to the top of the Language list.

The ReportUtil.dll assembly has resource files for English and Spanish. English is the default language. If the parameter passed to the LocalizedString method is any of the cultural variations of Spanish, the method uses the Spanish resource file to look up the text for the report title or a column heading. If anything else is passed to the LocalizedString method, the English resource file is used.

Modifying Reports from the Report Server

In addition to uploading a report definition to the report server, it is possible to download a report definition, modify it, and send your modifications back to the report server as an update. You only need to do this if you do not have a copy of the RDL file for a report that is on the report server and needs to be modified. If you already have the report in a report project, you can edit that report using the Report Designer and then redeploy it.

Downloading a Report Definition

For this example, imagine we do not have the RDL file for the SubReportTest report and need to make a change to the report. The first task we need to complete is to download this report's RDL file from the report server to our local computer. Follow these steps:

1. Open the Report Manager in your browser and navigate to the Chapter 09 folder.
2. In the previous section, when we wanted to view the Properties tab for a report, we first executed that report. Now, we use the Show Details button to get at the Properties tab another way. Click the Show Details button in the Contents tab toolbar. The detail view of the folder's contents appears.
3. Click the icon in the Edit column next to the SubReportTest report. The Properties tab for the SubReportTest report appears.
4. There is a Report Definition section on this page just above the buttons at the bottom. Click the Edit link in the Report Definition section. This causes the Report Manager to download a copy of the SubReportTest.rdl file so you can edit it. The File Download dialog box appears.
5. Click Save. The Save As dialog box appears.
6. Browse to an appropriate temporary location on your computer. Leave the filename as SubReportTest.rdl. Click Save to exit the Save As dialog box. The file is downloaded and saved in the specified location.

NOTE

If you have logon credentials stored in one or more data source definitions in the report, for security purposes, these are not saved in the resulting report definition file.

Editing the Report Definition

We now have the report definition file for the SubReportTest report moved from the report server to our local computer. However, an RDL file by itself is not useful. To edit it, we have to place it in a report project. Again, remember, for this example, we are imagining we do not already have the SubReportTest report in a report project. Here are the steps to follow:

1. Start Visual Studio or the Business Intelligence Development Studio.
2. Create a new report project in the MSSQLRS folder called **EditSubReportTest**. (Do not use the Report Wizard.)
3. Create a shared data source called **Galactic** for the Galactic database using **GalacticReporting** for the user name and **gds** for the password.
4. Right-click the Reports entry in the Solution Explorer, and select Add | Add Existing Item from the context menu. The Add Existing Item dialog box appears.
5. Navigate to the location where you stored the SubReportTest.rdl file in the previous section. Select the SubReportTest.rdl file, and click Add to exit the Add Existing Item dialog box.
6. Double-click the SubReportTest report to open it for editing. (If you encounter an error while trying to edit this report, save the project, close the Report Designer, restart it again, and reopen the EditSubReportTest project.)
7. Modify the Transports dataset to add the PurchaseDate field to the output.
8. Put the PurchaseDate in a text box to the right of the SerialNumber. Set the Format property for this text box to MM/dd/yyyy.
9. Use the Preview tab to make sure your changes were made properly.
10. Click Save All in the toolbar.
11. Close the Report Designer.

Uploading the Modified Report Definition

Now that the report definition changes are completed, we are ready to upload the modified report.

1. Return to the Report Manager. If you are not already there, navigate to the Properties tab for the SubReportTest report.
2. Click the Update link in the Report Definition section of the page. The Import Report page appears.
3. Click Browse. The Choose File dialog box appears.
4. Navigate to the EditSubReportTest folder to find the updated version of the SubReportTest.rdl file.

NOTE

Do not select the copy of SubReportTest.rdl you originally downloaded. The modified version is in the folder with the EditSubReportTest report project.

5. Select SubReportTest.rdl and click Open to exit the Choose File dialog box.
6. Click OK to upload the file.
7. Click the View tab to view the report, and then click the Report Refresh button in the Report Viewer toolbar. The purchase date is now shown for each transport.

Managing Items in Folders

You now know how to load items into folders on the report server. Of course, we live in a dynamic world, so things seldom stay where they are originally put. We need to be able to move items around as we come up with better ways of organizing them. We also need to be able to delete items as they are replaced by something better or are simply not needed anymore. Fortunately, the Report Manager provides ways for us to do this housekeeping in an efficient manner.

Moving Items Between Folders

As an example, let's create a more descriptive folder for our Nametags report and its supporting items. We begin by moving a single item to this new folder. Then, we look at a method for moving multiple items at the same time.

Moving a Single Item

Here are the steps to follow to move a single item:

1. Open the Report Manager in your browser, and navigate to the Galactic Delivery Services folder.
2. Click New Folder. The New Folder page appears.
3. Type **2009 Conference** for Name, and type **Materials for the 2009 User Conference** for Description.
4. Click OK to create the new folder.
5. Click Chapter 06 to view the contents of this folder.
6. Click Show Details.
7. Click the icon in the Edit column for the Nametags report. The Nametags report Properties tab appears.
8. Click Move. The Move Item page appears.
9. Select the 2009 Conference folder in the tree view.
10. Click OK to move the report to this folder.
11. Click the 2009 Conference link at the top of the page to view the contents of this folder.

Moving Multiple Items

You can see the Nametags report has been moved to the 2009 Conference folder. However, the report cannot function until the supporting items are also moved to this folder. Moving each item individually, as we did with the report, is rather time-consuming. Fortunately, there is another way.

1. Click the Galactic Delivery Services link at the top of the page.
2. Click Chapter 06 to view the contents of this folder.
3. Click Show Details to return to the detail view. In the detail view, you see check boxes next to each item in the folder. These check boxes work with the Delete and Move buttons in the Contents tab toolbar. When you click Delete, any checked items are deleted. Likewise, when you click Move, any checked items are moved.
4. Check the uppermost check box (the check box to the left of the word "Edit"). Checking this check box checks all items in the folder. Unchecking this check box unchecks all items in the folder. Because we are moving all the items in the folder, we want all the items to be checked.
5. Click Move in the Contents tab toolbar. The Move Multiple Items page appears.
6. Select the 2009 Conference folder in the tree view.
7. Click OK to move these items to this folder.

This method works for moving a single item, multiple items, or the entire contents of a folder. Just check the items you want to move and click the Move button. Remember, you need to be in the detail view when using this method.

This section demonstrated moving reports and supporting items. You can also move whole folders using the same techniques.

Deleting a Folder

The Chapter 06 folder is now empty and ready to be deleted. As with the Move function, you can accomplish this in two ways. The first way is to view the Properties tab for the folder you want to delete and then click the Delete button. Just for fun, we'll try the second method.

Deleting a Folder Using the Check Boxes and Toolbar

1. Click the Galactic Delivery Services link at the top of the page to view the contents of this folder.
2. Check the Chapter 06 folder.
3. Click Delete. The confirmation dialog box appears.
4. Click OK to confirm your deletion. The Chapter 06 folder is deleted.

Folders do not need to be emptied before they are deleted. If the Chapter 06 folder had contained reports, supporting items, or even other folders, these would have been deleted along with the folder.

Renaming a Folder

In addition to moving and deleting items, we may want to rename items. Let's give the Chapter 09 folder a more descriptive name.

1. Click the icon in the Edit column for the Chapter 09 folder. The Chapter 09 Properties tab appears.
2. Replace the contents of Name by typing **Rendering Test Reports**. Then type **Reports for testing the performance of various rendering types** for Description.
3. Click Apply.
4. Click the Galactic Delivery Services link at the top of the page.
5. Click Hide Details.

This same technique makes it just as easy to change the names and descriptions for reports and other items. Just because it is easy to make these changes does not mean you should do it often. Once users become familiar with a folder name, a report name, or a report's location within the folder structure, you should change it only if you have a good reason to do so.

You may have noted that we could have changed the name of the Chapter 06 folder rather than going through the move and delete processes of the previous sections. This is true; we could have simply changed the folder name. If we had done that, though, you would not know how to do moves and deletes!

Seek and Ye Shall Find: Search and Find Functions

The Report Manager provides two features to help users find information. The Search function helps the user locate a report within the report server folder structure, and the Find function enables the user to jump to a certain piece of information while viewing a report.

Searching for a Report

First, we look at the Search function. This function lets the user enter a portion of a word, a complete word, or a phrase. The Report Manager then searches the names and descriptions of items in the report server folder structure for occurrences of this text. The Report Manager does not search the contents of a report or supporting files.

For example, searching for "GDS Report" would find "The GDS Report" and "GDS Reporting." It would not find "Report GDS Income" or "GDS Accounting Report." This is strictly a search for the text exactly as it is entered—no Boolean logic, proximity searching, or other features you find in Internet search engines. Also, the search is not case-sensitive.

Follow these steps to use the Search function:

1. Open the Report Manager in your browser, and navigate to the Home folder.
2. Type **report** in the Search box in the upper-right corner of the screen, and then click the green arrow. The Search page is displayed with the search results.
3. The Report Manager finds five items: two folders, a text document, and two reports. No weighting or relevance is assigned to each result. They are simply displayed in alphabetical order. Click the Galactic Delivery Services folder. You see the contents of that folder.
4. Click your browser's Back button to return to the search results.
5. Click ReportReadMe.txt. You see the contents of this file.
6. Click your browser's Back button.
7. Click the SubReportTest report to execute this report. (Keep your browser on this report. We use it in the Find feature.)

Finding Text Within a Report

Next, we look at the Find function. This function also enables the user to enter a portion of a word, a complete word, or a phrase. The Report Manager then searches the contents of the current report for occurrences of this text. Next, it highlights the first occurrence and moves it to the top of the view. The user can use the Next button to move to the next occurrence.

As with the Search function, Find locates text just as it is entered—no Boolean logic or proximity searching. Also, Find is not case-sensitive.

We use the SubReportTest report to demonstrate the Find function. This report should be open in your browser. The SubReportTest report lists all the transports used by GDS. They are listed in transport number order. Suppose we want to look at just the Warp Hauler–type transports sprinkled throughout the report. Rather than skimming through the entire report, looking for what we are interested in, here is a better way:

1. Type **warp haul** in the entry area to the left of the words "Find | Next" in the Report Viewer toolbar.
2. Click Find. The first Warp Hauler transport (#1303) is brought to the top of the viewing area, and the Warp Haul portion of the transport type is highlighted.

3. Click Next. (Make sure you do not click Find. Clicking Find simply starts the find operation again from the top of the page.) The next Warp Hauler transport (#1307) is brought to the top of the viewing area.

4. Click Next. The report jumps to the next Warp Hauler transport (#1310). Click Next once more, and the report jumps to the next Warp Hauler transport (#1311). Click once more, and the report jumps to the next Warp Hauler transport (#1317) on Page 2 of the report.

Printing from Report Manager

No matter how convenient you make it for your users to access reports in a browser, and no matter how many interactive drilldown and drillthrough features you provide, your users always want to print their reports on paper. You can explain all the wonders of the multiple, cascading parameters you have created until you are blue in the face, but some users always need to touch and feel the numbers on paper. They need to be able to put something in a briefcase and take it home with them at night. It doesn't matter that they could receive up-to-date numbers through their virtual private network (VPN) at home. They want ink on paper.

Printing Options

Reporting Services provides several options for printing a report from Report Manager. Each provides some advantages and disadvantages for the user.

HTML Printing

These users could just click the Print button in their browser and get whatever type of printout HTML printing provides. As you are probably aware, HTML printing is not a good choice when formatting is important, as it usually is for reports. Lines of text can wrap in unusual ways or simply be cut off. A line of text at the bottom of the page can even be cut right in half, with the top half on one page and the bottom half on the next page.

Fortunately, the Report Manager provides a couple of alternatives to HTML printing.

Printing from a PDF Document or TIFF File

As discussed previously, a Portable Document Format (PDF) document or a Tagged Image File Format (TIFF) file does an excellent job of maintaining report format when a report is printed. Therefore, when users want to have a high-quality report printout, they can export the report to a PDF document or a TIFF file. Once this is complete, they can view the exported report using the appropriate viewer: Adobe Acrobat Reader for the PDF document or the Windows Picture and Fax Viewer for a TIFF file. The report can then be printed using the viewer.

This process provides the user with a quality printout. However, not all users are comfortable with saving a file to a local disk, finding that file and opening it in the appropriate viewer, and then printing the report. There is another printing alternative, which is even more straightforward.

Client-Side Printing

You may have noticed a button with a printer icon on the report toolbar. This button is for the client-side printing feature of Reporting Services. *Client-side printing* works through an ActiveX object downloaded to the user's computer. From then on, whenever the Client-Side Printing button is clicked, this ActiveX object provides the user interface and controls the printing.

The first time a user activates the client-side printing feature, they may be prompted with a security warning about the ActiveX download. After taking the appropriate precautions, such as making sure the ActiveX object is signed by Microsoft, the user should approve the download to enable client-side printing. Once the ActiveX object has been downloaded by this first use, it does not need to be downloaded again.

If a user has trouble downloading the ActiveX control, they may need to set the Report Manager as a trusted site in their browser. This is done on the Security tab of the Internet Options dialog box. The user should not lower their security setting for all sites in general to accomplish the ActiveX download.

Once downloaded, client-slide printing enables users to set various report attributes. These include margins, page size, and even page orientation. Users can also preview a report before putting it on paper.

Managing Reports on the Report Server

Now that you have moved some of your reports to the report server, you may be thinking your job is about done, but it is just beginning. Now you need to manage the reports and supporting materials to ensure the reports can be utilized properly by your users.

Two of the biggest concerns when it comes to managing reports are security and performance. Reports containing sensitive data must be secured so they are only accessed by the appropriate people. Reports must return information to users in a reasonable amount of time without putting undo stress on database resources. Fortunately, Reporting Services provides tools for managing both of these concerns. Security roles and item-level security give you extremely fine control over just who has access to each report and resource. Caching, snapshots, and history let you control how and when reports are executed.

Security

In Reporting Services, security was designed with both flexibility and ease of management in mind. Flexibility is provided by the fact that individual access rights can be assigned to each folder and to each item within a folder. An item is either a report or a resource. You can specify exactly who has rights to each item and exactly what those rights are. Ease of management is provided by security inheritance, security roles, and integration with Windows security. We begin our discussion with the last entry in this list.

NOTE

Remember, although we are creating and maintaining these role assignments using the Report Manager, the security rights apply to Reporting Services as a whole. No matter how you access folders and items—through the Report Manager or through the web service—these security rights are enforced.

Integration with Windows Security

Reporting Services does not maintain its own list of users and passwords. Instead, in its default configuration, it depends entirely on integration with Windows security. When a user accesses either the Report Manager web application or the web service, that user must authenticate with the report server. In other words, the user must have a valid domain user name and password, or a local user name and password, to log on to the report server. Both the Report Manager web application and the web service are set up requiring integrated Windows authentication to ensure this logon takes place.

NOTE

If it is impossible for each report user to have their own credentials on the report server, it is possible to configure Reporting Services to use forms-based security. This is discussed in detail in Chapter 12.

Once this logon occurs, Reporting Services utilizes the user name and the user's group memberships to determine what rights the user possesses. The user can access only those folders and items they have rights to. In the Report Manager, users do not even see the folders they cannot browse and reports they cannot run. There is no temptation for the user to try and figure out how to get into places they are not supposed to go, because they do not even know these places exist.

Local Administrator Privileges

In most cases, rights must be explicitly assigned to folders and items. One exception to this rule, however, is local administrator privileges. Any user who is a member of the local administrators group on the computer hosting the report server has content manager rights to all folders and all items. These automatic rights cannot be modified or removed.

Let's look at the security page.

1. Open the Report Manager in your browser, and navigate to the Home folder.
2. Click the Properties tab. You see the security page for the Home folder, as shown in Figure 10-16.

The report server maintains a security page for each item in the Report Catalog—every folder, every report, and every supporting item. The security page lists all the role assignments for an item. Each role assignment is made up of two things: a Windows user or group and a security role. The rights associated with the security role are assigned to the Windows user or group.

Initially, one role assignment is on the security page for each item. This entry assigns the Content Manager security role to the BUILTIN\Administrators group. This entry is a reminder that any user who is a member of the local administrators group has rights to manage the contents of this folder.

NOTE

You could delete the role assignment for BUILTIN\Administrators, and the members of the local administrators group would still have rights to manage the contents of this folder. These rights are hardwired into Reporting Services. The BUILTIN\Administrators assignment on the security page is, in most cases, just a reminder of the rights held by anyone in the local administrators group.

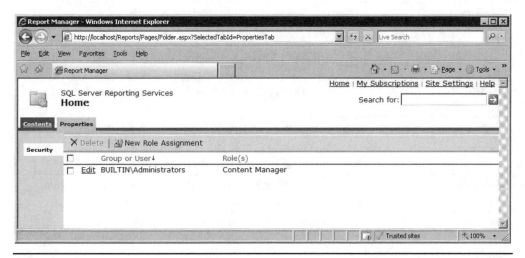

Figure 10-16 *The security page for the Home folder*

Tasks and Rights

You can perform a number of tasks in Reporting Services. Each task has a corresponding right to perform that task. For example, you can view reports. Therefore, a corresponding right exists to view reports. The tasks within Reporting Services are shown in Table 10-1.

You may not be familiar with some of these tasks. We discuss linked reports in the section "Linked Reports," and we discuss report history snapshots and subscriptions in Chapter 11. For now, you simply need to know these are tasks with associated rights within Reporting Services.

Task	Description
Consume reports	Read report definitions.
Create linked reports	Create linked reports and publish them to a report server folder.
Manage all subscriptions	View, modify, and delete any subscription, regardless of who owns it.
Manage data sources	Create and delete shared data source items; modify data source properties.
Manage folders	Create, view, and delete folders; view and modify folder properties.
Manage individual subscriptions	Each user can create, view, modify, and delete subscriptions that he or she owns.
Manage models	Create, view, and delete models; view and modify model properties.
Manage report history	Create, view, and delete report history snapshots; modify report history properties.
Manage reports	Create and delete reports; modify report properties.
Manage resources	Create, modify, and delete resources; modify resource properties.
Set security for individual items	View and modify security settings for reports, folders, resources, and shared data sources.
View data sources	View shared data sources items in the folder hierarchy; view data source properties.
View folders	View folder items in the folder hierarchy; view folder properties.
View models	View models in the folder hierarchy, use models as data sources for a report, and run queries against the model to retrieve data.
View reports	View reports and linked reports in the folder hierarchy; view report history snapshots and report properties.
View resources	View resources in the folder hierarchy; view resource properties.

Table 10-1 *Security Tasks Within Reporting Services*

Task	Description
Execute report definitions	Start execution from report definition without publishing it to the report server.
Generate events	Provides an application with the ability to generate events within the report server namespace.
Manage jobs	View and cancel running jobs.
Manage report server properties	View and modify properties that apply to the report server and to items managed by the report server.
Manage report server security	View and modify system-wide role assignments.
Manage roles	Create, view, modify, and delete role definitions.
Manage shared schedules	Create, view, modify, and delete shared schedules used to run reports or refresh a report.
View report server properties	View properties that apply to the report server.
View shared schedules	View a predefined schedule that has been made available to general use.

Table 10-2   *System-Wide Security Tasks Within Reporting Services*

In addition to the tasks listed in Table 10-1, there are system-wide tasks with associated rights. These system-wide tasks deal with the management and operation of Reporting Services as a whole. The system-wide tasks within Reporting Services are shown in Table 10-2.

Again, you may not be familiar with all the tasks in this list. We discuss jobs and shared schedules in Chapter 11.

Roles

The rights to perform tasks are grouped together to create *roles*. Reporting Services includes several predefined roles to help you with security management. In addition, you can create your own custom roles, grouping together any combination of rights that you like. The predefined roles and their corresponding rights are listed here.

The Browser Role   The *Browser* role is the basic role assigned to users who are going to view reports, but who are not going to create folders or upload new reports. The Browser role has rights to perform the following tasks:

▶   Manage individual subscriptions

▶   View folders

▶   View models

► View reports

► View resources

The Publisher Role   The *Publisher* role is assigned to users who are going to create folders and upload reports. The Publisher role does not have rights to change security settings or manage subscriptions and report history. The Publisher role has rights to perform the following tasks:

► Create linked reports

► Manage data sources

► Manage folders

► Manage models

► Manage reports

► Manage resources

The My Reports Role   The *My Reports* role is designed to be used only with a special folder called the My Reports folder. Within this folder, the My Reports role gives the user rights to do everything except change security settings. The My Reports role has rights to perform the following tasks:

► Create linked reports

► Manage data sources

► Manage folders

► Manage individual subscriptions

► Manage report history

► Manage reports

► Manage resources

► View data sources

► View folders

► View reports

► View resources

The Content Manager Role   The *Content Manager* role is assigned to users who are managing the folders, reports, and resources. All members of the Windows local administrators group on the computer hosting the report server are automatically members of the Content Manager role for all folders, reports, and resources. The Content Manager has rights to perform all tasks, excluding system-wide tasks.

The System User Role   The system-wide security tasks have two predefined roles. The *System User* role has rights to perform the following system-wide tasks:

▶ Execute report definitions

▶ View report server properties

▶ View shared schedules

The System Administrator Role   The *System Administrator* role provides the user with rights to complete any of the tasks necessary to manage the report server. All members of the Windows local administrators group on the computer hosting the report server are automatically members of the System Administrator role. This role has rights to perform the following system-wide tasks:

▶ Execute report definitions

▶ Manage jobs

▶ Manage report server properties

▶ Manage report server security

▶ Manage roles

▶ Manage shared schedules

Creating Role Assignments

As stated previously, role assignments are created when a Windows user or a Windows group is assigned a role for a folder, a report, or a resource. Role assignments are created on the security page for the folder, report, or resource. These role assignments control what the user can see within a folder and what tasks the user can perform on the folder, report, or resource.

Let's try creating role assignments for some of our folders and reports.

NOTE

To complete the next set of procedures, you need a user who has rights to log on to the report server, but who is not a member of the local administrators group on that computer. You should know the password for this user so you can log on as that user and view the results of your security settings.

Creating a Role Assignment for a Folder   Let's try creating a new role assignment for the Home folder.

1. Open the Report Manager in your browser. You should be viewing the contents of the Home folder.
2. Click the Properties tab. You see the security page for this folder.
3. Click New Role Assignment. The New Role Assignment page appears, as shown in Figure 10-17.
4. Type the name of a valid user for Group or User Name. If you are using a domain user or domain group, this must be in the format DomainName\UserName or DomainName\GroupName. If you are using a local user or local group, this must be in the format ComputerName\UserName or ComputerName\GroupName.
5. Check the check box for the Browser role.
6. Click OK to save your role assignment and return to the security page. Reporting Services makes sure you entered a valid user or group for the role assignment. If this is not a valid user or group, you receive an error message and your role assignment is not saved.

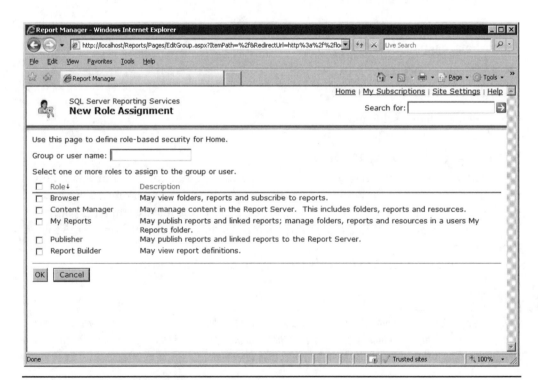

Figure 10-17 *The New Role Assignment page*

NOTE

A user needs to have at least viewing rights in the Home folder to view other folders and navigate to them.

Inherited Role Assignments   By default, folders (other than the Home folder), reports, and resources inherit their role assignments from the folder that contains them. You can think of the nested folders as branches of a tree, with the reports and resources as the leaves. *Inherited security* means you can make security changes to one folder and have those changes take effect for all the branches and leaves further along the tree.

This makes managing security easy. You can maintain security for all the reports and resources within a folder simply by modifying the role assignments for the folder itself. You can maintain security for an entire branch of the tree structure by modifying the role assignments for the folder that forms the base of that branch. Let's look at the security for the Galactic Delivery Services folder.

1. Click the Contents tab of the Home folder.
2. Select the Galactic Delivery Services folder to view its contents.
3. Click the Properties tab. You see the properties page for this folder.
4. Select Security on the left side of the page. You see the security page for this folder.

The Galactic Delivery Services folder is inheriting its role assignments from the Home folder. You did not add a role assignment giving Browser rights to your user in this folder and, yet, there it is! As soon as you added the role assignment to the Home folder, it appeared for all the items within the Home folder.

You gave your user Browser rights in the Home folder so they could view the contents of the Home folder and then navigate into other folders to find the reports they need. You may want to give this user additional rights in folders further along in the tree. Perhaps the user can manage the content of certain folders that belong to their department, but can only browse when in the Home folder.

To accomplish this task, you must first break the inherited security for the Galactic Delivery Services folder.

1. Click Edit Item Security. A dialog box with an inherited security message appears. The Report Manager is confirming you want to break that inheritance by creating your own role assignments for this folder.
2. Click OK to confirm you want to break the inherited security.

Now that you have broken the inherited security, you have new buttons on the toolbar for adding a new role assignment, deleting existing role assignments, and reverting to inherited security.

Now you can edit the role assignment for your user.

1. Click the Edit link next to the role assignment giving your user Browser rights. The Edit Role Assignment page appears.
2. Uncheck the check box for the Browser role.
3. Check the check box for the Content Manager role.
4. Click Apply to save the changes to your role assignment and return to the security page. The user now has Content Manager rights in the Galactic Delivery Services folder.
5. Click the Contents tab.
6. Select the Rendering Test Reports folder to view its content.
7. Click the Properties tab. You see the properties page for this folder.
8. Select Security on the left side of the page. You see the security page for this folder.

You can see the Rendering Test Reports folder is inheriting its role assignments from the Galactic Delivery Services folder.

NOTE

Although we do not do so in these exercises, you can check more than one role when creating or editing a role assignment. The user's rights are then the sum of the rights granted by each role.

Managing Role Assignments for Reports Now, let's try managing role assignments for reports.

1. Click the Contents tab.
2. Click Show Details.
3. Click the icon in the Edit column for the RenderingTest report. The properties page for this report appears.
4. Click Security on the left side of the page. The security page for this report appears.

Again, you can see this report is inheriting its role assignments from the folder that contains it—in this case, the Rendering Test Reports folder. Because the user has Content Manager rights for the folder, the user also has Content Manager rights for the report. This means the user can change any and all properties of this report and even delete the report altogether.

To continue our security example, we are going to suppose it is all right for the user to have Content Manager rights for the Rendering Test Reports folder, but not for the RenderingTest report. We need to edit the role assignment for your user. However, before we can do this, we must break the inheritance, as explained in the following steps.

1. Click Edit Item Security. The confirmation dialog box appears.
2. Click OK to confirm.
3. Click the Edit link next to the role assignment giving your user Content Manager rights. The Edit Role Assignment page appears.
4. Uncheck the check box for the Content Manager role.
5. Check the check box for the Browser role.
6. Click Apply to save the changes to your role assignment and return to the security page.
7. Click the Rendering Test Reports link at the top of the page.

Now we modify the rights granted to this user for the SubReportTest report. In our example, because this is a subreport, we assume the user should have limited rights to this report. In fact, they should only be able to review the report. In this case, the predefined Browser role has too many rights. We have to define our own custom role.

To do this, we need to use the SQL Server Management Studio. Follow these steps:

1. In the Windows Start menu, select Programs | SQL Server 2008 | Microsoft SQL Server Management Studio. The SQL Server Management Studio will start up, and the Connect to Server dialog box will appear.
2. Select Reporting Services from the Server type drop-down list, as shown in Figure 10-18.
3. Click Connect. The SQL Server Management Studio will connect to the report server.
4. Expand the Security entry in the Object Explorer window. Next, expand the Roles entry in the Object Explorer window. You will see the five default security roles, as shown in Figure 10-19.
5. Right-click the Roles entry in the Object Explorer window, and select New Role from the context menu. The New User Role dialog box appears.
6. Type **View Report** for Name.
7. Type **View Report Only** for Description.

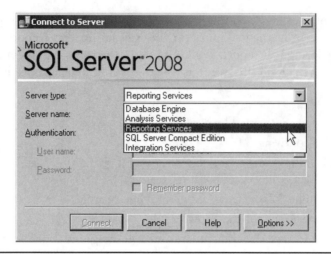

Figure 10-18 *The SQL Server Management Studio Connect to Server dialog box*

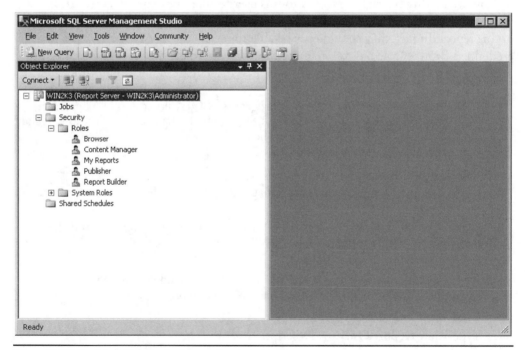

Figure 10-19 *The default Reporting Services security roles*

8. Check View Reports. The New User Role dialog box should appear as shown in Figure 10-20.

9. Click OK to save this new role.

10. Exit the SQL Server Management Studio, and return to the Report Manager in your browser.

11. Click the icon in the Edit column for the SubReportTest report. The properties page for this report appears.

12. Click Security on the left side of the page. The security page for this report appears.

13. Click Edit Item Security. Click OK to confirm.

14. Click the Edit link next to the role assignment giving your user Content Manager rights. The Edit Role Assignment page appears.

15. Uncheck the check box for the Content Manager role.

16. Check the check box for the View Report role.

17. Click Apply to save the changes to your role assignment and return to the security page. The user has rights to view the SubReportTest report, but no other rights with that report.

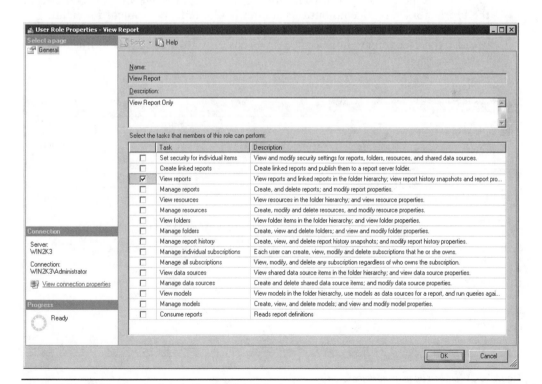

Figure 10-20 *The View Report role in the New User Role dialog box*

We make one more change to test security. We remove all rights assigned to this user for the DrillthroughTest report.

1. Navigate to the Rendering Test Reports folder.
2. Click the icon in the Edit column for the DrillthroughTest report. The properties page for this report appears.
3. Click Security on the left side of the page. The security page for this report appears.
4. Click Edit Item Security. Click OK to confirm.
5. Check the check box next to the role assignment giving your user Content Manager rights.
6. Click Delete. The confirmation dialog box appears.
7. Click OK to confirm the deletion.

You can now close your browser, log out of Windows, and log on with the user name you have been using in the role assignments. Let's test our security changes.

1. Open the Report Manager in your browser. You should be viewing the contents of the Home folder. Notice no buttons are in the Contents tab toolbar for creating folders and data sources or uploading files, as shown in Figure 10-21. That is because the user you are now logged on as has only Browser rights in this folder.

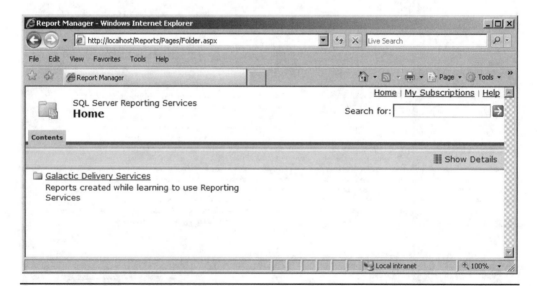

Figure 10-21 *Browser rights in the Home folder*

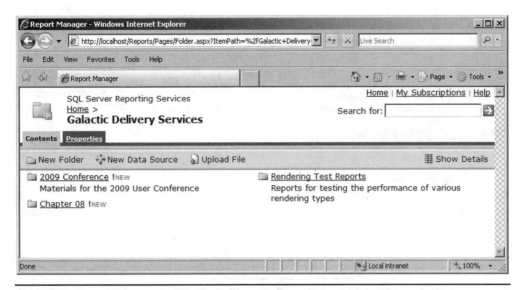

Figure 10-22 *Content Manager rights in the Galactic Delivery Services folder*

2. Select the Galactic Delivery Services folder to view its contents. When you are in this folder, the New Folder, New Data Source, Upload File, and Report Designer buttons have returned, as shown in Figure 10-22. In this folder, your user has Content Manager rights.

3. Select the Rendering Test Reports folder to view its contents.

4. Click Show Details.

5. Click the icon in the Edit column for the RenderingTest report. The properties page for this report appears. Note that Security doesn't appear on the left side of the page, as shown in Figure 10-23. Your user has Browser rights to this report, so you can view the report and its history and create subscriptions, but you cannot change its security. (Don't worry about what subscriptions are right now; we discuss them in Chapter 11.)

6. Click the link for the Rendering Test Reports folder at the top of the page.

7. Click the icon in the Edit column for the SubReportTest report. The properties page for this report appears. Now, the Subscriptions tab is gone, as shown in Figure 10-24. Your user has the rights from our custom View Report role for this report. You can view the report and its history, but you cannot create subscriptions.

8. Click the link for the Rendering Test Reports folder at the top of the page. Notice the DrillthroughTest report is nowhere to be seen because your user does not have any rights for this report, not even the rights to view it.

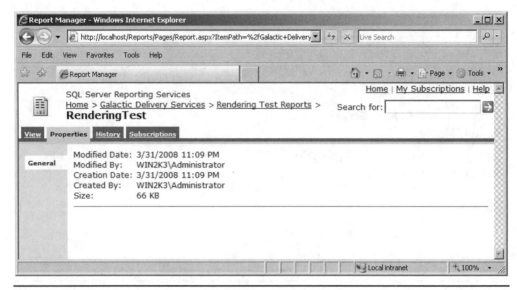

Figure 10-23 *Browser rights for the RenderingTest report*

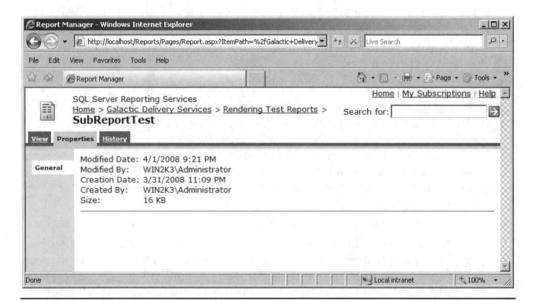

Figure 10-24 *View Report rights for the SubReportTest report*

9. Click the RenderingTest report to execute it.

10. Go to Page 2 of the report. Scroll down to the table below the graph where you see Custer, Inc.

11. The heading Custer, Inc. is a link to the DrillthroughTest report. The problem is that your user does not have any rights to the DrillthroughTest report. Clicking this link results in an insufficient rights error message, as shown in Figure 10-25.

Giving users only the rights they need is important. This prevents users from viewing data they should not see or from making modifications or deletions they should not be allowed to make. On the other hand, providing users with enough rights is important so their reports function properly. We don't want users to end up with an error message like the one shown in Figure 10-25 when they are trying to do legitimate work.

Role Assignments Using Windows Groups

As mentioned previously, role assignments can be made to Windows users or to Windows groups. If you create your role assignments using Windows users, you need to create a new set of role assignments every time a new user needs to access Reporting Services. This can be extremely tedious if you have a complex set of role assignments for various folders, reports, and resources.

In most cases, creating role assignments using Windows groups is better. Then, as new users come along, you simply need to add them to the Windows group that has the appropriate rights in Reporting Services. This is much easier!

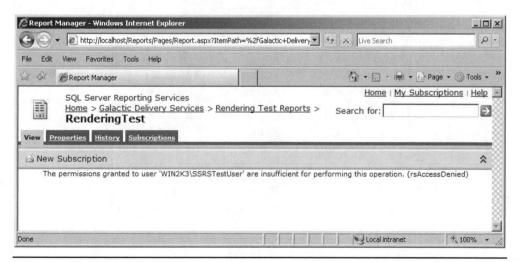

Figure 10-25 *Insufficient rights error message*

Linked Reports

In many cases, the security set up within Reporting Services restricts the folders a user can access. The sales department may be allowed to access one set of folders. The personnel department may be allowed to access another set of folders. The personnel department doesn't want to see sales reports and, certainly, some personnel reports should not be seen by everyone in the sales department.

This works well—a place for everything and everything in its place—until you come to the report that needs to be used by both the sales department and the personnel department. You could put a copy of the report in both places, but this gets to be a nightmare as new versions of reports need to be deployed to multiple locations on the report server. You could put the report in a third folder accessed by both the sales department and the personnel department, but that can make navigation in the Report Manager difficult and confusing.

Fortunately, Reporting Services provides a third alternative: the linked report. With a *linked report,* your report is deployed to one folder. It is then pointed to by links placed elsewhere within the Report Catalog, as shown in Figure 10-26. To the user, the links look just like a report. Because of these links, the report appears to be in many places. The sales department sees it in their folder. The personnel department sees it in their folder. The fact of the matter is the report is only deployed to one location, so it is easy to administer and maintain.

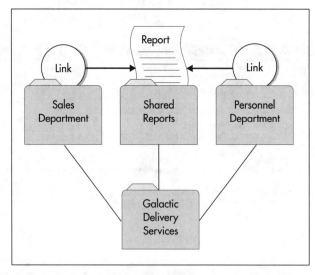

Report Catalog

Figure 10-26 *A linked report*

Creating a Linked Report

To demonstrate a linked report, we are going to make use of the Invoice-Batch Number Report from Chapter 4. This report shows the invoice amounts for companies in various cities. Galactic Delivery Services has sales offices in each of these cities, and each sales office has its own folder within the GDS Report Catalog.

A sales office should be able to access the Invoice-Batch Number Report in their own folder and see the invoices for customers in their city.

Deploying the Report to a Common Folder

We begin by deploying the report to a common folder. Here are the steps to follow:

1. Log in with a user name and password that has Content Manager rights in Reporting Services.
2. Start Visual Studio or the Business Intelligence Development Studio, and open the Chapter04 project.
3. Modify the properties of the Chapter04 project as follows:

Property	Value
TargetDataSourceFolder	Galactic Delivery Services/Data Sources
TargetReportFolder	Galactic Delivery Services/Shared Reports
TargetServerURL	http://ServerName/ReportServer

Replace ServerName with the appropriate server name or with localhost.
5. Deploy the Invoice-Batch Number Report.
6. Close the development environment.

Creating Linked Reports

Now that the report has been deployed to the Report Catalog, it is time to create our linked reports.

1. Open the Report Manager in your browser, and navigate to the Galactic Delivery Services folder.
2. Create a new folder. Type **Axelburg** for Name and **Axelburg Sales Office** for Description.
3. Create another new folder. Type **Utonal** for Name and **Utonal Sales Office** for Description.
4. Navigate to the Shared Reports folder.
5. Click Show Details.

6. Click the icon in the Edit column next to the Invoice-Batch Number Report.
7. Click Create Linked Report. The Create Linked Report page appears.
8. Type **Invoice-Batch Number Report** for Name and **Axelburg invoices in each batch** for Description.
9. Click Change Location. The Folder Location page appears.
10. Select the Axelburg folder, and click OK to return to the Create Linked Report page.
11. Click OK to create and execute this linked report in the Axelburg folder.
12. Type **01/01/2008** for Enter a Start Date and **12/31/2008** for Enter an End Date. Click View Report.
13. Click the link for the Axelburg folder at the top of the page.
14. Click Hide Details. You can see the linked report we just created looks like a regular report.
15. Navigate back to the Shared Reports folder.
16. Click Show Details.
17. Click the icon in the Edit column next to the Invoice-Batch Number Report.
18. Click Create Linked Report. The Create Linked Report page appears.
19. Type **Invoice-Batch Number Report** for Name and **Utonal invoices in each batch** for Description.
20. Click Change Location. The Folder Location page appears.
21. Select the Utonal folder, and click OK to return to the Create Linked Report page.
22. Click OK to create and execute this linked report in the Utonal folder.
23. Select Utonal from the Select a City drop-down list. Type **01/01/2008** for Enter a Start Date and **12/31/2008** for Enter an End Date. Click View Report.

We have now successfully created and tested our two linked reports.

Managing Report Parameters in Report Manager

We have our linked reports, but we have not quite fulfilled all the business needs stated for these linked reports. The Axelburg sales office is supposed to be able to see only their own invoice data. The same is true for the Utonal sales office. We can meet these business needs by managing the report parameters right in the Report Manager. Here are the steps to follow:

1. Navigate to the Axelburg folder. Note the small chain links on the icon for the Invoice-Batch Number Report. This indicates it is a linked report.
2. Click the icon in the Edit column next to the Invoice-Batch Number Report.

3. Click Parameters on the left side of the screen. The Parameter Management page appears. Note, the City parameter has a default of Axelburg. Because this is the Axelburg folder, we leave that default alone. What we modify is the user's ability to change this default value.

4. Uncheck the Prompt User check box in the City row. The user is no longer prompted for a city. Instead, the report always uses the default value. As you may have guessed, you can have a default value, you can prompt the user for the value, or you can do both. You must do at least one of these.

5. Check the Has Default check box in the StartDate row. Type **01/01/2008** for the default value for this row.

6. Check the Has Default check box in the EndDate row. Type **12/31/2008** for the default value for this row.

7. Click Apply to save your changes.

8. Click the View tab.

9. Notice you can no longer select a city. It is always Axelburg. Also, notice we now have default values for the date. Also worth noting is these default values are much easier to modify than the default values that are part of the report, because we can make changes without having to redeploy the report.

10. Navigate to the Utonal folder.

11. Click the icon in the Edit column next to the Invoice-Batch Number Report.

12. Click Parameters on the left side of the screen.

13. Change the City field's default parameter to Utonal.

14. Uncheck the Prompt User check box in the City row.

15. Check the Has Default check box in the StartDate row. Type **01/01/2008** for the default value for this row.

16. Check the Has Default check box in the EndDate row. Type **12/31/2008** for the default value for this row.

17. Click Apply to save your changes.

18. Click the View tab.

Now we have the linked reports working just the way we need them. Not only did we simplify things by not deploying the report in multiple places, but we also were able to hardcode parameter values for each linked report.

Delivering the Goods

In this chapter, you learned how to put the reports where your users could come and get them. Your users were set up to pull the reports off the report server. In the next chapter, you learn how to deliver the goods right to the users. In Chapter 11, the report server pushes the reports out to the users. The pull and push capabilities combine to give Reporting Services some powerful tools for putting information in the hands of the users, right where it needs to be.

Chapter 11

Delivering the Goods: Report Delivery

In This Chapter

- ▶ Caching In
- ▶ Execution Snapshots
- ▶ Report History
- ▶ Subscriptions
- ▶ Site Settings
- ▶ A Sense of Style
- ▶ Building On

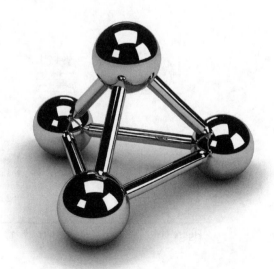

I n the previous chapter, we moved from the development environment to the report server. The report server enables us to make our reports available to end users. We reviewed the various ways reports and their supporting resources can be moved from the development environment to the report server. We also reviewed the security features the report server provides.

In addition to all this, we looked at the Report Manager interface, which provides users with one method of accessing reports on the report server. In this chapter, you learn about additional ways to take reports from the report server to the users. You also learn ways to manage how and when reports are executed. These features can be used to level out server load and to increase user response time.

Caching In

One of the best features of Reporting Services is that the data is requeried each time the report is executed. This is shown in Figure 11-1. The user is not viewing information from a static web page that is weeks or months old. Reporting Services reports include data that is accurate up to the second the report was run.

However, this feature can also be the source of one of the drawbacks of Reporting Services. The user is required to wait for the data to be requeried each time a report is run. If your query or stored procedure runs quickly, this may not be a problem.

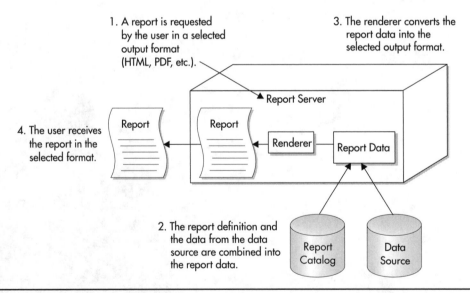

Figure 11-1   *Serving a report without caching*

However, even fairly quick queries can slow down a server if enough of them are running at the same time.

Fortunately, Reporting Services has a solution to this problem: report caching.

Report Caching

With many reports, it is not essential to have up-to-the-second data. You may be reporting from a data source that is only updated once or twice a day. The business needs of your users may only require data that is accurate as of the end of the previous business period, perhaps a month or a quarter. In these types of situations, it does not make sense to have the data requeried every time a user requests a report. Report caching is the answer.

Report caching is an option that can be turned on individually for each report on the report server. When this option is turned on, the report server saves a copy, or *instance*, of the report in a temporary location the first time the report is executed, as shown in Figure 11-2.

On subsequent executions, with the same parameter values chosen, the report server pulls the information necessary to render the report from the report cache, rather than requerying data from the database, as shown in Figure 11-3. Because these subsequent executions do not need to requery data, they are, in most cases, faster than the report execution without caching.

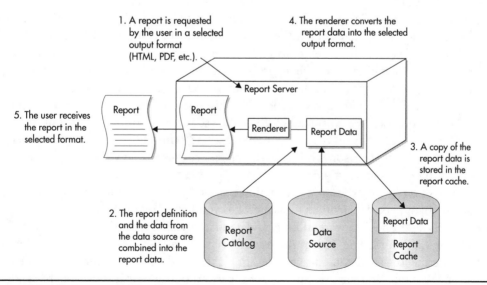

Figure 11-2   *Serving a report with caching, the first time*

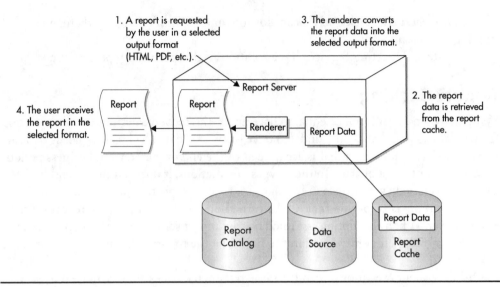

Figure 11-3 *Serving a report with caching, subsequent times*

Cached Report Expiration

Once an instance of the report is stored in the report cache, it is assigned an expiration date and time. The expiration date and time can be calculated in one of two ways. The expiration date can be calculated based on a certain number of minutes after the creation of the cached instance. For example, the cached instance of the report exists for 30 minutes, and then it is deleted. Or, the expiration date can be determined by a set schedule. For example, the cached instance of the report is deleted at 2:00 A.M. every Sunday morning.

The first type of expiration calculation is appropriate for a report that requires a large amount of database resources and is run often, but does not require up-to-the-second data. We can decrease the workload on the database server by fulfilling most of the requests for the report from the report cache. Every 30 minutes, we throw the cached report away. The next person who requests the report causes a new instance of the report, with updated data, to be placed in the report cache.

The second type of expiration calculation is appropriate for reports run against data that changes on a scheduled basis. Perhaps you have a report being run from your data warehouse. The data warehouse is updated from your transactional database each Sunday at 12:30 A.M. The data in the warehouse remains static in between these loads. The cached report is scheduled to expire right after the data load is completed. The next time the user requests the report after the expiration, a new instance of the report, with the updated data, is placed in the cache. This cached report contains up-to-date data until the next data load.

Cached Reports and Data Source Credentials

To create a cached instance of a report, the report must be using stored credentials. These can be credentials for either a Windows logon or a database logon, but they must be stored with the data source. If you think about this from a security standpoint, this is how it has to be.

Suppose for a minute that Reporting Services allowed a cached report to be created with Windows integrated security. The Windows credentials of the first person to run the report would be used to create a cached instance of the report. Subsequent users who request this report would receive this cached instance. However, this would mean the subsequent users are receiving data in the report created using the credentials from another user.

If the results of the database query or stored procedure that populates this report vary, based on the rights of the database login, we have the potential for a big problem. If the vice president of sales is the first person to run the report and create the cached instance, all subsequent users would receive information meant only for the VP! Conversely, if a sales representative is the first person to run the report and create the cached instance, when the VP comes along later and requests the report, he will not receive all the information he needs.

The same problem exists if the report prompts for credentials. The first person who runs the report and creates the cached instance is the one who supplies the credentials. Everyone who views the cached instance is essentially using someone else's logon to see this data.

The only way that caching works without creating the potential for a security problem is with credentials stored with the report. In this situation, the same credentials are used to access the database—whether it is the VP or a lowly sales representative running the report. There is no risk that the cached instance of the report will create a breach in database security.

Caching and Report Formats

As you can see in Figure 11-2, the report data, not the final format of the report, is stored in the report cache. The report data is a combination of the report definition and the data from the datasets. It is not formatted as a Hypertext Markup Language (HTML) page, a Portable Document Format (PDF) document, or other type of rendering format. It is an internal format ready for rendering.

Because the report data is stored in the report cache, the cached report can be delivered in any rendering format. The user who first requested the report and, thus, caused the cache instance to be created, may have received the report as an HTML document.

The next user may receive the cached instance of the report and export it to a PDF document. A third user may receive the cached instance of the report and export it to an Excel file. Caching the report data gives the report cache the maximum amount of flexibility.

Enabling Report Caching

Let's try enabling caching for one of our deployed reports. We have a report that is a good candidate for caching. The Weather report takes a long time to execute because of the calls to the web service. Also, the weather conditions returned by the web service are not going to change from minute to minute, so it is not essential to retrieve new information every time the report is executed. The Weather report works just fine if it is retrieved from the cache, as long as we expire the cached instance fairly often, say, every 45 minutes.

Enabling Report Caching for the Weather Report

Let's try enabling caching for the Weather report.

1. Open the Report Manager, and navigate to the Chapter 08 folder.
2. Click Show Details.
3. Click the icon in the Edit column for the Weather report. The Properties page for the Weather report appears.
4. Select Execution from the left side of the screen. The Execution Properties page appears, as shown in Figure 11-4.
5. Select the Cache a temporary copy of the report. Expire copy of report after a number of minutes.
6. Set the number of minutes to 45.
7. Click Apply.
8. Click the View tab. Select (Select All) in the Select Planets drop-down list, and click View Report. The Weather report runs.

The first time the Weather report runs after caching is turned on, the report needs to perform its regular execution process to gather the data for the intermediate format. This intermediate format is then copied to the report cache before it is rendered for you in the browser. Because the report goes through its regular execution process, it still takes a while to appear.

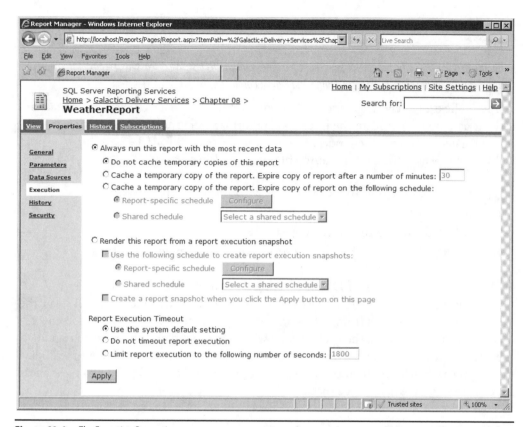

Figure 11-4   *The Execution Properties page*

Viewing the Report from the Report Cache

Now let's run the report again. Because a cached copy of the report has not expired, the report is rendered from the cached copy.

1. Click the Refresh Report button in the toolbar. The report appears almost immediately. That happened so fast, I bet you don't even believe it retrieved the report. Let's try it again another way.

2. Click the Chapter 08 link at the top of the page.

3. Click the WeatherReport link to run this report. Note, the Report Manager switched back to the non-detail, list view.

4. Select (Select All) in the Select Planets drop-down list, and click View Report.

NOTE

Be sure to make the same parameter selection each time you run this test. We discuss how report parameters affect caching in the section "Report Caching and Report Parameters."

Pretty slick! The report server doesn't need to retrieve any data, execute any expressions, call any assemblies, or create the intermediate format. All it needs to do is convert the intermediate format into the rendered format (in this case, HTML).

What happens if we ask for a different rendering format?

1. Select Acrobat (PDF) file from the Select a format drop-down list.
2. Click Export.
3. If a File Download dialog box appears, click Open.
4. Close the Adobe Acrobat Reader when you finish viewing the report.

A brief delay occurs as the PDF document is created and your Acrobat Reader is opened, but there is no delay to retrieve the information using the web service. Instead, the intermediate format comes from the report cache and is rendered into a PDF document.

If you wait 45 minutes, the cached copy will have expired and the report is again executed to create the intermediate format. If you want to try this, you can put the book down, go have lunch, and then come back and run the report. It's OK. You go right ahead. I'll be here waiting when you get back.

Cache Expiration on a Schedule

You have just learned the weather web service we are using for our Weather report is updated every hour, on the hour. It makes sense for us to set our cached copy of this report to expire on this same schedule. The cached copy should expire at five minutes past the hour so a new copy of the weather information shows up the next time the report is run after the web service information is updated.

1. Navigate to the Weather report in the Report Manager, if you are not already there.
2. Click the Properties tab. The Properties page appears.
3. Select Execution from the left side of the screen. The Execution Properties page appears.
4. Select Cache a temporary copy of the report. Expire copy of report on the following schedule.
5. Report-Specific Schedule is selected by default. Click Configure next to Report-Specific Schedule. The Schedule page appears, as shown in Figure 11-5.

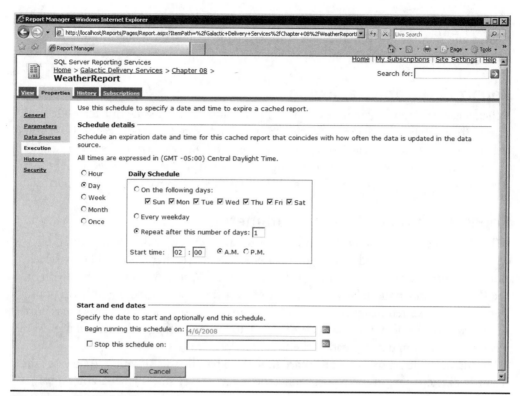

Figure 11-5   *The Schedule page*

6. You can specify hourly, daily, weekly, monthly, or one-time schedules. Select Hour.

7. Leave the Hourly Schedule set to run every 1 hours 00 minutes. Set Start Time to five minutes after the next hour. (If it is 2:30 P.M. now, set Start Time to 3:05 P.M.)

8. Today's date should be selected for Begin running this schedule on. Leave the Stop this schedule on blank. (You change these dates by clicking the calendar icon to the right of the entry area. You cannot type in the date directly.)

9. Click OK to return to the Execution Properties page. Note the description of the schedule you just created under Report-Specific Schedule.

10. Click Apply to save your changes to the report cache settings.

11. Click the View tab. Check (Select All) in the Select Planets drop-down list, and click View Report. The Weather report runs.

Again, the report takes longer to execute the first time as the intermediate format is created and put into the report cache. This cached instance of the report remains there until five minutes past the hour.

Report Cache and Deploying

When a cached report instance expires, either because of a schedule or because it has existed for its maximum length of time, it is removed from the report cache. One other circumstance can cause a cached report instance to be removed from the report cache. If a new copy of a report is deployed from the Report Builder or uploaded using the Report Manager, any cached instances of that report are removed from the report cache.

Report Caching and Report Parameters

What happens with our report caching if different users enter different parameters when the report is executed? Suppose one user runs the Weather report and only selects Borlaron from the Select Planets drop-down list. The Weather report is cached with only the Borlaron information. Now a second user runs the report, selecting only Stilation. Because a nonexpired instance of this report is in the report cache, it seems the report should come from the report cache. If this were to happen, though, the second user would receive the Borlaron data instead of the Stilation data.

Fortunately, the report server is smart enough to handle this situation. As part of the instance of the report in the report cache, the report server stores any parameter values used to create that cached instance, as shown in Figure 11-6. The cached instance is used

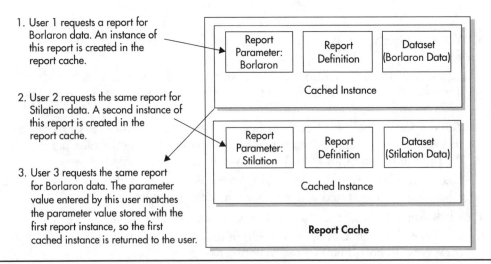

Figure 11-6 *Report caching with parameters*

to satisfy requests made by a subsequent user only if all the parameters used to create the cached instance match the parameters entered by the subsequent user.

Report Caching and Security

Not all users can change report-caching properties. To change the report caching properties for a report, you must have rights to the Manage Reports task. Of the four predefined security roles, the Content Manager, My Reports, and Publisher roles have rights to this task.

Execution Snapshots

Report caching is a great tool for improving the performance of reports with long execution times, but one problem still exists. The first user who requests the report after the cached instance has expired must wait for the report to be created from the underlying data. It would be nice if there were a way to have cached report instances created automatically so no user has to endure these wait times. Fortunately, Reporting Services can do this as well.

An *execution snapshot* is another way to create a cached report instance. Up to this point, we have discussed situations where cached report instances are created as the result of a user action. A user requests a report, and a copy of that report's intermediate format is placed in the report cache. With execution snapshots, a cached report instance is created automatically.

Execution snapshots can create cached report instances on a scheduled basis, or they can be created as soon as this feature is turned on for a particular report. If a schedule is used, each time the schedule is run, it replaces the current cached instance with a new one. Cached report instances created by an execution snapshot are used to satisfy user report requests the same as any other cached report instance.

Enabling Execution Snapshots

You can enable the creation of execution snapshots using two methods. Let's look at the manual method first.

Manually Creating an Execution Snapshot

Let's try enabling execution snapshots for the Weather report.

1. Navigate to the Weather report in the Report Manager, if you are not already there.
2. Click the Properties tab. The Properties page appears.

3. Select Execution from the left side of the screen. The Execution Properties page appears.

4. Select the Render this report from a report execution snapshot.

5. Check the Create a report snapshot when you click the Apply button on this page check box.

6. Click Apply. Note the error message that appears next to the execution snapshot option. When an execution snapshot is created, it is done as a background process, so no one will be available to select a value for the report parameter. Because this parameter has no default value, the report server does not know what value to use for the report parameter when the report is run by the schedule. Let's provide a default value for the parameter so we can proceed.

7. Select Parameters from the left side of the screen. The Parameters page appears.

8. Check the check box in the Has Default column.

9. Enter the following in the Default Value drop-down edit area:

   AFU

   BLN

   NOX

   RKM

   SLN

   SRA

   (We need to enter the values passed to the parameter—in this case, the planet abbreviations, not the planet names that are displayed in the drop-down list. Each value should be entered on a separate line.)

10. Click Apply to save the default value.

11. Let's try to set up snapshot execution again. Select Execution from the left side of the screen. The Execution Properties page appears.

12. Select the Render this report from a report execution snapshot option.

13. Check the Create a report snapshot when you click the Apply button on this page check box.

14. Click Apply. As soon as you click Apply, the report server executes the report and places an instance of the report in the report cache. Allow time for this process to complete.

15. Click the View tab.

The report is rendered from the cached report instance created by the execution snapshot.

Creating Execution Snapshots on a Schedule

Now let's try the scheduled approach to creating execution snapshots.

1. Click the Properties tab. The Execution Properties page should appear. If not, select Execution from the left side of the page.

2. Check the Use the following schedule to create report execution snapshots check box.

3. Report-specific schedule is selected by default. Click Configure next to Report-specific schedule. The Schedule page appears.

4. You can specify hourly, daily, weekly, monthly, or one-time schedules. The Day option should be selected by default. Leave this option selected.

5. Select the On the following days option.

6. Uncheck all the days except for today. (If you are reading this on Monday, for example, leave only Monday checked.)

7. Set the start time to five minutes from now.

8. Select today's date for Begin running this schedule on.

9. Check the Stop this schedule on check box, and then select tomorrow's date.

NOTE

I know this schedule does not fit the stated business requirements of refreshing the report at five minutes past the hour. However, you probably don't want to waste computer resources generating an execution snapshot of the Weather report hour after hour, day after day, so we use this schedule for the demonstration.

10. Click OK to return to the Execution Properties page. Note the description of the schedule you just created under Report-Specific Schedule.

11. Click Apply to save your changes to the execution snapshot settings. After five minutes, the scheduled execution snapshot will create a cached instance of the report.

12. Click the View tab after five minutes. (Go grab some caffeine while you are waiting. You wouldn't want to fall asleep while you are working through all this good stuff!) The Weather report runs and is rendered from the cached report instance created by your scheduled execution snapshot.

This type of execution snapshot schedule would be appropriate for a report whose underlying data is changed only periodically (again, think of a data warehouse updated from a transactional system). The execution snapshot would be scheduled to create a new cached instance of the report right after the new data is available in the warehouse.

Execution Snapshots and Security

Not all users can change execution snapshots. To change the execution snapshot properties for a report, you must have rights to the Manage Reports task. Of the four predefined security roles, the Content Manager, My Reports, and Publisher roles have rights to this task.

Report History

The *report history* feature of the Report Manager enables you to keep copies of a report's past execution. This lets you save the state of your data without having to save copies of the data itself. You can keep documentation of inventory levels, production schedules, or financial records. You can look back in time, using the report history, to do trend analysis or to verify past information.

Enabling Report History

To demonstrate the report history feature of Reporting Services, we need a report whose results change often. It just so happens we have such a report in our Chapter08 solution. The TransportMonitor report provides different values every time the report is run. We can move that report to the report server and then enable the report history.

1. Open the Report Manager, and navigate to the Chapter 08 folder.
2. Use the Upload File button to upload the TransportMonitor report from the Chapter 08 solution.
3. Select Show Details, if it is available in the report viewer toolbar. If it is unavailable, you are already in Show Details mode.
4. Click the icon in the Edit column for the TransportMonitor report. The Properties page appears.
5. Click Parameters on the left side of the page. The Parameters page appears.
6. Select the Has Default check box, and type **1304** for Default Value.
7. Click Apply.
8. Click Data Sources on the left side of the page. The Data Sources page appears.
9. Click Browse. The Data Source page appears.
10. Use the tree view to find the 2009 Conference folder in the tree structure. The 2009 Conference folder is inside the Galactic Delivery Services folder.
11. Select the Galactic shared data source, and click OK.
12. Click Apply.
13. Click History on the left side of the page. The History Properties page appears, as shown in Figure 11-7.

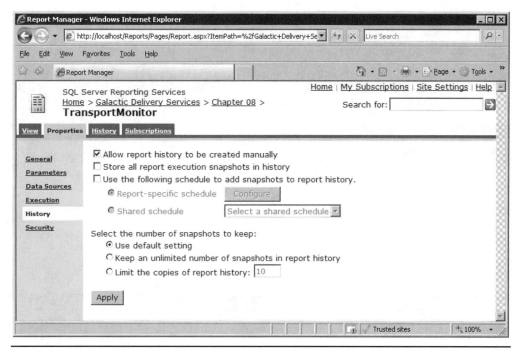

Figure 11-7   *The History Properties page*

14. Make sure the Allow report history to be created manually check box is checked. If it is not, check it and click Apply.

15. Click the View tab at the top of the page. Remember, this report has auto-refresh set. After a few seconds, the report refreshes and new data is displayed.

Manually Creating a Report History Snapshot

One way to create a report history is to do so manually. We can give this a try in the following example.

1. Click the History tab. (This is the History tab along the top, not the History link on the left side of the page.) The Create/View History page appears.

2. Click the New Snapshot button in the report viewer toolbar. An entry for a report history snapshot appears.

3. Click the New Snapshot button two more times to create two more report history snapshots, as shown in Figure 11-8.

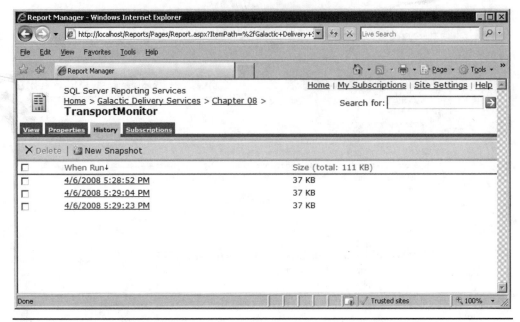

Figure 11-8   *The Create/View History page*

4. Click the link in the When Run column to the first report history snapshot you created. This report should appear in a new browser window.

5. Open the other two report history snapshots, and compare all three.

6. Close the three browser windows containing history snapshots.

As with the cached report instances, the report history snapshots store the intermediate format of the report. Because of this, you can export this report to any of the rendering formats.

1. Select one of your browser windows containing a report history snapshot.

2. Export the snapshot to the Acrobat (PDF) file format, and open it in Adobe Acrobat Reader.

3. Close Acrobat Reader and the browser windows containing your report history snapshots.

Report History Snapshots and Report Parameters

To make our TransportMonitor report work with report history snapshots, we had to provide a default value for the transport number parameter. These parameters cannot be changed when each snapshot is created. (They can be changed, however, if the report is run normally through the Report Manager.)

Essentially, we are saving report history snapshots for only one transport. To save report history snapshots for other transports, we need to create linked reports with parameters defaulted to the other transport numbers.

1. Click the Properties tab.
2. Click General on the left side of the page.
3. Click Create Linked Report.
4. Type **Transport 1305 Monitor** for Name and **The Transport Monitor Report for Transport 1305** for Description.
5. Click OK. The linked report executes.
6. Click the Properties tab.
7. Click Parameters on the left side of the page.
8. Change Default Value to **1305**.
9. Click Apply.
10. Click the History tab.
11. Click New Snapshot.
12. Click the entry for the new snapshot to view it. You can see this is a snapshot for transport number 1305.
13. Close the browser window containing your report history snapshot.

We can create as many linked reports as we need to collect report history snapshots for the different possible parameter values. Remember, linked reports all point back to a single report definition. If the TransportMonitor report is ever updated, it only needs to be deployed in one location, and all the linked reports will have the updated report definition.

Additional Methods for Creating Report History Snapshots

You can create report history snapshots in two other ways in addition to the manual method just described. You can instruct the report server to create a report history snapshot each time it creates an execution snapshot. With this setting turned on, any time the report server creates an execution snapshot—either manually or on a scheduled basis—a copy of that execution snapshot is saved as a report history snapshot.

You can also set up a schedule to create your report history snapshots. Let's give that a try.

1. Click the Chapter 08 link at the top of the page.
2. Click the icon in the Edit column for the TransportMonitor report (the original report, not the linked copy). The Properties page appears.
3. Click History on the left side of the page.
4. Check the Use the following schedule to add snapshots to report history check box.

5. The Report-specific schedule option is selected by default. Click Configure next to Report-specific schedule. The Schedule page appears.

6. Select Hour.

7. Change the Hourly Schedule to run every 0 hours 1 minutes. Set Start Time to five minutes from now.

8. Today's date should be selected for Begin Running This Schedule On.

9. Check the Stop This Schedule On check box, and set it to tomorrow's date.

10. Click OK to return to the History Properties page. Note the description of the schedule you just created under Report-specific schedule.

11. Click Apply to save your changes to the history snapshot settings.

12. Click the History tab.

As each minute passes beyond the time you chose for the schedule to start, a new report history snapshot is created. You need to refresh your browser to see the new history snapshots in the list.

Report History Snapshots and Security

Not all users can change report history snapshot properties. To change the report history snapshot properties for a report, you must have rights to the Manage Report History task. Of the four predefined security roles, the Content Manager and My Reports roles have rights to this task.

Managing Report History Snapshots

You will not usually have a report that requires a new report history snapshot every minute of the day, as we set up in our example. Even so, report history snapshots can start to pile up if you let them. Making business decisions about the number of history snapshots to save for each report is important. Even more important, then, is to implement those business decisions and manage the number of history snapshots being saved on the report server.

Setting Limits on the Number of Report History Snapshots

Reporting Services provides a way to limit the number of history snapshots saved for any given report. Let's take a look and put a limit on our TransportMonitor report snapshots at the same time.

1. Click the Properties tab.

2. In the Select the number of snapshots to keep section of the page, select the Limit the copies of report history option.

3. Set the limit to 5.

4. Click Apply to save your changes to the history snapshot settings.
5. Click OK in response to the warning dialog box.
6. Click the History tab.

If you waited long enough to accumulate more than five report history snapshots, you see the list was reduced to the five most recent history snapshots. The older history snapshots were automatically deleted. As each new history snapshot is created, the oldest history snapshot is deleted, so the total always remains at five. Again, remember you need to refresh your browser to see these changes as each minute passes.

We chose to set a limit on the number of history snapshots saved for this report. In addition to this option, you have two others to choose from (see Figure 11-7). You can keep an unlimited number of history snapshots, or you can use the default setting for history snapshot retention. You see how to change this default setting in the section "The General Site Settings Page."

Manually Deleting Report History Snapshots

In addition to using the history snapshot limit on the History Properties page, you can manually delete unwanted history snapshots.

1. Refresh your browser.

CAUTION

If you reached the limit of five history snapshots, the report server is automatically deleting old history snapshots as new ones are created. If your Create/View History page is not current, you could try to delete a history snapshot that has already been removed by the report server. This results in an error.

2. Check the check box in the Delete column for three of the snapshot history entries.
3. Click Delete in the History tab toolbar.
4. Click OK to confirm the deletion.

The report server again accumulates history snapshots for this report until it has reached our five snapshot limit. At that point, it again deletes the oldest history snapshot as each new one is created.

Disabling Report History Snapshot Creation

We can now disable the creation of report history snapshots for this report so we are not wasting valuable execution cycles.

1. Click the Properties tab.
2. Select History on the left side of the screen.

3. Uncheck the Use the following schedule to add snapshots to report history check box.
4. Click Apply.
5. Click the History tab.

New history snapshots are no longer created for this report on a scheduled basis. Note, however, that the existing history snapshots were not deleted. These history snapshots are still available for viewing, even though the schedule that created them was disabled.

Updating Report Definitions and Report History Snapshots

One of the best features of report history snapshots is this: They are not lost if the definition of the underlying report is changed. Let's see this in action.

1. Start Visual Studio or the Business Intelligence Development Studio, and open the Chapter 08 solution.
2. Open the TransportMonitor report layout.
3. In the Report Data window, right-click the entry for the TransportMonitor dataset, and select Dataset Properties from the context menu. The Dataset Properties dialog box appears.
4. Select the Filters page.
5. Click the Add button to add a filter.
6. Select [Item] from the Expression drop-down list. Select <> from the Operator drop-down list. Enter **Thruster** for the Value. This filter removes the thruster data from the report.
7. Click OK to exit the Dataset Properties dialog box.
8. Click the Preview tab. Check 1304 in the Transports drop-down list, and click View Report. Note the Thruster graph is missing.
9. Click Save All in the toolbar.
10. Right-click the TransportMonitor report in the Solution Explorer, and select Deploy from the context menu.
11. After the deployment has succeeded, close Visual Studio or the Business Intelligence Development Studio.
12. Return to the Report Manager in your browser.
13. Click the View tab for the TransportMonitor report. Note the report now includes our change, eliminating the thruster data from the report.
14. Click the History tab. We still have some report history snapshots based on the old report definition.

15. Click New Snapshot to manually create a report history snapshot based on the new report definition. Our five history snapshot limit is still in effect, so one of the old history snapshots may have to be deleted to make room for the new one.

16. Click the most recent history snapshot to view it. It does not contain thruster data because it is based on the new report definition.

17. Close this browser window.

18. Click the oldest history snapshot to view it. It does contain thruster data because it is based on the old report definition.

19. Close this browser window.

Just like the cached report instance, the report history snapshot contains both the report definition and the dataset. Therefore, it is unaffected by subsequent changes to the report definition.

Subscriptions

Up to this point, we have discussed only one way for users to receive reports. They log on to the Report Manager site, find the report they want, and execute it, which is known as *pull* technology. The user pulls the information out of Reporting Services by initiating the execution of the report.

Reporting Services also supports push technology for delivering reports. In a *push* technology scenario, Reporting Services initiates the execution of the report and then sends the report to the user. This is done through the report subscription.

Standard Subscriptions

Reporting Services supports several types of *subscriptions*. The first is the *standard* subscription, which is a request to execute a report once and push the result to a particular user or set of users. The standard subscription is usually a self-serve operation. A user logs on to the Report Manager site and finds the report they want. The user then creates the subscription by specifying the schedule for the push delivery and the delivery options.

Standard subscriptions have two delivery options: e-mail and file share. The *e-mail delivery* option, of course, sends an e-mail to the specified e-mail addresses with a link to the report or with the report itself either embedded as HTML or as an attached document. The *file share* option creates a file containing the report in a specified folder on a file share. The file share option can be used to place the report into a document store managed and/or indexed by another application, such as Microsoft's Office SharePoint Server.

Creating a Standard E-mail Subscription with an Embedded Report

You have been hired as the traffic manager for Galactic Delivery Services and are responsible for routing transport traffic. As part of your job, it is important to know what the weather is like at all the hubs. Rather than taking the time to go look at the Weather report on the Report Manager website, you want to have the report e-mailed to you hourly.

1. Open the Report Manager, and navigate to the Chapter 08 folder.
2. Click the entry for the Weather report.
3. Click the Subscriptions tab. The Create/View Subscriptions page appears.
4. Click New Subscription. The Subscription Properties page appears, as shown in Figure 11-9.
5. The Delivered by drop-down list defaults to E-Mail. Leave this set to the default setting.
6. Type your e-mail address for To. Note, you can enter multiple e-mail addresses, separated by a semicolon (;), and you can also enter e-mail addresses for Cc and Bcc.
7. Enter an e-mail address for Reply-To. This can be your own e-mail address, someone else's, or a dummy e-mail address that does not exist.
8. By default, the subject of the e-mail is the name of the report, followed by the time the report was executed. Change Subject to **@ReportName**.
9. Leave the Include Report check box checked. This includes the report in the e-mail. Uncheck the Include Link check box.
10. The Render Format drop-down list defaults to MHTML (web archive). Leave this selected.
11. Select High from the Priority drop-down list.
12. For Comment, type **This e-mail was sent from Reporting Services**.
13. Under the Run the subscription heading, select the When the scheduled report run is complete option.
14. Click Select Schedule. The Schedule page appears.
15. Select Hour.
16. Leave the schedule to run every 1 hour and 00 minutes. Set the start time to five minutes from now.
17. Today's date should be selected for Begin running this schedule on.
18. Check Stop this schedule on and select tomorrow's date.
19. Click OK to return to the Schedule Properties page.

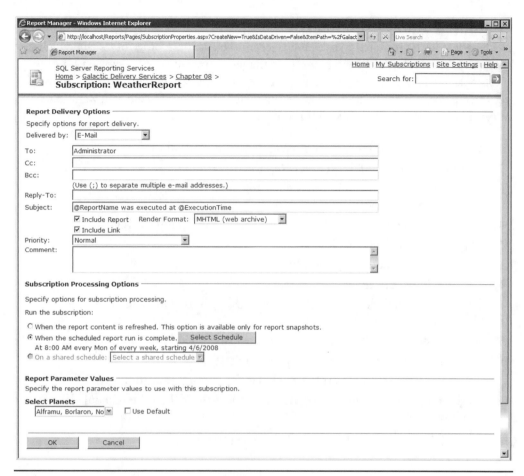

Figure 11-9 *The Subscription Properties page*

20. Note the default parameter values for this report appear in the Report Parameter Values section of this report. If necessary, you can specify parameters to use when running this subscription. Leave the parameter set to its default.

21. Click OK to create this standard subscription and return to the View/Edit Subscriptions page.

22. After the time specified by your schedule has passed, refresh this page. You should see the time of the execution in the Last Run column and Mail Sent To, followed by your e-mail address, in the Status column. You should also have a high-priority e-mail waiting for you in your mailbox.

23. Do not delete this subscription until you have had a chance to look at the My Subscriptions page in the section "My Subscriptions."

Creating a Standard E-mail Subscription with a Report Link

You have just been promoted to sales manager for the Axelburg office of Galactic Delivery Services. Congratulations! Being a good manager, you want to keep tabs on how your salespeople are doing. To do this, you want to view the Invoice-Batch Number Report each week to see how much you are invoicing your clients. As a memory aid, you want to receive an e-mail each week with a link to this report.

1. Open the Report Manager, and navigate to the Axelburg folder.
2. Click the Invoice-Batch Number Report to execute it.
3. Click New Subscription in the toolbar for the View tab. The Subscription Properties page appears.
4. Delivered by defaults to E-Mail. Leave this as the default setting.
5. Type your e-mail address for To.
6. Enter an e-mail address for Reply-To.
7. Change Subject to **@ReportName**.
8. Uncheck the Include Report check box. Leave the Include Link check box checked.
9. Render Format is not used because we are just embedding a link to the report.
10. Select High from the Priority drop-down list.
11. For Comment, type **Remember to check the invoice amounts**.
12. Under the Run the subscription heading, select the When the scheduled report run is complete option.
13. Click Select Schedule. The Schedule page appears.
14. Select Week.
15. Leave Repeat after this number of weeks set to 1.
16. Check today for On day(s). For example, check Mon if today is Monday. Uncheck all the other days.
17. Set the start time to five minutes from now.
18. Today's date should be selected for Begin running this schedule on.
19. Check Stop this schedule on and select tomorrow's date.
20. Click OK to return to the Schedule Properties page.
21. At the bottom of the Schedule Properties page, you see a list of the parameters for the selected report. Leave the default values for the parameters.
22. Click OK to create this standard subscription and return to the Report Viewer page.

When the scheduled time has passed, you will receive an e-mail with a link to this report.

Standard Subscriptions and Execution Snapshots

In addition to creating your own schedule for your standard subscriptions, you can synchronize your subscriptions with scheduled execution snapshots. For example, the Weather report is set to create an execution snapshot every hour. We want to receive an e-mail with the new version of the report after each new execution snapshot has been created.

One way to do this is to keep the schedule for the execution snapshot synchronized with the schedule for the subscription. The execution snapshot runs, and then the subscription runs one minute later. This can cause problems if the execution snapshot occasionally takes more than one minute to create or if one of the schedules is edited.

A better solution is to let the creation of the execution snapshot drive the delivery of the subscription. The When the Report Content Is Refreshed option does just that (refer to Figure 11-9). When this option is selected for a subscription, the subscription is sent out every time a new execution snapshot is created. Of course, this option is only available for reports that have execution snapshots enabled.

Multiple Subscriptions for One Report

Nothing prevents a user from creating more than one subscription for the same report. Perhaps you want a report delivered every Friday and on the last day of the month. You can't do this with one subscription, but you can certainly do it with two—a weekly subscription for the Friday delivery and a monthly subscription for delivery on the last day of the month.

Another reason for multiple subscriptions is to receive a report run for multiple sets of parameters. You saw it is possible to specify parameter values as part of the subscription properties. Using this feature, you could have one subscription send you a report with one set of parameters and another subscription send you the same report with a different set of parameters.

Embedded Report Versus Attached Report

When you choose to include the report along with the subscription e-mail, the report can show up either embedded in an HTML e-mail or as an attached document. If you select the Web Archive format, the report is embedded. If you select any of the other render formats, the report is sent as an attached document.

Having the report embedded in the e-mail makes it convenient for the user to view the report: It is simply part of the body of your e-mail. However, not all e-mail packages support HTML e-mail, so some users might be unable to view an embedded report. If a user is unsure of the capabilities of their e-mail package, they should choose the Acrobat (PDF) file format. This format is sent as an attachment and can be viewed by just about anyone.

Standard Subscriptions and Security

Not all users can create standard subscriptions. In fact, it is possible to view a report, but not be able to subscribe to it. To subscribe to a report or create a subscription for delivery to others, you must have rights to the Manage Individual Subscriptions task. Of the four predefined security roles, the Browser, Content Manager, and My Reports roles have rights to manage individual subscriptions.

Managing Your Subscriptions

An active user may subscribe to a number of reports scattered throughout a number of folders. Just remembering all the reports you subscribed to can be a big challenge. Managing all those subscriptions can be even tougher. Fortunately, the Report Manager provides a way to view all your subscriptions in one place.

My Subscriptions

The My Subscriptions page consolidates all your standard subscriptions in one place.

1. Click the My Subscriptions link at the top of the page. The My Subscriptions page appears, as shown in Figure 11-10.
2. You can click any heading to sort your list of subscriptions.
3. Click the Edit link next to WeatherReport. The Subscription Properties page appears.

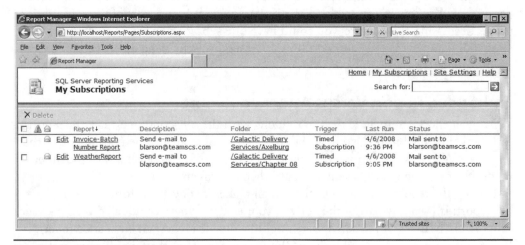

Figure 11-10 *The My Subscriptions page*

4. You can make changes to this subscription, if you desire. Click Cancel to return to the My Subscriptions page.
5. Click the WeatherReport link in the Report column. You jump to the Weather report.
6. Click your browser's Back button.
7. Click the text in the Folder column for the Invoice-Batch Number Report. You jump to the Axelburg folder.
8. Click your browser's Back button.

The My Subscriptions page lists all the standard subscriptions you created on this report server. This makes the subscriptions much easier to manage. You can sort the list several different ways to help you find and manage the subscriptions. You can also use the My Subscriptions page to delete unwanted subscriptions.

Let's delete these subscriptions so you do not waste computing power e-mailing reports.

1. Check the check box in the headings. This automatically checks the check box next to each subscription.
2. Click Delete in the toolbar.
3. Click OK to confirm the deletion.
4. Click the Home link at the top of the page. You return to the Home folder.

Data-Driven Subscriptions

A better name for a data-driven subscription might be "mass mailing." The data-driven subscription enables you to take a report and e-mail it to a number of people on a mailing list. The mailing list can be queried from any valid Reporting Services data source. The mailing list can contain fields in addition to the recipient's e-mail address, which are used to control the content of the e-mail sent to each recipient. As mentioned in Chapter 2, the Enterprise Edition of Reporting Services is required for you to use data-driven subscriptions.

Creating a Data-Driven Subscription

Transport 1305 has been acting up. Galactic Delivery Services (GDS) wants all its mechanics to have a good background on the types of problems this transport is having. To facilitate this, the results from the Transport 1305 Monitor report should be e-mailed to all mechanics every four hours. Employees holding the position of Mechanic I should receive the report as a high-priority e-mail. Employees holding the position of Mechanic II should receive the report as a normal-priority e-mail.

1. Open the Report Manager, and navigate to the Chapter 08 folder.
2. Click Show Details.
3. Click the icon in the Edit column for the Transport 1305 Monitor report.
4. Click the Subscriptions tab.
5. Click the New Data-Driven Subscription button. The first page of the Data-Driven Subscription process appears, as shown in Figure 11-11.
6. Type **Maintenance Watch on Transport 1305** for Description.
7. Select E-Mail from the Specify how recipients are notified drop-down list.
8. Select the Specify a shared data source option.

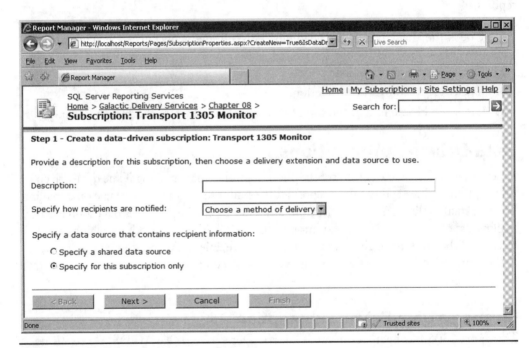

Figure 11-11 *Data-driven subscription process, first page*

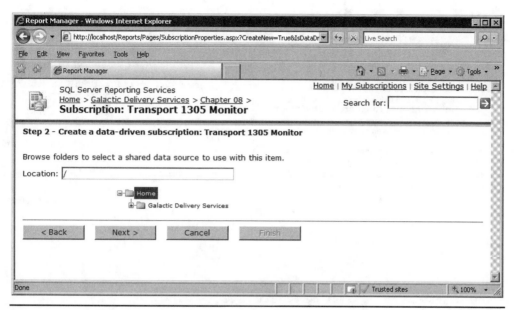

Figure 11-12 *Data-driven subscription process, Shared Data Source page*

9. Click the Next button. The Shared Data Source page appears, as shown in Figure 11-12.

10. Use the tree view to find the 2009 Conference folder in the Galactic Delivery Services folder.

11. Select the Galactic shared data source in the 2009 Conference folder.

12. Click the Next button. The Query page appears, as shown in Figure 11-13.

13. Type the following for the query:

```
EXEC stp_MechanicMailingList
```

14. Click Validate to make sure you don't have any typos or other problems.

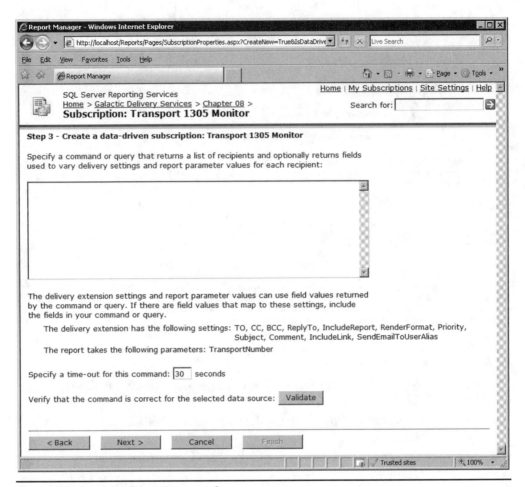

Figure 11-13 *Data-Driven Subscription process, Query page*

15. If the query does not validate successfully, look for the error in the query you typed. Otherwise, click Next. The Data Association page appears, as shown in Figure 11-14. Here, you can associate columns in the result set with fields in the subscription e-mail.

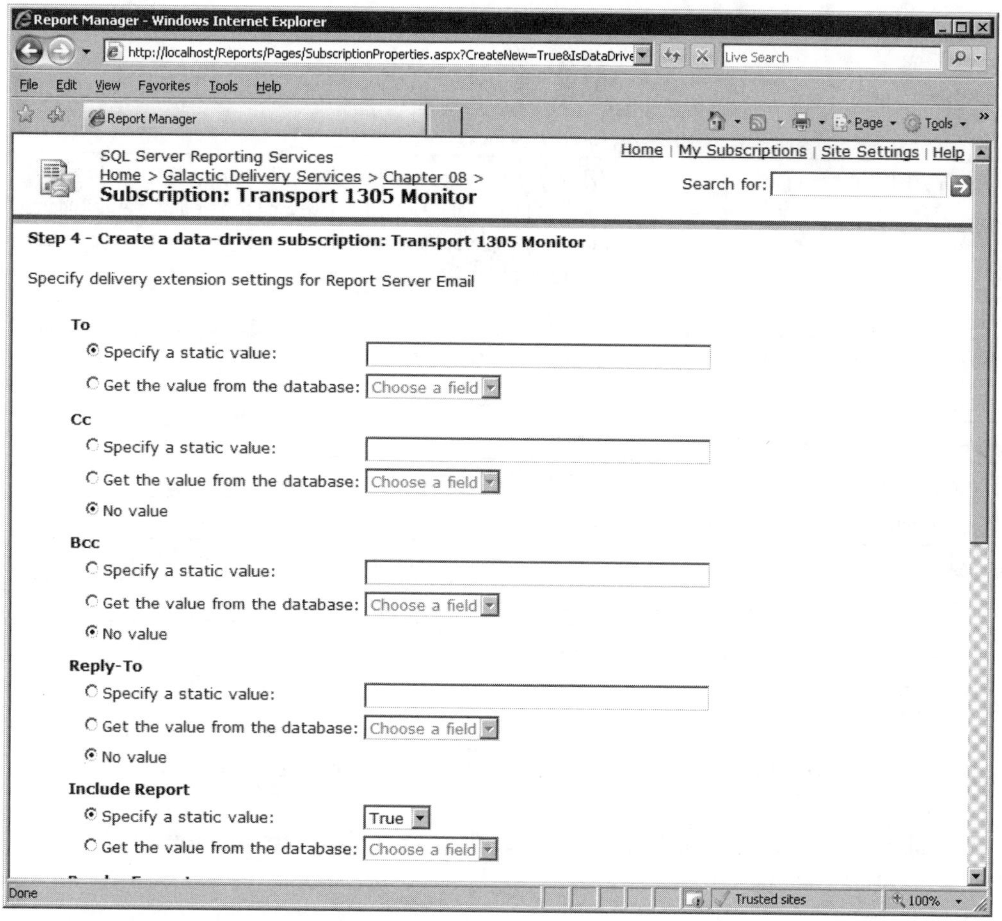

Figure 11-14   *Data-driven subscription process, Data Association page*

16. Set the following properties on this page:

Property	Value
To	Specify a static value.
Specify a static value (For To)	(Type your e-mail address here. Normally, you would select the e-mail address from a database field, but we want to have a valid e-mail address for our example. Because your system cannot send interplanetary e-mail, we have to use your e-mail address.)
Reply-To	Specify a static value
Specify a static value (Reply-To)	Reports@Galactic.SRA
Render Format	Specify a static value
Specify a static value (Render Format)	Acrobat (PDF) file
Priority	Get the value from the database
Get the value from the database (Priority)	Priority
Subject	Get the value from the database
Get the value from the database (Subject)	Subject
Include Link	Specify a static value
Specify a static value (Include Link)	False

17. Click the Next button. The Parameter Values page appears, as shown in Figure 11-15.

18. Click the Next button. The Notify Recipients page appears, as shown in Figure 11-16.

NOTE

Because we do not allow the user to change the TransportNumber parameter, the subscription does not allow us to change that default parameter value here. For a report that does include user-enterable parameters, the parameter values would be specified here. As with other items, parameter values can be static values or can come from the database.

19. Select the On a Schedule Created for This Subscription option.

20. Click the Next button. The Schedule page appears.

21. Select the Hour option.

22. Change the schedule to run every 4 hours 00 minutes.

23. Set the start time to five minutes from now.

24. Today's date should be selected for Begin Running This Schedule On.

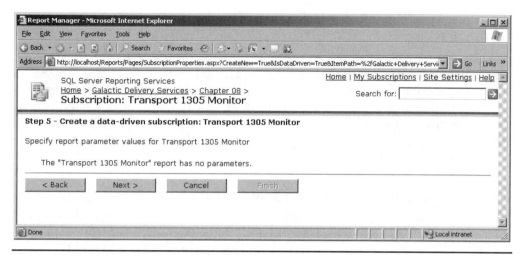

Figure 11-15 *Data-driven subscription process, Parameter Values page*

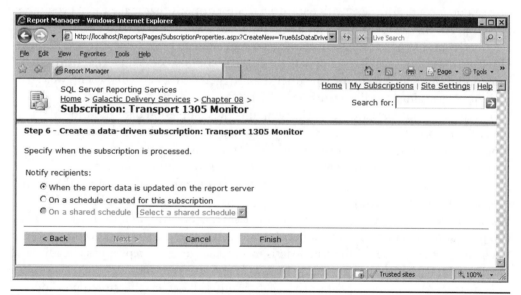

Figure 11-16 *Data-driven subscription process, Notify Recipients page*

25. Check Stop This Schedule On, and select tomorrow's date.

26. Click Finish.

27. Once the scheduled time for your subscription has passed, refresh this page. You should see the time of the execution in the Last Run column and Done: 8 processed of 8 total; 0 errors in the Status column. You should also receive eight e-mails (eight mechanics are in the database, and we sent an e-mail to each one) with the Transport 1305 Monitor report attached.

28. If you do not want to receive eight e-mails every four hours for the next day, you can delete this subscription.

Data-Driven Subscriptions and Security

Not all users can create data-driven subscriptions. To create a data-driven subscription for a report, you must have rights to the Manage All Subscriptions task. Of the four predefined security roles, only the Content Manager role has rights to this task.

Data-Driven Subscriptions and Event-Driven Behavior

You can do a couple of tricks with data-driven subscriptions that make them even more powerful. For instance, at times, you might not want a subscription sent out until after a certain event has occurred. For instance, you may want to e-mail a report to a number of recipients after a specific data update process has completed. While a data-driven subscription is a scheduled process, rather than triggered by a particular event, we can make it behave almost as if it were event-driven.

You need a field in a status table that contains the completion date and time of the last data load. You also need a field in a status table that contains the date and time when the report was last distributed. With these two flag fields in place, you can simulate event-driven behavior for your data-driven subscription.

First, you need to build a stored procedure that returns the mailing list for the report distribution. To this stored procedure, add logic that checks the date and time of the last data load against the date and time of the last report distribution. If the data load is complete and the report has not yet been distributed today, the stored procedure returns the mailing list result set. If the data load is incomplete, or if the report has already been distributed today, the stored procedure returns an empty result set.

Now you create a series of data-driven subscriptions based on this stored procedure. If the data load completes sometime between 1:00 A.M. and 3:00 A.M., you might schedule one data-driven subscription to execute at 1:00 A.M., another at 1:30 A.M., another at 2:00 A.M., and so on. When each data-driven subscription executes, the stored procedure determines whether the data load is complete and whether the report was already distributed. If the stored procedure returns a result set, the data-driven subscription e-mails the report to the mailing list. If the stored procedure returns an empty result set, the data-driven subscription terminates without sending any e-mails.

This same approach can be used to e-mail reports only when the report data has changed. You create a stored procedure that only returns a mailing list result set if the data has changed since the last time the report was e-mailed. This stored procedure is used to create a data-driven subscription. Now the data-driven subscription only sends out reports when the data has changed; otherwise, it sends nothing.

Data-Driven Subscriptions and Report Caching

If you looked closely, you may have noticed that the Specify How Recipients Are Notified drop-down list included the entry Null Delivery Provider. This doesn't seem to make much sense—why would you create a subscription and then not send it anywhere? This Null Delivery Provider is used to support report caching.

Suppose you have a report with a number of possible report parameter combinations that would benefit from caching. As you have seen, report parameter values must match for a report to be pulled from cache. How do we create cached copies of the report with all the possible parameter combinations? The answer is a data-driven subscription using the Null Delivery Provider.

The first step is to create a query that returns all the possible report parameter combinations (or at least the most popular ones) for this report. You then use this query to create a data-driven subscription to execute the report with each of these parameter combinations. If report caching is enabled, the data-driven subscription would cause a copy of the report to be cached with each of these parameter combinations. This is true even if the Null Delivery Provider is used and the report is never delivered anywhere by the subscription. Because the subscription created all these cached copies with the various parameter value combinations, no matter what combination of parameters a user enters the following day, the report is rendered from a cached copy.

Site Settings

When setting the limit for the number of report history snapshots kept for a given report, we encountered a setting that referred to using a default value. Each time you have the opportunity to specify a schedule for an execution snapshot, a subscription, or other feature, you have an option to select a shared schedule. The report history snapshot default value, the shared schedules, and several other site-wide settings are managed on the Site Settings page.

The General Site Settings Page

The main Site Settings page enables you to set several default values and configuration options. This page also acts as a front end for other configuration screens. You can access the Site Settings page by clicking the Site Settings link at the top of the page. The main Site Settings page is shown in Figure 11-17.

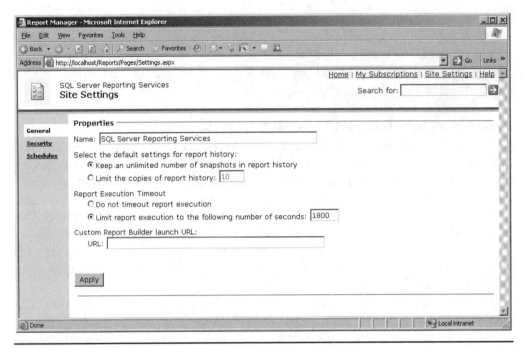

Figure 11-17 *The General Site Settings page*

We begin our examination of the site settings by looking at the configuration items and default values on the General Site Settings page.

Name

The value in the Name field appears at the top of each page in the Report Manager. You can change this to the name of your company or some other phrase that can help users identify this report server.

Report History Default

The report history default setting lets you specify a default value for the maximum number of report history snapshots to keep. This can be set to a specific number or set to allow an unlimited number of snapshots. Each report utilizing report history snapshots can either specify its own maximum number or use this default value.

Report Execution Timeout

The default for Report Execution Timeout enables you to specify a default value for the maximum amount of time a report may run before it times out. This can be a specific number of seconds or set to no timeout (unlimited execution time). Each report can either specify its own timeout value or use this default value.

NOTE

The report execution timeout is specified on the Execution Properties page for each report.

Custom Report Builder Launch URL

If you move the location of the Report Builder tool, you can specify the URL used to launch the Report Builder from its new location.

Other Pages Accessed from the Site Settings Page

In addition to the configuration options and default values managed on the General Site Settings page, there are two other pages available under the site settings. These pages enable you to manage the site-wide security configuration and the shared schedules. The following is a brief discussion of each area managed from the Site Settings pages.

Site-Wide Security

The Security page lets you assign Windows users and Windows groups to system-level roles. These system-level roles provide users with the rights to view and modify settings for the report server, such as those found on the Site Settings page. System Administrator and System User are the two predefined system-level roles.

For more information on system-level roles and system-level tasks, see Chapter 10.

Shared Schedules

Each time you had an option to create a schedule for a feature, such as report cache expiration or execution snapshot creation, it was accompanied by a choice to use a shared schedule. A *shared schedule* lets you use a single schedule definition in multiple places. A shared schedule is created through the same user interface used to create all the other schedules we have been looking at in this chapter.

Shared schedules are beneficial for situations where a number of events should use the same timing. For example, suppose you have ten reports that utilize execution snapshots, all pulling data from a data warehouse. That data warehouse is updated once a week. It makes sense to create one shared schedule that can be used to run the execution snapshots for all these reports.

Not only does this save the time that would otherwise be necessary to create the schedule ten times, but it also makes it easier if the timing of the data warehouse update is changed and the execution snapshot schedule must be changed. If you are using a shared schedule, you only need to make this change once in the shared location. Without the shared schedule, you would be forced to make this change ten times.

Managing Reporting Services Through the SQL Server Management Studio

In Chapter 10, we used the SQL Server Management Studio to help manage security on the report server. We created a new security role. We did this in the SQL Server Management Studio because this activity could not be done through the Report Manager. Let's look at a couple of other aspects of report server management that require the SQL Server Management Studio.

The Server Properties Dialog Box

Follow these steps to view the Server Properties dialog box in SQL Server Management Studio:

1. Start SQL Server Management Studio and connect to the report server as we did in Chapter 10.
2. Right-click the report server in the Object Explorer window, and select Properties from the context menu. The Server Properties dialog box appears, as shown in Figure 11-18.

As you can see, a number of the characteristics of the report server that can be managed through the Report Manager can also be controlled here. We will not discuss this ground that has already been covered; instead, we will cover the items that are unique to the Server Properties dialog box.

My Reports

The Enable a My Reports folder for each user option, on the General page of the Server Properties dialog box, turns on a feature giving each user their own private folder on the report server. When this option is enabled, a special folder called Users Folders is created in the Home folder. Only users assigned the System Administrator role can see this folder.

CAUTION

You should enable the My Reports option only if you intend to use it. Getting rid of the Users Folders folder and its content once it is created is a bit tricky. If you do create the folder and then need to delete it, turn off the My Reports option, go into each folder in the Users Folders folder, and give yourself Content Manager rights. Now you can delete the folders.

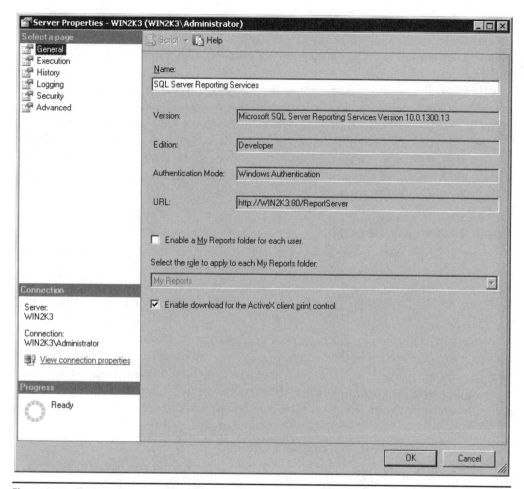

Figure 11-18 *The Server Properties dialog box in SQL Server Management Studio*

As each user logs on for the first time after the My Reports option is enabled, a new folder is created in the Users Folders folder. This new folder has the same name as the domain and logon name of the user signing in. The new folder is mapped to a folder called My Reports.

Let's discuss an example to make this clearer. Sally and José are two users in the Galactic domain. Shortly after the My Reports option is enabled, Sally accesses the report server using the Report Manager. A new folder is created in the Users Folders folder called Galactic Sally.

Sally is not assigned the System Administrator role, so she cannot see the Users Folders folder or the Galactic Sally folder inside of it. Instead, when Sally views her Home folder, she sees a folder called My Reports. Sally's My Reports folder is a mapping to the Galactic Sally folder.

When José accesses the report server using the Report Manager, a new folder is created in the Users Folders folder called Galactic José. José sees a folder called My Reports in his Home folder. José's My Reports folder is a mapping to the Galactic José folder.

José is assigned the System Administrator role. In addition to the My Reports folder, José can view the Users Folders folder. When José opens the Users Folders folder, he can see both the Galactic Sally and the Galactic José folders. In fact, José can open the Galactic Sally folder and view its contents.

Security and My Reports

Because the My Reports folder is for each user's personal reports, the users are granted more rights in the My Reports folder than they might be granted anywhere else on the site. On the Site Settings page, you decide which security role to assign to the user in their own My Reports folder. By default, users are assigned the My Reports role in their own My Reports folder.

A user can be granted broader rights in the My Reports folder, because they are the only one using the reports in this folder. No one else is going to set up caching and report history snapshots, for example, because no one else is going to use these reports. You want to be sure to assign the user to a role that has rights to publish reports; otherwise, each user will be unable to put reports in their own My Reports folder.

When to Enable the My Report Option

The My Reports option can be useful in two situations. First, if you have a number of individuals creating ad hoc reports for their own personal use, the My Reports folder provides a convenient spot for this to take place. If you do use the My Reports folder in this manner, you want to have some policies in place to ensure that each user's My Reports folder does not become an ad hoc dumping ground.

The second viable use of the My Reports folder is as a quality assurance (QA) testing area for report developers. The report developers can use their individual My Reports folders as a place to test a report in the server environment before it is deployed to a folder available to the users. This is convenient, because the system administrator can navigate through the Users Folders folder to access the report, after it has passed QA testing, and move it to its production location. Of course, having a dedicated quality assurance server for this purpose is far better, but in situations where this is not feasible, the My Reports folder can be considered as an option.

Report Execution Logging

The Enable Report Execution Logging option, on the Logging page of the Server Properties dialog box, determines whether information about each report execution is placed in the execution log. The execution log this option refers to is the ExecutionLogStorage table in the ReportServer database. This is not referring to any of the log text files created by the Report Server application. Along with turning logging off and on, you can specify how long the Report Server should keep these log entries.

The ExecutionLogStorage table uses cryptic globally unique identifier (GUID) strings to identify the reports being run. This is not going to be helpful when trying to figure out who has run the Invoice-Batch Number Report in the past month. Instead of querying the ExecutionLogStorage table directly, use the ExecutionLog2 view in the ReportServer database. This view decodes the GUID strings into the report paths and report names, making it much easier to work with.

Additional Settings

In addition to the configuration items on the Report Manager Site Settings page and the SQL Server Management Studio Server Properties dialog box, you can modify the functionality of the report server in other ways. In Chapter 12, we look at settings that can be changed using system properties. The system properties can be set through the Reporting Services Configuration Tool and through the SetSystemProperties method of the Reporting Services web service. See Chapter 12 for more details.

A Sense of Style

We do not have access to the source code of the Report Manager pages, so we cannot make changes to the way they function. However, because these pages are ultimately HTML pages sent to a browser, we can make changes to the way the pages look. This is done through a cascading style sheet (CSS).

The ReportingServices Style Sheet

The look of the Report Manager is controlled by the ReportingServices.css cascading style sheet. The default location for this file is

```
C:\Program Files\Microsoft SQL Server\MSRS10.MSSQLSERVER\Reporting Services\

                         ReportManager\Styles\ReportingServices.css
```

(There is also a cascading style sheet in this folder that controls the look of the web parts used to display reports in SharePoint.)

Let's take a look at the steps necessary to make a change to the cascading style sheet.

Modifying the ReportingServices Style Sheet

The following procedure changes the fonts for both the name displayed at the top of the Report Manager pages and the text showing the current folder.

1. Make a backup copy of the ReportingServices.css file.
2. Open the ReportingServices.css file in Notepad.
3. Locate the entry for msrs-lowertitle.
4. Change the font-size entry from 16px to 10px to decrease the size of the current folder text.
5. Locate the entry for msrs-uppertitle.
6. Change the font-size entry from x-small to large to increase the size of the name.
7. Add the following text immediately below the font-size entry:

   ```
   font-weight:bold;
   ```

8. Save your changes to the ReportingServices.css file, and exit Notepad.

NOTE

You need to remove any cached copies of the ReportingServices.css file from your browser before the changes to this style sheet can take effect.

9. Open the Report Manager in your browser, if it is not already open. If it is already open, navigate to a new folder in the Report Manager. You see the name at the top of the page now appears in large, bold text and the text showing the current folder is smaller.

Building On

In this chapter, you learned ways to deliver reports and control their execution from within the Report Manager. In the next chapter, we look at ways to customize report delivery by building on to Reporting Services. These techniques enable you to integrate Reporting Services reports with your own websites and custom applications.

Chapter 12

Extending Outside the Box: Customizing Reporting Services

In This Chapter

- ▶ **Using Reporting Services Without the Report Manager**
- ▶ **Custom Security**
- ▶ **Best Practices**
- ▶ **Where Do We Go from Here?**

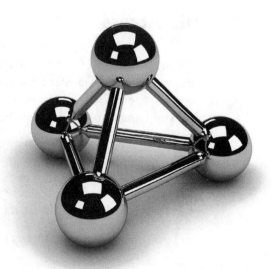

U p to this point, we have been using Reporting Services just as it comes out of the box (or off the installation CD, if you want to get technical). All our management of Reporting Services features and all our report execution have been through the Report Manager or the SQL Server Management Studio. Reporting Services, the Report Manager, and the SQL Server Management Studio do, after all, provide a feature-rich environment in their default configuration.

One of the best features of Reporting Services, however, is the capability to extend it beyond its basic operation. In this chapter, we do just that. You learn ways to execute reports without using the Report Manager interface. You look at ways to manage Reporting Services without using the Report Manager or the SQL Server Management Studio. Finally, you work through an example showing how to change the security mechanism used by Reporting Services.

All of this gives you a brief taste of what Reporting Services can do when you start extending outside the box.

Using Reporting Services Without the Report Manager

The Report Manager provides a nice interface for finding and executing reports. However, the Report Manager is not always the best way to deliver a report to your users. Perhaps the user is browsing your website or using a custom application and needs to view a report. In these situations, it does not make sense to force the user to jump to the Report Manager and begin navigating folders. We want to deliver the report to the user right where they are. In this section, we explore several ways to do just that.

URL Access

One way to execute a report without using the Report Manager is through Uniform Resource Locator (URL) access. URL access allows a browser or a program capable of issuing Hypertext Transfer Protocol (HTTP) requests to specify a URL and receive a report in the HTML report viewer. This URL can be built into a standard Hypertext Markup Language (HTML) anchor tag to allow a report to be displayed with one mouse click.

Basic URL Access

The basic URL used to access a report has two parts. The first part is the URL of the report server web service. In a default installation, this is

```
http://{computername}/ReportServer
```

where {computername} is the name of the computer hosting the report server. This is followed by a question mark and the path through the Reporting Services virtual folders to the report you want to execute. The Home folder is the root of this path, but it's not included in the path itself. The path must begin with a forward slash (/).

Let's try an example. We can execute the Invoice-Batch Number Report for the Axelburg office. This report is in the Axelburg folder inside the Galactic Delivery Services folder.

NOTE

In the examples used throughout the rest of this chapter, we assume Reporting Services is installed on your computer. The localhost name is used to access Internet Information Services (IIS) on this computer. If you have Reporting Services installed on a different computer, substitute the name of that computer in place of localhost in the following examples.

1. Start Internet Explorer.
2. Enter the following URL in the address bar:

```
http://localhost/ReportServer?/Galactic Delivery Services/Axelburg/
                                    Invoice-Batch Number Report
```

3. Click Go. The Invoice-Batch Number Report appears in the browser inside the HTML report viewer.

NOTE

When your URL is submitted, it is URL-encoded. Some of the characters in your URL may be replaced by other characters or by hexadecimal strings, such as %20. This ensures the URL can be interpreted correctly when it is sent to the web server.

As with Report Manager, Windows integrated security is being used when a user executes a report through URL access. The user must have rights to execute the report; otherwise, an error results. However, because the user is not browsing through the folder structure to get to the report, the user does not need to have any rights to the folder containing the report. You can use this fact to hide a report from non-administrative users who are browsing through folders in the Report Manager, while still making the report accessible to someone using URL access.

In addition to executing reports, you can view the contents of folders, resources, and shared data sources. Try the following:

1. Enter this URL in the address bar:

```
http://localhost/ReportServer?/Galactic Delivery Services
```

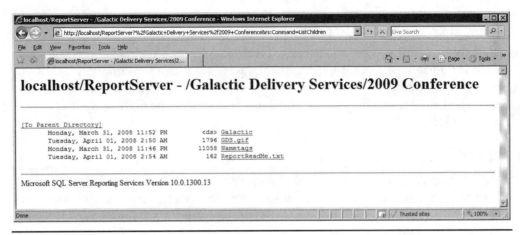

Figure 12-1 *Browsing folder contents using URL access*

2. Click Go. The contents of the Galactic Delivery Services folder appear.
3. Click the link for the 2009 Conference folder. The contents of the 2009 Conference folder appear, as shown in Figure 12-1.

Command Parameters

Look at the URL in the address bar. You see something has been added to the URL, namely &rs:Command=ListChildren. This is called a *command parameter*. It tells Reporting Services what to do with the item pointed to by the URL. The four possible values for the command parameter are listed in Table 12-1.

Looking at this table, you quickly realize that only one command parameter value applies to each type of item you can encounter in the Reporting Services virtual folders. Attempting to use a command parameter with the wrong type of item results in an error. If you do not include the command parameter, Reporting Services simply performs the one and only command that applies to the type of item you are targeting in your URL. Because specifying the command parameter is completely unnecessary, one can only assume this was put in place to allow for future growth.

Command Parameter	Applies To	Result
GetDataSourceContents	Data Source	Displays the data source definition as an Extensible Markup Language (XML) structure.
GetResourceContents	Resource Item	Displays the contents of the resource item in the browser.
ListChildren	Folder	Lists the contents of the folder with links to each content item.
Render	Report	Displays the report in the Report Viewer.

Table 12-1 *Values for the Command Parameter*

Passing Parameters

When you executed the Invoice-Batch Number Report through URL access, you received the default values for the start date and end date. You can change these dates in the Report Viewer, but only after waiting for the report to execute with the default values. It would be much better to get exactly what you want the first time around.

Fortunately, you have a way to do just that. You can pass the values for report parameters as part of the URL. On the URL, include an ampersand (&) followed by the name of the report parameter, an equals sign, and the parameter value. Try the following:

1. Enter the following URL in the address bar:

   ```
   http://localhost/ReportServer?/Galactic Delivery Services/Axelburg/
        Invoice-Batch Number Report&StartDate=11/1/2008&EndDate=11/30/2008
   ```

2. Click Go. The Invoice-Batch Number Report appears with data for November 2008.

It is possible to hide parameters from interactive report users, while still allowing values to be passed to those parameters through the URL or web service access. This is done through the Hide option for each parameter. Let's try the following:

1. Open the Report Manager and navigate to the /Galactic Delivery Services/ Axelburg folder.
2. Click Show Details.
3. Click the icon in the Edit column next to the Invoice-Batch Number Report.
4. Click Parameters on the left side of the screen. The Parameter Management page appears.
5. Check the Hide check box in the StartDate row. (Notice the default value for the StartDate parameter is 1/1/2008.)
6. Click Apply.
7. Click the View tab. Notice the Start Date prompt no longer appears in the parameter area.
8. Enter the following URL in the address bar:

   ```
   http://localhost/ReportServer?/Galactic Delivery Services/Axelburg/
        Invoice-Batch Number Report&StartDate=12/1/2008&EndDate=12/31/2008
   ```

9. Click Go. The Invoice-Batch Number Report appears with data for December 2008.

Even though the StartDate parameter does not appear in the parameters area, we can still specify a value for it other than the default value. The Hide check box is not checked for the City parameter. Instead, the Prompt User check box is unchecked. In this situation, you cannot specify a value for this parameter in the URL. The following URL is going to fail:

```
http://localhost/ReportServer?/Galactic Delivery Services/Axelburg/
          Invoice-Batch Number Report&City=Utonal&EndDate=12/31/2008
```

Controlling the Report Viewer

In addition to specifying report parameters in the URL, you can include parameters to control the format of the response from Reporting Services. You can specify which rendering format should be used for the report. Rather than using the Export drop-down list in the Report Viewer to export the report to a particular format, you can have it delivered in that format straight from Reporting Services.

Give this a try:

1. Enter the following URL in the address bar:

   ```
   http://localhost/ReportServer?/Galactic Delivery Services/
                        2009 Conference/Nametags&rs:Format=PDF
   ```

2. Click Go.
3. If you are prompted whether to open or save the file, click Open.
4. The Nametags report appears in PDF format in Adobe Acrobat Reader.
5. Close Adobe Acrobat Reader.

The valid format parameters are shown in Table 12-2.

Format Parameter	Result
CSV	Comma-separated value text file
EXCEL	Excel spreadsheet
HTML3.2	HTML page using the HTML 3.2 standard
HTML4.0	HTML page using the HTML 4.0 standard
IMAGE	BMP, EMF, GIF, JPEG, PNG, or TIFF Image
MHTML	Self-contained HTML document
NULL	None
PDF	Adobe PDF document
WORD	Microsoft Word document
XML	XML document

Table 12-2 *Values for the Format Parameter*

In addition to the rs:Command and rs:Format parameters, several other Report Server parameters use the rs: prefix. Table 12-3 shows these.

Device information parameters can also be passed as part of the URL. These *device information parameters* are specific to the format being used to render the report. Because they are rendering format-specific, device information parameters can also be thought of as renderer control parameters. Therefore, they use an rc: prefix.

Let's look at a couple of examples using device information parameters. When you receive a report rendered as HTML, you also receive the Report Viewer controls. This may not always be desirable. Several device information parameters enable you to specify what portion of the Report Viewer interface you want visible. For example:

1. Enter the following URL in the address bar:

   ```
   http://localhost/ReportServer?/Galactic Delivery Services/Axelburg/
        Invoice-Batch Number Report&StartDate=11/1/2008&EndDate=11/30/2008
        &rc:Parameters=false
   ```

2. Click Go. The Invoice-Batch Number Report appears with data for November 2008. The parameter portion of the Report Viewer is invisible, so the user cannot change the parameter values.

You can get rid of the entire Report Viewer interface as follows:

1. Enter the following URL in the address bar:

   ```
   http://localhost/ReportServer?/Galactic Delivery Services/Axelburg/
        Invoice-Batch Number Report&StartDate=11/1/2008&EndDate=11/30/2008
        &rc:Toolbar=false
   ```

Parameter	Valid Values	Function
rs:ClearSession	True False	When true, this parameter prevents a report from being pinned in cache by forcing the report to be re-rendered.
rs:ParameterLanguage	A valid culture identifier, such as "en-us"	Used to specify a language for the parameters passed in the URL that is different from the browser's language setting. This defaults to the browser's language setting when it is not specified.
rs:SessionID	A unique session identifier	Used to maintain session state when the report server has been configured not to use session cookies.
rs:Snapshot	The data and time of a valid snapshot for the specified report	Used to render the requested report from a history snapshot.

Table 12-3 *Report Server (rs) URL Parameters and Their Possible Values*

2. Click Go. The Invoice-Batch Number Report appears with data for November 2008.
3. Expand the 445 row heading and the Axelburg column heading.

Even when we expand the row and column headings, causing a new page to be sent from the report server, the Report Viewer does not reappear.

Table 12-4 shows the device information parameters for the comma-separated value (CSV) format.

Table 12-5 shows the device information parameters for the Excel format.

The device information parameters for the HTML formats are shown in Table 12-6.

Table 12-7 shows the device information parameters for the image format.

Setting	Valid Values	Function
rc:Encoding	ASCII UTF-7 UTF-8 Unicode	The character encoding scheme to use. The default is Unicode.
rc:ExcelMode	True False	If true, assumes the target output is to be loaded into Excel. The output may not be in true CSV format, but will be more suitable for loading into Excel. The default is true. "ExcelMode" will violate CSV compliance in order to make the output more suitable for import into Excel. Basically, it renders top-level peer data regions as their own "blocks" in CSV.
rc:FieldDelimiter		The field delimiter to use in the file. The default is a comma.
rc:FileExtension		The file extension for the file. The default is .CSV.
rc:NoHeader	True False	If true, no header is written with the data in the file. The default is false.
rc:Qualifier		The string qualifier to put around fields that contain the field delimiter. The default is a quotation mark.
rc:RecordDelimiter		The record delimiter to use in the file. The default is a carriage return and linefeed.
rc:SuppressLineBreaks	True False	If true, line breaks in the data are not included in the file. The default is false.
Rc:UseFormattedValues	True False	If true, formatted strings are put in the file. The default is true when ExcelMode is true; otherwise, the default is false.

Table 12-4 *CSV Format Device Information (rc) URL Parameters and Their Possible Values*

Setting	Valid Values	Function
rc:OmitDocumentMap	True False	If true, the document map for the rendered report is not included in the Excel file. The default is false.
rc:OmitFormulas	True False	If true, formulas are not included in the Excel file. The default is false.
rc:SimplePageHeader	True False	If true, the report page header is placed in the Excel page header. Otherwise, the report page header is placed in the first row of the worksheet. The default value is false.

Table 12-5 *Excel Format Device Information (rc) URL Parameters and Their Possible Values*

Table 12-8 shows the device information parameters for the MHTML format. The PDF format device information parameters are shown in Table 12-9. Table 12-10 shows the device information parameters for the Word format. Table 12-11 shows the device information parameters for the XML format.

Finally, you can specify the user name and password for data sources that prompt for credentials each time the report is run. This is done using the dsu and dsp prefixes. For example, to specify credentials for a data source called GalacticPrompt, you would add the following to the end of the URL:

```
dsu:GalacticPrompt=MyDBUser&dsp:GalacticPrompt=DBPassword
```

where MyDBUser is a valid database login and DBPassword is the password for that login.

URL Access Using an HTTP Post

The previous examples demonstrate the use of URL access using the HTTP Get method. This method has several limitations. First, all the parameter values are exposed in the URL itself. Second, the number of characters you can have in a URL is limited.

You can get around these limitations and still use URL access by employing the HTTP Post method. The *HTTP Post method* passes parameters as fields in an HTML form, so they are not exposed in the URL. Also, the HTTP Post is not subject to the same length restrictions as the HTTP Get.

Setting	Valid Values	Function
rc:BookmarkID	{BookmarkID}	Jumps to the specified Bookmark ID in the report.
rc:DocMap	True False	Specifies whether the document map is shown. The default is true.
rc:ExpandContent	True False	Determines whether the report is placed inside a table structure to limit its horizontal size.
rc:FindString	{TextToFind}	Searches for this text in the report and jumps to its first location.
rc:GetImage		A particular icon for the HTML Viewer user interface.
rc:HTMLFragment	True False	When this is set to true, the report is returned as a table rather than a complete HTML page. This table can then be placed inside your own HTML page. The default value is false.
rc:JavaScript	True False	If true, JavaScript is supported in the rendered report.
rc:LinkTarget	{TargetWindowName} _blank _self _parent _top	Specifies the target window to use for any links in the report.
rc:OnlyVisibleStyles	True False	If true, only shared styles for the currently rendered page are generated.
rc:Parameters	True False	Specifies whether to show the parameters section of the Report Viewer.
rc:Section	{PageNumber}	The page number of the report to render.
rc:StreamRoot	{URL}	The path used to prefix the value of the src attribute of any IMG tags in an HTML rendering of the report.
rc:StyleStream	True False	If true, styles and scripts are created as separate streams rather than in the document. The default is false.
rc:Toolbar	True False	Specifies whether the Report Viewer toolbar is visible.
rc:Zoom	Page Width Whole Page 500 200 150 100 75 50 25 10	The zoom percentage to use when displaying the report.

Table 12-6 *HTML Format Device Information (rc) URL Parameters and Their Possible Values*

Setting	Valid Values	Function
rc:ColorDepth	1 4 8 24 32	The color depth of the image created. The default is 24. This is only valid for the TIFF image type.
rc:Columns		The number of columns to use when creating the image.
rc:ColumnSpacing		The column spacing to use when creating the image
rc:DpiX		The number of dots per inch in the x-direction. The default is 96.
rc:DpiY		The number of dots per inch in the y-direction. The default is 96.
rc:EndPage		The last page to render. The default value is the value for the StartPage parameter.
rc:MarginBottom	An integer or decimal followed by "in" (the abbreviation for inches)	The bottom margin to use when creating the image.
rc:MarginLeft	An integer or decimal followed by "in" (the abbreviation for inches)	The left margin to use when creating the image.
rc:MarginRight	An integer or decimal followed by "in" (the abbreviation for inches)	The right margin to use when creating the image.
rc:MarginTop	An integer or decimal followed by "in" (the abbreviation for inches)	The top margin to use when creating the image.
rc:OutputFormat	BMP EMF GIF JPEG PNG TIFF	The graphics format to create.
rc:PageHeight	An integer or decimal followed by "in" (the abbreviation for inches)	The page height to use when creating the image.
rc:PageWidth	An integer or decimal followed by "in" (the abbreviation for inches)	The page width to use when creating the image.
rc:StartPage		The first page to render. A value of 0 causes all pages to be rendered. The default value is 1.

Table 12-7   *Image Format Device Information (rc) URL Parameters and Their Possible Values*

Setting	Valid Values	Function
rc:JavaScript	True False	If true, JavaScript is supported in the rendered report.
rc:MHTMLFragment	True False	When this is set to true, the report is returned as a table rather than a complete HTML page. This table can then be placed inside your own HTML page. The default value is false.

Table 12-8   *MHTML Format Device Information (rc) URL Parameters and Their Possible Values*

Setting	Valid Values	Function
rc:Columns		The number of columns to use when creating the PDF file.
rc:ColumnSpacing		The column spacing to use when creating the PDF file.
rc:EndPage		The last page to render. The default value is the value for the StartPage parameter.
rc:HumanReadablePDF	True False	Indicates whether the PDF source is in a more readable format. The default is false.
rc:MarginBottom	An integer or decimal followed by "in" (the abbreviation for inches)	The bottom margin to use when creating the PDF file.
rc:MarginLeft	An integer or decimal followed by "in" (the abbreviation for inches)	The left margin to use when creating the PDF file.
rc:MarginRight	An integer or decimal followed by "in" (the abbreviation for inches)	The right margin to use when creating the PDF file.
rc:MarginTop	An integer or decimal followed by "in" (the abbreviation for inches)	The top margin to use when creating the PDF file.
rc:PageHeight	An integer or decimal followed by "in" (the abbreviation for inches)	The page height to use when creating the PDF file.
rc:PageWidth	An integer or decimal followed by "in" (the abbreviation for inches)	The page width to use when creating the PDF file.
rc:StartPage		The first page to render. A value of 0 causes all pages to be rendered. The default value is 1.

Table 12-9   *PDF Format Device Information (rc) URL Parameters and Their Possible Values*

Setting	Valid Values	Function
rc:AutoFit	True False Never Default	If true, AutoFit is set to true on every Word table. If false, AutoFit is set to false on every Word table. If Never, AutoFit is not set on individual tables, so the behavior reverts to the Word default. If Default, AutoFit is set to true on all tables that are narrower than the physical drawing area.
rc:ExpandTools	True False	If true, all of the drilldown items are rendered in their expanded state. If false, all of the drilldown items are rendered in their collapsed state. The default is false.
rc:FixedPageWidth	True False	If true, the page width property in the resulting Word document is expanded to accommodate the width of the largest report page. If false, Word's default page width is used. The default is false.
rc:OmitHyperlinks	True False	If true, hyperlinks are not included in the resulting Word document. If false, hyperlinks are included. The default is false.
rc:OmitDrillThroughs	True False	If true, drill-through actions are not included in the resulting Word document. If false, drill-through actions are included. The default is false.

Table 12-10   *Word Format Device Information (rc) URL Parameters and Their Possible Values*

Setting	Valid Values	Function
rc:Encoding	ASCII UTF-8 Unicode	The character encoding scheme to use. The default is UTF-8.
rc:FileExtension		The file extension for the XML file. The default is .XML.
rc:Indented	True False	If true, the XML file is indented. The default is false.
rc:MIMEType		The MIME type of the XML file.
rc:OmitSchema	True False	If true, the schema name and XML Schema Definition (XSD) are not included in the XML file. The default is false.
rc:Schema	True False	If true, the XSD is rendered in the XML file. Otherwise, the report itself is rendered in the XML file. The default is false.
rc:UseFormattedValues	True False	If true, the formatted value of each text box is included in the XML file. Otherwise, the unformatted value of each text box is included.
rc:XSLT		The path in the report server namespace of an Extensible Stylesheet Language Transformation (XSLT) document to apply to the XML file. The XSLT must be a published resource on the report server, and it must be accessed through the report server itself.

Table 12-11   *XML Format Device Information (rc) URL Parameters and Their Possible Values*

The following HTML page uses the HTTP Post to request the Transport Monitor Report for Transport Number 1310 in the HTML 4.0, TIFF image, or Excel format:

```
<HTML>
<Head>
<title>
Reporting Services URL Post Demo
</title>
</Head>
<Body>
<FORM id="frmRender" action="http://localhost/ReportServer?
            /Galactic Delivery Services/Chapter 08/TransportMonitor"
            method="post" target="_self">
<H3>Transport Monitor Report</H3><br>
<b>For Transport 1310</b><br><br>
Render the Transportation Monitor Report in the following format:<br>
<Select ID="rs:Format" NAME="rs:Format" size=1>
<Option Value="HTML4.0">HTML 4.0</Option>
<Option VALUE="IMAGE">TIFF Image</Option>
<Option VALUE="EXCEL">Excel File</Option>
</Select>
<Input type="hidden" name="TransportNumber" value="1310">
<br><br>
<INPUT type="submit" value="Render Report">
</FORM>
</Body>
</HTML>
```

Not only can we use an HTML page like this on a website, we can also use it right within the Report Manager. As discussed in Chapter 10, we can upload any file to a report server folder, including an HTML page. This allows us to create a more polished user interface for gathering report parameters while still utilizing the organization, navigation, and security features of the Report Manager.

Let's give it a try:

1. Use a text editor to create a file called TransportMonitorFrontEnd.HTML that contains the code for the HTML page to do the HTTP Post.

2. Open the Report Manager in a browser and navigate to the Galactic Delivery Services/Chapter 08 folder.

3. Use the Upload File button in the Report Manager toolbar to upload the TransportMonitorFrontEnd.HTML file into the Chapter 08 folder. Set the Name to **Transport Monitor Front End**.

4. Select the Transport Monitor Front End in the Chapter 08 folder.

5. Select a rendering format from the drop-down list and click the Render Report button. You will see the Transport Monitor report for Transport 1310.

Now you could set the Hide in list view property of the Transport Monitor Report so the report itself is hidden in the list view of Chapter 08. Now the user must utilize the front-end HTML page to execute the report.

Web Service Access

In addition to URL and HTTP Post access, you can access reports by using the web service interface. This is the same interface used by the Report Manager web application to interact with Reporting Services. This means anything you can do in Report Manager, you can also do through the web service interface.

The web service interface provides additional functionality not available through URL access. For example, the web service interface enables you to specify a set of credentials to use when executing a report. This allows your custom application to use a set of hard-coded credentials to access reports through the web service interface. This can be a big benefit in situations where you want Reporting Services reports to be exposed on an Internet or extranet site where each user does not have a domain account.

Using a Web Service Call to Execute a Report

This example takes you through the steps necessary to execute a report using the web service interface. In this example, you build a web application that acts as a front end for the Axelburg Invoice-Batch Number Report.

NOTE

Some basic knowledge of ASP.NET programming is assumed in the following discussion.

Creating a Project and a Web Reference   First, you need to create an ASP.NET project with a reference to the Reporting Services web service.

1. Start up Visual Studio.
2. Create a new project.
3. Select Visual Basic in the Project Types area.
4. Select ASP.NET Web Application from the Templates area.
5. Type **AxelburgFrontEnd** for Name. Select an appropriate location for this project.
6. Click OK.
7. When the new project has been created, right-click the project folder for this new project in the Solution Explorer and select Add Service Reference from the context menu. The Add Service Reference dialog box appears.
8. Click the Advanced button. The Service Reference Settings dialog box appears.
9. Click the Add Web Reference button. The Add Web Reference dialog box appears.

10. Enter the following address for the web reference:

   `http://{computername}/ReportServer/ReportExecution2005.asmx`

   where {computername} is the name of the computer hosting the report server. Click Go.

11. When the ReportExecutionService Description appears in the dialog box, replace the Web reference name with **RptExecSvc**. Click Add Reference.

To use a web service, you need to create code that knows how to send data to and retrieve data from that web service. Fortunately, this code is generated for you by Visual Studio through the process of creating a web reference. Once the web reference is in place, you can call the methods of the web service the same way you call the methods of a local .NET assembly.

Creating the Web Form   Now, we need to create the web form that is going to serve as our user interface.

1. Change the name of Default.aspx to **ReportFrontEnd.aspx**.
2. Using the Design view of the ReportFrontEnd.aspx form, place three labels, two calendar controls, and a button on the web form, as shown in Figure 12-2.

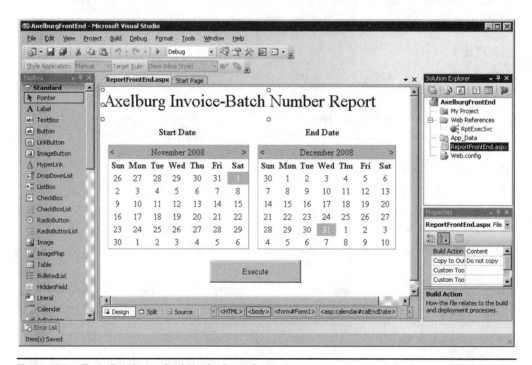

Figure 12-2   *The Axelburg Invoice-Batch Number Report front end*

3. Change the Text property of each label to match Figure 12-2.
4. Change the ID property of the left calendar control to **calStartDate**.
5. Set the SelectedDate property and the VisibleDate property of calStartDate to **November 1, 2008**.
6. Change the ID property of the right calendar control to **calEndDate**.
7. Set the SelectedDate property and the VisibleDate property of calEndDate to **December 31, 2008**.
8. Change the ID property of the button to **cmdExecute**.
9. Change the Text property of the button to **Execute**.
10. Double-click the cmdExecute button to open the code window.
11. Enter the following code for cmdExecute_Click:

```
Private Sub cmdExecute_Click(ByVal sender As System.Object, _
                            ByVal e As System.EventArgs) _
                            Handles cmdExecute.Click
    Dim report As Byte() = Nothing
    ' Create an instance of the Reporting Services
    ' Web Reference.
    Dim rs As RptExecSvc.ReportExecutionService _
                        = New RptExecSvc.ReportExecutionService
    ' Create the credentials that will be used when accessing
    ' Reporting Services. This must be a logon that has rights
    ' to the Axelburg Invoice-Batch Number report.
    ' *** Replace "LoginName", "Password", and "Domain" with
    '       the appropriate values. ***
    rs.Credentials = New _
            System.Net.NetworkCredential("LoginName", _
            "Password", "Domain")
    rs.PreAuthenticate = True

    ' The Reporting Services virtual path to the report.
    Dim reportPath As String = _
    "/Galactic Delivery Services/Axelburg/Invoice-Batch Number Report"

    ' The rendering format for the report.
    Dim format As String = "HTML4.0"

    ' The devInfo string tells the report viewer
    ' how to display with the report.
    Dim devInfo As String = _
        "<DeviceInfo>" + _
        "<Toolbar>False</Toolbar>" + _
        "<Parameters>False</Parameters>" + _
        "<DocMap>True</DocMap>" + _
        "<Zoom>100</Zoom>" + _
        "</DeviceInfo>"
```

```
' Create an array of the values for the report parameters
Dim parameters(1) As RptExecSvc.ParameterValue
Dim paramValue As RptExecSvc.ParameterValue _
                            = New RptExecSvc.ParameterValue
paramValue.Name = "StartDate"
paramValue.Value = calStartDate.SelectedDate
parameters(0) = paramValue
paramValue = New RptExecSvc.ParameterValue
paramValue.Name = "EndDate"
paramValue.Value = calEndDate.SelectedDate
parameters(1) = paramValue

' Create variables for the remainder of the parameters
Dim historyID As String = Nothing
Dim credentials() As RptExecSvc.DataSourceCredentials = Nothing
Dim showHideToggle As String = Nothing
Dim encoding As String
Dim mimeType As String
Dim warnings() As RptExecSvc.Warning = Nothing
Dim reportHistoryParameters() As _
                    RptExecSvc.ParameterValue = Nothing
Dim streamIDs() As String = Nothing

Dim execInfo As New RptExecSvc.ExecutionInfo
Dim execHeader As New RptExecSvc.ExecutionHeader
rs.ExecutionHeaderValue = execHeader
execInfo = rs.LoadReport(reportPath, historyID)
rs.SetExecutionParameters(parameters, "en-us")

Try
    ' Execute the report.
    report = rs.Render(format, _
                devInfo, "", mimeType, "", warnings, streamIDs)

    ' Flush any pending response.
    Response.Clear()

    ' Set the HTTP headers for a PDF response.
    HttpContext.Current.Response.ClearHeaders()
    HttpContext.Current.Response.ClearContent()
    HttpContext.Current.Response.ContentType = "text/html"
    ' filename is the default filename displayed
    ' if the user does a save as.
    HttpContext.Current.Response.AppendHeader( _
            "Content-Disposition", _
            "filename=""Invoice-BatchNumber.HTM""")

    ' Send the byte array containing the report
    ' as a binary response.
    HttpContext.Current.Response.BinaryWrite(report)
    HttpContext.Current.Response.End()
```

```
        Catch ex As Exception
            If ex.Message <> "Thread was being aborted." then
                HttpContext.Current.Response.ClearHeaders()
                HttpContext.Current.Response.ClearContent()
                HttpContext.Current.Response.ContentType = "text/html"
                HttpContext.Current.Response.Write( _
                        "<HTML><BODY><H1>Error</H1><br><br>" & _
                        ex.Message & "</BODY></HTML>")
                HttpContext.Current.Response.End()
            End If
        End Try
    End Sub
```

12. Click Save All on the toolbar.

13. Select Debug | Start from the main menu. This executes your program.

14. When the browser window opens with the web application front-end page, click Execute. The report appears using the dates selected on the front-end page.

15. Switch back to Visual Studio and select Debug | Stop Debugging from the main menu.

You can refer to the comments in the code sample for information on the purpose of each section of code. For additional information, refer to Appendix B.

NOTE

The items in the DeviceInfo XML structure are the same rendering-specific device information settings as those documented in the "URL Access" section of this chapter. Use the parameter name, minus the rc: prefix as the element name.

Managing Reporting Services Through Web Services

In addition to executing reports through the web service interface, you can manage Reporting Services using the web services. If you choose, you can write an application that completely replaces the Report Manager web application for controlling Reporting Services. Refer to Appendix B for more information on management capabilities of the web service interface.

The Report Viewer Control

The Report Server web service gives you a tremendous amount of control over report access. However, the web service simply provides our applications with a stream that contains the report. It is up to our applications to provide an appropriate method for viewing the content of that report stream.

The Report Viewer control in Visual Studio 2005 and Visual Studio 2008 takes things one step further. Not only does it provide access to the reports, it also provides a means to view them. In fact, the Report Viewer can even free you from the tether to the report server altogether. The Report Viewer control can be used in both Windows forms and web forms.

Displaying a Report from a Report Server

We first use the Report Viewer control to access a report on the report server. In this example, you build a Windows application that uses the Report Viewer to display the Axelburg Invoice-Batch Number Report. For this application to function properly, it must have access to the report server whenever a report is executed.

NOTE

The web service example in the previous section works in any version of Visual Studio .NET. The Report Viewer examples in this section require Visual Studio 2005 or Visual Studio 2008.

Creating a Project and an Instance of the Report Viewer   First, you need to create a Windows application project in Visual Studio.

1. Start up Visual Studio.
2. Create a new project.
3. Select Visual Basic | Windows in the Project Types area.
4. Select Windows Forms Application from the Templates area.
5. Enter **AxelburgRVFrontEnd** for Name. Select an appropriate location for this project.
6. Click OK. A Windows application project with a Windows form, called Form1, is created.
7. Expand Form1 so it covers the design surface.
8. Select the Toolbox window.
9. Locate the Reporting section of the Toolbox and, if it is not already expanded, expand it.
10. Drag the MicrosoftReportViewer control from the Toolbox and drop it on Form1 (see Figure 12-3).
11. Click the Dock in parent container link in the ReportViewer Tasks dialog box.

NOTE

If you plan to put other controls on the same form with the Report Viewer, do not dock the viewer in the parent container.

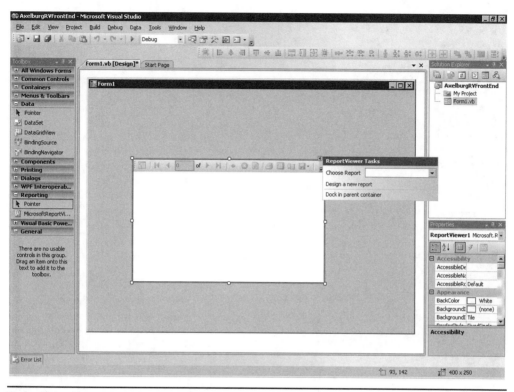

Figure 12-3 *Placing a Report Viewer control on a Windows form*

Configuring the Report Viewer Now we need to point the Report Viewer at a report. You need to make several selections from the ReportViewer Tasks dialog box. If this dialog box is invisible, click the small black triangle in the upper-right corner of the Report Viewer control, as shown in Figure 12-4.

1. In the ReportViewer Tasks dialog box, select <Server Report> from the Choose Report drop-down list.
2. Enter **http://{computername}/reportserver** for Report Server URL, where {computername} is the name of the server hosting Reporting Services.
3. Enter **/Galactic Delivery Services/Axelburg/Invoice-Batch Number Report** for Report Path.

NOTE

You can use the ServerReport.ReportServerUrl and ServerReport.ReportPath properties of the Report Viewer control to programmatically change the report that the Report Viewer displays. In this way, a single Report Viewer control can display different reports, depending on user selection.

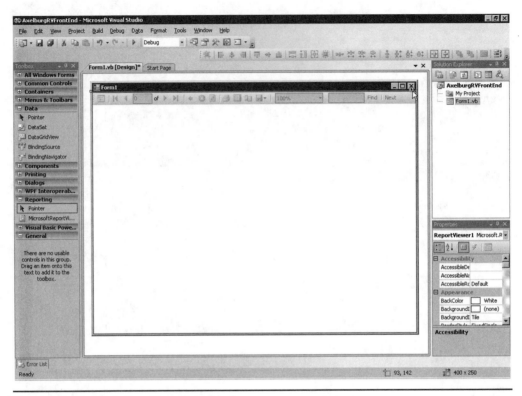

Figure 12-4 *Opening the ReportViewer Tasks dialog box*

4. Click Save All on the toolbar.
5. Select Debug | Start Debugging from the main menu. Form1 executes and displays the Invoice-Batch Number Report from the report server, as shown in Figure 12-5.

NOTE

The assembly necessary to support the ReportViewer control is not included in the standard Microsoft .NET framework. You need to download and install the ReportViewer redistributable on any computers that will be running applications utilizing the ReportViewer control that do not have Visual Studio installed. The ReportViewer redistributable is available, free of charge, from the Microsoft website.

Displaying a Local Report in the Report Viewer

So far, all the methods of accessing reports we looked at in this chapter have required a report server. The report server provides a number of advantages for managing reports, including centralized control for updating report definitions and maintaining security.

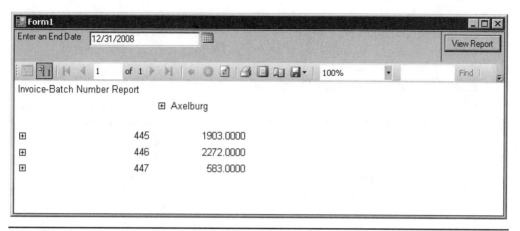

Figure 12-5 *The Report Viewer displaying a report with drilldown*

However, in some situations, it is impractical or undesirable for all installations of an application to pull reports from a report server.

The Report Viewer control provides an alternative. In addition to displaying reports rendered by a report server, the Report Viewer can render reports contained within the Visual Studio project. In this example, we create a simple report right in the Visual Studio project, and then display it with the Report Viewer.

Creating a Local Report We begin by creating a report in the Visual Studio project.

1. Close Form1 containing the report to return to Visual Studio, if you have not already done so.

2. Open the ReportViewer Tasks dialog box.

3. Click the Design a new report link. The Welcome page of the Report Wizard appears.

4. Click Next. The Choose a Data Source Type page of the Data Source Configuration Wizard appears.

5. Make sure Database is selected and click Next. The Choose Your Data Connection page of the Data Source Configuration Wizard appears.

6. Click New Connection. The Add Connection dialog box appears.

7. Create a connection to the Galactic database. Use SQL Server authentication with GalacticReporting as the user and gds as the password. Remember to check the Save my password check box. Test the connection to make sure you configured it correctly. When the connection passes the test, click OK to exit the Add Connection dialog box.

8. Select the radio button next to "Yes, include sensitive data in the connection string" and click Next. The Save the Connection String to the Application Configuration File page of the wizard appears.

9. In most cases, it makes sense to store the connection information in the configuration file to make maintenance easier. Leave the default setting of Yes and click Next. The Choose Your Database Objects page appears.

10. Expand the stored procedures node and place a check next to stp_EmployeeList. Enter **EmployeeList** for the DataSet name.

11. Click Finish. A typed dataset is created by the wizard for use with the report, and you are returned to the Select the Data Source page of the Report Wizard dialog box.

12. Select stp_EmployeeList and select Next. The Select the Report Type page of the Report Wizard appears.

13. Make sure Tabular is selected for the report type and click Next. The Design the Table page appears.

14. Click the Details button three times to place the LastName, FirstName, and EmployeeNumber fields in the Details area.

15. Click Finish. The Completing the Report Wizard page appears.

16. Enter **EmployeeList** for the name of the report. Click Finish again to exit the Report Wizard.

17. Your report layout should appear similar to the layout shown in Figure 12-6.

18. Click Save All on the toolbar.

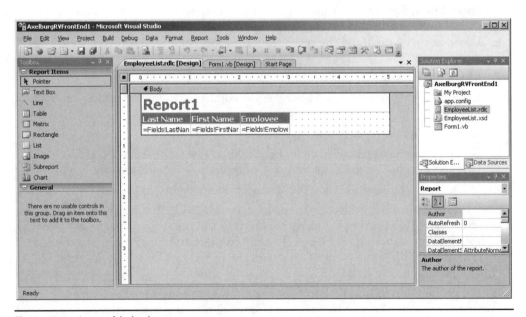

Figure 12-6 *Layout of the local report*

Point the Report Viewer at the Local Report   Now, we point the Report Viewer at the new local report.

1. Click the Form1.vb [Design] tab in the layout area of Visual Studio 2008.
2. Open the ReportViewer Tasks dialog box.
3. Select AxelburgRVFrontEnd.EmployeeList.rdlc from the Choose Report drop-down list.
4. Several items have been added to an area below the Form1 layout. If there is an entry for TableBinding, go to Step.
5. Right-click the entry for EmployeeList and select Edit in DataSet Designer from the context menu.
6. Right-click the stp_EmployeeList item and select Configure from the context menu. The Bind Commands to Existing Stored Procedures page of the TableAdapter Configure Wizard will appear.
7. Click Finish.
8. Close the EmployeeList.xsd tab.
9. A new section called AxelburgRVFrontEnd Components appears in the Toolbox. Drag the stp_EmployeeListTableAdapter item from this area of the Toolbox and drop it in the area below the Form1 layout. An entry called stp_EmployeeListTableAdapter1 is created.
10. Open the ReportViewer Tasks dialog box and click the Rebind Data Sources link.
11. Double-click the Form1 header to open the Form1.vb code window.
12. Type the following as the first line in the Form1_Load method:

    Me.Stp_EmployeeListTableAdapter1.Fill(Me.EmployeeList.stp_EmployeeList)
13. Click Save All on the toolbar.
14. Select Debug | Start Debugging from the main menu. Form1 executes and displays the local report. The local report you just created shows a list of all Galactic employees.
15. Close Form1 when you finish viewing this report.

When you compile the AxelburgRVFrontEnd project, the Report1.rdlc report definition is compiled as an embedded resource in the executable. Therefore, the data source is the only thing needed for the report to be rendered. The report always goes along with the application.

SharePoint Web Parts

We looked at a number of ways to integrate Reporting Services reports with applications, but we have one additional method yet to cover. Reporting Services provides a pair of web parts for use with SharePoint. The Report Explorer web part enables users to browse through the folders on the report server. The Report Viewer web part displays a rendered report. These web parts are designed for use with SharePoint, but they can be used as stand-alone components.

In addition to the Reporting Services web parts, there is a new method for delivering Reporting Services reports within SharePoint. This is the SharePoint integrated mode. In this configuration, the Report Catalog databases are hosted by the SharePoint server rather than by SQL Server. For more information on SharePoint integrated mode, see Appendix C.

Installing the Web Parts

The SharePoint web parts come with Reporting Services in the RSWebParts.cab file, ready for installation. The default location of this file is

```
C:\Program Files\Microsoft SQL Server\100\Tools\Reporting Services\SharePoint
```

This .cab file should be installed using the Stsadm utility. The Stsadm utility unpacks the web parts, installs them in the appropriate location, and creates entries in the SafeControls section of the web.config file for the SharePoint virtual server. Use the following command line to complete the installation using default locations:

```
C:\Program Files\Common Files\Microsoft Shared\web server extensions\
        60\BIN\STSADM.EXE -o addwppack -filename.
        "C:\Program Files\Microsoft SQL Server\100\Tools\
        Reporting Services\SharePoint\RSWebParts.cab"
```

NOTE

If you use the globalinstall switch with the Stsadm utility to install the web parts in the global assembly cache, you need to use the strong name for the assembly in place of the friendly name in the web.config file for the SharePoint virtual server.

Adding the Web Parts

Now that the web parts are installed, they need to be added to a web part page using the SharePoint window. Use the following steps:

1. Access the SharePoint site and click Create on the SharePoint toolbar.
2. Scroll down the page to the Web Pages section and click Web Part Page.
3. Type a name for the web part page and select a layout template.
4. Enter the location where your web part page is to be saved. The web part page appears.

5. Click Create at the bottom of the page.
6. Click Modify Shared Page. Point to Add Web Parts, and then click Browse.
7. Select the name of the gallery where you installed the Reporting Services web parts.
8. Select either Report Explorer or the Report Viewer from the list of web parts, and then drag it to an area of the web part page.

When both the Report Explorer and Report Viewer web parts are placed on the same web part page, you can connect them together. This enables the user to browse to a report in the Report Explorer web part, and then view the report in the Report Viewer web part. If the two web parts are not connected, selecting a report in the Report Explorer causes it to display in a new page. Use the following steps to connect the two web parts:

1. Click Modify Shared Web Part.
2. On the Report Explorer toolbar menu, click the down arrow, point to Connections, point to Show Report In, and then click Report Viewer.
3. Click OK.

Reporting Services Utilities

In addition to URL access, the web service interface, Report Viewer, and SharePoint web parts, you can interact with Reporting Services through several command-line utility programs. Like the other methods, these command-line utilities let you manage Reporting Services. These utilities enable you to control Reporting Services, as well as the encryption keys and encrypted values. The most capable of the utilities, the RS utility, lets you script and automate nearly any Reporting Services activity.

Each utility program is briefly described here. For more information, you can execute any of the utility programs followed by -? to view a listing of the valid parameters.

The RSKeyMgmt Utility

The *RSKeyMgmt utility* is used to administer the encryption key used by Reporting Services. You can use the RSKeyMgmt utility to back up the encryption key. You can also use RSKeyMgmt to delete encrypted data and create a new encryption key in case of a problem.

When Reporting Services is installed, sensitive information stored in the configuration files, such as logon credentials, is encrypted for security. Also, any user names and passwords stored in reports or shared data sources are encrypted. The encryption key used to decrypt the information is stored in the Report Catalog (ReportServer) database. Making certain changes can cause problems with the Reporting Services installation. These changes include the following:

▶ Modifying the user account used by the Reporting Services web service

▶ Modifying the name of the SQL server used to store the Report Catalog

▶ Modifying the name of the computer hosting Reporting Services

A backup copy of the encryption key made with the RSKeyMgmt utility helps recover your Reporting Services installation in these situations.

The backup copy of the encryption key is protected by a password. You specify this password as a parameter to the RSKeyMgmt utility when you create the backup. You must have this password when you use the backup copy of the key.

Creating a Backup of the Report Server Encryption Key   To make a backup of the report server encryption key, do the following:

1. Open a command window.
2. Enter the following at the command prompt, where {password} is the password used to protect the encryption key:

```
Rskeymgmt -e -f c:\temp\rsdbkey.txt -p {password}
```

3. Press ENTER.
4. When the backup process is complete, store the resulting file in a safe location.

Recovering a Reporting Services Installation   If your Reporting Services installation becomes disabled because of one of the situations described previously and you have a backup of the encryption key, follow this procedure:

1. Copy the backup of your encryption key onto the report server.
2. Open a command window.
3. Enter the following at the command prompt, where {password} is the password used to protect the encryption key:

```
Rskeymgmt -a -f c:\temp\rsdbkey.txt -p {password}
```

4. Press ENTER.

If your Reporting Services installation becomes disabled because of one of the situations described previously and you do not have a backup of the encryption key, follow this procedure:

1. Open a command window.
2. Enter the following at the command prompt:

```
Rskeymgmt -d
```

3. Press ENTER.
4. Use the RSConfig utility to specify the connection information to the Report Catalog.
5. Reenter the user names and passwords for all reports and shared data sources stored on this report server that use stored credentials.

The RSConfig Utility

The *RSConfig utility* is used to change the credentials used by Reporting Services to access the Report Catalog (ReportServer) database. These credentials are encrypted in the configuration file, so they cannot be edited directly.

The following example changes the credentials used to access the Report Catalog on a SQL server called RSServer to use a SQL Server logon called RSCatLogon with a password of rscat37:

```
Rsconfig -c -s RSServer -d ReportServer -a Sql -u RSCatLogon
                                                 -p rscat37
```

NOTE

The Report Server Configuration Manager, discussed in Chapter 2, can be used to perform the same functions as the RSKeyMgmt and RSConfig utility programs. The Configuration Manager provides a graphical user interface, which you may find preferable to the command-line interface of the other utility programs.

The RSReportServer.Config File

The RSConfig utility (as well as the Reporting Services Configuration Manager) modifies information stored in the RSReportServer.config file. Some of the information in this file, such as logon credentials, is encrypted for security purposes. This information must be edited using the utility program. Other configuration information in this file is in plain text and can be edited with Notepad or another text editor.

CAUTION

Always make a backup copy of the RSReportServer.config file before editing. The Reporting Services Windows service cannot restart if this configuration file is invalid.

The default location of this file is

```
C:\Program Files\Microsoft SQL Server\MSRS10.MSSQLSERVER
                                        \Reporting Services\ReportServer
```

Table 12-12 shows the values immediately under the Configuration element in the RSReportServer.config file. The settings are shown in the order they occur in the file.

Setting	Valid Values	Function
Report Server Database Connection Information	(Encrypted—use the RSConfig utility or the Reporting Services Configuration Tool to modify)	This is the information required by Reporting Services to access the ReportServer database. This includes DSN, LogonUser, LogonDomain, and LogonCred.
ConnectionType	Default Impersonate	The type of credentials being used by Reporting Services to access the ReportServer database.
InstanceID		The identifier for the Reporting Services instance. This is tied to a SQL Server instance.
InstallationID		A Globally Unique Identifier (GUID) to identify this Reporting Services installation.
SecureConnectionLevel	0 to 3	The degree of security for the web service connection. 0—All requests processed. 1—Requests made over insecure connections and passing sensitive information, such as credentials, are rejected. 2—All rendered reports and web service calls require a secure connection. 3—All calls made to the Reporting Services SOAP API require a secure connection.
CleanupCycleMinutes		The number of minutes after which old sessions and expired snapshots are removed from the ReportServer databases. A value of 0 disables the cleanup process. The default is 10.
SQLCommandTimeoutSeconds		This setting is not used.
MaxActiveReqForOneUser		The maximum number of simultaneous, in-progress connections a single user can have open. This setting is intended to thwart a denial of service (DoS) attack. A value of 0 indicates no limit. The default is 20.
DatabaseQueryTimeout		The number of seconds before a connection to the ReportServer database times out. A value of 0 results in no timeout. The default is 120.
RunningRequestsScavengerCycle		The number of seconds before orphaned and expired requests are canceled. The default is 60.

Table 12-12 *RSReportServer.config Configuration Elements*

Setting	Valid Values	Function
RunningRequestsDbCycle		The frequency, in seconds, at which the Manage Jobs page is updated and the running jobs are checked to determine if they have exceeded the report execution timeout. The default is 60.
RunningRequestsAge		The number of seconds after which a running job's status is changed from new to running. The default is 30.
MaxScheduleWait		The number of seconds Reporting Services waits for a schedule to be updated by the SQL Server Agent when a next run time is requested. The default is 5.
DisplayErrorLink	True False	If true, a link to the Microsoft Help and Support site is displayed when an error occurs. The default is true.
WebServiceUseFileShareStorage	True False	If true, the Reporting Services web service stores cached reports and temporary snapshots on the file system rather than in the ReportServerTempDB database. The default is false.
WatsonFlags		Specifies the type of dump sent with error reporting to Microsoft. 0x0430—Full dump 0x0428—Minidump 0x0002—No dump The default is 0x0428.
WatsonDumpOnExceptions		Do not change this setting.
WatsonDumpExcludeIfContainsExceptions		Do not change this setting.

Table 12-12 *RSReportServer.config Configuration Elements*

Below these items in the RSReportServer.config file are entries for URLReservations. These entries define the URLs used for HTTP access to the report server web service and the Report Manager web application. This information is created by your selections made through the Reporting Services Configuration Manager. You should *not* modify this information directly in the RSReportServer.config file. Instead, make all modifications using the Reporting Services Configuration Manager.

Table 12-13 shows the values in the Authentication section of the RSReportServer .config file. The settings are shown in the order they occur in the file.

Table 12-14 shows the values in the Service section of the RSReportServer.config file. The settings are shown in the order they occur in the file.

Table 12-15 shows the values in the UI section of the RSReportServer.config file. The settings are shown in the order they occur in the file.

Setting	Valid Values	Function
AuthenticationTypes	RSWindowsNegotiate RSWindowsKerberos RSWindowsNTLM RSWindowsBasic Custom	One or more authentication types used by the report server. When Custom is specified, none of the other types may be used. Removing the RSWindowsNTLM entry may cause some browsers to be unable to authenticate to the report server. See the following entries for an explanation of each valid value. The default values are RSWindowsNegotiate and RSWindowsNTLM.
RSWindowsNegotiate		The user security token is passed to the report server on the request.
RSWindowsNTLM		The report server accepts HTTP requests over an NTLM authenticated connection after the user identity is verified.
RSWindowsKerberos		The report server accepts Kerberos tokens.
RSWindowsBasic		Credentials are passed in the HTTP request in clear text. Secure Sockets Layer (SSL) encryption should always be used with this method of authentication.
Custom		This entry is used when a custom security extension is used.
LogonMethod	0 1 2 3	This entry specifies the logon type for RSWindowsBasic authentication. The valid logon types are: 0 - Interactive Logon (Default) 1 - Batch Logon 2 - Network logon 3 - Cleartext logon
Realm		This entry is used by RSWindowsBasic authentication to specify a resource partition that includes authorization and authentication features used to control access to protected resources.
DefaultDomain		This entry is used by RSWindowsBasic authentication to determine the domain to use.
EnableAuthPersistence	True False	If true, authentication is performed on connection and subsequent requests from that same connection impersonate the security context of the first request. If false, each request is authenticated separately. If you are using proxy server software such as ISA Server to access the report server, EnableAuthPersistence should be set to false to prevent all requests from impersonating the security context of the first request.

Table 12-13 *RSReportServer.config Authentication Elements*

Setting	Valid Values	Function
IsSchedulingService	True False	If true, a thread is dedicated to making sure the schedules in the ReportServer database match the schedules in the SQL Server Agent. The default is true.
IsNotificationService	True False	If true, a thread is dedicated to polling the notification table in the ReportServer database to determine if there are any pending notifications. The default is true.
IsEventService	True False	If true, Reporting Services processes events in the event queue. The default is true.
PollingInterval		The number of seconds between polls of the event table. The default is 10.
WindowsServiceUseFileShareStorage	True False	If true, the Report Server Windows service stores cached reports and temporary snapshots on the file system rather than in the ReportServerTempDB database. The default is false.
WorkingSetMaximum		The point after which no new memory allocations are granted to report server applications. By default, this is the amount of available memory on the server. This setting does not appear in the RSReportServer.config file unless it is added manually.
WorkingSetMinimum		The lower limit of memory usage by the report server. The report server will not release memory if overall use is below this limit. By default, this value is calculated at service startup. This setting does not appear in the RSReportServer.config file unless it is added manually.
MemorySafetyMargin		The percentage of the WorkingSetMaximum value that causes the report server to switch from using low memory pressure operating scenarios to using medium memory pressure operating scenarios.
MemoryThreshold		The percentage of the WorkingSetMaximum value that causes the report server to switch from using medium memory pressure operating scenarios to using high memory pressure operating scenarios. Under high memory pressure operating scenarios, the report server slows down request processing and changes the memory allocated to each server application.
RecycleTime		The number of minutes for the recycling of the report server application domain. After this interval has elapsed, all new requests are sent to a new instance of the Reporting Services application domain. The default is 720.

Table 12-14 *RSReportServer.config Service Elements*

Setting	Valid Values	Function
MaxAppDomainUnloadTime		The number of minutes the report server application domain is allowed to upload during a recycle operation. The default is 30.
MaxQueueThreads		The maximum number of threads dedicated to polling the event table in the ReportServer database. The default is 0.
UrlRoot		The URL root used by delivery extensions to create the URL for accessing items stored on the report server.
UnattendedExecutionAccount		The credentials for the Execution Account. See Chapter 2 for more information. These credentials are encrypted and should be set using the Reporting Services Configuration Tool.
PolicyLevel		The security policy configuration file for the report server.
IsWebServiceEnabled	True False	If true, the Report Server web service is enabled. This is set using the Surface Area Configuration for Reporting Services portion of Policy-Based Management. The default is true.
IsReportManagerEnabled	True False	If true, the Report Manager is enabled. The default is true.
FileShareStorageLocation		The path to the folder where cached reports and temporary snapshots are stored, if they are being stored on the file system. A Universal Naming Convention (UNC) path can be used, but it is not recommended. The default is C:\Program Files\Microsoft SQL Server\MSRS10.MSSQLSERVER\Reporting Services\RSTempFiles.

Table 12-14   *RSReportServer.config Service Elements (Continued)*

Setting	Valid Values	Function
ReportServerURL		The URL of the report server that the Report Manager connects to.
ReportBuilderTrustLevel	FullTrust	The trust level the Ad Hoc Report Builder runs under. This must be set to FullTrust.
PageCountMode	Estimate Actual	The method used by the Report Manager for calculating page count. If set to Estimate, the page count will be initially set to 2, but adjusts upward as the user pages through the report. If set to Actual, the entire report is processed to calculate the actual page count. This setting will increase the wait time for displaying the first page of lengthy reports. The default value is Estimate.

Table 12-15   *RSReportServer.config UI Elements*

The next sections of the RSReportServer.config file deal with extensions to the report server for delivery, rendering, data processing, semantic query processing, model generation, custom security, and event processing. These extensions are beyond the scope of this book, with the exception of the custom security extension, which is covered in the later section "Issues with Custom Security."

The RS Utility

The *RS utility* is used to execute scripts that can interact with Reporting Services. The scripting language supported by the RS utility is Visual Basic .NET. This scripting language supports the complete web service interface to Reporting Services.

The RS utility automatically creates a reference to the web service interface. This predefined reference, called rs, means you do not need to instantiate the web service interface; it is simply ready to go. All the Reporting Services classes and data types are also available.

The following sample code lists the contents of the Galactic Delivery Services virtual folder:

1. Enter the following into Notepad or some other text editor:

```
Public Sub Main()
    Dim items() As CatalogItem
    items = rs.ListChildren("/Galactic Delivery Services", False)

    Dim item As CatalogItem
    For Each item In items
        Console.WriteLine(item.Name)
    Next item
End Sub
```

2. Save this to a file called rstest.rss in a convenient folder on the report server.
3. Open a command window on the report server.
4. Change to the folder where you stored the rstest.rss file.
5. Enter the following at the command prompt, where {userID} is a logon with administrative rights on the report server and {password} is the password for that logon:

```
rs -i rstest.rss -s http://localhost/ReportServer
                                    -u {userID} -p {password}
```

6. Press ENTER. A list of the folders in the Galactic Delivery Services folder appears in the command window.

Using the RS Utility to Manage System Properties

In Chapter 11, we looked at the Site Settings page in the Report Manager. This page enables you to make configuration changes to Reporting Services system properties. In addition to the settings exposed on the Site Settings page, Reporting Services has a number of other configuration options. Table 12-16 lists all these Reporting Services system properties.

Property	Valid Values	Function
EnableClientPrinting	True False	If true, users may download the ActiveX object and use client-side printing. The default is true.
EnableExecutionLogging	True False	If true, the execution of each report is recorded in a log table. The default is true.
EnableIntegratedSecurity	True False	If true, integrated security may be used in data sources. The default is true.
EnableLoadReportDefinition	True False	If true, the report server will generate clickthrough reports in the Ad Hoc Report Builder. The default is true.
EnableMyReports	True False	If true, a MyReports folder is created for each report server user. The default is false.
EnableRemoteErrors	True False	If true, remote users will receive error information when a report fails. The default is false.
EnableReportDesignClientDownload	True False	If true, a user with appropriate rights may use the Edit link in the Report Definition section of the report properties to download a copy of the report definition. The default is true.
ExecutionLogDaysKept	0 to 2,147,483,647	The number of days of log information kept in the report execution log. A value of 0 means an unlimited number of days are kept in the log. The default is 60.
ExternalImagesTimeout		The maximum number of seconds the report server attempts to retrieve an external image. The default is 600.
MyReportsRole	{Security Role}	The security role to assign to each user with their MyReports folder. The default is My Reports.
SessionTimeout	An integer value	The number of seconds a session remains active without any activity. The default is 600.
SharePointIntegrated	True False	This is a read-only property indicating the current operational mode of the report server. If true, the report server is operating in SharePoint Integrated mode. If false, the report server is operating in native mode.
SiteName	A string up to 8,000 characters in length	The title displayed at the top of the Report Manager pages. The default is Microsoft Report Server.
SnapshotCompression	All None SQL	If All, report snapshots are compressed when stored in all locations, including both the ReportServer database and the file system. If None, report snapshots are not compressed. If SQL, report snapshots are only compressed when stored in the ReportServer database. The default is SQL.

Table 12-16 *Reporting Services System Properties*

Property	Valid Values	Function
StoredParametersLifetime	-1 to 2,147,483,647	The maximum number of days a stored parameter can be saved. The default is 180.
StoredParametersThreshold	-1 to 2,147,483,647	The maximum number of parameter values that can be stored by the report server. The default is 1500.
SystemReportTimeout	−1 to 2,147,483,647	The maximum number of minutes a given report may execute. This value can be overridden for an individual report. A value of −1 means reports may execute for an unlimited amount of time. The default is 5.
SystemSnapshotLimit	−1 to 2,147,483,647	The maximum number of snapshots that can be saved for a given report. A value of −1 means there is no limit.
UseSessionCookies	True False	If true, the report server uses session cookies to track each session. If false, the rs:SessionID report server parameter must be used to pass the session ID. The default is true.

Table 12-16 *Reporting Services System Properties (Continued)*

CAUTION

Using integrated security with a report exposes your SQL server to a security risk. If a user with administration rights on the SQL server executes a report with integrated security, that report then has administration rights on the server. A malicious query built into such a report could harm your SQL server when it is run with integrated security. This risk can be mitigated by using a careful QA testing process before each report is deployed to the report server. If this is impossible and you want to eliminate the risk of this type of attack, set the EnableIntegratedSecurity system property to false.

One of the easiest ways to query and set the system properties that are unavailable on the Site Settings page is through the RS utility. The following script prints all the system properties and their current values:

```
Public Sub Main()
    Dim SSRSProperties() As [Property]
    Dim SSRSProperty As [Property]

    SSRSProperties = rs.GetSystemProperties(Nothing)
    For Each SSRSProperty In SSRSProperties
        Console.WriteLine(SSRSProperty.Name & " - " & SSRSProperty.Value)
    Next
End Sub
```

This script sets the SystemReportTimeout property to ten minutes:

```
Public Sub Main()
    Dim SSRSProperties(0) As [Property]
    Dim SSRSProperty As New [Property]

    SSRSProperty.Name = "SystemReportTimeout"
    SSRSProperty.Value = 600
    SSRSProperties(0) = SSRSProperty

    rs.SetSystemProperties(SSRSProperties)
End Sub
```

Log Files

The report server creates a set of trace log files that can be helpful for managing and troubleshooting. These trace logs are text files that can be viewed with Notepad or any other text editor. In a default installation, the trace log files created by Reporting Services are stored in the following folder:

```
C:\Program Files\Microsoft SQL Server\MSRS10.MSSQLSERVER\
                            Reporting Services\LogFiles
```

In addition to these trace log files is an ExecutionLogStorage table in the Report Catalog (ReportServer) database. A record is created in this table each time a report is executed. The date and time of the execution, as well as the user name of the logged on user, are recorded. Unfortunately, the report being executed is identified by a globally unique identifier (GUID) rather than by the report name. Fortunately, there is a view called ExecutionLog2 that denormalizes these GUID references and makes it easy to query meaningful information from the ExecutionLogStorage table.

NOTE

Report Execution Logging must be turned on to use the logging features.

Custom Security

Another way to customize Reporting Services is through its security extension. By default, Reporting Services uses Windows integrated security. As you have seen, this means a user must have valid credentials (a user name and password) for either a local logon on the report server or for a domain logon on the domain containing the report server.

There are times, however, when creating Windows credentials for each Reporting Services user is not desirable or even feasible. You may want to expose reports on an Internet site or an extranet site. You may want to use the Report Manager as part of a web application that makes use of a different security model, such as forms authentication. In these situations, you can consider using the Reporting Services security extension to implement a security mechanism for the Report Manager and the Report Server web service that better fits your needs.

Authentication and Authorization

Before we discuss the security extension, let's look at the way security functions in Reporting Services. Security in Reporting Services has two parts: authentication and authorization. *Authentication* determines whether you can come in. *Authorization* determines what you can do once you are inside.

Authentication

Think of security like a trip to an amusement park, as shown in Figure 12-7. If you are a big amusement park fan like me (I can't get enough of those roller coasters!), you probably purchase the multiday pass. Because the pass can only be used by the person who originally purchased it, you must prove you are the rightful owner of that pass

Figure 12-7   *Authentication and authorization at the amusement park*

when you get to the main gate. You may even have to show a picture ID to prove you are who you say you are.

This is the process of authentication. You must prove you have the appropriate credentials to gain access. At the amusement park gate, you need two things to gain entrance: a pass and some type of identification to prove you have the right to use that pass. The same is true for authentication in the computer world. First, you need some type of pass that has rights to get you in the gate. This usually takes the form of a user name or, more accurately, a user account identified by a user name. You must have a valid user account to log on.

Second, you must have some way to prove you are the rightful owner of that user account. This is often done by specifying a password along with the user name. In areas where security needs to be tighter, this proof of ownership might take the form of an electronic card or a fingerprint scan.

In the default setup for Reporting Services, we are essentially outsourcing the main gate operations. Windows takes care of authenticating the user for us. If Windows says the user is okay, they must be okay. As you will see in a moment, when we implement custom security, we take back this job of authentication for ourselves.

Persisting Authentication

Because we are dealing with web interfaces—the Report Manager web application and the Report Server web service—we have one more authentication issue to deal with. Each time a user makes a request through either of these interfaces, the authentication has to be done again. This is just the nature of the HTTP requests we use with both web applications and web services. It is a bit like having to come in through the main gate of the amusement park every time you want to go on a different ride.

When we are using Windows authentication, the authentication process is completely transparent to the users. Because of this, having to redo the authentication each time a user requests a different Report Manager screen or executes a different report is not a big deal. However, if you create a logon screen as part of your custom security, this will be a different story. No user wants to reenter their user name and password each time they execute a report or navigate from one folder to another.

What we need is some way to remember we have already authenticated a particular user. We need the electronic equivalent of the ultraviolet-light-sensitive hand stamp used at the amusement park for exit and reentry. In computer terms, we need to *persist* the authentication.

In the "Creating a Custom Security Extension" section, we use a browser cookie to persist the authentication. If the cookie is not present in an HTTP request, the logon screen is displayed. This should happen only at the beginning of a user session. Once we authenticate the user, we can send the cookie information to the user's browser and instruct it to create a cookie. The browser sends this cookie along with all subsequent HTTP requests made to Reporting Services. If the cookie is present, the logon information is taken from the cookie and the user does not see the logon screen.

Authorization

Let's return to our amusement park analogy. You passed through the main gate and are ready to ride that killer coaster. However, some limitations exist on just who can go on each ride. You must be taller than a certain height to go on the wild rides. You must be shorter than a certain height to go on the kiddie rides.

This is the process of authorization. You must prove you have rights to perform a certain activity before you can do that activity. At the amusement park, you must prove to the ride operator that you are taller or shorter than the height marking painted on the sign. If your head does not come above the line, you do not have the right to perform the activity of riding the roller coaster.

As you saw in Chapter 10, Reporting Services uses role-based authorization. Your logon account is assigned to a certain role for each folder, report, or resource. This role includes rights to perform certain activities on that item. Being assigned to the Browser role for a report means you are authorized to view that report.

The role assignments are stored in the Report Catalog within Reporting Services. When using the default security setup, Reporting Services checks the role assignments in the Report Catalog each time you try to perform a task. It determines from these role assignments whether you are authorized to perform that task, and then either lets you proceed or brings the process to a screeching halt.

When we implement custom security, you must perform this authorization check yourself. Fortunately, Reporting Services enables you to continue to use the role information stored in the Report Catalog. Therefore, if you want, you can still use the screens in the Report Manager to create and edit role assignments, and you can have those changes stored in the Report Catalog. Your custom security implementation can then use the information in the Report Catalog to determine authorization. If this does not fit your needs, you can create your own method for determining what a user is authorized to do.

Issues with Custom Security

Before you see how to create and deploy a custom security extension, we need to discuss several issues related to custom security. Changing the security mechanism for an enterprise application should not be done lightly. Before implementing a custom security extension, make sure you cannot fulfill your business needs without it, and then look at each of the following issues.

Tried and True

Windows integrated security is the default security model for Reporting Services and is, in fact, the only security model that comes with the product. Reporting Services was designed with Windows integrated security in mind. Therefore, it is the only thoroughly tested security model and the only one proven to provide a secure environment.

If you implement your own custom security extension, you are taking the responsibility of creating a secure environment on your own shoulders. You are responsible for the design, testing, and implementation of an environment that ensures the proper security for your report server. Remember, a custom security extension includes both authentication and authorization. Not only do you need to keep out those people who are not allowed to enter your report server environment, but you also have to restrict the activities of those users you do let in.

All or Nothing

When you implement a custom security extension, you completely replace the security mechanism on a Reporting Services installation. You cannot use your custom security extension for some users and the default behavior for others. This is an all-or-nothing proposition. Once you replace the default security mechanism, *all* authentication and *all* authorization comes through your custom code.

Validate All User Input

Care should be taken to validate all user input to prevent problems. This is especially true when you are creating a security interface. You should take steps to ensure that your custom security extension is not vulnerable to invalid characters and buffer overruns as a means of gaining unauthorized entry.

In addition to serving as the means for a security attack, special characters can also cause a problem if you are using the MyReports feature. As discussed in Chapter 11, when the MyReports feature is enabled, a virtual user folder is created from the user name of each Reporting Services user. The MyReports folder is then mapped to the appropriate user folder as each user logs on. User names containing any of the following characters can cause problems with these virtual user folders:

```
: ? ; @ & = + $, \ * > < | . " / `
```

Using the Secure Sockets Layer

Anytime you are transmitting authentication information, you should use Secure Sockets Layer (SSL) to protect that transmission. When you use SSL, your data is encrypted before it is transmitted between the client and host computers. This helps prevent any interception or tampering with the authentication information while your data is in transit.

To use SSL, simply use https:// rather than http:// at the beginning of your URL. In addition, there is an SSL setting in the web application file. This setting can be used to require all users to utilize an SSL connection when accessing the Reporting Services web application and web service.

Changing Security Models

Changing security models on your Reporting Services installation is not something to be done lightly. Any role assignments you created under a previous security model are removed when you change to a new model. Only the default system administration rights are present.

Changing back from a custom security extension to the default Windows integrated security, although possible, is not generally recommended. If you do so, you may experience errors when accessing items that had security roles assigned to them under your custom security extension. In addition, if you cannot successfully change back to Windows integrated security, you must reinstall Reporting Services.

Creating a Custom Security Extension

To demonstrate custom security in Reporting Services, we need to create our own code for both authentication and authorization. This code takes the form of several custom classes that implement Reporting Services interfaces. In addition, we create an override for some of the methods in the web service wrapper class to implement the cookie processing and persist our authentication.

If the previous paragraph sounds like Greek to you, then the custom security extension is probably not for you. You need a firm grasp of object-oriented programming (OOP) to understand the code samples in this section. Don't feel bad if OOP is not your thing—many people lead happy and productive lives without knowing how to implement an interface or override a constructor!

We are going to look at a sample security extension that implements forms security for Reporting Services. *Forms security* enables you to present the user with a form on which they can enter their user name and password. You can then validate that user name and password against a database table or other data store where you are maintaining a list of valid user credentials. This sample can help you become familiar with the workings of a security extension in Reporting Services. The sample is based on Microsoft's Forms Authentication Sample for Reporting Services. The original sample was written in C#. I have translated it into Visual Basic for consistency with the other examples in this book. Some revisions were also made to better fit with the Galactic Delivery Services examples.

CAUTION

The code provided here is merely a sample to aid in your understanding of the custom security extension. It is not intended to be used in a production environment. Discuss any intended security changes with your organization's security manager, system administrator, or network administrator before proceeding.

Preparing the Sample Code

The forms security sample consists of a single solution called FormsSecurity. This solution contains two projects—the FormsSecurity project and the StoreRSLogon project. The *FormsSecurity project* contains all the classes that implement the security extension, along with the logon screens. The *StoreRSLogon project* contains code for a Windows application that enables you to assign user names and passwords to employees of Galactic Delivery Services.

First, three things need to be taken care of before we are ready to look through this sample code, so complete the following steps:

1. Download the FormsSecurity solution files and copy them to a test computer that contains both Reporting Services and Visual Studio 2008 with Visual Basic .NET.
2. Open the FormsSecurity solution.
3. Add a reference in the FormsSecurity project to the file Microsoft.ReportingServices .Interfaces.dll. The default location for this file is

```
C:\Program Files\Microsoft SQL Server\MSRS10.MSSQLSERVER\
            Reporting Services\ReportServer\bin
```

NOTE

In this example, it is assumed you are using a copy of Visual Studio 2008 that is running on your report server.

4. Add a web reference to the ReportService web service on this computer. The default URL for this web service is:

```
http://{computername}/ReportServer/ReportService2005.asmx
```

Name this web reference **RSWebService**. (Use the computer name rather than localhost when adding this reference. Testing has shown some unexpected results when using localhost for the web reference while building a custom security extension.)
5. Select Save All on the toolbar.

The AuthenticationExtension Class

The AuthenticationExtension class implements a Reporting Services interface called IAuthenticationExtension. The *AuthenticationExtension class,* along with a second class called CheckAuthentication, handles the authentication responsibilities. Some of the code from the AuthenticationExtension class is listed here (see the downloaded sample code for a complete listing):

```
Imports System
Imports System.Data
Imports System.Data.SqlClient
Imports System.Security.Principal
Imports System.Web
Imports Microsoft.ReportingServices.Interfaces

Namespace MSSQLRS.FormsSecurity
Public Class AuthenticationExtension : Implements _
                                               IAuthenticationExtension

    ' This function determines whether a user logon is valid.
    Public Function LogonUser(ByVal userName As String, _
                            ByVal password As String, _
                            ByVal authority As String) _
        As Boolean Implements IAuthenticationExtension.LogonUser
        Return CheckAuthentication.VerifyPassword(userName, password)
    End Function


    ' GetUserInfo is required by the implementation of
    ' IAuthenticationExtension.
    ' The Report Server calls the GetUserInfo method for each request to
    ' retrieve the current user identity.
    Public Sub GetUserInfo(ByRef userIdentity As IIdentity, _
                ByRef userId As IntPtr) _
                Implements IAuthenticationExtension.GetUserInfo
        ' If the current user identity is not null,
        ' set the userIdentity parameter to that of the current user.
        If (Not (HttpContext.Current Is Nothing)) And _
          (Not (HttpContext.Current.User.Identity Is Nothing)) Then
          userIdentity = HttpContext.Current.User.Identity
        Else
          userIdentity = Nothing
        End If

        userId = IntPtr.Zero
    End Sub
```

```vb
    ' This function is called by the Report Server when it sets
    ' security on an item. The function calls VerifyUser to make
    ' sure this is a valid user name.
    Public Function _
                IsValidPrincipalName(ByVal principalName As String) _
                As Boolean Implements _
                IAuthenticationExtension.IsValidPrincipalName
        Return VerifyUser(principalName)
    End Function

    ' Look up the user name in the database to make sure it is valid.
    Public Shared Function VerifyUser(ByVal userName As String) _
                As Boolean
        Dim isValid As Boolean = False
        Dim conn As SqlConnection = New SqlConnection(ConnectionString)
        Dim cmd As SqlCommand = New SqlCommand("stp_LookupUser", conn)
        Dim sqlParam As SqlParameter
        Dim reader As SqlDataReader

        ' Look up the user name in the Employee table
        ' in the Galactic database.
        cmd.CommandType = CommandType.StoredProcedure
        sqlParam = cmd.Parameters.Add("@UserName", SqlDbType.VarChar, 255)
        sqlParam.Value = username

        Try
            conn.Open()
            reader = cmd.ExecuteReader

            ' If a row was returned, the user is valid.
            If reader.Read() Then
                isValid = True
            End If
        Catch ex As Exception
            Throw New Exception("Exception verifying password. " & _
                                                    ex.Message)

        Finally
            conn.Close()
        End Try

        Return isValid
    End Function
End Class
End Namespace
```

GetUserInfo Method   The *GetUserInfo method* of the AuthenticationExtension
class is called by Reporting Services to determine the identity of the current user. This
method reads the user's credentials that are being persisted in the cookie. Going back to
our amusement park analogy, the GetUserInfo method puts our user's hand under the
ultraviolet light to see if it has been stamped.

If GetUserInfo does not find a cookie with credential information, it returns an empty
identity. When this occurs, the user is redirected to the logon page. The user then supplies
the credentials, and the authorization process can continue. If everything is working
correctly, this should only occur once, at the beginning of the session.

Remember, GetUserInfo is simply extracting the credentials from the cookie. It is
not determining the validity of those credentials. That is left to the LogonUser method.

LogonUser Method   Once you have the credentials, either from the cookie or from
the logon page, they must be verified. Reporting Services calls the LogonUser method
to do this verification. In our implementation, *LogonUser* calls the VerifyPassword
method in the CheckAuthentication class.

VerifyPassword looks up the user name in the Employee table of the Galactic database.
It encrypts the password supplied as part of the user's credentials and compares it with
the encrypted password stored in the Employee table. If the two encrypted passwords
match, the logon is valid. The result of this password match is returned to the LogonUser
method, and then returned to Reporting Services.

IsValidPrincipalName and VerifyUser Methods   The *IsValidPrincipalName*
and *VerifyUser* methods are used to determine whether a user name is valid. The
IsValidPrincipalName method simply calls the VerifyUser method to perform this task.
The VerifyUser method looks for the user name in the Employee table of the Galactic
database. If the user name is found in the table, it is valid.

The VerifyUser method is called by a method in the AuthorizationExtension class.
This is done to validate the user name in a configuration file. The IsValidPrincipalName
method is called from Reporting Services whenever you create a new role assignment.
This is done to validate the user name entered for that role assignment, before the
assignment is saved in the Report Catalog.

The AuthorizationExtension Class

The *AuthorizationExtension* class implements a Reporting Services interface called
IAuthorizationExtension. The AuthorizationExtension class handles the authorization
responsibilities. Some of the code from the AuthorizationExtension class is listed here
(see the downloaded sample code for a complete listing):

```
Imports System
Imports System.IO
Imports System.Collections
```

```vb
Imports System.Collections.Specialized
Imports System.Globalization
Imports System.Runtime.Serialization
Imports System.Runtime.Serialization.Formatters.Binary
Imports Microsoft.ReportingServices.Interfaces
Imports System.Xml


Namespace MSSQLRS.FormsSecurity
Public Class AuthorizationExtension : Implements _
                                    IAuthorizationExtension

    Private Shared m_adminUserName As String

    Public Function CheckAccess(ByVal userName As String, _
                        ByVal userToken As IntPtr, _
                        ByVal secDesc() As Byte, _
                        ByVal requiredOperation As FolderOperation) _
        As Boolean Implements IAuthorizationExtension.CheckAccess
        Dim acl As AceCollection
        Dim ace As AceStruct
        Dim aclOperation As FolderOperation

        ' If the user is the administrator, allow unrestricted access.
        ' Because SQL Server defaults to case-insensitive, we have to
        ' perform a case insensitive comparison.
        If String.Compare(userName, m_adminUserName, True, _
                        CultureInfo.CurrentCulture) = 0 Then
            Return True
        End If

        acl = DeserializeACL(secDesc)
        For Each ace In acl
            ' First check to see if the user has an access control
            ' entry for the item.
            If String.Compare(userName, ace.PrincipalName, True, _
                            CultureInfo.CurrentCulture) = 0 Then
                ' If an entry is found, return true if the given
                ' required operation is contained in the ACE structure
                For Each aclOperation In ace.FolderOperations
                    If aclOperation = requiredOperation Then
                        Return True
                    End If
                Next
```

```vb
          End If
      Next

      Return False
  End Function


  ' Overload for an array of folder operations
  Public Function CheckAccess(ByVal userName As String, _
                       ByVal userToken As IntPtr, _
                       ByVal secDesc() As Byte, _
                       ByVal requiredOperations As FolderOperation()) _
                As Boolean Implements IAuthorizationExtension.CheckAccess

      Dim operation As FolderOperation
      For Each operation In requiredOperations
         If Not CheckAccess(userName, userToken, secDesc, operation) Then
             Return False
         End If
      Next

      Return True
  End Function

  ' This subroutine implements SetConfiguration as required
  ' by IExtension
  Public Sub SetConfiguration(ByVal configuration As String) _
              Implements IAuthorizationExtension.SetConfiguration
      ' Retrieve the admin user and password from the config settings
      ' and verify it.
      Dim doc As XmlDocument = New XmlDocument
      Dim child As XmlNode

      doc.LoadXml(configuration)

      If doc.DocumentElement.Name = "AdminConfiguration" Then
         For Each child In doc.DocumentElement.ChildNodes
            If child.Name = "UserName" Then
               m_adminUserName = child.InnerText
            Else
               Throw New Exception("Unrecognized configuration element.")
            End If
         Next
```

```
        If _
         MSSQLRS.FormsSecurity.AuthenticationExtension.VerifyUser( _
                                             m_adminUserName) _
                                                 = False Then
            Throw New Exception("An attempt was made to load an " & _
            "Administrative user for the Report Server that is not valid.")
         End If
      Else
         Throw New Exception("Error loading config data.")
      End If
   End Sub

End Class
End Namespace
```

SetConfiguration Method   The *SetConfiguration* method reads a section of XML
from the RSReportServer.config file. This XML information specifies the user name of
the administrative user. This user name is stored in the m_adminUserName property of
the AuthorizationExtension class.

The CheckAccess methods give this user all rights to all items. This ensures at least
one user has rights to administer Reporting Services. This is necessary because when
you initially switch to your custom security extension, no role assignments exist for any
of the items in Reporting Services.

CheckAccess Methods   The AuthorizationExtension class has several *CheckAccess*
methods, which are overloaded based on the last parameter, requiredOperation. The
correct method is called, depending on which type of access is being checked.

For example, if the user is trying to delete a folder, the CheckAccess method is
called with a requiredOperation parameter of type FolderOperation. The version of
CheckAccess that checks rights on folder operations is executed. If the user is using the
check boxes on the Report Manager View Details page to delete several folders at once,
the CheckAccess method is called with a requiredOperation parameter that is an array
of the FolderOperation type. The version of CheckAccess that checks rights on an array
of folder operations is executed.

Only two of the CheckAccess methods—the method for a folder operation and the
method for an array of folder operations—are printed here. The CheckAccess methods

for reports, resources, and other types of report items are similar to the CheckAccess methods shown here for folder operations. You can refer to the source code to view the other overloads of the CheckAccess methods.

The CheckAccess method is called by Reporting Services to verify the user's right to perform operations. It may be called once if the user is performing a specific operation. In other cases, the CheckAccess method may be called many times during the painting of a single screen. For example, if the user is viewing the Home folder, the CheckAccess method must be called for each item in the Home folder to determine if the user has rights to view that item.

The CheckAccess method first determines if the current user is the administrative user. If they are, the CheckAccess method returns true, indicating this user has rights to do whatever operation is being requested. The operation is then completed by Reporting Services.

If this is not the administrative user, the CheckAccess method walks through the security descriptor collection until it finds an entry for this particular user. It then walks through a second collection, which contains the rights assigned to this user. If it finds the rights to the requested operation, it returns true, allowing the operation to be completed. If it does not find the rights to the requested operation, it returns false, causing the operation to be aborted.

Deploying a Custom Security Extension

This section contains a process for deploying a custom security extension on a report server. If you want to complete this process solely for educational purposes, you should do so on a test installation of Reporting Services. That way, if anything goes wrong, either in deploying the custom security extension or in reverting back to Windows integrated security, you can reinstall Reporting Services without harming a production environment.

This process should not be tested on a production installation of Reporting Services with the intent to revert to Windows integrated security at its conclusion. As stated earlier, changing to a custom security extension and then changing back to Windows integrated security is not generally recommended. You have been warned. Don't come crying to me if you screw up your production server!

Preparation

> **CAUTION**
>
> *Create a backup of all configuration files as directed in the following procedure. Without these backups, you may be unable to return to a working environment if the custom security extension fails.*

To create a backup for all configuration files, follow these steps:

1. Add the reference and the web reference as instructed in the section "Preparing the Sample Code."
2. Create a folder called RSSecurityBackup on the report server. This folder can be anywhere it will not be accidentally deleted. This folder will hold a backup copy of your Reporting Services configuration files for backing up your custom security extension.
3. In the RSSecurityBackup folder, create a folder called ReportServer and a folder called ReportManager.
4. Copy the following files from the Reporting Services\ReportManager folder to the RSSecurityBackup\ReportManager folder:

```
rsmgrpolicy.config
Web.config
```

The default location for the Reporting Services\ReportManager folder is

```
C:\Program Files\Microsoft SQL Server\MSRS10.MSSQLSERVER\Reporting
              Services\ReportManager
```

5. Copy the following files from the Reporting Services\ReportServer folder to the RSSecurityBackup\ReportServer folder:

```
RSReportServer.config
rssrvpolicy.config
Web.config
```

The default location for the Reporting Services\ReportServer folder is

```
C:\Program Files\Microsoft SQL Server\MSRS10.MSSQLSERVER\Reporting
              Services\ReportServer
```

Compiling and Deploying the Custom Security Assembly and Logon Pages

Now that you have created backup copies of your Reporting Services configuration files, you can compile and deploy the custom security assembly and the logon pages.

1. Open the FormsSecurity solution in Visual Studio 2008.
2. Select Build | Build Solution from the main menu to build the assembly and the executable in this solution.

3. Copy the resulting MSSQLRS.FormsSecurity.dll assembly and the MSSQLRS
   .FormsSecurity.pdb debug database to the ReportManager\bin folder. The default
   location for this folder is

   ```
   C:\Program Files\Microsoft SQL Server\MSRS10.MSSQLSERVER\Reporting
                      Services\ReportManager\bin
   ```

4. Copy the same MSSQLRS.FormsSecurity.dll assembly and the MSSQLRS
   .FormsSecurity.pdb debug database to the ReportServer\bin folder. The default
   location for this folder is

   ```
   C:\Program Files\Microsoft SQL Server\MSRS10.MSSQLSERVER\Reporting
                      Services\ReportServer\bin
   ```

5. Copy the UILogon.aspx file to the ReportManager\Pages folder. The default
   location for this folder is

   ```
   C:\Program Files\Microsoft SQL Server\MSRS10.MSSQLSERVER\Reporting
                      Services\ReportManager\Pages
   ```

6. Copy the Logon.aspx file to the ReportServer folder. The default location for this
   folder is

   ```
   C:\Program Files\Microsoft SQL Server\MSRS10.MSSQLSERVER\Reporting
                      Services\ReportServer
   ```

Modifying the Reporting Services Configuration

In addition to placing the assembly and the logon pages in the appropriate location, you
need to modify several Reporting Services configuration files to enable your custom
security extension.

1. You begin by modifying two Report Manager configuration files. These two files
   can be found in the following folder:

   ```
   C:\Program Files\Microsoft SQL Server\MSRS10.MSSQLSERVER\Reporting
                      Services\ReportManager
   ```

2. Open the rsmgrpolicy.config file in a text editor, such as Notepad. This file
   contains the code access security configuration for the Report Manager.

3. Find the code group for the MyComputer zone. Change the permission set from
   Execution to FullTrust, as shown here:

   ```
   <CodeGroup
           class="FirstMatchCodeGroup"
           version="1"
           PermissionSetName=" FullTrust"
           Description="This code group grants MyComputer code Execution
                                           permission. ">
   ```

```
<IMembershipCondition
    class="ZoneMembershipCondition"
    version="1"
    Zone="MyComputer" />
```

This change is necessary to allow the custom security extension to access the database and to look up user information.

CAUTION

As with all XML documents, the config files are case-sensitive. Pay close attention to the case of each entry you make in these configuration files.

4. Save your changes and exit.

5. Open the Web.config file in your text editor. This file contains the standard configuration information for the Report Manager web application.

6. Locate the <identity impersonate="true"/> entry. Change this entry to "false" as shown:

```
<identity impersonate=" false"/>
```

7. Save your changes and exit.

8. Next, you modify three report server configuration files. These three files can all be found in the following folder:

```
C:\Program Files\Microsoft SQL Server\MSRS10.MSSQLSERVER\Reporting
                Services\ReportServer
```

9. Open the RSReportServer.config file in your text editor. This file contains custom configuration information for the Report Server web service.

10. Find the <AuthenticationTypes> entry and modify it as shown:

```
<Authentication>
    <AuthenticationTypes>
        <Custom/>
    </AuthenticationTypes>
    <EnableAuthPersistence>true</EnableAuthPersistence>
</Authentication>
```

11. Find the <UI> entry and add the following, replacing {computername} with the name of your report server computer:

```
<UI>
 <CustomAuthenticationUI>
        <loginUrl>/Pages/UILogon.aspx</loginUrl>
        <UseSSL>False</UseSSL>
 </CustomAuthenticationUI>
 <ReportServerUrl>http://{computername}/ReportServer</ReportServerUrl>
<PageCountMode>Estimate</PageCountMode>
 </UI>
```

This entry tells the Report Manager where to redirect a user who has not been authenticated. If you have SSL available on this server, change the <UseSSL> setting from False to True.

12. Find the <Security> and <Authentication> entries under <Extensions> and modify them as shown:

```
<Security>
        <Extension Name="Forms"
                   Type="MSSQLRS.FormsSecurity.AuthorizationExtension,
                                       MSSQLRS.FormsSecurity">
                <Configuration>
                        <AdminConfiguration>
                                <UserName>Stanley</UserName>
                        </AdminConfiguration>
                </Configuration>
        </Extension>
</Security>
<Authentication>
        <Extension Name="Forms"
                   Type="MSSQLRS.FormsSecurity.AuthenticationExtension,
                                       MSSQLRS.FormsSecurity"/>
</Authentication>
```

These entries tell the Report Server web service what classes to use for authentication and authorization and which assembly contains those classes. The <Configuration> entry here contains the configuration information read by the SetConfiguration method, as discussed previously. Stanley is the administrative user.

13. Save your changes and exit.

14. Open the rssrvpolicy.config file in your text editor. This file contains the code access security configuration for the Report Server.

15. Add a code group for the custom security assembly, as shown here:

```
<CodeGroup
        class="UnionCodeGroup"
        version="1"
        PermissionSetName="FullTrust">
    <IMembershipCondition
            class="UrlMembershipCondition"
            version="1"
            Url="$CodeGen$/*"
    />
</CodeGroup>
<CodeGroup
        class="UnionCodeGroup"
        version="1"
        Name="SecurityExtensionCodeGroup"
        Description="Code group for the sample security extension"
        PermissionSetName="FullTrust">
```

```
<IMembershipCondition
        class="UrlMembershipCondition"
        version="1"
        Url="C:\Program Files\Microsoft SQL
Server\MSRS10.MSSQLSERVER\Reporting
                    Services\ReportServer\bin\MSSQLRS.FormsSecurity.dll"
    />
</CodeGroup>
```

NOTE

The line beginning with Url= should be consolidated onto one line in the rssrvpolicy.config file.

This code group uses URL membership to assign Full Trust rights to the custom security assembly. If Reporting Services is not installed in the default location, change the URL path as necessary.

16. Save your changes and exit.

17. Open the Web.config file in your text editor. This file contains the standard configuration information for the Report Server web service.

18. Locate the <identity impersonate="true"/> entry. Change this entry to "false" as shown:

```
<identity impersonate=" false"/>
```

19. Locate the <authentication mode="Windows"/> entry. Replace it with the following:

```
<authentication mode="Forms">
  <forms loginUrl="logon.aspx" name="sqlAuthCookie" timeout="60"
                                          path="/"></forms>
</authentication>
```

20. Add the following <authorization> entry immediately below the <authentication> entry:

```
<authorization>
  <deny users="?"/>
</authorization>
```

21. Save your changes and exit.

Reporting Services is now configured to use the custom security extension.

Restarting Reporting Services

Anytime you make a change to the Reporting Services configuration files or to the custom security assembly, you need to restart Reporting Services for these changes to take effect. Stop and start the Reporting Services Windows service to load the custom security settings.

Using the Custom Security Extension

To test the custom security extension, simply open your browser and go to the Report Manager. Rather than seeing the Report Manager, you see the logon page. Enter a user name and password, and then click Logon to log on to Reporting Services.

Two logons are set up in the Employee table of the Galactic database:

User Name	Password	Administrative User
Stanley	SR	Yes
Ellen	EH	No

The logon for Ellen does not have any security role assignments. Use the Stanley administrative logon to assign security roles to the Ellen logon.

NOTE

For the cookie to function properly, you need to access the Report Manager using the computer name rather than using localhost.

Creating Logons

You can create additional nonadministrative logons using the StoreRSLogon application. You created this executable when you built the FormsSecurity solution. To create a new logon, do the following:

1. Run StoreRSLogon.exe.
2. Select a Galactic Delivery Services employee from the Employee drop-down list.
3. Enter a user name and password for this employee.
4. Click Save to save these credentials in the Employee table of the Galactic database. The password is stored in the Employee table as an encrypted value.
5. Exit the StoreRSLogon program.

Debugging the Custom Security Assembly

In some cases, the custom security code does not work perfectly on the first try. Hard to believe, but true. You have two tools to help you in this situation: the log files and the Visual Studio debugger.

The *log files* are helpful because they record any exceptions that might occur. Because we deployed the debug database file (PDB) along with the assembly file (DLL), the log file even contains the method name and line number where the exception occurred. If an exception occurs, check the most recent log files.

You can also use the Visual Studio debugger to set breakpoints and step through the custom assembly code. Debugging should only be done on a test or development server, never on a production server. To use the debugger, do the following:

1. Start Visual Studio 2008 and open the FormsSecurity solution.
2. Open Internet Explorer and navigate to the Report Manager. The logon page appears. Do not log on yet.
3. Return to Visual Studio and set the desired breakpoints in your code.
4. Select Debug | Attach to Process from the main menu. The Attach to Process dialog box appears.
5. Check the Show process from all users check box.
6. From the list of processes, select the ReportingServicesService.exe process and then click Attach.
7. Switch to Internet Explorer, enter the user name and password, and click Logon.
8. When one of your breakpoints is encountered, the debugger stops execution and changes focus to Visual Studio.
9. You can now view variables and step through the code as you do with any other Visual Basic program.
10. When you complete your debugging session, click Stop Debugging in Visual Studio, and then close Internet Explorer.

Changing Back to Windows Integrated Security

If your custom security extension does not function properly or, if despite all the warnings, you want to change from your custom security extension back to Windows integrated security, use the following procedure:

1. Remove all role assignments you created using the forms security user names.
2. Copy all the files in the RSSecurityBackup\ReportManager folder to the ReportManager folder. Replace the existing files. The default location of the ReportManager folder is

    ```
    C:\Program Files\Microsoft SQL Server\MSRS10.MSSQLSERVER\Reporting
                    Services\ReportManager
    ```

3. Copy all the files in the RSSecurityBackup\ReportServer folder to the ReportServer folder. Replace the existing files. The default location of the ReportServer folder is

    ```
    C:\Program Files\Microsoft SQL Server\MSRS10.MSSQLSERVER\Reporting
                    Services\ReportServer
    ```

4. Stop and start the Reporting Services Windows service.

Other Extensions

In addition to the custom security extension, Reporting Services offers other APIs that enable you to extend its default functionality. You can develop your own data access extensions, rendering extensions, and delivery extensions. Examples showing how to utilize some of these extensions are included with Reporting Services. A number of third-party developers are using these APIs to create some capable add-ons for Reporting Services.

Best Practices

Before finishing, let's consider a few items that can make Reporting Services more efficient and easier to manage. These best practices are general rules of thumb that help things run smoother in most Reporting Services installations. As with all rules of thumb, exceptions always exist. However, as you create your Reporting Services installation and the business practices to go with it, consider these practices and the benefits that go with them.

Report-Authoring Practices

The following practices can make your report-authoring process more efficient and more consistent. A standard look and feel is usually desirable as users move from one report to the next. The ability to be responsive to your users and create reports in a timely manner is always a plus.

Use Report Templates

A number of tasks in report authoring can be repetitive, such as placing the company name and logo at the top of the page and placing the page number and date of execution at the bottom. Rather than wasting time creating these items afresh on each report, use one or more report templates. The report templates enable you to start your report layout with these redundant items already present.

In addition, the report templates let you provide a common look and feel to your reports. Templates can help ensure that certain style elements, such as a logo image or a page number in a certain location, are always present. The templates can help to enforce this common look and feel across a number of report authors.

Use Source Control

Because the report-authoring environment for Reporting Services is also a development environment, seamless support for source control is built right in. Use it! It takes very little additional time and effort to manage your reports using source control.

Source control has two advantages. First, no one has to wonder who has the latest source code for a report. This is especially important when modifying and then deploying reports to the report server. You do not want to have a report author deploy an old version of a report on top of a newer version. Second, source control provides versioning of your report source code. If you decide you don't like the latest changes to a report, you can roll back to an older version. If an older version of an RDL file is pulled off of the report server on top of your newer version, source control can save the day.

Use Shared Data Sources

Shared data sources can help cut down on management headaches. They centralize the storage of database credentials. If a database is moved to a new server, fewer places exist to change the connection information. If the database logon credentials are changed, fewer locations must be modified.

Shared data sources also facilitate the use of production and development database servers. Report development can be done using a shared data source pointing to the development database server. A shared data source with the same name can exist on the production report server pointing to the production database server. With the Overwrite Data Sources option turned off, the shared data source from the development environment does not overwrite the shared data source in the production environment. Instead, the report goes seamlessly from querying development data in the development environment to querying production data in the production environment. Isn't that the way it's supposed to work?

Use Views and Stored Procedures

Give your report authors rights to query views and execute stored procedures. Avoid giving them rights to the underlying tables. Having them operate with views and stored procedures makes it easier to enforce security and maintain privacy. It also prevents accidental data modifications and deletions.

Use Navigation Features

Take advantage of the document map, bookmark, drilldown, and drillthrough capabilities to make your reports more usable. These navigation features make it easier for your users to find the information they are looking for. *Drilldown* and *drillthrough* make it possible to hide complex detail until your user specifically requests it. Finally, drillthrough allows several reports to be linked together into a working unit.

Remember, the goal of reporting is to convey information to the end user. This is done best when a user can quickly navigate to desired information and follow the data intuitively from one level of detail to another or from one report to another. The Reporting Services navigation features make this possible.

Report Deployment Practices

The practices listed here can help you move reports from the development environment to the production report server. You need to make sure there is some level of control over which reports can access your production data. You also need to control who can do what on your production report server.

Create a Backup of the Encryption Key

This tip is not a report deployment practice, but it does help protect all the reports and shared data sources you have deployed to the report server. Occasionally, the key used to encrypt all the sensitive information stored on the report server becomes corrupt. When this happens, all that sensitive information is no longer accessible. The report credentials stored with each shared data source can no longer be decrypted and used. Worse yet, the credentials stored in the RSReportServer.config file cannot be decrypted, so the Report Server Windows service can no longer connect to the Report Catalog. In short, everything comes to a screeching halt.

If you do not have a backup copy of the encryption key, the only way to recover from this situation is to create a new encryption key and then reenter all the credential information. That is why the encryption key backup can be so important. With an encryption key backup, recovery from a corrupt key is trivial!

Review Reports Before Deploying

It is generally a good idea to have reports reviewed before they are put into production. This is especially true if you have nondevelopers creating their own reports. You need to make sure efficient queries are being used to extract the data so an undue burden is not placed on the database server. You also need some level of assurance the information the report claims to present is the information being pulled from the database.

Use Linked Reports

Rather than deploying duplicate copies of the same report to your report server, use linked reports. Each linked report can have its own default parameters and its own security. At the same time, updates to that report are done in one centralized location. This helps prevent the confusion that can arise from having multiple versions of the same report running in the production environment at the same time.

Use Folders and Descriptions to Organize Reports

If your Reporting Services installation is as successful as we all hope, soon, tens or even hundreds of reports will reside on your report server. With this number of reports, organizing the reports properly to aid both the end users and the administrators is important. Otherwise, both the users and the administrators can become frustrated.

Organize your reports into logical groupings in folders. Use the tree structure of the folders to create a multiple-level structure. You should create enough folders so no folder contains too many reports, but not so many folders that the structure becomes cumbersome.

Use meaningful report names and add informational descriptions to each report. Remember, both the report name and the description are searchable in Report Manager. Then make sure your users know how to use this search function.

Assign Security at the Folder Level

Make your security role assignments at the folder level. Let the reports inherit their security from the folders they reside in. Assigning individual security roles to individual reports is cumbersome and easily leads to errors. Your security practices should be relatively easy to implement; otherwise, they will not be followed.

Assign Security to Domain Groups

By the same token, it makes more sense to assign roles to domain groups than try to assign roles to each individual user. Just as with assigning security at the report level, making assignments at the user level causes things to become very complex very rapidly. The simpler security policy is usually better, because it is the one more likely to be followed.

Assign Only the Rights Needed

Only give each user the rights they need to complete their required tasks. Assigning broad rights rather than narrow is easier, but this can lead to security breaches and problems managing the report server. Take the time to create custom security roles that provide users with only those rights they need. Then use these custom roles as you are granting access to domain groups. The additional time taken during setup is more than made up for in the time saved not having to clean up after users who were doing things they shouldn't have been able to do in the first place.

Hide Items

Keep the folders looking as clean and uncluttered as possible. Use "Hide in list view" to hide items the user does not need to interact with. This might include shared data sources or subreports. If the user should not click an item, then the user has no reason to see it in the folder.

Remember, however, this is not a security measure. The user can easily click Show Details to reveal any of these hidden items. Security rights provide security; "Hide in list view" is a means of keeping things neat.

Deploy Supporting Items to the Report Server

The report server has the capability to store and serve supporting information. Documentation for your reports should be created as HTML pages, Word documents, PDF documents, Excel spreadsheets, and even PowerPoint presentations. These items can then be deployed to the report server right in the folders with the reports. This makes it easier for your users to understand the content and appropriate use of each report.

Use Caching and Snapshots

Use caching and snapshots to reduce the load on your report server and increase performance. Set up scheduled snapshots to execute long-running reports during off-hours. Believe me, users will not care if their data is eight hours old when they can get their reports back in seconds!

Where Do We Go from Here?

As Reporting Services continues to mature over the coming years, little doubt exists that it will remain an exciting product. With this new version of Reporting Services in SQL Server 2008, and third parties releasing alternative report-authoring environments and Reporting Services extensions, it is safe to say Reporting Services will continue to be in the news for some time to come. Based on current interest, it also looks like Reporting Services is going to have a rapidly growing user community.

It may be difficult to say exactly where Reporting Services is going from here, but all the signs point in a positive direction. It might be easier to answer the question, "Where does my business information go from here?" With a tool as capable, flexible, and extensible as Reporting Services, the answer is, "Anywhere you need it to go!"

Part IV

Appendixes

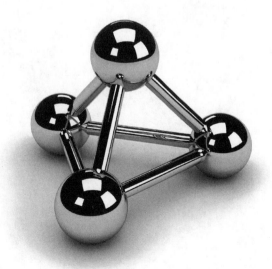

Appendix A

Report Item Reference

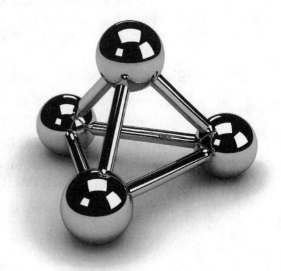

Report Objects

The first section of this appendix lists the report objects available in Reporting Services. These include the layout areas, the data regions, and the remaining report items. This section describes each object, including whether the object has its own Custom Properties dialog box, and lists all the properties for that object. Properties can be set in the Properties window or in the Custom Properties dialog box. The font of each property lets you know if the property can be set in the Properties window, the Custom Properties dialog box, or both. (See the following key.)

Layout Areas

KEY:

Property in Properties Window Only

Property in Properties Window and Custom Properties Dialog Box

Property in Custom Properties Dialog Box Only

Body

Description: The layout area containing the bulk of the report content.

Custom Properties Dialog Box: Yes

Properties: BackgroundColor, BackgroundImage, BorderColor, BorderStyle, BorderWidth, Size

Notes: If the Size: Width of the Body item added to the Margins: Left and Margins: Right of the report item is wider than the PageSize: Width of the report item, your report will span multiple pages horizontally.

Page Footer

Description: The layout area repeated at the bottom of each page. Can be enabled and disabled in the Report Properties dialog box or on the Report menu.

Custom Properties Dialog Box: Yes

Properties: BackgroundColor, BackgroundImage, BorderColor, BorderStyle, BorderWidth, Height, PrintOnFirstPage, PrintOnLastPage

Notes: You cannot include field values in the Page Footer.

Page Header

Description: The layout area repeated at the top of each page. Can be enabled and disabled in the Report Properties dialog box or on the Report menu.

Custom Properties Dialog Box: Yes

Properties: BackgroundColor, BackgroundImage, BorderColor, BorderStyle, BorderWidth, Height, PrintOnFirstPage, PrintOnLastPage

Notes: You cannot include field values in the Page Header.

Report

Description: The report is not a layout area itself, but rather, is a container for the other layout areas.

Custom Properties Dialog Box: Yes

Properties: Assemblies, Author, AutoRefresh, BackgroundColor, BackgroundImage, BorderColor, BorderStyle, BorderWidth, **Classes,** Code, Columns, ConsumeContainerWhitespace, *CustomCode,* **CustomProperties,** DataElementName, DataElementStyle, **DataSchema, DataTransform,** DeferVariableEvaluation, **Description,** DescriptionLocID, InteractiveSize, Language, **Margins, PageSize, Variables,** Width

Notes: If the Size: Width of the Body item added to the Margins: Left and Margins: Right of the report item is wider than the PageSize: Width of the report item, your report will span multiple pages horizontally.

Data Regions

KEY:

Property in Properties Window Only

Property in Properties Window and Custom Properties Dialog Box

Property in Custom Properties Dialog Box Only

Chart

Description: A business graphic, such as a line graph or a pie chart. The chart data region cannot contain other report items.

Custom Properties Dialog Box: Yes

Properties: BackgroundColor, BackgroundGradientEndColor, BackgroundGradientType, BackgroundImage, **BackgroundPatternType,** Bookmark, **BorderColor, BorderSkin, BorderStyle, BorderWidth,** Calendar, ChartAreas, CustomPaletteColors, CustomProperties, DataElementName, DataElementOutput, **DataSetName,** Direction, DocumentMapLabel, DynamicHeight, DynamicWidth, **Filters, Hidden,** LabelLocID, Language, Legends, Location, **Name,** NoDataMessage, NumeralLanguage, NumeralVariant, **PageBreak, Palette,** PalettePatternBehavior, Parent, Size, Titles, **ToggleItem, ToolTip,** ZIndex

Chart Area

Description: Controls the charting area of the chart.

Custom Properties Dialog Box: Yes

Properties: AlignOrientation, AlignType, AlignWithChartArea, **Area3DStyle, BackgroundColor, BackgroundGradientEndColor, BackgroundGradientType,** BackgroundImage, BackgroundPatternType, **BorderColor, BorderStyle, BorderWidth,** CategoryAxes, CustomInnerPlotPosition, CustomPosition, EquallySizedAxesFonts, **Hidden,** Name, **ShadowColor, ShadowOffset,** ValueAxes

Chart Axis

Description: Controls an axis placed on the chart.

Custom Properties Dialog Box: Yes

Properties: AllowLabelRotation, Arrows, CrossAt, HideEndLabels, HideLabels, IncludeZero, Interlaced, InterlacedColor, Interval, IntervalOffset, IntervalOffsetType, IntervalType, LabelInterval, LabelIntervalOffset, LabelIntervalOffsetType, LabelIntervalType, LabelsAngle, LabelsAutoFitDisabled, LabelsColor, **LabelsFont,** LabelsFormat, **LabelTextDecoration,** LineColor, LineStyle, LineWidth, LogBase, LogScale, MajorGridLines, MajorTickMarks, Margin, MarksAlwaysAtPlotEdge, MaxFontSize, Maximum, MinFontSize, Minimum, MinorGridLines, MinorTickMarks, OffsetLabels, PreventFontGrow, PreventFontShrink, PreventLabelOffset, PreventWordWrap, Reverse, Scalar, ScaleBreakStyle, StripLines, **Title, TitleAlignment,** TitleColor, TitleFont, TitleTextDecoration, TitleTextOrientation, VariableAutoInterval, Visible

Chart Category/Series Group

Description: Controls the category groupings on the chart. These usually form the X axis of the chart.

Custom Properties Dialog Box: Yes

Properties: DataElementName, DataElementOutput, *Filters, GroupExpressions,* **Label**, Name, *Sorting, Variables*

Chart Gridlines

Description: Controls the grid lines in a charting area.

Custom Properties Dialog Box: Yes

Properties: Enabled, **Interval**, IntervalOffset, IntervalOffsetType, **IntervalType**, **LineColor, LineStyle, LineWidth**

Chart Legend

Description: Controls a title placed on the chart.

Custom Properties Dialog Box: Yes

Properties: AutoFitTextDisabled, **BackgroundColor**, **BackgroundGradientEndColor**, **BackgroundGradientType**, BackgroundImage, BackgroundPatternType, **BorderColor, BorderStyle, BorderWidth**, Color, CustomPosition, **DockOutsideChartArea, DockToChartArea**, EquallySpacedItems, **Font, Hidden**, InterlacedRows, InterlacedRowsColor, **Layout**, MaxAutoSize, MinFontSize, **Name, Position**, Reversed, **ShadowColor**, **ShadowOffset, TextDecoration**, TextWrapThreshold, TitleAlignment, TitleBackgroundColor, TitleColor, TitleFont, TitleSeparator, TitleSeparatorColor, TitleTextDecoration

Chart Series

Description: Controls the values placed on the chart

Custom Properties Dialog Box: Yes

Properties: Action, BackgroundGradientEndColor, **BackgroundGradientType**, BackgroundImage, **BackgroundPatternType**, **BorderColor, BorderStyle, BorderWidth, CategoryAxisName**, *CategoryField,* **ChartAreaName**, Color, CustomAttributes, DataPoint, EmptyPoint, **Hidden, HideInLegend**, Label, **LegendName, LegendText, Marker**, Name, **ShadowColor, ShadowOffset**, SmartLabels, ToolTip, Type, *Value,* **ValueAxisName**

Chart Title

Description: Controls a title placed on the chart.

Custom Properties Dialog Box: Yes

Properties: Action, BackgroundColor, BackgroundGradientEndColor, BackgroundGradientType, BackgroundImage, **BackgroundPatternType, BorderColor, BorderStyle, BorderWidth, Caption,** Color, CustomPosition, **DockOffset, DockOutsideChartArea, DockToChartArea, Font, Hidden,** Name, **Position, ShadowColor, ShadowOffset, TextDecoration,** TextEffect, TextOrientation, ToolTip

Gauge Label

Description: Adds text to a gauge panel.

Custom Properties Dialog Box: Yes

Properties: Action, Angle, BackgroundColor, BackgroundGradientEndColor, BackgroundGradientType, BackgroundPatternType, BackgroundShadowOffset, **BorderColor, BorderStyle, BorderWidth, Font, Height, Hidden, Left,** Name, **ParentItem,** ResizeMode, **Text, TextAlign,** TextColor, **TextDecoration, TextShadowOffset,** ToolTip, **Top,** UseFontPercent, **VerticalAlign, Width,** ZIndex

Gauge - Linear

Description: A thermometer-style gauge.

Custom Properties Dialog Box: Yes

Properties: Action, AspectRatio, *BackFill,* **BackFrame,** ClipContent, **Height,** Hidden, **Left, Name, Orientation,** ParentItem, Scales, **ToolTip, Top,** TopImage, **Width,** ZIndex

Gauge Panel

Description: A graphic, such as a thermometer or dashboard gauge. The gauge data region cannot contain other report items.

Custom Properties Dialog Box: Yes

Properties: *Action,* AntiAliasing, **AutoLayout,** BackFrame, **BackgroundColor,** Bookmark, **BorderColor, BorderStyle, BorderWidth,** Calendar,

CustomProperties, DataElementName, DataElementOutput, **DataSetName**, Direction, DocumentMapLabel, *Filters*, **Hidden**, LabelLocID, Labels, Language, LinearGauges, Location, **Name**, NumeralLanguage, NumeralVariant, **PageBreak**, Parent, RadialGauges, ShadowIntensity, Size, TextAntiAliasingQuality, **ToggleItem**, **ToolTip**, ToolTipLocID, TopImage, ZIndex

Gauge Pointer - Linear

Description: The pointer on a linear gauge.

Custom Properties Dialog Box: Yes

Properties: Action, BarStart, **BorderColor**, **BorderStyle**, **BorderWidth**, **DistanceFromScale**, **FillColor**, **FillGradientEndColor**, **FillGradientType**, **FillPatternType**, Hidden, MarkLength, MarkStyle, Name, **Placement**, PointerImage, **ShadowOffset**, SnappingEnabled, SnappingInterval, Thermometer, ToolTip, **Type**, **Value**, **Width**

Gauge Pointer - Radial

Description: The pointer on a radial gauge.

Custom Properties Dialog Box: Yes

Properties: Action, BarStart, **BorderColor**, **BorderStyle**, **BorderWidth**, **DistanceFromScale**, **FillColor**, **FillGradientEndColor**, **FillGradientType**, **FillPatternType**, Hidden, MarkLength, MarkStyle, Name, **NeedleStyle**, **Placement**, **PointerCap**, PointerImage, **ShadowOffset**, SnappingEnabled, SnappingInterval, ToolTip, **Type**, **Value**, **Width**

Gauge - Radial

Description: A dashboard-style gauge.

Custom Properties Dialog Box: Yes

Properties: Action, AspectRatio, *BackFill*, **BackFrame**, ClipContent, **Height**, Hidden, **Left**, **Name**, ParentItem, **PivotX**, **PivotY**, Scales, **ToolTip**, **Top**, TopImage, **Width**, ZIndex

Gauge Range

Description: Denotes a range on a gauge.

Custom Properties Dialog Box: Yes

Properties: **Action, BorderColor, BorderStyle, BorderWidth, DistanceFromScale**, EndValue, EndWidth, **FillColor, FillGradientEndColor, FillGradientType, FillPatternType**, Hidden, InRangeBarPointerColor, InRangeLabelColor, InRangeTickMarkColor, Name, **Placement, ShadowOffset**, StartValue, StartWidth, ToolTip

Gauge Scale - Linear

Description: The scale on a linear gauge.

Custom Properties Dialog Box: Yes

Properties: **Action, BorderColor, BorderStyle, BorderWidth**, CustomLabels, **EndMargin, FillColor, FillGradientEndColor, FillGradientType, FillPatternType**, Hidden, **Interval, IntervalOffset, LabelStyle, Logarithmic, LogarithmicBase, MajorTickMark**, MaximumPin, **MaximumValue**, MinimumPin, **MinimumValue, MinorTickMark, Multiplier**, Name, Pointers, **Position**, Ranges, **Reversed, ShadowOffset, StartMargin**, TickMarksOnTop, ToolTip, **Width**

Gauge Scale - Radial

Description: The scale on a radial gauge.

Custom Properties Dialog Box: Yes

Properties: **Action, BorderColor, BorderStyle, BorderWidth**, CustomLabels, **FillColor, FillGradientEndColor, FillGradientType, FillPatternType, Hidden, Interval, IntervalOffset, LabelStyle, Logarithmic, LogarithmicBase, MajorTickMark**, MaximumPin, **MaximumValue**, MinimumPin, **MinimumValue, MinorTickMark, Multiplier**, Name, Pointers, **Radius**, Ranges, **Reversed, ShadowOffset, StartAngle, SweepAngle**, TickMarksOnTop, ToolTip, **Width**

Tablix

Description: A tabular layout for viewing row and column data.

Custom Properties Dialog Box: Yes

Properties: BackgroundColor, BackgroundImage, Bookmark, BorderColor, BorderStyle, BorderWidth, Calendar, Color, CustomProperties, DataElementName, DataElementOutput, **DataSetName**, DocumentMapLabel, **Filters, FixedColumnHeaders, FixedRowHeaders**, Font, Format, GroupsBeforeRowHeaders, **Hidden, KeepTogether**, LabelLocID, LayoutDirection, LineHeight, Location, **Name**, NoRowsMessage, NumeralLanguage, NumeralVariant, OmitBorderOnPageBreak, Padding,

PageBreak, Parent, **RepeatColumnHeaders**, **RepeatRowHeaders**, Size, SortExpressions, TextAlign, TextDecoration, **ToggleItem**, **ToolTip**, ToolTipLocID, UnicodeBiDi, VerticalAlign, WritingMode, ZIndex

Tablix Column/Row

Description: Defines the appearance of a column in a tablix.

Custom Properties Dialog Box: No

Properties: BackgroundColor, BackgroundImage, Bookmark, BorderColor, BorderStyle, BorderWidth, Calendar, CanGrow, CanShrink, Color, DataElementName, DataElementOutput, DataElementStyle, Direction, DocumentMapLabel, Font, Format, Hidden, HideDuplicates, InitialToggleState, KeepTogether, LabelLocID, Language, LineHeight, Location, Name, NumeralLanguage, NumeralVariant, Padding, Parent, RepeatWith, Size, SpaceAfter, SpaceBefore, TextAlign, TextDecoration, ToggleItem, ToolTip, UnicodeBiDi, Value, ValueLocID, VerticalAlign, WritingMode, ZIndex

Tablix Group

Description: Defines the data that makes up a group of columns or rows in a tablix.

Custom Properties Dialog Box: Yes

Properties: *DocumentMap, Filters, GroupExpressions, Hidden, Name, PageBreak, Sorting, ToggleItem, Variables*

Report Items

KEY:

Property in Properties Window Only

Property in Properties Window and Custom Properties Dialog Box

Property in Custom Properties Dialog Box Only

Image

Description: Places a graphic on the report.

Custom Properties Dialog Box: Yes

Properties: Action, Bookmark, BorderColor, BorderStyle, BorderWidth, CustomProperties, DocumentMapLabel, **Hidden**, LabelLocID, Location, MIMEType, **Name**, Padding, Parent, **RepeatWith, Size, Sizing, Source, ToggleItem, ToolTip**, ToolTipLocID, **Value**, ZIndex

Line

Description: Places a line on the report.

Custom Properties Dialog Box: No

Properties: Bookmark, CustomProperties, DocumentMapLabel, EndPoint, Hidden, LabelLocID, LineColor, LineStyle, LineWidth, Location, Name, Parent, RepeatWith, ToggleItem, ZIndex

Rectangle

Description: Places a rectangle on the report.

Custom Properties Dialog Box: Yes

Properties: BackgroundColor, BackgroundImage, Bookmark, BorderColor, BorderStyle, BorderWidth, CustomProperties, **DataElementName**, DataElementOutput, DocumentMapLabel, **Hidden, KeepTogether,** LabelLocID, LinkToChild, Location, **Name, OmitBorderOnPageBreak, PageBreak**, Parent, RepeatWith, Size, **ToggleItem**, ToolTip, ToolTipLocID, ZIndex

Subreport

Description: Inserts one report into another.

Custom Properties Dialog Box: Yes

Properties: Bookmark, **BorderColor, BorderStyle, BorderWidth**, Calendar, Color, CustomProperties, DataElementName, DataElementOutput, DocumentMapLabel, Font, Format, **Hidden**, KeepTogether, LabelLocID, Language, LineHeight, Location, MergeTransactions, **Name**, NoRowsMessage, NumeralLanguage, NumeralVariant, **OmitBorderOnPageBreak**, Padding, **Parameters**, Parent, **ReportName**, Size, TextAlign, **ToggleItem**, ToolTip, ToolTipLocID, UnicodeBiDi, VerticalAlign, WritingMode, ZIndex

Text Box

Description: Places a text box on the report.

Custom Properties Dialog Box: Yes

Properties: Action, BackgroundColor, BackgroundImage, Bookmark, **BorderColor, BorderStyle, BorderWidth**, Calendar, **CanGrow, CanShrink,**

Color, CustomProperties, DataElementName, DataElementOutput, DataElementStyle, Direction, DocumentMapLabel, **Font**, **Format**, **Hidden**, HideDuplicates, **InitialToggleState**, KeepTogether, LabelLocID, Language, **LineHeight**, Location, **Name**, NumeralLanguage, NumeralVariant, **Padding**, Parent, **RepeatWith**, Size, SpaceAfter, SpaceBefore, **TextAlign**, **ToggleItem**, **ToolTip**, **UserSort**, **Value**, ValueLocID, **VerticalAlign**, **WritingMode**, ZIndex

Property Reference

This section describes the properties of the report objects. The property is listed only once, even if it is a property of several objects. If the property can be set in a Custom Properties dialog box, the explanation notes the tab where this property appears.

Some properties serve as a summary of several properties in the Properties window. BackgroundImage and BorderColor are two examples of these summary properties. A plus sign (+) to the left of a property in the Properties window tells you it is a summary property and has several detail properties beneath it. Click the plus sign to expand the summary property so you can view and change the value of the detail properties.

In this section, the **Detail Properties:** entry signals this property is a summary property, which contains several detail properties. The detail properties are explained in the **Notes:** entry for the summary property.

Properties

Action

Description: Specifies which type of hyperlink action this item will execute.

When to Use: The report item causes the Report Viewer to navigate to a bookmark in this report, to another report, or to a website.

Notes: Linking to a bookmark or to another report works only in the Report Viewer or in the HTML and MHTML rendering formats. Linking to a website works only in the Report Viewer and the HTML, MHTML, PDF, and Excel rendering formats.

Property Of: Chart Series, Chart Title, Gauge Label, Gauge - Linear, Gauge Panel, Gauge Pointer- Linear, Gauge Pointer- Radial, Gauge - Radial, Gauge Range, Gauge Scale - Linear, Gauge Scale - Radial, Image, Text Box

AlignOrientation

Description: Specifies how this chart area is aligned with another chart area in the same chart.

When to Use: Two or more chart areas are used in a chart, and the values charted in the two areas must be aligned with one another.

Notes: The other chart area in the alignment pair is specified by the AlignWithChartArea property.

Property Of: Chart Area

AlignType

Description: Specifies which parts of a chart area are to be aligned with another chart area.

When to Use: Two or more chart areas are used in a chart, and the values charted in the two areas must be aligned with one another.

Notes: The other chart area in the alignment pair is specified by the AlignWithChartArea property.

Property Of: Chart Area

Detail Properties: AxesView, InnerPlotPosition, Position

AlignWithChartArea

Description: Specifies the chart area to which this chart area is to be aligned.

When to Use: Two or more chart areas are used in a chart, and the values charted in the two areas must be aligned with one another.

Notes: The specifics of the chart area alignment are specified by the AlignOrientation and AlignType properties.

Property Of: Chart Area

AllowLabelRotation

Description: Specifies how chart axis labels may be rotated when they are auto-fit along the axis.

When to Use: The rotation of the chart axis labels must be controlled during the auto-fit process.

Notes: This property can also be used to prevent chart axis label rotation.

Property Of: Chart Axis

Angle

Description: Adjusts the angle of a label on a gauge.

When to Use: A label is placed on a chart, and the label needs to be rotated to an orientation other than horizontal.

Property Of: Gauge Label

AntiAliasing

Description: The method used to smooth diagonal lines and curves in gauges on a gauge panel.

When to Use: Gauge-rendering performance needs to be improved by reducing the anti-aliasing calculations done during rendering.

Property Of: Gauge Panel

Area3DStyle

Description: Controls the three-dimensional behavior of a chart area.

When to Use: A chart area needs to have a three-dimensional appearance.

Property Of: Chart Area

Detail Properties: Clustered, DepthRatio, Enabled, GapDepth, Inclination, Perspective, ProjectionMode, Rotation, Shading, WallThickness

Arrows

Description: Places an arrow on the end of a chart axis.

When to Use: An arrow must be placed on the end of a chart axis.

Property Of: Chart Axis

AspectRatio

Description: Controls the ratio of width to height of a gauge.

When to Use: The proportion of a gauge's width to height needs to be a constant ratio.

Property Of: Gauge - Linear, Gauge - Radial

Assemblies

Description: The external .NET assemblies referenced by a report.

When to Use: Code from an external .NET assembly needs to be utilized within a report.

Property Of: Report

Author

Description: Records the author of the report.

When to Use: The author's name needs to be stored with the report.

Property Of: Report

AutoFitTextDisabled

Description: Turns off the auto-fit feature in a chart legend.

When to Use: The chart legend auto-fit is producing an undesirable layout.

Property Of: Chart Legend

AutoLayout

Description: The flag controlling whether the gauges on a gauge panel are to be laid out automatically.

When to Use: Auto-layout needs to be turned off to allow manual layout of gauges in a gauge panel.

Property Of: Gauge Panel

AutoRefresh

Description: Sets the number of seconds for the report to automatically reexecute when being displayed in the Report Viewer.

When to Use: The report shows constantly changing information and is viewed in the Report Viewer.

Notes: AutoRefresh only works in the Report Viewer in Report Manager. AutoRefresh does not work on the Visual Studio Preview tab or in any of the export formats.

Property Of: Report

BackFill

Description: The color used to fill the background of a gauge.

When to Use: The background color of a gauge needs to be modified.

Notes: The BackFill property is the same as the BackgroundColor detail property within the BackFrame property.

Property Of: Gauge - Linear, Gauge - Radial

BackFrame

Description: The characteristics of a gauge background.

When to Use: The background of a gauge needs to be customized.

Property Of: Gauge - Linear, Gauge Panel, Gauge - Radial

Detail Properties: BackgroundColor, BackgroundGradientEndColor, BackgroundGradientType, BackgroundPatternType BorderColor, BorderStyle, BorderWidth, FrameColor, FrameGradientEndColor, FrameGradientType, FrameHatchType, FrameImage: ClipImage, FrameImage: HueColor, FrameImage: MIMEType, FrameImage: Source, FrameImage: TransparentColor, FrameImage: Value, FrameShape, FrameStyle, GlassEffect, ShadowOffset,

BackgroundColor

Description: Sets the fill color for the item.

When to Use: An item needs to have its own fill color.

Notes: This also serves as the background gradient start color, if a gradient fill is used.

Property Of: Body, Chart, Chart Area, Chart Legend, Chart Title, Gauge Label, Gauge Panel, Page Header, Page Footer, Rectangle, Report, Tablix, Tablix Column/Row, Text Box

BackgroundGradientEndColor

Description: The ending color of a gradient fill.

When to Use: An item needs to use a gradient fill for its background.

Property Of: Chart, Chart Area, Chart Legend, Chart Series, Chart Title, Gauge Label

BackgroundGradientType

Description: The type and direction of a gradient fill.

When to Use: An item needs to use a gradient fill for its background.

Property Of: Chart, Chart Area, Chart Legend, Chart Series, Chart Title, Gauge Label

BackgroundImage

Description: Selects a graphic to fill the background of an item.

When to Use: An item needs to have its own fill provided by a graphic.

Notes: The Source detail property specifies whether the image is embedded, external, in a database, or from a URL. The Value detail property contains the name of the image. The MIMEType detail property contains the MIME type of the image. The BackgroundRepeat detail property specifies how the image is repeated, if it does not fill the entire report object.

Property Of: Body, Chart, Chart Area, Chart Legend, Chart Series, Chart Title, Page Header, Page Footer, Rectangle, Report, Tablix, Tablix Column/Row, Text Box

Detail Properties: Source, Value, MIMEType, BackgroundRepeat, TransparentColor, Position

BackgroundPatternType

Description: The pattern to use in the background of an item.

When to Use: An item needs to use a pattern fill for its background.

Notes: The BackgroundGradientEndColor is used as the second color in the pattern and must be different from the BackgroundColor in order for the BackgroundPatternType to show.

Property Of: Chart, Chart Area, Chart Legend, Chart Series, Chart Title, Gauge Label

BackgroundShadowOffset

Description: The number of points a shadow is offset from the gauge label background.

When to Use: The gauge label needs to have a drop shadow behind its background.

Notes: This controls the shadow of the gauge label's background, not the shadow of the text itself. The gauge label's background color must be set to something other than transparent in order for the shadow to appear correctly. Setting this property to **0pt** turns off the shadow.

Property Of: Gauge Label

BarStart

Description: The starting location of a bar pointer.

When to Use: A bar pointer is being used on a gauge.

Property Of: Gauge Pointer- Linear, Gauge Pointer- Radial

Bookmark

Description: Creates a named bookmark in a report.

When to Use: A chart value, image, or text box is to serve as a hyperlink to this report item.

Notes: The Bookmark serves as the target for a hyperlink jump within the same report. Clicking a chart value, image, or text box whose JumpToBookmark property matches this report item's Bookmark property causes the Report Viewer to jump to this report item. Bookmarks work only in the HTML and MHTML rendering formats.

Property Of: Chart, Gauge Panel, Image, Line, Rectangle, Subreport, Tablix, Tablix Column/Row

BorderColor

Description: The color of the border around the outside of the report item.

When to Use: A non-black border needs to be around this report item.

Notes: The value in the Default detail property is used as the value for the Left, Right, Top, and Bottom detail properties, unless a value is specified for the detail property itself. The Left, Right, Top, and Bottom detail properties control the color of the individual sides of the report object.

Property Of: Body, Chart, Chart Area, Chart Legend, Chart Series, Chart Title, Gauge Label, Gauge Panel, Gauge Pointer- Linear, Gauge Pointer- Radial, Gauge Range, Gauge Scale - Linear, Gauge Scale - Radial, Image, Page Header, Page Footer, Rectangle, Report, Subreport, Tablix, Tablix Column/Row, Text Box

Detail Properties: Default, Left, Right, Top, Bottom

BorderSkin

Description: A set of properties controlling the border of a chart.

When to Use: The chart border is to be given a 3-D effect border.

Property Of: Chart

Detail Properties: BackgroundColor, BackgroundGradientEndColor, BackgroundGradientType, BackgroundImage: Source, BackgroundImage: Value, BackgroundImage: MIMEType, BackgroundImage: BackgroundRepeat, BackgroundImage: TransparentColor, BackgroundImage: Position, BackgroundPatternType, BorderColor, BorderStyle, BorderWidth, PageColor, SkinType

BorderStyle

Description: The style (none, solid, dotted, dashed, and so forth) of the border around the outside of the report item.

When to Use: A border needs to be around this report item.

Notes: A border is displayed only when the BorderStyle property is set to a value other than None. Some of the more complex border styles, such as double and groove, are not clearly visible, unless the corresponding BorderWidth property is set to a value larger than 1 point. The value in the Default detail property is used as the value for the Left, Right, Top, and Bottom detail properties, unless a value is specified for the detail property itself. The Left, Right, Top, and Bottom detail properties control the style for the individual sides of the report object.

Property Of: Body, Chart, Chart Area, Chart Legend, Chart Series, Chart Title, Gauge Label, Gauge Panel, Gauge Pointer - Linear, Gauge Pointer - Radial, Gauge Range, Gauge Scale - Linear, Gauge Scale - Radial, Image, Page Header, Page Footer, Rectangle, Report, Subreport, Tablix, Tablix Column/Row, Text Box

Detail Properties: Default, Left, Right, Top, Bottom

BorderWidth

Description: The width of the border around the outside of the report item.

When to Use: A border needs to be around this report item with a width other than 1 point.

Notes: The value in the Default detail property is used as the value for the Left, Right, Top, and Bottom detail properties, unless a value is specified for the detail property itself. The Left, Right, Top, and Bottom detail properties control the width for the individual sides of the report object.

Property Of: Body, Chart, Chart Area, Chart Legend, Chart Series, Chart Title, Gauge Label, Gauge Panel, Gauge Pointer - Linear, Gauge Pointer - Radial, Gauge Range, Gauge Scale - Linear, Gauge Scale - Radial, Image, Page Header, Page Footer, Rectangle, Report, Subreport, Tablix, Tablix Column/Row, Text Box

Detail Properties: Default, Left, Right, Top, Bottom

Calendar

Description: The calendar to use when dealing with date values in this report item.

When to Use: A calendar other than the Gregorian calendar is to be used with date values in this report item.

Property Of: Chart, Gauge Panel, Subreport, Tablix, Tablix Column/Row, Text Box

CanGrow

Description: Specifies whether a text box can grow vertically to display the entire contents of the Value property.

When to Use: The expected length of the Value property contents is not known or may vary.

Notes: Text boxes can grow in the vertical direction, but not in the horizontal direction.

Property Of: Tablix Column/Row, Text Box

CanShrink

Description: Specifies whether a text box can shrink vertically to remove any blank lines after the content of the Value property is displayed.

When to Use: The expected length of the Value property contents is not known or may vary.

Property Of: Tablix Column/Row, Text Box

Caption

Description: The text to be displayed as the title.

When to Use: A title needs to be added to a chart.

Property Of: Chart Title

CategoryAxes

Description: The collection of category axes used for this chart area.

When to Use: The chart area needs to have one or more category axes.

Property Of: Chart Area

CategoryAxisName

Description: The name of the category axis associated with this chart series.

When to Use: There is more than one category axis for a chart area, and the chart series must be associated with one of them.

Property Of: Chart Series

CategoryField

Description: The field used to create the items on the category axis for a chart series.

When to Use: The chart series needs to have items along the category axis.

Property Of: Chart Series

ChartAreaName

Description: The name of the chart area.

When to Use: Multiple chart areas will be placed in a single chart.

Property Of: Chart Series

ChartAreas

Description: The collection of chart areas in a chart.

When to Use: The chart needs to have multiple chart areas.

Property Of: Chart

Classes

Description: The classes (assemblies) referenced by this report, which include nonshared properties or methods.

When to Use: Nonshared properties or methods from an assembly need to be referenced by one or more expressions in the report.

Notes: The ClassName detail property contains a list of classes, contained in external assemblies, referenced by this report. The InstanceName detail property contains the name of an object (or instance) created from this class.

Property Of: Report

Detail Properties: ClassName, InstanceName

ClipContent

Description: Determines if the gauge content is clipped to the gauge bounds or its frame.

When to Use: The clipping behavior of the gauge needs to be controlled.

Property Of: Gauge - Linear, Gauge - Radial

Code

Description: Visual Basic functions to be utilized within the report.

When to Use: One or more calculations have become too complex to conveniently edit within an expression window, or the same calculation must be used in multiple places in a report.

Property Of: Report

Color

Description: The foreground color.

When to Use: A foreground color other than black needs to be used.

Property Of: Chart Legend, Chart Series, Chart Title, Subreport, Tablix, Tablix Column/Row, Text Box

Columns

Description: The number of columns in the report body.

When to Use: The report body needs to have multiple columns.

Property Of: Report

ConsumeContainerWhitespace

Description: Controls whether extra white space on the report body is removed. White space is removed when this property is set to true. The default value is false.

When to Use: Extra white space should be removed from the report body.

Property Of: Report

CrossAt

Description: The point where one chart axis is crossed by another chart axis.

When to Use: One chart axis should cross the other at its maximum value rather than at its minimum value.

Property Of: Chart Axis

CustomAttributes

Description: Additional attributes of a chart series specific to its chart type.

When to Use: Specific behaviors of a chart series need to be modified.

Property Of: Chart Series

Detail Properties: Detail properties vary by chart type.

CustomCode

Description: Visual Basic functions and subroutines to be embedded in the report.

When to Use: The report requires Visual Basic code too complex to put in a property value.

Property Of: Report

CustomInnerPlotPosition

Description: Determines the position of the inner plot area.

When to Use: The position of the inner plot area needs to be manually adjusted.

Property Of: Chart Area

Detail Properties: Enabled, Height, Left, Top, Width

CustomLabels

Description: A collection of custom labels on a gauge scale.

When to Use: The gauge scale needs to include custom labels.

Property Of: Gauge Scale - Linear, Gauge Scale - Radial

CustomPaletteColors

Description: A collection of custom palette colors for a chart.

When to Use: A custom set of palette colors needs to be defined for a chart.

Property Of: Chart

CustomPosition

Description: Determines the position of the item within the chart.

When to Use: The position of the item needs to be manually adjusted.

Property Of: Chart Area, Chart Legend, Chart Title

Detail Properties: Enabled, Height, Left, Top, Width

CustomProperties

Description: Custom information to be passed to the report-rendering engine.

When to Use: Additional custom values need to be passed to control the manner in which a custom-rendering extension renders the report item.

Property Of: Chart, Gauge Panel, Image, Line, Rectangle, Report, Subreport, Tablix, Text Box

Detail Properties: Name, Value

DataElementName

Description: The name to use for the element or attribute when exporting to the Extensible Markup Language (XML)-rendering format.

When to Use: The report needs to be exported using the XML-rendering format.

Property Of: Chart, Chart Category/Series Group, Gauge Panel, Rectangle, Report, Subreport, Tablix, Tablix Column/Row, Text Box

DataElementOutput

Description: Specifies whether this item is output when exporting to the XML-rendering format.

When to Use: The report needs to be exported using the XML-rendering format.

Property Of: Chart, Chart Category/Series Group, Gauge Panel, Rectangle, Subreport, Tablix, Tablix Column/Row, Text Box

DataElementStyle

Description: Specifies whether this item is output as an element or an attribute when exporting to the XML-rendering format.

When to Use: The report needs to be exported using the XML-rendering format.

Property Of: Report, Tablix Column/Row, Text Box

DataPoint

Description: The attributes of the data points created for a chart series.

When to Use: The appearance of the data points must be modified.

Property Of: Chart Series

Detail Properties: Action, AxisLabel, BackgroundGradientEndColor, BackgroundGradientType, BackgroundPatternType, BorderColor, BorderStyle, BorderWidth, Color, CustomAttributes, DataElementName, DataElementOutput, Label, LegendAction, LegendText, LegendToolTip, Marker, Tooltip

DataSchema

Description: The schema name used when exporting to the XML-rendering format.

When to Use: The report needs to be exported using the XML-rendering format.

Property Of: Report

DataSetName

Description: The name of the dataset to be used with the data region.

When to Use: A dataset is to be used with a data region.

Property Of: Chart, Gauge Panel, Tablix,

DataTransform

Description: The name of a transform (XSLT document) to be applied after the report has been exported using the XML-rendering format.

When to Use: The XML document created by the export is to be transformed into another document format.

Property Of: Report

DeferVariableEvaluation

Description: Determines whether to evaluate variables prior to or as part of report rendering.

When to Use: Variable values should not be evaluated until used in the report.

Property Of: Report

Description

Description: The description of the report.

When to Use: The report's description needs to be stored with the report.

Property Of: Report

DescriptionLocID

Description: The localization identifier (language and culture, for example: "en-us") for a description property.

When to Use: The report's description has been localized.

Property Of: Report

Direction

Description: The writing direction to use with this item, either left-to-right or right-to-left.

When to Use: A character set that is written right-to-left is being used in this item.

Property Of: Chart, Gauge Panel, Tablix Column/Row, Text Box

DistanceFromScale

Description: The distance a gauge pointer or gauge range should be from the gauge scale.

When to Use: The distance between the gauge pointer or gauge range and the gauge scale needs to be adjusted.

Property Of: Gauge Pointer - Linear, Gauge Pointer - Radial, Gauge Range

DockOffset

Description: The offset distance to use between the top of the chart and the chart title.

When to Use: The position of the chart title needs to be changed.

Property Of: Chart Title

DockOutsideChartArea

Description: Determines whether the chart legend or chart title is docked inside or outside the chart area.

When to Use: The chart legend or chart title is to be forced to dock outside of the charting area.

Notes: The DockToChartArea must be turned on before this property will have any effect.

Property Of: Chart Legend, Chart Title

DockToChartArea

Description: Determines whether the chart legend or chart title is docked to the chart area.

When to Use: The title should stay in position relative to the chart area.

Property Of: Chart Legend, Chart Title

DocumentMapLabel

Description: The field used to create document map entries for this item.

When to Use: The user should be able to jump directly to this location in the report by clicking on a document map entry.

Property Of: Chart, Gauge Panel, Image, Line, Rectangle, Subreport, Tablix, Tablix Column/Row, Tablix Group

DynamicHeight

Description: The height to which the chart is to grow or shrink.

When to Use: A limit must be placed on the chart's change in size.

Property Of: Chart

DynamicWidth

Description: The width to which the chart is to grow or shrink.

When to Use: A limit must be placed on the chart's change in size.

Property Of: Chart

EmptyPoint

Description: Defines the way an empty point is represented in the chart series.

When to Use: The rendering of an empty point in the chart series needs to be modified.

Property Of: Chart Series

Detail Properties: Action, AxisLabel, BackgroundGradientEndColor, BackgroundGradientType, BackgroundPatternType, BorderColor, BorderStyle, BorderWidth, Color, Label, LegendAction, LegendText, LegendToolTip, Marker, Tooltip

Enabled

Description: Controls the visibility of chart gridlines.

When to Use: The chart grid lines need to be turned off.

Property Of: Chart Gridlines

EndMargin

Description: The distance between the end of the gauge scale and the top or side of the gauge.

When to Use: The position of the end of the gauge scale needs to be adjusted.

Notes: EndMargin is expressed as a percent of the total gauge height for horizontal gauges or total gauge width for vertical gauges.

Property Of: Gauge Scale - Linear

EndPoint

Description: The coordinates of the end of the line.

When to Use: A line needs to be positioned on the report.

Notes: The Horizontal and Vertical detail properties specify the location of the end of the line.

Property Of: Line

Detail Properties: Horizontal, Vertical

EndValue

Description: The properties of the end of the radial gauge range.

When to Use: The formatting of the end of the radial gauge range needs to be modified.

Property Of: Gauge Range

Detail Properties: AddConstant, DataElementName, DataElementOutput, Formula, MaxPercent, MinPercent, Multiplier, Value

EndWidth

Description: The width of the radial gauge range at its end.

When to Use: The width of the radial gauge range needs to be modified.

Property Of: Gauge Range

EquallySizedAxesFonts

Description: If true, the same size font will be used for all auto-fit axes on this chart area.

When to Use: The auto-fit text on the chart area axes needs to be the same size.

Property Of: Chart Area

EquallySpacedItems

Description: If true, the legend items are to be equally spaced.

When to Use: The legend items must be equally spaced.

Property Of: Chart Legend

FillColor

Description: Sets the fill color for the item.

When to Use: An item needs to have its own fill color.

Notes: This also serves as the fill gradient start color, if a gradient fill is used.

Property Of: Gauge Pointer - Linear, Gauge Pointer - Radial, Gauge Range, Gauge Scale - Linear, Gauge Scale - Radial

FillGradientEndColor

Description: The ending color of a gradient fill.

When to Use: An item needs to use a gradient fill for its background.

Property Of: Gauge Pointer - Linear, Gauge Pointer - Radial, Gauge Range, Gauge Scale - Linear, Gauge Scale - Radial

FillGradientType

Description: The type and direction of a gradient fill.

When to Use: An item needs to use a gradient fill for its background.

Property Of: Gauge Pointer- Linear, Gauge Pointer- Radial, Gauge Range, Gauge Scale - Linear, Gauge Scale - Radial

FillPatternType

Description: The pattern to use in the background of an item.

When to Use: An item needs to use a pattern fill for its background.

Notes: The FillGradientEndColor is used as the second color in the pattern and must be different from the FillColor in order for the FillPatternType to show.

Property Of: Gauge Pointer - Linear, Gauge Pointer - Radial, Gauge Range, Gauge Scale - Linear, Gauge Scale - Radial

Filters

Description: One or more expressions to exclude certain records from the dataset.

When to Use: The dataset contains records not desired in the data region, and these records cannot or should not be removed by the dataset query.

Notes: The detail properties combine to build a set of filter expressions. Only records in the dataset that satisfy this set of filter expressions are included in the data region or grouping.

Property Of: Chart, Chart Category/Series Group, Gauge Panel, Tablix, Tablix Group

Detail Properties: Expression, Operator, Value, And/Or

FixedColumnHeader

Description: Flag to freeze column headers on the screen during scrolling.

When to Use: The column headers should not scroll off the screen.

Property Of: Tablix

FixedRowHeaders

Description: Flag to freeze row headers on the screen during scrolling.

When to Use: The row headers should not scroll off the screen.

Property Of: Tablix

Font

Description: The specification of the font to be used to render text within this item.

When to Use: A font other than Normal, Arial, 10 point is desired.

Notes: The FontStyle detail property specifies whether the font is normal or italicized. The FontFamily detail property contains the name of the font. The FontSize detail property specifies the size of the font in points. The FontWeight detail property specifies the thickness of the font and is used to create bold text. (Underlining is controlled by the TextDecoration property.)

Property Of: Chart Legend, Chart Title, Gauge Label, Subreport, Tablix, Tablix Column/Row, Text Box

Detail Properties: FontStyle, FontFamily, FontSize, FontWeight

Format

Description: A formatting string to control the appearance of a value.

When to Use: An appearance other than the default appearance of a value is required for better readability.

Property Of: Subreport, Tablix, Tablix Column/Row, Text Box

GroupExpressions

Description: The grouping expressions

When to Use: Data is to be grouped when displayed by this tablix.

Property Of: Chart Category/Series Group, Tablix Group

GroupsBeforeRowHeaders

Description: The number of columns to appear to the left of the row headers (reverse this if you're using a right-to-left matrix).

When to Use: The row headers need to appear in the matrix, rather than to the left (or right) of it.

Property Of: Tablix

Height

Description: The coordinate of the left edge of a gauge or gauge label.

When to Use: The layout of the gauge or gauge label within the gauge panel must be changed manually.

Notes: The AutoLayout property of the gauge panel must be set to false in order for this property to take effect.

Property Of: Gauge Label, Gauge - Linear, Gauge - Radial, PageFooter, PageHeader

Hidden

Description: Controls the visibility of an item.

When to Use: The item should not be visible on the report.

Notes: Often used with the ToggleItem property to facilitate drilldown.

Property Of: Chart, Chart Area, Chart Legend, Chart Series, Chart Title, Gauge Label, Gauge - Linear, Gauge Panel, Gauge Pointer - Linear, Gauge Pointer - Radial, Gauge - Radial, Gauge Range, Gauge Scale - Linear, Gauge Scale - Radial, Image, Line, Rectangle, Subreport, Tablix, Tablix Column/Row, Tablix Group

HideDuplicates

Description: Specifies whether to hide duplicate values when the text box is repeated in a table column.

When to Use: The value in the text box is to act as a group header, even though it is within the table detail rather than the group header.

Property Of: Tablix Column/Row, Text Box

HideEndLabels

Description: Specifies whether the starting and ending labels of an axis should be displayed.

When to Use: The chart is more readable if the starting and ending labels are not present.

Property Of: Chart Axis

HideInLegend

Description: Determines whether a chart series is represented in the chart legend.

When to Use: The chart series should not be included in the chart legend.

Note: This is often used when a given chart series represents a maximum, minimum, or goal value and should not be included with the other chart series in the chart legend.

Property Of: Chart Series

HideLabels

Description: Determines whether the chart axis labels are visible.

When to Use: The chart axis labels are not required for the proper interpretation of the chart.

Property Of: Chart Axis

IncludeZero

Description: Determines whether zero will be used as the minimum value for the chart axis.

When to Use: Zero should not be the minimum value for the chart axis.

Notes: If IncludeZero is true, Minimum is set to Auto, and all of the axis values are positive, zero will be used as the minimum value for the chart axis. If Minimum is set to a value rather than Auto, that value will be used for the minimum. In all other cases, the lowest value being charted on this chart axis will be the minimum value.

Property Of: Chart Axis

InitialToggleState

Description: The initial state of the toggle graphic associated with this text box.

When to Use: This text box is used to control the visibility of another report item.

Property Of: Tablix Column/Row, Text Box

InRangeBarPointerColor

Description: The color of a bar pointer within this gauge range.

When to Use: The bar point should change color to accentuate the fact it is within this range on the gauge scale.

Notes: This setting only affects bar pointers, not needle pointers.

Property Of: Gauge Range

InRangeLabelColor

Description: The color of the scale labels that overlap this gauge range.

When to Use: The scale label color should change to accentuate values within this range on the gauge scale.

Property Of: Gauge Range

InRangeTickMarkColor

Description: The color of the scale tick marks that overlap this gauge range.

When to Use: The scale tick mark color should change to accentuate values within this range on the gauge scale.

Property Of: Gauge Range - Linear, Gauge Range - Radial

InteractiveSize

Description: The default page size of the report when it is viewed in an interactive renderer.

When to Use: The page size of the report should be different when viewed in an interactive renderer than when viewed in a printed or fixed-page format.

Property Of: Report

Interlaced

Description: Turns on interlaced, alternating colors for this chart axis.

When to Use: The chart should have alternating color bars across its background corresponding to the major grid lines of this chart axis.

Notes: This setting is used with the InterlacedColor setting.

Property Of: Chart Axis

InterlacedColor

Description: The color to use for interlaced, alternating colors for this chart axis.

When to Use: The chart should have alternating color bars across its background corresponding to the major grid lines of this chart axis.

Notes: The interlaced color will alternate with the background color of the chart area.

Property Of: Chart Axis

InterlacedRows

Description: Turns on interlaced, alternating colors for this chart legend.

When to Use: The chart legend should have alternating color bars across its background.

Notes: This setting is used with the InterlacedRowsColor setting.

Property Of: Chart Legend

InterlacedRowsColor

Description: The color to use for interlaced, alternating colors for this chart legend.

When to Use: The chart legend should have alternating color bars across its background.

Notes: The interlaced color will alternate with the background color of the chart legend.

Property Of: Chart Legend

Interval

Description: The interval between major grid lines or tick marks.

When to Use: The frequency of major grid lines or tick marks must be adjusted from the interval automatically determined.

Property Of: Chart Axis, Chart Gridlines, Gauge Scale - Linear, Gauge Scale - Radial

IntervalOffset

Description: The amount the major grid lines or tick marks should be offset from the minimum value.

When to Use: The interval between the minimum value and the next major grid line or tick mark needs to be different from the interval between the other major grid lines or tick marks.

Notes: Interval offset is not reflected on the design tab for chart axis items, but it does affect the look of the chart when it is rendered.

Property Of: Chart Axis, Chart Gridlines, Gauge Scale - Linear, Gauge Scale - Radial

IntervalOffsetType

Description: The type of units used to express the interval offset.

When to Use: The units used to express the interval type differ from the units used to express the interval.

Notes: For example, this would be used when the interval is expressed in years or hours and the interval offset is expressed in months or minutes.

Property Of: Chart Axis, Chart Gridlines

IntervalType

Description: The units used to express the interval.

When to Use: The chart rendering must make better automatic formatting decisions through knowledge of the type of values it is dealing with on the axis.

Notes: This is especially helpful for axes expressing time.

Property Of: Chart Axis, Chart Gridlines

KeepTogether

Description: Specifies whether to attempt to keep this data region on one page.

When to Use: The data region needs to be kept on one page for better readability and analysis.

Property Of: Rectangle, Subreport, Tablix, Tablix Column/Row, Text Box

Label

Description: The document map label for this item.

When to Use: The report needs to include a document map, and this item needs to be linked to one item in the document map.

Notes: The document map works only in the Report Viewer and in the PDF- and Excel-rendering formats.

Property Of: Chart Category/Series Group, Chart Series

LabelInterval

Description: The interval between chart axis labels.

When to Use: Chart axis labels should not appear with every major grid line or should appear in between major grid lines.

Property Of: Chart Axis

LabelIntervalOffset

Description: The amount the chart axis labels should be offset from the minimum value.

When to Use: The interval between the minimum value and the next label needs to be different from the interval between labels.

Property Of: Chart Axis

LabelIntervalOffsetType

Description: The type of units used to express the label interval offset.

When to Use: The units used to express the label interval type differ from the units used to express the label interval offset.

Notes: For example, this would be used when the label interval is expressed in years or hours and the label interval offset is expressed in months or minutes.

Property Of: Chart Axis

LabelIntervalType

Description: The units used to express the label interval.

When to Use: The chart rendering must make better automatic formatting decisions through knowledge of the type of values it is dealing with on the axis.

Notes: This is especially helpful for axes expressing time.

Property Of: Chart Axis

LabelLocID

Description: The localization identifier (language and culture, for example: "en-us") for a document map label.

When to Use: The document map label has been localized.

Property Of: Chart, Gauge Panel, Image, Line, Rectangle, Subreport, Tablix, Tablix Column/Row, Text Box

Labels

Description: The collection of chart labels on a label panel.

When to Use: Labels need to be added to a graph panel to add meaning to the data.

Property Of: Gauge Panel

LabelsAngle

Description: The angle of the labels on a chart axis.

When to Use: The label text on a chart axis needs to be something other than horizontal.

Notes: The LabelAutoFitDisabled property must be set to true for this property to take effect.

Property Of: Chart Axis

LabelsAutoFitDisabled

Description: Controls the automatic layout of labels on a chart axis.

When to Use: The label layout on a chart axis needs to be controlled manually to improve clarity.

Property Of: Chart Axis

LabelsColor

Description: The color of the chart axis labels.

When to Use: The chart axis labels need to appear in a color other than black.

Property Of: Chart Axis

LabelsFont

Description: The font formatting for a chart axis label.

When to Use: The label font formatting for a chart axis needs to be controlled manually to improve clarity.

Notes: The LabelAutoFitDisabled property must be set to true for this property to take effect.

Property Of: Chart Axis

LabelsFormat

Description: A formatting string to control the appearance of the chart axis labels.

When to Use: An appearance other than the default appearance of a value is required for better readability.

Property Of: Chart Axis

LabelStyle

Description: The formatting applied to the labels on a gauge scale.

When to Use: An appearance other than the default appearance of the labels is required for better readability.

Property Of: Gauge Scale - Linear, Gauge Scale - Radial

Detail Properties: DistanceFromScale, Font: FontFamily, Font: FontSize, Font: FontStyle, Font: FontWeight, FontAngle, FormatString, Hidden, Interval, IntervalOffset, Placement, ShowEndLabels, TextColor, TextDecoration, UseFontPercent

LabelTextDecoration

Description: The decoration (underline or line through) applied to the chart axis label.

When to Use: The text is to be underlined or struck through.

Property Of: Chart Axis

Language

Description: The language used to display values within this report item.

When to Use: The language used needs to be something other than the default language on the computer.

Property Of: Chart, Gauge Panel, Subtotal, Report, Tablix Column/Row, Text Box

Layout

Description: The layout used to arrange the items in a chart legend.

When to Use: The layout of the chart legend must be modified for greater clarity or to better fit the legend onto the chart.

Property Of: Chart Legend

LayoutDirection

Description: The direction in which matrix columns are built: either left-to-right or right-to-left.

When to Use: A matrix must be built from right-to-left.

Property Of: Tablix

Left

Description: The coordinate of the left edge of a gauge or gauge label.

When to Use: The layout of the gauge or gauge label within the gauge panel must be changed manually.

Notes: The AutoLayout property of the gauge panel must be set to false in order for this property to take effect.

Property Of: Gauge Label, Gauge - Linear, Gauge - Radial

LegendName

Description: The name of the legend this chart series should appear in.

When to Use: The chart area has more than one chart legend associated with it.

Property Of: Chart Series

Legends

Description: A collection of legends on a chart.

When to Use: The chart needs to include one or more legends.

Property Of: Chart

LegendText

Description: The text to be displayed in the chart legend for this chart series.

When to Use: Text other than that which results from the expression that created the chart series should appear in the chart legend.

Property Of: Chart Series

LinearGauges

Description: The collection of linear gauges in a gauge panel.

When to Use: One or more linear gauges need to appear in a gauge panel.

Property Of: Gauge Panel

LineColor

Description: The color of the line.

When to Use: The line must be a color other than black.

Property Of: Chart Axis, Chart Gridlines, Line

LineHeight

Description: The height of a line of text within this report item.

When to Use: The report item needs to use a nonstandard line height.

Property Of: Subreport, Tablix, Tablix Column/Row, Text Box

LineStyle

Description: The style of the line (solid, dashed, dotted, and so forth).

When to Use: The line must be a style other than solid.

Property Of: Chart Axis, Chart Gridlines, Line

LineWidth

Description: The width of the line in points.

When to Use: The line must be a width other than 1 point.

Property Of: Chart Axis, Chart Gridlines, Line

LinkToChild

Description: The report item within the rectangle that will be the ultimate target of a document map entry that points to the rectangle.

When to Use: A rectangle containing several report items is the target of a document map entry.

Property Of: Rectangle

Location

Description: The location of the report item within the layout area.

When to Use: Every time an item is placed in a layout area.

Notes: The Left and Top detail properties specify the position of the upper-left corner of the report item in the layout area.

Property Of: Gauge Panel, Image, Line, Rectangle, Subreport, Tablix, Tablix Column/Row, Text Box

Detail Properties: Chart, Left, Top

Logarithmic

Description: Determines whether a logarithmic scale is used for this gauge scale.

When to Use: A gauge needs to use a logarithmic scale to better display the value being represented.

Notes: Works with the LogarithmicBase property.

Property Of: Gauge Scale - Linear, Gauge Scale - Radial

LogarithmicBase

Description: The base of a logarithmic scale used for this gauge scale.

When to Use: A gauge needs to use a logarithmic scale to better display the value being represented.

Notes: Works with the LogarithmicBase property.

Property Of: Gauge Scale - Linear, Gauge Scale - Radial

LogBase

Description: The base of a logarithmic scale used for this chart axis.

When to Use: A chart needs to use a logarithmic scale to better display the values being represented.

Notes: Works with the LogScale property.

Property Of: Chart Axis

LogScale

Description: Determines whether a logarithmic scale is used for this chart axis.

When to Use: A chart needs to use a logarithmic scale to better display the values being represented.

Notes: Works with the LogBase property.

Property Of: Chart Axis

MajorGridLines

Description: Controls the formatting of the major grid lines for a chart axis.

When to Use: The major grid lines need to be formatted to improve chart readability.

Property Of: Chart Axis

Detail Properties: Enabled, Interval, IntervalOffset, IntervalOffsetType, IntervalType, LineColor, LineStyle, LineWidth

MajorTickMark

Description: Controls the formatting of the major tick marks for a gauge scale.

When to Use: The major tick marks need to be formatted to improve gauge readability.

Property Of: Gauge Scale - Linear, Gauge Scale - Radial

Detail Properties: Enabled, Interval, IntervalOffset, IntervalOffsetType, IntervalType, Length, LineColor, LineStyle, LineWidth, Type

MajorTickMarks

Description: Controls the formatting of the major tick marks for a chart axis.

When to Use: The major tick marks need to be formatted to improve chart readability.

Property Of: Chart Axis

Detail Properties: Enabled, Interval, IntervalOffset, IntervalOffsetType, IntervalType, Length, LineColor, LineStyle, LineWidth, Type

Margin

Description: Controls whether the maximum value plotted on the chart is at the top of the chart or if there is a margin above the maximum value.

When to Use: The Maximum property of the chart axis is set to Auto and you want the chart axis scale to extend slightly beyond the maximum value being charted.

Notes: If the Minimum property of the chart axis is set to a value other than Auto, then the Margin property is ignored.

Property Of: Chart Axis

Margins

Description: The size of the margins on the report page.

When to Use: The margins are to be something other than one inch.

Notes: If the body width plus the left and right margins are greater than the report page width, the report will span more than one page horizontally. The Left, Right, Top, and Bottom detail properties specify the size of each margin in inches.

Property Of: Report

Detail Properties: Left, Right, Top, Bottom

Marker

Description: The formatting of the data point markers for this chart series.

When to Use: The data points on the chart need to be individually marked with a symbol.

Property Of: Chart Series

Detail Properties: BorderColor, BorderWidth, Color, Image: BackgroundRepeat, Image: MIMEType, Image: Parent, Image: Position, Image: PropertyStore, Image: Source, Image: TransparentColor, Image: Value, MarkerType, Size

MarkerStyle

Description: The style of marker shown on the gauge.

When to Use: Used on every gauge to set the type of marker being used.

Property Of: Gauge Pointer - Linear, Gauge Pointer - Radial

MarkLength

Description: The length of the marker used for a gauge pointer.

When to Use: The length of the marker needs to be manually set.

Notes: This property only affects marker-type gauge pointers, not bar- or thermometer-type gauge pointers.

Property Of: Gauge Pointer - Linear, Gauge Pointer - Radial

MarksAlwaysAtPlotEdge

Description: Determines whether axis labels and tick marks are rendered at the edge of the plot area or on the axis line.

When to Use: The position of the axis labels and tick marks needs to be manually controlled for this chart axis.

Property Of: Chart Axis

MaxAutoSize

Description: The maximum size of the legend auto-position.

When to Use: The size of the auto-positioning of a chart legend must be adjusted.

Notes: The value is interpreted as a percent.

Property Of: Chart Legend

MaxFontSize

Description: The maximum font size used in the chart axis or chart legend.

When to Use: The font size selected by the auto-format process must be modified.

Notes: This setting applies to an auto-formatted chart axis or auto-formatted chart legend.

Property Of: Chart Axis, Chart Legend

Maximum

Description: The largest value displayed on the chart axis.

When to Use: The top value on the chart axis needs to be set to a fixed value rather than allowed to float based on the data values.

Property Of: Chart Axis

MaximumPin

Description: The properties of the maximum pin on the gauge scale.

When to Use: The maximum pin needs to be placed on the gauge to show the maximum travel of the pointer.

Notes: The Location property determines the location of the pin relative to the end of the scale. A positive Location value places the pin beyond the end of the scale. A negative Location value places the pin on the scale.

Property Of: Gauge Scale - Linear, Gauge Scale - Radial

Detail Properties: BorderColor, BorderStyle, BorderWidth, DistanceFromScale, Enable, EnableGradient, FillColor, GradientDensity, Hidden, Length, Location, PinLabel, Placement, Shape, TickMarksImage, Width

MaximumValue

Description: The properties used to determine the largest value displayed on the gauge scale.

When to Use: The characteristics of the top value on the gauge scale need to be modified.

Property Of: Gauge Scale - Linear, Gauge Scale - Radial

Detail Properties: AddConstant, DataElementName, DataElementOutput, Formula, MaxPercent, MinPercent, Multiplier, Value

MergeTransactions

Description: Combines any transactions from a subreport with the transactions of the parent report.

When to Use: The queries in both the parent report and the subreport initiate data modifications that should be committed only if both are successful.

Notes: Both reports must use the same data source.

Property Of: Subreport

MIMEType

Description: The MIME type of the graphic used to populate the image item.

When to Use: The MIME type must be selected only when using an external image source, such as a database. The MIME type is automatically detected for embedded images.

Property Of: Image

MinFontSize

Description: The minimum font size used in the chart axis or chart legend.

When to Use: The font size selected by the auto-format process must be modified.

Notes: This setting applies to an auto-formatted chart axis or auto-formatted chart legend.

Property Of: Chart Axis, Chart Legend

Minimum

Description: The smallest value displayed on the chart axis.

When to Use: The bottom value on the chart axis needs to be set to a fixed value rather than allowed to float based on the data values or to default to zero.

Property Of: Chart Axis

MinimumPin

Description: The properties of the minimum pin on the gauge scale.

When to Use: The minimum pin needs to be placed on the gauge to show the maximum travel of the pointer.

Notes: The Location property determines the location of the pin relative to the beginning of the scale. A positive Location value places the pin before the beginning of the scale. A negative Location value places the pin on the scale.

Property Of: Gauge Scale - Linear, Gauge Scale - Radial

Detail Properties: BorderColor, BorderStyle, BorderWidth, DistanceFromScale, Enable, EnableGradient, FillColor, GradientDensity, Hidden, Length, Location, PinLabel, Placement, Shape, TicksMarksImage, Width

MinimumValue

Description: The properties used to determine the smallest value displayed on the gauge scale.

When to Use: The characteristics of the bottom value on the gauge scale need to be modified.

Property Of: Gauge Scale - Linear, Gauge Scale - Radial

Detail Properties: AddConstant, DataElementName, DataElementOutput, Formula, MaxPercent, MinPercent, Multiplier, Value

MinorGridLines

Description: Controls the formatting of the minor grid lines for a chart axis.

When to Use: The minor grid lines need to be formatted to improve chart readability.

Property Of: Chart Axis

Detail Properties: Enabled, Interval, IntervalOffset, IntervalOffsetType, IntervalType, LineColor, LineStyle, LineWidth

MinorTickMark

Description: Controls the formatting of the minor tick marks for a gauge scale.

When to Use: The minor tick marks need to be formatted to improve gauge readability.

Property Of: Gauge Scale - Linear, Gauge Scale - Radial

Detail Properties: Enabled, Interval, IntervalOffset, IntervalOffsetType, IntervalType, Length, LineColor, LineStyle, LineWidth, Type

MinorTickMarks

Description: Controls the formatting of the minor tick marks for a chart axis.

When to Use: The minor tick marks need to be formatted to improve chart readability.

Property Of: Chart Axis

Detail Properties: Enabled, Interval, IntervalOffset, IntervalOffsetType, IntervalType, Length, LineColor, LineStyle, LineWidth, Type

Multiplier

Description: The amount by which a scale's values are multiplied before being displayed.

When to Use: The values being represented by a gauge must be multiplied by a factor in order to be interpreted properly.

Notes: The multiplier can be a whole number or a decimal.

Property Of: Gauge Scale - Linear, Gauge Scale - Radial

Name

Description: The name of the report item.

When to Use: The report item will be referenced by another item in the report (for example, to control visibility).

Notes: Report item names must be unique within a report.

Property Of: Chart, Chart Area, Chart Category/Series Group, Chart Legend, Chart Series, Chart Title, Gauge Label, Gauge - Linear, Gauge Panel, Gauge Pointer - Linear, Gauge Pointer - Radial, Gauge - Radial, Gauge Range, Gauge Scale - Linear, Gauge Scale - Radial, Image, Line, Rectangle, Subreport, Tablix, Tablix Column/Row, Tablix Group, Text Box

NeedleStyle

Description: The type of needle used on a radial gauge.

When to Use: Always used to set the type of needle on a radial gauge.

Property Of: Gauge Pointer - Radial

NoDataMessage

Description: The properties of the message displayed when a chart has no data to graph.

When to Use: A message needs to be displayed to let the user know there is no data to graph.

Property Of: Chart

Detail Properties: Action, BackgroundColor, BackgroundGradientEndColor, BackgroundGradientType, BackgroundImage, BackgroundPatternType, BorderColor, BorderStyle, BorderWidth, Caption, Color, CustomPosition, DockOffset, DockOutsideChartArea, DockToChartArea, Font, Hidden, Name, Position, ShadowColor, ShadowOffset, TextDecoration, TextEffect, TextOrientation, ToolTip

NoRowsMessage

Description: The message displayed in place of a data region when that data region's dataset contains no rows.

When to Use: A data region's dataset may be empty.

Property Of: Subreport, Tablix

NumeralLanguage

Description: The language to use when applying formatting to numeric output.

When to Use: The numeral language needs to be something other than the default for the computer.

Property Of: Chart, Gauge Panel, Subreport, Tablix, Tablix Column/Row, Text Box

NumeralVariant

Description: The variant of the numeral language to use when applying formatting to numeric output.

When to Use: The numeral language variant needs to be something other than the default for the computer.

Property Of: Chart, Gauge Panel, Subreport, Tablix, Tablix Column/Row, Text Box

OffsetLabels

Description: Determines whether labels for the chart axes are shown with an offset.

When to Use: Labels on a vertical axis must alternate between two columns, or labels on a horizontal axis must alternate between two rows.

Notes: LabelsAutoFitDisabled must be set to true to use this property.

Property Of: Chart Axis

OmitBorderOnPageBreak

Description: Determines whether borders should appear around a report item if it spans multiple pages.

When to Use: The border around the report item causes an undesirable report appearance when the item crosses a page break.

Property Of: Rectangle, Subreport, Tablix

Orientation

Description: Controls whether a linear gauge is vertical or horizontal.

When to Use: A linear gauge needs to be changed from vertical to horizontal.

Property Of: Gauge - Linear

Padding

Description: The amount of empty space left around the sides of an item.

When to Use: The amount of empty space needs to be changed to improve the report's presentation and readability.

Notes: The Left, Right, Top, and Bottom detail properties specify in points the white space on each side of the report item.

Property Of: Image, Subreport, Tablix, Tablix Column/Row, Text Box

Detail Properties: Left, Right, Top, Bottom

PageBreak

Description: Specifies whether a forced page break is inserted before or after this report item.

When to Use: A page break needs to be forced to meet report-formatting needs.

Property Of: Chart, Gauge Panel, Rectangle, Tablix, Tablix Group

PageSize

Description: The size of the report page.

When to Use: The report will be printed or exported to the PDF- or TIFF-rendering formats.

Notes: The Width detail property specifies the width of the report in inches. The Height detail property specifies the height of the report in inches.

Property Of: Report

Detail Properties: Width, Height

Palette

Description: The color scheme to use for a chart.

When to Use: A nondefault set of colors needs to be used when creating a chart.

Property Of: Chart

PalettePatternBehavior

Description: Determines how patterns are applied to the chart data series.

When to Use: The behavior of a pattern must be controlled.

Property Of: Chart

Parameters

Description: The parameter values to be passed to a subreport.

When to Use: The subreport needs to receive values from the parent report to control the subreport's content.

Notes: The Parameter Name detail property contains a list of parameters for the selected subreport. The Parameter Value detail property contains a list of values to be assigned to each of those parameters.

Property Of: Subreport

Detail Properties: Parameter Name, Parameter Value

Parent

Description: The report item that contains this item.

When to Use: This is a read-only property controlled by the item's location on the report layout.

Property Of: Chart, Gauge Panel, Image, Line, Rectangle, Subreport, Tablix, Tablix Column/Row, Text Box

ParentItem

Description: The parent item of an item in a gauge panel.

When to Use: A gauge or gauge label must be linked to the coordinate system of a parent item for layout purposes.

Property Of: Gauge Label, Gauge - Linear, Gauge - Radial

PivotX

Description: The horizontal position on a radial gauge around which the radial pointer is to rotate.

When to Use: The radial pointer should pivot on a point other than the center of the gauge.

Notes: PivotX is expressed as a percentage of the width of the gauge.

Property Of: Gauge - Radial

PivotY

Description: The vertical position on a radial gauge around which the radial pointer is to rotate.

When to Use: The radial pointer should pivot on a point other than the center of the gauge.

Notes: PivotY is expressed as a percentage of the height of the gauge.

Property Of: Gauge - Radial

Placement

Description: Determines the position of a gauge pointer relative to a gauge range or the position of a gauge range relative to a gauge scale.

When to Use: The position of the gauge pointer or gauge range needs to be modified.

Property Of: Gauge Pointer - Linear, Gauge Pointer - Radial, Gauge Range

PointerCap

Description: The properties of a radial gauge pointer cap.

When to Use: The appearance of the radial gauge pointer cap needs to be modified.

Property Of: Gauge Pointer - Radial

Detail Properties: CapImage, CapStyle, FillColor, FillGradientEndColor, FillGradientType, FillPatternType, Hidden, OnTop, Reflection, Width

PointerImage

Description: The properties of the image used to create a gauge pointer.

When to Use: An image will provide the representation of the gauge pointer.

Property Of: Gauge Pointer - Linear, Gauge Pointer - Radial

Detail Properties: HueColor, MIMEType, OffsetX, OffsetY, Source, Transparency, TransparentColor, Value

Pointers

Description: The collection of pointers used by a gauge scale.

When to Use: Always used to contain the pointer or pointers used to indicate the value's position on a gauge scale.

Property Of: Gauge Scale - Linear, Gauge Scale - Radial

Position

Description: The position of the chart value labels or the matrix subtotal.

When to Use: The chart value label needs to be placed in a position other than directly above the data point, or the matrix subtotal needs to be placed above or before the detail, rather than below or after it.

Property Of: Chart Legend, Chart Title

PreventFontGrow

Description: Controls whether the label font can be made larger during the auto-fit process.

When to Use: The labels on a chart axis should not use a larger font size as a result of the auto-fit process.

Property Of: Chart Axis

PreventFontShrink

Description: Controls whether the label font can be made smaller during the auto-fit process.

When to Use: The labels on a chart axis should not use a smaller font size as a result of the auto-fit process.

Property Of: Chart Axis

PreventLabelOffset

Description: Controls the use of label offset by the auto-fit process.

When to Use: The labels on a chart axis should not be offset as a result of the auto-fit process.

Property Of: Chart Axis

PreventWordWrap

Description: Controls the use of label wrapping by the auto-fit process.

When to Use: The labels on a chart axis should not wrap as a result of the auto-fit process.

Property Of: Chart Axis

PrintOnFirstPage

Description: Specifies whether the page header or page footer should print on the first page of the report.

When to Use: The report contains a page header or footer that is not to be printed on the first page of the report.

Property Of: Page Header, Page Footer

PrintOnLastPage

Description: Specifies whether the page header or page footer should print on the last page of the report.

When to Use: The report contains a page header or footer that is not to be printed on the last page of the report.

Property Of: Page Header, Page Footer

RadialGauges

Description: The collection of radial gauges in a gauge panel.

When to Use: One or more radial gauges need to appear in a gauge panel.

Property Of: Gauge Panel

Radius

Description: The radius of a radial gauge scale.

When to Use: The size of a radial gauge scale needs to be manually adjusted.

Notes: The value is a percent of the gauge size.

Property Of: Gauge Scale - Radial

Ranges

Description: A collection of ranges used by the gauge scale.

When to Use: One or more ranges need to be used with a gauge scale.

Property Of: Gauge Scale - Linear, Gauge Scale - Radial

RepeatColumnHeaders

Description: Specifies whether the column headers should be repeated on each new page spanned by the tablix.

When to Use: A tablix contains column headers that need to be repeated on every page spanned by the tablix.

Property Of: Tablix

RepeatRowHeaders

Description: Specifies whether row headers should be repeated on each new page spanned by the tablix.

When to Use: A tablix contains row headers that need to be repeated on every page spanned by the tablix.

Property Of: Tablix

RepeatWith

Description: The data region this report item should repeat with across multiple pages.

When to Use: This report item is part of a heading that needs to be repeated with a data region that spans multiple pages.

Property Of: Image, Line, Rectangle, Tablix Column/Row, Text Box

ReportName

Description: The name of the report to be displayed in this subreport item.

When to Use: The report name is always required when using a subreport item.

Property Of: Subreport

ResizeMode

Description: Determines if the font size of a gauge label is to be automatically changed so the text always fills the label.

When to Use: The font of the label text should not be auto-sized, but should always use the font size specified.

Property Of: Gauge Label

Reverse

Description: Determines whether the order of items on a chart axis should be reversed.

When to Use: The items on a chart axis should appear in the sorted order, from right to left or top to bottom, rather than left to right or bottom to top.

Property Of: Chart Axis

Reversed

Description: Determines whether the order of items in a chart legend or on a gauge scale should be reversed.

When to Use: The items in a chart legend or on a gauge scale should appear in the sorted order, from right to left or top to bottom, rather than left to right or bottom to top.

Property Of: Chart Legend, Gauge Scale - Linear, Gauge Scale - Radial

Scalar

Description: Indicates the chart axis represents a continuum of values.

When to Use: The values on a chart axis are scalar values, and therefore, missing values must be included on the axis, even if there are no data points for that value.

Property Of: Chart Axis

ScaleBreakStyle

Description: The properties controlling the appearance of a scale break.

When to Use: A chart axis has values that vary widely or has a few outlier values, so scale breaks make the chart more readable.

Property Of: Chart Axis

Detail Properties: BorderColor, BorderStyle, BorderWidth, BreakLineType, CollapsibleSpace Threshold, Enabled, IncludeZero, MaxNumberOfBreaks, Spacing

Scales

Description: A collection of scales used on a gauge.

When to Use: A gauge needs to contain one or more gauge scales.

Property Of: Gauge - Linear, Gauge - Radial

ShadowColor

Description: The color of the shadow.

When to Use: An item needs to have a drop shadow.

Notes: This property is used along with the ShadowOffset property to create a drop shadow effect.

Property Of: Chart Area, Chart Legend, Chart Series, Chart Title

ShadowIntensity

Description: The intensity of shadows on this gauge panel.

When to Use: Items on a gauge panel need to have shadows.

Property Of: Gauge Panel

ShadowOffset

Description: The offset of the shadow.

When to Use: An item needs to have a drop shadow.

Notes: This property is used along with the ShadowColor property to create a drop shadow effect.

Property Of: Chart Area, Chart Legend, Chart Series, Chart Title, Gauge Pointer - Linear, Gauge Pointer - Radial, Gauge Range, Gauge Scale - Linear, Gauge Scale - Radial

Size

Description: The size of the report item.

When to Use: Every time an item is placed in a layout area.

Notes: The Width detail property contains the width of the report object in inches. The Height detail property contains the height of the report object in inches.

Property Of: Body, Chart, Gauge Panel, Image, Rectangle, Subreport, Tablix, Tablix Column/Row, Text Box

Detail Properties: Width, Height

Sizing

Description: The technique used to size a graphic within an image report item.

When to Use: The graphic needs to be sized using a technique other than the fit technique.

Notes: The *AutoSize* technique changes the size of the image report item so the graphic completely fills it at its normal size. The *Fit* technique stretches the graphic to fit the dimensions of the image report item. The *FitProportional* technique shrinks or magnifies the graphic to fit the image report item, but retains its proportions of height to width. The *Clip* technique displays as much of the graphic at its normal size as will fit within the image report item; the remainder is clipped off.

Property Of: Image

SmartLabels

Description: The properties of smart labels for a chart series.

When to Use: The appearance of the labels for a chart series needs to be adjusted.

Property Of: Chart Series

Detail Properties: AllowOutSidePlotArea, CalloutBackColor, CalloutLineAnchor, CalloutLineStyle, CalloutLineWidth, CalloutStyle, Disabled, MarkerOverlapping, MaxMovingDistance, MinMovingDistance, NoMoveDirections, ShowOverlapped.

SnappingEnabled

Description: Enables the snapping of the gauge pointer position to a certain interval.

When to Use: The gauge pointer should round the value according to the specified interval when calculating its position on the gauge scale.

Notes: This is used with the SnappingInterval property.

Property Of: Gauge Pointer - Linear, Gauge Pointer - Radial

SnappingInterval

Description: The interval used when snapping is enabled.

When to Use: The gauge pointer should round the value according to the specified interval when calculating its position on the gauge scale.

Notes: This is used with the SnappingEnabled property.

Property Of: Gauge Pointer - Linear, Gauge Pointer - Radial

SortExpressions

Description: A collection of sorting expressions.

When to Use: The data in a tablix must be sorted in the report.

Property Of: Tablix

Sorting

Description: The expression used to order the dataset or data grouping.

When to Use: The dataset or data grouping is to be presented in a sort order that is not provided by the dataset query.

Notes: The Expression detail property contains a list of expressions used to sort the contents of the data region or grouping. The Direction detail property specifies whether each sort is in ascending or descending order.

Property Of: Chart Category/Series Group, Tablix Group

Detail Properties: Expression, Direction

Source

Description: The source of the graphic.

When to Use: A source must be specified for each image report item.

Notes: A database image is extracted from a binary large object (BLOB). An embedded image is stored in the report itself. An external image is stored in the report project and deployed to the Report Manager with the report.

Property Of: Image

SpaceAfter

Description: The amount of space following a paragraph.

When to Use: The amount of space following a paragraph is to be controlled when using rich formatting.

Property Of: Tablix Column/Row

SpaceBefore

Description: The amount of space before a paragraph.

When to Use: The amount of space before a paragraph is to be controlled when using rich formatting.

Property Of: Tablix Column/Row

StartAngle

Description: The angle at which a radial gauge scale should begin.

When to Use: The starting point of a radial gauge scale needs to be manually adjusted.

Notes: The angle is calculated from a position at the bottom of the radial gauge and proceeds in a clockwise direction.

Property Of: Gauge Scale - Radial

StartMargin

Description: The distance between the start of the gauge and the start of the scale.

When to Use: The location of the start of a linear gauge scale needs to be manually adjusted.

Notes: This value is a percentage of the total gauge height for vertical gauges or the total gauge width for horizontal gauges.

Property Of: Gauge Scale - Linear

StartValue

Description: The properties of the start of the radial gauge range.

When to Use: The formatting of the start of the radial gauge range needs to be modified.

Property Of: Gauge Range

Detail Properties: AddConstant, DataElementName, DataElementOutput, Formula, MaxPercent, MinPercent, Multiplier, Value

StartWidth

Description: The width of the radial gauge range at its start.

When to Use: The width of the radial gauge range needs to be modified.

Property Of: Gauge Range

StripLines

Description: A collection of strip lines linked to the chart axis.

When to Use: A set of strip lines separated by a given interval needs to be added to a chart axis.

Notes: Strip lines can only be added to a chart axis using the dialog box associated with this property.

Property Of: Chart Axis

SweepAngle

Description: The circular distance covered by a radial gauge scale.

When to Use: The circular distance covered by a radial gauge scale needs to be modified.

Notes: This property is a number of degrees that proceeds in a clockwise direction from the scale start.

Property Of: Gauge Scale - Radial

Text

Description: The text to display in a gauge label.

When to Use: A gauge label needs to be added to a gauge panel.

Property Of: Gauge Label

TextAlign

Description: The horizontal position of the text within a report item.

When to Use: The text needs to be centered or right-justified.

Property Of: Gauge Label, Subreport, Tablix, Tablix Column/Row, Text Box

TextAntiAliasingQuality

Description: The method used to smooth diagonal lines and curves in text on a gauge panel.

When to Use: Gauge-rendering performance needs to be improved by reducing the anti-aliasing calculations done during rendering.

Property Of: Gauge Panel

TextColor

Description: The color of the text in a gauge label.

When to Use: A gauge label needs to be added to a gauge panel.

Property Of: Gauge Label

TextDecoration

Description: The decoration (underline, overline, or line through) applied to the text.

When to Use: The text needs to be underlined, overlined, or struck through.

Property Of: Chart Legend, Chart Title, Gauge Label, Tablix, Tablix Column/Row

TextEffect

Description: A special effect added to a chart title.

When to Use: A special effect needs to be added to a chart title to improve its appearance.

Property Of: Chart Title

TextOrientation

Description: The rotation of a chart title.

When to Use: The chart title needs to be rotated for a better fit within the chart.

Property Of: Chart Title

TextShadowOffset

Description: The offset of the text shadow.

When to Use: The gauge text needs to have a drop shadow.

Property Of: Gauge Label

TextWrapThreshold

Description: The preferred number of characters in the chart legend text; characters beyond this threshold will wrap.

When to Use: The text-wrapping behavior of the chart legend needs to be manually adjusted.

Notes: Setting this property to zero will disable text wrapping.

Property Of: Chart Legend

Thermometer

Description: The properties controlling a thermometer-type gauge pointer.

When to Use: A thermometer-type gauge pointer is being used on a linear gauge.

Property Of: Gauge Pointer - Linear

Detail Properties: BackgroundColor, BackgroundGradientEndColor, BackgroundGradientType, BackgroundPatternType, BulbOffset, BulbSize, ThermometerStyle

TickMarksOnTop

Description: Determines whether the tick marks should appear on top of the pointer.

When to Use: The tick marks of a gauge scale should appear on top of the pointer.

Property Of: Gauge Scale - Linear, Gauge Scale - Radial

Title

Description: The title of a chart axis.

When to Use: A chart axis needs to be given a title to aid in the proper interpretation of the chart.

Property Of: Chart Axis

TitleAlignment

Description: The alignment of a chart axis title or chart legend title.

When to Use: The alignment of a chart axis title needs to be something other than centered, or the alignment of the chart legend title needs to be something other than left-justified.

Property Of: Chart Axis, Chart Legend

TitleBackgroundColor

Description: The background color of the chart legend title.

When to Use: The chart legend title should have a background color.

Property Of: Chart Legend

TitleColor

Description: The color of the chart axis title or chart legend title.

When to Use: The chart axis title or chart legend title should use a color other than black.

Property Of: Chart Axis, Chart Legend

TitleFont

Description: The font of the chart axis title or chart legend title.

When to Use: The appearance of the chart axis title or chart legend title needs to be modified.

Property Of: Chart Axis, Chart Legend

Detail Properties: FontFamily, FontSize, FontStyle, FontWeight

Titles

Description: A collection of titles on a chart.

When to Use: The chart needs to be given one or more titles to provide better understanding of the data it contains.

Property Of: Chart

TitleSeparator

Description: The separator between legend title and the content of the chart legend.

When to Use: The chart legend needs to have a title with a separator to offset the title from the content of the legend.

Property Of: Chart Legend

TitleSeparatorColor

Description: The color of the separator between the legend title and the content of the chart legend.

When to Use: The chart legend needs to have a title with a separator to offset the title from the content of the legend.

Property Of: Chart Legend

TitleTextDecoration

Description: The text decoration of a chart axis title or chart legend title.

When to Use: The chart axis title or the chart legend title needs to be underlined or struck-through.

Property Of: Chart Axis, Chart Legend

TitleTextOrientation

Description: The rotation of the chart axis title.

When to Use: The chart axis title needs to be rotated for a better fit within the chart.

Property Of: Chart Axis

ToggleItem

Description: The report item that will toggle the hidden property of this item.

When to Use: A report item needs to be hidden in the report until the user clicks another report item to toggle the hidden property.

Property Of: Chart, Gauge Panel, Image, Line, Tablix, Tablix Column/Row, Rectangle, Subreport, Tablix Group

ToolTip

Description: The tool tip displayed for this report item.

When to Use: The user needs to be provided with additional information concerning a report item when interacting with the report.

Property Of: Chart, Chart Series, Chart Title, Gauge Label, Gauge - Linear, Gauge Panel, Gauge Pointer - Linear, Gauge Pointer - Radial, Gauge - Radial, Gauge Range, Gauge Scale - Linear, Gauge Scale - Radial, Image, Rectangle, Subreport, Tablix, Tablix Column/Row, Text Box

ToolTipLocID

Description: The localization identifier (language and culture, for example: "en-us") for a ToolTip.

When to Use: The ToolTip has been localized.

Property Of: Gauge Panel, Image, Rectangle, Subreport, Tablix

Top

Description: The coordinate of the top edge of a gauge or gauge label.

When to Use: The layout of the gauge or gauge label within the gauge panel must be changed manually.

Notes: The AutoLayout property of the gauge panel must be set to false in order for this property to take effect.

Property Of: Gauge Label, Gauge - Linear, Gauge - Radial

TopImage

Description: The properties of an image to be placed over the top of the gauge.

When to Use: An image needs to be rendered over the top of the gauge to give the gauge a custom appearance.

Notes: In most cases, the transparent color property will need to be used so some or all of the gauge can be seen through the image.

Property Of: Gauge - Linear, Gauge Panel, Gauge - Radial

Detail Properties: HueColor, MIMEType, Source, TransparentColor, Value

Type (for Chart Series)

Description: The type of chart used to represent this chart series.

When to Use: A chart type must be specified for all chart series.

Property Of: Chart Series

Type (for Gauge Pointer)

Description: The type of gauge pointer.

When to Use: A type must be specified for all gauge pointers.

Property Of: Gauge Pointer - Linear, Gauge Pointer - Radial

UnicodeBiDi

Description: The technique used for handling text rendered right-to-left embedded in a line of text rendered left-to-right or vice versa.

When to Use: Multiple languages need to be included in the same text box, with one language rendered left-to-right and the other rendered right-to-left.

Property Of: Subreport, Tablix, Tablix Column/Row

UseFontPercent

Description: Determines whether the font size is calculated as a percent of the parent or is taken from the Font: FontSize property.

When to Use: The font size of the gauge label text should not be determined by the percentage calculation, but should come from the Font: FontSize property.

Property Of: Gauge Label

UserSort

Description: The properties to facilitate a dynamic sort within the report.

When to Use: The report is to include dynamic sorting.

Notes: The SortExpression detail property contains the expression that will be used for sorting. The SortExpressionScope detail property specifies the scope to which the sort is applied. The SortTarget detail property specifies the data region object, grouping, or dataset to which the sort is applied.

Property Of: Text Box

Detail Properties: SortExpression, SortExpressionScope, SortTarget

Value

Description: Chart Series—An expression to determine the values to be charted; Gauge Pointer - Linear and Gauge Pointer - Radial—An expression to determine the value to be represented on the gauge; Image—The name of the graphic to be placed in the image item; Tablix Column/Row—An expression to determine grouping of a tablix column or tablix row; Text Box—The text to be displayed in the text box.

When to Use: A value is required for a chart value, an image, or a text box.

Property Of: Chart Series, Gauge Pointer - Linear, Gauge Pointer - Radial, Image, Tablix Column/Row, Text Box

ValueAxes

Description: The collection of value axes used for this chart area.

When to Use: The chart area needs to have one or more value axes.

Property Of: Chart Area

ValueAxisName

Description: The name of the value axis associated with this chart series.

When to Use: There is more than one value axis for a chart area, and the chart series must be associated with one of them.

Property Of: Chart Series

ValueLocID

Description: The localization identifier (language and culture, for example: "en-us") for a value.

When to Use: The value has been localized.

Property Of: Tablix Column/Row, Text Box

VariableAutoInterval

Description: Determines how the number of intervals is determined for a chart axis.

When to Use: The number of intervals should be allowed to vary rather than being fixed at around five intervals.

Notes: When the property is false, the chart axis will always have about five intervals. When this property is true, the number of intervals will vary, depending on the axis length and label font size.

Property Of: Chart Axis

Variables

Description: A collection of variables.

When to Use: One or more variables need to be used to aid calculations or report formatting.

Property Of: Report, Chart Category/Series Group, Tablix Group

VerticalAlign

Description: The vertical position of the text within a report item.

When to Use: The text needs to be located in the middle or at the bottom of a report item.

Property Of: Gauge Label, Subreport, Tablix, Tablix Column/Row, Text Box

Visible

Description: Determines whether a chart axis is visible.

When to Use: A chart axis is not needed for the proper interpretation of a chart and, therefore, should not be displayed.

Property Of: Chart Axis

Width

Description: The width of the report item.

When to Use: The width of the report item must be modified.

Property Of: Gauge Label, Gauge - Linear, Gauge Pointer - Linear, Gauge Pointer - Radial, Gauge - Radial, Gauge Scale - Linear, Gauge Scale - Radial, Report

WritingMode

Description: Indicates whether the text is written left-to-right/top-to-bottom or top-to-bottom/right-to-left.

When to Use: A character set that is written top-to-bottom/right-to-left needs to be used.

Property Of: Subreport, Tablix, Tablix Column/Row, Text Box

ZIndex

Description: Specifies the drawing order of the report items.

When to Use: This is an internal, read-only property.

Property Of: Chart, Gauge Label, Gauge - Linear, Gauge Panel, Gauge - Radial, Image, Line, Rectangle, Subreport, Tablix, Subreport, Tablix Column/Row

Appendix B

Web Service Interface Reference

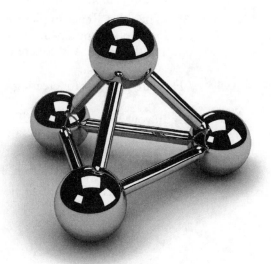

Reporting Services Web Service

Creating a Web Reference

To use a web service, you need to create code that knows how to send data to and retrieve data from that web service. Fortunately, this code is generated for you by Visual Studio through the process of creating a web reference. Once the web reference is in place, you can call the methods of the web service the same way you call the methods of a local .NET assembly.

Two web service interfaces are provided for Reporting Services: the ReportService2005 web service and the ReportExecution2005 web service. The ReportService2005 web service enables you to manage Reporting Services. The ReportExecution2005 web service lets you execute reports.

Here are the steps for creating a web reference in Visual Studio 2005:

1. In your Visual Basic .NET or C# project (not a Report project), right-click the project entry in the Solution Explorer and select Add Web Reference from the Context menu. The Add Web Reference dialog box appears.

2. Enter one of the following Uniform Resource Locators (URLs) for the web reference:

   ```
   http://{computername}/ReportServer/ReportExecution2005.asmx
   ```

   or

   ```
   http://{computername}/ReportServer/ReportService2005.asmx
   ```

   where {computername} is the name of the computer hosting the report server.

3. When the "ReportingService2005" Description or "ReportExecutionService" Description appears in the dialog box, enter an appropriate web reference name, and then click Add Reference.

Here are the steps for creating a web reference in Visual Studio 2008:

1. In your Visual Basic .NET or C# project (not a Report project), right-click the project entry in the Solution Explorer and select Add Service Reference from the Context menu. The Add Service Reference dialog box appears.

2. Click the Advanced button. The Service Reference Settings dialog box appears.

3. Click the Add Web Reference button. The Add Web Reference dialog box appears.

4. Enter one of the following URLs for the web reference:

   `http://{computername}/ReportServer/ReportExecution2005.asmx`

   or

   `http://{computername}/ReportServer/ReportService2005.asmx`

   where {computername} is the name of the computer hosting the report server and click Go.

5. When the "ReportingService2005" Description or "ReportExecutionService" Description appears in the dialog box, enter an appropriate web reference name, and then click Add Reference.

The computer name is used as the first portion of the namespace for the web services. Therefore, the ReportService2005 web service uses {computername}. ReportService2005 as its namespace and the ReportExecution2005 web service uses {computername}.ReportExecution2005 as its namespace.

Credentials

Most ReportService2005 and ReportExecution2005 methods require logon credentials to be authenticated prior to their execution. This is accomplished by creating a network credential object and assigning it to the Credentials property of the web service object. In the following code, a logon is accomplished prior to the execution of the ListChildren method. The *ListChildren method* returns an array with one element for each report item found in the specified folder (the Home folder in this example). The array only contains those items the specified credentials have the right to view.

```
Dim rs As ReportServer.ReportService2005
Dim LogonCredentials As System.Net.NetworkCredential
Dim items As localhost.CatalogItem()

rs = New localhost.ReportingService
LogonCredentials = New _
   System.Net.NetworkCredential("LogonName", "Password", "Domain")
rs.Credentials = LogonCredential
rs.PreAuthenticate = True

items = rs.ListChildren("/", False)
```

Of course, if you were to use this sample code, you would need to replace LogonName, Password, and Domain with the appropriate logon name, password, and domain name for a valid domain logon. Also, this code sample assumes you created a web reference to the ReportService2005 web service running on a server called ReportServer and you called this web reference ReportService2005, as described in the previous section.

When the PreAuthenticate property is True, the credentials are sent with the first web service request. When the PreAuthenticate property is False, the credentials are not sent to the server until the server issues an authentication challenge. In other words, when the PreAuthenticate property is False, the credentials are not sent to the server until the server requires a login. Setting the PreAuthenticate property to True can save one roundtrip between the server and the client, but as long as you have the Credentials property initialized to a valid logon, either setting for the PreAuthenticate property (True or False) works.

Compatibility

The web services in SQL Server 2008 Reporting Services are designed to be compatible with the .NET 2.0 Report Viewer control available in Visual Studio 2005 and with the .NET 3.5 Report Viewer control available in Visual Studio 2008. Therefore, all of the properties and methods from the SQL Server 2005 Reporting Services web services are still present in the SQL Server 2008 Reporting Services web services. Additional functionality has been added in two different ways.

In the report execution web service, when additional functionality is required to support new 2008 functionality, a second version of a method is present, with a "2" added to the end. For example, there is now a LoadReport method and a LoadReport2 method. For the report service web service, a second web service, called ReportService2006, has been added. The ReportService2005 and ReportService2006 have only a few differences. We will look at the ReportExecution2005 and ReportService2005 web services first, and then discuss how the ReportService2006 web service differs.

ReportExecution2005 Properties

The ReportExecution2005 class inherits from the HttpWebClientProtocol class, the SoapHttpClientProtocol class, and the WebClientProtocol class. The following public properties are defined in the ReportExecution2005 class itself.

ExecutionHeaderValue

Description: This property holds information about the state of the current report server session. This state information is contained in an Execution-Header object. The ExecutionHeader inherits from the SoapHeader object.

ServerInfoHeaderValue

Description: This property holds information about the current version of the report server.

TrustedUserHeaderValue

Description: This property holds a TrustedUserHeader object, which contains the user name and security token for the trusted user account. This property supports the Reporting Services infrastructure and is not intended to be directly accessed by user code.

ReportExecution2005 Methods

The ReportExecution2005 class inherits from the HttpWebClientProtocol class, the SoapHttpClientProtocol class, and the WebClientProtocol class. The following public methods are defined in the ReportExecution2005 class itself.

FindString

Description: This method finds occurrences of a string within a report. This method returns an integer indicating the page of the report where the string was found.

Parameters:

Name	Type	Description
StartPage	Integer	The page of the report on which to begin the search
EndPage	Integer	The page of the report on which to end the search
FindValue	String	The string for which to search

GetDocumentMap

Description: This method returns a representation of the document map for the execution. This method returns a DocumentMapNode object.

Parameters: None

GetExecutionInfo

Description: This method returns information about the report execution. This method returns an ExecutionInfo object.

Parameters: None

GetExecutionInfo2

Description: This method returns information about the report execution. This method returns an ExecutionInfo2 object.

Parameters: None

GetRenderResource

Description: This method gets a resource for the specified rendering extension. This method returns a byte array containing a base-64 encoding of the requested resource.

Parameters:

Name	Type	Description
Format	String	The rendering extension format (for example, Portable Document Format [PDF] or Extensible Markup Language [XML]).
DeviceInfo	String	A device-specific setting for the specified rendering format.
MimeType	String	The Multipurpose Internet Mail Extensions (MIME) type of the resource. (This parameter must be called ByRef.)

ListRenderingExtensions

Description: This method lists the rendering extension formats available on this report server. This method returns an array of Extension objects.

Parameters: None

ListSecureMethods

Description: This method lists the ReportExecution2005 web service methods that require a secure connection. This method returns an array of strings containing the method names.

Parameters: None

LoadDrillthroughTarget

Description: This method creates a report execution from a drillthrough from the current execution to a new report. This method returns an ExecutionInfo object.

Parameters:

Name	Type	Description
DrillthroughID	String	The ID of the item that is the target of the drillthrough.

LoadDrillthroughTarget2

Description: This method creates a report execution from a drillthrough from the current execution to a new report. This method returns an ExecutionInfo2 object.

Parameters:

Name	Type	Description
DrillthroughID	String	The ID of the item that is the target of the drillthrough.

LoadReport

Description: This method creates a new execution from a report on the report server. This method returns an ExecutionInfo object.

Parameters:

Name	Type	Description
Report	String	The folder path and name of the report to load.
HistoryID	String	The ID of the history snapshot from which to render the report. (Set this to Nothing if the report should not be rendered from a history snapshot.)

LoadReport2

Description: This method creates a new execution from a report on the report server. This method returns an ExecutionInfo2 object.

Parameters:

Name	Type	Description
Report	String	The folder path and name of the report to load.
HistoryID	String	The ID of the history snapshot from which to render the report. (Set this to Nothing if the report should not be rendered from a history snapshot.)

LoadReportDefinition

Description: This method creates a report execution from a report definition supplied by the client. This method returns an ExecutionInfo object.

Parameters:

Name	Type	Description
Definition	Array of Bytes	The Report Definition Language (RDL) defining the new report in base-64 binary.
Warnings	Array of Warning Objects	A list of warnings generated when the report definition was loaded. (This parameter must be called ByRef.)

LoadReportDefinition2

Description: This method creates a report execution from a report definition supplied by the client. This method returns an ExecutionInfo2 object.

Parameters:

Name	Type	Description
Definition	Array of Bytes	The Report Definition Language (RDL) defining the new report in base-64 binary.
Warnings	Array of Warning Objects	A list of warnings generated when the report definition was loaded. (This parameter must be called ByRef.)

Logoff

Description: This method logs off the current user making requests of the ReportExecution2005 web service. This method must be called using a Hypertext Transfer Protocol Secure (HTTPS) Secure Sockets Layer (SSL) request. This method does not return a value.

Parameters: None

LogonUser

Description: This method logs a user on to the ReportExecution2005 web service. This method does not return a value.

Parameters:

Name	Type	Description
UserName	String	The user name to use for the logon.
Password	String	The password to use for the logon.
Authority	String	The authority to use when authenticating this user. This parameter is optional.

NavigateBookmark

Description: This method navigates to a specified bookmark. This method returns an integer that corresponds to the bookmark ID. This method returns zero if the specified bookmark ID is invalid or is not found.

Parameters:

Name	Type	Description
BookmarkID	String	The ID of the bookmark to navigate to.
UniqueName	String	The unique name of the report item pointed to by the bookmark. (This parameter must be called ByRef.)

NavigateDocumentMap

Description: This method navigates to a specified document map entry. This method returns an integer that corresponds to the document map ID. This method returns zero if the specified document map ID is invalid or is not found.

Parameters:

Name	Type	Description
DocMapID	String	The ID of the document map entry to navigate to.

Render

Description: This method renders the specified report. This method returns a byte array containing the rendered report.

Parameters:

Name	Type	Description
Format	String	The rendering format to be used.
DeviceInfo	String	An XML structure to control the behavior of the renderer.
MimeType	String	The MIME type of the rendered report. (This parameter must be called ByRef.)
Encoding	String	The encoding used for the contents of the report. (This parameter must be called ByRef.)
Warnings	An Array of Warning Objects	An array containing any warnings that resulted from the rendering of the report. (This parameter must be called ByRef.)
StreamIDs	String	A stream identifier used by the RenderStream method. This is used to render an external resource, such as an image. (This parameter must be called ByRef.)

Render2

Description: This method renders the specified report. This method returns a byte array containing the rendered report.

Parameters:

Name	Type	Description
Format	String	The rendering format to be used.
DeviceInfo	String	An XML structure to control the behavior of the renderer.
PaginationMode	PageCountMode Enumeration	An enumeration with values of Actual or Estimate.
Extension	String	The file extension to use if the report is saved to a file. (This parameter must be called ByRef.)
MimeType	String	The MIME type of the rendered report. (This parameter must be called ByRef.)
Encoding	String	The encoding used for the contents of the report. (This parameter must be called ByRef.)
Warnings	An Array of Warning Objects	An array containing any warnings that resulted from the rendering of the report. (This parameter must be called ByRef.)
StreamIDs	String	A stream identifier used by the RenderStream method. This is used to render an external resource, such as an image. (This parameter must be called ByRef.)

RenderStream

Description: This method obtains the contents of an external resource used by a rendered report. This method returns a byte array containing the external resource.

Parameters:

Name	Type	Description
Format	String	The rendering format to be used.
StreamID	String	The ID of the stream for the main report.
Encoding	String	The encoding used for the contents of the report. (This parameter must be called ByRef.)
MimeType	String	The MIME type of the rendered report. (This parameter must be called ByRef.)

ResetExecution

Description: This method resets the current execution. This method returns an ExecutionInfo object.

Parameters: None

ResetExecution2

Description: This method resets the current execution. This method returns an ExecutionInfo2 object.

Parameters: None

SetExecutionCredentials

Description: This method sets the credentials associated with the current execution. This method returns an ExecutionInfo object.

Parameters:

Name	Type	Description
Credentials	Array of DataSourceCredentials Objects	The credentials to set.

SetExecutionCredentials2

Description: This method sets the credentials associated with the current execution. This method returns an ExecutionInfo2 object.

Parameters:

Name	Type	Description
Credentials	Array of DataSourceCredentials Objects	The credentials to set.

SetExecutionParameters

Description: This method sets the parameter property for the current execution. This method returns an ExecutionInfo object.

Parameters:

Name	Type	Description
Parameters	An Array of ReportParameter Objects	An array of information on report parameter properties.
ParameterLanguage	String	The language and culture identifier for the parameter (for example, "en-us").

SetExecutionParameters2

Description: This method sets the parameter property for the current execution. This method returns an ExecutionInfo2 object.

Parameters:

Name	Type	Description
Parameters	An Array of ParameterValue Objects	An array of information on report parameter properties.
ParameterLanguage	String	The language and culture identifier for the parameter (for example, "en-us").

Sort

Description: This method applies or removes a sort based on user action. This method returns an integer providing the page number where the item indicated by the ReportItem parameter now falls.

Parameters:

Name	Type	Description
SortItem	String	The ID of the item.
Direction	SortDirectionEnum	The direction of the sort. Valid values are Ascending, Descending, and None.
Clear	Boolean	True if all other sorts on this item should be cleared.
ReportItem	String	The ID of the item on the page being used to position the view. (This parameter must be called ByRef.)
NumPages	Integer	The new total number of pages after the sort.

Sort2

Description: This method applies or removes a sort based on user action. This method returns an integer providing the page number where the item indicated by the ReportItem parameter now falls.

Parameters:

Name	Type	Description
SortItem	String	The ID of the item.
Direction	SortDirectionEnum	The direction of the sort. Valid values are Ascending, Descending, and None.
Clear	Boolean	True if all other sorts on this item should be cleared.
PaginationMode	PaginationCountMode enumeration	An enumeration with values of Actual or Estimate.

Name	Type	Description
ReportItem	String	The ID of the item on the page being used to position the view. (This parameter must be called ByRef.)
ExecutionInfo	ExecutionInfo2 Object	A report execution object.

ToggleItem

Description: This method toggles the show/hide property of a report item. This method returns a Boolean that is True if the item is found.

Parameters:

Name	Type	Description
ToggleID	String	ID of the report item to toggle.

ReportService2005 Properties

The ReportService2005 class inherits from the HttpWebClientProtocol class, the SoapHttpClientProtocol class, and the WebClientProtocol class. The following public properties are either inherited properties used in the code samples in this book or properties defined in the ReportService2005 class itself.

BatchHeaderValue

Description: This property is used to hold a unique, system-generated batch ID. This batch ID serves to group multiple method calls from the ReportService2005 web service into a single batch. The batch ID is created by calling the CreateBatch method. The batch is committed by calling the ExecuteBatch method. The batch is rolled back by calling the CancelBatch method.

Credentials

Description: This property is used to hold the logon credentials used by the client application to authenticate on the ReportService2005 web service. Most ReportService2005 methods require authentication before they execute.

ItemNamespaceHeaderValue

Description: This property determines how items are retrieved with the GetProperties method. Items can be retrieved by passing an item identifier or the full path of the item.

PreAuthenticate

Description: When the PreAuthenticate property is True, the credentials are sent with the first web service request. When the PreAuthenticate property is False, the credentials are not sent to the server until the server issues an authentication challenge.

ServerInfoHeaderValue

Description: This property holds information about the current version of the report server.

ReportService2005 Methods

The ReportService2005 class inherits from the HttpWebClientProtocol class, the SoapHttpClientProtocol class, and the WebClientProtocol class. The following public methods are defined in the ReportService2005 class itself.

CancelBatch

Description: This method cancels the current batch of ReportService2005 method calls. The current batch is specified by the BatchHeader object and must be assigned to the BatchHeaderValue property of the ReportingService object. If the batch is cancelled, none of the method calls in the batch are executed.

This method does not return a value.

Parameters: None

CancelJob

Description: This method cancels an executing job. This method returns True if the job was cancelled; otherwise, it returns False.

Parameters:

Name	Type	Description
JobID	String	The ID of the job to cancel.

CreateBatch

Description: This method creates a batch ID that can be used to group ReportService2005 method calls into a batch. If an error occurs in one of the method calls in the batch, all previous operations performed by the batch are rolled back and subsequent operations are not attempted. This is useful when you have one ReportingService method call that depends on the successful completion of a prior ReportingService method call. For instance, you may call the CreateFolder method to create a new folder, and then call the CreateReport method to create a report in your new folder. You do not want to attempt to create the report if the folder cannot be created.

This method returns a batch ID string. This batch ID must be assigned to the batchID property of a BatchHeader object. The BatchHeader object must be assigned to the BatchHeaderValue property of the ReportService2005 object. The methods in the batch are not executed until the ExecuteBatch method is called to commit the batch.

Parameters: None

CreateDataDrivenSubscription

Description: This method creates a data-driven subscription for a report. This method returns a string containing the subscription ID.

Parameters:

Name	Type	Description
Report	String	The folder path and name of the report to which to subscribe.
ExtensionSettings	ExtensionSettings Object	An object containing the settings for the delivery extension (for example, e-mail delivery) used by this subscription.
DataRetrievalPlan	DataRetrievalPlan Object	An object containing the information necessary to connect to and retrieve the data used for the data-driven subscription.
Description	String	The description of this subscription.
EventType	String	Either TimedSubscription for a subscription triggered by a schedule or SnapshotUpdated for a subscription triggered by the updating of a snapshot.
MatchData	String	Information used to implement the event type.
Parameters	An Array of ParameterValueOrFieldReference Objects	An array of the values used for the report's parameters.

CreateDataSource

Description: This method creates a new shared data source. This method does not return a value.

Parameters:

Name	Type	Description
DataSource	String	The name of the data source.
Overwrite	Boolean	True if this data source should overwrite an existing data source; otherwise, False.
Parent	String	The path to the folder where the shared data source is created.
Definition	DataSourceDefinition Object	An object containing the connection information for the shared data source.
Properties	An Array of Property Objects	An array of property settings for the shared data source.

CreateFolder

Description: This method creates a new Reporting Services folder in the specified folder. This method does not return a value.

Parameters:

Name	Type	Description
Folder	String	The name of the new folder.
Parent	String	The path to the folder where the new folder is created.
Properties	An Array of Property Objects	An array of property settings for the folder.

CreateLinkedReport

Description: This method creates a new linked report in the specified folder. This method does not return a value.

Parameters:

Name	Type	Description
Report	String	The name of the new linked report.
Parent	String	The path to the folder where the new linked report is created.
Link	String	The folder path and name of the report to which the new linked report should be linked.
Properties	An Array of Property Objects	An array of property settings for the new linked report.

CreateModel

Description: This method creates a model for use with the Report Builder. This method returns an array of Warning objects.

Parameters:

Name	Type	Description
Model	String	The name of the new model.
Parent	String	The path to the folder where the new model is created.
Definition	An Array of Bytes	The model definition of this model.
Properties	An Array of Property Objects	The properties of this model.

CreateReport

Description: This method creates a new report in the specified folder. This method returns an array of Warning objects.

Parameters:

Name	Type	Description
Report	String	The name of the new report.
Parent	String	The path to the folder where the new report is created.
Overwrite	Boolean	True if an existing report with the same name in the same folder is to be replaced with the new report; otherwise, False.
Definition	An Array of Bytes	The Report Definition Language (RDL) defining the new report in base-64 binary.
Properties	An Array of Property Objects	An array of property settings for the report.

CreateReportHistorySnapshot

Description: This method creates a history snapshot of a specified report. The snapshot is created immediately, not at a scheduled time. This method call fails if report history is not enabled for the specified report.

This method returns a string representing the date and time at which the history snapshot was created.

Parameters:

Name	Type	Description
Report	String	The Reporting Services folder and the name of the report from which the history snapshot is created.
Warnings	An Array of Warning Objects	An array of warning messages generated when creating this report history snapshot. (This parameter must be called ByRef.)

CreateResource

Description: This method creates a new resource entry in the specified folder. This method does not return a value.

Parameters:

Name	Type	Description
Resource	String	The name of the new resource.
Parent	String	The path to the folder where the new resource is created.
Overwrite	Boolean	True if an existing resource with the same name in the same folder is to be replaced with the new resource; otherwise, False.
Contents	An Array of Bytes	The contents of the resource in base-64 binary.
MimeType	String	The MIME type of the resource (260 characters maximum).
Properties	An Array of Property Objects	An array of property settings for the resource.

CreateRole

Description: This method creates a new Reporting Services security role. This method does not return a value.

Parameters:

Name	Type	Description
Name	String	The name of the new role.
Description	String	The description of the new role.
Tasks	An Array of Task Objects	An array of Reporting Services tasks that may be executed by this role.

CreateSchedule

Description: This method creates a new shared schedule. This method returns a string containing the schedule ID.

Parameters:

Name	Type	Description
Name	String	The name of the schedule.
ScheduleDefinition	ScheduleDefinition Object	An object containing the information necessary to define a schedule.

CreateSubscription

Description: This method creates a new subscription for a report. This method returns a string containing the subscription ID.

Parameters:

Name	Type	Description
Report	String	The folder path and name of the report to which to subscribe.
ExtensionSettings	ExtensionSettings Object	An object containing the settings for the delivery extension (for example, e-mail delivery) used by this subscription.
Description	String	The description of this subscription.
EventType	String	Either TimedSubscription for a subscription triggered by a schedule or SnapshotUpdated for a subscription triggered by the updating of a snapshot.
MatchData	String	Information used to implement the event type.
Parameters	An Array of ParameterValue Objects	An array of the values used for the report's parameters.

DeleteItem

Description: This method removes an item from a Reporting Services folder. This can be a report, a resource, a shared data source, or a Reporting Services folder. If a report is deleted, any subscriptions and snapshots associated with that report are also deleted. This method does not return a value.

You cannot use this method to delete the My Reports folder or the Users folders created when the My Reports option is enabled.

Parameters:

Name	Type	Description
Item	String	The folder path and name of the item to be deleted.

DeleteReportHistorySnapshot

Description: This method removes a specified history snapshot. This method does not return a value.

Parameters:

Name	Type	Description
Report	String	The folder path and name of the report from which the history snapshot is to be deleted.
HistoryID	String	The ID of the history snapshot to delete.

DeleteRole

Description: This method removes a Reporting Services security role. This also removes all security assignments involving the deleted security role. This method does not return a value.

Parameters:

Name	Type	Description
Name	String	The name of the security role to delete.

DeleteSchedule

Description: This method removes a shared schedule. In addition, any snapshots or subscriptions using this schedule are also deleted. This method does not return a value.

Parameters:

Name	Type	Description
ScheduleID	String	The schedule ID of the schedule to delete.

DeleteSubscription

Description: This method removes a subscription from a report and it does not return a value.

Parameters:

Name	Type	Description
SubscriptionID	String	The subscription ID of the subscription to delete.

DisableDataSource

Description: This method disables a shared data source. Any reports and data-driven subscriptions that use this shared data source will not execute. This method does not return a value.

Parameters:

Name	Type	Description
DataSource	String	The folder path and name of the shared data source to be disabled.

EnableDataSource

Description: This method enables a shared data source and it does not return a value.

Parameters:

Name	Type	Description
DataSource	String	The folder path and name of the shared data source to be enabled.

ExecuteBatch

Description: This method executes all method calls associated with the current batch. (See the CreateBatch method.) The method calls in the batch are not executed until the ExecuteBatch method is called. This method does not return a value.

Parameters: None

FindItems

Description: This method finds reports, resources, shared data sources, and folders whose name or description satisfies the search conditions. The contents of the specified folder and all the folders contained within that folder are searched. This method returns an array of CatalogItem objects that satisfy the search conditions.

Parameters:

Name	Type	Description
Folder	String	The folder path and name of the folder that serves as the root of the search.
BooleanOperator	BooleanOperatorEnum	AND if all the search conditions must be True; otherwise, OR if only one of the search conditions must be True.
Conditions	An Array of SearchCondition Objects	An array containing the search conditions.

FireEvent

Description: This method triggers a Reporting Services event. You can use the ListEvents method to get an array of valid events and their parameters. This method does not return a value.

Parameters:

Name	Type	Description
EventType	String	The name of the event.
EventData	String	The values for the parameters associated with this event.

FlushCache

Description: This method clears any cached copies of the specified report. This includes cached copies created both by caching and by execution snapshots. It does not clear history snapshots. This method does not return a value.

Parameters:

Name	Type	Description
Report	String	The folder path and name of the report whose cache is to be flushed.

GenerateModel

Description: This method generates a default model based on a shared data source. This method returns an array of Warning objects containing any warning messages that may result from this operation.

Parameters:

Name	Type	Description
DataSource	String	The name of the data source upon which the model is to be created.
Model	String	The name of the model to be generated.
Parent	String	The name of the folder into which the new model should be placed.
Properties	Array of Property	The properties to be set on the model.

GetCacheOptions

Description: This method checks whether there is a cached copy of the specified report. If a cached copy of the report exists, the expiration time or the scheduled expiration information for the cached copy is returned in the Item parameter. This method returns a Boolean, which is True if caching is enabled for the report; otherwise, it returns False.

Parameters:

Name	Type	Description
Report	String	The folder path and name of the report whose cache options are to be checked.
Item	ExpirationDefinition Object	An object containing the expiration information for the cached copy of the report. (This parameter must be called ByRef.)

GetDataDrivenSubscriptionProperties

Description: This method gets information from the specified data-driven subscription. The data-driven subscription information is returned in several reference parameters. This method returns a string containing the ID of the owner of the specified data-driven subscription.

Parameters:

Name	Type	Description
DataDrivenSubscriptionID	String	The data-driven subscription ID of the data-driven subscription whose information is to be returned.
ExtensionSettings	ExtensionSettings Object	An object containing the extension settings. (This parameter must be called ByRef.)
DataRetrievalPlan	DataRetrievalPlan Object	An object containing the data source and query used to select data for the data-driven subscription. (This parameter must be called ByRef.)
Description	String	The description of the data-driven subscription. (This parameter must be called ByRef.)
Active	ActiveState Object	An object containing the active state of the data-driven subscription. (This parameter must be called ByRef.)
Status	String	The status of the data-driven subscription. (This parameter must be called ByRef.)
EventType	String	The event type associated with the data-driven subscription. (This parameter must be called ByRef.)
MatchData	String	The parameter data for the event type associated with the data-driven subscription. (This parameter must be called ByRef.)
Parameters	An Array of ParameterValueOrFieldReference Objects	An array of parameter information for the report associated with the data-driven subscription. (This parameter must be called ByRef.)

GetDataSourceContents

Description: This method gets the information for the specified shared data source. This method returns a DataSourceDefinition object containing the information for the shared data source.

Parameters:

Name	Type	Description
DataSource	String	The folder path and name of the shared data source whose information is to be returned.

GetExecutionOptions

Description: This method gets the execution options for the specified report. This method returns an ExecutionSettingEnum value of either Live, indicating the report is to be executed, or Snapshot, indicating the report is to be rendered from a history snapshot.

Parameters:

Name	Type	Description
Report	String	The folder path and name of the report whose execution option is to be returned.
Item	ScheduleDefinitionOrReference Object	An object containing a schedule definition or a reference to a shared schedule. (This parameter must be called ByRef.)

GetExtensionSettings

Description: This method gets the parameter information for the specified delivery extension. This method returns an array of ExtensionParameter objects containing the parameter information.

Parameters:

Name	Type	Description
Extension	String	The name of the delivery extension.

GetItemDataSourcePrompts

Description: This method gets the prompt strings for all the data sources tied to the specified item. This method returns an array of DataSourcePrompt objects.

Parameters:

Name	Type	Description
Item	String	The folder path and name of the item whose data source prompts are to be returned.

GetItemDataSources

Description: This method gets the data sources tied to the specified item. This method returns an array of DataSource objects.

Parameters:

Name	Type	Description
Item	String	The folder path and name of the item whose data sources are to be returned.

GetItemType

Description: This method gets the type of the specified Reporting Services item. This method returns an ItemTypeEnum value, as shown here:

Value	Description
Unknown	Invalid Item Path or Item of Unknown Type.
Folder	This item is a folder.
Report	This item is a report.
Resource	This item is a resource.
LinkedReport	This item is a linked report.
DataSource	This item is a shared data source.
Model	This item is a report model.

Parameters:

Name	Type	Description
Item	String	The folder path and name of the item whose type is to be returned.

GetModelDefinition

Description: This method gets the definition of the specified model. This method returns an array of bytes.

Parameters:

Name	Type	Description
Model	String	The folder path and name of the model whose definition is to be returned.

GetModelItemPermissions

Description: This method gets the permissions associated with the specified model item. This method returns an array of strings.

Parameters:

Name	Type	Description
Model	String	The folder path and name of the model that contains the item whose permissions are to be returned.
ModelItemID	String	The ID of the model item whose permissions are to be returned. If omitted, the permissions of the model root are returned.

GetModelItemPolicies

Description: This method gets the Reporting Services security policies associated with the specified model item. This method returns an array of Policy objects.

Parameters:

Name	Type	Description
Model	String	The folder path and name of the model that contains the item whose policies are to be returned.
ModelItemID	String	The ID of the model item whose policies are to be returned. If omitted, the policies of the model root are returned.
InheritParent	Boolean	True if the policies are inherited from the parent folder; otherwise, False. (This parameter must be called ByRef.)

GetPermissions

Description: This method gets the tasks that may be executed on the specified Reporting Services item by the logon credentials currently being used to access the ReportService2005 web service. This method returns an array of strings, with each string containing the name of one task the logon credentials have permission to execute.

Parameters:

Name	Type	Description
Item	String	The folder path and the name of the item whose permissions are to be returned.

GetPolicies

Description: This method gets the Reporting Services security policies associated with the specified Reporting Services item and returns an array of Policy objects.

Parameters:

Name	Type	Description
Item	String	The folder path and the name of the item whose policies are to be returned.
InheritParent	Boolean	True if the policies are inherited from the parent folder; otherwise, False. (This parameter must be called ByRef.)

GetProperties

Description: This method gets the values of each specified property of the Reporting Services item and returns an array of Property objects.

Parameters:

Name	Type	Description
Item	String	The folder path and the name of the item whose properties are to be returned.
Properties	An Array of Property Objects	An array of the properties whose values you want returned.

GetRenderResource

Description: This method gets a resource for the specified rendering extension. This method returns a byte array containing a base-64 encoding of the requested resource.

Parameters:

Name	Type	Description
Format	String	The rendering extension format (for example, PDF or XML).
DeviceInfo	String	A device-specific setting for the specified rendering format.
MimeType	String	The MIME type of the resource. (This parameter must be called ByRef.)

GetReportDefinition

Description: This method gets the definition for the specified report and returns a byte array with the report definition as a base-64–encoded RDL structure.

Parameters:

Name	Type	Description
Report	String	The folder path and name of the report whose definition is to be returned.

GetReportHistoryLimit

Description: This method gets the maximum number of history snapshots that may be saved for the specified report. This method returns an integer representing the history snapshot limit.

Parameters:

Name	Type	Description
Report	String	The folder path and name of the report whose snapshot history limit is to be returned.
IsSystem	Boolean	True if the report history snapshot limit comes from the system limit; otherwise, False. (This parameter must be called ByRef.)
SystemLimit	Integer	The system limit for report history snapshots. (This parameter must be called ByRef.)

GetReportHistoryOptions

Description: This method gets the report history snapshot options and properties for the specified report. This method returns a Boolean value that is True if a history snapshot is enabled and False otherwise.

Parameters:

Name	Type	Description
Report	String	The folder path and name of the report whose snapshot history options are to be returned.
KeepExecutionSnapshots	Boolean	True if a history snapshot is enabled; otherwise, False. (This parameter must be called ByRef.)
Item	ScheduleDefinitionOrReferenceObject	An object that contains information about a schedule definition or a reference to a shared schedule used to create the history snapshot. (This parameter must be called ByRef.)

GetReportLink

Description: This method gets the name of the report to which the specified linked report is tied. This method returns a string containing the folder path and the name of the report.

Parameters:

Name	Type	Description
Report	String	The folder path and name of the linked report whose underlying report is to be returned.

GetReportParameters

Description: This method gets the report parameter properties for the specified report. This method returns an array of ReportParameter objects.

Parameters:

Name	Type	Description
Report	String	The folder path and name of the report whose parameter properties are to be returned.
HistoryID	String	Set this parameter to a history ID to retrieve the parameters for a history snapshot; otherwise, set it to Nothing (Null for C#).
ForRendering	Boolean	Set this parameter to True to return the parameter properties used during the creation of the specified history snapshot; otherwise, set it to False.
Values	An Array of ParameterValue Objects	An array of the values to be validated for the report.
Credentials	An Array of DataSourceCredentials Objects	An array specifying data source credentials to be used when validating parameters.

GetResourceContents

Description: This method gets the contents of a Reporting Services resource and returns a byte array containing the base-64-encoded contents of the resource.

Parameters:

Name	Type	Description
Resource	String	The folder path and name of the resource whose contents are to be returned.
MimeType	String	The MIME type of the resource. (This parameter must be called ByRef.)

GetRoleProperties

Description: This method gets a description of the specified role, along with the tasks this role is able to complete. This method returns an array of Task objects.

Parameters:

Name	Type	Description
Name	String	The name of the role whose description and tasks are to be returned.
Description	String	The description of the role. (This parameter must be called ByRef.)

GetScheduleProperties

Description: This method gets the properties of the specified shared schedule. This method returns a Schedule object.

Parameters:

Name	Type	Description
ScheduleID	String	The schedule ID of the schedule to be returned.

GetSubscriptionProperties

Description: This method gets the properties of the specified subscription. This method returns a string containing the ID of the owner of this subscription.

Parameters:

Name	Type	Description
SubscriptionID	String	The subscription ID of the subscription whose properties are to be returned.
ExtensionSettings	An ExtensionSettings Object	An object containing the settings for the delivery extension associated with this subscription. (This parameter must be called ByRef.)
Description	String	The description of the subscription. (This parameter must be called ByRef.)
Active	An ActiveState Object	An object containing the active state of the subscription. (This parameter must be called ByRef.)
Status	String	The status of the subscription. (This parameter must be called ByRef.)
EventType	String	Either TimedSubscription for a subscription triggered by a schedule or SnapshotUpdated for a subscription triggered by the updating of a snapshot. (This parameter must be called ByRef.)
MatchData	String	Information used to implement the event type. (This parameter must be called ByRef.)
Parameters	An Array of ParameterValue Objects	An array of the values used for the report's parameters. (This parameter must be called ByRef.)

GetSystemPermissions

Description: This method gets the system permissions assigned to the logon credentials currently being used to access the ReportService2005 web service. This method returns an array of strings that contain the system permissions.

Parameters: None

GetSystemPolicies

Description: This method gets the system policy for this Reporting Services installation. This method returns an array of Policy objects.

Parameters: None

GetSystemProperties

Description: This method gets the value of each specified system property. This method returns an array of Property objects.

Parameters:

Name	Type	Description
Properties	An Array of Property Objects	An array of properties and their values.

GetUserModel

Description: This method gets the semantic portion of a model for which the current user has access permission. This method returns an array of bytes.

Parameters:

Name	Type	Description
Model	String	The folder path and name of the model whose user model is to be retrieved.
Perspective	String	The ID of the perspective whose user model is to be retrieved.

InheritModelItemParentSecurity

Description: This method sets the mode to inherit its security from its parent. As a result, any policies assigned specifically for this model are deleted. This method does not return a value.

Parameters:

Name	Type	Description
Model	String	The folder path and name of the model that contains the item whose policies are to be inherited.
ModelItemID	String	The ID of the model item whose policies are to be inherited.

InheritParentSecurity

Description: This method sets the Reporting Services item to inherit its security from its parent folder. As a result, any role assignments made specifically for this item are deleted. This method does not return a value.

Parameters:

Name	Type	Description
Item	String	The folder path and name of the item whose security is to be inherited.

ListChildren

Description: This method lists all the Reporting Services items that are children of the specified folder. The list includes only those items that the logon credentials currently being used to access the ReportService2005 web service have a right to view. This method returns an array of CatalogItem objects.

Parameters:

Name	Type	Description
Item	String	The folder path and name of the folder whose children are to be listed.
Recursive	Boolean	True if the list should recurse down the folder tree; otherwise, False.

ListDependentItems

Description: This method lists all the Reporting Services items dependent on the specified item. This method returns an array of CatalogItem objects.

Parameters:

Name	Type	Description
Item	String	The folder path and name of the folder whose dependents are to be listed.

ListEvents

Description: This method lists the events supported by this Reporting Services installation and returns an array of Event objects.

Parameters: None

ListExtensions

Description: This method lists the extensions of the specified type defined for this Reporting Services installation. It returns an array of Extension objects.

Parameters:

Name	Type	Description
ExtensionType	ExtensionTypeEnum	Delivery for delivery extensions, Render for rendering extensions, Data for data access extensions, or All for all of the above.

ListJobs

Description: This method lists the jobs currently running on this Reporting Services installation and returns an array of Job objects.

Parameters: None

ListModelDrillthroughReports

Description: This method lists the reports tied to a specific entity in a model. It also returns an array of ModelDrillthroughReport objects.

Parameters:

Name	Type	Description
Model	String	The folder path and name of the model that contains the item whose drillthrough reports are to be listed.
ModelItemID	String	The ID of the model item whose drillthrough reports are to be listed.

ListModelItemChildren

Description: This method lists all the children of the specified model item. This method returns an array of ModelItem objects.

Parameters:

Name	Type	Description
Model	String	The folder path and name of the model that contains the item whose children are to be listed.
ModelItemID	String	The ID of the model item whose children are to be listed. If omitted, the children of the model root of the model are listed.
Recursive	Boolean	True if the list should recurse through the model tree; otherwise, False.

ListModelPerspective

Description: This method lists the perspectives of the specified model and it returns an array of ModelCatalogItem objects.

Parameters:

Name	Type	Description
Model	String	The folder path and name of the model whose perspectives are to be listed.

ListReportHistory

Description: This method lists the history snapshots and their properties for the specified report. It also returns an array of ReportHistorySnapshot objects.

Parameters:

Name	Type	Description
Report	String	The folder path and name of the report whose history snapshots are to be listed.

ListRoles

Description: This method lists the roles defined for this Reporting Services installation. This method returns an array of Role objects.

Parameters:

Name	Type	Description
SecurityScope	SecurityScopeEnum	The security scope of the roles to be listed. Valid values are All, Catalog, Model, and System.

ListScheduledReports

Description: This method lists the reports using the specified shared schedule and returns an array of CatalogItem objects.

Parameters:

Name	Type	Description
ScheduleID	String	The schedule ID of the shared schedule whose reports are to be listed.

ListSchedules

Description: This method lists all the shared schedules and returns an array of Schedule objects.

Parameters: None

ListSecureMethods

Description: This method lists all the ReportService2005 web service methods that require a secure connection. This method returns an array of strings containing the method names.

Parameters: None

ListSubscriptions

Description: This method lists the subscriptions a specified user has created for a specified report. It also returns an array of Subscription objects.

Parameters:

Name	Type	Description
Report	String	The folder path and name of the report whose subscriptions are to be listed.
Owner	String	The name of the owner whose subscriptions are to be retrieved.

ListSubscriptionsUsingDataSource

Description: This method lists the subscriptions using the specified shared data source and returns an array of Subscription objects.

Parameters:

Name	Type	Description
DataSource	String	The folder path and name of the shared data source whose subscriptions are to be listed.

ListTasks

Description: This method lists the tasks defined for this Reporting Services installation and returns an array of Task objects.

Parameters:

Name	Type	Description
SecurityScope	SecurityScopeEnum	The security scope of the tasks to be listed. Valid values are All, Catalog, Model, and System.

Logoff

Description: This method logs off the current user making requests of the ReportService2005 web service. It must be called using an HTTPS (SSL) request. This method does not return a value.

Parameters: None

LogonUser

Description: This method logs a user on to the Report Server web service. It does not return a value. An authentication cookie is passed back in the header of the HTTPS request.

Parameters:

Name	Type	Description
UserName	String	The user name to use for the logon.
Password	String	The password to use for the logon.
Authority	String	The authority to use when authenticating this user. This parameter is optional.

MoveItem

Description: This method moves the specified Reporting Services item to the specified folder path. It does not return a value.

Parameters:

Name	Type	Description
Item	String	The folder path and name of the item to be moved.
Target	String	The folder path to which this item is to be moved.

PauseSchedule

Description: This method pauses the execution of the specified schedule. It does not return a value.

Parameters:

Name	Type	Description
ScheduleID	String	The ID of the schedule to pause.

PrepareQuery

Description: This method determines the fields to be returned by the specified query running against the specified data source. This information can be used by the CreateDataDrivenSubscription and SetDataDrivenSubscriptionProperties methods. This method returns a DataSetDefinition object.

Parameters:

Name	Type	Description
DataSource	DataSource Object	An object containing the data source information.
DataSet	DataSetDefinition Object	An object containing the query to return the fields for the data-driven subscription.
Changed	Boolean	True if the dataset passed in the DataSet parameter is different from the dataset returned in the DataSetDefinition object; otherwise, False. (This parameter must be called ByRef.)

RegenerateModel

Description: This method updates a default model based on a shared data source. The regeneration will make updates based on changes to the data source schema. This method returns an array of Warning objects containing any warning messages that may result from this operation.

Parameters:

Name	Type	Description
Model	String	The name of the model to be regenerated.

RemoveAllModelItemPolicies

Description: This method deletes all policies associated with the items in the specified model. It does not return a value.

Parameters:

Name	Type	Description
Model	String	The folder path and name of the model.

ResumeSchedule

Description: This method resumes a schedule that has been paused. It does not return a value.

Parameters:

Name	Type	Description
ScheduleID	String	The ID of the schedule to resume.

SetCacheOptions

Description: This method sets the caching options for the specified report. It does not return a value.

Parameters:

Name	Type	Description
Report	String	The folder path and name of the report whose caching options are to be set.
CacheReport	Boolean	True if each execution of the report is to be cached; otherwise, False.
Item	ExpirationDefinition Object	An object containing information telling when the cached report is to expire.

SetDataDrivenSubscriptionProperties

Description: This method sets the properties of a data-driven subscription. It does not return a value.

Parameters:

Name	Type	Description
DataDrivenSubscriptionID	String	The ID of the data-driven subscription whose properties are to be set.
ExtensionSettings	ExtensionSettings Object	An object containing the settings for the delivery extension (for example, e-mail delivery) used by this subscription.
DataRetrievalPlan	DataRetrievalPlan Object	An object containing the information necessary to connect to and retrieve the data used for the data-driven subscription.
Description	String	The description of this subscription.
EventType	String	Either TimedSubscription for a subscription triggered by a schedule or SnapshotUpdated for a subscription triggered by the updating of a snapshot.
MatchData	String	Information used to implement the event type.
Parameters	An Array of ParameterValueOrFieldReference Objects	An array of the values used for the report's parameters.

SetDataSourceContents

Description: This method sets the properties of a shared data source. It does not return a value.

Parameters:

Name	Type	Description
DataSource	String	The name of the data source.
Definition	DataSourceDefinition Object	An object containing the connection information for the shared data source.

SetExecutionOptions

Description: This method sets the execution options (either Live or Snapshot) of the specified report. It does not return a value.

Parameters:

Name	Type	Description
Report	String	The folder path and name of the report whose execution option is to be set.
ExecutionSetting	ExecutionSettingEnum	Either Live if the report is to be executed from the data sources or Snapshot if the report is to come from an execution snapshot.
Item	ScheduleDefinitionOrReference Object	An object containing the information for a schedule or a reference to a shared schedule. This schedule is used to create the execution snapshot and is valid only if the ExecutionSetting is Snapshot.

SetItemDataSources

Description: This method sets the properties for data sources associated with the specified item. It does not return a value.

Parameters:

Name	Type	Description
Item	String	The folder path and name of the item for which the data source properties are to be set.
DataSources	An Array of DataSource Objects	An array of data sources and their properties.

SetModelDefinition

Description: This method sets the model definition of the specified model. This method returns an array of Warning objects containing any warning messages that may result from this operation.

Parameters:

Name	Type	Description
Model	String	The folder path and name of the model for which the model definition is to be set.
Definition	An Array of Bytes	A byte array containing the model definition in base-64 binary.

SetModelDrillthroughReports

Description: This method associates a set of drill-through reports with the specified model. It does not return a value.

Parameters:

Name	Type	Description
Model	String	The folder path and name of the model.
ModelItemID	String	The ID of the model item.
Reports	Array of ModelDrillthroughReport Objects	The drill-through reports to set for the model item.

SetModelItemPolicies

Description: This method sets the security policies for the specified model item. It does not return a value.

Parameters:

Name	Type	Description
Model	String	The folder path and name of the model.
ModelItemID	String	The ID of the model item.
Policies	An Array of Policy Objects	An array of security policy information.

SetPolicies

Description: This method sets the security policies for the specified report. It does not return a value.

Parameters:

Name	Type	Description
Item	String	The folder path and name of the Reporting Services item for which the security policies are to be set.
Policies	An Array of Policy Objects	An array of security policy information.

SetProperties

Description: This method sets the properties of the specified Reporting Services item. This method does not return a value.

Parameters:

Name	Type	Description
Item	String	The folder path and name of the Reporting Services item for which the properties are to be set.
Properties	An Array of Property Objects	An array of properties and their values.

SetReportDefinition

Description: This method sets the report definition of the specified report. It returns an array of Warning objects containing any warning messages that may result from this operation.

Parameters:

Name	Type	Description
Report	String	The folder path and name of the report for which the report definition is to be set.
Definition	An Array of Bytes	A byte array containing the Report Definition Language (RDL) in base-64 binary.

SetReportHistoryLimit

Description: This method sets the limit for the number of history snapshots that may be saved for the specified report. It does not return a value.

Parameters:

Name	Type	Description
Report	String	The folder path and name of the report for which the history snapshot limit is to be set.
UseSystem	Boolean	True if the system default history snapshot limit is to be used with this report; otherwise, False.
HistoryLimit	Integer	The limit for the number of history snapshots saved for this report.

SetReportHistoryOptions

Description: This method sets the options specifying when a history snapshot is created for the specified report. This method does not return a value.

Parameters:

Name	Type	Description
Report	String	The folder path and name of the report for which the history snapshot options are to be set.
EnableManualSnapshotCreation	Boolean	True if snapshots can be created using the CreateReportHistorySnapshot method; otherwise, False.
KeepExecutionSnapshots	Boolean	True if execution snapshots are saved as history snapshots; otherwise, False.
Item	ScheduleDefinitionOrReference Object	An object containing the information for a schedule or a reference to a shared schedule. This schedule is used to create the history snapshot.

SetReportLink

Description: This method sets the report to which the specified linked report should be linked. It does not return any value.

Parameters:

Name	Type	Description
Report	String	The folder path and name of the linked report.
Link	String	The folder path and name of the report to which this should be linked.

SetReportParameters

Description: This method sets the parameter property for the specified report. It does not return a value.

Parameters:

Name	Type	Description
Report	String	The folder path and name of the report whose parameter property should be set.
Parameters	An Array of ReportParameter Objects	An array of information on report parameter properties.

SetResourceContents

Description: This method sets the contents of a Reporting Services resource. It does not return a value.

Parameters:

Name	Type	Description
Resource	String	The folder path and name of the resource whose contents are to be set.
Contents	An Array of Bytes	The contents of the resource in base-64 binary.
MimeType	String	The MIME type of the resource. This is optional and is returned through an out parameter.

SetRoleProperties

Description: This method sets the properties of a security role. This method does not return a value.

Parameters:

Name	Type	Description
Name	String	The folder path and name of the security role whose properties are to be set.
Description	String	The description of the security role.
Tasks	An Array of Task Objects	An array of Reporting Services tasks that may be executed by this role.

SetScheduleProperties

Description: This method sets the properties of a shared schedule. It does not return a value.

Parameters:

Name	Type	Description
Name	String	The name of the shared schedule.
ScheduleID	String	The ID of the shared schedule whose properties are to be set.
ScheduleDefinition	ScheduleDefinition Object	An object containing the information necessary to define a schedule.

SetSubscriptionProperties

Description: This method sets the properties of a subscription. It does not return a value.

Parameters:

Name	Type	Description
SubscriptionID	String	The ID of the subscription whose properties are to be set.
ExtensionSettings	ExtensionSettings Object	An object containing the settings for the delivery extension (for example, e-mail delivery) used by this subscription.
Description	String	The description of this subscription.
EventType	String	Either TimedSubscription for a subscription triggered by a schedule or SnapshotUpdated for a subscription triggered by the updating of a snapshot.
MatchData	String	Information used to implement the event type.
Parameters	An Array of ParameterValue Objects	An array of the values used for the report's parameters.

SetSystemPolicies

Description: This method sets the system policies for this Reporting Services installation. It does not return a value.

Parameters:

Name	Type	Description
Policies	An Array of Policy Objects	An array of the values used to set the system policies.

SetSystemProperties

Description: This method sets the specified system properties. It does not return a value.

Parameters:

Name	Type	Description
Properties	An Array of Property Objects	An array of properties and their values.

UpdateReportExecutionSnapshot

Description: This method updates the report execution snapshot for the specified report. It does not return a value.

Parameters:

Name	Type	Description
Report	String	The folder path and name of the report whose execution snapshot is to be updated.

ValidateExtensionSettings

Description: This method validates the settings for a Reporting Services extension and returns an array of ExtensionParameter objects.

Parameters:

Name	Type	Description
Extension	String	The name of the extension.
ParameterValues	An Array of ParameterValueOrFieldReference Objects	An array of parameter values to be validated.

ReportService2006

One new property and three new methods have been added to the ReportService2006 web service.

TrustedUserHeaderValue Property

Description: This property holds a TrustedUserHeader object, which contains the user name and security token for the trusted user account. This property supports the Reporting Services infrastructure and is not intended to be directly accessed by user code.

ListMySubscriptions Method

Description: This method lists the subscriptions created by the current user for the given site. This method returns an array of Subscription objects.

Parameters:

Name	Type	Description
Site	String	The site where the subscriptions come from.

ListParents Method

Description: This method lists the parent items for a given item. This method returns an array of CatalogItem objects.

Parameters:

Name	Type	Description
Item	String	The item whose parents are to be returned.

ListReportSubscriptions Method

Description: This method lists the subscriptions created for the given report. This method returns an array of Subscription objects.

Parameters:

Name	Type	Description
Report	String	The path and name of the report.

Items Removed

The following properties have been removed from the ReportService2006 web service:

- ▶ BatchHeaderValue
- ▶ ItemNamspaceHeaderValue

The following methods have been removed from the ReportService2006 web service:

- ▶ CancelBatch
- ▶ CreateBatch
- ▶ CreateLinkedReport
- ▶ CreateRole
- ▶ DeleteRole
- ▶ ExecuteBatch
- ▶ FindItems
- ▶ GetRenderResource
- ▶ GetReportLink
- ▶ GetSystemPolicies
- ▶ ListAllSubscriptions

- ▶ ListSubscriptions
- ▶ ListSubscriptionsUsingDataSource
- ▶ Logoff
- ▶ LogonUser
- ▶ SetReportLink
- ▶ SetRoleProperties
- ▶ SetSystemPolicies

ReportService2005 and ReportExecution2005 Web Service Classes

The Namespace for Reporting Services Web Service Classes

The namespace for Reporting Services web service classes is the same as the namespace used for web services themselves. If the ReportService2005 web service has a namespace of

```
{ComputerName}.ReportService
```

then the namespace for each web service class associated with the ReportService2005 web service would be

```
{ComputerName}.{ClassName}
```

Where {ComputerName} is the name of the computer hosting the web service and {ClassName} is the name of one of the classes. The description for each class will tell you whether it is a class of the ReportService2005 web service or the ReportExecution2005 web service.

The "Specified" Properties

Many of the properties for these classes have a corresponding property of the same name, with "Specified" on the end. These properties are used to let any code using the class know if a value was specified for this property or if it was left with no value specified. In most cases, these "specified" properties are added to correspond to class properties with data types of Boolean, date, and others that cannot easily represent an empty state.

For example, the DataSourceDefinition class has a property named Enabled. When this property is set to True, the data source is enabled. When this property is set to False, the data source is disabled. If you do not specify a value for this property, it defaults to False and the data source is disabled. To prevent this from happening, a property called

EnabledSpecified of type Boolean has been added to the DataSourceDefinition class. This additional property lets the code using this class know whether the value for the Enabled property should be used because it was specified by the user or if it should be ignored because it was not specified.

As the developer, you must make sure these "specified" properties are set properly. Any time you provide a value for a property with a corresponding "specified" property, you need to set that "specified" property to True. If you do not take care of this in your code, these property values will be ignored by the methods using these classes.

In some cases, "specified" properties were added for read-only class properties. This seems to make no sense, because you cannot specify a value for a read-only property. Nevertheless, there they are. In these cases, the "specified" properties can be safely ignored.

ActiveState

Description: An object of the ActiveState class type is returned by the GetSubscriptionProperties method to provide information on various error conditions that may be present in a specified subscription. In addition to the properties listed here, this class includes a "specified" property for each of the properties shown. These "specified" properties can be ignored. This is a class of the ReportService2005 web service.

Properties:

Property	Type	Description
DeliveryExtensionRemoved	Boolean	True if the delivery extension used by the subscription has been removed; otherwise, False. (Read-only.)
InvalidParameterValue	Boolean	True if a parameter value saved with a subscription is invalid; otherwise, False. (Read-only.)
MissingParameterValue	Boolean	True if a required parameter value is not saved with a subscription; otherwise, False. (Read-only.)
SharedDataSourceRemoved	Boolean	True if a shared data source used with a subscription has been removed; otherwise, False. (Read-only.)
UnknownReportParameter	Boolean	True if a parameter name saved with a subscription is not recognized as a parameter for this report; otherwise, False. (Read-only.)

BatchHeader

Description: This class contains the Batch ID for a batch of web-service method calls. This is a class of the ReportService2005 web service.

Properties:

Property	Type	Description
BatchID	String	The identifier for a batch.

CatalogItem

Description: This class contains information about a single item in the Report Catalog. This may be a Reporting Services folder, a report, a shared data source, or a resource. This is a class of the ReportService2005 web service.

Properties:

Property	Type	Description
CreatedBy	String	The name of the user who created the item. (Read-only.)
CreationDate	Date	The date and time the item was created. (Read-only.)
CreationDateSpecified	Boolean	True if a value for CreationDate is specified; otherwise, False.
Description	String	The description of the item.
ExecutionDate	Date	The date and time a report item was last executed. (Valid only for report items.) (Read-only.)
ExecutionDateSpecified	Boolean	True if a value for ExecutionDate is specified; otherwise, False.
Hidden	Boolean	True if the item is hidden; otherwise, False.
HiddenSpecified	Boolean	True if a value for Hidden is specified; otherwise, False.
ID	String	The ID of the item. (Read-only.)
MimeType	String	The MIME type of a resource item. (Valid only for resource items.) (Read-only.)
ModifiedBy	String	The name of the user who last modified the item. (Read-only.)
ModifiedDate	Date	The date and time the item was last modified. (Read-only.)
ModifiedDateSpecified	Boolean	True if a value for ModifiedDate is specified; otherwise, False.
Name	String	The name of the item.
Path	String	The folder path to the item. (Read-only.)
Size	Integer	The size of the item in bytes. (Read-only.)
SizeSpecified	Boolean	True if a value for Size is specified; otherwise, False.
Type	ItemTypeEnum	The type of the item. Valid values are Unknown, Folder, Report, Resource, LinkedReport, and Datasource. (Read-only.)
VirtualPath	String	The virtual path to the item. This is populated only when viewing items under the MyReports folder. (Read-only.)

DailyRecurrence

Description: This class contains the time that must elapse, in days, before a schedule recurs. This class inherits from RecurrencePattern. This is a class of the ReportService2005 web service.

Properties:

Property	Type	Description
DaysInterval	Integer	The number of days before a schedule recurs.

DataRetrievalPlan

Description: This class is used to define the data to be selected for a data-driven subscription. This is a class of the ReportService2005 web service.

Properties:

Property	Type	Description
DataSet	DataSetDefinition	Defines the dataset to use with the data-driven subscription.
Item	DataSourceDefinitionOrReference	Defines the data source to use with the data-driven subscription.

DataSetDefinition

Description: This class contains the information necessary to define a dataset. This is a class of the ReportService2005 web service.

Properties:

Property	Type	Description
AccentSensitivity	SensitivityEnum	True if this dataset is sensitive to accents. False if this dataset is not sensitive to accents. Auto if the sensitivity setting should be determined from the data provider.
AccentSensitivitySpecified	Boolean	True if a value for AccentSensitivity is specified; otherwise, False.
CaseSensitivity	SensitivityEnum	True if this dataset is case-sensitive. False if this dataset is not case-sensitive. Auto if the sensitivity setting should be determined from the data provider.
CaseSensitivitySpecified	Boolean	True if a value for CaseSensitivity is specified; otherwise, False.
Collation	String	The locale used when sorting the data in the dataset. (Uses the SQL Server collation codes.)
Fields	An Array of Field Objects	An array containing the field information.

Property	Type	Description
KanatypeSensitivity	SensitivityEnum	True if this dataset is kanatype-sensitive. False if this dataset is not kanatype-sensitive. Auto if the sensitivity setting should be determined from the data provider. (This is used only for some Japanese character sets.)
KanatypeSensitivitySpecified	Boolean	True if a value for KanatypeSensitivity has been specified; otherwise, False.
Name	String	The name of the dataset.
Query	QueryDefinition Object	An object containing the query used to retrieve the data.
WidthSensitivity	SensitivityEnum	True if this dataset is width-sensitive. False if this dataset is not width-sensitive. Auto if the sensitivity setting should be determined from the data provider.
WidthSensitivitySpecified	Boolean	True if a value for WidthSensitivity is specified; otherwise, False.

DataSource

Description: This class contains either a reference to a shared data source or an object with the information necessary to define a data source. This is a class of the ReportService2005 web service.

Properties:

Property	Type	Description
Item	A DataSourceReference Object or a DataSourceDefinition Object	If the data source is referencing a shared data source, this is a DataSourceReference object; otherwise, this is a DataSourceDefinition object.
Name	String	The name of the data source.

DataSourceCredentials

Description: This class contains the credentials used to access a data source. This is a class of the ReportExecution2005 and ReportService2005 web service.

Properties:

Property	Type	Description
DataSourceName	String	The name of the data source that uses these credentials.
Password	String	The password used to connect to the data source.
UserName	String	The user name used to connect to the data source.

DataSourceDefinition

Description: This class contains the information necessary to define a data source. This class inherits from DataSourceDefinitionOrReference. This is a class of the ReportService2005 web service.

Properties:

Property	Type	Description
ConnectString	String	The connection string.
CredentialRetrieval	CredentialRetrievalEnum	Prompt if the user is to be prompted for credentials when accessing this data source. Store if the credentials are stored in the data source definition. Integrated if Windows Authentication is to be used to access the data source. None if no credentials are required.
Enabled	Boolean	True if the data source is enabled; otherwise, False.
EnabledSpecified	Boolean	True if a value for Enabled is specified; otherwise, False.
Extension	String	The name of the data source extension. Valid values include SQL, OLEDB, ODBC, and a custom extension.
ImpersonateUser	Boolean	True if the report server is to impersonate the user after a connection has been made to the data source; otherwise, False.
ImpersonateUserSpecified	Boolean	True if a value for ImpersonateUser is specified; otherwise, False.
Password	String	The password when the credentials are stored in the data source definition.
Prompt	String	The message used when prompting the user for credentials.
UseOriginalConnectString	Boolean	True if the data source should revert to the original connection string; otherwise, False.
UserName	String	The user name when the credentials are stored in the data source definition.
WindowsCredentials	Boolean	True if the stored credentials are Windows credentials. False if the stored credentials are database credentials.

DataSourceDefinitionOrReference

Description: This class serves as a parent class. Any class that inherits from the DataSourceDefinitionOrReference class can be used where a Data SourceDefinitionOrReference type object is required. This is a class of the ReportService2005 web service.

Classes Inheriting from This Class:

Class Name	Description
DataSourceDefinition	Used when a data source definition is to be specified.
DataSourceReference	Used when a reference to a shared data source is to be specified.

DataSourcePrompt

Description: This class contains information about the message displayed to the user when prompting for data source credentials. This is a class of the ReportExecution2005 and ReportService2005 web services.

Properties:

Property	Type	Description
DataSourceID	String	The unique ID of a data source.
Name	String	The name of the data source.
Prompt	String	The prompt message.

DataSourceReference

Description: This class contains a reference to a shared data source. This class inherits from DataSourceDefinitionOrReference. This is a class of the ReportService2005 web service.

Properties:

Property	Type	Description
Reference	String	The folder path and name of the shared data source.

DaysOfWeekSelector

Description: This class contains information for the days of the week on which a schedule runs. This is a class of the ReportService2005 web service.

Properties:

Property	Type	Description
Friday	Boolean	True if the schedule is to run on Friday; otherwise, False.
Monday	Boolean	True if the schedule is to run on Monday; otherwise, False.
Saturday	Boolean	True if the schedule is to run on Saturday; otherwise, False.
Sunday	Boolean	True if the schedule is to run on Sunday; otherwise, False.
Thursday	Boolean	True if the schedule is to run on Thursday; otherwise, False.
Tuesday	Boolean	True if the schedule is to run on Tuesday; otherwise, False.
Wednesday	Boolean	True if the schedule is to run on Wednesday; otherwise, False.

DocumentMapNode

Description: This class contains the definition of a single node in a document map. This is a class of the ReportExecution2005 web service.

Properties:

Property	Type	Description
Children	Array of DocumentMapNode Objects	The children of the document map node.
Label	String	The label of the document map node.
UniqueName	String	The unique name of the report item or grouping pointed to by this document map node.

ExecutionInfo

Description: This class describes the state of the current report execution. This is a class of the ReportExecution2005 web service.

Properties:

Property	Type	Description
AllowQueryExecution	Boolean	True if the user can provide values for the parameters used in the query.
CredentialsRequired	Boolean	True if the report requires credentials to be supplied.
DataSourcePrompts	Array of DataSourcePrompt Objects	The prompt strings for each data source used by the report.
Execution	DateTime DateTime	The date and time the snapshot associated with the execution was created.
ExecutionID	String	The unique identifier of this report execution.
ExpirationDateTime	DateTime	The date and time this execution expires.
HasDocumentMap	Boolean	True if the report has a document map.
HasSnapshot	Boolean	True if data has been retrieved and processed for the report.

Property	Type	Description
HistoryID	String	Contains the history ID of the report, if the report is from a report history snapshot.
NeedsProcessing	Boolean	True if the snapshot for this execution needs to be created or reprocessed.
NumPages	Integer	The number of logical pages, including soft page breaks, in the report.
Parameters	Array of ReportParameter	The parameters for the execution.
ParametersRequired	Boolean	True if the report requires parameter values.
ReportPath	String	The folder path to the report on the report server.

ExecutionInfo2

Description: This class describes the state of the current report execution. This is a class of the ReportExecution2005 web service.

Properties:

Property	Type	Description
AllowQueryExecution	Boolean	True if the user can provide values for the parameters used in the query.
AutoRefreshInterval	Integer	The rate, in seconds, at which a report page rendered as Hypertext Markup Language (HTML) is automatically refreshed.
CredentialsRequired	Boolean	True if the report requires credentials to be supplied.
DataSourcePrompts	Array of DataSourcePrompt Objects	The prompt strings for each data source used by the report.
ExecutionDateTime	DateTime DateTime	The date and time the snapshot associated with the execution was created.
ExecutionID	String	The unique identifier of this report execution.
ExpirationDateTime	DateTime	The date and time this execution expires.
HasDocumentMap	Boolean	True if the report has a document map.
HasSnapshot	Boolean	True if data has been retrieved and processed for the report.
HistoryID	String	Contains the history ID of the report, if the report is from a report history snapshot.
NeedsProcessing	Boolean	True if the snapshot for this execution needs to be created or reprocessed.
NumPages	Integer	The number of logical pages, including soft page breaks, in the report.
Parameters	Array of ReportParameter	The parameters for the execution.
ParametersRequired	Boolean	True if the report requires parameter values.
ReportPageSettings	Array of PageSettings	The report page settings for the current execution.
ReportPath	String	The folder path to the report on the report server.

ExpirationDefinition

Description: This class serves as a parent class. Any class that inherits from the ExpirationDefinition class can be used where an ExpirationDefinition type object is required. This is a class of the ReportService2005 web service.

Classes Inheriting from This Class:

Class Name	Description
ScheduleExpiration	Used when a date and time are to be specified for the expiration.
TimeExpiration	Used when an elapsed time, in minutes, should be specified for the expiration.

Extension

Description: This class represents a Reporting Services extension. This is a class of the ReportExecution2005 and ReportService2005 web services.

Properties:

Property	Type	Description
ExtensionType	ExtensionTypeEnum	Delivery for a delivery extension, Render for a rendering extension, Data for a data-processing extension, or All to represent all extension types. (Read-only.)
LocalizedName	String	The localized name of the extension for display to the user. (Read-only.)
Name	String	The name of the extension. (Read-only.)
Visible	Boolean	True if the extension is visible to the user interface; otherwise, False.

ExtensionParameter

Description: This class contains information about a setting for a delivery extension. This is a class of the ReportService2005 web service.

Properties:

Property	Type	Description
DisplayName	String	The name of the extension parameter.
Encrypted	Boolean	True if the Value property should be encrypted; otherwise, False. (Read-only.)
Error	String	An error message describing a problem with the value specified for this extension parameter. (Read-only.)

Property	Type	Description
IsPassword	Boolean	True if the value for this parameter should not be returned in Simple Object Access Protocol (SOAP) responses (this prevents passwords from being sent in clear text); otherwise, False. (Read-only.)
Name	String	The name of the device information setting. (Read-only.)
ReadOnly	Boolean	True if this extension parameter is read-only; otherwise, False. (Read-only.)
Required	Boolean	True if this extension parameter is required; otherwise, False. (Read-only.)
RequiredSpecified	Boolean	True if a value for Required is specified; otherwise, False.
ValidValues	An Array of ValidValue Objects	An array of valid values for this extension parameter.
Value	String	The value of this extension parameter.

ExtensionSettings

Description: This class contains information for a delivery extension. This is a class of the ReportService2005 web service.

Properties:

Property	Type	Description
Extension	Extension Object	An object representing a Reporting Services extension.
ParameterValues	An Array of ParameterValueOfFieldReference Objects	An array of parameter values for this extension.

Field

Description: This class contains information for a field within a dataset. This is a class of the ReportService2005 web service.

Properties:

Property	Type	Description
Alias	String	The alias of a field in a report.
Name	String	The name of a field in a query.

ItemNamespaceHeader

Description: This is used to determine how property information is retrieved with GetProperty. It inherits from SoapHeader. The following property is not inherited, but it is defined in the ItemNamespaceHeader class. This is a class of the ReportService2005 web service.

Properties:

Property	Type	Description
ItemNamespace	ItemNamespaceEnum	The method used for retrieving properties. Valid values are GUIDBased and PathBased.

MinuteRecurrence

Description: This class contains the time that must elapse, in minutes, before a schedule recurs. This class inherits from RecurrencePattern. This is a class of the ReportService2005 web service.

Properties:

Property	Type	Description
MinutesInterval	Integer	The number of minutes before a schedule recurs.

ModelCatalogItem

Description: This class contains information about a model. This is a class of the ReportService2005 web service.

Properties:

Property	Type	Description
Description	String	The description of a model catalog item.
Model	String	The folder path and name of the model catalog item.
Perspectives	Array of ModelPerspective Objects	The perspectives of the model catalog item.

ModelDrillthroughReport

Description: This class contains information about a model drillthrough report. This is a class of the ReportService2005 web service.

Properties:

Property	Type	Description
Path	String	The full path and name of the drillthrough report.
Type	ModelDrillthroughTypeEnum	The type of the data presented by the drillthrough report. Valid values are Detail and List.

ModelItem

Description: This class contains a semantic definition of a model item. This is a class of the ReportService2005 web service.

Properties:

Property	Type	Description
Description	String	The description of a model item.
ID	String	The ID of a model item.
ModelItems	Array of ModelItem Objects	The children of a model item.
Name	String	The name of the model item.
Type	ModelItemTypeEnum	The type of the model item. Valid values are Attribute, Entity, Entity Folder, Field Folder, Model, and Role.

ModelPerspective

Description: This class contains information about a model perspective. This is a class of the ReportService2005 web service.

Properties:

Property	Type	Description
Description	String	The description of a perspective.
ID	String	The ID of a perspective.
Name	String	The name of a perspective.

MonthlyDOWRecurrence

Description: This class contains the days of the week, the weeks of the month, and the months of the year on which a schedule runs. This class inherits from RecurrencePattern. This is a class of the ReportService2005 web service.

Properties:

Property	Type	Description
DaysOfWeek	DaysOfWeekSelector Object	An object that determines the days of the week on which the schedule runs.
MonthsOfYear	MonthsOfYearSelector	An object that determines the months of the year on which the schedule runs.
WhichWeek	WeekNumberEnum	FirstWeek if the schedule is to run the first week of the month, SecondWeek if the schedule is to run the second week of the month, ThirdWeek if the schedule is to run the third week of the month, FourthWeek if the schedule is to run the fourth week of the month, or LastWeek if the schedule is to run the last week of the month.
WhichWeekSpecified	Boolean	True if a value for WhichWeek has been specified; otherwise, False.

MonthlyRecurrence

Description: This class contains the days of the month and the months of the year on which a schedule runs. This class inherits from RecurrencePattern. This is a class of the ReportService2005 web service.

Properties:

Property	Type	Description
Days	String	The days of the month on which the schedule recurs.
MonthsOfYear	MonthsOfYearSelector	An object that determines the months of the year on which the schedule recurs.

MonthsOfYearSelector

Description: This class contains information on the months of the year in which a schedule runs. This is a class of the ReportService2005 web service.

Properties:

Property	Type	Description
April	Boolean	True if the schedule is to run in April; otherwise, False.
August	Boolean	True if the schedule is to run in August; otherwise, False.
December	Boolean	True if the schedule is to run in December; otherwise, False.

Property	Type	Description
February	Boolean	True if the schedule is to run in February; otherwise, False.
January	Boolean	True if the schedule is to run in January; otherwise, False.
July	Boolean	True if the schedule is to run in July; otherwise, False.
June	Boolean	True if the schedule is to run in June; otherwise, False.
March	Boolean	True if the schedule is to run in March; otherwise, False.
May	Boolean	True if the schedule is to run in May; otherwise, False.
November	Boolean	True if the schedule is to run in November; otherwise, False.
October	Boolean	True if the schedule is to run in October; otherwise, False.
September	Boolean	True if the schedule is to run in September; otherwise, False.

NoSchedule

Description: This class is used when no schedule is associated with an execution snapshot or a history snapshot. This class inherits from Schedule DefinitionOrReference. It does not contain any properties. This is a class of the ReportService2005 web service.

ParameterFieldReference

Description: This class represents a field in a dataset used to supply the value for a parameter. This class inherits from ParameterValueOrFieldReference. This is a class of the ReportService2005 web service.

Properties:

Property	Type	Description
FieldAlias	String	The alias of a field.
ParameterName	String	The name of a field.

ParameterValue

Description: This class represents the actual value for a parameter. This class inherits from ParameterValueOrFieldReference. This is a class of the ReportExecution2005 and the ReportService2005 web services.

Properties:

Property	Type	Description
Label	String	The label used for this parameter.
Name	String	The name of the parameter.
Value	String	The value of the parameter.

ParameterValueOrFieldReference

Description: This class serves as a parent class. Any class that inherits from the ParameterValueOrFieldReference class can be used where a ParameterValueOrFieldReference type object is required. This is a class of the ReportExecution2005 and the ReportService2005 web services.

Classes Inheriting from This Class:

Class Name	Description
ParameterFieldReference	Used when a reference to a field is to be specified.
ParameterValue	Used when a parameter value is to be specified.

Policy

Description: This class represents a domain user or domain group and the security roles assigned to that user or group. This is a class of the ReportService2005 web service.

Properties:

Property	Type	Description
GroupUserName	String	The name of a domain user or domain group.
Roles	An Array of Role Objects	An array of security roles.

Property

Description: This class represents a property of a Reporting Services item. This is a class of the ReportService2005 web service.

Properties:

Property	Type	Description
Name	String	The name of the property.
Value	String	The value of the property.

QueryDefinition

Description: This class contains information to define a query used for a dataset or a data-driven subscription. This is a class of the ReportService2005 web service.

Properties:

Property	Type	Description
CommandText	String	The query text (usually a SELECT statement).
CommandType	String	The type of query supplied in the CommandText property. (For data-driven subscriptions, this always has a value of Text.)
Timeout	Integer	The number of seconds the query may execute before it times out.
TimeoutSpecified	Boolean	True if a value for Timeout has been specified; otherwise, False.

RecurrencePattern

Description: This class serves as a parent class. Any class that inherits from the RecurrencePattern class can be used where a RecurrencePattern type object is required. This is a class of the ReportService2005 web service.

Classes Inheriting from This Class:

Class Name	Description
MinuteRecurrence	Used when the schedule is to recur in minutes.
DailyRecurrence	Used when the schedule is to recur on a daily basis.
WeeklyRecurrence	Used when the schedule is to occur on certain days of the week and to recur on a weekly basis.
MonthlyRecurrence	Used when the schedule is to occur on certain days of the month and certain months of the year.
MonthlyDOWRecurrence	Used when the recurrence is to occur on a day of the week, week of the month, and month of the year.

ReportHistorySnapshot

Description: This class contains information defining a history snapshot. This is a class of the ReportService2005 web service.

Properties:

Property	Type	Description
CreationDate	Date	The date and time the history snapshot was created. (Read-only.)
HistoryID	String	The ID of the history snapshot. (Read-only.)
Size	Integer	The size (in bytes) of the history snapshot. (Read-only.)

ReportParameter

Description: This class contains information about a report parameter. This is a class of the ReportExecution2005 and the ReportService2005 web services. Properties vary between the two web services.

Properties:

Property	Type	Description
AllowBlank	Boolean	True if this report parameter can be empty; otherwise, False. (Read-only.)
AllowBlankSpecified	Boolean	True if a value for AllowBlank was specified; otherwise, False.
DefaultValues	String	The default value of the report parameter.
DefaultValuesQueryBased	Boolean	True if the default value comes from a query; otherwise, False. (Read-only.)
DefaultValuesQueryBasedSpecified	Boolean	True if a value for DefaultValuesQueryBased is specified; otherwise, False.
Dependencies	An Array of Strings	An array showing which other report parameters are depended on by the query used to provide the default value and the query used to provide valid values. Used only if the default value or the valid values come from a parameterized query. (Read-only.)
ErrorMessage	String	Any error messages describing errors with this report parameter.
MultiValue	Boolean	True if the parameter can be a multivalued parameter. (Read-only.)
MultiValueSpecified	Boolean	True if a value for MultiValue is specified; otherwise, False.
Name	String	The name of the parameter. (Read-only.)
Nullable	Boolean	True if the report parameter may be null; otherwise, False.
NullableSpecified	Boolean	True if a value for Nullable is specified; otherwise, False.
Prompt	String	The message displayed to the user when prompting for a value for this parameter.

Property	Type	Description
PromptUser	Boolean	True if the user is to be prompted for this report parameter; otherwise, False.
PromptUserSpecified	Boolean	True if a value for PromptUser has been specified; otherwise, False.
QueryParameter	Boolean	True if this parameter is used in a data source query; otherwise, False. (Read-only.)
QueryParameterSpecified	Boolean	True if a value for QueryParameter is specified; otherwise, False.
State		HasValidValue if the report parameter has a valid value, MissingValidValue if a valid value for the report parameter does not exist, HasOutstandingDependencies if other report parameters depended on by this report parameter are not yet specified, or DynamicValuesUnavailable if no values were returned by a query designated to provide the list of valid values. (Read-only.)
StateSpecified	Boolean	True if a value for State is specified; otherwise, False.
Type		Boolean if type boolean, DateTime if type datetime, Float if type float, Integer if type integer, or String if type string. (Read-only.)
TypeSpecified	Boolean	True if a value for Type is specified; otherwise, False.
ValidValues	An Array of ValidValue Objects	An array of the valid values for this report parameter.
ValidValuesQueryBased	Boolean	True if the valid values come from a query; otherwise, False.
ValidValuesQueryBased Specified	Boolean	True if a value for ValidValuesQueryBased is specified; otherwise, False.

Role

Description: This class contains information about a security role. This is a class of the ReportService2005 web service.

Properties:

Property	Type	Description
Description	String	The description of the role.
Name	String	The name of the role.

Schedule

Description: This class contains information about a schedule. This is a class of the ReportService2005 web service.

Properties:

Property	Type	Description
Creator	String	The name of the user who created the schedule. (Read-only.)
Definition	ScheduleDefinition Object	The definition of the schedule.
Description	String	The description of the schedule.
LastRunTime	Date	The date and time the schedule was last run. (Read-only.)
LastRunTimeSpecified	Boolean	True if a value for LastRunTime is specified; otherwise, False.
Name	String	The name of the schedule.
NextRunTime	Date	The date and time the schedule will run next. (Read-only.)
NextRunTimeSpecified	Boolean	True if a value for NextRunTime is specified; otherwise, False.
ReferencesPresent	Boolean	True if this is a shared schedule and it is referenced by reports and subscriptions.
ScheduleID	String	The ID of the schedule. (Read-only.)
State	ScheduleStateEnum	Running if one or more reports associated with this schedule are currently running, Ready if one or more reports associated with this schedule are ready to run, Paused if the schedule is paused, Expired if the end date for this schedule has passed, or Failing if an error has occurred and the schedule has failed.

ScheduleDefinition

Description: This class contains information for defining a schedule. This class inherits from ScheduleDefinitionOrReference. This is a class of the ReportService2005 web service.

Properties:

Property	Type	Description
EndDate	Date	The end date and time for the schedule.
EndDateSpecified	Boolean	True if a value for EndDate has been specified; otherwise, False.
Item	RecurrencePattern Object	An object containing information about when the schedule should run.
StartDateTime	Date	The start date and time for the schedule.

ScheduleDefinitionOrReference

Description: This class serves as a parent class. Any class that inherits from the ScheduleDefinitionOrReference class can be used where a ScheduleDefinitionOrReference type object is required. This is a class of the ReportService2005 web service.

Classes Inheriting from This Class:

Class Name	Description
NoSchedule	Used when no schedule is to be specified.
ScheduleDefinition	Used when a schedule definition is to be specified.
ScheduleReference	Used when a reference to a shared schedule is to be specified.

ScheduleExpiration

Description: This class defines when a cached copy of a report should expire. This class inherits from ExpirationDefinition. This is a class of the ReportService2005 web service.

Properties:

Property	Type	Description
Item	ScheduleDefinitionOrReference Object	Either a schedule definition or a reference to a shared schedule.

ScheduleReference

Description: This class contains a reference to a shared schedule. This class inherits from ScheduleDefinitionOrReference. This is a class of the ReportService2005 web service.

Properties:

Property	Type	Description
Definition	ScheduleDefinition Object	The definition of the schedule.
ScheduleID	String	The ID of the shared schedule.

SearchCondition

Description: This class provides information on a search within the Report Catalog. This is a class of the ReportService2005 web service.

Properties:

Property	Type	Description
Condition	ConditionEnum	Contains if the search must match only a portion of the property's value to be considered a match; Equals if the search must match all the property's value to be considered a match.
ConditionSpecified	Boolean	True if a value for Condition has been specified; otherwise, False.
Name	String	The name of the property being searched.
Value	String	The value to find.

ServerInfoHeader

Description: This class contains information on the current version of the report server. This is a class of the ReportExecution2005 and the ReportService2005 web services.

Properties:

Property	Type	Description
ReportServerEdition	String	A read-only property containing the edition of the report server.
ReportServerVersion	String	A read-only property containing the version of the report server.
ReportServerVersionNumber	String	A read-only property containing the version number of the report server.

Subscription

Description: This class contains information to define a subscription. This is a class of the ReportService2005 web service.

Properties:

Property	Type	Description
Active	ActiveState Object	The active state of the subscription. (Read-only.)
DeliverySettings	ExtensionSettings Object	The settings specific to the delivery extension.
Description	String	A description of the format and the delivery method.
EventType	String	The type of event that triggers the subscription.
IsDataDriven	Boolean	True if the subscription is data-driven; otherwise, False.
LastExecuted	Date	The date and time the subscription was last executed. (Read-only.)
LastExecutedSpecified	Boolean	True if a value for LastExecuted is specified; otherwise, False.
ModifiedBy	String	The name of the user who last modified the subscription. (Read-only.)

Property	Type	Description
ModifiedDate	Date	The date and time of the last modification to the subscription. (Read-only.)
Owner	String	The user name of the owner of the subscription. (Read-only.)
Path	String	The full path and name of the report associated with the subscription.
Report	String	The name of the report associated with the subscription.
Status	String	The status of the subscription. (Read-only.)
SubscriptionID	String	The ID of the subscription.
VirtualPath	String	The virtual path to the report associated with the subscription. This is populated only if the associated report is under the MyReports folder.

Task

Description: This class contains information about a Reporting Services task. This is a class of the ReportService2005 web service.

Properties:

Property	Type	Description
Description	String	The description of this task. (Read-only.)
Name	String	The name of this task. (Read-only.)
TaskID	String	The ID for this task. (Read-only.)

TimeExpiration

Description: This class contains the time that must elapse, in minutes, before a cached copy of a report expires. This class inherits from ExpirationDefinition. This is a class of the ReportService2005 web service.

Properties:

Property	Type	Description
Minutes	Integer	The number of minutes before expiration.

ValidValue

Description: This class contains information on a valid value for an extension parameter or a report parameter. This is a class of the ReportExecution2005 and the ReportService2005 web services.

Properties:

Property	Type	Description
Label	String	The label for the valid value.
Value	String	The valid value for the setting.

Warning

Description: This class contains information on a warning message or an error message. This is a class of the ReportExecution2005 and the ReportService2005 web services.

Properties:

Property	Type	Description
Code	String	The error or warning code. (Read-only.)
Message	String	The error or warning message. (Read-only.)
ObjectName	String	The name of the object associated with the warning or error. (Read-only.)
ObjectType	String	The type of the object associated with the warning or error. (Read-only.)
Severity	String	Warning if this is a warning; Error if this is an error.

WeeklyRecurrence

Description: This class contains the days of the week on which a schedule runs and the number of weeks to elapse before each recurrence. This class inherits from RecurrencePattern. This is a class of the ReportService2005 web service.

Properties:

Property	Type	Description
DaysOfWeek	DaysOfWeekSelector Object	An object that determines the days of the week on which the schedule runs.
WeeksInterval	Integer	The number of weeks before a schedule runs again.
WeeksIntervalSpecified	Boolean	True if a value for WeeksInterval is specified; otherwise, False.

Appendix C

Ad Hoc Reporting

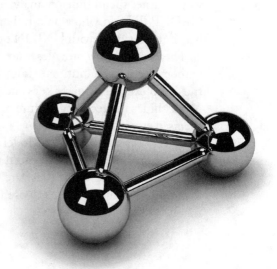

The previous sections of this book were aimed at report authors creating reports to be used over and over again. These types of reports are often referred to, rather ignominiously, as "canned" reports. While not a glamorous moniker, it is rather fitting. These reports are prepared ahead of time, packaged, and stored for later execution by the user.

At times, however, rather than opening a can, cooking from scratch is more appropriate. A user may need some information on short notice, so a report author has no time to create a report. An analyst may need a bit of data for a one-time analysis, so a report development effort is hard to justify. In cases such as these, it would be beneficial to have a way for a knowledgeable user to quickly create a report or explore the data to find the desired information.

Fortunately, SQL Server 2008 Reporting Services provides such a mechanism with Report Models and the Ad Hoc Report Builder. Report Models provide an easy-to-understand view of the database structure. The Ad Hoc Report Builder provides a straightforward and readily available tool for creating reports. Together, they offer the means for users to quickly and easily gain access to the information they need.

The Report Model

One of the biggest hurdles for nondatabase professionals to overcome when creating reports is the creation of the dataset. Unless data is being pulled from a ready-made view or stored procedure, dataset creation is going to involve the creation of a SQL SELECT statement, with all the INNER JOINs and WHERE clauses that go along with it. For those who want to get the full benefits of the Reporting Services environment, becoming conversant in the SQL dialect is worthwhile. For others who would rather spend time on analyzing data than learning the in's and out's of the GROUP BY, and who would rather concentrate on aiding their organizations than becoming intimate with UNION queries, there is the Report Model.

The *Report Model* provides a nontechnical user with a view of database content without requiring an intimate knowledge of relational theory and practice. It hides all the complexity of primary keys and foreign key constraints. In other words, the Report Model hides the technical nature of the database and enables the users to concern themselves with the data.

Once created, the Report Model serves as the basis for report creation with the Ad Hoc Report Builder. First, we need to have one or more Report Models built over the top of our database. Once these are created and deployed to the report server, we can turn a select number of users loose to create ad hoc reports and do data analysis on the fly.

Creating a Report Model

The following sections walk through the creation of a Report Model for the Galactic database. This model is then used to construct ad hoc reports with the Ad Hoc Report Builder in the second part of this appendix. Like reports, Report Models are created in Visual Studio 2008 or the Business Intelligence Development Studio, and then deployed to a report server to be used. Unlike reports, Report Models can have security rights assigned to different pieces of their structure to provide the fine-grained security often required in ad hoc reporting situations.

We use the Report Model Wizard to create the Report Model, and then do some manual tweaking to make it more usable. We deploy the Report Model to the report server. Finally, we look at the method for setting security within the model itself.

NOTE

Before defining a Report Model from a relational database, it is important that the database exhibit good design and implementation practices. Tables should have explicitly declared primary keys. Also, all foreign keys should be maintained by foreign key constraints.

Create a Report Model Project in the Business Intelligence Development Studio

Follow these steps to create a Report Model project in Visual Studio 2008 or the Business Intelligence Development Studio.

1. Start up Visual Studio 2008 or the Business Intelligence Development Studio and create a new project.
2. Select Report Model Project in the Templates area of the New Project dialog box (see Figure C-1).
3. Type **GDS Model** for the Name and select the MSSQLRS folder for the location.
4. Click OK to continue.

Create a Data Source

As with reports, Report Models require a data source to provide the information and credentials for connecting to a database. The following steps enable us to create a data source in the Report Model project.

1. Right-click the Data Sources folder in the Solution Explorer window and select Add New Data Source from the Context menu. The Data Source Wizard dialog box appears.
2. Click Next. The Select How to Define the Connection page appears.

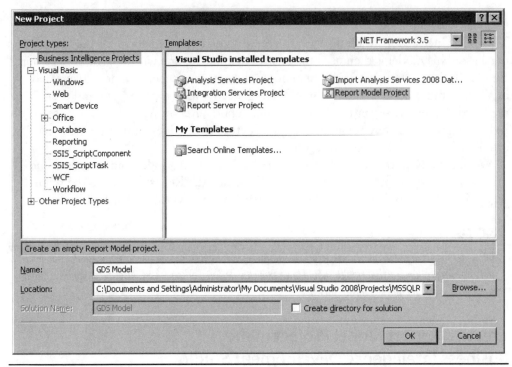

Figure C-1   *Creating a Report Model project*

3.   If a connection to the Galactic database already exists in the Data Connections list, select this connection and go to Step 12. If there is no connection, click New. The Connection Manager dialog box appears.

4.   Type the name of the Microsoft SQL Server database server hosting the Galactic database, or select it from the drop-down list. If the Galactic database is hosted by the computer you are currently working on, you may type **(local)** for the server name.

5.   Click the Use SQL Server Authentication radio button.

6.   Type **GalacticReporting** for the user name.

7.   Type **gds** for the password.

8.   Click the Save my password check box.

9.   Select Galactic from the Select or enter a database name drop-down list.

10.   Click Test Connection. If a Test Connection Succeeded message appears, click OK. If an error message appears, make sure the name of your database server, the user name, the password, and the database were entered properly. If your test connection still does not succeed, make sure you have correctly installed the Galactic database.

11. Click OK. You return to the Data Source Wizard dialog box.

12. Click Next. The Completing the Wizard page appears.

13. Make sure the Data source name is Galactic. Click Finish.

Create a Data Source View

In addition to the data source, the Report Model requires a data source view. The *data source view* is simply a selected subset of the tables from the data source itself. In many cases, we do not want our model to include data from all the tables in the database. Some tables might be used for logging or a temporary holding place for other operations. The data source view enables us to exclude these types of tables from the Report Model.

The following steps create a data source view for the tables in the Galactic database.

1. Right-click the Data Source Views folder in the Solution Explorer window and select Add New Data Source View from the Context menu. The Data Source View Wizard dialog box appears.

2. Click Next. The Select a Data Source page appears.

3. Select the Galactic data source and click Next. The Select Tables and Views page appears.

4. Move all the tables *except* the dtproperties, TransMonitorI, TransMonitorQ, and TransportMonitor into the Included objects list. Do *not* include any of the views in the Included objects list. The dtproperties table is a system table, so it should not be included. The other three tables are used for temporary processing and do not hold any meaningful data for ad hoc reporting.

5. Click Next. The Completing the Wizard page appears.

6. Make sure the Data source view name is Galactic. Click Finish.

Create a Report Model

With the preliminaries done, the following steps utilize the Report Model Wizard to create the Report Model.

1. Right-click the Report Models folder in the Solution Explorer window and select Add New Report Model from the Context menu. The Report Model Wizard appears.

2. Click Next. The Select Data Source View page appears.

3. Select the Galactic data source view and click Next. The Select Report Model Generation Rules page appears (see Figure C-2). This page enables you to select the rules to apply during the first pass and the second pass through the tables in the data source view. The default settings work for most data models, so we will leave the default settings. You can also select the language to use when creating your data model. The figures here use a data model generated in English.

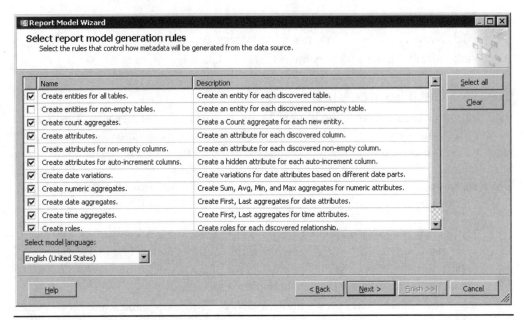

Figure C-2   *The Select Report Model Generation Rules page of the Report Model Wizard*

4. Click Next. The Collect Model Statistics page appears.

5. The data model generation process uses the database statistics in the data source view. To create a data model that best reflects the current database and how it is used, we recommend you select the Update Statistics Before Generating radio button. Therefore, leave the Update model statistics before generating radio button selected. Click Next. The Completing the Wizard page appears.

6. Make sure the report model name is Galactic. Click Run. The wizard creates the model.

7. The wizard page shows the actions taken during each pass of the model generation process (see Figure C-3). When the process is complete, click Finish.

8. You may receive a message stating the data source view file has been modified outside of the editor and asking if you want it reloaded. If this message appears, click Yes.

The Report Data Model Parts and Pieces

Let's first take a look at the model that resulted from the wizard. Double-click the Galactic.smdl file entry in the Solution Explorer window to open it, if it is not already open. The model appears as shown in Figure C-4. You can see each of the tables in the Galactic database has become an entity in the model. An *entity* is simply a set of things, events, or concepts of interest to us in the data world. Each individual thing, event, or concept is an instance of an entity.

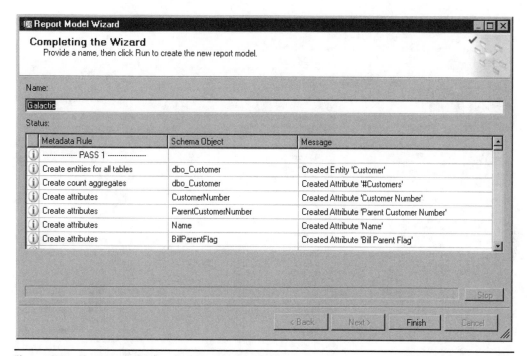

Figure C-3   *The Report Model Wizard creating the report model*

The fields from our database become attributes of our entities, as shown in Figure C-5 and Figure C-6. *Attributes* are bits of information about each instance of an entity—the name of a particular company or the address of a particular employee, for example. Attributes may also be referred to as *fields*. The field, or set of fields, that uniquely identifies a particular instance of an entity is called the *identifying field*. This is the primary key from the database.

The attribute type is identified in Figure C-5 and Figure C-6 by the icon to the left of each attribute name. The # notes a numeric attribute. The *a* notes an alphanumeric attribute. The calendar identifies a date/time attribute. The check box identifies a bit or Boolean attribute. Numeric attributes also include sum, average, minimum, and maximum aggregates. Date/time attributes also include the date parts of day, month, year, and quarter, along with aggregates for the first and last date.

NOTE

The Report Model contains some attributes that provide a count of the number of instances of an entity. For example, Figure C-5 shows an attribute called #Customers, which provides a count of the number of customer entities. Do not confuse the # icon, which indicates the attribute type with the # that is used at the beginning of the attribute name.

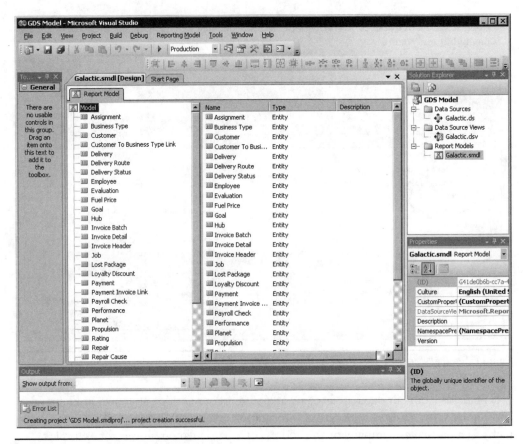

Figure C-4 *Entities in the Galactic Report Model*

Finally, in the model, entities can have various roles. *Roles* are created by the foreign key constraints in the database. The roles link one entity to other entities in the model. A role can be a one-to-many, many-to-one, or one-to-one relationship. For example, in Figure C-6, a customer may have many invoice headers associated with it. This is a one-to-many relationship. On the other hand, an Account Rep Employee is an account representative for many customers. From the customer entity's point of view, this is a many-to-one relationship. Finally, a customer may have no more than one loyalty discount. This is a one-to-one relationship. Note the differing icons associated with each of these types of relationship.

Anyone familiar with entity relationship diagrams (ERD) immediately recognizes this terminology. A database designer often creates an ERD first, and then designs the database from the ERD. We are now working this same process in the reverse direction.

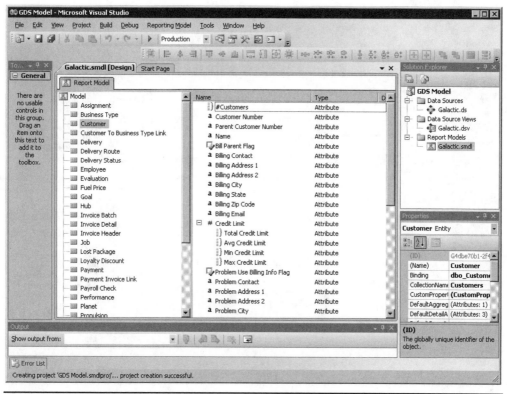

Figure C-5   *Attributes of the Customer entity in the Galactic Report Model*

Cleaning Up the Report Model

Creating the Report Model using the Report Model Wizard is only half the battle. The wizard does a great job of creating the model for us. However, a number of refinements still need to be made to the model by hand to get it ready for the users.

Here are the tasks that must be accomplished to clean up the Report Model:

▶   Remove any numeric aggregates that don't make sense.

▶   Remove attributes that should not be present.

▶   Rename entities with cryptic names.

▶   Set the default attributes for the entities.

▶   Use folders to organize entities, attributes, and roles.

▶   Rearrange the entity, attribute, and role order.

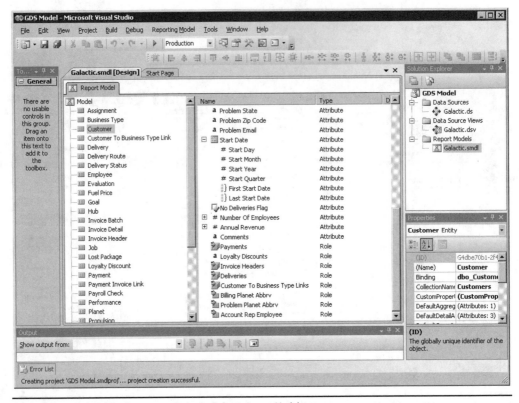

Figure C-6   *Roles of the Customer entity in the Galactic Report Model*

▶ Manually create calculated attributes.

▶ Add descriptions.

▶ Create perspectives coinciding with business areas.

This appendix does not provide step-by-step instructions to clean up the entire Galactic Report Model. Instead, it provides a single example of each of these cleanup tasks using the Galactic Report Model. Of course, these cleanup tasks should be applied exhaustively to your own production models.

Remove Any Numeric Aggregates That Don't Make Sense   As stated earlier, the Report Model Wizard creates aggregates for all numeric attributes. In the case of a numeric identifying field, such as the Invoice Number, these aggregates are complete nonsense and should be removed from the model. We do not want a user using the average of the invoice numbers when they think they are getting the average of the invoice amounts! Let's keep our users out of trouble and remove these aggregates that simply don't add up.

1. Select the Invoice Header entity.
2. Expand the Invoice Number attribute.
3. Select the Total Invoice Number, Avg Invoice Number, Min Invoice Number, and Max Invoice Number attributes.
4. Press DELETE.
5. Click OK to confirm the deletion.

Remove Attributes That Should Not Be Present Spotting numeric aggregates that don't make sense is a fairly easy exercise. Finding other attributes that do not belong is a bit harder. After all, each of these attributes comes from a database field and if the information in a particular field is not useful, what is it doing in the database in the first place? Still, there may be fields in the database for system tasks, housekeeping chores, or security purposes that should not be available to end users.

The Galactic Report Model provides an example in the Employee entity. There are fields to hold a user name and the pieces necessary for password encryption. Nothing good can come from having these exposed to prying eyes!

1. Select the Employee entity.
2. Select the User Name, Password Hash, and Password Salt attributes.
3. Press DELETE.
4. Click OK to confirm the deletion.

Rename Entities with Cryptic Names The whole reason for the Report Model is to make it easy for users to create ad hoc reports without having to know the technical in's and out's of the database. Therefore, we want to make sure our entities, attributes, and roles have names that are obvious to the users. Any names that include acronyms and abbreviations that are not well known to the users should be changed.

I will give myself a pat on the back here and state that the names used in the Galactic database are pretty self-explanatory, so the entity, attribute, and role names in the model are as well. This is an endorsement for good database design. However, here is one example of a name generated by the wizard that could be improved upon.

1. Select the Customer entity.
2. Right-click the Account Rep Employee role and select Rename from the context menu.
3. Type **Accounts for this Account Rep** as the new name and press ENTER.

Set the Default Attributes for the Entities   When an entity is placed on an ad hoc report, one or more attributes are automatically placed on the report to identify this entity. These are the default attributes for each entity. The Report Model Wizard makes its best guess as to which attributes should be used as the default attributes for each entity. As with other best guesses, sometimes the Report Wizard's choices are not the best possible choices available. You will greatly streamline the ad hoc reporting process by taking the time to assign sensible default attributes to each entity in the Report Model.

Here we set the default attributes for the Delivery entity to the Delivery Number and the Pickup Date Time.

1. Select the Delivery entity.
2. In the Properties window, select the DefaultDetailAttributes entry. Click the ... button that appears. The AttributeReference Collection Editor dialog box appears.
3. Remove each of the four attributes in the Members column.
4. Click Add. The Default Detail Attributes dialog box appears.
5. Select Delivery Number and Click OK.
6. Click Add again.
7. Scroll down and select Pickup Date Time. Click OK.
8. Click OK to exit the AttributeReference Collection Editor.

Use Folders to Organize Entities, Attributes, and Roles   We can create folders to help organize our entities and attributes. Not only can these folders help us with organization, but we can also assign specific security roles to these folders. Entities and attributes that should have more restricted access, therefore, should be put in their own folders.

We put the entities related to the employee evaluations in a separate folder to make it easier to assign security later. We put the contact-related attributes in separate folders in the Customer entity to keep things more organized.

1. In the tree view in the left-hand pane, right-click the Model entry and select New | Folder from the Context menu. A new folder is added at the bottom of the tree view.
2. Rename the new folder **Employee Evaluation**.
3. Select the Model entry at the top of the left-hand pane again.
4. Select the Evaluation, Goal, Performance, and Rating entities in the right-hand pane.
5. Drag these entities to the Employee Evaluation folder.
6. In the tree view in the left-hand pane, right-click the Customer entry and select New | Folder from the context menu. A new folder is created in the Customer entity. Expand the Customer entry to view this new folder.

7. Rename the new folder **Billing Contact Info**.

8. Select the Customer entity in the left-hand pane again. Select all the billing contact–related attributes in the right-hand pane.

9. Drag these to the Billing Contact Info folder.

10. In the tree view in the left-hand pane, right-click the Customer entry and select New | Folder from the context menu. A new folder is created in the Customer entity.

11. Rename the new folder **Problem Contact Info**.

12. Select the Customer entity in the left-hand pane again. Select all the problem contact–related attributes in the right-hand pane.

13. Drag these to the Problem Contact Info folder.

Rearrange the Entity, Attribute, and Role Order   Entities and attributes can be arranged in any desired order in the model. By default, entities appear in the model in alphabetical order, while attributes and roles appear in the order in which the fields and foreign key relationships are encountered in the database. This may not be the most appropriate order.

You may want to group your entities together into related groups. This is a bit difficult in the Galactic model because so many entities are interrelated. Instead, let's keep the entities arranged alphabetically. However, several of the items we moved around are not in alphabetical order, so we still have some rearranging to do. In the Delivery entity, it might make more sense to have the Pickup Date Time attribute right before the pickup contact and address information. The same is true with the Delivery Date Time.

1. Select the Delivery entity.

2. Click the Pickup Date Time attribute and hold down the mouse button. Drag the Pickup Date Time attribute up until it is immediately above the Pickup Contact attribute.

3. Use the same process to put the Delivery Date Time attribute immediately above the Delivery Contact attribute.

Manually Create Calculated Attributes   The Report Model Wizard created some calculated attributes containing counts, aggregates, and date parts. Some additional calculated attributes may be helpful. These calculated attributes could contain arithmetic calculations or even string concatenations. We look at an example of each of these.

1. Right-click the Delivery entity and select New | Expression from the context menu. The Define Formula dialog box appears.

2. In the Entities list, select Service Type.

3. Drag the Cost field from the Fields list to the Formula for each Delivery area.

4. Click the minus (–) button below the Formula for each Delivery area.

5. In the Entities list, select Delivery.

6. Drag the Discount field from the Fields list and drop it after the minus sign in the Formula area.

7. Click OK. The NewExpression attribute will appear at the bottom of the list.

8. Rename the NewExpression attribute you just created to **Net Cost**.

9. Right-click the Employee entity and select New | Expression from the context menu. The Define Formula dialog box appears.

10. Drag the First Name field from the Fields list to the Formula area.

11. Click the ampersand (&) button below the Formula for each Delivery area.

12. Type " " and click the ampersand button.

13. Drag the Middle Initial field from the Fields list and drop it after the ampersand.

14. Click the ampersand button.

15. Type " " and click the ampersand button.

16. Drag the Last Name field from the Fields list and drop it after the ampersand.

17. Click OK.

18. Rename the NewExpression attribute you just created to **Full Name**.

19. In the Properties window, set the Nullable property of the Full Name attribute to True.

Add Descriptions   Perhaps the most helpful thing you can do during this entire cleanup process is to add descriptions to each entity, attribute, role, and folder. These descriptions are displayed to the users when they hover the mouse over an item during report creation. The descriptions enable you to provide a detailed explanation of each item. These detailed descriptions can ensure the users are selecting the correct items and getting exactly the information they are looking for. We are only entering one description as an example here. In your production Report Model, descriptions should be entered for all entities, attributes, roles, and folders.

1. Select the Employee entity.

2. Select the Full Name attribute you just created.

3. In the Properties window, enter **The first name, middle initial, and last name of the employee.** for the Description property of the Full Name attribute.

Create Perspectives Coinciding with Business Areas   *Perspectives* hide some of the complexity of the complete data model by grouping entities into logical units. Perspectives organize entities into sets that are likely to be used together by a given set of ad hoc report users. As you have seen, entity folders can also be used to group entities, but with two major differences. More on those differences in a moment.

Let's consider the groupings first used to introduce the Galactic database in Chapter 3. The tables were presented in four diagrams, each relating to a different functional area of Galactic Delivery Services: Accounting Information, Package Tracking, Personnel Information, and Transport Maintenance. We use these four groupings to create four perspectives in the Report Model.

Someone working in the accounting department is most likely to run reports from the tables in the Accounting Information diagram. Conversely, someone in the package tracking area will have little interest in the Accounting tables, but will primarily report from the Package Tracking tables. Both of these people are interested in the content of the Customer table, however. This means both want the Customer table to show up in their perspective. Fortunately, an entity can appear in multiple perspectives.

This, then, is the first difference between perspectives and entity folders. A single entity can show up in multiple perspectives, but it can only reside in one entity folder. The second difference between perspectives and entity folders is security roles can be assigned to entity folders, but they cannot be assigned to perspectives.

Let's create our four perspectives.

1. Select Model at the top of the left-hand pane.
2. Right-click and select New | Perspective from the context menu.
3. Click Clear All.
4. Select the following entities:

   Business Type

   Customer

   Customer To Business Type Link Invoice Batch

   Invoice Detail

   Invoice Header

   Loyalty Discount

   Payment

   Payment Invoice Link

NOTE

Other entities related to the entities you select are implicitly checke and marked with a dark gray check mark in a light gray check box. Explicitly check all of the entities listed here so they are marked with a black check mark in a white check box. After you make all the explicit selections, leave the implicit selections as they are.

5. Click OK.
6. Rename the new perspective **Accounting Information**.

7. Right-click Model in the left-hand pane and select New | Perspective from the context menu.

8. Click Clear All.

9. Select the following entities:

   Customer

   Delivery

   Hub

   Lost Package

   Planet

   Service Type

   Transport

10. Click OK.

11. Rename the new perspective **Package Tracking**.

12. Right-click Model in the left-hand pane and select New | Perspective from the context menu.

13. Click Clear All.

14. Select the following entities:

    Assignment

    Employee

    Job

    Payroll Check

    Time Entry

    Employee Evaluation (This is the folder we created earlier.)

15. Click OK.

16. Rename the new perspective **Personnel Information**.

17. Right-click Model in the left-hand pane and select New | Perspective from the context menu.

18. Click Clear All.

19. Select the following entities:

    Fuel Price

    Propulsion

    Repair

    Repair Cause

    Repair Work Done Link

Scheduled Maint

Transport

Transport Type

Work Done

20. Click OK.

21. Rename the new perspective **Transport Maintenance**.

22. Click Save All in the toolbar.

Deploy the Model

Once you have the Report Model looking the way it should, it can be deployed to the report server. This is done in a manner similar to the process for deploying reports.

1. Right-click the entry for the GDS Model Project in the Solution Explorer window and select Properties from the context menu. The GDS Model Property Pages dialog box appears.

2. Enter **Galactic Delivery Services/Shared Reports** for the TargetDataSourceFolder. This causes the Report Model to use the Galactic shared data source that already exists in this folder.

3. Enter **Galactic Delivery Services/Models** for the TargetModelFolder. This creates a new folder to contain the Report Model itself.

4. Enter **http://{ReportServer}/ReportServer** for the TargetServerURL, where {ReportServer} is the name of the report server.

5. Click OK to exit the dialog box.

6. Right-click the entry for the GDS Model Project and select Deploy from the context menu. The model deploys to the server. You receive one warning stating that the shared data source cannot be deployed because it already exists.

Secure the Model

The number of people who have access to the Report Model for ad hoc reporting is probably larger than the number of people who have access to the database for report authoring. This wider audience and increased exposure makes security doubly important. Personal information, such as Social Security numbers, pay rates, and employee's health care information, must be protected. In addition, important financial information, which should not be widely disbursed, may be in the data.

Let's first take a look at the Report Model using the Report Manager. Open Report Manager and browse to the /Galactic Delivery Services/Models folder where the model was deployed. As you can see in Figure C-7, the entry in the folder for the Galactic model looks much like the entries we have seen for reports and shared data sources. Clicking the Galactic model opens the Properties tab for the model.

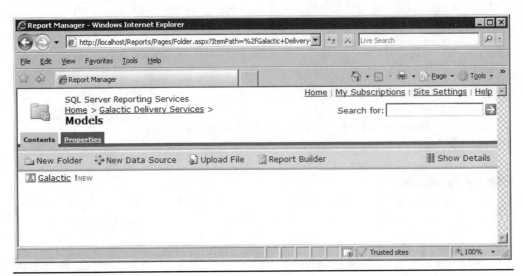

Figure C-7   *The Galactic Report Model deployed to the report server*

The General page, the Data Sources page, and the Security page on the Properties tab for the Report Model look and function almost identical to their counterparts for a report. The Clickthrough page and the Model Item Security page are specific to Report Models. It is assumed that you can determine the function of the General, Data Sources, and Security pages, with one additional note of explanation. The Security page allows you to make security role assignments on the Report Model as a whole. To make security role assignments for individual parts of the model, you need to use the Model Item Security page.

Clickthrough   The Clickthrough page requires a bit of background information. When users are looking at Ad Hoc Report Builder reports, they are able to click items to follow foreign key relationships within the Report Model. For example, when looking at a report of customers, users can click an aggregate showing the number of deliveries to see detail information about each delivery. Users can also click the name of the parent customer to see detail information about it. When this clickthrough occurs, the report server automatically generates a new report to display the clickthrough data. The first situation, clicking an aggregate to see multiple records, creates a *multiple instance report*. The second situation, clicking an entry to see detail from a single record, creates a *single instance report*.

The clickthrough report feature requires the Enterprise Edition of SQL Server. If you do not see the Clickthrough page link, or if you do not have clickthrough functionality when viewing Ad Hoc Report Builder reports, you are using a SQL Server edition other than the Enterprise Edition or Developer Edition.

Rather than having the report server create generic clickthrough reports on the fly, you can create your own reports to be used for this purpose. These reports must be created through the Ad Hoc Report Builder. They must also have the Allow users to drill to this report from other reports property check box checked in the Report Properties dialog box.

Once you have created an Ad Hoc Report Builder report to use as a clickthrough report, you must link the report to an entity in the report model. This is done using the Clickthrough page shown in Figure C-8. Note, you provide different reports for a single instance report and for a multiple instance report.

Report Model Item Security   As stated earlier, it is important to properly secure the information in your Report Model. This is done by applying security to individual items within the Report Model itself. This is accomplished on the Model Item Security page shown in Figure C-9. Once the Secure individual model items independently for this model check box is checked, you can assign read permissions for individual entities or attributes to individual users or groups.

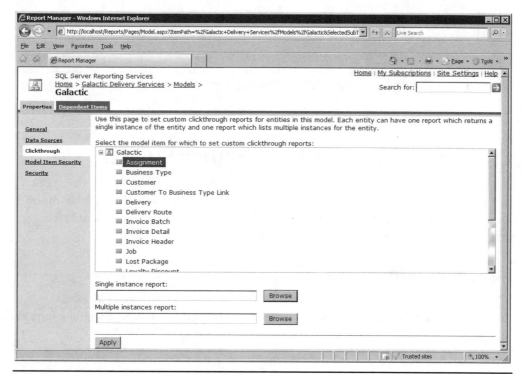

Figure C-8   *The Clickthrough page of the Report Model Properties tab*

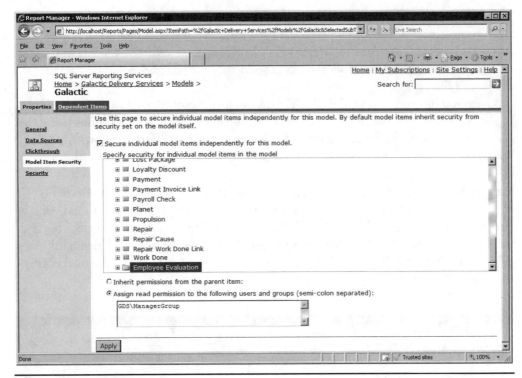

Figure C-9 *The Model Item Security page of the Report Model Properties tab*

Creating Reports with the Report Builder

Now that a Report Model is in place on the server, users can create reports based on that model using the Report Builder. Three types of report layouts are available in the Report Builder: the table report, the matrix report, and the chart. We look at brief examples of all three reports; but first, let's go over some of the basics.

Report Builder Basics

The Report Builder is a special type of Windows program known as a *ClickOnce application*, which is installed on your computer by following a link or clicking a button on a web form. The application is launched in the same way.

Launching the Ad Hoc Report Builder Application

You launch the Ad Hoc Report Builder by bringing up Report Manager in a browser, and then clicking the Report Builder button in the toolbar. You can also launch the Ad Hoc Report Builder without first going to the Report Manager. This is done using the following URL:

```
http://{ReportServer}/ReportServer/ReportBuilder/ReportBuilder.application
```

where {ReportServer} is the name of your report server.

The Microsoft Ad Hoc Report Builder launches and begins creating a new report. The Task pane is displayed on the right side of the screen. You must select a data source for the report (see Figure C-10). Instead of basing your report on the entire Report Model, you can select a perspective from within the model. As you learned earlier, a perspective is a subset of the information in the model. Usually, a perspective coincides with a particular job or work area within an organization.

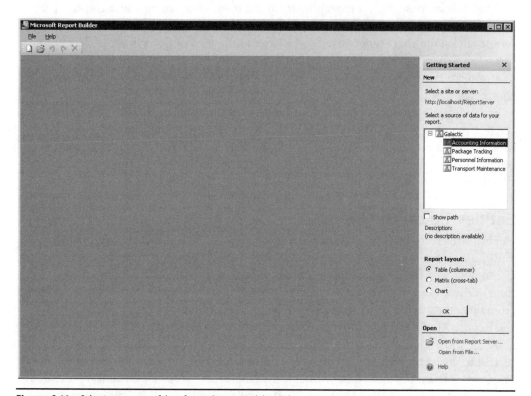

Figure C-10   *Selecting a source of data from a Report Model with four perspectives*

If a plus (+) sign is to the left of the model, then the model contains one or more perspectives. Click the plus sign to view the perspectives. If you select one of these perspectives as the data source for your report, only the entities in that perspective are available to your report. Because perspectives reduce the number of entities you have to look through to find the data you need on your report, it is usually a good idea to choose a perspective rather than using the entire Report Model.

You must also select a report layout. The Task pane shows the three types of report layouts available in Report Builder. The *table report* creates a report with rows and columns. This is the most familiar report layout. In a table report, the columns are predefined by the report layout and we will not know the number of rows until the data is selected at run time.

The *matrix report* creates a report containing what is known as either a cross-tab or a pivot table. We do not know how many columns or rows will be in the matrix in advance, because it uses data selected at run time to define both. The matrix report can be somewhat confusing the first time you encounter it, but an example usually helps. If you are fuzzy on how a matrix works, be sure to check out the sample matrix report.

The *chart* creates a business graphic from the data. This can be a line graph, a bar chart, or a pie chart, among other things. While you can create a basic chart with a few mouse clicks, the chart report itself has a large number of options that enable you to format the chart just the way you want it.

If you are creating a new report, select the Report Model or the perspective that should serve as the data source along with the report layout and click OK. If you want to edit an existing report, click the Open button in the toolbar. You can then navigate the report server folder structure to find the Ad Hoc Report Builder report you want to edit. You cannot use the Ad Hoc Report Builder to edit reports that were created or edited using the Report Builder in Visual Studio 2005 or the Business Intelligence Development Studio.

Entities, Roles, and Fields

Reports are created in the Ad Hoc Report Builder using entities, roles, and fields. Entities are simply the objects or processes our data know something about. Employees, Customers, and Deliveries are all examples of entities in the Galactic Report Model used in these examples. A single report may contain information from a single entity or from several related entities. Entities can be grouped together in entity folders within the Report Model or perspective to help keep things organized.

Roles show us how one entity relates to another entity. For example, a delivery is related to a customer through its role as a delivery of a package for that customer. An employee is related to a customer through the employee's role as an account representative for that customer. A delivery hub is related to a delivery through its role as a stop on a delivery route.

Roles enable us to show information from multiple entities together on a single report in a meaningful manner. This may seem a bit confusing as you read about it, but remember the roles are already defined for you by the Report Model. If the model has been created properly, you should find they are natural to the way you think about your business processes. Information from different entities should combine on your reports just as you expect, without having to get caught up in the technical structure behind the relationships.

The information about the entities is stored in fields. A field is simply one bit of information: a first name, an invoice number, a hiring date. Fields are what we place on our reports to spit out these bits of information.

The Entities List

Once the data source and report layout are selected, you click the OK button to display the main Ad Hoc Report Builder. When creating a new report with the Accounting Information perspective chosen as the source, the Ad Hoc Report Builder appears similar to Figure C-11. Let's take a look at each of the windows that make up this screen.

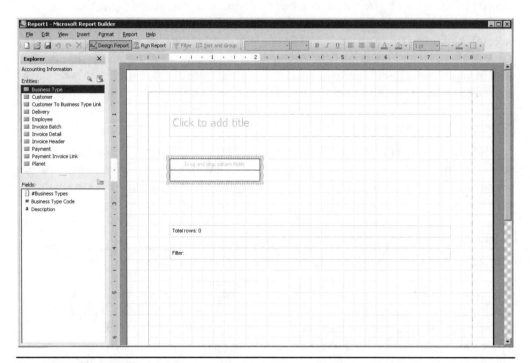

Figure C-11 *The Ad Hoc Report Builder screen*

The *Entities list*, in the upper-left corner, shows the entities and entity folders in the selected Report Model or perspective. All the data in a Report Builder report comes from the entities displayed in this window. Once an entity has been selected and placed on the report, the Entities list shows that entity along with its roles.

The Fields List

The *Fields list*, in the lower-left corner, shows the fields available for the selected entity. Some of these fields contain information coming directly from the database, while others contain information calculated by the report. The icon to the left of the field identifies the type of data being stored in the field. A pound sign (#) indicates a field contains numeric data. A small letter *a* indicates a field containing alphanumeric data. A check box indicates a field that contains yes or no, true or false data. A calendar indicates a date and time. A grouping of three yellow boxes indicates a calculated field that combines values from a number of items into one value—for example, the sum of all invoice amounts for a customer.

You can create your own calculated fields by clicking the New Field button at the upper-right corner of the Fields list. This displays the Define Formula dialog box shown in Figure C-12. Use this dialog box to define your calculated field. You can create expressions by dragging existing fields to the Formula area. The fields' values can be combined using the arithmetic and string operator buttons below the formula area. You can also use the Functions tab to reference a large number of functions that can be used in your expressions. Once you click OK to create the calculated field, it is displayed in the Fields list of the Report Builder.

Clickthrough Reports

As discussed earlier, entities are related through roles in our data model. Sometimes it can be helpful, as you are analyzing your data, to follow these role relationships through your data. The Ad Hoc Report Builder enables you to do this by using clickthrough reports.

NOTE

The SQL Server 2008 Enterprise Edition is required for the clickthrough reports feature.

Clickthrough reports are automatically created when you click a role relationship to move from one entity to another. The clickthrough reports are defined on the fly according to the data in the model for the entity being reported on. Each clickthrough report can lead to other clickthrough reports. Using clickthrough reports, you can continue to follow your data wherever it may lead to perform in-depth analysis.

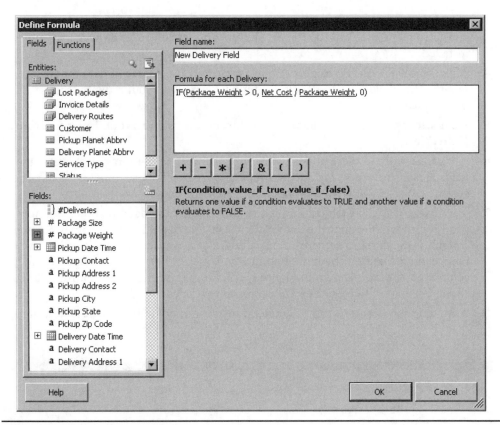

Figure C-12   *The Define Formula dialog box*

Creating a Table Layout Report

We begin by creating a table layout report showing customers and their deliveries. We create the basic report, modify the report to show monthly information, and then add additional formatting.

Creating the Basic Table Layout Report

We start by creating the basic report.

1. Open a browser and bring up the Report Manager using the following URL:

    ```
    http://{ReportServer}/Reports
    ```

    where {ReportServer} is the name of your Reporting Services report server.

2. Click the Report Builder button in the Report Manager toolbar.

3. Click the appropriate responses to any security warning dialog boxes that may appear to allow the Ad Hoc Report Builder application to be downloaded and installed.

4. Make sure the Galactic Report Model is selected as a source of data for your report. Also, make sure the Table (columnar) Report Layout radio button is selected. Click OK.

5. Double-click the Click to add title text box on the report layout. Enter **Customer Deliveries**.

6. Click Customer in the Entities list. Drag Customer to the Drag and drop column fields area of the report layout. A grouping is created for Customer with three columns: Name, Customer Number, and Billing Contact.

7. The string of X's in each column is the template for the data. It shows you how wide and in what format the data will appear. The data in the Customer Number column is much narrower than the heading. To save space, let's make this a two-line heading. Position the mouse pointer so you can drag the Customer Number column narrower, as shown in Figure C-13. Drag the column just narrow enough so the Customer Number heading wraps to two lines.

8. Now, drag the headings row tall enough to accommodate the two-line heading.

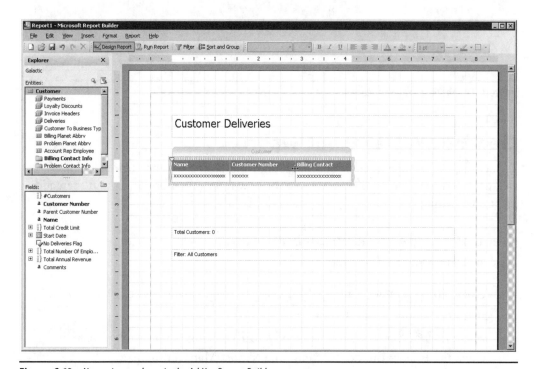

Figure C-13   *Narrowing a column in the Ad Hoc Report Builder*

9. The Customer Number is helpful in our report, but Billing Contact is not necessary. Right-click the Billing Contact column and select Delete from the context menu. The Billing Contact column will be removed from the report.

10. Next, you want to use the date of pickup to identify each delivery. If you are familiar with the Report Model, you can use the Entities list and the Fields list to find the appropriate field. If you are not familiar with the Report Model, you may need some assistance. Click the magnifying glass in the upper-right corner of the Explorer pane to get that assistance. The Search dialog box appears.

11. Enter **delivery date** for the Search text. Select Entire data source to search the entire Report Model rather than the current item only. (The current item would be the Customer entity, because that was the last entity placed on the report.) Click Find.

12. You see a list of all fields in the Report Model that contain "delivery date." Note, the search is not case-sensitive. Scroll down until you find the Delivery Date Time field with a location of Customer/Deliveries in the search result. (Make sure you select the Delivery Date Time field from the correct location!) Select this item and click OK. You jump to the Delivery Date Time field in the Fields list.

13. Click the Delivery Date Time field and drag it onto the report layout, over the top of the Customer Number column. You see a blue insert bar, as shown in Figure C-14. Drop the field to create a new column at the location of the insert bar.

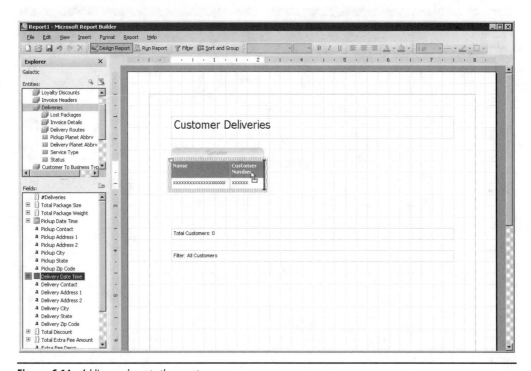

Figure C-14 *Adding a column to the report*

14. There is a template for the content of the Delivery Date Time column. It shows the date portion will be displayed, but the time portion will not. With a package delivery, both the date and time are important. To change this formatting, right-click the Delivery Date Time column and select Format from the context menu. The Format dialog box appears.

15. Select the Number tab. (Why this is called Number when it contains other formatting options as well is beyond me.)

16. You can see a number of available formats for the Delivery Date Time column. Select a format that contains both the date and the time. Click OK to return to the report layout.

17. Expand the Delivery Date Time column so the template and the heading do not wrap.

18. Now let's add the cost of each delivery. The cost is in the Service Type entity, because cost is based on the type of service used. In the Entities list, click Service Type. The Fields list now shows the fields for the Service Type entity. Select Total Cost and drag it onto the report layout. Note, as you drag the Total Cost field over the existing layout, you could put it in between any of the existing columns. For this layout, drop it on the right side. Your report layout should appear as shown in Figure C-15.

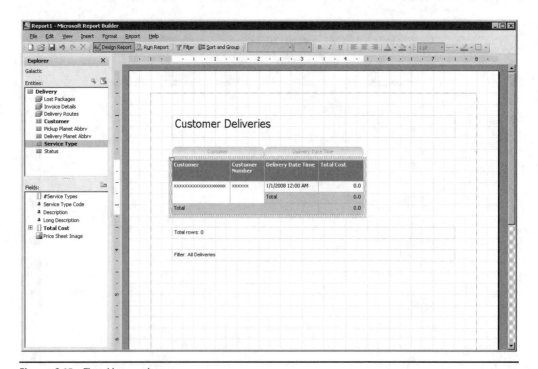

Figure C-15 *The table report layout*

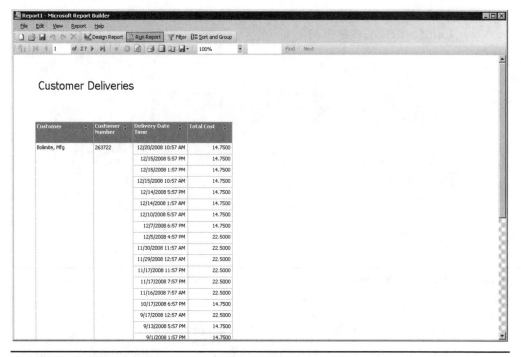

Figure C-16 *The table report preview*

19. Let's preview the report and see what we have so far. Click Run Report in the Report Builder toolbar. The report should appear as shown in Figure C-16.

Modify the Report to Show Monthly Information

Let's add some basic formatting to the report and modify our grouping so the report shows monthly information.

1. You can see the Total Cost column has four decimal places, which is not how we usually like to see dollar amounts. Click Design Report in the Ad Hoc Report Builder toolbar to return to the report layout.

2. Right-click the template in the Total Cost column on the report layout. Take a moment to look at the options available in the context menu shown in Figure C-17:

    ▶ **Format**   Displays the Format dialog box to modify the colors, borders, and formatting of the column content.

    ▶ **Edit Formula**   Displays the Define Formula dialog box to modify the content of the column.

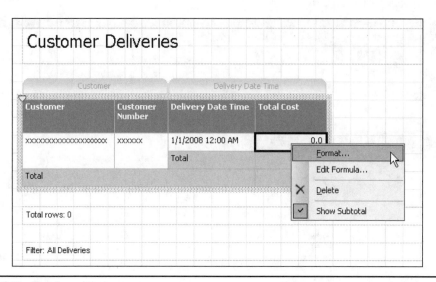

Figure C-17 *The column context menu*

> ► **Delete**   Removes this column from the report.

> ► **Show Subtotal**   Unchecking this option removes all the subtotaling from the report.

3. Select Format from the context menu. The Format dialog box appears.

4. Select the format that includes the dollar sign and click OK.

5. Repeat this for each field in the Total Cost column. You can use SHIFT to select and change the format of both remaining fields at the same time.

6. Looking at the cost for every delivery is a bit overwhelming for the user. Instead, let's look at the cost for each month. To do this, you need a field that contains the year and month from the Delivery Date Time field. Select Delivery in the Entities list, and then click the New Field button above the Fields list. The Define Formula dialog box appears.

7. Enter **Delivery Month** for Field name.

8. Select the Functions tab and expand the Conversion entry. Double-click the TEXT function. This function converts a numeric or date value to text.

9. Select the Fields tab. Expand the Delivery Date Time entry in the Fields list. Double-click the Delivery Date Time Year field, which is the third entry under Delivery Date Time. Notice this field was placed inside the TEXT function. The formula takes the year portion of the Delivery Date Time and converts it from a number to text.

10. Press END to move the cursor to the end of the formula. Click the ampersand button.

11. Select the Functions tab and expand the Text entry. (This is the Text entry with the folder icon, not the TEXT entry with the *fx* icon.) Double-click the RIGHT function. This function returns the rightmost characters of a string.

12. Replace the highlighted text with " " and click the ampersand button.

13. Double-click the TEXT function. The TEXT function you just added is nested inside the RIGHT function. Functions may be nested up to seven levels deep.

14. Click the Fields tab. Double-click the Delivery Date Time Month field. This is the second entry under Delivery Date Time. This field is placed inside of the TEXT function.

15. Replace the yellow-highlighted word "length" with **2**. This second part of the formula appends the month number as a string after the year. The RIGHT function adds a space before single-digit month numbers so they sort properly with the two-digit month numbers. When complete, your formula should match the formula shown in Figure C-18.

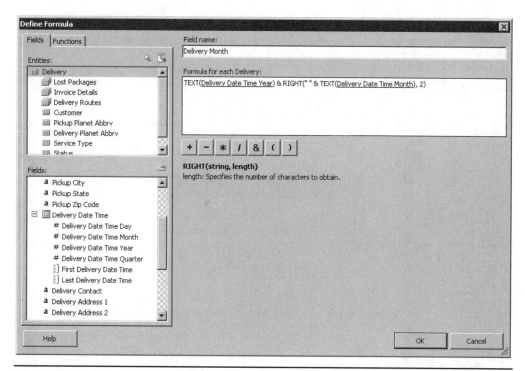

Figure C-18 *The Delivery Month field formula*

16. Click OK to exit the Define Formula dialog box. The new Delivery Month calculated field appears at the top of the Fields list.

17. Drag the Delivery Month field from the Fields list to the left of the Delivery Date Time field in the report layout.

18. Right-click the Delivery Date Time column in the report layout and select Delete from the context menu.

19. Click the Total Cost field, drag and drop it between the Delivery Month column and its current position. This serves to combine the Delivery Month and Total Cost columns into a single group. The report layout appears as shown in Figure C-19.

20. Click Run Report to preview the report.

Add More Formatting

Now, let's add more formatting, filtering, and sorting.

1. Note, there are entries from both 2007 and 2008. Let's look at only 2008 deliveries. Click Design Report in the Report Builder toolbar to return to the report layout.

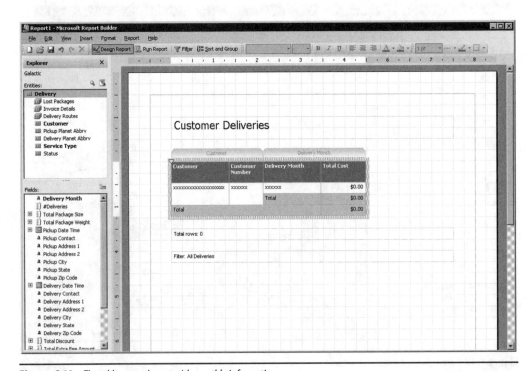

Figure C-19   *The table report layout with monthly information*

2. Click Filter in the Report Builder toolbar. The Filter Data dialog box appears.

3. Select Delivery in the Entities list of the Filter Data dialog box, and then expand Delivery Date Time in the Fields list. Double-click Delivery Date Time Year in the Fields list of the Filter Data dialog box. Enter **2008** for the Equals value (see Figure C-20).

4. While we are filtering, let's also limit the report to only those deliveries made to the city of Axelburg. Double-click the Delivery City field in the Fields list of the Filter Data dialog box.

5. Notice how the Report Builder creates a drop-down list of all unique values in the Delivery City field. Select Axelburg from this drop-down list.

6. The Filter Data dialog box should appear as shown in Figure C-20.

7. Click OK to exit the Filter Data dialog box.

8. Let's also change the sort order so we can see the most recent month first. Click Sort and Group in the Report Builder toolbar. The Sort dialog box appears.

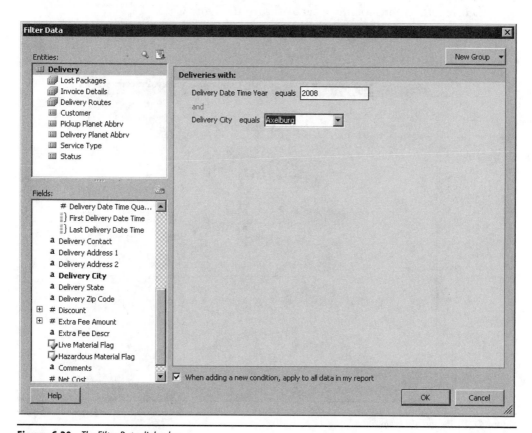

Figure C-20 *The Filter Data dialog box*

9. Select the Delivery Month group in the Select Group list. Select Delivery Month from the Sort by drop-down list and select Descending for this sort. The dialog box should appear as shown in Figure C-21.

10. Click OK to exit the Sort dialog box.

11. Click Run Report to preview the report. Note, there are now only entries for 2008 and the months are in descending order.

12. Click Design Report. We'll try one more modification. Suppose now that we have seen the information in this report, we want to analyze not only which companies are sending packages to Axelburg, but also where those packages are originating from. We need to look at the location of each company. We use the city from the billing address to make that determination.

13. Select Customer in the Entities list, and then select the Billing Contact Info folder under Customer in the Entities list.

14. Click the Billing City field in the Fields list and drag it to the *left* of the Customer column in the report layout. A new grouping is created for Billing City. Your report layout should appear as shown in Figure C-22.

15. Click Run Report. The report should appear similar to Figure C-23.

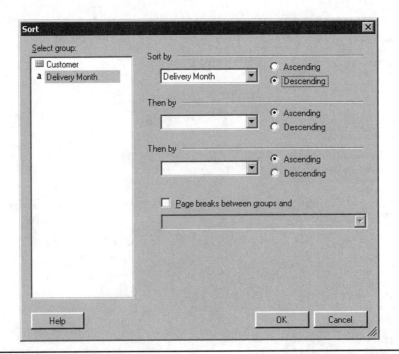

Figure C-21 *The Sort dialog box*

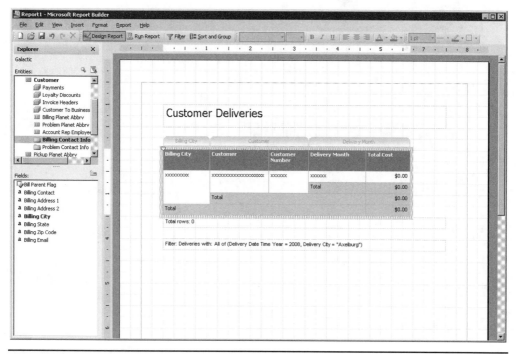

Figure C-22 *The completed table report layout*

Clickthrough Reports and Saving the Report Builder Report

You have seen how the Report Builder enables us to quickly build a table report. You have also seen how you can enhance that report to gain more information as you conduct your ad hoc analysis. Beyond this, exploring related information during ad hoc analysis is often helpful. Further, once you have a report that works well, you may want to share that report with others.

Let's look at how to do both of these tasks. If you not running either the Enterprise Edition or Developer Edition of SQL Server, you will not see the clickthrough behavior, so jump to Step 8.

1. Click Run Report, if the report is not running.

2. Hover the mouse pointer over Landmark, Inc. on Page 1 of the report. The mouse pointer changes from an arrow to a hand. This indicates a clickable link is at this location in the report.

3. Go ahead and click this link. A report showing information about the customer, Landmark, Inc., appears. This is a clickthrough report. This report did not exist before you clicked the link. Instead, it was built on the fly when you asked for it.

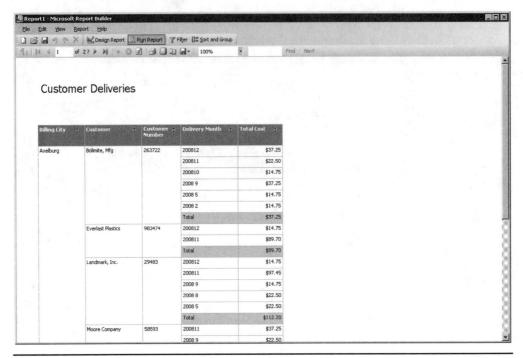

Figure C-23   *The completed table report preview*

4. Click the 2 across from # Invoice Headers. A clickthrough report showing the two invoice headers appears.

5. Click the 10 under # Invoice Details. A clickthrough report showing the ten invoice detail lines for this invoice appears.

6. Click the 7 under Line Number. A clickthrough report showing the information from invoice detail line 7 appears. As long as there is related information, you can continue to navigate to new reports using the clickthrough links.

7. Click the Back to Parent Report arrow in the Report Viewer toolbar to navigate back through the clickthrough reports. The back arrow is shown in Figure C-24. Continue going back until you get to the original Customer Deliveries table report.

8. Click Save in the Ad Hoc Report Builder toolbar. The Save As Report dialog box appears. The Save Report dialog box starts at the Models folder on the Report Server.

9. Click the button with the folder and the green arrow in the dialog box to navigate to the parent folder. This takes you to the Galactic Delivery Services folder.

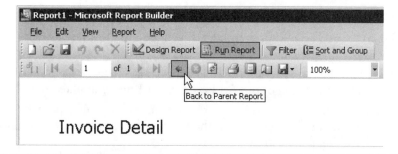

Figure C-24 *The Back to Parent Report arrow in the Report Viewer*

10. Double-click Shared Reports. Enter **Customer Table Report** for Name, and then click Save. (To open an existing Ad Hoc Report Builder report, click Open on the Ad Hoc Report Builder toolbar.)

11. Return to the Report Manager running in your browser and navigate to the Shared Reports folder. An entry for the Customer Table Report is in the Shared Reports folder. This entry was created when you saved the report. In fact, the only way to save a Report Builder report is to place it in a folder on the Report Server.

12. Click the entry for the Customer Table Report to run the report. You see it looks exactly the same as when you ran the report in the Report Builder. You can even click items to jump to clickthrough reports.

Once you have a report in the Report Manager, you can save the report definition to a file in your file system and edit it in a report project with Visual Studio. This makes it possible for an ad hoc report to serve as a starting point for the authoring of a standard report. To do this, click the Properties tab while you are viewing the Customer Table Report in the Report Manager. The Edit link under Report Definition enables you to save this report definition to a file. See Chapter 10 for more information.

If you do edit an Ad Hoc Report Builder report in Visual Studio, you may have to modify the data source and query used in the dataset of the report. Once these changes have been made, the report cannot be edited in the Ad Hoc Report Builder. You may be able to make some minor formatting changes without previewing the report in Visual Studio, save the report back to the Report Manager, and still edit the report in the Ad Hoc Report Builder.

Creating a Matrix Layout Report

Next, we look at a Report Builder report that functions a bit differently. This is the matrix layout report. As mentioned earlier, a matrix layout report is the same as what other tools call a pivot table or crosstab report. Let's see how it works.

Creating the Basic Matrix Report

1. Return to the Ad Hoc Report Builder, if you are not already there. Click Design Report, if the previous report is still being run.
2. Click New in the Ad Hoc Report Builder toolbar. The Getting Started window appears on the right side of the Ad Hoc Report Builder application.
3. We use one of the perspectives from the data model for this report. Expand the Galactic Report Model entry in the Getting Started window and select the Package Tracking perspective.
4. Select Matrix (cross-tab) for the report layout in the Getting Started window.
5. Click OK in the Getting Started window.
6. Double-click the Click to Add Title text box.
7. Enter **Deliveries by Customer by Service Type** into this text box as the report title.
8. Select Customer in the Entities list.
9. Drag the Name field from the Fields list to the Drag and drop row groups area of the report layout.
10. In the Entities list, select Deliveries. Also in the Entities list, select Service Type under Deliveries.
11. Drag the Description field from the Fields list to the Drag and drop column groups area of the report layout.
12. Drag the #Deliveries field from the Fields list to the Drag and drop totals area of the report layout.
13. Click Run Report. Just that quickly, you have a report showing the number of deliveries of each type for each customer.

Adding Groupings to the Matrix

Let's add more grouping levels to the matrix.

1. Click Design Report.
2. Drag the Pickup City field from the Fields list to the left of Customer in the matrix. This creates a grouping on the pickup city.
3. Click Run Report. Note how the report now has a row grouping for each pickup city. You can expand a pickup city to see the row groupings for the customers within it.
4. Click Design Report.
5. Because this report grows horizontally, it should use a landscape page layout. Right-click somewhere on the page layout area that is not occupied by a report item. Select Page Setup from the context menu. The Page Setup menu appears.

6. Select Landscape and click OK.

7. Expand Pickup Date Time in the Fields list. Drag the Pickup Date Time Year field from the Fields list to below the Service Type (#Deliveries) column heading, as shown in Figure C-25. This creates a column grouping for each year with columns within each year for each service type.

8. Click Run Report. Note the new column grouping.

9. Click Save in the Report Builder toolbar. The Save As Report dialog box appears.

10. Click the button in the dialog box for navigating to the parent folder. This takes you to the Galactic Delivery Services folder.

11. Double-click Shared Reports. Enter **Deliveries by Customer by Service Type Report** for Name. Click Save. This report is now available in the Shared Reports folder on the Report Server.

Creating a Chart Layout Report

Finally, we look at an Ad Hoc Report Builder report that creates a business chart.

Creating the Chart Layout Report

1. Return to the Ad Hoc Report Builder, if you are not already there. Click Design Report, if the previous report is still being run.

2. Click New in the Ad Hoc Report Builder toolbar. The Getting Started window opens on the right side of the Ad Hoc Report Builder application.

3. Select the Galactic Report Model.

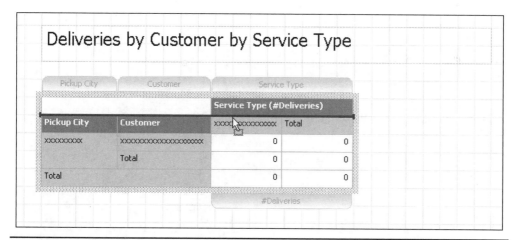

Figure C-25 *Adding a new column grouping to the matrix*

4. Select Chart for Report layout and click OK.

5. Right-click somewhere on the page layout area that is not occupied by a report item. Select Page Setup from the context menu. The Page Setup menu appears.

6. Select Landscape and click OK.

7. Charts like lots of space. Click the chart. Click the sizing handle on the right side of the chart and drag the chart as wide as the page. This is shown in Figure C-26.

8. Select the text box containing the word "Filter:" and drag this text box down to the bottom of the page.

9. Click the chart. Click the sizing handle on the bottom of the chart and drag the bottom of the chart so it is just above the Filter text box.

10. Select Customer in the Entities list. Drag the Name field from the Fields list to the Drag and drop category fields.

11. Select Deliveries in the Entities list. Drag the #Deliveries field from the Fields list to the Drag and drop data value fields.

12. Expand the Pickup Date Time field in the Fields list. Drag the Pickup Date Time Year field from the Fields list to the Drag and drop series fields.

13. Right-click the chart and select Chart Options from the context menu. The Chart Options dialog box appears.

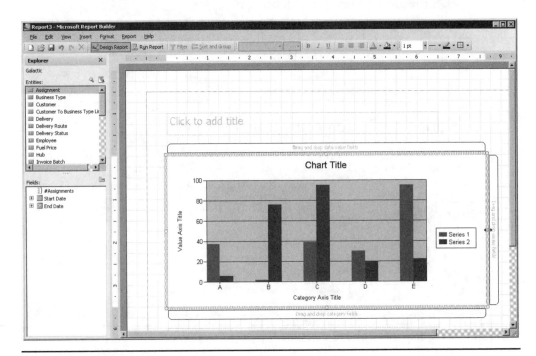

Figure C-26 *Expanding the chart report item*

14. The Chart Type tab of the dialog box enables us to change the type of chart being used to display the data. We use the default chart type, the Column chart. Click the Titles tab.

15. Enter **Deliveries by Customer by Year** for Chart title. Enter **Customers** for Category title. This is the label on the *X* axis of the chart. Enter **Number of Deliveries** for Value title. This is the label on the *Y* axis of the chart.

16. Click the 3-D Effect tab.

17. Check the Display dhart with 3-D visual effect check box. Also, check the Orthographic check box.

18. Click OK to exit the Chart Options dialog box.

19. Click Run Report. Your report should appear as shown in Figure C-27.

20. Click Save in the Report Builder toolbar. The Save As Report dialog box appears.

21. Click the button in the dialog box for navigating to the parent folder. This takes you to the Galactic Delivery Services folder.

22. Double-click Shared Reports. Enter **Deliveries by Customer by Year Chart** for Name. Click Save. This report is now available in the Shared Reports folder on the report server.

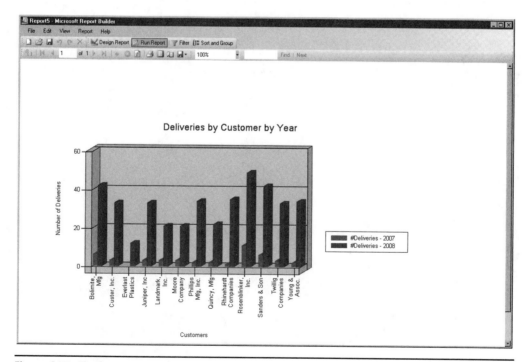

Figure C-27   *The chart report preview*

Give It a Try

As with most skills, the best way to become proficient at creating reports with the Ad Hoc Report Builder is to do it. Use the model built on the Galactic database to practice your data analysis. Better yet, have one or more models created from your own organization's data and jump right in.

Remember, you can't break anything, so give it a try.

Index

— (minus) signs, 317, 320
& operator, 194, 257
@DynamicQuery variable, 436
@TransportNumber stored procedure parameter, 436
+ (plus) signs, 316, 320
3 D Effect, 250
3-D stacked column charts, 252–257

A

<A href></A> tag, 424
AccentSensitivity property, DataSetDefinition class, 760
AccentSensitivitySpecified property, DataSetDefinition class, 760
Access report import tool, 437
Account Rep Employee role, Customer entity, 791
accounting, GDS, 87
Accounting Information diagram, 794
Acrobat Reader, 450, 506, 544, 576
Action page, 431
action property, 647
Active parameter
    GetDataDrivenSubscriptionProperties method, 732
    GetSubscriptionProperties method, 739
Active property, Subscription class, 778
ActiveState web service class, 758
ActiveX object, 507
ad hoc reporting
    Report Builder
        chart layout reports, 819–821
        clickthrough reports, 804–805
        defined, 10
        Entities list, 803–804
        entities, roles, and fields, 802–803
        Fields list, 804
        infinite clickthrough reports feature, 28
        launching, 801–802
        matrix layout reports, 817–819
        narrowing columns, 806
        overview, 800
        table layout reports, 805–817

Report Model
    cleaning up, 789–797
    creating, 785–786
    creating project in BIDS, 783
    data sources, 783–785
    overview, 782
    parts and pieces, 786–789
    securing, 797–800
Add Existing Item dialog box, 501
Add Language dialog box, 499
Add New Chart Area option, context menu, 230
Add New Data Source, 783
Add New Item dialog box, 305–306, 324–325
Add New Report command, Report Wizard, 139
Add New Report Model, Context menu, 785
Add Parameter, 401
Add Reference dialog box, 400, 405
Add Service Reference dialog box, 585, 710
Add Table dialog box, Graphical Query Designer, 123
Add Title text box, 818
Add Web Reference dialog box, 585, 710
administration utilities, 25–26
administrative rights, Reporting Services, 60
Administrative Tools, 438
Adobe Acrobat Reader, 450, 506, 544, 576
Adobe Portable Document Format (PDF) presentation
    format. *See* PDF
Adobe Professional, 452
Adobe Standard, 452
advanced server support feature, Enterprise Edition, 28
AdventureWorks database, 27
aggregate functions, 106, 227, 321–323, 340
alias, 82, 182
Alias property, Field class, 767
AlignOrientation property, 648
AlignType property, 648
AlignWithChartArea property, 648
AllMembershipCondition
    file, 398, 495
    security class, 493

AllowBlank property, ReportParameter class, 774
AllowBlankSpecified property, ReportParameter class, 774
AllowLabelRotation property, 648–649
AllowQueryExecution property
    ExecutionInfo class, 764
    ExecutionInfo2 class, 765
Amount field, InvoiceDetail dataset, 426
Analysis Services, 404, 408, 411
anchor tag, 572
angle property, 649
AntiAliasing property, 649
Application Configuration File page, 594
April property, MonthsOfYearSelector class, 770
Area3DStyle property, 649
areas, chart, 230–231, 235
Areas of Excellence text box, Design tab, 418
AreasForImprovement field, 417, 418, 421, 424
AreasOfExcellence field, 416, 418, 420, 422
arrows property, 649
AspectRatio property, 649
ASP.NET Web Application, Templates area, 585
assemblies property, 650
Attach to Process dialog box, 628
attached reports, versus embedded reports, 553
AttributeReference Collection Editor dialog box, 792
attributes, 70, 360, 787
August property, MonthsOfYearSelector class, 770
<authentication mode="Windows"/> entry, 626
<Authentication> entry, 625
<authentication> entry, 626
AuthenticationExtension class, 615–617
AuthenticationTypes authentication element,
    RSReportServer.config, 602
<AuthenticationTypes> entry, 624
author property, 650
Authority parameter, LogonUser method, 716, 745
<authorization> entry, 626
AuthorizationExtension class, 617–621
Auto Execute toolbar, 409
AutoFitTextDisabled property, 650
Auto-Hide feature, 182
AutoLayout property, 650, 667, 676, 704
AutoRefresh property, 437, 650
AutoRefreshInterval property, ExecutionInfo2 class, 765
AutoSize technique, 696
Available Values drop-down list, 403
Available Values page, 368, 387
AVG( ) aggregate function, 106
Avg( ) aggregate function, 322
AvgWeight field, 407, 410
Axelburg Invoice-Batch Number Report, 586

AxelburgRVFrontEnd project, 595
AxelburgRVFrontEnd.EmployeeList.rdlc file, 595
Axis Title Properties dialog box, 233–234, 241–242, 255

B

<B></B> tag, 424
Back to Parent Report button, Report Viewer toolbar, 432
BackFill property, 651
BackFrame property, 651
BackgroundColor property, 281, 651, 652
BackgroundGradientEndColor property, 651, 652
BackgroundGradientType property, 652
BackgroundImage property, 647, 652
BackgroundPatternType property, 652
BackgroundRepeat detail property, 652
BackgroundShadowOffset property, 652–653
backspace key, 370
Backup button, 57
BarStart property, 653
basic reports
    Repair Count By Type report
        creating data source, 197–200
        creating dataset, 197–200
        formatting, 202–205
        Matrix item, 200–202
        overview, 197
    Transport Information Sheet
        creating data source, 206–207
        List item, 212–218
        overview, 206
        TransportInfo dataset, 207–211
        TransportSNs dataset, 206–207
    Transport List report
        creating data source, 173–178
        creating dataset, 178–182
        formatting, 188–195
        overview, 172–173
        Table item, 182–188
BatchHeader object, 722, 723
BatchHeader web service class, 758–759
BatchHeaderValue property, 721, 722, 723
BatchID property, BatchHeader class, 759
Begin Running This Schedule On option, Schedule page, 546, 560
begin tags, RDL, 359–360
BeginWorkDate field, MAX( ) aggregate function, 182
best practices
    report deployment practices, 631–633
    report-authoring practices, 629–630
BI. *See* business intelligence (BI)
Billing City field, 814

Billing Contact Info folder, 793, 814
BillingContact text box, 284
binary large object (BLOB), 697
Bind Commands to Existing Stored Procedures page, 595
BLOB (binary large object), 697
body layout area, 638
Bolimite row, 443
Bookmark property, 653
BookmarkID parameter, NavigateBookmark
    method, 717
bookmarks, 452
Boolean attribute, 787
Boolean expressions, 330
BooleanOperator parameter, ExecuteBatch method, 730
border properties, 281
BorderColor property, 647, 653
BorderColor: Top property, 413
BorderSkin property, 654
BorderStyle property, 654
BorderWidth: Bottom property, 413
BorderWidth property, 654–655
Bottom detail property, 680
broken-link X symbol, 487
Browser role, 511–512, 514, 516, 517
built-in fields, 304
BUILTIN\Administrators group, 509
business intelligence (BI)
    project type, 11–12
    sharing
        advantages of Reporting Services, 8–10
        need for, 5–6
        solutions, 6–8
Business Intelligence Development Studio, 11, 27, 472, 498,
    501, 525, 548
        creating new project in, 114–116
        creating Report Model project in, 783
business need
    business type distribution chart, 247
    conference nametags, 275
    conference place cards, 282
    days in maintenance chart, 251
    deliveries versus lost packages chart, 221
    digital dashboard, 257
    employee list report, 324
    employee mailing labels report, 335–336
    employee time report, 307
    fuel price chart, 236, 244
    overtime report, 343
    rate sheet report, 288
    report template, 299
    revised employee time report, 351

C

cached data. *See* data caching during preview
CacheReport parameter, SetCacheOptions method, 747
caching, report
    data source credentials, 533
    data-driven subscriptions and, 563–566
    enabling
        deploying, 538
        expirations, 536–538
        parameters, 538–539
        security, 539
        viewing reports, 535–536
        weather reports, 534–535
    expirations, 532
    formats, 533–534
    overview, 530–531
calculated fields, 101–104
Calculated Member Builder dialog box, 407
Calculated Members pane, 407
calendar property, 655
calEndDate property, 587
calStartDate property, 587
CancelBatch method, 721, 722
CancelJob method, 722
CanGrow property, 655
CanShrink property, 655
caption property, 656
cardinality of relations, 73–76
cascading style sheet (CSS), 569
CaseSensitivity property, DataSetDefinition class, 760
CaseSensitivitySpecified property, DataSetDefinition class, 760
CatalogItem objects, 729
CatalogItem web service class, 759
category axes in charts, 227, 242–243
Category Group Properties dialog box, 249–250, 253
Category pane, 370
category scope, 256
CategoryAxes property, 656
CategoryAxisName property, 656
CategoryField property, 656
Cause group, 380
Change button, 57–58
Change Credentials button, 54
Change Data Source dialog box, 119
Change Database button, 54
Changed parameter, PrepareQuery method, 746
chart area data region, 640
Chart Area Properties dialog box, 249
chart axis, 694
chart axis data region, 640

chart axis title, 702
chart category/series group data region, 640–641
chart data region, 639–640
chart gridlines data region, 641
chart layout reports, creating, 819–821
chart legend data region, 641
chart legend title, 702
Chart Options dialog box, 820, 821
Chart Properties dialog box, 435
chart report, expanding, 820
chart report item, 220
chart report preview, 821
chart series data region, 641
chart title data region, 642
Chart Title Properties dialog box, 241
Chart Type tab, 821
ChartAreaName property, 656
ChartAreas property, 656
charts
    business type distribution chart, 247–250
    days in maintenance chart
        business need, 251
        creating new report, 251–257
        dataset, 251–257
        features highlighted, 250
        placing chart item on report and populating it,
          251–257
        task overview, 251
    deliveries versus lost packages chart
        alternate ways to present, 227–236
        business need, 221
        creating new report, 221–222
        creating project, 221–222
        datasets, 221–222
        features highlighted, 220–221
        placing chart item on report and populating it,
          222–227
        shared data source, 221–222
        task overview, 221
    fuel price chart
        business need, 236
        creating new report, 236–237
        datasets, 236–237
        features highlighted, 236
        placing chart item on report and populating it,
          238–240
        refining chart, 240–244
        task overview, 236
        version 2, 244–247
    overview, 220
    similarity to gauges, 267

check in, VSS, 363
check out, VSS, 363
Check Syntax dialog box, 407
CheckAccess methods, 620–621
CheckAuthentication class, 615, 617
child tables, 72
Children property, DocumentMapNode class, 764
Choose a Data Source Type page, 593
Choose File dialog box, 480, 488, 489, 490, 501, 502
Choose Report drop-down list, 595
Choose the Deployment Location page, Report Wizard, 130
Choose the Table Layout page, Report Wizard, 146
Choose the Table Style page, Report Wizard, 129
Choose Your Data Connection page, 593
Choose Your Database Objects page, 594
Classes area, Report Properties dialog box, 400
classes property, 657
ClassName detail property, 657
CleanupCycleMinutes element, 600
Clear parameter, Sort method, 720
Clear parameter, Sort2 method, 720
ClickOnce application, 800
Clickthrough page, 798–799
clickthrough reports, 804–805, 815–817
client-side printing, 507
Clip technique, 696
ClipContent property, 657
cmdExecute button, 587
cmdExecute_Click code, 587
code access, 491
Code Access Modifications folder, 398
code access security, 491–494
Code Group portion, 494
Code Groups file, 398
code property, 657
Collation property, DataSetDefinition class, 760
Collect Model Statistics page, 786
color property, 657
Column cells, 384
columns, 67–70
    employee mailing labels report, 340–342
    grouping, 819
    header, 310
    static and dynamic, 357
Columns cell, Tablix Properties dialog box, 434
Columns property, 342
columns property, 658
command parameter, 574
command window, 598, 599
CommandText property, QueryDefinition class, 773
CommandType property, QueryDefinition class, 773

Comma-Separated Values (CSV), 442, 460–461
compatibility, web services, 712
composite primary keys, 70
computer memory, 34
ComputerName property, 469, 498
concatenation operator (&), 194
Condition property, SearchCondition class, 778
Conditions parameter, ExecuteBatch method, 730
ConditionSpecified property, SearchCondition class, 778
conference nametags
    business need, 275
    creating new report, 276–282
    dataset, 276–282
    features highlighted, 275
    placing report items on report, 276–282
    task overview, 276
conference place cards
    business need, 282
    creating new report, 282–287
    dataset, 282–287
    features highlighted, 282
    placing report items on report, 282–287
    task overview, 282
Configuration drop-down list, 478
configuration element, 599
configuration files, Report Manager, 623
<Configuration> entry, 625
confirmation dialog box, 503
Connect button, 60
Connect to Server dialog box, 517
Connect Using options, 485, 486, 487
Connection Manager dialog box, 784
Connection Properties dialog box, 117, 406
Connection String text box, 406, 481
connection strings, 118–119
ConnectionType element, RSReportServer.config
    configuration, 600
ConnectString property, DataSourceDefinition class, 762
constant fields, 101–104
constant vbCrLf, 194
constraints, 70
Consume reports task, 510
ConsumeContainerWhitespace property, 658
Content Manager, 509, 512–513, 516, 517, 519, 520, 521, 525, 539, 562
Contents parameter
    CreateResource method, 726
    SetResourceContents method, 753
Contents tab, 469, 470, 471, 500, 503, 520
    Hide Details button, 485
    New Data Source button, 481
    Show Details, 516
    Show Details button, 484
    Upload File, 488, 489
    Upload File button, 480
    Upload File page, 490
Context menu
    Add New Report Model, 785
    Add Service Reference dialog box, 710
    Add Web Reference dialog box, 710
Control Panel, 438
controls, Toolbox, 16
CONVERT( ) function, 308
cookies, 627
COUNT( ) aggregate function, 106
Count( ) aggregate function, 202, 227, 322, 381, 384
CountDistinct( ) aggregate function, 322
CountRows( ) aggregate function, 322
Create Linked Report page, 526
Create linked reports task, 510
CreateBatch method, 722–723
CreateDataDrivenSubscription method, 723
CreateDataSource method, 723–724
CreatedBy property, CatalogItem class, 759
CreateFolder method, 723, 724
CreateLinkedReport method, 724
CreateModel method, 725
CreateReport method, 723, 725
CreateReportHistorySnapshot method, 725–726
CreateResource method, 726
CreateRole method, 726
CreateSchedule method, 727
CreateSubscription method, 727
Create/View History page, 543, 544, 547
Create/View Subscriptions page, 550
CreationDate property
    CatalogItem class, 759
    ReportHistorySnapshot class, 774
CreationDateSpecified property, CatalogItem class, 759
Creator property, Schedule class, 776
CredentialRetrieval property, DataSourceDefinition class, 762
credentials, 485–487, 711–712
Credentials parameter, 482
    GetReportParameters method, 738
    SetExecutionCredentials method, 719
    SetExecutionCredentials2 method, 719
Credentials property, 721
CredentialsRequired property
    ExecutionInfo class, 764
    ExecutionInfo2 class, 765
criteria pane, Graphical Query Designer, 123
CrossAt property, 658
crosstab (pivot table report), 153
CSS (cascading style sheet), 569

CStr( ) function, 194
CSV (Comma-Separated Values), 442, 460–461
CSV Format Device Information (rc), 578
CSV format parameter, 576
Cube Selection dialog box, 408
Custom authentication element, 602
Custom Properties dialog box, 638, 639, 647
custom security
    authentication, 609–611
    authorization, 611
    issues with, 611–613
    other extensions, 629
    overview, 608–609
CustomAttributes property, 658
CustomCode property, 658
Customer Deliveries table report, 816
Customer drop-down list, 376
Customer entity, 791
    attributes of, 789
    roles of, 790
customer list reports, 386–389
    begin new project, 114–116
    choosing layout, 127–137
    creating data source, 116–120
    creating dataset, 121–127
    overview, 113
Customer List.rdl entry, 386
Customer Number column, 806, 807
Customer Table Report, 817
Customer-Invoice report
    choosing layout, 145–152
    creating data source, 139–144
    creating dataset, 139–144
    creating new project in, 138–144
    overview, 137
CustomerInvoices dataset, 429
CustomerName attribute, Results pane, 407
CustomerName field, 410, 429, 431
CustomerNumber parameter, 368, 370
CustomInnerPlotPosition property, 659
customizing Reporting Services
    best practices
        report deployment practices, 631–633
        report-authoring practices, 629–630
    custom security
        creating extensions, 613–621
        deploying extensions, 621–626
        using extensions, 627–628
    security, 608–629
        authentication, 609–611
        authorization, 611
        issues with, 611–613

    using without Report Manager
        Report Viewer control, 589–595
        Reporting Services utilities, 597–599
        RSReportServer.config file, 599–608
        SharePoint web parts, 595–597
        URL access, 572–585
        web service access, 585–589
CustomLabels property, 659
CustomPaletteColors property, 659
CustomPosition property, 659
CustomProperties property, 659

D

DailyRecurrence property, RecurrencePattern class, 773
DailyRecurrence web service class, 760
dashboard. *See* digital dashboard
Data Association page, 558, 559
data caching during preview
    employee list report
        business need, 324
        creating new report and dataset, 324–325
        features highlighted, 324
        floating header, 332–335
        interactive sorting, 332–335
        report layout, 325–332
        task overview, 324
    employee mailing labels report
        adding multiple columns, 340–342
        business need, 335–336
        creating mailing label content, 336–339
        features highlighted, 335
        report header, 340–342
        task overview, 336
    overtime report
        business need, 343
        creating new report, 343–345
        datasets, 343–345
        features highlighted, 343
        report layout, 345–351
        task overview, 343
    overview, 323
    revised employee time report
        business need, 351
        copying and renaming existing report, 352–358
        features highlighted, 351
        modifying dataset, 352–358
        modifying layout, 352–358
        task overview, 351
data definition, 13–14
data exchange formats
    CSV, 460–461

overview, 460
XML, 461–464
data label expression scope, 256
Data Mining Expression (DMX), 14, 408
data providers, 19
data regions, 14, 196, 639–645
Data Source Configuration Wizard, 593
data source credentials, 120, 533
Data Source Properties dialog box, 176, 405, 406
Data Source Properties page, 483, 485, 486
Data Source View Wizard dialog box, 785
Data Source Views folder, 785
data source views, Report Model, 785
Data Source Wizard dialog box, 783, 785
data sources
Customer List Report, 116–120
Customer-Invoice report, 139–144
Invoice-Batch Number report, 153–155
paid invoices report, 438–439
Report Model, 783–785
Transport List report, 173–178
Data Sources link, 483, 497
Data Sources page, 542, 798
database credentials, 38
database files, images stored in, 274
database server, 36
Database Structure
cardinality of relations, 73–76
normalization, 70–72
overview, 66
primary keys, 70
relations, 72–73
retrieving data
inner joins, 76–77
joining multiple tables, 81
outer joins, 77–80
self-joins, 81–82
sorting, 83–84
tables, rows, and columns, 67–70
DatabaseQueryTimeout element, 600
data-driven subscriptions
creating, 555–562
Enterprise Edition, 28
event-driven behavior and, 562–563
report caching and, 563
security and, 562
DataDrivenSubscriptionID parameter
GetDataDrivenSubscriptionProperties method, 732
SetDataDrivenSubscriptionProperties method, 748
DataElementName property, 461, 464, 660
DataElementOutput property, 464, 660

DataElementStyle property, 464, 660
DataPoint property, 660
DataRetrievalPlan parameter
CreateDataDrivenSubscription method, 723
GetDataDrivenSubscriptionProperties method, 732
SetDataDrivenSubscriptionProperties method, 748
DataRetrievalPlan web service class, 760
DataSchema property, 660
dataset names, spaces and, 165
DataSet parameter, PrepareQuery method, 746
Dataset Properties dialog box, 165, 388, 406, 407, 548
business type distribution charts, 248
conference nametags, 276
conference place cards, 283
days in maintenance chart, 251–252
deliveries versus lost packages chart, 221–222
digital dashboard gauges, 258
fuel price chart, 236–237, 245
overtime report, 344
rate sheet report, 288–289
DataSet property, DataRetrievalPlan class, 760
DataSetDefinition web service class, 760–761
DataSetName property, 661
datasets, 13
business type distribution chart, 248
conference nametags, 276–282
conference place cards, 282–287
customer list reports, 121–127, 387–389
customer-invoice report, 139–144
days in maintenance chart, 251–257
deliveries versus lost packages chart, 221–222
delivery analysis reports, 405–409
delivery status reports, 367–368
digital dashboard, 258–262, 267–273
employee evaluation reports, 412–418
employee list report, 324–325
employee time report, 307–308
fuel price chart, 236–237, 245–247
invoice front-end reports, 429–430
invoice reports, 425–428
Invoice-Batch Number report
lost delivery reports, 378–380
overtime report, 343–345
Parameterized Invoice-Batch Number report, 161–165
payroll checks, 390–392
rate sheet report, 288–292
revised employee time report, 352–358
Transport Information Sheet, 206–211
Transport List report, 178–182
transport monitor reports, 433–437

DataSource parameter
  CreateDataSource method, 724
  DisableDataSource method, 729
  EnableDataSource method, 729
  GenerateModel method, 731
  GetDataSourceContents method, 732
  ListSubscriptionsUsingDataSource method, 744
  PrepareQuery method, 746
  SetDataSourceContents method, 748
DataSource value, GetItemType method, 734
DataSource web service class, 761
DataSourceCredentials web service class, 761
DataSourceDefinition class, 757–758
DataSourceDefinition property, DataSourceDefinitionOrReference
    class, 763
DataSourceDefinition web service class, 762
DataSourceDefinitionOrReference web service class, 762–763
DataSourceID property, DataSourcePrompt class, 763
DataSourceName property, DataSourceCredentials class, 761
DataSourcePrompt web service class, 763
DataSourcePrompts property
  ExecutionInfo class, 764
  ExecutionInfo2 class, 765
DataSourceReference property, DataSourceDefinitionOrReference
    class, 763
DataSourceReference web service class, 763
DataSources parameter, SetItemDataSources method, 749
DataTransform property, 661
DATEADD( ) function, 162–163
date-formatting code, 244
DATEPART( ) function, 308
Date/time attributes, 787
days in maintenance chart
  business need, 251
  creating new report, 251–257
  dataset, 251–257
  features highlighted, 250
  placing chart item on report and populating it, 251–257
  task overview, 251
Days property, MonthlyRecurrence class, 770
DaysInterval property, DailyRecurrence class, 760
DaysOfWeek property, MonthlyDOWRecurrence class, 770
DaysOfWeek property, WeeklyRecurrence class, 780
DaysOfWeekSelector web service class, 763–764
DBPassword password, 579
Debug configuration, 477, 478
debug database file (PDB), 627
Debug menu, 479
debugging, 306–307, 627–628
DebugLocal configuration, 477
December property, MonthsOfYearSelector class, 770
default configuration settings, 48

Default Detail Attributes dialog box, 792
Default detail property, 653, 654, 655
Default Value drop-down edit area, 540
Default Values page, 369
Default.aspx file, 586
DefaultDetailAttributes entry, Properties window, 792
DefaultDomain authentication element, 602
DefaultValues property, ReportParameter class, 774
DefaultValuesQueryBased property, ReportParameter class, 774
DefaultValuesQueryBasedSpecified property, ReportParameter
    class, 774
DeferVariableEvaluation property, 661
Define Formula dialog box, 794, 804, 805, 809, 811
Define Query Parameters dialog box, 258, 268
Definition parameter
  CreateDataSource method, 724
  CreateModel method, 725
  CreateReport method, 725
  LoadReportDefinition method, 715
  LoadReportDefinition2 method, 716
  SetDataSourceContents method, 748
  SetModelDefinition method, 749
  SetReportDefinition method, 751
Definition property
  Schedule class, 776
  ScheduleReference class, 777
Delete button, 58
Delete Legend, 435
DELETE query, 88–89
Delete Title, 435
DeleteItem method, 727–728
DeleteReportHistorySnapshot method, 728
DeleteRole method, 728
DeleteSchedule method, 728
DeleteSubscription method, 729
deleting
  folders, 503–504
  report history snapshots, 547
deliveries versus lost packages chart
  alternate ways to present, 227–236
  business need, 221
  creating new report, 221–222
  creating project, 221–222
  datasets, 221–222
  features highlighted, 220–221
  placing chart item on report and populating
      it, 222–227
  shared data source, 221–222
  task overview, 221
delivering reports
  caching
      data source credentials, 533

enabling, 534–539
    expirations, 532
    formats, 533–534
    overview, 530–531
execution snapshots, 539–542
report history snapshots, 542–549
ReportingServices style sheet, 569–570
site settings
    Site Settings page, 563–565
    SQL Server Management Studio, 566–569
subscriptions, 549–563
    data-driven subscriptions, 555–563
    My Subscriptions page, 554–555
    standard subscriptions, 549–554
delivery analysis reports, 404–411, 491, 498
Delivery City field, 813
Delivery Date Time attribute, 793
Delivery Date Time column, 808
Delivery Date Time entry, 810
Delivery Date Time field, 807, 810
Delivery Date Time Month field, 811
Delivery Date Time Year, 813
Delivery Date Time Year field, 810
Delivery entity, 792
Delivery measure group, 407
Delivery Month field, 811
Delivery Month field formula, 811
Delivery Month group, 814
Delivery Status Report layout, 373
Delivery Status Report preview, 374, 376
delivery status reports, 367–377
Delivery_Count field, 410
DeliveryAnalysis report, 405, 498, 499
DeliveryCount field, 410
DeliveryDateTime field, 372
DeliveryDetail report, 425, 427
DeliveryExtensionRemoved property, ActiveState class, 758
DeliveryInfo dataset, 410
DeliveryNumber column, 372
DeliveryNumber datatype, 462
DeliveryNumber field, 370–371, 377, 378
DeliveryPlanet field, 372
DeliveryQuarter attribute, Results pane, 407
DeliveryQuarter field, 410
DeliverySettings property, Subscription class, 778
DeliveryStatus dataset, 370, 377, 425
DeliveryType datatype, 462
denormalizing, 77
Dependencies property, ReportParameter class, 774
deploying reports, 17–18
    to common folders, 525
    report caching and, 538

using Report Designer
    in Chapter09 project, 472–473
    creating folders while deploying, 474
    overview, 472
    Property Pages dialog box, 477–479
    shared data sources, 474–477
    single report, 474
    working through web service, 474
Description drop-down list, 407, 495
Description parameter
    CreateDataDrivenSubscription method, 723
    CreateRole method, 726
    CreateSubscription method, 727
    GetDataDrivenSubscriptionProperties method, 732
    GetRoleProperties method, 739
    GetSubscriptionProperties method, 739
    SetDataDrivenSubscriptionProperties method, 748
    SetRoleProperties method, 753
    SetSubscriptionProperties method, 754
description property, 661
Description property
    CatalogItem class, 759
    Full Name attribute, 794
    ModelCatalogItem class, 768
    ModelItem class, 769
    ModelPerspective class, 769
    Role class, 775
    Schedule class, 776
    Subscription class, 778
    Task class, 779
DescriptionLocID property, 661
Design Mode toolbar, 409
Design Report, 812, 814, 818
design surface, 15
Design the Matrix page, 156
Design the Table page, 128, 145, 594
details groups, 315
Developer Edition, 28–29
device information parameters, 577, 578, 579
DeviceInfo parameter
    GetRenderResource method, 714, 736
    Render method, 717
    Render2 method, 718
DeviceInfo XML structure, 589
diagram pane, Graphical Query Designer, 122
dialog boxes
    changing properties of, 259
    property, 236, 262–267
digital dashboard
    adding second gauge, 267–273
    business need, 257
    creating new report, 258–262

digital dashboard (*Continued*)
    dataset, 258–262
    features highlighted, 257
    modifying dataset, 267–273
    overview, 257
    presenting data on gauge, 258–262
    refining appearance of gauge, 262–267
    task overview, 258
Direction detail property, 697
Direction parameter, 720
direction property, 661–662
DisableDataSource method, 729
disk space, 34
DisplayErrorLink element, 601
DisplayName property, ExtensionParameter class, 766
DistanceFromScale property, 662
DISTINCT query, 92, 94
distributed installation, 31, 36, 44
<DIV></DIV> tag, 424
DMX (Data Mining Expression), 14, 408
DockOffset property, 662
DockOutsideChartArea property, 662
DockToChartArea property, 662
DocMapID parameter, NavigateDocumentMap method, 717
document map, 431
documentation, 27
DocumentMapLabel property, 663
DocumentMapNode object, 713
DocumentMapNode web service class, 764
domain user accounts, 38
downloading report definitions, 500
drilldown feature, 630
    employee time report, 313–317
    Report Wizard, 137
drillthrough, 630
DrillthroughID parameter
    LoadDrillthroughTarget method, 714
    LoadDrillthroughTarget2 method, 715
DrillthroughTest report, 520, 521, 523
drop areas, chart, 223–225
drop-down lists, 350–351
dummy groups, 332
duplicate data, 70–71
dynamic query, 389
dynamic rows and columns, 357
DynamicHeight property, 663
DynamicWidth property, 663

E

Edit Item Security
    dialog box, 515, 517
    page, 519, 520

Edit link, 500, 516, 554
Edit Role Assignment page, 516, 517, 519
editing
    Report Definition Language, 361
    report definitions, 500–501
EditSubReportTest folder, 501
e-mail delivery option, 549
Email field, 388
e-mail server, 36
E-mail Settings page, Reporting Services Configuration Manager, 55–56
embedded images, 274–275, 287
embedded reports
    versus attached reports, 553
    creating standard subscriptions with, 550–551
Employee entity, 791, 794
Employee Evaluation Detail Report layout, 413
Employee Evaluation folder, 792
employee evaluation reports, 412–424
Employee Evaluations Report preview, 417
Employee field text box, 421
employee list report
    business need, 324
    creating new report and dataset, 324–325
    features highlighted, 324
    floating header, 332–335
    interactive sorting, 332–335
    report layout, 325–332
    task overview, 324
employee mailing labels report
    adding multiple columns, 340–342
    business need, 335–336
    creating mailing label content, 336–339
    features highlighted, 335
    report header, 340–342
    task overview, 336
employee time report. *See also* revised employee time report
    adding drilldown capability, 313–317
    adding totaling, 317–323
    business need, 307
    creating new report, 307–308
    creating project, 307–308
    dataset, 307–308
    features highlighted, 307
    populating report layout, 308–313
    shared data source, 307–308
    task overview, 307
EmployeeEval report, 413
EmployeeList, 595
EmployeeName field, 414
EmptyPoint property, 663
Enable Report Execution Logging option, 569
EnableAuthPersistence authentication element, 602

EnableClientPrinting property, Reporting Services, 606
enabled property, 663
EnableDataSource method, 729
EnabledSpecified class, 758
EnabledSpecified property, DataSourceDefinition class, 762
EnableExecutionLogging property, Reporting Services, 606
EnableIntegratedSecurity property, Reporting Services, 606
EnableLoadReportDefinition property, Reporting Services, 606
EnableManualSnapshotCreation parameter,
    SetReportHistoryOptions method, 752
EnableMyReports property, Reporting Services, 606
EnableRemoteErrors property, Reporting Services, 606
EnableReportDesignClientDownload property, Reporting
    Services, 606
Encoding parameter
        Render method, 717
        Render2 method, 718
        RenderStream method, 718
Encrypted property, ExtensionParameter class, 766
encrypting Reporting Services information, 36–37
encryption key, 597–598
encryption key backup, 630
Encryption Keys page, Reporting Services Configuration Manager,
    57–59
end tags, RDL, 359–360
EndDate property, ScheduleDefinition class, 776
EndDateSpecified property, ScheduleDefinition class, 776
EndMargin property, 664
EndPage parameter, 713
EndPoint property, 664
EndValue property, 664
EndWidth property, 664
Enterprise Edition, 28, 44
entities, Report Builder, 802–803
entity relationship diagrams (ERD), 788
EquallySizedAxesFonts property, 664–665
EquallySpacedItems property, 665
equals signs, 349
ERD (entity relationship diagrams), 788
error page, 481
Error property, ExtensionParameter class, 766
ErrorMessage property, ReportParameter class, 774
errors in reports
        adding drilldown capability, 313–317
        adding totaling, 317–323
        business need, 307
        creating new report, 307–308
        creating project, 307–308
        dataset, 307–308
        features highlighted, 307
        overview, 306–307

        populating report layout, 308–313
        shared data source, 307–308
        task overview, 307
ES folder, 491
EvalDetail field, 415
EvalDetail report, 412, 413
EvalPerformance dataset, 413, 418
EvalRatings report, 412
Evaluation Edition, 27–28
EvaluatorEmployeeNumber group, 412
EventData parameter, FireEvent method, 730
event-driven behavior, data-driven subscriptions
    and, 562–563
EventType parameter
        CreateDataDrivenSubscription method, 723
        CreateSubscription method, 727
        FireEvent method, 730
        GetDataDrivenSubscriptionProperties method, 732
        GetSubscriptionProperties method, 739
        SetDataDrivenSubscriptionProperties method, 748
        SetSubscriptionProperties method, 754
EventType property, Subscription class, 778
Excel Format Device Information (rc)
        rc:OmitDocumentMap parameter, 579
        rc:OmitFormulas parameter, 579
        rc:SimplePageHeader parameter, 579
EXCEL format parameter, 576
Excel presentation format
        features not supported by, 456
        features supported by, 455–456
        overview, 455
        viewing documents, 455
        when to use, 457
Execute permissions, 497
Execute report definitions task, 511
ExecuteBatch method, 721, 723, 729
Execution Account page, Reporting Services Configuration
    Manager, 56–57
execution cache, 27
Execution permission, 493
Execution Properties page, 534, 535, 536, 537, 540, 541, 565
Execution property, ExecutionInfo class, 764
execution snapshots
        creating on schedule, 541
        manually creating, 539–541
        security and, 542
        standard subscriptions and, 553
ExecutionDate property, CatalogItem class, 759
ExecutionDateSpecified property, CatalogItem class, 759
ExecutionDateTime property, ExecutionInfo2 class, 765
Execution-Header object, 712

ExecutionHeaderValue property, 712
ExecutionID property
    ExecutionInfo class, 764
    ExecutionInfo2 class, 765
ExecutionInfo object, 713
ExecutionInfo parameter, Sort2 method, 721
ExecutionInfo web service class, 764–765
ExecutionInfo2 object, 713
ExecutionInfo2 web service class, 765
ExecutionLogDaysKept property, Reporting Services, 606
ExecutionLogStorage table
    Report Catalog, 608
    ReportServer database, 569
ExecutionSetting parameter, SetExecutionOptions method, 749
ExecutionTime global field, 304
ExpirationDateTime property
    ExecutionInfo class, 764
    ExecutionInfo2 class, 765
ExpirationDefinition web service class, 766
expirations, 532, 536–538
exporting reports
    data exchange formats
        CSV, 460–461
        overview, 460
        XML, 461–464
    overview, 441–444
    presentation formats
        Excel, 455–457
        overview, 445–447
        PDF, 450–452
        printed, 459–460
        TIFF, 447–450
        web archive, 452–455
        Word, 458–459
    printing reports, 445
    viewing exported reports, 444
Expression detail property, 697
Expression dialog box, 190, 191, 369, 370, 375, 378, 379, 391, 395
    business type distribution charts, 249
    days in maintenance chart, 252–253, 255
    employee list reports, 328–329, 333
    employee mailing labels report, 337–340
    fuel price chart, 241–242
    overtime report, 346–347
    page footers, 302
    rate sheet report, 290
    revised employee time report, 353–356
    Value property, 194
Expression drop-down list, 548
expressions, delivery status reports, 374–377
Extensible Markup Language (XML), 14, 359–361, 397, 442, 494, 660

Extension parameter
    GetExtensionSettings method, 733
    Render2 method, 718
    ValidateExtensionSettings method, 755
Extension property
    DataSourceDefinition class, 762
    ExtensionSettings class, 767
Extension web service class, 766
ExtensionParameter web service class, 766–767
<Extensions> entry, 625
ExtensionSettings parameter
    CreateDataDrivenSubscription method, 723
    CreateSubscription method, 727
    GetDataDrivenSubscriptionProperties method, 732
    GetSubscriptionProperties method, 739
    SetDataDrivenSubscriptionProperties method, 748
    SetSubscriptionProperties method, 754
ExtensionSettings web service class, 767
ExtensionType parameter, ListExtensions method, 742
ExtensionType property, Extension class, 766
external report images, uploading, 487–489
ExternalImagesTimeout property, Reporting Services, 606

F

Fax Viewer, 447, 448, 507
Feature Selection Page
    Reporting Services distributed installation and scale-out
        installation, 44
    Reporting Services full installation, 41
    Reporting Services report author installation, 43
    Reporting Services server installation, 41–42
Feature Selection screen, server components not on, 60
February property, MonthsOfYearSelector class, 771
FIELD LIST, 90, 92–93, 94, 101–102
Field Selector, 185, 224, 388
Field web service class, 767
FieldAlias property, ParameterFieldReference class, 771
fields, 787
    case-sensitivity, 190
    Report Builder, 802–803
Fields entries, Expression dialog box, 328
Fields list, Report Builder, 804
Fields property, DataSetDefinition class, 760
File Download dialog box, 500, 536
file share option, 549
FileShareStorageLocation service element, 604
FillColor property, 665
FillGradientEndColor property, 665
FillGradientType property, 665
FillPatternType property, 665–666

Filter Data dialog box, 813
Filter Expression column, 407
Filter pane, 407, 409
Filter text box, 820
filters, 349–351
filters property, 666
FindItems method, 729–730
FindString method, 713
FindValue parameter, FindString method, 713
FireEvent method, 730
First( ) aggregate function, 322, 377
first match code group, 492
Fit technique, 696
FitProportional technique, 696
FixedColumnHeader property, 666
FixedRowHeaders property, 666
floating headers, employee list report, 332–335
FlushCache method, 730
Folder Location page, 526
folder names, invalid characters, 116
Folder parameter
    CreateFolder method, 724
    ExecuteBatch method, 730
Folder value, GetItemType method, 734
Folder.aspx page, 469
FolderOperation type, requiredOperation parameter, 620
folders
    adding using Report Manager, 470–471
    creating role assignments for, 514
    creating while deploying reports, 474
    deleting, 503–504
    moving items between, 502–503
    overview, 468–470
    renaming, 504
font property, 213, 666–667
<FONT></FONT> tag, 424
FontFamily detail property, 666
FontFamily property, 188, 462
FontSize detail property, 666
FontSize property, 188, 705
FontStyle detail property, 666
FontStyle property, 188
FontWeight detail property, 666
FontWeight property, 186, 188, 430
footer, page, 301–305
footer rows, 310–312, 318–319
foreign key constraints, 783, 788
foreign keys, 72, 783
Form1_Load method, 595
Form1.vb [Design] tab, 595
format code MMM, 244

Format dialog box, 808, 809
Format parameter
    GetRenderResource method, 714, 736
    Render method, 717
    Render2 method, 718
    RenderStream method, 718
format property, 667
formats, report caching and, 533–534
formatting
    Repair Count By Type report, 202–205
    Transport List report, 188–195
Forms security, 613
FormsSecurity project, 614
FormsSecurity solution, 614, 622, 627, 628
ForRendering parameter, GetReportParameters
    method, 738
Friday property, DaysOfWeekSelector class, 764
FROM clause, 90–92
Front-End report, 429, 431
fuel price chart
    business need, 236
    creating new report, 236–237
    datasets, 236–237
    features highlighted, 236
    placing chart item on report and populating it, 238–240
    refining chart, 240–244
    task overview, 236
    version 2, 244–247
full installation, 29, 41–42
Full Name attribute, 794
Full Trust right, 626
FullTrust permission, 494
FullTrust rights, 497, 623
Functions tab, 804, 811
fx button, 194

G

Galactic data source, 401, 438
Galactic database, 112
Galactic Delivery Services (GDS), 112, 367, 412, 473
    accounting, 87
    package tracking, 85–86
    personnel, 86–87
    transport maintenance, 87–88
Galactic Delivery Services link, 503, 504
Galactic Report Model, 806
    deployed to the report server, 798
    entities in, 788
Galactic Report Model entry, 818
Galactic shared data source, 425, 429, 438, 483, 497

GalacticDeliveriesDataMart cube, 404, 407
GalacticOLAP project, 405, 406
GalacticPrompt data source, 579
GalacticReporting, 438, 593
gauge label data region, 642
gauge panel data region, 642–643
gauge pointer data regions, 643
gauge - radial data region, 643
gauge range data region, 643–644
gauge scale - linear data region, 644
gauge scale - radial data region, 644
gauges
    adding second, 267–273
    business need, 257
    creating new report, 258–262
    dataset, 258–262
    features highlighted, 257
    modify dataset, 267–273
    overview, 257
    presenting data on, 258–262
    refining appearance of, 262–267
    task overview, 258
GDS. *See* Galactic Delivery Services (GDS)
GDS logo, 487
GDSReport template, 390, 400, 405, 412, 429
GDSServer code access group, 493
General Site Settings page, 564
Generate events task, 511
GenerateModel method, 731
Generic Query Designer, 90, 387, 389
    business type distribution charts, 248
    conference nametags, 276
    conference place cards, 283
    days in maintenance chart, 251–252
    deliveries versus lost packages chart, 221–222
    digital dashboard gauges, 258
    fuel price chart, 237, 245
    modifying gauge, 268
    rate sheet report, 288–289
Generic Query Designer window, 207
Get Latest Version feature, VSS, 363
GetCacheOptions method, 731
GetDataDrivenSubscriptionProperties method, 731–732
GetDataSourceContents command parameter, 574
GetDataSourceContents method, 732
GetDocumentMap method, 713
GetExecutionInfo method, 713
GetExecutionInfo2 method, 713
GetExecutionOptions method, 733
GetExtensionSettings method, 733
GetItemDataSourcePrompts method, 733
GetItemDataSources method, 733–734

GetItemType method, 734
GetModelDefinition method, 734
GetModelItemPermissions method, 734–735
GetModelItemPolicies method, 735
GetPermissions method, 735
GetPolicies method, 735–736
GetProperties method, 721, 736
GetRenderResource method, 714, 736
GetReportDefinition method, 736
GetReportHistoryLimit method, 737
GetReportHistoryOptions method, 737
GetReportLink method, 737–738
GetReportParameters method, 738
GetResourceContents command parameter, 574
GetResourceContents method, 738
GetRoleProperties method, 738–739
GetScheduleProperties method, 739
GetSubscriptionProperties method, 739, 758
GetSystemPermissions method, 740
GetSystemPolicies method, 740
GetSystemProperties method, 740
Getting Started window, 818, 819
GetUserInfo method, 617
GetUserModel method, 740
GetWeather method, 400, 403, 497
Global Assembly Cache, 400
global fields, 304
globalinstall switch, 596
globally unique identifier (GUID), 569, 608
Goal field, 412
GoalComment field, 412
Graphical Query Designer, 162, 222, 387
graphics. *See also* charts; images
    digital dashboard
        adding second gauge, 267–273
        business need, 257
        creating new report, 258–262
        dataset, 258–262
        features highlighted, 257
        modifying dataset, 267–273
        overview, 257
        presenting data on gauge, 258–262
        refining appearance of gauge, 262–267
        task overview, 258
    overview, 220
GROUP BY clause, 90, 104–107, 181–182, 782
Group Properties dialog box, 203, 313–315, 328–329, 390, 391, 430
group sorting, 332
group totals, 317–319
GroupExpressions property, 667
grouping fields in charts, 240
Grouping pane, 16

GroupLevel0 tablix, 439
groups, dynamic, 357
GroupsBeforeRowHeaders property, 667
GroupUserName property, Policy class, 772
GUID (globally unique identifier), 569, 608

H

hardware requirements, 34–35
HasDocumentMap property
    ExecutionInfo class, 764
    ExecutionInfo2 class, 765
HasSnapshot property
    ExecutionInfo class, 764
    ExecutionInfo2 class, 765
HAVING clause, 90, 107–108
header columns, 310
header rows, 310–312
headers
    employee mailing labels report, 340–342
    floating, in employee list report, 332–335
    page, in report template, 299–301
height property, 667
hidden property, 668
Hidden property, CatalogItem class, 759
HiddenSpecified property, CatalogItem class, 759
Hide Details button, Contents tab, 485
Hide option, 575
HideDuplicates property, 668
HideEndLabels property, 668
HideInLegend property, 668
HideLabels property, 669
History Of dialog box, 363–364
History Options dialog box, 363
History Properties page, 542, 546, 547
History tab, 543, 545, 547, 548
HistoryID parameter
    DeleteReportHistorySnapshot method, 728
    GetReportParameters method, 738
    LoadReport method, 715
    LoadReport2 method, 715
HistoryID property
    ExecutionInfo class, 765
    ExecutionInfo2 class, 765
    ReportHistorySnapshot class, 774
HistoryLimit parameter, SetReportHistoryLimit method, 751
<Hn></Hn> tag, 424
Hoc Report Builder application, 806
Home folder, 471
    Browser rights, 520
    security page, 509
horizontal chart axes, 227

Horizontal detail property, 664
Hourly Schedule option, Schedule page, 546
HoursWorked field, 392
HTML, 424
HTML BI sharing solution, 6–7
HTML Format Device Information (rc), 580
HTML formatting tags, 424
HTML printing, 506
HTML3.2 format parameter, 576
HTML4.0 format parameter, 576
HTTP post, URL access using, 579–585
HttpWebClientProtocol class, 712, 713, 721, 722
Hub field, 370, 378, 380

I

<I></I> tag, 424
ID property, 587
    CatalogItem class, 759
    ModelItem class, 769
    ModelPerspective class, 769
identifying field, 787
<identity impersonate="true"/> entry, 624, 626
IDEs (integrated development environments), 11
IIF( ) function, 330–332, 358
IIS (Internet Information Services), 4, 60, 61, 573
Image Format Device Information (rc), 581
IMAGE format parameter, 576
Image Properties dialog box
    conference nametags, 279
    conference place cards, 285
    rate sheet report, 289, 291
    report template, 299
images
    conference nametags
        business need, 275
        creating new report, 276–282
        dataset, 276–282
        features highlighted, 275
        placing report items on report, 276–282
        task overview, 276
    conference place cards
        business need, 282
        creating new report, 282–287
        dataset, 282–287
        features highlighted, 282
        placing report items on report, 282–287
        task overview, 282
    overview, 273–275
    rate sheet report
        business need, 288
        creating new report, 288–292

images (*Continued*)
dataset, 288–292
features highlighted, 288
placing report items on report, 288–292
refining report layout, 293–294
task overview, 288
ImpersonateUser property, DataSourceDefinition class, 762
ImpersonateUserSpecified property, DataSourceDefinition class, 762
Import Report page, 501
import tool, 437–439
IN operator, 436
IncludeZero property, 669
IndexOf method, 404
infinity sign, 85
inherited role assignments, 515–516
InheritModelItemParentSecurity method, 740–741
InheritParent parameter
GetModelItemPolicies method, 735
GetPolicies method, 736
InheritParentSecurity method, 741
InitialToggleState property, 669
INNER JOIN clause, 782
inner joins, 76–77
InRangeBarPointerColor property, 669
InRangeLabelColor property, 670
InRangeTickMarkColor property, 670
INSERT query, 88
Installation Error 2755, Reporting Services, 60–61
Installation Log File, Reporting Services, 61
InstallationID element, 600
installing
Reporting Services Configuration Manager
E-mail Settings page, 55–56
Encryption Keys page, 57–59
Execution Account page, 56–57
Menu Bar, 60
overview, 49–50
Report Manager URL page, 55
Report Server Database page, 53–55
Scale-out Deployment page, 59
Server Status page, 51
Service Account page, 51–52
Web Service URL page, 52–53
SharePoint web parts, 596
SQL Server 2008
completing the SQL Server Installation Wizard, 49
Feature Selection Page, 41–44
Instance Configuration page, 45–46
overview, 39–40
preliminaries, 41
Reporting Services Configuration page, 47–49
Server Configuration page, 46

Instance Configuration page, 45–46
InstanceID element, 600
InstanceName detail property, 660
Insufficient rights error message, 523
integrated development environments (IDEs), 11
integrated security, 486–487, 607
Integration Services packages, 11
interacting with reports
invoice front-end reports, 429–432
overview, 428
transport monitor reports, 432
interactive presentation rendering formats, 442
interactive sorting, employee list report, 332–335
InteractiveSize property, 670
Inter-galactic-net, 432
Interlaced property, 670
InterlacedColor property, 670–671
InterlacedColor setting, 670
InterlacedRows property, 671
InterlacedRowsColor property, 671
InterlacedRowsColor setting, 670
intermediate reporting. *See also* data caching during preview
handling errors in reports
adding drilldown capability, 313–317
adding totaling, 317–323
business need, 307
creating new report, 307–308
creating project, 307–308
dataset, 307–308
features highlighted, 307
overview, 306–307
populating report layout, 308–313
shared data source, 307–308
task overview, 307
overview, 298
Report Definition Language, 359–361
report template
business need, 299
copying to report project directory, 305–306
creating template project, 299–301
features highlighted, 299
overview, 298–299
page footer, 301–305
page header, 299–301
task overview, 299
Visual SourceSafe, 361–364
Internet, images obtained through, 274–275, 301
Internet Information Services (IIS), 4, 60, 61, 573
Internet Options dialog box, 499, 507
interval property, 671
IntervalOffset property, 671–672
IntervalOffsetType property, 672

IntervalType property, 672
InvalidParameterValue property, 758
Invoice Detail table, 69
invoice front-end reports, 429–432
Invoice Header entity, 790
Invoice Header table, 69
Invoice Number attribute, 790
invoice reports, 424–428
Invoice-Batch Number report
 choosing layout, 155–160
 creating data source, 153–155
 creating dataset
 overview, 153
InvoiceDate field, Data row, 429
InvoiceDetail dataset, 426
InvoiceHeader dataset, 426
InvoiceInfo.mdb file, 437, 438
InvoiceNumber field, Data row, 429
IP addresses, 52
IsDataDriven property, Subscription class, 778
IsEventService service element, 603
IsNotificationService service element, 603
ISNULL( ) function, 104, 105
IsPassword property, ExtensionParameter class, 767
IsSchedulingService service element, 603
IsSystem parameter, GetReportHistoryLimit method, 737
IsValidPrincipalName method, 617
IsWebServiceEnabled service element, 604
Item parameter
 DeleteItem method, 728
 GetCacheOptions method, 731
 GetExecutionOptions method, 733
 GetItemDataSourcePrompts method, 733
 GetItemDataSources method, 734
 GetItemType method, 734
 GetPermissions method, 735
 GetPolicies method, 736
 GetProperties method, 736
 GetReportHistoryOptions method, 737
 InheritParentSecurity method, 741
 ListChildren method, 741
 ListDependentItems method, 741
 ListParents method, 756
 MoveItem method, 745
 SetCacheOptions method, 747
 SetExecutionOptions method, 749
 SetItemDataSources method, 749
 SetPolicies method, 750
 SetProperties method, 751
 SetReportHistoryOptions method, 752
 SetReportLink method, 752

Item property
 DataRetrievalPlan class, 760
 DataSource class, 761
 ScheduleDefinition class, 776
 ScheduleExpiration class, 777
ItemNamespace property, ItemNamespaceHeader class, 768
ItemNamespaceHeader web service class, 768
ItemNamespaceHeaderValue property, 721
ItemTypeEnum value, 734

J

January property, MonthsOfYearSelector class, 771
JobID parameter, CancelJob method, 722
JOIN clause, 90, 93–97
Join Context menu, 142
joining multiple tables, 81
joins, 76
July property, MonthsOfYearSelector class, 771
June property, MonthsOfYearSelector class, 771

K

KanatypeSensitivity property, DataSetDefinition class, 761
KanatypeSensitivitySpecified property, DataSetDefinition class, 761
KeepExecutionSnapshots parameter, GetReportHistoryOptions
 method, 737
KeepExecutionSnapshots parameter, SetReportHistoryOptions
 method, 752
KeepTogether property, 672
Kerberos, 487
key symbol, 85

L

Label field, 370
Label Properties dialog box, 266, 271
Label property, 370, 403
 DocumentMapNode class, 764
 ParameterValue class, 772
 ValidValue class, 780
LabelAutoFitDisabled property, 674, 675
LabelInterval property, 673
LabelIntervalOffset property, 673
LabelIntervalOffsetType property, 673
LabelIntervalType property, 673
LabelLocID property, 673–674
labels, 214, 250, 257, 342
labels property, 674
LabelsAngle property, 674
LabelsAutoFitDisabled property, 674, 687
LabelsColor property, 674

LabelsFont property, 674–675
LabelsFormat property, 675
LabelStyle property, 675
LabelTextDecoration property, 675
Language global field, 304
Language Preference dialog box, 499
language property, 675
Last( ) aggregate function, 322
Last Run column, 551
LastExecuted property, Subscription class, 778
LastExecutedSpecified property, Subscription class, 778
LastRunTime property, Schedule class, 776
LastRunTimeSpecified property, Schedule class, 776
latest report versions, VSS, 363
layout
        employee list report, 325–332
        overtime report, 345–351
        rate sheet report, 293–294
        revised employee time report, 352–358
layout areas, 638–639
layout property, 676
LayoutDirection property, 676
Left detail property, 678, 680
left outer joins, 79
left property, 676
Legend Properties dialog box, 253–254
LegendName property, 676
legends property, 676
LegendText property, 677
Length property, 404
<LI></LI> tag, 424
line graphs, 223
line report item, 646
line with markers graphs, 239–240
LineAmount field, 391, 392, 393, 395
linear gauge data region, 642
linear gauge pointer data region, 643
Linear Gauge Properties dialog box, 269
Linear Scale Properties dialog box, 271
Linear Scale Range Properties dialog box, 270–271
LinearGauges property, 677
LineColor property, 281, 677
LineHeight property, 677
LineNumber field, InvoiceDetail dataset, 426
LineStyle property, 677
LineWidth property, 677
Link parameter, CreateLinkedReport method, 724
linked reports, 524–527
LinkedReport value, GetItemType method, 734
linking tables, 75
LinkToChild property, 678

List item, 212–218
list reports, 205
list tablix, 392
ListChildren command parameter, 574
ListChildren method, 711, 741
ListDependentItems method, 741
ListEvents method, 742
ListExtensions method, 742
ListJobs method, 742
ListModelDrillthroughReports method, 742
ListModelItemChildren method, 742–743
ListModelPerspective method, 743
ListMySubscriptions method, 755
ListParents method, 755–756
ListRenderingExtensions method, 714
ListReportHistory method, 743
ListReportSubscriptions method, 756
ListRoles method, 743
ListScheduledReports method, 744
ListSchedules method, 744
ListSecureMethods method, 714, 744
ListSubscriptions method, 744
ListSubscriptionsUsingDataSource method, 744
ListTasks method, 745
LoadDrillthroughTarget method, 714
LoadDrillthroughTarget2 method, 714–715
LoadReport method, 712, 715
LoadReport2 method, 712, 715
LoadReportDefinition method, 715
LoadReportDefinition2 method, 716
local administrator privileges, security, 508–509
local service account, 38
local system account, 38
localization, 410, 499
localization identifier, 661, 704
LocalizedName property, Extension class, 766
LocalizedString method, 410, 411, 499
location property, 678
lock icon, VSS, 363
log files, 608, 627
logarithmic property, 678
LogarithmicBase property, 678
LogBase property, 679
Logging page, 569
logical page presentation formats, 442
login accounts, 37–38
Logoff method, 716, 745
Logon.aspx file, 623
LogonMethod authentication element, 602
logons, 627
LogonUser method, 617, 716, 745

LogScale property, 679
lost delivery reports, 377–385
lost packages. *See* deliveries versus lost packages chart
LostDelivery dataset, 384

M

m_adminUserName property, AuthorizationExtension class, 620
Macromedia's ColdFusion, 6
Mail Sent To column, 551
mailing labels. *See* employee mailing labels report
maintainability of stored procedures, 345
maintenance. *See* days in maintenance chart
MajorGridLines property, 679
MajorTickMark property, 679
MajorTickMarks property, 680
Manage All Subscriptions task, 510, 562
Manage data sources task, 510
Manage folders task, 510
Manage individual subscriptions task, 510, 554
Manage jobs task, 511
Manage models task, 510
Manage report history task, 510, 546
Manage report server properties task, 511
Manage report server security task, 511
Manage reports task, 510, 539
Manage resources task, 510
Manage roles task, 511
Manage shared schedules task, 511
many-to-many relation, 74
March property, MonthsOfYearSelector class, 771
margin property, 680
margins, 342
margins property, 680
marker property, 680–681
MarkerStyle property, 681
MarkLength property, 681
MarksAlwaysAtPlotEdge property, 681
MatchData parameter
    CreateDataDrivenSubscription method, 723
    CreateSubscription method, 727
    GetDataDrivenSubscriptionProperties method, 732
    GetSubscriptionProperties method, 739
    SetDataDrivenSubscriptionProperties method, 748
    SetSubscriptionProperties method, 754
Matrix item, 200–202
matrix layout reports
    adding groupings to, 818–819
    creating, 818
    overview, 817

matrix reports, 172, 802
    Invoice-Batch Number report
        choosing layout, 155–160
        creating data source, 153–155
        creating dataset
        overview, 153
matrix, tablix functioning as, 196
matrix1_RowGroup2_Collection tag, 462
MAX( ) aggregate function, 106, 182
MaxActiveReqForOneUser element, 600
MaxAppDomainUnloadTime service element, 604
MaxAutoSize property, 681
MaxFontSize property, 681–682
maximum property, 682
MaximumPin property, 682
MaximumValue property, 682
MaxQueueThreads service element, 604
MaxScheduleWait element, 601
May property, MonthsOfYearSelector class, 771
MDX (Multidimensional Expression), 14, 404
MDX Query Designer, 405–409
MemorySafetyMargin service element, 603
MemoryThreshold service element, 603
Menu Bar, Reporting Services Configuration Manager, 60
merged cells, 353–354
MergeTransactions property, 683
Message property, Warning class, 780
Me.Stp_EmployeeListTableAdapter1.Fill file, 595
Metadata Browser pane, 408
Metadata pane, 406, 408
.mhtml extension, 452
MHTML Format Device Information (rc), 582
MHTML format parameter, 576
Microsoft SQL Server 2008 Reporting Services.
    See Reporting Services
Microsoft Word format, 457
MicrosoftReportViewer control, 590
MIMEType detail property, 652
MimeType parameter
    CreateResource method, 726
    GetRenderResource method, 714, 736
    GetResourceContents method, 738
    Render method, 717
    Render2 method, 718
    RenderStream method, 718
    SetResourceContents method, 753
MIMEType property, 683
MimeType property, CatalogItem class, 759
MIN( ) aggregate function, 106, 211
MinFontSize property, 683
Minimum property, 680, 683

MinimumPin property, 683–684
MinimumValue property, 684
MinorGridLines property, 684
MinorTickMark property, 684
MinorTickMarks property, 685
minus (— signs, 317, 320
MinuteRecurrence property, RecurrencePattern class, 773
MinuteRecurrence web service class, 768
Minutes property, TimeExpiration class, 779
MinutesInterval property, MinuteRecurrence class, 768
MissingParameterValue property, ActiveState class, 758
MMM format code, 244
Model entry, 792
Model Item Security page, 799, 800
Model parameter
    CreateModel method, 725
    GenerateModel method, 731
    GetModelDefinition method, 734
    GetModelItemPermissions method, 735
    GetUserModel method, 740
    InheritModelItemParentSecurity method, 741
    ListModelDrillthroughReports method, 742
    ListModelItemChildren method, 743
    ListModelPerspective method, 743
    RegenerateModel method, 746
    RemoveAllModelItemPolicies method, 747
    SetModelDefinition method, 749
    SetModelDrillthroughReports method, 750
    SetModelItemPolicies method, 750
Model property, ModelCatalogItem class, 768
Model value, GetItemType method, 734
ModelCatalogItem web service class, 768
ModelDrillthroughReport web service class, 768–769
ModelItem web service class, 769
ModelItemID parameter
    GetModelItemPermissions method, 735
    GetModelItemPolicies method, 735
    InheritModelItemParentSecurity method, 741
    ListModelDrillthroughReports method, 742
    ListModelItemChildren method, 743
    SetModelDrillthroughReports method, 750
    SetModelItemPolicies method, 750
ModelItems property, ModelItem class, 769
ModelPerspective web service class, 769
Modified Date column heading, 485
ModifiedBy property
    CatalogItem class, 759
    Subscription class, 778
ModifiedDate property
    CatalogItem class, 759
    Subscription class, 779
ModifiedDateSpecified property, CatalogItem class, 759

Modify Shared Page, 597
Modify Shared Web Part, 597
Monday property, DaysOfWeekSelector class, 764
MonthlyDOWRecurrence property, RecurrencePattern class, 773
MonthlyDOWRecurrence web service class, 769–770
MonthlyRecurrence property, RecurrencePattern class, 773
MonthlyRecurrence web service class, 770
MonthsOfYear property, 770
MonthsOfYearSelector web service class, 770–771
Move Item page, 502
Move Multiple Items page, 503
MoveItem method, 745
MSSQLRS folder, 783
MSSQLRS.FormsSecurity.pdb debug database, 623
MSSQLRS.FormsSecurity.dll assembly, 623
Multidimensional Expression (MDX), 14, 404
multiple instance report, 798
multiple property dialog boxes, 236, 262–267
multiple tables, joining, 81
multiplier property, 685
MultiValue property, ReportParameter class, 774
MultiValueSpecified property, ReportParameter class, 774
My Reports folder, 566–568
My Reports option, 566, 567, 568, 727
My Reports role, 512, 539
My Subscriptions page, 551, 554–555
MyComputer zone, 399, 623
MyDBUser database login, 579
MyReports feature, 612
MyReportsRole property, Reporting Services, 606

N

Name field, 564
Name parameter
    CreateRole method, 726
    CreateSchedule method, 727
    DeleteRole method, 728
    GetRoleProperties method, 739
    SetRoleProperties method, 753
    SetScheduleProperties method, 753
name property, 685
Name property
    CatalogItem class, 759
    DataSource class, 761
    DataSourcePrompt class, 763
    Extension class, 766
    ExtensionParameter class, 767
    Field class, 767
    ModelItem class, 769
    ModelPerspective class, 769
    ParameterValue class, 772

Property class, 772
ReportParameter class, 774
Role class, 775
Schedule class, 776
SearchCondition class, 778
Task class, 779
Name text box, 285
named permission sets, 491, 493–494
Named Permission Sets file, 398
namespace, for ReportService2005 and ReportExecution2005 web
    service classes, 757
nametags, conference
    business need, 275
    creating new report, 276–282
    dataset, 276–282
    features highlighted, 275
    placing report items on report, 276–282
    task overview, 276
Nametags report, 480, 481, 487, 488, 502, 503
    Adobe Acrobat Reader, 576
    Properties tab, 483
Native mode default configuration option, 48
NavigateBookmark method, 716–717
NavigateDocumentMap method, 717
navigation, invoice front-end reports, 430–432
NeedleStyle property, 685
NeedsProcessing property, 765
.NET assemblies, uploading reports using
    code access security, 491–494
    copying .NET assembly to report server, 491
    deploying, 498–499
    localization, 499
    modifying security configuration, 494–497
    overview, 491
    uploading report, 497–498
network service account, 38
New Calculated Member, 407
New Data Source button, 481
New Data Source page, 482, 521
New Data-Driven Subscription button, 556
New Field button, 804, 810
New Folder button, 470
New Folder page, 470, 471, 502, 521
New Item command, Solution Explorer window, 175
New Project dialog box, 12, 174, 783
New Role Assignment page, 514
New Snapshot button, 543, 549
New User Role dialog box, 517, 519
NewExpression attribute, 794
Next Page button, 150
NextRunTime property, Schedule class, 776

NextRunTimeSpecified property, Schedule class, 776
NoDataMessage property, 686
normalization, 70–72
NoRows property, 351
NoRowsMessage property, 686
NoSchedule property, ScheduleDefinitionOrReference class, 777
NoSchedule web service class, 771
Notepad, 461, 489
Nothing permission, 493
Notify Recipients page, 560, 561
November property, MonthsOfYearSelector class, 771
NT AUTHORITY\LOCAL SERVICE account, 38
NT AUTHORITY\NETWORK SERVICE account, 38
NT AUTHORITY\SYSTEM account, 38
Null Delivery Provider, 563
NULL format parameter, 576
NULL values, 103
Nullable property
    Properties window, 794
    ReportParameter class, 774
NullableSpecified property, ReportParameter class, 774
NumeralLanguage property, 686
NumeralVariant property, 686
Numeric attributes, 787
NumPages parameter, Sort method, 720
NumPages property, 765

O

Object Explorer window, 517, 566
ObjectName property, Warning class, 780
ObjectType property, Warning class, 780
October property, MonthsOfYearSelector class, 771
ODBC (Open Database Connectivity), 438
OffsetLabels property, 687
<OL></OL> tag, 424
OmitBorderOnPageBreak property, 687
one-to-many relation, 73
one-to-one relation, 73–74
Open Database Connectivity (ODBC), 438
Open dialog box, 438
Operator drop-down list, 402, 548
ORDER BY clause, 90, 99–101, 247, 325
orientation property, 687
outer joins, 77–80
Output window, 498
Outside Border toolbar button, 215
overtime report
    business need, 343
    creating new report, 343–345
    datasets, 343–345

overtime report (*Continued*)
    features highlighted, 343
    report layout, 345–351
    task overview, 343
overview, 27–28
Overwrite Data Sources option, 630
Overwrite parameter
    CreateDataSource method, 724
    CreateReport method, 725
    CreateResource method, 726
OverwriteDataSources property, 475, 476, 498
Owner parameter, ListSubscriptions method, 744
Owner property, Subscription class, 779

P

<P></P> tag, 424
package tracking, GDS, 85–86
padding property, 687
page breaks, 332, 455
page footers, 301–305, 638
page headers, 299–301, 639
Page Setup menu, 818, 820
PageBreak property, 393, 455, 687–688
PageCountMode UI element, 604
PageNumber global field, 304
Pages/Folder.aspx web page, 469
PageSize property, 688
PaginationMode parameter
    Render2 method, 718
    Sort2 method, 720
paid invoices report, 437–439
palette property, 688
PalettePatternBehavior property, 688
Parameter Management page, 527, 575
Parameter Name detail property, 688
Parameter pane, 370
Parameter Value detail property, 688
parameter values, 560
Parameter Values page, 560, 561
ParameterFieldReference property,
    ParameterValueOrFieldReference class, 772
ParameterFieldReference web service class, 771
Parameterized Invoice-Batch Number report
    adding parameters to query in dataset, 161–164
    creating second dataset, 164–165
    customizing parameters, 165–169
    overview, 160
ParameterLanguage parameter
    SetExecutionParameters method, 719
    SetExecutionParameters2 method, 720
ParameterName property, ParameterFieldReference class, 771

Parameters entries, Expression dialog box, 328
Parameters entry, Report Data window, 394, 410
Parameters page, 415, 427, 540
Parameters parameter
    CreateDataDrivenSubscription method, 723
    CreateSubscription method, 727
    GetDataDrivenSubscriptionProperties method, 732
    GetSubscriptionProperties method, 739
    SetDataDrivenSubscriptionProperties method, 748
    SetExecutionParameters method, 719
    SetExecutionParameters2 method, 720
    SetReportParameters method, 752
    SetSubscriptionProperties method, 754
Parameters property, 688, 765
parameters, report, 330
ParametersRequired property, 765
ParameterValue property, ParameterValueOrFieldReference
    class, 772
ParameterValue web service class, 771–772
ParameterValueOrFieldReference web service class, 772
ParameterValues parameter, ValidateExtensionSettings
    method, 755
ParameterValues property, ExtensionSettings class, 767
Parent parameter
    CreateDataSource method, 724
    CreateFolder method, 724
    CreateLinkedReport method, 724
    CreateModel method, 725
    CreateReport method, 725
    CreateResource method, 726
    GenerateModel method, 731
parent property, 689
ParentItem property, 689
ParentName field, 430, 432
Password parameter, LogonUser method, 716, 745
Password property
    DataSourceCredentials class, 761
    DataSourceDefinition class, 762
Path property
    ModelDrillthroughReport class, 769
    Subscription class, 779
PauseSchedule method, 746
payroll checks, 389
PDB (debug database file), 627
PDF (Portable Document Format), 8, 450, 506–507, 533
    features not supported by, 452
    features supported by, 450–451
    overview, 450
    viewing documents, 450
    when to use, 452
PDF BI sharing solution, 7

PDF Format Device Information (rc), 582
PDF format parameter, 576
Peer Evaluations text box, 415
permission sets, 494
persisting authentication, 610–611
personnel, GDS, 86–87
Perspective parameter, GetUserModel method, 740
Perspectives property, ModelCatalogItem class, 768
physical page presentation formats, 442
Pickup City field, 818
Pickup Date Time attribute, Delivery entity, 793
pivot table report (crosstab), 153
PivotX property, 689
PivotY property, 689
place cards, conference
    business need, 282
    creating new report, 282–287
    dataset, 282–287
    features highlighted, 282
    placing report items on report, 282–287
    task overview, 282
placeholders, 187, 421–422
placement property, 689–690
PlanetaryWeather class, 400
plus (+) signs, 316, 320
Pointer Properties item, context menu, 264
PointerCap property, 690
PointerImage property, 690
pointers property, 690
Policies parameter
    SetModelItemPolicies method, 750
    SetPolicies method, 750
    SetSystemPolicies method, 754
policy web service class, 772
PolicyLevel service element, 604
PollingInterval service element, 603
populating
    business type distribution chart, 249–250
    days in maintenance chart, 251–257
    deliveries versus lost packages chart, 222–227
    employee time report, 308–313
    fuel price chart, 238–240
Portable Document Format. *See* PDF
position property, 690
PostScript description language, 450
PowerPoint, 489
PreAuthenticate property, 712, 722
PrepareQuery method, 746
preprocessing, 344
presentation formats
    Excel, 455–457
    overview, 445–447

PDF, 450–452
printed, 459–460
TIFF, 447–450
web archive, 452–455
Word, 458–459
PreventFontGrow property, 691
PreventFontShrink property, 691
PreventLabelOffset property, 691
PreventWordWrap property, 691
preview. *See* data caching during preview
previous versions, retrieving, 363–364
primary keys, 70
Print dialog box, 445
Print Layout button, Report Designer, 445
Print Layout Mode, 305
printed presentation format
    features not supported by, 460
    features supported by, 460
    overview, 459–460
    viewing documents, 460
    when to use, 460
printing, 445
    from Report Manager
        client-side, 507
        HTML, 506
        overview, 506
        PDF format, 506–507
        TIFF format, 506–507
PrintOnFirstPage property, 691
PrintOnLastPage property, 692
Priority drop-down list, 550
Problem Contact Info folder, 793
ProblemContact field, 372
ProblemEMail field, 372
processors, 34
Production configuration, 477
production manager, 5–6
program-authoring software, 11
project directory, copying report template to, 305–306
Project Property Pages dialog box, 478
Project Types area, 585
ProjectItems\ReportProjects folder, 305
Prompt property
    DataSourceDefinition class, 762
    DataSourcePrompt class, 763
    ReportParameter class, 774
PromptUser property, ReportParameter class, 775
PromptUserSpecified property, ReportParameter class, 775
properties
    action, 647
    AlignOrientation, 648
    AlignType, 648

properties (*Continued*)
AlignWithChartArea, 648
AllowLabelRotation, 648–649
angle, 649
AntiAliasing, 649
Area3DStyle, 649
arrows, 649
AspectRatio, 649
assemblies, 650
author, 650
AutoFitTextDisabled, 650
AutoLayout, 650
AutoRefresh, 650
BackFill, 651
BackFrame, 651
BackgroundColor, 651
BackgroundGradientEndColor, 651
BackgroundGradientType, 652
BackgroundImage, 652
BackgroundPatternType, 652
BackgroundShadowOffset, 652–653
BarStart, 653
Bookmark, 653
BorderColor, 653
BorderSkin, 654
BorderStyle, 654
BorderWidth, 654–655
calendar, 655
CanGrow, 655
CanShrink, 655
caption, 656
CategoryAxes, 656
CategoryAxisName, 656
CategoryField, 656
ChartAreaName, 656
ChartAreas, 656
classes, 657
ClipContent, 657
code, 657
color, 657
columns, 658
ConsumeContainerWhitespace, 658
CrossAt, 658
CustomAttributes, 658
CustomCode, 658
CustomInnerPlotPosition, 659
CustomLabels, 659
CustomPaletteColors, 659
CustomPosition, 659
CustomProperties, 659
DataElementName, 660
DataElementOutput, 660

DataElementStyle, 660
DataPoint, 660
DataSchema, 660
DataSetName, 661
DataTransform, 661
DeferVariableEvaluation, 661
description, 661
DescriptionLocID, 661
direction, 661–662
DistanceFromScale, 662
DockOffset, 662
DockOutsideChartArea, 662
DockToChartArea, 662
DocumentMapLabel, 663
DynamicHeight, 663
DynamicWidth, 663
employee list reports, 325
employee mailing labels report, 336–338
employee time reports, 308–309, 311–312
EmptyPoint, 663
enabled, 663
EndMargin, 664
EndPoint, 664
EndValue, 664
EndWidth, 664
EquallySizedAxesFonts, 664–665
EquallySpacedItems, 665
FillColor, 665
FillGradientEndColor, 665
FillGradientType, 665
FillPatternType, 665–666
filters, 666
FixedColumnHeader, 666
FixedRowHeaders, 666
font, 666–667
format, 667
GroupExpressions, 667
GroupsBeforeRowHeaders, 667
height, 667
hidden, 668
HideDuplicates, 668
HideEndLabels, 668
HideInLegend, 668
HideLabels, 669
IncludeZero, 669
InitialToggleState, 669
InRangeBarPointerColor, 669
InRangeLabelColor, 670
InRangeTickMarkColor, 670
InteractiveSize, 670
Interlaced, 670
InterlacedColor, 670–671

properties (*Continued*)
InterlacedRows, 671
InterlacedRowsColor, 671
interval, 671
IntervalOffset, 671–672
IntervalOffsetType, 672
IntervalType, 672
KeepTogether, 672
label, 672
LabelInterval, 673
LabelIntervalOffset, 673
LabelIntervalOffsetType, 673
LabelIntervalType, 673
LabelLocID, 673–674
labels, 674
LabelsAngle, 674
LabelsAutoFitDisabled, 674
LabelsColor, 674
LabelsFont, 674–675
LabelsFormat, 675
LabelStyle, 675
LabelTextDecoration, 675
language, 675
layout, 676
LayoutDirection, 676
left, 676
LegendName, 676
legends, 676
LegendText, 677
LinearGauges, 677
LineColor, 677
LineHeight, 677
LineStyle, 677
LineWidth, 677
LinkToChild, 678
location, 678
logarithmic, 678
LogarithmicBase, 678
LogBase, 679
LogScale, 679
MajorGridLines, 679
MajorTickMark, 679
MajorTickMarks, 680
margin, 680
margins, 680
marker, 680–681
MarkerStyle, 681
MarkLength, 681
MarksAlwaysAtPlotEdge, 681
MaxAutoSize, 681
MaxFontSize, 681–682
maximum, 682

MaximumPin, 682
MaximumValue, 682
MergeTransactions, 683
MIMEType, 683
MinFontSize, 683
minimum, 683
MinimumPin, 683–684
MinimumValue, 684
MinorGridLines, 684
MinorTickMark, 684
MinorTickMarks, 685
multiplier, 685
name, 685
NeedleStyle, 685
NoDataMessage, 686
NoRowsMessage, 686
NumeralLanguage, 686
NumeralVariant, 686
OffsetLabels, 687
OmitBorderOnPageBreak, 687
orientation, 687
overtime report, 346–347
padding, 687
page footer, 301–303
page header, 300–301
PageBreak, 687–688
PageSize, 688
palette, 688
PalettePatternBehavior, 688
parameters, 688
parent, 689
ParentItem, 689
PivotX, 689
PivotY, 689
placement, 689–690
PointerCap, 690
PointerImage, 690
pointers, 690
position, 690
PreventFontGrow, 691
PreventFontShrink, 691
PreventLabelOffset, 691
PreventWordWrap, 691
PrintOnFirstPage, 691
PrintOnLastPage, 692
RadialGauges, 692
radius, 692
ranges, 692
rate sheet report, 289–291, 293
RepeatColumnHeaders, 692
RepeatRowHeaders, 693
RepeatWith, 693

properties (*Continued*)
    ReportName, 693
    ResizeMode, 693
    reverse, 693
    reversed, 694
    revised employee time report, 353–354
    scalar, 694
    ScaleBreakStyle, 694
    scales, 694
    setting for fields, 214
    ShadowColor, 694–695
    ShadowIntensity, 695
    ShadowOffset, 695
    size, 695
    sizing, 695–696
    SmartLabels, 696
    SnappingEnabled, 696
    SnappingInterval, 696
    SortExpressions, 697
    sorting, 697
    source, 697
    SpaceAfter, 697
    SpaceBefore, 697–698
    StartAngle, 698
    StartMargin, 698
    StartValue, 698
    StartWidth, 698
    StripLines, 699
    SweepAngle, 699
    text, 699
    TextAlign, 699
    TextAntiAliasingQuality, 699
    TextColor, 700
    TextDecoration, 700
    TextEffect, 700
    TextOrientation, 700
    TextShadowOffset, 700
    TextWrapThreshold, 700–701
    thermometer, 701
    TickMarksOnTop, 701
    title, 701
    TitleAlignment, 701
    TitleBackgroundColor, 702
    TitleColor, 702
    TitleFont, 702
    titles, 702
    TitleSeparator, 702
    TitleSeparatorColor, 703
    TitleTextDecoration, 703
    TitleTextOrientation, 703
    ToggleItem, 703
    ToolTip, 703

    ToolTipLocID, 704
    top, 704
    TopImage, 704
    type (for chart series), 704
    type (for gauge pointer), 704
    UnicodeBiDi, 705
    UseFontPercent, 705
    UserSort, 705
    value, 705
    ValueAxes, 706
    ValueAxisName, 706
    ValueLocID, 706
    VariableAutoInterval, 706
    variables, 706
    VerticalAlign, 707
    visible, 707
    width, 707
    WritingMode, 707
    ZIndex, 707
Properties dialog box, 424
Properties page, 534, 539, 545
Properties Pages dialog box, 474
Properties parameter
    CreateDataSource method, 724
    CreateFolder method, 724
    CreateLinkedReport method, 724
    CreateModel method, 725
    CreateReport method, 725
    CreateResource method, 726
    GenerateModel method, 731
    GetProperties method, 736
    GetSystemProperties method, 740
    SetProperties method, 751
    SetSystemProperties method, 754
Properties tab, 490, 497, 500, 502, 516, 536, 547, 817
    Create Linked Report, 545
    Hide in List View check box, 489
    Nametags report, 483
    New Role Assignment page, 514
Properties window, 16, 371, 435, 462, 463, 638, 647
    conference nametags, 277–280
    conference place cards, 284–286
    days in maintenance chart, 252
    digital dashboard gauges, 259
    employee time reports, 318–319
    fuel price chart, 242–243
    Nullable property, 794
    overtime report, 348
    Property Pages button, 205
    Text Box Properties dialog box, 203
property dialog boxes, 236, 262–267
Property Pages button, 205

Property Pages dialog box, 477–479, 498
property web service class, 772
Public Assemblies folder, 400, 491
PublicKeyBlob, 495
Publisher role, 512, 539
publishing reports, 17–18
pull technology, 549
PurchaseDate field, 501
push technology, 549

Q

quality assurance (QA) testing, 568
queries, versus stored procedures, 344–345
Query Designer
    business type distribution charts, 248
    conference nametags, 276
    conference place cards, 283
    days in maintenance chart, 251–252
    deliveries versus lost packages chart, 221–222
    digital dashboard gauges, 258
    fuel price chart, 237, 245
    modifying gauge, 268
    rate sheet report, 288–289
    revised employee time report, 352
Query entry area, Dataset Properties dialog box, 237
QueryDefinition web service class, 773
Querying Data
    FROM Clause, 90–92
    Constant and Calculated Fields, 101–104
    FIELD LIST, 92–93
    GROUP BY Clause, 104–107
    HAVING Clause, 107–108
    JOIN Clause, 93–97
    ORDER BY Clause, 99–101
    overview, 88–89
    SELECT Query, 90–108
    WHERE Clause, 97–99
QueryParameter property, ReportParameter class, 775
QueryParameterSpecified property, ReportParameter class, 775

R

radial gauge pointer data region, 643
Radial Pointer Properties dialog box, 264
Radial Scale Properties dialog box, 262–263
Radial Scale Range Properties dialog box, 265
RadialGauges property, 692
RadialPointer1 item, gauge, 260
RadialPointer2 item, gauge, 261
Radial-Two Scales gauge, 259–262
radius property, 692

ranges, gauge, 264–267
ranges property, 692
rate sheet report
    business need, 288
    creating new report, 288–292
    dataset, 288–292
    features highlighted, 288
    placing report items on report, 288–292
    refining report layout, 293–294
    task overview, 288
Rating field, 412
rc: prefix parameter, 577, 589
rc:AutoFit parameter, Word Format Device Information, 583
rc:BookmarkID parameter, HTML Format Device Information, 580
rc:ColorDepth parameter, Image Format Device Information, 581
rc:Columns parameter, Image Format Device Information, 581
rc:Columns parameter, PDF Format Device Information, 582
rc:ColumnSpacing parameter, Image Format Device Information, 581
rc:ColumnSpacing parameter, PDF Format Device Information, 582
rc:DocMap parameter, HTML Format Device Information, 580
rc:DpiX parameter, Image Format Device Information, 581
rc:DpiY parameter, Image Format Device Information, 581
rc:Encoding parameter, CSV Format Device Information, 578
rc:Encoding parameter, XML Format Device Information, 583
rc:EndPage parameter, Image Format Device Information, 581
rc:EndPage parameter, PDF Format Device Information, 582
rc:ExcelMode parameter, CSV Format Device Information, 578
rc:ExpandContent parameter, HTML Format Device Information, 580
rc:ExpandTools parameter, Word Format Device Information, 583
rc:FieldDelimiter parameter, CSV Format Device Information, 578
rc:FileExtension parameter, CSV Format Device Information, 578
rc:FileExtension parameter, XML Format Device Information, 583
rc:FindString parameter, HTML Format Device Information, 580
rc:FixedPageWidth parameter, Word Format Device Information, 583
rc:GetImage parameter, HTML Format Device Information, 580
rc:HTMLFragment parameter, HTML Format Device Information, 580
rc:HumanReadablePDF parameter, PDF Format Device Information, 582
rc:Indented parameter, XML Format Device Information, 583
rc:JavaScript parameter, HTML Format Device Information, 580
rc:JavaScript parameter, MHTML Format Device Information, 582
rc:LinkTarget parameter, HTML Format Device Information, 580
rc:MarginBottom parameter, Image Format Device Information, 581
rc:MarginBottom parameter, PDF Format Device Information, 582
rc:MarginLeft parameter, Image Format Device Information, 581
rc:MarginLeft parameter, PDF Format Device Information, 582
rc:MarginRight parameter, Image Format Device Information, 581
rc:MarginRight parameter, PDF Format Device Information, 582

rc:MarginTop parameter, Image Format Device Information, 581
rc:MarginTop parameter, PDF Format Device Information, 582
rc:MHTMLFragment parameter, MHTML Format Device Information, 582
rc:MIMEType parameter, XML Format Device Information, 583
rc:NoHeader parameter, CSV Format Device Information, 578
rc:OmitDocumentMap parameter, Excel Format Device Information, 579
rc:OmitDrillThroughs parameter, Word Format Device Information, 583
rc:OmitFormulas parameter, Excel Format Device Information, 579
rc:OmitHyperlinks parameter, Word Format Device Information, 583
rc:OmitSchema parameter, XML Format Device Information, 583
rc:OnlyVisibleStyles parameter, HTML Format Device Information, 580
rc:OutputFormat parameter, Image Format Device Information, 581
rc:PageHeight parameter, Image Format Device Information, 581
rc:PageHeight parameter, PDF Format Device Information, 582
rc:PageWidth parameter, Image Format Device Information, 581
rc:PageWidth parameter, PDF Format Device Information, 582
rc:Parameters parameter, HTML Format Device Information, 580
rc:Qualifier parameter, CSV Format Device Information, 578
rc:RecordDelimiter parameter, CSV Format Device Information, 578
rc:Schema parameter, XML Format Device Information, 583
rc:Section parameter, HTML Format Device Information, 580
rc:SimplePageHeader parameter, Excel Format Device Information, 579
rc:StartPage parameter, Image Format Device Information, 581
rc:StartPage parameter, PDF Format Device Information, 582
rc:StreamRoot parameter, HTML Format Device Information, 580
rc:StyleStream parameter, HTML Format Device Information, 580
rc:SuppressLineBreaks parameter, CSV Format Device Information, 578
rc:Toolbar parameter, HTML Format Device Information, 580
rc:UseFormattedValues parameter, CSV Format Device Information, 578
rc:UseFormattedValues parameter, XML Format Device Information, 583
rc:XSLT parameter, XML Format Device Information, 583
rc:Zoom parameter, HTML Format Device Information, 580
RDL (Report Definition Language), 14, 359–361, 386, 461, 479
ReadOnly property, ExtensionParameter class, 767
Realm authentication element, 602
rectangle report item, 646
RecurrencePattern web service class, 773
Recursive parameter
    ListChildren method, 741
    ListModelItemChildren method, 743
RecycleTime service element, 603
Reference property, DataSourceReference class, 763
ReferencesPresent property, Schedule class, 776
Refresh Report button, 488, 489, 535

Refresh toolbar button, 323–324
RegenerateModel method, 746
relations, 72–73
remote administration, 26
RemoveAllModelItemPolicies method, 747
renaming folders, 504
Render command parameter, 574
Render Format drop-down list, 550
Render method, 717
Render Report button, 584
Render2 method, 718
renderers, 19
Rendering Test Reports folder, 516, 520, 521
RenderingTest report, 443, 447, 450, 455, 460, 462, 473, 516, 521, 523
    browser rights, 522
    document map exported to Excel file, 456
    exported to Excel file, 457
    exported to PDF file, 451
    exported to TIFF file, 449
    exported to web archive file, 453
    exported to Word document, 459
    Preview tab, 446
RenderStream method, 718
Repair Count By Type report
    creating data source, 197–200
    creating dataset, 197–200
    formatting, 202–205
    Matrix item, 200–202
    overview, 197
Repair table, Transport table and, 181
RepeatColumnHeaders property, 692
RepeatRowHeaders property, 693
RepeatWith property, 693
report author installation, 30–31, 43
report authoring architecture
    BI project type, 11–12
    overview, 10–11
    Report Designer
        design surface, 15
        Grouping pane, 16
        overview, 14–15
        Preview tab, 15
        Properties Window, 16
        Report Data Window, 15
        Toolbox, 16
    Standalone Report Builder, 16–17
    structure
        data definition, 13–14
        overview, 12–13
        RDL, 14
        report layout, 14

Report Builder, 418, 538
    chart layout reports, 819–821
    clickthrough reports, 804–805
    entities, 802–803
    Entities list, 803–804
    Export toolbar button, 442
    fields, 802–803
    Fields list, 804
    launching, 801–802
    matrix layout reports
        adding groupings to, 818–819
        creating, 818
        overview, 817
    overview, 800
    roles, 802–803
    table layout reports, 805–817
        adding formatting, 812–815
        clickthrough reports, 815–817
        creating, 805–809
        modifying to show monthly information, 809–812
Report Builder button, 801, 805
Report Builder toolbar, 819, 821
    Design Report, 812
    Filter Data dialog box, 813
    Run Report tab, 809
Report Catalog, 18–19, 26, 468, 486, 509, 524, 596, 608, 611, 630
Report Catalog folders, 469
report container, 639
report data source, 475
Report Data window, 15, 161, 368, 388, 391, 401, 405, 406, 410, 439, 548
    adjusting size of, 168
    conference place cards, 283–285, 287
    Data Source Properties dialog box, 176
    Design tab, 387
    Parameters entry, 394
Report Definition Language (RDL), 14, 359–361, 386, 461, 479
Report Definition section, 500
report definitions
    downloading, 500
    editing, 500–501
    uploading modified, 501–502
report delivery
    Report Manager website, 20
    SharePoint, 21
    subscription delivery, 21
    web service interface, 21–22
report deployment practices, 631–633
Report Designer, 10–11, 15, 386, 389, 408, 418, 437, 438, 442, 443, 458, 481, 498, 500
    deploying reports

        in Chapter09 project, 472–473
        creating folders while deploying, 474
        overview, 472
        Property Pages dialog box, 477–479
        shared data sources, 474–477
        single report, 474
        working through web service, 474
    design surface, 15
    Grouping pane, 16
    overview, 14–15
    Preview tab, 15, 445, 446
    Properties Window, 16
    Report Data Window, 15
    Toolbox, 16
Report Designer folder, 397, 405
Report Execution Logging feature, 569, 608
Report Execution Timeout setting, 565
Report Explorer, 21, 597
Report Formatting toolbar, 347
report history feature
    enabling, 542–546
    managing, 546–548
report layout, 12, 14, 820
report links, creating standard subscriptions with, 552
Report Manager, 440, 443, 464, 487, 570, 573, 575, 584, 609, 627, 797
    configuration files, 623
    deploying reports using Report Designer, 472–479
    finding text within reports, 505–506
    folders
        adding new, 470–471
        deleting, 503–504
        moving items between, 502–503
        overview, 468–470
        renaming, 504
    linked reports, 524–527
    modifying reports from report server, 501–502
    overview, 467–468
    printing from, 506–507
    Report Builder button, 805
    roles
        Browser, 511–512
        Content Manager, 512–513
        creating, 513–523
        My Reports, 512
        Publisher, 512
        System Administrator, 513
        System User, 513
    searching for reports, 504–505
    security, 508–511
    Site Settings page, 569

Report Manager (*Continued*)
   uploading
      external report images, 487–489
      reports, 479–487
      reports using .NET assemblies, 491–499
      supporting materials, 489–491
   using Reporting Services without
      Report Viewer control, 589–595
      Reporting Services utilities, 597–599
      RSReportServer.config file, 599–608
      SharePoint web parts, 595–597
      URL access, 572–585
      web service access, 585–589
   View Details page, 620
Report Manager URL page, 55
Report Manager website, 9, 20
Report Model
   cleaning up, 789–797
   creating, 785–786
   creating project in BIDS, 783
   data source views, 785
   data sources, 783–785
   overview, 782
   parts and pieces, 786–789
   securing, 797–800
Report Model Wizard, 783, 785, 789, 790, 792, 793
   creating report model, 787
   selecting source of data, 801
report objects
   data regions, 639–645
   layout areas, 638–639
   report items, 645–647
Report parameter
   CreateDataDrivenSubscription method, 723
   CreateLinkedReport method, 724
   CreateReport method, 725
   CreateReportHistorySnapshot method, 726
   CreateSubscription method, 727
   DeleteReportHistorySnapshot method, 728
   FlushCache method, 730
   GetCacheOptions method, 731
   GetExecutionOptions method, 733
   GetReportDefinition method, 736
   GetReportHistoryOptions method, 737
   GetReportLink method, 738
   GetReportParameters method, 738
   ListReportHistory method, 743
   ListReportSubscriptions method, 756
   ListSubscriptions method, 744
   LoadReport method, 715
   LoadReport2 method, 715
   SetCacheOptions method, 747

SetExecutionOptions method, 749
SetReportDefinition method, 751
SetReportHistoryLimit method, 751
SetReportHistoryOptions method, 752
SetReportLink method, 752
SetReportParameters method, 752
UpdateReportExecutionSnapshot method, 755
Report Parameter Properties dialog box, 166, 212, 387, 394, 395, 401, 410, 433
   employee list reports, 327–328
   fuel price chart, 238, 246
   overtime report, 345–346
Report Parameter Values section, 551
Report Parameters dialog box, 169, 368, 369
report processors, 19
report project directory, copying report template to, 305–306
Report Project template, 12
Report Project Wizard template, 12
Report Properties dialog box, 303–304, 341, 395, 405, 414, 417
   Classes area, 400
   Code page, 396
   Page Header, 639
Report property, Subscription class, 779
Report Refresh button, 502
Report Server
   data providers, 19
   modifying reports from, 501–502
   renderers, 19
   Report Catalog, 18–19
   report processor, 19
   request handler, 19
Report Server Configuration Manager, 599
Report Server database, 26–27
Report Server Database page, Reporting Services Configuration Manager, 53–55
Report Server Temp DB database, 26–27
Report Server Windows service, 630
Report tag, 462
report template
   business need, 299
   copying to report project directory, 305–306
   creating template project, 299–301
   features highlighted, 299
   overview, 298–299
   page footer, 301–305
   page header, 299–301
   task overview, 299
Report Viewer
   displaying local report in Report Viewer, 592–595
   displaying report from Report Server, 590–592
   overview, 589–590
   URL access, 576–579

Report Wizard, 593
   Customer List report
      begin new project in Business Intelligence
         Development Studio or Visual Studio, 114–116
      choosing layout, 127–137
      creating data source, 116–120
      creating dataset, 121–127
      overview, 113
   dialog box, 594
   Galactic database, 112
   interactive table reports
      choosing layout, 145–152
      creating data source, 139–144
      creating dataset, 139–144
      creating new project, 138–139
      overview, 137
   matrix reports
      choosing layout, 155–160
      creating data source, 153–155
      creating dataset
      overview, 153
   report parameters
      adding parameters to query in dataset, 161–164
      creating second dataset, 164–165
      customizing parameters, 165–169
      overview, 160
report-authoring practices, 629–630
ReportBuilderTrustLevel UI element, 604
ReportExecution2005 methods
   FindString, 713
   GetDocumentMap, 713
   GetExecutionInfo, 713
   GetExecutionInfo2, 713
   GetRenderResource, 714
   ListRenderingExtensions, 714
   ListSecureMethods, 714
   LoadDrillthroughTarget, 714
   LoadDrillthroughTarget2, 714–715
   LoadReport, 715
   LoadReport2, 715
   LoadReportDefinition, 715
   LoadReportDefinition2, 716
   Logoff, 716
   LogonUser, 716
   NavigateBookmark, 716–717
   NavigateDocumentMap, 717
   Render, 717
   Render2, 718
   RenderStream, 718
   ResetExecution, 719
   ResetExecution2, 719

SetExecutionCredentials, 719
SetExecutionCredentials2, 719
SetExecutionParameters, 719
SetExecutionParameters2, 720
Sort, 720
Sort2, 720–721
ToggleItem, 721
ReportExecution2005 properties, 712–713
ReportExecutionService Description, 586
ReportFolder global field, 304
ReportFrontEnd.aspx file, 586
ReportHistorySnapshot web service class, 773–774
reporting
   import tool, 437–439
      overview, 437
      paid invoices report, 437–439
   interacting with reports
      invoice front-end reports, 429–432
      overview, 428
      transport monitor reports, 432
   overview, 365–366
   subreports
      employee evaluation reports, 412–424
      invoice reports, 424–428
      overview, 411
   Visual Basic .NET code
      customer list reports, 386–389
      delivery analysis reports, 404–411
      delivery status reports, 367–377
      lost delivery reports, 377–385
      overview, 366
      payroll checks, 389
      weather reports, 397–404
Reporting Catalog, and encrypted data, 59
Reporting Services, 424, 437, 440, 442
   administrative rights, 60
   advantages of, 8–10
   components of
      administration utilities, 25–26
      AdventureWorks database, 27
      Business Intelligence Development Studio, 27
      documentation, 27
      Report Server database, 26–27
      Report Server Temp DB database, 26–27
      sample reports, 27
      SQL Server 2005/2008, 26
      SQL Server Agent, 26
      Standalone Report Builder, 27
      Visual Studio, 27
      Windows service, 25
   default security roles, 518

Reporting Services (*Continued*)
    editions of
        Developer Edition, 28–29
        Enterprise Edition, 28
        overview, 27–28
        Standard Edition, 28
        Workgroup Edition, 28
    EnableClientPrinting property, 606
    EnableExecutionLogging property, 606
    EnableIntegratedSecurity property, 606
    EnableLoadReportDefinition property, 606
    EnableMyReports property, 606
    EnableRemoteErrors property, 606
    EnableReportDesignClientDownload property, 606
    encryption key, 57
    ExecutionLogDaysKept property, 606
    ExternalImagesTimeout property, 606
    and IIS on the same server, 61
    Installation Error 2755, 60–61
    Installation Log File, 61
    installing
        considerations for, 35–39
        Reporting Services Configuration Manager, 49–60
        requirements for, 34–35
        SQL Server 2008, 39–49
        types of installations, 29–34
    MyReportsRole property, 606
    overview, 4–5, 24
    security tasks, 510
    server components not on Feature Selection screen, 60
    SessionTimeout property, 606
    SharePointIntegrated property, 606
    SiteName property, 606
    SnapshotCompression property, 606
    StoredParametersLifetime property, 607
    StoredParametersThreshold property, 607
    SystemReportTimeout property, 607
    SystemSnapshotLimit property, 607
    system-wide security tasks, 511
    UseSessionCookies property, 607
Reporting Services Books Online, 437
Reporting Services Configuration Connection dialog box, 50
Reporting Services Configuration Manager, 25
    E-mail Settings page, 55–56
    Encryption Keys page, 57–59
    Encryption Keys page:backing up the encryption key, 58–59
    Execution Account page, 56–57
    Menu Bar, 60
    overview, 49–50
    Report Manager URL page, 55
    Report Server Database page, 53–55

    Scale-out Deployment page, 59
    Server Status page, 51
    Service Account page, 51–52
    SMTP, 36
    Web Service URL page, 52–53
Reporting Services Configuration Manager authentication
    element, 601
Reporting Services Configuration page, 47–49
Reporting Services Configuration Tool, 569
Reporting Services distributed installation and scale-out
    installation, 44
Reporting Services full installation, 41
Reporting Services Installation Wizard, 49
Reporting Services report author installation, 43
Reporting Services server installation, 41–42
Reporting Services utilities
    RSConfig utility, 599
    RSKeyMgmt utility, 597–599
ReportingService method, 723
ReportingServices style sheet, 569–570
ReportingServices.css file, 569, 570
ReportingServicesService.exe process, 628
ReportItem parameter, 720, 721
ReportName global field, 304
ReportName property, 693
ReportPageSettings property, ExecutionInfo2 class, 765
ReportParameter web service class, 774–775
ReportPath property, ExecutionInfo class, 765
ReportPath property, ExecutionInfo2 class, 765
ReportReadMe.txt file, 489, 490, 505
Reports folder, 386, 438
Reports parameter, SetModelDrillthroughReports method, 750
ReportServerEdition property, ServerInfoHeader class, 778
ReportServerUrl global field, 304
ReportServerURLI UI element, RSReportServer.config, 604
ReportServerVersion property, ServerInfoHeader class, 778
ReportServerVersionNumber property, ServerInfoHeader class, 778
ReportService2005 and ReportExecution2005 web service classes
    ActiveState, 758
    BatchHeader, 758–759
    CatalogItem, 759
    DailyRecurrence, 760
    DataRetrievalPlan, 760
    DataSetDefinition, 760–761
    DataSource, 761
    DataSourceCredentials, 761
    DataSourceDefinition, 762
    DataSourceDefinitionOrReference, 762–763
    DataSourcePrompt, 763
    DataSourceReference, 763
    DaysOfWeekSelector, 763–764

DocumentMapNode, 764
ExecutionInfo, 764–765
ExecutionInfo2, 765
ExpirationDefinition, 766
Extension, 766
ExtensionParameter, 766–767
ExtensionSettings, 767
Field, 767
ItemNamespaceHeader, 768
MinuteRecurrence, 768
ModelCatalogItem, 768
ModelDrillthroughReport, 768–769
ModelItem, 769
ModelPerspective, 769
MonthlyDOWRecurrence, 769–770
MonthlyRecurrence, 770
MonthsOfYearSelector, 770–771
namespace for, 757
NoSchedule, 771
ParameterFieldReference, 771
ParameterValue, 771–772
ParameterValueOrFieldReference, 772
policy, 772
property, 772
QueryDefinition, 773
RecurrencePattern, 773
ReportHistorySnapshot, 773–774
ReportParameter, 774–775
role, 775
schedule, 776
ScheduleDefinition, 776
ScheduleDefinitionOrReference, 777
ScheduleExpiration, 777
ScheduleReference, 777
SearchCondition, 777–778
ServerInfoHeader, 778
"specified" properties, 757–758
subscription, 778–779
task, 779
TimeExpiration, 779
ValidValue, 779–780
Warning, 780
WeeklyRecurrence, 780
ReportService2005 methods
CancelBatch, 722
CancelJob, 722
CreateBatch, 722–723
CreateDataDrivenSubscription, 723
CreateDataSource, 723–724
CreateFolder, 724
CreateLinkedReport, 724
CreateModel, 725
CreateReport, 725
CreateReportHistorySnapshot, 725–726
CreateResource, 726
CreateRole, 726
CreateSchedule, 727
CreateSubscription, 727
DeleteItem, 727–728
DeleteReportHistorySnapshot, 728
DeleteRole, 728
DeleteSchedule, 728
DeleteSubscription, 729
DisableDataSource, 729
EnableDataSource, 729
ExecuteBatch, 729
FindItems, 729–730
FireEvent, 730
FlushCache, 730
GenerateModel, 731
GetCacheOptions, 731
GetDataDrivenSubscriptionProperties, 731–732
GetDataSourceContents, 732
GetExecutionOptions, 733
GetExtensionSettings, 733
GetItemDataSourcePrompts, 733
GetItemDataSources, 733–734
GetItemType, 734
GetModelDefinition, 734
GetModelItemPermissions, 734–735
GetModelItemPolicies, 735
GetPermissions, 735
GetPolicies, 735–736
GetProperties, 736
GetRenderResource, 736
GetReportDefinition, 736
GetReportHistoryLimit, 737
GetReportHistoryOptions, 737
GetReportLink, 737–738
GetReportParameters, 738
GetResourceContents, 738
GetRoleProperties, 738–739
GetScheduleProperties, 739
GetSubscriptionProperties, 739
GetSystemPermissions, 740
GetSystemPolicies, 740
GetSystemProperties, 740
GetUserModel, 740
InheritModelItemParentSecurity, 740–741
InheritParentSecurity, 741
ListChildren, 741
ListDependentItems, 741

ReportService2005 methods (*Continued*)
    ListEvents, 742
    ListExtensions, 742
    ListJobs, 742
    ListModelDrillthroughReports, 742
    ListModelItemChildren, 742–743
    ListModelPerspective, 743
    ListReportHistory, 743
    ListRoles, 743
    ListScheduledReports, 744
    ListSchedules, 744
    ListSecureMethods, 744
    ListSubscriptions, 744
    ListSubscriptionsUsingDataSource, 744
    ListTasks, 745
    Logoff, 745
    LogonUser, 745
    MoveItem, 745
    PauseSchedule, 746
    PrepareQuery, 746
    RegenerateModel, 746
    RemoveAllModelItemPolicies, 747
    ResumeSchedule, 747
    SetCacheOptions, 747
    SetDataDrivenSubscriptionProperties, 747–748
    SetDataSourceContents, 748
    SetExecutionOptions, 748–749
    SetItemDataSources, 749
    SetModelDefinition, 749
    SetModelDrillthroughReports, 750
    SetModelItemPolicies, 750
    SetPolicies, 750
    SetProperties, 750–751
    SetReportDefinition, 751
    SetReportHistoryLimit, 751
    SetReportHistoryOptions, 751–752
    SetReportLink, 752
    SetReportParameters, 752
    SetResourceContents, 753
    SetRoleProperties, 753
    SetScheduleProperties, 753
    SetSubscriptionProperties, 753–754
    SetSystemPolicies, 754
    SetSystemProperties, 754
    UpdateReportExecutionSnapshot, 754–755
    ValidateExtensionSettings, 755
ReportService2005 properties, 721–722
ReportService2006 methods, 755–757
ReportService2006 property, 755
report-serving architecture
    overview, 17–18

report delivery
    Report Manager website, 20
    SharePoint, 21
    subscription delivery, 21
    web service interface, 21–22
Report Server
    data providers, 19
    renderers, 19
    Report Catalog, 18–19
    report processor, 19
    request handler, 19
Report-Specific Schedule, 537, 541
Report-specific schedule option, Schedule page, 546
ReportUtil assembly, 405, 410, 411
ReportUtil.dll assembly, 405, 491, 493, 494, 499
ReportViewer Tasks dialog box, 590, 591, 592, 593, 595
request handler, 19
requiredOperation parameter, FolderOperation type, 620
RequiredSpecified property, ExtensionParameter class, 767
ResetExecution method, 719
ResetExecution2 method, 719
ResizeMode property, 693
Resource parameter
    CreateResource method, 726
    GetResourceContents method, 738
    SetResourceContents method, 753
Resource value, GetItemType method, 734
Restore button, 57
result sets, 77, 247
results pane, 125
Results pane, 407, 408, 409
ResumeSchedule method, 747
retrieving data
    inner joins, 76–77
    joining multiple tables, 81
    outer joins, 77–80
    self-joins, 81–82
    sorting, 83–84
reusability of stored procedures, 345
reverse property, 693
reversed property, 694
revised employee time report
    business need, 351
    copying and renaming existing report, 352–358
    features highlighted, 351
    modifying dataset, 352–358
    modifying layout, 352–358
    task overview, 351
rich formatting, 419–424
Right detail property, 680
RIGHT function, 811

right outer joins, 79
rights, 510–511
role web service class, 775
role-based authorization, 611
roles
  Browser, 511–512
  Content Manager, 512–513
  creating assignments
    for folders, 514
    inherited, 515–516
    managing for reports, 516–523
    overview, 513
    using Windows groups, 523
  My Reports, 512
  Publisher, 512
  Report Builder, 802–803
  System Administrator, 513
  System User, 513
Roles property, Policy class, 772
Rosetta project, 4
Row Group pane, 390
Row Groups pane, 188, 430, 463
RowNumber( ) running aggregate function, 323, 339
rows, 67–70
  header and footer, 310–312, 318–319
  static and dynamic, 357
RS utility, 605–608
RSCatLogon SQL Server logon, 599
rs:ClearSession parameter, 577
rs:Command parameter, 577
RSConfig utility, 599
rs:Format parameter, 577
RSKeyMgmt utility, 597–599
rs:ParameterLanguage parameter, 577
RSPreviewPolicy.config file, 397, 398
RSReportServer.config, 602–604
RSReportServer.config file, 624, 630
  log files, 608
  overview, 599–605
  RS utility, 605–608
RSSecurityBackup folder, 622
RSSecurityBackup\ReportManager folder, 628
RSSecurityBackup\ReportServer folder, 628
rs:SessionID parameter, 577
rs:Snapshot parameter, 577
rssrvpolicy.config file, 494, 497, 625
RSWebParts.cab file, 596
RSWindowsBasic authentication element, 602
RSWindowsKerberos authentication element, 602
RSWindowsNegotiate authentication element, 602
RSWindowsNTLM authentication element, 602
Run Report tab, 809, 814

RunningRequestsAge element, 601
RunningRequestsDbCycle element, 601
RunningRequestsScavengerCycle element, 600
RunningValue( ) running aggregate function, 323

S

<S></S> tag, 424
sample reports, 27
Saturday property, DaysOfWeekSelector class, 764
scalar property, 694
scale breaks, 228, 235
scale, gauge, 262–263
ScaleBreakStyle property, 694
scale-out deployment feature, Enterprise Edition, 28
Scale-out Deployment page, Reporting Services Configuration
  Manager, 59
scale-out installation, 32–34, 36, 44
scales property, 694
Schedule page, 537, 541, 550, 552
  Begin Running This Schedule On option, 546, 560
  Hourly Schedule option, 546
  Report-specific schedule option, 546
  On a Schedule Created for This Subscription option, 560
  Stop This Schedule On check box, 546
Schedule Properties page, 550, 552
schedule web service class, 776
ScheduleDefinition parameter
  CreateSchedule method, 727
  SetScheduleProperties method, 753
ScheduleDefinition property, ScheduleDefinitionOrReference
  class, 777
ScheduleDefinition web service class, 776
ScheduleDefinitionOrReference web service class, 777
ScheduledMaint table, 211
ScheduleExpiration property, ExpirationDefinition class, 766
ScheduleExpiration web service class, 777
ScheduleID parameter
  DeleteSchedule method, 728
  GetScheduleProperties method, 739
  GetSubscriptionProperties method, 739
  ListScheduledReports method, 744
  PauseSchedule method, 746
  ResumeSchedule method, 747
  SetScheduleProperties method, 753
  SetSubscriptionProperties method, 754
ScheduleID property
  Schedule class, 776
  ScheduleReference class, 777
ScheduleReference property, ScheduleDefinitionOrReference
  class, 777
ScheduleReference web service class, 777

Search box, Report Manager, 505
SearchCondition web service class, 777–778
searching for reports, 504–505
"Second Code-Access Security Insert.txt" file, 399
secondary chart axes, 232–233, 235
Secondary Value Axis Properties dialog box, 233–234
Secure Sockets Layer (SSL), 36, 612–613, 716
SecureConnectionLevel element, 600
security
    custom extensions
        creating, 613–621
        debugging, 627–628
        deploying, 621–626
        using, 627–628
    data-driven subscriptions and, 562
    execution snapshots and, 542
    integration with Windows security, 508
    local administrator privileges, 508–509
    My Reports folder and, 568
    report caching and, 539
    report history feature and, 546
    Report Model item, 799–800
    standard subscriptions and, 554
    task and rights, 510–511
security classes, 493
Security page, 565, 798
<Security> entry, 625
SecurityScope parameter
    ListRoles method, 743
    ListTasks method, 745
Select a Shared Data Source page, 483, 497
Select bookmark drop-down list, 431
Select Chart Type dialog box, 223, 435
Select Data Source View page, 785
Select How to Define the Connection page, 783
Select Planets drop-down list, 402, 534, 535, 537, 538
SELECT queries, 66, 89, 90–108
Select Report Model Generation Rules page, 785, 786
Select Service Types drop-down list, 410
SELECT statement, 90–91, 435, 782
    @DynamicQuery variable, 436
    deliveries versus lost packages chart, 222
    employee list reports, 325
    fuel price chart, 245–247
    GROUP BY clause, 106–107
    HAVING clause, 107–108
    with JOIN clauses, 93–97
    modifying gauge, 268, 273
Select the Data Source page, 594
Select the Report Type page, 127, 594
Select URL drop-down list, 431

SelectedDate property, 587
self-joins, 81–82
September property, MonthsOfYearSelector class, 771
SerialNumber field, 501
Series Group Properties dialog box, 252
series groups in charts, 240
Series Properties dialog box, 225–226, 230–232
series scope, 256–257
Server Configuration page, 46
server installation, 29–30, 41–42
Server Properties dialog box, 566, 567, 569
Server Status page, Reporting Services Configuration
    Manager, 51
ServerInfoHeader web service class, 778
ServerInfoHeaderValue property, 712, 722
ServerName, 525
ServerReport.ReportPath property, Report Viewer, 591
ServerReport.ReportServerUrl property, Report Viewer, 591
Service Account page, Reporting Services Configuration
    Manager, 51–52
Service Pack 1 (SP1), 470
Service Pack 2 (SP2), 470
Service Reference Settings dialog box, 585
Service Type drop-down list, 407
Service Type entity, 808
Services snap-in, 52
ServiceType field, 371
SessionTimeout property, Reporting Services, 606
Set security for individual items task, 510
SetCacheOptions method, 747
SetConfiguration method, 620
SetDataDrivenSubscriptionProperties method, 747–748
SetDataSourceContents method, 748
SetExecutionCredentials method, 719
SetExecutionCredentials2 method, 719
SetExecutionOptions method, 748–749
SetExecutionParameters method, 719
SetExecutionParameters2 method, 720
SetItemDataSources method, 749
SetModelDefinition method, 749
SetModelDrillthroughReports method, 750
SetModelItemPolicies method, 750
SetPolicies method, 750
SetProperties method, 750–751
SetReportDefinition method, 751
SetReportHistoryLimit method, 751
SetReportHistoryOptions method, 751–752
SetReportLink method, 752
SetReportParameters method, 752
SetResourceContents method, 753
SetRoleProperties method, 753

SetScheduleProperties method, 753
SetSubscriptionProperties method, 753–754
SetSystemPolicies method, 754
SetSystemProperties method, 569, 754
Severity property, Warning class, 780
ShadowColor property, 694–695
ShadowIntensity property, 695
ShadowOffset property, 695
shared data sources
    creating using Report Manager, 481–483
    deliveries versus lost packages chart, 221–222
    delivery status reports, 367–368
    deploying, 474–477
    employee time report, 307–308
shared images, 275
Shared Reports folder, 525, 817
shared schedules, 565–566
SharedDataSourceRemoved property, ActiveState class, 758
SharePoint, 21, 468, 595–597
SharePointIntegrated property, Reporting Services, 606
sharing BI
    advantages of Reporting Services, 8–10
    need for
        chief executive officer, 6
        production manager, 5–6
        vice president of sales, 6
    solutions
        HTML, 6–7
        PDF, 7
        third-party reporting environment, 7–8
Show Axis Title, 435
Show Details button, 484, 500, 503
Show Details mode, 542
Show Empty Cells toolbar, 409
Simple Mail Transfer Protocol (SMTP) server, 36
Simple Object Access Protocol (SOAP), 22
simplicity, stored procedure, 344–345
single instance report, 798
Site parameter, ListMySubscriptions method, 755
Site Settings page, 563–565, 568, 605, 607
SiteName property, 606
size property, 695
Size property
    CatalogItem class, 759
    ReportHistorySnapshot class, 774
SizeSpecified property, CatalogItem class, 759
sizing property, 695–696
SmartLabels property, 696
SMTP (Simple Mail Transfer Protocol) server, 36
SnappingEnabled property, 696
SnappingInterval property, 696

SnapshotCompression property, Reporting Services, 606
SOAP (Simple Object Access Protocol), 22
SoapHttpClientProtocol class, 712, 713, 721, 722
software requirements, 35
Solution Configuration drop-down list, 478
Solution Explorer window, 227
    adjusting size of, 168
    Data Source Views folder, 785
    DeliveryAnalysis report, 498
    New Item command, 175
Sort dialog box, 813, 814
Sort method, 720
Sort2 method, 720–721
SortExpression detail property, 705
SortExpressions property, 697
SortExpressionScope detail property, 705
sorting, 83–84, 332–335
sorting property, 697
SortItem parameter, 720
source code, 630
source control, 361–364, 629–631
Source detail property, 652
source property, 697
SP1 (Service Pack 1), 470
SP2 (Service Pack 2), 470
SpaceAfter property, 697
SpaceBefore property, 697–698
Spacing property, 342
<SPAN></SPAN> tag, 424
"specified" properties, 757–758
Specify How Recipients Are Notified drop-down list, 563
SQL GROUP BY clause, 193
SQL pane, Generic Query Designer, 222, 237
SQL pane, Graphical Query Designer, 124
SQL Server 2005, 26
SQL Server 2008, 26
    Feature Selection Page
        Reporting Services distributed installation and
          scale-out installation, 44
        Reporting Services full installation, 41
        Reporting Services report author installation, 43
        Reporting Services server installation, 41–42
    Instance Configuration page, 45–46
    preliminaries, 41
    Reporting Services Configuration page, 47–49
    Reporting Services Installation Wizard, 49
    Server Configuration page, 46
SQL Server Agent, 26
SQL Server aggregate functions, 322
SQL Server Books Online, 27
SQL Server Installation Program, 39

SQL Server login, 38
SQL Server Management Studio, 517, 566–569
SQL Server Management Studio Connect to Server
 dialog box, 518
SQLCommandTimeoutSeconds element, 600
SSL (Secure Sockets Layer), 36, 612–613, 716
Standalone Report Builder, 10, 16–17, 27
Standard Edition, 28
standard subscriptions
 creating with embedded report, 550–551
 creating with report link, 552
 embedded reports versus attached reports, 553
 execution snapshots and, 553
 multiple for one report, 553
 overview, 549
 security and, 554
Start Debugging button, 479
StartAngle property, 698
StartDate parameter, 575
StartDate row, 527
StartDateTime property, ScheduleDefinition class, 776
StartMargin property, 698
StartPage parameter, FindString method, 713
StartValue property, 698
StartWidth property, 698
State property
 ReportParameter class, 775
 Schedule class, 776
StateSpecified property, ReportParameter class, 775
static rows and columns, 357
static text, 422
static values, 560
Status parameter
 GetDataDrivenSubscriptionProperties method, 732
 GetSubscriptionProperties method, 739
Status property, Subscription class, 779
StatusName field, 371, 374, 377
StDev( ) aggregate function, 322
StDevP( ) aggregate function, 322
stored procedures, 126, 344, 562–563
StoredParametersLifetime property, Reporting Services, 607
StoredParametersThreshold property, Reporting Services, 607
StoreRSLogon application, 627
StoreRSLogon project, 614
stp_CustomerInvoices stored procedure, 429
stp_DeliveryDetail stored procedure, 425
stp_DeliveryStatus stored procedure, 425
stp_EmployeeList stored procedure, 594, 595
stp_EmployeeListTableAdapter stored procedure, 595
stp_EvalPerformance stored procedure, 413
stp_EvalRatings stored procedure, 412

stp_InvoiceDetail stored procedure, 426
stp_InvoiceHeader stored procedure, 426
stp_LostDeliveries stored procedure, 378
stp_PayrollChecks stored procedure, 390
stp_TransportList stored procedure, 433
stp_TransportMonitor stored procedure, 433
stp_WeekNumbers stored procedure, 390
StreamID parameter, RenderStream method, 718
StreamIDs parameter
 Render method, 717
 Render2 method, 718
string constants, 98
string literals, 98
StripLines property, 699
StrongNameMembershipCondition security class, 493
structures, 126
Stsadm utility, 596
subreport item, 411
Subreport Properties dialog box, 415, 416, 427
subreport report item, 646
subreports, 411
 employee evaluation reports, 412–424
 invoice reports, 424–428
 overview, 411
SubReportTest report, 500–501, 505, 517, 519, 521, 522
SubReportTest.rdl file, 500, 501
subscription delivery, 21
Subscription Properties page, 550, 551, 552, 554
subscription web service class, 778–779
SubscriptionID parameter, DeleteSubscription
 method, 729
SubscriptionID property, Subscription class, 779
subscriptions, 549–563
 data-driven subscriptions, 555–563
 My Subscriptions page, 554–555
 standard subscriptions, 549–554
Subscriptions tab, 550, 556
SUM( ) aggregate function, 106, 256
Sum( ) aggregate function, 201, 227, 321–322, 391
summary property, 647
Sunday property, DaysOfWeekSelector class, 764
supporting materials, uploading, 489–491
SweepAngle property, 699
Switch( ) function, 358
System Administrator role, 513, 565, 568
System ODBC data source, 438
system properties, 607
System User role, 513, 565
SystemLimit parameter, GetReportHistoryLimit method, 737
SystemReportTimeout property, Reporting Services, 607
SystemSnapshotLimit property, Reporting Services, 607

T

Table item, 182–188
table layout reports
    adding formatting, 812–815
    clickthrough reports, 815–817
    creating, 805–809
    modifying to show monthly information, 809–812
TableAdapter Configure Wizard, 595
TableBinding, 595
tables, 67–70, 81
tablix, 195–196
    conference nametags, 277–280
    deliveries versus lost packages chart, 220
    delivery status reports, 370–374
    employee evaluation reports, 412–413
    employee list reports, 326–327
    employee mailing labels report, 336–338
    employee time reports, 309–311
    fuel price chart, 236
    lost delivery reports, 378–385
    overtime report, 347–348
    payroll checks, 390–394
    rate sheet report, 291
    revised employee time report, 356–357
    weather reports, 401–404
tablix column/row data region, 645
tablix data region, 644–645
tablix group data region, 645
Tablix group dialog box, 370, 378, 379
    employee list reports, 328–329
    employee time reports, 309
    revised employee time report, 353–356
Tablix Properties dialog box, 328, 348, 402, 434
Tablix to rep, delivery analysis reports, 409–411
Tagged Image File Format. *See* TIFF images
tags, RDL, 359–360
Target parameter, MoveItem method, 745
TargetDataSourceFolder folder, 472, 797
TargetDataSourceFolder property, 476, 477, 498
TargetModelFolder property, 797
TargetReportFolder property, 472, 476, 477, 498
TargetServerURL folder, 472, 797
TargetServerURL property, 477, 498
task web service class, 779
TaskID property, Task class, 779
Tasks parameter, CreateRole method, 726
Tasks parameter, SetRoleProperties method, 753
TaxDeductions function, 396
TCP (Transmission Control Protocol) port, 52
template, report
    business need, 299

copying to report project directory, 305–306
creating template project, 299–301
features highlighted, 299
overview, 298–299
page footer, 301–305
page header, 299–301
task overview, 299
templates, 12, 629
Test Connection button, 119
Test Connection Succeeded message, 784
text alignment property, 213
Text Box Properties dialog box, 192, 391, 392, 393, 430, 431
    employee list reports, 327, 333
    employee mailing labels report, 340
    employee time reports, 317–318
    Interactive Sort page, 334–335
    Properties window, 203
text box report item, 646–647
text boxes
    conference place cards, 284–287
    employee list reports, 325
    employee mailing labels report, 336–337
    employee time reports, 308–309
    overtime report, 346–347
    rate sheet report, 289–291, 293
Text entry, 811
TEXT function, 810, 811
Text property, 587, 699
TextAlign property, 187, 281, 699
TextAntiAliasingQuality property, 699
Textbox: Text Box Properties, 430
TextColor property, 700
TextDecoration property, 186, 700
TextEffect property, 700
TextOrientation property, 700
TextShadowOffset property, 700
TextWrapThreshold property, 700–701
thermometer property, 701
third-party reporting environment, 7–8
Three Color Range gauge, 269–273
Thursday property, DaysOfWeekSelector class, 764
TickMarksOnTop property, 701
TIFF (Tagged Image File Format) images, 8
    features not supported by, 449–450
    features supported by, 447–449
    overview, 447
    printing, 506–507
    viewing documents, 447
    when to use, 450
TIFF image viewer, 446
Time dimension, Metadata pane, 407

Time In cell, 375
Time In text box, 371
Time Out cell, 375
Time Out text box, 371
time reports. *See* employee time report
TimeExpiration property, ExpirationDefinition class, 766
TimeExpiration web service class, 779
Timeout property, QueryDefinition class, 773
TimeoutSpecified property, QueryDefinition class, 773
title property, 701
TitleAlignment property, 701
TitleBackgroundColor property, 702
TitleColor property, 702
TitleFont property, 702
titles, delivery status reports, 368–370
titles property, 702
TitleSeparator property, 702
TitleSeparatorColor property, 703
TitleTextDecoration property, 703
TitleTextOrientation property, 703
ToggleID parameter, ToggleItem method, 721
ToggleItem method, 721
ToggleItem property, 667, 703
toggling properties, 315–317, 319–320
Toolbar, deleting folders using, 503–504
Toolbox, 16, 182, 391, 411, 590
ToolTip property, 703
ToolTipLocID property, 704
Top detail property, 678, 680
top property, 704
TopImage property, 704
Total Cost column, 809, 810
Total Cost field, 808, 811
TotalAmount field, Data row, 429
TotalPages global field, 304
Transact-Structured Query Language (T-SQL), 14
Transmission Control Protocol (TCP) port, 52
transparent color property, 704
Transport Information Sheet
    creating data source, 206–207
    List item, 212–218
    overview, 206
    TransportInfo dataset, 207–211
    TransportSNs dataset, 206–207
Transport List report
    creating data source, 173–178
    creating dataset, 178–182
    formatting, 188–195
    overview, 172–173
    Table item, 182–188
transport maintenance, GDS, 87–88

Transport Monitor, 404, 432, 436, 584
Transport table, 181
Transport telemetry, 436
TransportDetail dataset, 211
TransportInfo dataset, 207–211
TransportList dataset, 433
TransportMonitor dataset, 434
TransportMonitor report, 433, 542, 544, 545, 546, 548
TransportNumber field, 434, 436
TransportNumber Report Parameter, 433
TransportSNs dataset, 206–207
TrustedUserHeader object, 713
TrustedUserHeaderValue property, 713, 755
T-SQL (Transact-Structured Query Language), 14
Tuesday property, DaysOfWeekSelector class, 764
type (for chart series) property, 704
type (for gauge pointer) property, 704
Type column heading, 484
Type drop-down list, 119, 405
Type property
    CatalogItem class, 759
    ModelDrillthroughReport class, 769
    ModelItem class, 769
    ReportParameter class, 775
TypeSpecified property, ReportParameter class, 775

U

<U></U> tag, 424
<UI> entry, 624
UILogon.aspx file, 623
<UL></UL> tag, 424
UnattendedExecutionAccount service element, 604
UNC (Universal Naming Convention) path, 61
UnicodeBiDi property, 705
Uniform Resource Locator (URL) access
    command parameters, 574
    controlling Report Viewer, 576–579
    passing parameters, 575–576
    using HTTP post, 579–585
Uniform Resource Locator access. *See* URL access
union code group, 492
UNION operator, 247
UNION queries, 782
unioned result sets, 247
UniqueName parameter, NavigateBookmark method, 717
UniqueName property, DocumentMapNode class, 764
Universal Naming Convention (UNC) path, 61
Unknown value, GetItemType method, 734
UnknownReportParameter property, ActiveState
    class, 758

UPDATE query, 88
UpdateReportExecutionSnapshot method, 754–755
updating report definitions, 548–549
Upload File button, 542
    Contents tab, 480
    Report Manager, 584
Upload File page, 480, 521
    Contents tab, 489, 490
    Contents tab toolbar, 488
uploading, 479
    external report images using Report Manager, 487–489
    modified report definitions, 501–502
    reports using .NET assemblies
        code access security, 491–494
        copying .NET assembly to report server, 491
        deploying, 498–499
        localization, 499
        modifying security configuration, 494–497
        overview, 491
        uploading report, 497–498
    reports using Report Manager
        in Chapter06 project, 480–481
        connecting using options, 485–487
        creating shared data sources, 481–483
        hiding items, 483–485
        overview, 479
    supporting materials using Report Manager, 489–491
URL (Uniform Resource Locator) access
    basic, 572–574
    command parameters, 574
    controlling Report Viewer, 576–579
    passing parameters, 575–576
    using HTTP post, 579–585
UrlMembershipCondition security class, 493
UrlRoot service element, 604
UseFontPercent property, 705
UseOriginalConnectString property, DataSourceDefinition
    class, 762
UserID global field, 304
User!Language global variable, 411
User!Language parameter, 499
UserName parameter, LogonUser method, 716, 745
UserName property
    DataSourceCredentials class, 761
    DataSourceDefinition class, 762
Users Folders folder, 566, 567
UserSort property, 705
UseSessionCookies property, Reporting Services, 607
<UseSSL> entry, 625
UseSystem parameter, SetReportHistoryLimit method, 751
utility program, 597

V

ValidateExtensionSettings method, 755
ValidValue web service class, 779–780
ValidValues property
    ExtensionParameter class, 767
    ReportParameter class, 775
ValidValuesQueryBased property, ReportParameter class, 775
ValidValuesQueryBased Specified property, ReportParameter
    class, 775
value axes in charts, 227, 243
Value Axis Properties dialog box, 228, 234, 243, 435
Value detail property, 652
Value field, 370, 435
value property, 705
Value property
    Expression dialog box, 194
    ExtensionParameter class, 767
    ParameterValue class, 772
    ParameterValueOrFieldReference class, 772
    Property class, 772
    SearchCondition class, 778
    ValidValue class, 780
ValueAxes property, 706
ValueAxisName property, 706
ValueLocID property, 706
Values parameter, GetReportParameters method, 738
Var( ) aggregate function, 322
VariableAutoInterval property, 706
variables property, 706
VarP( ) aggregate function, 322
VerifyPassword, 617
VerifyUser method, 617
vertical chart axes, 227
Vertical detail property, 664
VerticalAlign property, 281–282, 707
View Code, PaidInvoices report, 439
View data sources task, 510
View folders task, 510
View models task, 510
viewing
    cached reports, 535–536
    documents
        Excel presentation format, 455
        PDF format, 450
        printed presentation format, 460
        TIFF format, 447
        web archive presentation format, 453
        Word presentation format, 458
    exported reports, 444
virtual private network (VPN), 506

VirtualPath property
    CatalogItem class, 759
    Subscription class, 779
visibility properties, 315–317, 319–320
visible property, 707
VisibleDate property, 587
Visual Basic .NET code
    customer list reports, 386–389
    delivery analysis reports, 404–411
    delivery status reports, 367–377
    lost delivery reports, 377–385
    overview, 366
    payroll checks, 389
    weather reports, 397–404
Visual SourceSafe (VSS), 361–364
Visual Studio, 11, 27, 39, 114–116, 472, 475, 498, 585
VPN (virtual private network), 506
VSS (Visual SourceSafe), 361–364

W

Warning web service class, 780
Warnings parameter
    CreateReportHistorySnapshot method, 726
    LoadReportDefinition method, 715
    LoadReportDefinition2 method, 716
    Render method, 717
    Render2 method, 718
Warp Hauler transport, 505–506
WatsonDumpExcludeIfContainsExceptions element, 601
WatsonDumpOnExceptions element, 601
WatsonFlags element, 601
weather reports, 397–404, 534–535
WeatherInfo assembly, 400–401
WeatherInfo.dll assembly, 397, 400, 491, 492, 493, 494
WeatherInfo.GetWeather method, 497
WeatherReport link, 497, 535, 555
WeatherReport report, 400
WeatherReport.rdl file, 497
web archive presentation format
    features not supported by, 454
    features supported by, 453–454
    overview, 452
    viewing documents, 453
    when to use, 454–455
web service access, 585–589
web service interface, 21–22
Web Service URL page, Reporting Services Configuration
    Manager, 52–53
web services
    compatibility, 712
    creating, 710–711

credentials, 711–712
defined, 21
ReportExecution2005 methods, 713–721
ReportExecution2005 properties, 712–713
ReportService2005 and ReportExecution2005 web service
    classes
        ActiveState, 758
        BatchHeader, 758–759
        CatalogItem, 759
        DailyRecurrence, 760
        DataRetrievalPlan, 760
        DataSetDefinition, 760–761
        DataSource, 761
        DataSourceCredentials, 761
        DataSourceDefinition, 762
        DataSourceDefinitionOrReference, 762–763
        DataSourcePrompt, 763
        DataSourceReference, 763
        DaysOfWeekSelector, 763–764
        DocumentMapNode, 764
        ExecutionInfo, 764–765
        ExecutionInfo2, 765
        ExpirationDefinition, 766
        Extension, 766
        ExtensionParameter, 766–767
        ExtensionSettings, 767
        Field, 767
        ItemNamespaceHeader, 768
        MinuteRecurrence, 768
        ModelCatalogItem, 768
        ModelDrillthroughReport, 768–769
        ModelItem, 769
        ModelPerspective, 769
        MonthlyDOWRecurrence, 769–770
        MonthlyRecurrence, 770
        MonthsOfYearSelector, 770–771
        namespace for, 757
        NoSchedule, 771
        ParameterFieldReference, 771
        ParameterValue, 771–772
        ParameterValueOrFieldReference, 772
        policy, 772
        property, 772
        QueryDefinition, 773
        RecurrencePattern, 773
        ReportHistorySnapshot, 773–774
        ReportParameter, 774–775
        role, 775
        schedule, 776
        ScheduleDefinition, 776
        ScheduleDefinitionOrReference, 777
        ScheduleExpiration, 777

web services (*Continued*)
    ScheduleReference, 777
    SearchCondition, 777–778
    ServerInfoHeader, 778
    "specified" properties, 757–758
    subscription, 778–779
    task, 779
    TimeExpiration, 779
    ValidValue, 779–780
    Warning, 780
    WeeklyRecurrence, 780
  ReportService2005 methods
    CancelBatch, 722
    CancelJob, 722
    CreateBatch, 722–723
    CreateDataDrivenSubscription, 723
    CreateDataSource, 723–724
    CreateFolder, 724
    CreateLinkedReport, 724
    CreateModel, 725
    CreateReport, 725
    CreateReportHistorySnapshot, 725–726
    CreateResource, 726
    CreateRole, 726
    CreateSchedule, 727
    CreateSubscription, 727
    DeleteItem, 727–728
    DeleteReportHistorySnapshot, 728
    DeleteRole, 728
    DeleteSchedule, 728
    DeleteSubscription, 729
    DisableDataSource, 729
    EnableDataSource, 729
    ExecuteBatch, 729
    FindItems, 729–730
    FireEvent, 730
    FlushCache, 730
    GenerateModel, 731
    GetCacheOptions, 731
    GetDataDrivenSubscriptionProperties, 731–732
    GetDataSourceContents, 732
    GetExecutionOptions, 733
    GetExtensionSettings, 733
    GetItemDataSourcePrompts, 733
    GetItemDataSources, 733–734
    GetItemType, 734
    GetModelDefinition, 734
    GetModelItemPermissions, 734–735
    GetModelItemPolicies, 735
    GetPermissions, 735
    GetPolicies, 735–736

GetProperties, 736
GetRenderResource, 736
GetReportDefinition, 736
GetReportHistoryLimit, 737
GetReportHistoryOptions, 737
GetReportLink, 737–738
GetReportParameters, 738
GetResourceContents, 738
GetRoleProperties, 738–739
GetScheduleProperties, 739
GetSubscriptionProperties, 739
GetSystemPermissions, 740
GetSystemPolicies, 740
GetSystemProperties, 740
GetUserModel, 740
InheritModelItemParentSecurity, 740–741
InheritParentSecurity, 741
ListChildren, 741
ListDependentItems, 741
ListEvents, 742
ListExtensions, 742
ListJobs, 742
ListModelDrillthroughReports, 742
ListModelItemChildren, 742–743
ListModelPerspective, 743
ListReportHistory, 743
ListRoles, 743
ListScheduledReports, 744
ListSchedules, 744
ListSecureMethods, 744
ListSubscriptions, 744
ListSubscriptionsUsingDataSource, 744
ListTasks, 745
Logoff, 745
LogonUser, 745
MoveItem, 745
PauseSchedule, 746
PrepareQuery, 746
RegenerateModel, 746
RemoveAllModelItemPolicies, 747
ResumeSchedule, 747
SetCacheOptions, 747
SetDataDrivenSubscriptionProperties, 747–748
SetDataSourceContents, 748
SetExecutionOptions, 748–749
SetItemDataSources, 749
SetModelDefinition, 749
SetModelDrillthroughReports, 750
SetModelItemPolicies, 750
SetPolicies, 750
SetProperties, 750–751

web services (*Continued*)
   SetReportDefinition, 751
   SetReportHistoryLimit, 751
   SetReportHistoryOptions, 751–752
   SetReportLink, 752
   SetReportParameters, 752
   SetResourceContents, 753
   SetRoleProperties, 753
   SetScheduleProperties, 753
   SetSubscriptionProperties, 753–754
   SetSystemPolicies, 754
   SetSystemProperties, 754
   UpdateReportExecutionSnapshot, 754–755
   ValidateExtensionSettings, 755
  ReportService2005 properties, 721–722
  ReportService2006 property and methods, 755–757
WebClientProtocol class, 712, 713, 721, 722
Web.config file, 624, 626
WebServiceUseFileShareStorage element, 601
Wednesday property, DaysOfWeekSelector class, 764
Week Number drop-down list, 395
WeeklyRecurrence property, RecurrencePattern class, 773
WeeklyRecurrence web service class, 780
WeekNumber entry, 394
WeekNumber parameter, 394
WeekNumbers dataset, 390
WeeksInterval property, WeeklyRecurrence class, 780
WeeksIntervalSpecified property, WeeklyRecurrence class, 780
Welcome to the Report Wizard page, 116
When Run column, 544
When the Report Content Is Refreshed option, 552
WHERE clause, 90, 97–99, 162, 164, 404, 782
WhichWeek property, MonthlyDOWRecurrence class, 770
WhichWeekSpecified property, MonthlyDOWRecurrence class, 770
Width detail property, 688
width property, 707
WidthSensitivity property, DataSetDefinition class, 761

WidthSensitivitySpecified property, DataSetDefinition class, 761
Windows Forms Application, 590
Windows groups, creating role assignments using, 523
Windows integrated security, 628
Windows Picture, 447, 448, 507
Windows security, 508
Windows service, 25
Windows service account, 37–38
WindowsCredentials property, DataSourceDefinition class, 762
WindowsServiceUseFileShareStorage service element, 603
Word Format Device Information (rc), 583
WORD format parameter, 576
Word presentation format, 458–459
WorkDate field, 392
Workgroup Edition, 28
WorkingSetMaximum service element, 603
WritingMode property, 287, 707

X

XML (Extensible Markup Language), 14, 359–361, 397, 442, 494, 660
XML data exchange format
  customizing, 462–464
  overview, 461–462
XML Format Device Information (rc), 583
XML format parameter, 576
XML-rendering format, 660

Y

Year drop-down list, 376
Year parameter, 370, 420

Z

ZIndex property, 707
ZoneMembershipCondition file, 399, 495